GEORGE L. LEFFLER taught for many years at The Pennsylvania State University. During his lifetime, he was recognized as one of the country's leading authorities on securities markets. His writings and research continue to be a major contribution to the academic and financial communities.

LORING C. FARWELL is Associate Professor of Finance at Northwestern University. He completed his undergraduate work at the Massachusetts Institute of Technology, and received his master's and doctor's degrees from Northwestern University. Dr. Farwell has for several years taught the training course for securities organization personnel in the Chicago area sponsored by the New York Stock Exchange. He has also been the instructor on "Stock Exchange Operations" in the Investment Bankers Association course on the securities business offered nationally.

THE
STOCK MARKET

By the Late
George L. Leffler
THE PENNSYLVANIA STATE UNIVERSITY

THIRD EDITION

Revised by
Loring C. Farwell
NORTHWESTERN UNIVERSITY

THE RONALD PRESS COMPANY • NEW YORK

Library of Congress Catalog Card Number: 63–10640

To

THE LATE GEORGE L. LEFFLER

Preface to the Third Edition

Significant changes in the stock market, since publication of the Second Edition, provide the fundamental reason for this edition. Current conditions, practices, and procedures are its subject. New chapters on investment banking and foreign stock markets and a section on corporation finance have been added. The outline of chapters has been changed slightly to bring more clearly together those relating to exchanges, securities houses and their customers, regulation, and investment practices. the goal, however, is not changed. The book is a study of the stock market as it operates and functions today.

While rewriting the book, the author had, as Professor Leffler also did, the fullest cooperation from people in the securities business. A listing of all of them would take pages. The contribution of Robert M. Bishop and David D. Huntoon, and their colleagues in the Department of Member Firms Liaison of the New York Stock Exchange, must be acknowledged. They undertook to see that each chapter had a critical reading from one or more individuals expert in the subject of the chapter. Nor can one fail to acknowledge the critical reviews and additional data provided by Jonathan A. Brown, and his colleagues, in the Division of Research and Statistics at the Exchange. Mr. H. Vernon Lee, American Stock Exchange, gave graciously to the preparation of the chapter on that exchange. Others to whom I am particularly indebted for their willingness to give freely of their specialized knowledge are Stuart Scott, Jr., Carlisle & Jacquelin; Edwin Lefevre, Jr., De Coppett & Doremus; and Herbert Filer, Sr., Filer, Schmidt & Company. Some twenty officers and staff members of the New York Stock Exchange reviewed segments of the book critically. One cannot acknowledge sufficiently the degree of care they took in these reviews nor the value of the changes in text that resulted from them. Finally, it should be recalled that the contributions of all the persons whom Professor Leffler named in the Preface to the Second Edition have carried forward into the present one.

I am aware of a responsibility and an opportunity in the preparation of the present edition. Professor Leffler's careful work and thoughful statements of complex subjects made the two editions he prepared of value to many readers. I have preserved as far as practicable his work in the form in which he presented it. This is particularly true of the material in the section on Investing Practices and Special Instruments. Errors and omissions in this edition, however, are clearly my responsibility. It is my hope that those familiar with the book will find the new edition worthy of its predecessors, and that new readers will find their interest rewarded.

LORING C. FARWELL

Evanston, Illinois
January, 1963

Preface to the Second Edition

This is a study of the stock market as it operates and functions today. It is written for the serious observer and student of the market, whether he be an investor or trader, a staff member of a brokerage firm, or a college student.

The reader will find in the book a thoroughly up-to-date description of all operations of the stock exchange. The chief relationships between the customer and his brokerage firm are covered in detail. All aspects of investing and trading in stocks are considered, from the opening of an account with a brokerage firm to the most advanced trading practices.

In the few years since the first edition of this book was published, a number of substantial changes have occurred in the stock market. The Second Edition incorporates these changes and reflects current conditions in the securities market. Many chapters have been completely rewritten. The others have been brought up to date in every respect. Additional material includes new chapters or sections on the investment merits of securities, construction and management of security portfolios, technical analysis of stock prices, and investing and trading in common stocks. The material on investment plans and formulas has been expanded substantially.

The goal of the Second Edition is the same as that of the first: a comprehensive and objective description of the stock market and its operations. This book contains no magic, "get-rich-quick" formulas for easy profits in the stock market. In the opinion of the author there are no such formulas. The science and art of investment in stocks are techniques requiring careful study, long experience, extreme caution, and staunch courage. Frustrating failure often accompanies pleasant success. There is no smooth road to wealth anywhere. And the author makes no pretense at stating the final word on the securities markets. An attempt was made, however, to cover in as exhaustive a manner as possible all aspects of the stock market. Although highly technical operations of the market are included in the book, the author at all times has sought to reduce them to clear, nontechnical descriptions understandable to readers not directly employed in the securities business.

College instructors in courses in the stock market or the securities markets will find that the book is organized for use as a text for a one-semester course. The material has been refined and tested thoroughly for classroom use. Both practice and theory are combined in such a way as to find maximum usefulness for college teaching.

The student will find in the book a complete description of the entire securities market. Particular attention has been given to the economic functions performed by such markets and their place in the economic life of which we are a part. Special emphasis has been placed upon the relations between the government and the securities business. The sections of the book which deal with the history of the market bring into sharp contrast conditions as they existed in the old market with those of today. The student is shortly to become a business or professional man; he will then become a potential investor or trader in stocks and bonds. It is therefore of the highest practical importance that he know the essential relationships between customers and brokers and the way trading and investing in stocks are carried on. He should know how the securities business operates, if for no other reason than to avoid the pitfalls which ensnare so many unwary followers of the market.

The staff member of a brokerage or investment firm should also find much of value and importance in the book. Many of the technical aspects of the operation of the stock exchange and its member firms are covered in great detail. While revising the book, the author was privileged to work with a number of officials of the two leading exchanges in New York and was thus able to incorporate in it the latest and most accurate details on the operations of the stock exchanges. The book was especially designed to be of service to those workers in the financial district who are interested in an over-all picture of the entire securities market, including the work of the exchange and member firms, and also of the over-the-counter market.

No one writes alone. In the preparation of this section the author had the ever-helpful assistance of many officials of the New York Stock Exchange, the American Stock Exchange, partners of brokerage firms, bank officials, executives of investment houses, and colleagues in the teaching profession.

The men and organizations to whom the author is particularly indebted include G. Keith Funston, C. MacCoy, Phillip L. West, Edward DeLaura, Frank J. Coyle, John W. O'Reilly, and John H. Kirvin of the New York Stock Exchange; H. Vernon Lee and Arthur A. Bellone of the American Stock Exchange; Victor Cook, James F. MacLennan, James Corbett, and

R. J. Ciullo of Merrill Lynch, Pierce, Fenner & Beane; Morris Goldstein of Francis J. Du Pont & Company; Dr. G. Wright Hoffman of the University of Pennsylvania; Edward B. Norton of *Barron's;* J. George Zipp of De Coppet & Doremus; Sander Landfield of Carlisle & Jacquelin; Francis B. Bowman of Chase Manhattan Bank; Roy Rierson and Edwin J. Dikeman of Bankers Trust Company; Harold Z. Schreder of Distributors Group, Incorporated; Edmund L. Vogelius of Moody's Investors Service; Louis Brand of Standard and Poor's Corporation; and John G. Becker of Fitch Publishing Company.

Finally, the author wishes to express his sincere appreciation to Miss Alice E. Warne for her excellent technical assistance in the preparation of the manuscript.

GEORGE L. LEFFLER

University Park, Pennsylvania
January, 1957

Contents

Part III

WORK OF THE SECURITIES HOUSES

Part IV

REGULATION

Part V

INVESTING PRACTICES AND SPECIAL INSTRUMENTS

I

FUNDAMENTAL INFORMATION

1

Security Markets
and Security Owners

This book is about stock markets and the way they work. Before discussing market mechanisms and investment practices, however, the variety of security markets and of the securityholders who buy and sell in them deserves consideration.

KINDS OF MARKETS

The securities business in the United States is handled in two broad classes of markets: the organized securities exchange market and the over-the-counter market.

National Securities Exchanges. The Securities Exchange Act of 1934 provided that all formally organized securities exchanges must apply for registration with the Securities and Exchange Commission (hereafter called the SEC).[1] After compliance with the provisions of the Act and the regulations of the SEC, an exchange is registered to do business as a "national securities exchange." In 1962 fourteen such exchanges were registered (Table 1–1). The two largest were in New York City, while twelve regional exchanges operated in various parts of the country.

Small, local exchanges are permitted exemption from registration under the Act upon application to the SEC. The Commission may exempt such exchanges if it believes that their business is purely local and their volume of transactions is so small that it is impractical or unnecessary in the public interest to register them. In 1962 there were four such exchanges,

[1] Securities Exchange Act of 1934, Sec. 6.

at Colorado Springs, Honolulu, Richmond, and Wheeling. Their combined volume of business was under $30 million in 1961 and 95 per cent of that was business transacted on the Honolulu exchange. This total volume was less than 0.04 per cent of that on the registered national securities exchanges.

Volume of Exchange Business. A breakdown of the volume of business done on the fourteen national securities exchanges during 1961 is shown in Table 1–1. The volume of business done in bond transactions was very small. The amounts shown are for stock transactions.

Table 1–1. Comparative Volume of Stocks Sold on National
Securities Exchanges, 1961

Exchange	Per Cent of Dollar Volume	Per Cent of Share Volume
New York	82.60	64.28
American	10.58	26.13
Combined	93.18	90.41
Boston	.50	.31
Chicago Board of Trade*	–	–
Cincinnati	.07	.04
Detroit	.38	.32
Midwest	2.76	2.18
National*	–	–
Pacific Coast	2.00	3.52
Philadelphia-Baltimore	1.04	.80
Pittsburgh	.06	.05
Salt Lake	.00	.97
San Francisco Mining	.00	1.00
Spokane	.01	.40
Combined	6.82	9.59

* Inactive in 1961.
Source: SEC, *Statistical Bulletin,* February, 1962, p. 10.

It will be noted that the New York Stock Exchange is by far the most important organized market in the country. It accounted for 83 per cent of the dollar volume of stock sales and 64 per cent of the share volume in 1961. The American Stock Exchange accounted for 11 per cent of the dollar volume and 26 per cent of the share volume of stock sales in that year. The rather high ratio of share volume on this exchange reflects low average prices for the shares traded on it. The two major exchanges, therefore, accounted for 93 per cent of the dollar volume and 90 per cent of the share volume in stock sales on all registered exchanges.

The Midwest Stock Exchange clearly was the most active of the regional exchanges. In 1961 it accounted for 2.8 per cent of the dollar volume on all exchanges. Some of the other regional exchanges did an immense volume of business on a share basis because many low-priced or "penny stock" issues traded. The aggregate dollar volume was low. This was particularly true of the Salt Lake Stock Exchange and the San Francisco Mining Exchange.

Over the last several decades there has been no indication that any one securities exchange was growing more rapidly in importance than others. The major New York exchanges continue to dominate the market, but their share of the market has been very stable over the years.

Over-the-Counter Market. The over-the-counter market is that vast, informally organized market which handles securities sales off the organized exchanges. Over 5,500 brokers and dealers were registered with the SEC to do business in this market in 1961.[2] A number of unregistered individuals and firms also were active.

There are no data to show the dollar or share volume of business done in this market. It has been estimated, however, that more than 40,000 stock and bond issues are traded in this market in a year and that probably 16,000 issues are traded in any three-month period.

The market clearly accounts for about two-thirds of all security resales in this country. Practically 100 per cent of all sales of federal, state, and municipal obligations are handled in it. It accounts for about four-fifths of all corporate bond sales and perhaps one-third of all stock sales. Although it is primarily a market for stock issues not listed on organized exchanges, a substantial volume of business is done in these issues also.

STOCKHOLDERS

Number. Until 1952 reliable data on the number of stockholders in the United States were not available. In 1951, however, the New York Stock Exchange employed a well-know research organization to conduct a study and provide a reasonably sound estimate of their number. The results were published in 1952.[3] Since then the Exchange has conducted its own censuses through sampling. Reports were published in 1957, 1960, and 1962.[4]

There are two kinds of data on shareownership. One is the number of book stockholders. This includes the total number of names that appear on the stock record books of all corporations. In this number, if Mr. A

[2] *Twenty-Seventh Annual Report of the SEC*, 1961, p. 74.

[3] Lewis H. Kimmel, *Share Ownership in the United States* (Washington, D.C.: The Brookings Institution, 1952).

[4] *1956 Census of Shareowners* (New York: New York Stock Exchange, 1957); *Shareownership in America: 1959* (New York: New York Stock Exchange, 1960); *1962 Census of Shareowners in America* (New York: New York Stock Exchange, 1962).

owns stock in five companies his name is counted five times. Obviously, a large amount of duplication arises if a simple count of names on the stock record books is used as a count of stockholders. The studies referred to above employed methods that permitted estimates of the unduplicated number of shareowners, or the number of individual shareholders.

The number thus obtained has risen sharply over the years studied. It was 6.5 million in 1951, 8.6 million in 1956, 12.5 million in 1959, and 17.0 million in 1962. The very substantial spread of interest in stocks during the decade of the 1950's is clearly indicated. The number of shareholders nearly tripled in the decade covered.

The number of book stockholders, for comparison, was 30.3 million in 1951 and 45.5 million in 1962. The "average" shareowner—a nebulous notion—held shares of 4.7 issues in the earlier year and 3.4 issues in the later year. The decline in this number reflects the great number of new shareowners holding stock in one or two issues.

These numbers are estimates of shareownership in "public companies," those with at least one stock issue listed on a national stock exchange or with stock outstanding in the hands of at least 300 owners. A substantial additional number of persons hold stock in corporations excluded from this count, but the marketability of their stock is questionable and thus not counted.

General Characteristics.[5] These New York Stock Exchange studies also yield information about shareowners. In 1962 two-thirds of them owned at least one stock traded on the New York Stock Exchange; another fifth owned stock traded on one of the other exchanges or over-the-counter but did not own any listed on the New York Stock Exchange; and the remainder, 2,165,000, owned only investment company shares.

One out of six adults in the United States owned stock in 1962. The median age—half the shareowners were older, half younger—was forty-eight. A larger proportion of people aged forty-five to fifty-four owned stock than did those in other age classifications. The next highest ratios of ownership were in the age groups above this one, fifty-five to sixty-four and sixty-five or older. New shareholders were younger; the median age was thirty-nine. Shareownership, however, was clearly a feature of the middle and later years of life.

There is a definite correlation between education and stock ownership. The percentage of groups defined by the amount of education the members had increases sharply with the number of years of schooling. This has been persistently true through the years covered by these studies. Only a small proportion of people who did not finish high school own stocks. The percentage is very much larger for those who attended

[5] *Ibid.* Based primarily on the 1962 study.

college. It is still larger for those who completed at least four years of college or university training.

A distinct relationship between occupation and shareownership is also apparent. Business proprietors and managers show a very high proportion of shareholding. More than one in four owns some stock. Very nearly as great a ratio of professional and semiprofessional people have chosen this investment medium also. Over one-fifth of clerical and sales personnel own stock. One-half as great a percentage of the persons in the classifications of non-employed adult men (including retired persons) and housewives or non-employed women own stock The lowest ratio of ownership, 1.4 per cent, is found among farmers and farm workers. Only slightly higher percentages characterize manufacturing and service workers.

As these comments on shareownership and occupation suggest, a relationship also exists between place of residence and stockholding. Substantially higher proportions of people living in New England and the Middle Atlantic states own stock than is true elsewhere. The next highest ratios are found among people in the Pacific region and those living abroad. The ratio is lowest in the South Central states. New York State and California have the largest number of shareowners, but the ratio of shareownership to population is greater in the District of Columbia, Connecticut, Delaware, New Jersey, and Vermont. Stockholding is about equally frequent in cities of 500,000 or more and cities of 100,000 to 500,000. It is slightly less frequent in cities of smaller size, but the figures remain substantially greater than those for rural areas. The proportion in large cities of population owning stock is highest in San Francisco, followed by Pittsburgh, and then by St. Louis, Cincinnati, Baltimore, and Washington, D.C.

Women outnumber men as shareholders. However, since they also outnumber men in the total population, it is interesting to note that slightly higher percentages of men than women own stock. There has been an increase in shareownership by women over the years. The 1951 study indicated slightly less numbers of women than of men shareholders. In 1962 direct ownership of shares was greater for men than for women; the former held 24 per cent and the latter held 19 per cent of the outstanding stock of public corporations. Another 7 per cent was held in joint accounts.

These data for direct ownership indicate that half the outstanding shares of public corporations are owned by individuals. The other half is held by foreigners and institutional investors: fiduciaries, brokers and dealers, nominees, and other institutions. It is estimated that 120,000,000 people own stock indirectly through claims on institutions.

Household income is another factor related to shareownership. Most shareholders are in the $5,000 to $7,500 income group. The proportion of people in higher income groups who invest in stock is substantially greater, however, than for the group just mentioned. Nearly one of two persons in households where income is $25,000 or more invests in stock. The ratio rises with income from one in forty for the group with incomes under $3,000 to the one-to-two ratio.

Other investments usually are made by stock owners. In 1962 the New York Stock Exchange study showed that stockholders generally had funds invested in other ways. Of the total, 87 per cent had life insurance, 86 per cent had savings accounts, 77 per cent owned their homes, 56 per cent held U. S. Government savings bonds, and 50 per cent had equities in pension funds.

Reasons for Stock Ownership. The New York Stock Exchange carried out surveys in 1954 and 1959 to gain more insight into the way people thought about stock ownership.[6] Among stockholders, the advantages of stock ownership were placed in the following order: long-term capital gains, good dividends, good to have when general prices are going up, and opportunity for a quick profit. They indicated strongly a belief that common stock provided good protection against inflation.

Adults who did not own stock reversed the order of the advantages and said they didn't know whether common stock provided good protection against inflation.

The answers from stockholders suggest that about equal numbers seek capital gains, good dividends, or an inflation hedge. Most of them would invest more money—if they had it—in stock, but a substantial fraction indicated a preference for fixed value investment as a next use of funds.

A reason why more people do not own stock is apparent from the responses of non-owners. Four-fifths of them were unable to say what common stock was, two-thirds of them did not wish to know more than they did about common stock, and only two-fifths of them thought that more people should own common stock. Ninety per cent had never talked to a broker. A smaller proportion invested in other kinds of securities or savings than was true of the stock owner group. However, within the large group of people who did not own stock there was a subgroup, of about 13 million, who did evince interest and did indicate that when they could they would invest in stock. Within this subgroup the concept of stock ownership as a way to quick profit was less widely

---

[6] *The Public Speaks to the Exchange Community* (New York: New York Stock Exchange, 1955); *The Investors of Tomorrow* (New York: New York Stock Exchange, 1960).

held than in the non-owner group as a whole. They placed more stress than the others on good dividends and the advantage of stock owner-ship when general prices go up. Risk of losing money, irregularity of dividend income, and low yield are undoubtedly concepts that affect the attitudes of the non-owner group. Perhaps the whole matter of why some individuals prefer other investments to common stock can be summed up by saying that they believe these other investments are safer and they know more about them.

Trading Practices. Some individual shareholders are traders, inter-ested only in short-term profits, while others buy and hold stocks for long periods of time. In a study of public transactions in September, 1961, the New York Stock Exchange found that 9.5 per cent of the public transactions were closed out within thirty days; 28.5 per cent, between thirty days and six months; and 62.0 per cent, sometime after six months had passed.[7] Any transaction closed out in a period only slightly over six months may be a speculative transaction. The purpose for the invest-ment may be gain from price action rather than fundamental interest in the underlying corporate prospects. The figures above, unfortunately, do not indicate how large a proportion of the transactions were closed out within a short period after six months had passed and the long-term capital gain provision of the income tax regulations had become a factor in the investor's decisions. Nevertheless, the large proportion of the transactions covering the longer period suggests that a good deal of investor interest is directed to acquiring securities to hold for investment returns through dividends and eventual capital gains. This seems more likely because of the order of reasons for owning stock discussed above. The first three such reasons fit long-term investment. The proportion of trading on very short turnover is clearly low.

Institutional Stockholders. About half the stock of publicly owned corporations is held by institutional investors. Some of this, to be sure, is held by trustees for funds established by individuals or by firms acting as custodians for securities owned by their clients. Other institutions—such as insurance companies, pension funds, mutual savings banks, invest-ment companies, and common trust funds—that own stock provide indirect ownership to individual policy holders, account holders, shareholders, or trustors. Some idea of the distribution of stockholdings among different kinds of institutional investors is given by the data of Table 1–2. Supple-mentary data in a memorandum from the New York Stock Exchange indicates that the largest holdings in the "financial institutions and other institutions" class in an earlier year, 1959, were those of investment com-

---

[7] *Eleventh Public Transaction Study, September 13, 1961* (New York: New York Stock Exchange, 1961), p. 4.

panies. Next in importance, and increasing rapidly, were those of non-insured corporate pension funds. Third were holdings of a group of non-profit organizations, such as university and college endowment funds and foundations. Stockholdings of life insurance companies, common trust funds, and mutual savings banks are relatively small. This order of commitment to stock ownership by institution investors probably remained true for 1962.

Table 1–2. Distribution of Stock Ownership in the United States, Publicly Owned Companies, 1962

Type of Holder	Per Cent of Total Shares Outstanding
Individuals and joint accounts	52.0
Financial institutions and other institutions	17.5
Nominees	13.7
Brokers and dealers	7.6
Fiduciary individuals	4.0
Fiduciary institutions	2.6
Foreign citizens and institutions	2.6
Total	100.0

Source: *1962 Census of Shareowners in America* (New York: New York Stock Exchange, 1962), p. 36.

The activities of institutional investors also are significant in trading volume. The transactions studies referred to above show that about one-fourth of the volume of transactions on the New York Stock Exchange on the days studied over the past decade involved institutional buyers and sellers. More than half this volume arose from transactions of commercial banks and investment companies.

POPULAR STOCKS

Blue Chips. Purchasers of stock vary in their preferences. Some favor the so-called "blue chips," a term doubtless borrowed long ago from the gambling tables. These stocks are the general favorites of the more conservative type of individual or institution. They are the choicest of issues. Enjoying a broad and active market, they are the issues of strong and stable companies, which enjoy long earnings and dividend records. Usually the leaders in their respective fields, their earning power is protected by such things as excellent management, fine patents, valuable goodwill, good products, extensive markets, and a continuous growth in demand for their goods or services. The more stable the company and the less subject to cyclical fluctuations, the better it qualifies for this category.

The high popularity enjoyed by these stocks with both individuals and investors has one decided disadvantage. They sell at very high prices and at very low yields.

Growth Stocks. One of the most popular stock categories in recent years is growth stocks. These are stocks that have shown the ability to grow much more rapidly over a period of time than the average issue, often twice as rapidly. Although characterized by low yields, their high rate of appreciation makes them especially popular with institutions and with those investors who prefer appreciation to income. They are extensively treated in Chapter 31.

Traders on the Exchange. There are many lists of stocks popular with American securityholders. The first such list to be considered here is that of buyers and traders of stocks listed on the New York Stock Exchange. Over a long period of time, going back to 1917, four such stocks have been outstanding. In order of importance, they rank as follows: United States Steel, General Motors, Radio Corporation of America, and New York Central. Year after year these stocks come close to the top of the list of market leaders on that exchange.

Small Stockholders. Perhaps the best way to indicate the preferences of small stockholders is to list the corporations that have the largest number of stockholders. This list changes, of course, from time to time. The ten companies listed on the New York Stock Exchange with the greatest number of stockholders in 1962 were, in descending order: American Telephone and Telegraph, General Motors, Standard Oil Company (New Jersey), General Electric, General Telephone & Electronics, United States Steel, Ford, Bethlehem Steel, Socony Mobil, and du Pont. American Telephone and Telegraph had more than 2 million shareholders.

Monthly Investment Plan. The monthly investment plan, sponsored by the New York Stock Exchange and its member firms, is a means of encouraging potential stockholders to buy stocks with regular monthly or quarterly payments. It is described more fully in Chapter 31. The ten most popular stocks for the investors using the investment plan in November, 1961, were, in descending order: General Motors, International Business Machines, American Telephone and Telegraph, General Electric, Minnesota Mining & Manufacturing, Dow Chemical, Tri-Continental, Standard Oil Company (New Jersey), General Telephone & Electronics, and Pfizer.

Investment Institutions. At regular intervals, a list of the stocks most popular with one thousand or more leading investment institutions and funds is published. The ten leading stocks of these institutional owners in 1961 were, in descending order: Standard Oil Company (New Jersey),

General Motors, General Electric, American Telephone and Telegraph, du Pont, Texas Company, Union Carbide, United States Steel, Philips Petroleum, and Socony Mobil. The duplication in these three lists of the popular stock issues is clear.

BONDHOLDERS

Number. Unfortunately, there are no recent estimates on the number of bondholders in the United States, except for savings bonds. The number of individuals who own bonds, exclusive of federal obligations, was estimated for 1948 at six million by the Federal Reserve Board.[8] Some forty million persons held Series E savings bonds at the close of 1954.[9] It is evident, therefore, that more individuals own bonds than stocks. Even these figures are dwarfed by the ownership of insurance policies. About 115 million Americans held life insurance policies in 1959.[10]

Institutional Ownership. While most stocks are owned by individuals, rather than institutions, the reverse is true for bonds, disregarding Series E savings bonds. Approximately three-fourths of the federal debt is held by commercial banks, non-bank private associations and corporations, United States Government agencies, Federal Reserve Banks, and state and local governments.

An immense volume of non-federal bonds is held by life insurance companies, savings banks, commercial banks, endowed institutions, foundations, investment companies, and fire and casualty insurance companies. Indirectly, millions of individuals have an interest in these obligations because of ownership of checking accounts, life insurance policies, saving accounts, shares of investment institutions, and the like, as well as through employment by these institutions.

Both directly and indirectly, therefore, the American nation has a vast interest in stocks and bonds, their market value, and their income.

---

[8] *Survey of Consumer Finances,* 1948, p. 10.
[9] *The New York Times,* May 1, 1956.
[10] American Bankers Association, *Statistics on the Savings Market, 1960,* p. 10.

2

Corporate Securities

Investors and brokers surely should know the basic characteristics of the securities available in the market. The analysis of investments and of investment portfolios is complex. Well-informed advisors or investors spend years in mastering these subjects. This chapter can serve only as an introduction to a fascinating field. It can, however, be a basis for understanding the fundamental nature of the securities that investors may buy and from ownership of which they may profit.

CORPORATION FINANCE

The stock market is a market for corporate securities. The rights of ownership in other forms of business organization are not marketable in the same sense. Other forms of organization, the United States government and municipalities for example, supply bonds to the securities markets, but they do not issue stock. Corporation finance, then, is significant in the stock market. An understanding of securities is increased by an understanding of corporate finance. In the next several paragraphs an outline of this subject is sketched in broad strokes. More complete discussion is left to other texts and other times.[1] Also in this chapter, however, is detailed description of different types of securities and their investment merits.

Requirements for Funds. Business activity depends on the availability of goods and services under the control of individual business managements. Raw materials and services with which to produce goods for sale

[1] For example: Harry G. Guthmann and Herbert E. Dougall, *Corporate Financial Policy* (4th ed.; Englewood Cliffs, N.J.: Prentice-Hall, Inc., 1962); R. Miller Upton and Bion B. Howard, *Introduction to Business Finance* (New York: McGraw-Hill Book Co., Inc., 1953).

13

are purchased, for the most part, as they are needed. The money received from sale of goods is used to pay for the additional raw materials and services as they are purchased. In a successful business the flow of funds from sales matches most requirements for funds. Goods and services are combined in finished products. The finished goods are sold, receivables are collected, and the money is used to buy more goods and services for production of more finished goods.

In contrast, however, some of the goods needed by business concerns must be stockpiled. To make sales, for example, an inventory of products usually must be on hand so that deliveries may be made. To produce requiries inventories of raw materials and of goods in the process of manufacture. The process of manufacture requires tools, equipment, machinery, transportation facilities, and buildings. The useful life of these may extend over many years. Sales are made almost universally on credit, and a group of receivables in process of collection must be held by the business concern pending collection. Good sense requires the holding of a certain amount of cash, the universal form of purchasing power, for use as unexpected events occur and unexpected needs for funds arise. This reason for holding cash is reinforced by conventions in relationships between business concerns and their creditors. Thus, the process of business imposes the need to acquire and maintain the level of investment in assets: cash, accounts receivable, inventory, plant and equipment. The extent of the requirement for investment in assets by business concerns is indicated in the left-hand column on the following balance sheet, which is *typical* in the sense that it is a combined balance sheet for all United States manufacturing corporations at the end of the year, 1961.[2]

Two accounts, "Other current assets" and "Other non-current assets" represent for the most part special claims on other individuals or businesses. These claims may have arisen in the process of doing business but some of them arise owing to special circumstances in individual concerns.

The amount of the plant, property, and equipment account is reduced by the reserves for depreciation and depletion before the net investment is shown in the column of totals. These reserves are an accumulation of charges that companies have made in past periods against the income they derived from sales of the products made in these plants and with this equipment. The charge is one included in the price customers pay for the products of the manufacturers to compensate for the use of these assets in the production process. Eventually, of course, over a number

[2] Federal Trade Commission–Securities and Exchange Commission, *Quarterly Financial Report for Manufacturing Corporations, Fourth Quarter, 1961* (Washington, D.C.: Government Printing Office, 1962).

United States Manufacturing Corporations, Balance Sheet, December 31, 1961, (in millions of dollars)

Cash	$ 28,083	Trade accounts and		
Accounts Receivable	44,921	notes		$ 24,697
Inventories	62,800	Bank loans		7,681
Other current assets	6,795	Accrued taxes		9,706
Total current		Current portion of		
assets	$142,599	long-term debt		2,325
Plant, property, and		Other current		
equipment	$206,824	liabilities		13,047
Reserves for depreci-		Total current		
ation and depletion	101,122 $105,702	liabilities		57,456
Other non-current		Long-term debt		33,934
assets	23,174	Other non-current		
		liabilities		4,238
		Total liabilities.		$ 95,628
		Net worth:		
		Capital stock		
		accounts	$ 68,540	
		Unclassified		
		reserves	1,982	
		Retained earnings		
		and reserves	105,325	
		Total net		
		worth and		$175,847
Total assets	$271,475	liabilities		$271,475

of years the full cost of individual assets is met by these charges against income. Maintenance of productive capacity requires the continuing expenditure of money to buy new plant, property, and equipment. Annual requirements for such purchases almost equal annual charges of cost against income. The ratio of the accumulation of charges under the listing "Reserves . . ." to the original cost figures accumulated in the property accounts is quite stable through time. On the average, United States manufacturers have plant, property, and equipment investments about equal to one-half the purchase price of the items on their accounting records. New items are continuously added, and old items are retired as they are paid for by the customers in successful businesses. The maintenance of a net investment in plant, property, and equipment, however, provides a continuing requirement for funds.

Sources of Funds. The stockpiling of goods requires the use of funds, as the amounts invested in assets indicate. Corporate management, in general, has three types of sources from which it can obtain funds: (1) short-term creditors, (2) long-term creditors, and (3) owners.

The principal kinds of short-term credit are shown by the items in the current liability section, in the right-hand column, of the balance sheet above. The first is "Trade accounts and notes." Just as most concerns sell to their customers on credit terms, they buy on such terms. Nearly all business concerns have trade credit, or accounts payable, on their books at any given time. Further credit is obtained by borrowing from financial institutions—commercial banks, commercial finance companies—and the use of this source is shown above as "Bank loans" and as part of "Other current liabilities." The present conventions in tax accounting show another source of short-term credit to be the governments that wait a short time to receive payments of taxes based on current incomes earned by individual concerns. The balance sheet shows that some credit is extended in other ways but the great significance of trade credit, borrowing, and tax accrual is clear. To the extent that businesses obtain these kinds of credit, the need to draw on other sources is reduced. However, the terms used for trade credit, the conventions used by lenders, and the provisions of tax law make it unusual for the amounts of funds supplied by these sources to become large. The amounts of trade and tax credit arise automatically from the processes of doing business and are not open to much modification by management decision. Borrowing is affected more by management, but creditors are loath to grant short-term credits in large amounts. For United States manufacturing corporations in 1961 the sum of the short-term liabilities was 40 per cent of the current asset requirements and a little more than 21 per cent of the total asset requirements.

The balance of funds is obtained on long terms. The sources of long-term loans are, again, the financial institutions—commercial banks, commercial finance companies, insurance companies—and, to a small degree, individual investors. Some of the long-term obligations of corporations are bought and sold in the securities markets, but the proportion is small. Most of the transactions involve direct negotiation with one lending institution or a small group of them. The availability in the market of some credit instruments of corporations is a reason, however, for describing them in more detail later in this chapter. The proportion of funds obtained through long-term credit extended to the United States manufacturing corporations in 1961 was 14 per cent of total asset requirements. The proportion of total liabilities, of all credit sources, was 35 per cent.

The investment by owners, the net worth of the business concerns, is as long term as business itself. It is the first source to be drawn on at the formation of a corporation and the last to be compensated if the concern is liquidated and dissolved. The capital stocks of corporations are the instruments of greatest interest in the stock market. In 1961 the owners' interest in United States manufacturing corporations supplied 65 per cent of the funds needed to meet asset requirements. The owners supplied two dollars for each dollar obtained from a credit source.

Corporate Financial Policy. A principal problem for financial management of a corporation is determination of the amounts and kinds of long-term securities and of short-term borrowings to use and the ratio to be maintained between debt and ownership equity. The policies adopted by individual managements affect the position of stockholders. Choice among the sources depends on concepts of risk, income, and control. From the point of view of corporate management and stockholders, debt increases risk but also increases income and control. Ownership equity decreases each of them.

Some ratio between debt and equity—and a ratio that may be expected to differ among management groups—yields enhanced income and control but not sufficiently to overcome the increased risk of added debt. For businesses that are inherently risky, such as the machine tool, textile, or mining industries, the voluntary use of any debt is nonsense. For others, particularly the highly stable industries like finance, as much debt may be incurred as creditors are willing to permit. To the stockholder the significant fact is the appropriateness of the balance of debt to equity chosen by the management of a firm in which he holds stock. His expectation of reward is affected by the willingness to accept risk by using credit sources so long as the added risk is adequately compensated by added income.

A special case of decision about use of ownership funds arises in successful businesses. A source of funds mentioned above but not fully discussed is the customer. As customers buy and pay for goods they provide funds in excess of the amounts currently disbursed to pay for services and raw materials. This excess equals approximately the net profit of the business. Once earned, these funds are part of the ownership equity, the net worth of the business. The managers may choose to retain them and increase the proportionate use of ownership investment or disburse them as dividends, or elect some combination. The kind of choices made among the sources will affect this decision.

Management may decide, for example, that growth should be financed with equity funds. It may do so by retaining the funds obtained from successful sale of products or by issuing additional stock. Let us consider a simplified illustration. A concern is operating with a 10 per cent per year return on net worth. Net worth equals two-thirds of the total asset requirements. Growth of total assets to sustain increased levels of business is expected to be 3 per cent per year—the average level of growth for the economy over the last several decades. The management of this concern could choose to limit dividends to 5½ per cent on net worth and retain funds sufficient to finance the growth. It might choose, however, to pay a larger dividend—for example, 10 per cent on net worth —and finance the growth by new issues of stock. The larger dividend

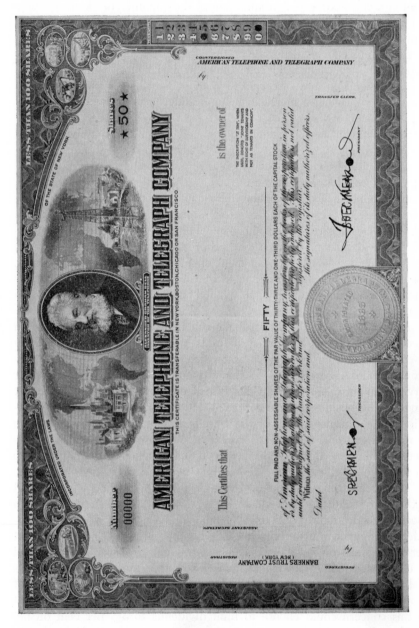

Fig. 2–1. A common stock certificate.

would enhance the willingness of the market to acquire the additional stock. International Business Machines and American Telephone and Telegraph provide interesting contrasts on this point. International Business Machines has chosen to finance growth almost entirely by retention of earnings and without new issues of stock; American Telephone and Telegraph has chosen to pay out annually a very high proportion of earnings and finance growth almost exclusively through new issues of stock.

In summary, then, corporation finance requires decisions about (1) the amounts of funds that must be invested in assets to permit successful operation of a concern, (2) the amounts and kinds of sources from which to obtain the total sum required, and (3) the policy for management of funds generated internally through the operation of the business. These sets of decisions involve concepts of risk, income, and control. The management and the stockholders must decide whether the choice among the wide range of opportunities to draw funds from creditor and owner institutions or individuals is appropriate to the concern. To appreciate the breadth of choice more fully and the nature of the instruments that are traded in the stock market, the features of stock and debt contracts are considered in more detail in the following paragraphs.

COMMON STOCKS

Nature. All corporations issue common stock. It is the first security to be issued and the last to be retired. A corporation must have common stock outstanding to represent the chief ownership of the company. Common stock has the greatest management control over the company. It has the last claim on earnings; all other securities must be paid first. While the existence of senior securities increases the risk, it also enhances the possibility of profit, since other obligations generally have fixed claims and do not participate in earnings over and above such claims. Common stock has the last claim on assets. Although this risk may be shared equally with the preferred stock in some cases, no other security holder has a junior claim on assets.

Transfer of Stock. Stock certificates issued by the company represent the number of shares owned by stockholders. These certificates are evidence of ownership and indicate the number of shares (Fig. 2–1). When a stockholder buys a certain number of shares he is entitled to such a certificate. The purchase is recorded on a stock record book of the transfer agent, who notes the number of shares and the new owner. The certificate of the former stockholder is then canceled. The new certificate then goes to a registry office or registrar which ordinarily is another bank or trust company specializing in business of this kind. The registrar checks the entire transaction to see that the transfer office has made no error. In due time the new security owner receives his new certificate. The expense of the transfer is always borne by the corporation.

This procedure is used by the large companies whose securities are listed. The small company may be its own transfer agent and have no registrar.

Treasury Stock. The average investor is not much concerned with treasury stock. This is stock that has been issued as fully paid and non-assessable and has come back into the company treasury in some manner. It is entirely different from other common stock in that it has no voting power; it receives no dividends; it can be sold at any price by the company; it can be exchanged for other assets or given away, as for bonus payments. It may be held in the treasury indefinitely, reissued to the public, or retired. It is acquired sometimes by purchase. In such cases the company may have had an excess of uninvested cash, or it may have wanted to increase the price of the stock in the market. It may have been purchased to buy out owners of a close corporation or to be distributed among officers and employees. In other cases the stock may have been donated to the company by stockholders for the purpose of raising additional working capital. This was especially true in earlier days before non-par stock became a common method of financing. Once treasury stock is reissued it takes on the identical characteristics of the other outstanding shares.

Par Value Stock. The par value of a stock is a face value. The certificate states on its face that the stock has a par value; for example, $100. The American Telephone and Telegraph certificate in Figure 2–1 shows it to have a par value of $33⅓ per share. The original purpose of par value was to insure that the company issued the stock for cash, services, or property equivalent in amount. The assets received were considered part of a sort of trust fund which the directors were to protect for the stockholders. In actual practice this seldom worked out in any meaningful way. The term "par value" was found to have less and less significance as time passed. Par value today means in practice only two things: first, it places a lower limit on the price at which new shares may be issued, and second, it may restrict dividend payment, if there is a deficit in earned surplus.

Par value is likely to lead to a fallacious concept of stock value in that the assets of the company may be valued either too high or too low in relation to their economic worth and thus distort the meaning of the par value assigned to the offsetting stock. In many cases par value does not represent the amount paid in by the original stockholders or any other significant fact. Earnings or losses increase or reduce the market value of stock almost as soon as it is issued. The par value figure, therefore, is an artificial price tag that investors do not accept as a measure of worth.

The par value attached today to various classes of stocks varies considerably. Among the principal railroad stocks \$100, \$50, and \$25 are common.[3] No principal industrial or utility common stock carries a \$100 par value. Among the utilities \$10 and \$5 are usual; among the industrials \$1 par value is most often chosen. Many odd par values now exist. Examples include such unusual figures as \$0.16⅔, \$0.40, \$8.25, \$14²⁄₇, and \$33⅓.

Table 2–1 shows the lack of relationship between par and market values for an arbitrary selection of ten stocks traded in 1961.

Table 2–1. Comparison of Par, Book, and Market Values for Selected Stocks, 1961

Company	Par Value	Approximate Book Value at End of Year, 1961	Market Range, 1961
American Motors Corp.	1.67	12	17⅜– 15⅛
Armour & Co.	5.00	37	53⅝– 37¾
Chicago & North Western Ry.	No	222	26¼– 13¾
Chrysler Corp.	25.00	81	57⅝– 37⅜
Commonwealth Edison	12.50	18	50⅜– 34⅛
Federated Department Stores	1.25	15	59½– 34¾
First National Bank of Boston	12.50	54	103½– 61⅝
International Business Machines	5.00	43	607 –387
United Fruit Co.	No	34	29¼– 17¼
United States Steel Corp.	16.67	57	91¼– 75¼

Source: Standard & Poor's, *Stock Guide,* April, 1962; *Value Line Investment Service* (as published in June, 1962).

Book Value. Some investors are concerned with the book value of their stocks. Book value may be defined as the stated value of assets behind each share of stock. It can be found by adding the stated value of the common stock on the company's balance sheet to the surplus and dividing by the number of common shares. The concept of book value formerly received much attention from investors who believed that the only safe common stock was one well secured by a substantial volume of assets. The depression of the 1930's largely destroyed confidence in any remaining fragments of this theory, since many large and respected companies entered the depression with excellent book values only to find that their stock declined to a fraction of book value. This was par-

[3] "Principal" in this chapter in this context means the stocks chosen for Standard & Poor's *Stock Guide,* August, 1961.

ticularly true of railroads. Today the shrewd investor is more interested in earning power per share, since it is that alone which makes dividends possible, not the book value of assets.

Book, par, and market value may coincide momentarily when the first issue of stock is made, provided the stock is transferred for assets placed on the books at values precisely equal to par. This is in fact an unlikely event. Book and market values should be equal when stock is issued, but equivalence with a par value is rare. Once issued, the market value is influenced by investor opinions about the future; book value reflects only the past. There is no reason to assume that equivalence of these values will then exist. In a few instances, such as electric public utility and bank stock issues, the near future for income is related closely to the present book value of the stock because there are practical limitations in law or custom enforcing such a relationship. Even so, the market may value longer-term forecasts and separate book and market values.

Table 2–1 illustrates the lack of relationship in a selected group of issues. Extremes are found in the Chicago & North Western Railway issue, for which market is 10 per cent of book, and the International Business Machines issue, for which market is 15 times book. Book values, therefore, may be ignored by investors. Forecasts of earnings and dividends are more significant. Some investors, however, prefer to take book value into account in an analysis. Their hypothesis is simply that whatever it is about the mixture of assets that produces the earnings, this will continue to be related to the amount of assets. Thus, change in book value is evidence of changed ability to earn and, more particularly, an upward trend in book value provides a reason for forecasting an upward trend in earnings. This hypothesis is not proved but, as one of a number that an analyst may hold, it need not be ignored.

No-Par Stock. No-par stock is stock without face value. It was first legalized in this country by New York in 1912, after many years of agitation for its use. During the 1920's it became extremely popular; 80 to 90 per cent of the new industrial and public utility issues were of this type. In 1929 about 40 per cent of all stocks, other than railroad, on the New York Stock Exchange were of this type. After 1930 this type of stock declined in popularity as companies sought to cut down on capitalization and to reduce transfer taxes for their stockholders. In 1961 about 10 per cent of all principal industrial common stocks were of the no-par type. The ratio for railroads was 45 per cent; for public utilities, 22 per cent.

No-par stocks are of two types. The first is the true no-par type, which may be issued at any price and whose value for balance sheet purposes may be fixed by the directors. The other is the type which the law requires must be issued at a certain minimum figure and must be listed on the balance sheet with a minimum stated value, which is low, $1 being a common figure. In this latter type no face value is stated on the stock certificate, but the law requires that it must nevertheless be sold at or above a certain minimum.

The main advantage to a company issuing a no-par stock is flexibility in pricing. It can be sold at any price. Other advantages include some conformity to actual facts, since we have seen that par value has little real significance; a warning to purchasers to investigate real values; and a limitation of the stockholder's liability to the subscription price. The corporation directors sometimes become involved in accounting difficulties because of the faint dividing line between capital and surplus which results from no-par stock financing. For example, a company may sell a no-par share for $20 and, if it sees fit, place $1 per share in the capital stock account and $19 in paid-in surplus. This tends to mislead stockholders as to the true situation, and even directors may be tempted to charge dividends against this surplus.

From the stockholder's point of view, there is little difference between par value and no-par value stocks. No-par stocks can be just as good or worthless as any par value stocks.

Classified Common Stock. Infrequently, the investor will come across classified common stocks. These are usually called Class A or Class B stocks. This means that the company has divided its common stock into two classes. The Class A stock is sold to the public, and the Class B stock is usually retained by the management or controlling stockholders.

Historically, Class A stock was without voting power. It usually had a preference over Class B as to dividends. This preference was cumulative and the Class A might have rights to further participation in additional dividends if they were declared. Often the stock was callable. Under these circumstances the Class B stock held voting control and the rights to the residual values of the business. It provided a device by which a relatively small investment by a group of promoters could lay claim to the substantial gains to be obtained from success in a new venture.

Classified common stock became very popular in the 1920's with investment bankers because it enabled them to retain complete control over a company and yet to raise money from outside interests. It was popular with management for the same reason. It was a new idea and possessed sales appeal. The stockholder, who was not particularly concerned with voting rights, thought the stock attractive in that it appeared to have the speculative possibilities of a common stock and at the same time the stability of a preferred stock. As a matter of fact, it did have many of the characteristics of a weak preferred issue.

A storm of criticism arose against this type of stock in the mid-1920's. It was argued that such issues gave the management complete control with little or no investment. It gave power without responsibility, and this was true in many cases. In 1924 the New York Stock Exchange refused to list any more classified common stocks. Because of this fact and the widespread criticism which continued to grow, the stock declined in popularity. Many companies which formerly issued the stock recapitalized, eliminated such issues, and went back to the conventional type of common stock.

Thus, the picture has changed today. Only a few classified common issues exist. Stock without voting power is not listed. Recent issues of Class A stock have a slight preference over Class B stock—cash dividends may be paid to Class A without payment to the B stock, but not vice versa. Differences in assigned par values or in the relative number of shares may give voting control to the Class B, but most issues have been created to limit dividend payout for management. In other respects the claims of the two series are identical.

The stockholder, in buying a classified common stock, will do well to examine carefully its characteristics and preferences. The weight of investment opinion is that such stocks usually are not desirable.

Watered Stock. Common stock that has been issued without the company's receiving an honest equivalent of the par value in cash, services, or property is called "watered." Its value has been diluted. The term originated in the New York cattle trade, where—as the story goes— Daniel Drew, later a famous manipulator in stocks, made a practice of driving stock to the market without water, allowing them to consume salt with their feed, and afterward watering them heavily.

The issuing of watered stock was a common practice in many of the combinations in the period from 1875 to the early 1900's. All the common stock and much of the preferred stock of the United States Steel Corporation was watered when the company was organized in 1901.[4] The practice became infrequent in later years, partly because of sounder financial practices, partly because of government regulations, and partly because the use of low- or no-par stock made such a practice unnecessary.

At one time the use of watered stock was severely condemned. It was believed to be bad from the standpoint of corporation credit and bondholder protection. It was thought that it discriminated against public stockholders, since the watered stock usually went to favored "insiders." The public outcry was loudest, however, in the field of pricing. It was believed that watered stock meant high prices for goods and

---

[4] Eliot Jones, *The Trust Problem in the United States* (New York: The Macmillan Co., 1921), p. 186.

services of those corporations, which would be compelled to pay large dividends on the overcapitalized structure. But this idea of high prices could not stand up under theoretical analysis, however popular it might have been in the public press. A corporation charges what it can get regardless of its capitalization.

Today the concept of watered stock is of little importance to stockholders. The value of a common stock is now judged by its earnings rather than by its book assets. Some of the best-secured common stocks of years ago have turned out to be great disappointments; the railroads have been conspicuous examples. On the other hand, corporations with apparently inadequate assets have made fine profits for their owners. Through excellent management, valuable patents, well-known brand names, skillful advertising campaigns, and other intangible factors, companies have returned large profits, regardless of the real or stated value of the assets.[5]

Stock Splits. A stock split occurs when a company divides its shares. Thus, a company with five million shares outstanding might divide its stock by two-for-one and increase the number to ten million. A stock split has no effect on the net worth of the company. A common way to split a stock is to reduce its par value. Thus, in 1961 H. J. Heinz Company split its stock three-for-one by reducing the par value from $25.00 to $8.33; stockholders retained the original certificates and received two additional shares for each old share owned. A split may also be accomplished by canceling outstanding no-par shares and issuing par value shares or by canceling par value shares and issuing no-par shares.

Stock splitting becomes very popular during periods of high stock prices, such as in the late 1920's and after World War II. Splits of two-for-one and three-for-one are the most popular types, but occasionally there are larger splits. There have been splits as high as 2,000-for-one in closed corporations desiring to offer stock in the public market.

Three chief purposes seem to dictate stock splits. The principal one is to reduce the market value of the stock. Many corporations dislike to have their issues sell above $100 and will split as soon as this level is exceeded, although a few companies will not split until their issues exceed the $200 level. The prevailing practice appears to be to split the stock so that its new value will range between $30 and $60, which is apparently a very popular price range for most stockholders. This reduction in market value makes the stock more marketable and frequently results in a substantial gain in the number of stockholders.

[5] For an extended discussion, see: Benjamin Graham and D. L. Dodd, *Security Analysis* (3d ed.; New York: McGraw-Hill Book Co., Inc., 1951).

Another reason for splitting a stock is to permit the company to pay additional dividends without increasing the dividend rate. Few companies like to pay high dividends per share. If the stock is split, moderate dividends can be paid, but the total payments can be substantially increased. This is a common occurrence. A final reason for splitting a stock is to prepare for future financing. Getting the stock down to a popular price level makes it more attractive when additional shares are sold under a privileged subscription.

Stock splits, theoretically, have no effect on stockholders, since each stockholder maintains the same equity in the company as before. Actually, he usually gains by an improvement in market price and an increase in total dividends received. Stock splits accompanied by dividend in-increase often have a bullish influence on stock prices.

Dividend Policies. Owners of common stock are greatly concerned over dividends paid. Many factors determine the amount of cash dividends paid by a particular company, such as its cash position, the stage of the business cycle, the age of the corporation, its need for new capital, its credit standing, competition, and its stability of earnings.

The amount of a company's net profits allocated to dividends varies greatly from corporation to corporation. Each company seems to be a law unto itself. In the same industry one company may be very generous; its closest competitor may be very conservative. During the 1920's it was a common practice for an industrial company to pay out about 70 per cent of its net earnings as dividends. For a period after World War II the ratio fell to slightly under 50 per cent. Corporations had great need for expansion capital in a period of inflation. More recently the ratio has returned to the levels characteristic of the 1920's.

A few companies such as American Telephone and Telegraph, pride themselves on a regular dividend policy. The same dividend is paid year after year. This policy, first popularized by United States Steel, was considered highly proper by many corporations in the 1920's. During the depression nearly all corporations dropped the practice as being unrealistic. Today dividends are paid on an interim basis, which means that they are determined by directors on the basis of current earnings and financial needs. If earnings rise, the dividend is increased; if they fall, the dividend is cut. A common practice is to pay three rather small dividends during the first three quarters of the year and to pay a substantial year-end dividend.

Stockholders need not be unduly concerned as to whether or not a company pays a regular dividend. The main thing is how much does the stockholder receive in dividends over a period of time. The regular dividend policy, however, has the effect of giving a better credit standing to the company's bonds and to its stock. By thus making the stock a more stable investment, its market price tends to increase and its yield to decrease. In other words, investors pay more for the stable or regular dividend policy.

Kinds of Dividends. Corporations distribute three kinds of dividends: cash, stock, and property. The cash dividends is by far the most important.

Stock dividends are issued in the stock of the company distributing the dividends. They may accompany cash dividends. A few companies distribute a small stock dividend along with the cash dividend and continue this policy for long periods. A stock dividend is accounted for by capitalizing the surplus of the company, which removes a certain sum from the surplus account and places it in the stock account. Stock dividends became popular in this country after the Supreme Court in 1920 declared them non-taxable for income tax purposes.

The chief purpose of a stock dividend is said to be conservation of the cash of the company while acknowledging to the stockholders that earnings are accumulating. This is questionable. The dividend has the effect of lowering the price per share of the stock, and may be used to reduce the amount of earnings and dividends per share shown in published reports. It may satisfy stockholders, who see large earnings but are not receiving correspondingly large cash dividends.

The rates on stock dividends range from one to more than 1000 per cent. Because they are so similar in nature to stock splits, the New York Stock Exchange has arbitrarily ruled that distributions under 25 per cent are to be accounted stock dividends.

A stock dividend has no effect on a stockholder. He owns the same percentage of the outstanding stock and he receives the same percentage of the dividends paid. His taxes are not increased. If he sells his additional stock, he is merely selling a part of his equity in the company. From a practical standpoint, he may be benefited by an increase in the total dividends received and by a subsequent rise in the value of his total holdings. He has been given the option to determine whether to have cash, from sale of the stock dividend shares, or to reinvest in the same company, by retaining the stock dividend shares.

Property dividends consist of real or personal property paid out by the company to stockholders. In nearly all cases, these dividends consist of securities held by the company for purposes of investment or control. In World War I many companies, overloaded with Liberty bonds, distributed these as property dividends. In the last 20 years a number of corporations have distributed property dividends in the form of common stocks because of the breakup of holding companies. The top companies owned stock in subsidiaries. When the holding company was broken up, such as under the Public Utility Holding Company Act of 1935, the stockholders received the stock of subsidiaries. A very famous example of a property dividend took place when the federal government required General Electric and Westinghouse to sever their relations with Radio Corporation. Stockholders in these two companies received stock in Radio Corporation on a pro rata basis.

Guaranteed Stock. There are a limited number of guaranteed common stocks on the market. These are typically found in the railroad field. They developed during the early years of railroading when large systems were being welded together. The parent company would take over a small line and turn it into its subsidiary. In doing so, it would guarantee the dividend rate on the stock of the subsidiary. The two roads were tied together by a lease or consolidation. The guaranteed stock then took on something of the characteristics of a preferred stock. The dividends became fixed charges of the operating company. Many such stocks sell on the same basis as preferred stocks and bonds, so great is their popularity with investors.

Stock Yields. The yields on common stock are of great importance to investors. This aspect is treated at length in Chapter 3.

Investment Merits. The investment merits of common stocks have long been a controversial subject in the field of finance. On the one hand, there are authorities who contend that common stocks should never be considered as investments, but only as speculations.[6] This view is supported by the thesis that an investment should possess safety of principal and stability of income, neither of which is possessed by the common stock.

There are others who contend that common stocks are the best of investments, since greater profits are made from them than from any other type of securities. Their higher yields and appreciation possibilities more than offset their admitted qualities of insecurity of principal and instability of return.

The chief motive for most stockholders in buying stocks is to obtain the appreciation from ownership; income is secondary. This is speculation—the hope of buying at a given price and later selling at a higher price. Technically, this is not investment in the traditional meaning of the word. It implies risk. Yet the purchase of the "safest" bonds also subjects the holder to risk, which in periods of inflation becomes extreme. There is no such thing as a riskless investment, if by such definition one means both safety of principal and stability of purchasing power.

---

[6] An early presentation of this view is found in: Lawrence Chamberlain and George W. Edwards, *The Principles of Bond Investment* (New York: Henry Holt & Co., Inc., 1927).

A 100 per cent rise in the price level reduces the purchasing power of the strongest government bond by exactly half. The riskiest investments in periods of inflation are the choicest fixed return obligations.

There are a number of reasons to support the argument that common stocks are good investments. The first is that common stocks have a higher yield than either preferred stocks or bonds. The exact difference is hard to state precisely, since it depends on the sample of stocks and bonds being compared and because the spread changes over a period of time. There is no question that common stock is substantial except during the peak of bull stock markets. The Dow-Jones industrial average from 1946 to 1961 yielded 4.8 per cent, or much above the best-rated bonds.

The second reason in support of common stock ownership is that these stocks have greater appreciation possibilities than other types of investments. This is particularly true if one is fortunate enough to buy growth stocks. Many studies have been made to indicate the long-run appreciation of common stocks. The minimum annual appreciation found is about 3 per cent. Add this to the 5 per cent annual return and the total gain becomes 8 per cent. At this rate, money doubles in nine years, disregarding taxes and commissions.

A third reason for buying common stocks is that they provide a form of hedge against inflation. In this they share honors with real estate. Bonds and preferred stocks are hedges against deflation, but common stocks by reason of a long-term upward trend are far superior in protection against inflation. Over a long period of American history, inflation has been a greater danger to the investor than deflation. "If one wants to maintain stability of purchasing power, the common stock is more likely to be a safe investment than the bond."

A fourth reason for common stock investment is that their management requires less of the owner's attention than do many other types of investments, such as real estate. All security investments share in this quality. In real estate investments, many dislike the constant supervision entailed, such as keeping the property rented, insured, maintained, and serviced.

A final advantage for some stocks is liquidity, the ability to sell quickly at little variation from the market price. Many securities other than common stocks, of course, possess this quality, but few are superior to the actively traded common stock.

Is it more profitable to own common stocks than bonds? There have been many opinions. One must realize that, inherently, common stocks are subject to high risk, more so than preferred stocks and bonds. In spite of this risk, which no one will deny, many contend that the common stock—all things considered—is still the best security to buy. One of the earliest advocates of the purchase of common stocks as long-run investments was Edgar L. Smith, who through eleven tests examined common stock and bond performances during the period 1866 to 1922.[7] In ten of these tests he found that stock showed a superior performance to bonds. In only one test did the bonds show an advantage over stocks. That was from 1866 to 1885, when the nation was in a period of deflation. The intense interest aroused by his study stimulated many writers at later dates to make similar investigations.

Perhaps the best study which followed up Smith's original study was that of Winthrop B. Walker.[8] His comparisons covered the period 1923 to 1951. He used twelve tests covering four different periods of time. Thirty stocks were used, selection being made by three different methods. In each test, $1,000 was invested in each of ten stocks and $10,000 in long-term government bonds. In ten of his twelve tests, stocks proved more advantageous investments than bonds. The total profit of stocks over bonds was $17,500. His study showed substantially the same conclusions as those which Smith made many years earlier.

Certain conclusions can be drawn concerning the purchase of common stocks. One must be willing and able to assume a considerable amount of risk in order to obtain the greater yields and higher appreciation possibilities as compared with bonds. If stocks are purchased for the long-term view, rather than for the short-run, they offer an advantage over the purchase of bonds. One's portfolio of stocks should be well diversified by companies and industries. Commitments should be limited to the stronger companies as shown by their historical performance. Care should be taken to avoid large commitments during periods of high stock prices, when stocks sell at very low yields and high price/earnings ratios. Lower-than-average yields are justified if the stocks offer growth opportunities with greater-than-average appreciation.

PREFERRED STOCKS

Nature. Preferred stocks represent a form of compromise or hybrid security. They partly resemble bonds in that they have a stated rate of return, and partly resemble common stock in that they are an ownership or equity security with some voting power. They have a favored position over common stock in that they have a preference as to income, usually a priority as to assets, and a stated rate of return. On the other hand, they have decided weaknesses and limitations, as compared to

[7] E. L. Smith, *Common Stocks as Long Term Investments* (New York: The Macmillan Co., 1924).

[8] W. B. Walker, *A Re-Examination of Common Stocks as Long-Term Investments* (Portland: The Anthoensen Press, 1954).

common, in that their return is limited, their participation in management is restricted, and their right to buy new securities is also limited.

Par Value. Most preferred stocks have a par value, the amount of which is usually $100. The next most important denomination is $50. Other values are found, but not frequently. The par value determines the size of the dividend, which is a percentage of such value, such as 4, 5, or 6 per cent. It also measures the priority as to assets in cases of liquidation.

A minority of issues have no-par value. About 10 per cent of the principal industrials are no-par issues. There are no railroad issues of this type, but about 10 per cent of the utility preferred stocks are no-par issues. No-par preferred stocks are issued in order that the company may sell them at whatever price that market conditions dictate at the time of issue, such as 97, 99, 99½, or 100, for example. Dividends on no-par issues are stated in dollars, such as $4.50, $5, or $7. Asset priority is also stated in dollars, such as $50 or $100. The stock is a paradox in that it is no-par at the time of issue and is thereafter, in effect, a par value issue.

Historical Reasons for Issue. Railroad preferred stocks, which typically carry the low rate of 4 per cent, were issued in great numbers in the 1880's and 1890's, when many railroads were being reorganized in bankruptcy courts. Such financing eliminated fixed charges by the issue of preferred stock with contingent charges. The reason that industrials originally issued preferred stock was to enable them to sell a stock with greater dividend regularity than common stock. This would appeal to investors who wanted less risk than common stock but greater returns than were possible from bond ownership.

The preferred contract has gone through an interesting evolution in complexity. The first issues were nothing more than common stocks with priority as to dividends. The contracts became more and more complex as time went on. The bankers added one new clause after another. The purpose of this growing complexity was largely one of salesmanship. It sought to give the stock the speculative possibilities of a common stock, plus all of the apparent safety of a bond. Obviously, such a thing is financially impossible. This evolution explains the endless variations found in modern preferred issues.

Cumulative Provisions. The typical preferred stock carries a cumulative clause, which means that the dividends accumulate if they are not paid. The stockholders are entitled to the dividend, whether or not it is earned. If it is not paid in a particular year but is "passed" by the directors, the lapsed dividend must be made up at a future time before any dividend can be paid on the common. The stockholder is entitled only to the exact amount of the accumulated dividends, such as $6 per year, and not to any interest or compensation for the forced delay.

The early issues of railroad stocks were usually non-cumulative, since they were not offered for sale. But in later years they have generally carried the cumulative clause to make them more marketable. About 60 per cent of the railroad issues on the New York Stock Exchange carry the cumulative clause. It was a common practice in the nineteenth century for industrials to issue non-cumulative preferred stocks, but after 1925, practically without exception, such issues carried the clause. Over 90 per cent of the industrials on the New York Stock Exchange have the provision. Perhaps half of the public utility preferred stocks issued before 1920 had the clause, but since that date the practice has been universal.[9]

Frequently back dividends pile up on preferred stock during a period of depression or low earnings. The stronger companies generally pay them up during periods of increased prosperity if they are not too large; but not infrequently the company attempts to sidestep its obligation. Many methods have been tried to avoid the payment of back dividends, such as issuing new stock to the extent of the dividends, refunding the stock into a new issue paying immediate dividends, and reorganization. The protection afforded by the cumulative clause is often of doubtful value. If the dividends are earned, they are usually paid. If they are not earned for a long period, the stockholders often lose them.

Non-cumulative Preferred Stock. In a non-cumulative preferred stock, the holder of the stock is supposed to get the dividends if they are earned; but he is not to get them if they are not earned. The company cannot pay dividends to common stock in a given year if the preferred stock receives no dividends.

There has been much legal dispute about the position of non-cumulative dividends. No dispute arises where the dividend has not been earned. It is, of course, gone forever. The disputes arise in case the dividend has been earned, in whole or in part, but the directors have not paid it. The legal view of the United States Supreme Court now seems to be that, if the directors apply the profits to capital improvements and no dividend is declared, the claim for dividends is gone and cannot be claimed at a later date, despite the possibility of abuse by the directors.[10]

Non-cumulative preferred stocks may fall into any one of three common patterns. First, the contract may give the directors complete discretion to pay. Even if the dividend is earned, they need not pay. Second,

---

[9] A. S. Dewing, *The Financial Policy of Corporations* (5th ed.; New York: The Ronald Press Co., 1953), p. 138.

[10] *Wabash Railway Co. v. Barclay*, 280 U. S. 197 (1930).

the contract may provide that the company must pay whatever is earned, when there are earnings. Third, the company must pay whatever is earned before anything is paid on the common. The last type is really a cumulative preferred stock with the amount of the cumulative dividend being only the amount actually earned, not the full dividend.

Purchasers of preferred stock will do well to investigate thoroughly the cumulative aspects of their contemplated purchases, as well as the dividend record of the company over a period of years.

Participating Preferred Stock. A participating preferred stock is one that receives a stipulated dividend—for example, 7 per cent—and then shares in the earnings available for the common. It not only has a prior claim to earnings but also is allowed to share in additional earnings, which would normally go to the common stock. There is a considerable amount of legal dispute as to whether a preferred stock is participating, in the absence of a charter provision giving such rights. Ordinarily, however, this is no legal problem, since lawyers, in the clearest possible language, always insert into the contract the rights of the stock in this regard.

Participation is rare in preferred stocks, especially in the stronger companies. In a study of 1,094 preferred stocks which applied for listing on the New York Stock Exchange over a period of nearly fifty years, only 133, or 12 per cent, were participating.[11] It is unwise for a company to put in a participating clause unless it is absolutely necessary in order to sell the stock, since such a clause operates to the disadvantage of the common stockholders who control the company. Hence, only very weak companies ordinarily issue such stocks, and these may be avoided by the well-informed investor.

There are many methods of computing participation. The most common is the plan of simple or full participation, in which the preferred stock receives its stated dividend—for example, $7 per share. Then the common receives a like amount and, next, both classes participate equally, share for share, in the balance. Another method is immediate participation, in which the preferred receives its stated dividend—for example, $7—and immediately participates with the common stock on a pro rata basis, share for share.

Preference as to Assets. The provision entitles the preferred stockholder, upon liquidation of the company, to receive assets up to the stated or par value of the stock before anything is paid to the common stockholders. There is some legal dispute in various states as to whether the preferred stock carries this right in the absence of a statement to

---

11 W. H. S. Stevens, "Stockholders' Participating in Profits," *Journal of Business of the University of Chicago,* April, 1936, pp. 114–32.

that effect in the contract. In practice the lawyers take no chances and write into the contract the exact views of the organizers of the corporation. Generally speaking, it is very rare for a railroad stock to carry such a priority. A majority of utility stocks, however, carry the provision, and nearly all industrials do. In the public utility and industrial issues, the clause is inserted as a selling point to make the stock look more secure. Actually the provision probably has little worth. A solvent company seldom goes out of business and distributes its assets. The insolvent company either reorganizes or liquidates. In the latter case, there are seldom any assets left after the creditors have received their due.

Dividend Rates. It is probable that the dividend rate of the preferred stock contract is its most vital provision. Dividends are real, but many of the other provisions are merely selling gadgets, inserted to attract the unwary investor. Typically, the dividend rates on a preferred stock are higher than the interest rates on the bonds of the same company. They are often 1 or 2 per cent higher because of the greater risk and smaller protection afforded the junior issue.

Historically, railroads have paid the lowest rates, usually 5 per cent, because such issues were given out at the time reorganization rather than because of their investment strength. During the 1920's public utility rates were quite high, often 6 to 7 per cent, but in recent years rates have fallen sharply, following the decline in interest rates in general. Preferred stocks of such companies on the New York Stock Exchange now range from 2.1 per cent upward.

Industrial preferred stocks carry the greatest variation in dividend rates. During the 1920's the typical rate was 7 per cent, which exceeded all other rates combined. In recent years industrial companies have been able to issue stock with much lower rates, such as the May Department Stores preferred with 3⅗ per cent and Beatrice Foods preferred with 3⅜ per cent. A number of 3½ and 3¾ per cent industrial preferred issues have been listed on the New York Stock Exchange.

Protective Provisions. Many companies add to their preferred stock contracts various provisions that give additional safeguards to the issue. The purpose is to make the stock more salable and to give it some of the respectability of a well-secured bond. Sometimes the contract may carry a provision in which the stock is protected against future issues of bonds or additional preferred stock. Such issues may have to be approved by the preferred stockholders. In other cases sinking funds are required to pay off the stock; this has been a common practice since the 1920's for industrials. The company may have to maintain a dividend reserve, or it may be required to keep the volume of working capital equal to, or more than, the volume of preferred stock.

Such provisions are given reluctantly by corporations. Where they are of real value, the stockholder pays for their insertion in the contract by paying more for the stock or by getting a lower dividend rate.

Redemption Provisions. The redemption clause of a preferred stock contract gives the company the right or option to call in the stock and retire it at a specified price. The stock is often called "callable stock" because of this feature. Although the provision is rare in railroad stocks, it is almost universal in public utility and industrial stocks because of their recurring capital needs. Such rights of redemption are usually exercised by companies during boom periods, when the companies have substantial cash balances for redemption purposes.

The technique for redemption is for the company to give an advance notice of its action, usually one or two months. Redemption takes place on the regular quarterly dividend date with the company paying the redemption price plus all back dividends. Public utility preferred stocks are called at the par value plus a premium of 5 to 10 per cent, usually the latter. Industrial stocks carry a premium of 10 to 20 per cent, usually the former. The premium is supposed to compensate the owner for the inconvenience of turning in his old security and purchasing another, which often turns out to be less attractive than the one surrendered.

In some cases the contract requires compulsory redemption by the company on an annual basis. This is done to hold up the price of the issue and to insure its payment within a reasonable time.

The redemption clause adds nothing to the value of a preferred stock and is really a liability to the owner. Non-callable preferred stocks often sell at very high prices because of this fact; a well-known example is the United States Steel Corporation 7 per cent preferred.

Classified and Serial Preferred Stocks. Some companies, particularly public utilities, issue preferred stocks in different series or classes. Hence the company may have Class A, Class B, Class C, etc., or the issues may be labeled as I preferred, II preferred, III preferred, etc. These series are issued at different times and may have different dividend rates, different priorities as to assets, different claims on earnings, and different voting rights.

In spite of the efforts of the company to issue such classes of stock, each with an apparently different security, there is not much fundamental difference among classes other than the rate of dividend. If the company goes into bankruptcy, all issues are usually treated the same. Hence, if the company continues solvent, the essential difference is merely the amount of dividend paid per share.

Convertible Preferred Stock. Some preferred stocks carry in their contracts the convertible provision, which allows the owners, under certain circumstances, to convert their stock into common stock. The holder may retain his preferred stock, or he may convert it into common stock if the alternative is more profitable. The provision is very frequently found in industrial preferreds and in a few public utility preferreds, but rarely in railroad issues. One thorough study found that 47 per cent of all industrial preferreds issued between 1933 and 1952 carried this provision, while only 11 per cent of the utility issues did so. Only one railroad preferred stock was issued during that entire period, and it was convertible.[12]

Convertible preferred stocks are treated in detail in Chapter 27.

Voting Rights. Preferred stocks vary greatly in their voting rights, and the owner must carefully read his contract to determine its provisions. In the absence of a specific limitation in the charter and bylaws, the preferred stock ordinarily has been considered to have the same voting rights as the common. Except in Illinois, however, the company may limit the voting rights of the stock, and this is usually done in practice.

Some stocks carry full voting rights with the common stock. This is the usual practice for railroads, but is found in only a minority of public utility and industrial issues. Even here, the preferred is nearly always outvoted by the larger number of common shares; hence the privilege is less valuable than it would appear on the surface.

Public utility and industrial preferred stocks usually have restricted voting power. This is the typical practice. They vote only under certain circumstances. This often takes the form of contingent voting power. For example, the company may pass the dividends from four to six quarters, in which case the preferred stock is given full voting power or sometimes complete control of the company. Other cases of restricted voting power might be called veto or denial voting power. Here the stockholder votes on certain proposals which greatly affect the welfare of the preferred stockholders, such as the issue of bonds, issue of more preferred, or a change in the preferred contract. The preferred stockholders are then given the right to veto such proposals if they are believed not to be in the best interests of the stockholders.

Other voting plans are sometimes found. It is rare to deny all voting rights on all occasions to the preferred stockholders. Sometimes the preferred stock is given the right of unusual voting power, such as a number of votes per share; the preferred stockholders may be given the right to elect a certain percentage of the board of directors, such as 25 per cent.

---

[12] C. James Pilcher, *Raising Capital with Convertible Securities* (Ann Arbor: University of Michigan, 1955), p. 20.

The average stockholder is not much concerned with the voting rights of his preferred stock. He usually signs the proxy mailed out by the company and drops it in the nearest mailbox.

Investment Merits. The investment standing of preferred stocks has been subject to considerable dispute over the years. Many investment authorities are frankly critical of them, maintaining that they have the limited income of the bond without its greater security and the risk of ownership of the common stock without its possibilities of appreciation and higher yield. Industrial preferred stocks performed very badly in the period 1915 to 1923, registering a decline of about 30 per cent in that interval.[13]

Again, during the depression of the 1930's substantial declines took place. In 1934, when the depression was near its worst level, 30 per cent of the preferred stocks of leading industrials were paying no dividends. Even such a solid company as United States Steel was paying only $2 instead of the customary $7 per share. Many companies accumulated huge arrears during the depression that were carried for years afterward. As late as 1945 there were sixty-two companies on the New York Stock Exchange with total arrearages of $984 million. This was down to 10 issues and $29 million by 1961. Strong companies eventually pay off such arrearages. Weak ones, however, often find it impossible or undesirable to do so. Compromises with the preferred shareholders then become the order of the day.

It is probably unwise to condemn or praise preferred stocks as a group. They stand in an intermediary position between common stocks and bonds. Some are as safe as the best bonds, while others are as weak as the most speculative common stocks. The investor must use the careful judgment in buying them that is necessary in all security purchasing. His best investments will be in those preferred issues that have no bonds ahead of them.

BONDS

General Form. A bond may be defined as a promise given under a seal to pay a definite sum of money. It is a formal evidence of debt and represents the senior security issued by the corporation (Fig. 2–2). Bonds are issued under legal agreements between the corporation and the bondholders. These agreements are commonly called indentures, or deeds of trust. The agreement gives in detail the rights and duties of the company, the trustee, and the bondholders.

[13] A. S. Dewing, "The Role of Economic Profits in the Return on Investments," *Harvard Business Review*, I, 462.

Fig. 2–2. A bond.

The promise-to-pay clause of the bond is one of its most important parts. This is usually an unconditional promise to pay a definite sum of money at maturity plus interest at fixed intervals. This statement has certain exceptions in that some bonds are perpetual and some bonds have a contingent interest clause. The promise-to-pay clause clearly distinguishes the bond from the stock or equity security.

Denominations range from $50 to $10,000, but by far the most common denomination is $1,000. The reason for this rather large denomination is that bonds are sold chiefly to large financial institutions or wealthy investors who prefer this size. Although there are certain advantages in smaller par values, such as a possibly larger market and steadier price, the higher costs of issue and handling make the larger size the more favored by the corporation.

Bonds are either of the coupon or the registered type. In the coupon bond the title is transferred by hand-to-hand delivery since the bond carries no owner name. It is easy to transfer title, although there is some danger of theft or loss if the owner is careless. The owner receives his interest periodically by clipping the current coupon and depositing it at a local bank or mailing into the company paying office; this is one of the most enjoyable forms of exercise permitted the bondholder. Registered bonds are registered with the company in the name of the owner, and the interest is paid by check to him.

Nearly all bonds pay interest semiannually, such as June 30 and December 31. The next most common interval is once a year.

Interest Rates. The interest rate on a bond is a fixed charge for the debtor corporation and is always paid as long as the corporation is solvent. This is true of all bonds except income or adjustment bonds. Interest rates on bonds run as low as 2.5 per cent except for railroad equipment bonds, which have even lower rates. The coupon rate depends on many things, such as the credit standing of the company at the time the bond was issued, interest rates when the bond was issued, whether the bond was originally sold at a premium or discount, its convertible provisions, the investment standing of the industry, the security behind the bond, and its popularity with investors.

In recent years there has been a great decline in interest rates in general and hence in the coupon rates of bonds. Triple-A bonds yielded 5.1 per cent in 1920, 4.7 per cent in 1929, 3.0 per cent in 1939, and 2.5 per cent in 1945. Since then interest rates have hardened and through the years 1959 to 1961 were up to 4.4 per cent. The important thing in buying bonds is the yield rather than the coupon rate; for if the coupon rate is high the bond will sell at a premium, and if it is low the bond will sell at a discount.

In buying a particular bond as of a given date, it is well to always remember one of the oldest, simplest, and best tests of the investment standing of a bond: The lower the yield, the better the security.

Maturity of Bonds. The investor has a choice of many different maturities. He may buy those that mature in a few days after he purchases them, or he may buy perpetual issues. Most maturities fall within these extreme limits. Authorities on bonds usually divide them into classes based on maturities.

Short-term bonds are usually considered to be those maturing within five years. They are either secured or unsecured. They are commonly found in industrial financing but are rare for public utilities and railroads, which issue longer maturities. Of course, as a long-term bond approaches maturity it becomes a short-term bond.

Medium-term bonds are those that run from about five to twenty years. They are nearly always secured, ordinarily by a real estate mortgage, although they may be backed by other securities. This type of bond is usual in railroad and utility financing.

Long-term bonds may be said to be those that run twenty years or more. Their greatest use is in railroad and utility financing. A large majority of the country's railroads have issued them at some time or another. Large numbers of them were issued many years ago during periods of reorganization, when the railroads realized that they would never be able to retire their debts in full. Any kind of long-term obligation is rare in industrial financing. However, both Standard Oil Company (New Jersey) and Bethlehem Steel Corporation have issued one-hundred-year bonds in the past.

Mortgage Bonds. Mortgage bonds are those secured by a lien or mortgage upon real estate. The lien may be a first, second, or subsequent mortgage. The importance of the mortgage is that it prevents other creditors from preceding the mortgage in case of financial difficulty. First mortgage bonds are the best secured of all mortgage bonds and have a first claim upon earnings and assets of the company, compared with other creditors and security holders. The name "First Mortgage" has great prestige in financial circles and is always boldly displayed in the sale of such bonds.

The strength of the mortgage and its characteristics vary considerably from bond issue to bond issue. Some bonds are backed by mortgages, with after-acquired clauses in which the mortgages cover not only all the property owned at the time the bond was issued but also all property to be acquired in the future. Some mortgages are open and some are closed. The open-end mortgage permits the corporation to issue more bonds on the same mortgage under certain conditions protecting the bondholders; the closed mortgage forbids further issue of bonds with the same priority. Open-end mortgage bonds would appear to be less secure than closed mortgage bonds, but this is not necessarily so. Covenants under open-end mortgages require that, if further bonds are issued under the mortgage, they must be adequately secured by property and earnings, and that the stockholders must make proportional contributions to the invested capital of the company, either through reinvested profits or sale of additional stock. Although open-end mortgage bonds are unusual for industrials, they are very common for railroads and are the almost universal type for public utilities.

Special Kinds of Senior Mortgage Bonds. Not all senior mortgage bonds are called first mortgage bonds. There are a number of special types available for investment. Divisional bonds have a special place in railroad financing. These are first lien bonds on railroad divisions, which are the operating units of a railroad. They vary from very strong to very weak, depending on the importance of the particular division.

Prior lien bonds are senior mortgage bonds that have been placed ahead of first mortgage bonds, usually during a period of reorganization, when the corporation needed new money for rehabilitation. Consent of the first mortgage bondholders is necessary for their issue.

Special direct lien or joint bonds are frequently encountered. They are first lien issues based on some special form of property, such as a railroad terminal, bridge, and docks. The name "joint bond" comes from the fact that often two or more companies jointly own and operate the property and guarantee the bonds. They are issued because railroads have after-acquired clauses, which are troublesome in financing new bonds, and because no one company wants to assume the entire responsibility for financing and operating the property used as security. Their strength or weakness depends on the value of the operating property. Single companies may issue special direct lien bonds; for example, a theater holding company may place a special direct lien on one theater that is owned by a subsidiary.

Junior Mortgage Bonds. Junior mortgage bonds are those that are secondary in claim to other mortgage bonds, both as to earnings and assets. They are common in railroad finance, which is noted for its multiplicity of mortgages. They may be very strong if the first mortgage is not too large, and they may be very weak if their backing is poor.

Since the phrase "second mortgage" is taboo in finance, these issues usually bear some such vague and high-sounding title as "consolidated mortgage," "general mortgage," or "refunding mortgage."

Collateral Trust Bonds. These are bonds based upon securities deposited with a trustee. Either stocks or bonds may serve as collateral, but no real estate is involved. They have been issued frequently in both railroad and public utility financing. Ordinarily the reasons for issue were that the company wished to consolidate many small issues for a better market, or as a cheap method of controlling subsidiaries, or to avoid difficulties in issuing mortgage bonds.

The bonds are backed up by collateral which is worth substantially more than the face value of the bonds. As a rule, the collateral is worth from 25 to 33 per cent more than the par value of the bonds, and this margin must be maintained by the borrowing company. In most cases the security deposited is the stocks and bonds of the owned subsidiaries. The parent company may withdraw the collateral and substitute other collateral provided that it maintains the required margin of protection to the bonds. The issuing company, of course, receives the interest and dividends on the pledged collateral and votes the pledged stock, thereby continuing its control of its subsidiaries.

Collateral trust bonds vary all the way from top investment quality to very poor, depending on the value of the pledged collateral, the earning power of pledged securities, and the strength of the issuing corporation.

Railroad Equipment Obligations. These contracts represent financing for railroads upon the pledge of specific rolling stock. They are a unique method of financing which is very economical to the borrowing road. It is now the cheapest of all methods of obtaining new capital for railroads, regardless of the underlying credit of the borrowing road. Equipment obligations have the added advantage of avoiding the after-acquired clause so common in railroad mortgages. The amount of these obligations runs into the hundreds of millions of dollars with nearly a billion dollars of such certificates being outstanding at one time.

The security pledged is new rolling stock—either a single class, such as freight cars, or mixed, such as part passenger cars and part locomotives. Down payments (often called advanced rentals) vary from 20 to 25 per cent of the cost of equipment. Recently a large life insurance company has been advancing as much as 80 to 90 per cent of the cost of the equipment and requiring down payments of only 10 to 20 per cent. The contracts usually run about fifteen years to maturity. A feature of them is that they are paid off in serial form faster than the property depreciates; hence, the longer the bonds are outstanding the safer they become.

There are three forms of sale: the Philadelphia or lease plan, the conditional sale, and the equipment mortgage. The first plan involves a lease in which the buying company pays a substantial advance rental of 20 to 25 per cent and then pays a yearly rental sufficient to pay the interest on the outstanding certificates and to retire each year a given series of the certificates. At the end of fifteen years the entire debt, for example, $15 million, is liquidated. The railroad does not have any semblance of title until the debt is liquidated. This has long been the usual method of financing new equipment. Equipment financed under the conditional sale plan and the equipment mortgage follows the usual procedure of financing any type of movable property by these methods. In times past they were not as favored as the lease plan in that they did not give so strong a protection to the bondholders.

The railroad equipment certificate enjoys an investment standing possessed by few other corporate securities. Before the depression of the 1930's, there were only a few repossessions of leased equipment, and only one issue resulted in a loss to investors. The reasons are obvious. The equipment is always worth more than the outstanding notes; the equipment is new or nearly so; it is easier for the railroad to continue to make payment than to secure additional equipment; the notes are paid off faster than the equipment depreciates; and bankruptcy courts have been very careful to preserve the rights of the bondholders. As a result, yields have been relatively low. In 1961 they were running from 3.9 to 5.0 per cent.

Income or Adjustment Bonds. These are hybrid securities, half bond and half preferred stock. There is a definite promise to pay the principal, but the interest is to be paid only when and if earned. The holders have no power to enforce their claims against the corporation for unpaid interest. This type of bond developed many years ago as an outgrowth of railroad reorganizations. The bonds were given to junior bondholders by the bankrupt companies in order to cut down fixed charges. The interest on the bonds may or may not be cumulative, and it is usually paid to the nearest one-half of one per cent if not fully earned. In many cases the big problem has been whether or not the interest charges were earned, since the interest is figured after all fixed charges and depreciation allowances have been deducted. In a sense the bond is really a preferred stock with security and income superior to any preferred stock already issued by the company. The term "income bond" is not popular, so the phrase "adjustment bond" is often used instead. Some bonds are used by newly organized companies and are not the result of bankruptcy. This is a sound procedure from the standpoint of the new company, whose earnings are uncertain, but the practice is not popular with investors; therefore, such issues of industrials are rare.

Assumed and Guaranteed Bonds. Assumed bonds are found largely in railroad finance. They are the result of a large railroad taking over a small one during a period of merger or consolidation. The small company merges with the large corporation and is dissolved. The large company assumes liability for the bonds of the smaller organization. The bonds are, therefore, secured not only by the initial lien upon specific property but also by the promise-to-pay clause of the large railroad.

Guaranteed bonds arise from similar conditions. The small railroad, however, continues its legal existence. The larger or parent company guarantees the interest and principal of the bonds of the smaller company. The guaranty may be made through the terms of rental of the operating property, through an endorsement of the bonds, or through a special convenant between the two roads. The value of the guaranty varies from strong to weak, depending on the earning power of the property and the willingness and ability of the larger road to continue the guaranty.

Debenture Bonds. Debenture bonds are those issued upon the general credit of the corporation. There is no pledge of real estate, personal property, or securities. The company, of course, makes a definite promise to pay both interest and principal; thus the interest becomes a fixed charge of the company. The bonds are superior in every way to the preferred stock of the company, but they are inferior to secured bonds. In case of bankruptcy the bonds represent an unsecured debt and therefore rank on a par with other unsecured debts of private creditors.

There are various uncertainties involved in such bonds; chief among these is that the company might put secured debts ahead of them. Protection against this danger is often given by the company to the investors who own the bonds. It agrees to protect the bonds by a lien in case mortgage bonds are to be issued.

These bonds have never been as popular in railroad finance as mortgage bonds. This has been because of the attitude of investors and often because of state laws on the so-called "legal investments" which have at times made unsecured bonds ineligible for purchase by fiduciaries. In recent years these bonds have attained some popularity in public utility financing, and some companies with very excellent credit, such as the American Telephone and Telegraph Company, have issued them with marked success. In industrial finance they are the usual type. Mortgage bonds are not as necessary in the industrial field as in the railroad field, since there is seldom more than one issue of bonds involved and the matter of priorities is not a matter of concern. The chief backing behind an industrial bond is a lien not upon specific assets but upon earnings. If earnings are adequate, the bonds are secure. If the company fails because of lack of earnings, the property often has little value because of its specialized character.

Debenture bonds are often made convertible to increase their attractiveness. This feature permits the holders under certain conditions to exchange their bonds for a certain number of shares of common stock. The bond, therefore, appears to have the security of a bond, plus the speculative possibilities of the common stock. This added feature, if it is of any value, is of course reflected in a higher price or a lower coupon rate, although this fact may not be apparent to the purchaser. These convertible issues are considered in more detail in Chapter 37.

Participating Bonds. These bonds participate or share in the earnings of the company over and above the stipulated rate of interest. For example, the bond may receive a fixed rate of interest of 6 per cent, and in addition may participate up to an additional 2 per cent if the earnings are sufficient. Participating bonds, therefore, have some of the characteristics of common stock. They are very weak bonds and are usually issued only by companies with very poor credit. Conspicuous issuers have been bridge companies. No strong company will issue them because common stockholders desire to retain for themselves all earnings over and above the fixed rate promised the bondholders.

Sinking Fund Bonds. These are not a special type of bond in themselves, but merely a type of bond in which a sinking fund provision has been inserted in the contract. Any type of bond may be given this feature by the issuing company. The corporation, for any one of a number of reasons, merely decides to set aside each year a certain amount of money to retire systematically its bonds. The feature may be added to make the bonds sell better, to retire the bonds in an orderly manner, to avoid loss because of the exhaustion of wasting asset, or to give higher credit to the bonds. Most companies dislike sinking fund issues, since the provision imposses the heavy burden of meeting sinking fund instalments each year. In many cases companies also believe in the advantage of a permanent debt structure; in other cases, such as railroads, they are unable to pay off their indebtedness.

At one time the sinking fund clause was very common in railroad financing, but its popularity declined after the wave of reorganizations in the late nineteenth century. Some recent railroad issues have carried the provision at the insistence of the federal government. A minority of public utility issues carry the provision; utilities ordinarily prefer a substantial bonded indebtedness because it enables them to secure capital funds at moderate cost. Perhaps a third of utility issues have this feature. Sinking funds are common in industrial issues with perhaps one-half of such issues carrying the provision. Industrial bonds are often difficult to sell, and the feature adds to their investment status.

There is no assurance that any industrial will be in business at the end of twenty or thirty years; the quicker it pays off its debts, the better it is for the investors and the company.

The owner of sinking fund bonds will find there are many methods by which the company determines the annual instalment paid into the fund. Fixed annual instalments are common for industrials; the corporation either pays in a fixed number of dollars each year or retires a fixed amount of par value. Proportional instalments, under which the company retires a definite percentage of the outstanding bonds each year, such as 5 per cent, are popular in public utility finance. Instalments may also be based on the fluctuations of the business, such as gross receipts, net earnings, or dividends paid. Some weak sinking fund agreements may even make the instalments optional, although a minimum instalment may be required.

In the usual sinking fund arrangement, the company pays in the agreed instalment to the sinking fund agent, which is, as a rule, the trustee of the bond issue. The agent then retires bonds equal to the amount of the instalment. If necessary, these bonds are called in by the company to meet the instalment. The bonds, however, may be purchased on the open market, if the price is advantageous. Then the typical procedure is for the company to cancel the called or purchased bonds and thereby reduce its debt and fixed charges.

Serial Bonds. Serial bonds are those in which the bond issue is divided into series, instead of the whole debt maturing on a given date. One series matures each year. The company agrees to pay each series in order. The bonds may be callable, although ordinarily they are not. The usual practice is for the bonds to be sold with the same coupon rate, but at varying prices. The early maturities, being most attractive to certain institutional buyers, sell the best and have the lowest yield. Some issues have different coupon rates for different series, the low coupon rates being for the earlier maturities and the higher rates for the distant maturities. In either type the yields are always lower for the earlier maturities.

There are two types of serial bonds. One is the straight-line issue, in which the company divides the total issue into series of equal size, such as $500,000 per year. In the annuity or amortized type, the size of each series differs; it begins small and increases in later years; thus the total burden to the company for principal and interest is equalized over the entire life of the issue.

Serial bonds have certain advantages to the issuer, such as greater public confidence and less interest cost. They have long proved their worth in the field of municipal bonds. In the field of corporation finance, however, they are rarely found outside of railroad equipment obligations, where special conditions have made them desirable. There are listing and marketing difficulties in issuing such bonds. In addition, there is the ever-present burden of meeting annual instalments of principal, which can be very embarrassing in poor years. Many companies actually prefer to remain permanently in debt; hence the serial bond is a rarity in the investment market.

3

Reading the Financial Page

The stock market reflects news. Transactions are made by individuals acting on the kinds of information each has. The financial page of the daily newspaper is a significant source of such information for many of them. This chapter deals with some technical aspects of the financial page and the raw material and interpretation of financial news.

STOCK PRICES

Daily Stock Transactions. The daily report on the stock market occupies more space and attracts more interest and attention than any other part of the financial section of the newspaper. The report is presented in two forms: the stock table and the interpretative column. Although the leading financial pages cover not only the transactions of the New York Stock Exchange but also those of the American Stock Exchange and a number of leading regional exchanges, those of the largest exchange are of most interest; they dominate the entire securities market.

Stock Points. Stocks and bonds are quoted in the principal markets in "points." The term is used differently for each type of security. In stocks it means one dollar. For stocks selling at $1 or more per share, there are seven fractional points: $\frac{1}{8}$, $\frac{1}{4}$, $\frac{3}{8}$, $\frac{1}{2}$, $\frac{5}{8}$, $\frac{3}{4}$, and $\frac{7}{8}$, each $\frac{1}{8}$ point being 12½¢. Thus, a stock selling at 25⅝ is valued at $25.62½. Active stocks fluctuate between an $\frac{1}{8}$ and a $\frac{1}{4}$ point between sales; larger fluctuations occur in periods of rapid change.

For stocks selling below $1 per share, smaller fractional points are permitted. Theoretically, the smallest fractional point recognized by the commission schedule of the New York Stock Exchange is $\frac{1}{256}$th of a point. No one has ever seen a stock sold so low. Very few stocks on the New York Stock Exchange ever sell under one point.

Stock rights often sell for small fractional points. In practice, the lowest fractional point for rights is $\frac{1}{64}$. Rights selling at more than $1 are often quoted in $\frac{1}{32}$ of a point, such as $2\frac{5}{32}$.

The Day's Transactions. To give a full understanding of stock tables, a sample section from the market report of the *Wall Street Journal* of June 28, 1962, is presented in Table 3–1. This tabulation is a complete record of the significant facts about the previous day's trading in all stocks sold on the New York Stock Exchange.

Table 3–1. Transactions on the New York Stock Exchange, June 28, 1962

Thursday's Volume, 5,440,000 Shares

Volume since Jan. 1:	1962	1961	1960
Total sales	487,176,209	569,459,101	392,831,921

MOST ACTIVE STOCKS

	Open	High	Low	Close	Chg.	Volume
Polaroid	97⅛	101½	96⅝	98	+ 2¼	101,400
Xerox	109¼	117	109	115½	+ 6½	84,100
Litton Ind	89¾	95	88⅝	93½	+ 6	80,000
Am Tel & Tel ..	103½	105	102⅝	104⅝	+ 2⅝	71,300
Korvette	38½	39⅛	37⅜	38⅝	+ 2½	69,100
Zenith	48¼	49⅞	47⅜	49¼	+ 2⅞	66,600
U S Steel	41⅞	43¼	41⅞	43⅛	+ 1⅜	63,700
Magnavox	30⅞	31⅞	30	31⅜	+ 2⅛	60,100
I B M	338	348½	335¼	344	+11	54,500
Amer Photo ...	17½	17⅝	16⅛	16¼	— ⅞	53,600

Average closing price of most active stocks: 93.42

A

–1962– High	Low	Stocks	Div.	Sales in 100s	Open	High	Low	Close	Net Chg
55	36	Abacus Fd	1.25t	1	36¾	36¾	36¾	36¾	+ ¼
81¾	60¾	Abbott L	1.80a	18	63½	63½	62⅜	63	....
21⅞	13	ABC Vend	.50b	7	13⅝	13⅝	13⅜	13½	+ ¼
75⅛	52¼	ACF Ind	2.50	10	56	58	56	58	+2½
21	10½	Acme Stl		30	10⅝	10⅞	10⅜	10⅝	+ ⅛
33⅜	22½	Adams Ex	.30e	26	23⅞	24⅜	23⅞	24¼	+1¼
23¾	10	Ad Millis	.72	3	13	13	12¾	13	+ ⅛
90¾	47⅝	Addressog	.90b	157	52	52⅞	50¾	51¾	+1¾
19⅝	11⅛	Admiral		41	11⅞	12⅛	11¾	11¾	....
35⅜	20⅛	Aeroquip	.40b	20	20½	22	20½	22	+1⅝
18⅜	10	Air Control	.50e	14	14¼	14⅜	13¾	14¼	+ ⅜
84¼	41¼	Air Prod	.20b	46	46¼	47¾	45⅞	47¾	+2¾
70⅛	45⅛	Air Reduc	2.50	38	49⅛	49⅜	48¼	48⅞	+ ¼

Source: *Wall Street Journal,* June 29, 1962.

Range for the Year. Complete stock tables usually begin with a column giving the year's high and low prices. This is called the range.

Throughout January and February this column carries the range for all of the previous year and the current year to date, in order to give a longer view of recent prices of the stock. Sometime in March the range for the previous year is dropped and only the current year is quoted. The date of this change varies from paper to paper; it is generally between the ninth and twenty-third of the month.

The significance of this column is that it shows how a stock stands today as compared with recent months; an interpretation of current strength or weakness may then be possible. This column also enables one to tell whether a given stock is making a new high or low for the year. Finally, the column may be used to compare a given stock's behavior with that of the rest of the market. If a given stock is making a new low while many other issues are making new highs, the comparison may be significant.

Dividend Rates. The abbreviated name of the issue is always followed by the dividend rate being paid on the stock. This is always in dollars and never in percentages and represents the annual dividend. This apparently simple figure is the most difficult part of the stock table to compute and is only an approximation. In some cases, such as American Telephone and Telegraph, the newspaper or financial service can state the rate with finality and authority; it is $3.60 per year. Such a statement may be made of any company that has paid a regular dividend for some time, such as $0.75 per quarter. The editor of the table merely multiplies the quarterly dividend by four. In companies that have an irregular or interim dividend policy, the problem becomes very complex, since no one knows from quarter to quarter what the dividend will be. Let us suppose that a given company last year paid these dividends by quarters: $0.50, $0.50, $0.75, and $1.25. In the first quarter of the current year it paid $1. What is the annual dividend? There are four possible answers. First, take the total dividends paid for the last twelve months; this is $3.50 and is probably the best solution. Second, report the amount of dividends paid last year; this is $3. Third, give the dividend for the first quarter of the current year only and state that this is the amount paid so far this year; this is $1. Fourth, multiply the dividend for the first quarter by four; this is $4. Each option has some weakness.

Stocks are quoted flat; the expression means that the buyer pays nothing additional for accumulated dividends. Any future dividend is included in the price as quoted. This contrasts with bond prices, for which the buyer pays the quoted price plus any accumulated interest.

The Day's Sales. Sales may be given in full, such as 12,500. Usually, as in Table 3–1, they are given in hundreds, such as 125, for space condensation. The figure represents the number of reported shares sold and not the number of separate transactions, for which there is no record. The volume figure indicates the activity in the issue. For active stocks the number runs from one hundred shares up. For stocks that are traded in ten-share units (page 168), volume may be reported in total, such as ten, twenty, or fifty shares.

The day's sales are reported both for the market as a whole and for each individual stock sold. The all-time high for total sales on the New York Stock Exchange was on October 29, 1929, when 16,410,030 shares were sold. This was nearly reached on May 29, 1962, when volume was 14,750,000 shares. The dollar volumes for the two days were far from comparable, however. Average share price in 1962 was about one-half that of 1929.

The average daily volume in 1961 was 4 million shares. The daily volume is of considerable interest to students of the technical condition of the market, who show an acute concern with the axiom, "Volume goes with the trend." Briefly, this is the theory that a genuine rise or fall in prices is accompanied by a substantial increase in the volume of shares sold. Brokerage firms also have an interest in daily volume. A common opinion is that the break-even point in such an organization is its usual share in a daily volume of 2½ million shares.

Unusual situations often create records in volume for individual stocks. The day's record for a single stock up to mid-1962 was 941,100 shares of Alleghany Corporation traded on April 4, 1961, during a proxy battle. Typical news events in recent years that have created very high daily sales for individual stocks have included a market tip by a well-known news commentator, announcement of an unexpected split in a stable issue, and news about a facsimile machine assumed to have wide application.

Some stocks, mostly high-priced preferred issues, are sold in trading units of ten shares. There were 198 of these traded at Post 30, the trading post on the New York Stock Exchange floor for inactive issues, in early 1962. A few inactive issues are traded elsewhere on the Exchange floor. Volume, as might be expected, is often low, such as 10, 20, or 50 shares in a day. It is usually reported in full. The *Wall Street Journal* reports volume in these shares preceded by a "z."

The Day's Prices. There are four of the day's prices in most stock tables. The "open" represents the first sale of the day without regard to the time of day when it was made. The "high" is the highest price at which the stock sold during the trading session. The "low" is the bottom price for the day. The "close" or "last" is the final sale made during the trading day, whether it occurred near the closing hour of the market or not.

Net Change. The term "net change" is highly significant and is often misunderstood. It is the difference between the closing price of a given day and the close of the last session in which the stock was sold. For the majority of stocks the net change represents a twenty-four-hour change, or from the close of one session to the close of the next previous one, but in less active stocks it may represent a change over several days or weeks, even a month. The direction of change is indicated by a plus or minus sign, such as —½, which indicates that today's close was $0.50 under that of yesterday. No change is indicated by two periods (..).

Measurement of change is affected by dividend payments. When directors of a corporation pay dividends, a certain date is set as the "date of record" or the day that "the books are closed." Stockholders of record on that date will receive the next dividend on the stock. Technically, the stock is traded ex-dividend, according to the rules of the New York Stock Exchange, on the third full business day before the list of stockholders is taken off. Hence, if the dividend was payable to stockholders of record on Thursday, March 15, the stock would be sold ex-dividend on Monday, March 12. The reason is that the Exchange uses "four-day delivery," which means that a stock is not delivered until four days after it is sold. Hence, it is not possible to get a new stockholder's name on the books if the stock is sold three days before the date established by the directors—in this case, March 15.

When it goes ex-dividend, a stock falls in price by the amount of the dividend. If General Motors sells at 45 before it goes ex-dividend, it will sell at 44½ on the day it goes "ex," since it is worth $0.50 less at that time. The stock is reported as showing "no change" if the price falls by the exact amount of the dividend. In the example just cited, General Motors would be reported "no change" if the stock closed on the ex-dividend date at 44½ but would be reported "—½" if it closed at 44.

Number of Issues. Most, but not all, of the stocks listed on the New York Stock Exchange are sold each day. In 1961 a typical day's trading involved about 1,300 issues and a week's trading, 1,450 issues. The total number of issues listed at that time was slightly over 1,500. About 85 per cent of the issues were active enough to be sold daily. The number of issues sold daily is considered by many to be an indication of the strength of interest and, hence, the significance of trend in the market. Some consider it superior to the averages as an indicator. In a strong market 1,300 to 1,400 issues may be traded; 800 may advance and 200 may decline with 300 remaining unchanged.

Up to 1950, the all-time high in number of issues sold in one day was on June 26 of that year at the outbreak of the Korean War, when 1,260 issues traded. This record has been broken many times since. On May 29, 1962, trading took place in 1,399 issues.

Bid and Asked Quotations. About 200 to 300 issues are not sold on a typical day. In order to indicate current values in such stocks, many financial pages give quotations for them secured from the specialists. These quotations consist of the current bid and asked prices. They are illustrated in Table 3–2.

Table 3–2. Bid and Ask Quotations, June 28, 1962

New York Stock Exchange

Closing Bid and Asked Prices of Stocks Not Traded

	Bid	Asked		Bid	Asked		Bid	Asked
Aldens pf	90	91½	Harb Wk pf	126	127½	Ph El 4.68pf	102½	104
Alleg & W	89	90	Hat Cp pf	38½	39⅞	Ph El 4.30pf	97	98½
Allied Kid	12⅛	12¼	Heinz pf	85	87	Pillsby pf	98	100
Amal Sug	16⅝	16⅞	Helme pf	37½	38	PitCoke pf	76½	78
Am Airl pf	91	99	Herc Pdr A	52	60	PitCoke4.80pf	70½	77
Am Bk N pf	62	63½	Hey N pf A	69	70½	Pit Ft W pf	130½	132
Am Con Ind	22	22½	Hill Cp	6	6¼	Pit Yng&A pf	118	122
Am Cry pf	89	90½	Hilton H pf	24¾	25	Plough wi	24⅜	24¾
Am Inv pf	102	102½	Holly S pf	30½	31½			
Am Smelt pf	145	146½	Hook Ch pf	87½	88½	Scott P 4 pf	95½	98
Am Snuff	23½	24½	Hotel Cp pf	14½	15	Scott P 3.40 pf	85	85½
Am Snuff pf	125½	128½	HousF4.40pf	93½	96	Scovill pf	74	80
Am WW 7 pf	26¼	26¾	HousF 4 pf	85½	88	Shahmoon Ind	7	7¾

Source: *Wall Street Journal*, June 29, 1962.

Preferred Stocks. All stocks are considered as common stocks in the stock tables unless otherwise indicated. Preferred stocks are reported as the name of the stock, followed by the letters "pf" and the annual dividend.

Over-the-Counter Stocks. There are approximately 3,000 common and preferred stock issues handled on all the registered and exempt stock exchanges in the country. Many thousands more transfer in the over-the-counter market. The trading in these stocks is done largely through telephone and teletype communications. No sales figures are ever reported by the more than 4,000 brokers and dealers in the market. The newspapers, however, each day systematically gather from dealers and reporting agencies a list of several hundred of the more important issues being sold in the market. Typical lists include bank stocks, insurance company stocks, industrial and utility issues, mutual funds, and guaranteed stocks. All reports are given as quotations. As a rule, these are not the highest and lowest figures, but representative bids and offers, which are indicators but not precise measures of conditions in the market. In general, the bid price is a price that a stockholder might expect to obtain if he tried to sell his stock in this market, but the asking price is only a rough approximation for the price that would be paid by a purchaser in this market. Several examples of bids and asking prices as reported in *The New York Times,* June 28, 1962, are given below:

	Bid	*Asked*
First National City Bank	78½	82¼
Aetna Life Insurance	94	110
Wellington Fund	10.53	11.45
United Servomation	14	15⅜

Stock Yields. The current yield on a stock is computed as follows:

$$\text{Current yield} = \frac{\text{Annual dividend}}{\text{Current market price}}$$

For example, a stock paying an annual dividend of $2.40 and selling at 50 yields 4.8 per cent. In computing the annual dividend most investors and investment services take the amount of dividends paid in the last four quarters.

The question is often asked: What is the average yield on a common stock? The answer one gets depends on two things: (1) what stocks are used as a sample, and (2) what period of time is chosen. Any number of answers may be obtained by changing these two variables.

The average yield of the thirty-stock Dow-Jones industrial average, computed quarterly, from 1946 to 1961 was 4.8 per cent. The range for this period was from 3.07 to 6.72 per cent. During 1961 this average showed a yield of 3.3 per cent and the range of quarterly data was 3.07 to 3.67 per cent.

Yields vary with the type of corporation chosen for the sample. For example, in 1961 the stocks used by the Moody Service showed this variation in yields:

125 industrials	3.0%
24 public utilities	3.1
25 railroads	4.9
15 banks	3.2
10 insurance companies	2.3
All issues	3.1%

An examination of current yields in the newspaper will reveal striking variations in size. Some will be as low as 0, or 1 or 2 per cent, while others exceed 6 per cent. In general, the explanation is popularity; the more popular the stock the lower its yield.

Common stocks in recent years with low yields often have been growth stocks. Because of high rates of appreciation they became extremely popular with individual investors and institutions, and were bid up to high price levels. Certain drug, electronic, and office equipment issues in this category showed yields from 0.5 to 3.5 per cent in 1961. Income stocks, held primarily for yield rather than appreciation, during the same period showed substantially higher yields even in the cases of very strong companies. In summary, the growth stock carries a typically low yield.

For preferred stock, quality means safety of income and principal. For these twin virtues the investor will pay a high price and take a yield but little higher than that on good bonds. A good example is Eastman Kodak $3.60 preferred, which usually carries a yield of about 3.6 per cent.

High yields on a common stock may be symptoms of risk, danger, and lack of desirability. Earnings and dividends may be uncertain. Again, the company may be small and unknown and not considered a good investment for these reasons. Often a very high yield, such as 10 per cent, is a clear warning signal that dividends are in danger and will be reduced shortly. A good example was Chrysler in 1954, when the yield for a short time exceeded 10 per cent.

The question may well be asked: Are stocks with very low yields worth the price? The answer depends on the investment objectives of the buyer. If one is interested primarily in appreciation rather than income, they may be. Growth stocks have shown wonderful gains to many buyers in the past twenty years. On the other hand, if one does not want to take the inherent risk of growth stock and is interested in income, such stocks are not appropriate. One may wait as long as ten years to obtain a reasonable income on his investment. One easily may pay too much for the growth factor.

A final question on yields is of importance: Can or should yields be ignored at any time in the purchase of common stocks? The answer is that yield can and should be ignored if the buyer intends to hold on to the stock less than one year. During the course of twelve months every common stock fluctuates by more than the amount of the annual dividend. The change in price becomes more important than the amount of the dividend. Hence, for short-term trading, dividends can be ignored; the profit is made on price fluctuation.

Market Leaders. These are the most actively traded stocks in any given trading period, such as one day, one week, or one year. The best-known reports on them are the daily lists published by newspapers; they include typically, fifteen, or twenty stocks (as, for example, in Table 3–1).

The items on such lists are considered significant by traders because (1) they help to indicate the trend of the market and (2) they show the direction of speculative interest in the period covered.

Numerous factors may boost a stock into the limelight of market leadership. The size of the company and its national prominence often explain leadership over a long period, as in the case of General Motors, United States Steel, or American Telephone and Telegraph. Large railroads like the New York Central and the Pennsylvania are also important for this reason. Special factors usually account for temporary leadership, such as unusual earnings, very favorable prospects, changed dividends, unusual sales, merger possibilities, and radical changes in management. As soon as these factors cease to be important, the company stock drops from the very active list.

More than 150 issues have been on annual lists of the 20 most active stocks in one or more years since 1924. The unquestioned leaders from 1924 to 1961 were: General Motors, which was on the list in thirty-six of the thirty-eight years; United States Steel, thirty-four years; and Radio Corporation of America, thirty years. A different list is drawn from the record of activity for the shorter five-year period, 1956–60. During that period the 5 most active issues were: General Motors, Standard Oil Company (New Jersey), Sperry Rand, Bethlehem Steel, and Royal Dutch Petroleum.

Market leaders are not so important as they once were. In 1917 the 20 most active stocks accounted for 67 per cent of reported volume activity on the New York Stock Exchange. In 1929 the ratio had dropped to 29 per cent. By 1955 it had dropped to 14 per cent, and this has been approximately characteristic of the years since then. There is less concentration of speculation today in market favorites. The market is more selective and has more investment characteristics. More companies have become well established and well known to the investing public. To be sure, there have been flurries of speculation in small issues and stocks of unknown corporations in some markets; but, on the whole, changing investment tastes, information, and responsible corporate management have combined to lessen the importance of market leaders and to increase the significance of a broader list of stocks.

Market leaders reflect the concentration of popular enthusiasms in the market somewhat more than other lists of stocks. In 1961, for example, the average high price among market leaders, the 20 most active issues, was 46 per cent above the average low price. In that year the high for the Dow-Jones industrial average was 20 per cent above its low and the range for *The New York Times* industrial average was 21 per cent.

Market Averages and Indexes. Most followers of the market pay particular attention to the "market averages." These are computed from prices for carefully selected lists of representative stocks. Some have been computed over many years by financial services and newspapers. The averages reflect market directions and day-to-day fluctuations. When plotted on charts, they show more clearly the course of the market than do the basic figures from which they are derived. Since no service cares to calculate averages based on over 1,500 stocks on the Exchange, the expedient alternative has been to pick leading industrial, railroad, and public utility stocks and combine them into averages and indexes based on lists ranging in size from 15 to 500 issues.

Among the better-known market averages and indexes appearing daily or weekly are the 65-stock averages of the Dow-Jones Company; the 50-stock averages of *The New York Times;* the 100-stock averages of the *New York Herald Tribune;* the 60-stock averages of the Associated Press; the 500-stock indexes of the Standard and Poor's Corporation; and the 256-stock indexes of the SEC. A detailed examination of averages and indexes is made in Chapter 29.

Most leading financial pages carry a special table of market averages and indexes. A typical example is that of *The New York Times* given in Table 3–3.

BOND PRICES

Bond Points and Prices. Bonds are quoted in points, but the bond point is 1 per cent and not $1, as in stocks. This reduces all bonds, regardless of denomination, to a common measure of price. All are quoted as though they had a $100 denomination (see Table 3–4), although actually most bonds have a $1,000 denomination. A price of 95 would mean 95 per cent of par; this would be $475 on a $500 bond, $950 on a $1,000 bond, etc. For other than United States government bonds, the fractional bond points begin at $1/8$ and go up to $7/8$; no smaller fractional points are used to indicate changes in price. On federal obligations quotes are in fractional points of $1/32$. For example, if United States Treasury 4¼'s were quoted 103.12, this might read $103 \frac{12}{32}$ or $103\frac{3}{8}$. In dollars the bid is $1,033.75 on a $1,000 par value bond.

Maturity dates are always given for bonds, such as " '69," which means that the bond matures in 1969. In government bonds the call date is also shown; it is the earlier of the two dates. The obligor has the privilege of calling in and paying off the bond at the call date but not before. If no call date in indicated, which is the typical situation for a corporate bond, the company may be allowed to call in the security at any time. An examination of the basic indenture, or contract, agreement must be made to ascertain just what the company's privilege is.

Table 3–3. Market Averages of *The New York Times,*
Wednesday, June 27, 1962

THE NEW YORK TIMES AVERAGE

STOCKS

	High	Low	Last	Net Chge.
25 rails	86.68	84.79	86.00	— .42
25 industrials	498.78	489.48	496.50	+ .02
50 combined	292.73	287.13	291.25	— .20

DOMESTIC BONDS

20 Rails	10 Indust.	10 Utils.	Comb.
72.80 —.20	94.78 —.05	78.01 —.34	79.60 —.20

DOW-JONES STOCK AVERAGES

	High	Low	Last	Net Chge.
30 industrials ..	539.28	528.73	536.98	+ 1.22
20 rails	116.66	114.23	115.94	— .11
15 utilities	104.17	102.13	103.93	+ .60
65 stocks	188.66	184.92	187.86	+ .45

STANDARD & POOR'S INDEX

	High	Low	Last	Net Chge.
425 industrials	55.33	54.22	55.10	+ .30
25 rails	26.93	26.41	26.81	— .04
50 utilities	50.88	49.87	50.62	+ .31
500 composite	52.83	51.77	52.60	+ .28

Daily, Monthly and Yearly Range of Times Averages

DAILY RANGE OF 50 STOCKS

	High	Low	Last	Net Chge.
June 26	297.65	289.65	291.45	— .02
June 25	294.89	286.09	291.47	— 2.43
June 22	301.06	293.04	293.90	— 5.83
June 21	306.79	299.44	299.73	— 6.79
June 20	311.81	305.47	306.52	— 4.50
June 19	312.61	308.12	311.02	— 1.03
June 18	316.64	308.49	312.05	— 2.00

DAILY RANGE OF 25 INDUSTRIALS

June 26	507.36	493.59	496.48	— .15
June 25	502.55	487.37	496.63	— 4.10
June 22	513.67	499.20	500.73	—10.52
June 21	523.95	510.81	511.25	—12.00

DAILY RANGE OF 25 RAILS

June 26	87.94	85.72	86.42	+ .11
June 25	87.24	84.82	86.31	— .77
June 22	88.46	86.89	87.08	— 1.13
June 21	89.63	88.07	88.21	— 1.59

MONTHLY RANGE OF 50 STOCKS

1962	High	Date	Low	Date	Last	Chge.
June ..	341.24	1	286.09	25	291.25	—47.55
May ..	374.62	2	305.51	29	338.80	—27.71
Apr. ..	392.04	2	364.30	30	366.51	—24.26
Mar. ..	402.87	16	388.67	30	390.77	— 2.00
Feb. ..	401.01	15	386.54	1	392.77	+ 3.86
Jan. ..	405.37	4	382.04	26	388.91	—11.48
1961.						
Dec. ..	405.45	28	391.02	21	400.39	+ 5.31
Nov. ..	411.17	15	390.10	1	395.08	+ 3.09

					Net Chge.
Oct. ..	398.01	6	384.93	3	391.99	+ 2.12
Sept. ..	407.32	7	382.30	26	389.87	—10.80
Aug. ..	405.57	22	391.29	1	400.67	+ 7.28
July ..	395.67	31	373.98	19	393.39	+12.27
June ..	394.04	9	375.75	27	381.12	— 6.06

YEARLY RANGE OF 25 RAILROADS

	High	Date	Low	Date	Last
1962......	110.70	Feb. 1	84.79	June 27	86.00
1961......	114.28	Oct. 12	93.82	Jan. 3	106.83

YEARLY RANGE OF 25 INDUSTRIALS

	High	Date	Low	Date	Last
1962......	700.11	Jan. 7	487.37	June 25	496.50
1961......	709.46	Nov.15	586.29	Jan. 3	693.95

YEARLY RANGE OF 50 STOCKS

	High	Date	Low	Date	Last
1962......	405.37	Jan. 4	286.09	June 25	291.25
1961......	411.17	Nov.15	340.05	Jan. 3	400.37
1960......	420.14	Jan. 4	315.94	Oct. 25	341.14
1959......	427.89	Aug. 3	354.60	Feb. 9	413.70
1958......	368.41	Dec. 31	265.21	Apr. 10	366.57
1957......	347.74	July 16	261.07	Dec. 23	268.02
1956......	354.18	Aug. 9	307.62	Jan. 23	335.39

DAILY RANGE OF DOMESTIC BONDS

June 26......	79.80 —.12	June 21......	80.07 —.29
June 25......	79.92 —.11	June 20......	80.36 +.04
June 22......	80.03 —.04	June 19......	80.32 —.03

YEARLY RANGE OF DOMESTIC BONDS

1962......	81.71	May 16	78.94	Jan. 2	79.60
1961......	81.72	Mar. 13	78.50	Sept. 26	78.77
1960......	88.36	Dec. 28	82.48	Jan. 4	88.17
1959......	87.18	Apr. 27	82.23	Dec. 29	82.32
1958......	86.54	June 16	83.27	Sept. 18	34.86

Bonds usually are quoted "with interest." The purchaser pays the quoted market price *plus* the interest on the bond at the time of purchase. Interest payments typically occur at six-month intervals; interest accumulates between such payment dates and must be paid by the new owner to the date at which he assumes ownership. Bonds may be quoted flat if they are income bonds or in default. In this case the purchaser's price is the quoted price.

Bond Yields. Computation of bond yields is mysterious to most laymen. They can be computed in a few minutes, but an untrained person is unlikely to get the right answer. The best way to ascertain yield

Table 3–4. Bond Quotations

	Bid	*Asked*
Barium cvdb 5½ '69	53	60
Burlgt Ind cv 4¼ '75	105	110
Cdn Pac cv 3½ '66	83	87
Cdn Pac Ry cv 4 '69	82¼	85¾
Carrier Corp 4⅛ '82	96½	101
Collins Radio 4¾ '80	90	93½
Daytn Rub cv 5¼ '72	75	81½
Duke Power 4½ '92	103¾	105¾
El Paso NG cv 5¼ '77	103½	106½
Food Fair Pr 5½ '75	76	81
Freuhauf Tr cv 4 '76	89	93½
Hilton Hotel 6 '84 ww	95	101
Hotel St Geo 4½ '60	88	92½
Keyes sbcvdb 5¼ '85	106	..
Lowenst cvdb 4⅜ '81	66	69½
Mid-Am sbdb 6½ '80	101	104

Source: *Wall Street Journal,* June 29, 1962.

on a given bond is to look it up in a bond table, some form of which is available in any broker's office. The reason for complexity in computation is that the formula for finding a bond yield takes into account five separate factors: maturity date, market price, coupon rate, deviation of price from par, and investment value of coupons remaining for payment before maturity. Yields, however, are seldom identical with coupon rates. A 4 per cent bond is quite unlikely to be a 4 per cent investment for a buyer. It may yield more or less, and the buyer should investigate before acting.

Railroad Equipment Certificates. Most bonds are quoted in terms of points, such as 100, 101½, or 102.22. However, in certain types of bonds, such as railroad equipment certificates, quotations are in terms of yields. Buyers want low prices, so they give high-yield bids. Sellers want high prices for their bonds, so they quote low-yielding offers. The important thing in both cases is the yield rather than the price of the issue. Several examples are given below, taken from *The New York Times* of June 28, 1962.

	Maturities	*Rate*	*Bid*	*Asked*
Atlantic Coast Line	'62–'72	2½–4¼	4.40	4.25
Chesapeake & Ohio	'62–'74	1⅞–4⅝	4.20	4.10
Erie RR.	'62–'72	1⅝–4¾	5.50	5.25
Southern Ry.	'62–'68	2⅜–4⅛	4.25	4.15

This method of quoting is also used in the market for United States Treasury bills.

THE NEWS

The Averages and Indexes. A careful student of the market will do well to follow one of the leading stock averages or indexes just discussed. One's choice may depend on the newspaper read or the type of average or index best fitted to one's need.

Individual Stocks. It is well to select a small but representative list of stocks and to follow them regularly. A stockholder will always watch prices on his own investments, but this is not necessarily the best list of stocks to follow in keeping abreast of market changes. The following list is a useful one: United States Steel, General Motors, General Electric, Standard Oil (New Jersey), du Pont, New York Central, and Atchison, Topeka and Santa Fe. Some analysts feel that a good picture of market action can be obtained by watching the price of General Motors alone.

Business Indicators. There is such a bewildering flow of business news items that the average market follower finds it hard to make an intelligent selection. There are, however, a number of basic indicators which are of value in the interpretation of business conditions. Since the stock market is heavily influenced by traders and investors who attempt to forecast business conditions, a careful study of the economic situation will do much to reveal basic causes of stock market trends.

Steel production figures are highly significant statistics. Released each week by the American Iron and Steel Institute, they cover the tonnage produced for the week. Their great importance is indicated by the fact that 40 per cent of all manufactured goods employ steel as a raw material.

Automobile production figures are also highly important, since the automobile industry is one of the key industries of the country, not only as a leading consumer of steel and a leading employer but also as an indicator of consumer demand. These figures are released weekly by *Ward's Automobile Reports* and *Automotive News*.

Department store sales, gathered and released weekly by Federal Reserve districts, are the best and quickest data available on retail trade. They are an index of consumer demand. The surveys of consumer spending plans published by the Federal Reserve Board and by the University of Michigan have provided better indexes recently.

Data on carloadings are released weekly by the Association of American Railroads. These data cover the number of freight cars loaded by district and major freight classifications. They are guides for appraisal of the volume of traffic moving in industrial and commercial channels, as well as significant indicators of earnings of the railroads.

The F. W. Dodge Corporation releases data on building contracts awarded in forty-eight states each month. In a basic industry that is greatly influenced by business fluctuations and that, in turn, has a tremendous influence itself, this series is highly important, since the industry employs millions of workers and furnishes a great demand for building materials, appliances, furnishings, and equipment. Extremely important are the data on contracts for industrial or heavy construction, since these reflect the planning of thousands of corporations and are, therefore, a sign of either business confidence or the lack of it on the part of the country's corporate leaders. Building permit data are no longer of significance.

The McGraw-Hill Publishing Company and the SEC both provide data on business plans for capital spending. These data give an opportunity for anticipation of changes likely to occur in construction and sales of durable goods.

Electric power production figures are compiled by the Edison Institution and issued weekly. These figures show changes in the kilowatt-hour output of the country. They have shown a strong growth for many years. Since they reflect industrial, commercial, and consumer demands, they need extremely careful interpretation when used as an index of business activity.

Wholesale price data, released weekly by the Bureau of Labor Statistics, should be examined carefully for signs of inflation and deflation, as well as for changes in the supply and demand for basic industrial commodities. If they are properly interpreted, they become valuable tools for the study of business conditions. They are released in two forms: (1) weekly index of primary wholesale prices and (2) a daily index of wholesale commodity prices. The latter is a very small but very sensitive index of basic commodities, primarily agricultural products and minerals. Both indexes use 1947–49 as 100. Many other wholesale price data, of course, appear on the financial page.

Imports and exports are compiled by the Department of Commerce and released about six weeks after the close of any given month. They are significant in the analysis of business conditions in many lines of industry, commerce, and agriculture that depend upon foreign trade for a substantial part of their business.

Data on employment, payrolls, and unemployment, released by various government agencies, are useful indicators of rising and falling national income, production, and consumption.

There are a number of well-known indexes of physical production. The best-known and most complete one is the index of physical production of the Federal Reserve Board. It uses 1957 as 100 and is a very accurate gauge of changes in the physical production of the nation. It is released about fifteen days after the close of a calendar month.

The monthly crop reports on production and prices of the Department of Agriculture are important in judging farm prosperity. Each crop is handled on a somewhat different basis; reports vary from seven to twenty-four times a year. Farm prices indicate the buying power of a very substantial segment of the nation's economy.

At one time, bank clearings were accorded great attention as business indicators. They are seldom mentioned today because of the presence of superior indexes of business conditions. Some students of business have shifted their interest to data on changes in the money supply and the turnover of the money stock.

Business forecasters pay much attention to the statistics on business inventories. Data on these have grown rapidly in accuracy and prestige in recent years, due to the activities of the Department of Commerce. Changes in the inventory policies of business firms can often turn recession into prosperity or vice versa. Many a business boom is no more than a strong buildup of inventories.

The monthly reports of the National Association of Purchasing Agents are attracting more and more attention in the press. These agents, who are very close to the pulse of business activity, report regularly through their central office their analyses of business conditions, particularly prices and production. These are of great value.

The study of business conditions in recent years has been revolutionized by the development of studies on the Gross National Prduct, which is the total market value of all goods and services produced in the nation. Compiled by the Department of Commerce, using elaborate statistical techniques, these figures are invaluable in the study of current economic conditions.

In 1959 the Federal Reserve Board began publishing quarterly summaries of the major flows of funds and savings in the United States. This addition to the volume of information about significant factors in general economic activity is a basis for improved and amplified analysis of business conditions.

There are many banking data to watch, but one needs skill for sound interpretation. The volume of business loans, reported weekly, is a useful indicator of changes in bank credit and lending policies. The rate of interest on prime commercial paper is of equal importance. Call loan rates to brokers have only minor significance today as compared with many years ago. The credit policies and rediscount rates of the Federal Reserve System should be watched with great care, since these are powerful weapons for control of business activity.

Corporate earnings fill many columns of the financial page over a period of time. Each day brings a stream of individual corporate reports, which becomes a flood during periods when quarterly reports are being released. These should be watched with care in view of the popular belief that stock prices are determined more by changes in earnings and dividends than by any other factors.

All experienced readers of the financial page realize the interdependence of business news. No one industry operates in a vacuum. The prosperity of one industry spreads to many others like ripples from rocks thrown into a mill pond. The prosperity of the automobile industry affects the demand for steel, rubber, glass, paint, accessories, parts, copper, nickel, and aluminum. Employment and trade are affected over wide areas. Similarly, a decline in construction means a reduction in the demand for lumber, paint, brick, cement, tile, steel, electrical equipment, appliances, glass, furnishings, and many other products. A drop in farm prices and in income lowers the demands for farm machinery, consumer goods, automobiles, mail order sales, fertilizer, and the many other products and services sold to farmers. Such ever-present phenomena explain why so many groups of stocks tend to move up and down in sympathy.

Political News. The reader of the financial page who overlooks the political news of the day will have a decidedly unbalanced picture of the stock market. The market is swayed today much more than it was many years ago by political developments; they are almost as fundamental as business conditions. Central governments today in all countries play a major role in the economic life of their nation through taxation, expenditures, and economic control. The theory that the central government is responsible for the prosperity of the country has grown so strong in recent years that it is doubtful if government will ever again play a minor role in the nation's economic existence. Hence, policies of the President, acts of Congress, federal court decisions, decrees of commissions—all must be properly weighed in an analysis of the stock market.

War, both "hot" and "cold," has been of vast importance for years. With the likelihood of a continuous struggle between the communist and free worlds for many years to come, the reader of the financial page must be ever watchful of the reaction of the market to political news. Often it even overshadows the economic developments of the day.

Source of News. The news which appears on the financial pages of a newspaper comes from many and varied sources. It is gathered largely by the great press associations, such as the Associated Press and United Press International, and by Dow-Jones and Company, which publishes the *Wall Street Journal* and the Dow-Jones news ticker service. Many of the larger metropolitan papers have extensive business newsstaffs of their own. These agencies, in turn, gather their financial and business news from corporations, trade associations, research organizations, business executives, and government agencies. In general, such agencies do an excellent job of compiling, editing, classifying, and sorting out the most useful items in the endless stream of such reports. No paper can hope to publish all the material released today.

Much of the news is purely factual and constitutes no problem; it can be acepted at face value. The problem here is selectivity and interpretation. The reader, however, must be constantly on his guard against certain kinds of news stories. These are often called "inspired" by the gentlemen of the fourth estate. These stories are released by interested parties to show the favorable side of a picture, to convey an impression favorable to the source which releases the report, to impress the readers, to conceal unfavorable facts, to cover up a premature rumor, or to sway an audience to an unexpressed point of view. A corporation president in his report will seldom play up the unfavorable prospects of his company; rather, he will stress the hopes for the future or the profits of the past. A financier will deny rumors of a merger until its final details have been approved. A labor leader will present only his side of a labor dispute. Never in history have business leaders been so acutely aware of the importance of favorable public relations. The desire to present to the public at all times a "good story" of company affairs has become a major objective of management. The intelligent reader will do well to evaluate corporate reports at all times to see if they are complete, unbiased, and objective.

Market Reaction to News. A reader may cram his brain with endless facts, statistics, statements, reports, and forecasts; he may be well informed through a careful, continuous, and systematic study of the financial page and the numerous other reports of economic conditions. What then? The most difficult job in reading the financial page is not the finding of news; it is in interpretation.

The student of the stock market must realize that he is not dealing with a machine; one does not feed a mass of statistics into the market and see a reaction similar to pressing one's foot on the starter of a well-maintained automobile. The market is not an automaton. Rather it is a composite of all the hopes, fears, generalizations, forecasts, guesses, and analyses of the thousands upon thousands of individuals, firms, and corporations that deal in the market each day.

The market may or may not react to news as expected. A good piece of news may affect the market days or weeks before it reaches the news tickers; it may influence the market the instant it becomes known; it may produce results a day or two afterward; or it may never make the least difference in the price of the stock. All this is mysterious to the layman. There is no easy road to the interpretation of financial or political news in terms of stock market trends.

The easiest way to interpret the market is to assume that it reacts only to so-called "spot news." Some stock market commentators fall into this superficial method of analysis. If the market falls today, it is because the bad news outweighs the good news of the day; if the market is buoyant, the good news forces prices up. For example, a major coal strike is in the making: if the market breaks, there is pessimism about its settlement; if the market rises, the speculators are hopeful of a quick adjustment; if the market does nothing, traders are adopting a "wait and see" attitude. Too often such an analysis proves spurious, since many underlying forces influence the market. These forces are often as obscure to brokers close to the market, even on the floor of the Exchange, as they are to the outside observer. An underlying bull market may be in progress; but the most mature analysts do not perceive its growth until some time has lapsed and then opinion may be strongly divided as to when it will terminate. To interpret such a trend purely on the basis of "spot news" is apt to lead one to many false conclusions and financial losses. One of the most remarkable things about the market it its ability to absorb bad news without damage during strong markets and its incapacity to recover on good news during bear markets. This tendency has resulted in many Wall Street axioms; for example, "Never sell on strike news."

There are many spot news stories used to explain the daily changes in the prices of individual stocks. The one given the most prominence by the editors of the daily columns interpreting the market is on dividend actions.

Discounted News. Certain news items of importance cause substantial changes in the level of stock prices; others of equal importance cause no change. The explanation in many cases is based upon the principle of "discounted" and "non-discounted news."

Discounted news is that which has been successfully forecast or discounted before it reaches the ears of the general public or the financial pages of the daily paper. For example, well-informed traders and investors may predict the increase or reduction of a dividend, a stock split, a favorable or unfavorable earnings report, a rate increase, a change in prices, or a corporate merger. Acting on this forecast, often reinforced by inside information not available generally, a substantial amount of buying or selling of stock in the company affected takes place. The stock mysteriously rises or declines. By the time the news has reached the press, the market has fully discounted the news and nothing happens. If the news was good, the stock may have risen 5, 10, or 15 points before there was full realization of what was taking place. The amateur trader is apt to buy too late in such a situation. The market has already advanced as far as the situation justified.

A few examples of discounted news will clarify the point. In 1953 Chrysler stock was selling at 96. By January, 1954, it was down to 59, even though the dividend was unchanged and sales and earnings for 1953 were at a record level. By August, 1954, however, the dividend was down to $3, a cut discounted far in advance. Further indication of investor sophistication in evaluation of Chrysler was apparent in later years. In 1961, for example, announcement of a substantial deficit in first quarter earnings had no influence on price; it had been anticipated. Again, in 1953 Studebaker was selling at 43½. By January, 1954, it was down to 21⅜. The dividend was cut in that month from $0.75 to $0.40. So successfully had the reduction been discounted that the stock showed only a nominal change after the dividend change was announced. A third illustration is found in the decline in price of Polaroid in 1960–61. When announcement of declining earnings was made in January, 1961, little if any price action ensued.

In contrast to discounted news is non-discounted news. This is news that was not forecast at all or, in some cases, wrongly forecast in advance. It comes without warning, like the proverbial "bolt from the blue." Or the news story may be in direct contrast to the expectations. The stock may then react sharply; this depends on whether or not the news is good or bad. For example, a corporation may announce a stock split, a change in dividend, a merger, or a large order. A government official, judge, or commission may announce a significant policy or decision. A highly important political event may take place unexpectedly. Since the news story was carefully concealed until public disclosure to the news services, the market reacts at that time in accordance with the weight of opinion as to the ultimate effects of the news upon stock values.

A few examples will illustrate the effect of non-discounted news. In June, 1950, the Korean war broke out; *The New York Times* industrial average fell 13 points the first day. In September, 1955, President Eisenhower suffered a heart attack; the industrial average dropped 41 points. As a contrast, his decision to run again in February, 1956, was well discounted days in advance. In November, 1955, the directors of the Union Pacific Railroad announced a five-for-one split. The action, not discounted in advance, caused a rise of 16½ points, 11 of them on the first day following the report. In December, 1959, a similar move by the directors of American Telephone and Telegraph was the cause of a 22-

point jump. In 1961, an unanticipated Supreme Court decision requiring du Pont to divest itself entirely of its stock in General Motors was reflected in a 23-point drop over the next two trading days.

The ability of the market followers to discount the news successfully can prove to be very profitable. Rare, indeed, is the trader who can do it well and consistently.

Optimism and the Market. The stock market and those who make a living from it, directly and indirectly, thrive on optimism. Everyone likes to hear good news about the market, whether he is trader, investor, stockholder, newspaper editor, broker, politician, businessman, housewife, farmer, or the well-known "man-in-the street." Hence, there is a great tendency for all those who produce, gather, edit, and distribute the news to look for the favorable side of the news and to minimize the unfavorable. The "bulls" in the market probably outnumber the "bears." For this reason, many readers of the financial page and many followers of the market tend to be carried away by the rosy glow of false hopes. No greater error can be made by the intelligent trader or investor.

The Market Can Do Anything. The student of the market who tries to explain everything in terms of rational causes will find much to mystify him. No truer characterization has been made of the market than that it can do anything. On occasion it can show sharp gains with no discernible cause. At other times it will break widely with no news event to justify such action. No full explanation of market action exists.

II

WORK OF
THE STOCK EXCHANGES

4

Stock Exchange Functions

This chapter deals with the functions performed by the stock exchanges of the country. Particular stress will be given to the ability of the New York Stock Exchange to perform such functions, since it is the dominant organized market in the business. The Exchange justifies its existence on the basis of its ability to furnish useful services to the securities business, securities owners, listed corporations, and the economic life of the nation. The American Stock Exchange and the regional exchanges perform the same services in their respective spheres of operation.

Creation of a Continuous Market. Without question, the creation of a continuous market for individual security issues is one of the most important functions of the stock exchanges. A continuous market is one in which securities are bought and sold in volume with little variation in current market price as trades succeed one another. Four tests may be used to indicate continuity in the market for a given stock: (1) frequency of sales, (2) narrow spread between bids and offers, (3) prompt execution of orders, and (4) minimum price changes between transactions as they occur.

What makes a continuous market? Several conditions tend to create it. A large number of stockholders in a given company will do so, although some companies with very large stockholder lists have less continuous markets than do companies with smaller lists. The size of the company also has significance, but many very large companies have a less continuous market than do some smaller ones. Speculative interest in a given company undoubtedly makes a market more continuous. Heavy speculation implies frequent, fast sales and, usually, narrow spreads. In many cases this factor is more important than the number of stockholders or the size of the company in making a continuous market, especially over short periods. Margin buying and short selling increase the volume, frequency, and speed of sales, and probably make for smaller fluctuations between sales.

The benefits of a continuous market are principally two, although minor benefits may be added: (1) it creates marketable, liquid investments; and (2) hence, it facilitates collateral lending. Investors may place and withdraw funds rapidly. An institution, such as a bank, insurance company, or mutual fund, may keep its funds invested at all times; it may switch investments and it may withdraw such funds immediately upon need. Similar advantages accrue to the individual who may have funds to invest or may need to withdraw them for personal or business use, for payment of taxes, or to meet emergencies. Other things being equal, listed stocks are better collateral for security loans than unlisted ones. They have a higher collateral value for hypothecation purposes, which benefits the borrower; the lender also benefits by having behind the loan a liquid security which may be quickly sold if the loan becomes jeopardized.

The question of how continuous the market in stocks really is cannot be answered simply. Some stocks, such as the 50 most active stocks on the New York Stock Exchange, have a remarkably continuous market. These stocks on the average provide about 25 per cent of all sales on the Exchange. The first 20 leaders alone provide about 14 per cent of all Exchange activity. Well over half of Exchange sales are concentrated in the activity of the 100 most popular issues.

In 1961 there were slightly over 1,500 stocks listed on the New York Stock Exchange. The exact figure for January 2, 1962, was 1,542. In January, 1962, an average day's trading involved 1,298 issues, while an average week's trading included 1,471 issues. Stated another way, 84 per cent of all issues were sold daily and 95 per cent were sold weekly. How continuous was the market? The issues sold daily enjoyed a continuous market. To a lesser extent, those sold weekly enjoyed a fairly continuous market. But what about the 71 issues not sold even weekly? It is true that these 71 issues did not enjoy frequent sales. They failed, therefore, one of the tests of a continuous market. On the other hand, because of the system of specialists on the Exchange any stock may be sold or purchased at any time, and very quickly, if there is a demand for a transaction. In this sense, therefore, every stock on the Exchange may be said to have a continuous market to some degree. On the less active issues, however, the spread between bid and asked prices and the fluctuations between sales are apt to be greater (for some, much greater) than those of the 50 market leaders.

Three criticisms have been made of the performance of this function on the Exchange in the past. The first has been that sales for many issues are not frequent enough to assure a close, continuous market. This situation has just been reviewed. In fairness to the Exchange, it is doubtful whether activity in the less popular issues should be stimulated merely to create a more continuous market. A stock does not become a fundamentally better investment simply because some shares are sold daily rather than weekly.

A second criticism of the performance of this function has been that the Exchange, in creating a continuous market, permitted excessive activity detrimental to the best interest of the market. This criticism was voiced strongly many years ago when speculation in certain issues ran to extreme lengths. For example, in 1931 the entire capital of J. I. Case Company was turned over 68 times.[1] Again, in 1929 when the pool in Radio Corporation of America was at its peak of activity, sales of the stock in one day were equal to 10 per cent of all listed shares of the corporation. There is no doubt that in the old, unregulated market of the past, market activity in certain stocks exceeded all necessary requirements for making marketable, liquid investments. This was particularly so when there was so much manipulation in the market and artificial market activity was an important implement in attaining a pool objective of higher prices. With today's substantial controls over the market by the SEC and the Exchange, it is unlikely that another J. I. Case situation of 1931 or a Radio Corporation of America operation of 1929 will again take place. Manipulation and pool activity are largely ghosts of the past. However, speculation can and does still have its effect on the market from time to time. In August, 1960, for example, 16 per cent of the outstanding stock of TelAutograph and 13 per cent of Comptometer changed hands on a single day. The markets for these issues were disorganized for several days. In late 1960 and 1961 speculative activity in stocks of new, unknown corporations was evident and had its effect on the volume of trading, especially on the American Stock Exchange.

To illustrate contrasts in the present extent of activity in the market, let us take the cases of Studebaker-Packard and General Motors in 1961. In that year Studebaker-Packard was the leader in sales on the Exchange with a volume of 10.4 million shares. It had about 12.2 million shares outstanding. The turnover was 85 per cent. General Motors was the fourth most active issue with sales of 9.1 million shares. This volume provided a turnover of only 3 per cent of the 284 million shares outstanding.

Instead of excessive market turnover, today the opposite is more generally true. In 1961 the average turnover of stocks on the Exchange was only 15 per cent, a rate that in the opinion of many made for a very

---

[1] John T. Flynn, *Security Speculation* (New York: Harcourt, Brace & World, Inc., 1934), p. 303.

thin market as a whole. This has been true of the market for several years. During the period of high volume of activity in early 1961, turnover for the whole list reached 19 per cent, but this was within the range for the previous decade. In contrast, one may recall that in 1928 when speculation was rampant the turnover of stock was 132 per cent and in 1929, 119 per cent.

A third criticism of the performance of this function made in the past has been that the continuity of liquidity in the market was more apparent than real. If everyone tried to liquidate his investments this characteristic of the market would disappear; there would be not enough buyers and the market would collapse as in 1929. While there may be liquidity as long as there are only a few sellers disposing of their securities, this characteristic may disappear under pressure. It is, of course, true that in severe market breaks buying power is weaker than selling pressure and liquidity may vanish temporarily. The very rapid response to the selling pressure on September 26, 1955, after President Eisenhower's heart attack, suggests that the argument is not very strong, however. On that day delays in opening on most issues did not exceed two hours and all orders in the market were executed during the day. Buying power was found quickly; sellers found liquidity in the sense that they were able to exchange their securities for cash with little delay. This response was repeated on May 29, 1962.

In fairness to the exchanges, too, it should be pointed out that lack of liquidity is not a characteristic unique to the stock market in times of crisis. The same situation in the past has prevailed in banking, commodities, and real estate. At the depth of the Great Depression of the 1930's, our entire banking system collapsed; 40 per cent of the banks disappeared in the process. Basic raw materials and real estate found few buyers even at drastic price reductions.

Under normal conditions, the New York Stock Exchange provides for stocks of established companies a market that is reasonably continuous. The ability of the Exchange to provide a continuous market for seasoned stocks, thus creating marketable, liquid issues, is one of the two outstanding functions which it performs. All things considered, it does a better job of this function for stocks than does the over-the-counter market.

The Exchange specializes in making a market for strong, nationally known companies backed by substantial assets and earnings; the shares are "seasoned" before being listed. The American Stock Exchange and the regional exchanges do more to create a market for the newer, "unseasoned" issues. Continuity of liquidity in these markets is less definite but still assuredly usual.

Fair Price Determination. As important as the creation of a continuous market is the performance of the function of fair price determination. Prices are not fixed by the exchanges or their members; prices are determined on the exchanges by matching buy and sell orders.

The stock exchanges facilitate the bringing together of buyers and sellers from all over the nation and often from foreign countries. Bids and offers of these buyers and sellers in an auction market determine the prices as of the moment. Specialists on the exchanges play a temporary, facilitating part in this determination; through time, however, prices are fixed only by the effective demand and supply from the investing public and securities issuers. The result is as near a market for free competition as can be found in this country; the commodity markets, of course, are similar in operation. In a day when price fixing or price control by private business or government agency is a dominant factor in price determination all over the world, the exchanges still create one of the freest markets in existence.

Two criticisms have been leveled at the performance of this function of the market. One has been that, in the past at least, prices were not determined fairly but were manipulated; they were driven up by pools and manipulators who used every trick in the business to create artificial valuations; they were pushed down by "bear raiders" without regard to fundamental values. There is, of course, truth in the indictment that much manipulation did exist in the market, and that the markets have been largely free of such operations only within comparatively recent years.

Price determination by manipulation is indefensible, without doubt. It is not in the best interests of the exchanges in the long run, nor in those of the public. An organized exchange today that permitted manipulation, even if the SEC did not stop it, would be rendering a great disservice to the securities market.

A second criticism made of the performance of this function is that speculation tends to send prices above investment worth at times and below it at other times. It is true, of course, that prices do show very large fluctuations. They were too high in 1929, too low in 1932. It is all very well to say that stocks should sell at "investment values" or "intrinsic worth," but what do these terms mean? There is no recognized standard for measuring the investment value of a stock. As we saw in Chapter 2, for example, there is little obvious relationship between book value, par value, and market value for many stock issues. Investment value reflects opinions of people about a future which is not clearly seen and which no man has predicted with certainty.

It is sometimes stated that stock prices should be capitalized on the basis of earnings; for example, stocks should sell at, say, ten times earnings. We know that the market has never operated under any such precise formula. From 1939 to 1961, the Dow-Jones industrial stocks have sold at an average price/earnings ratio of better than 13/1. However, this ratio has soared to more than 23/1 and to less than 8/1 in that period. Similarly, current yields averaged 4.7 per cent in the period, but ranged from as high as 6.7 per cent to as low as 3.0 per cent. What then is the "real value" of a typical Dow-Jones industrial in terms of price/earnings and yield? There is no exact standard.

About all that we can conclude under these conditions is that a stock is worth what it will bring. If it sells below net quick assets, as many did in 1932, that is what it is worth; if it sells at twenty times earnings, that is its value. Stock prices are not fixed by mathematical rules and ratios; they are determined by what buyer and seller are willing to bid and offer. Perhaps the most important factor is public confidence, and this cannot be measured.

Stock prices should be influenced neither by manipulation nor by speculative excess. They are not so influenced to any considerable extent today. Other than this, fair price determination is accomplished by matching what buyers bid and sellers offer in a free market and agree upon as reasonable.

Aid in Financing Industry. Industry receives most of its new capital by retention of earnings and sales of securities off the stock exchanges. The exchanges render a different service for the most part.

Insofar as industry raises capital by selling securities, it usually does so through the over-the-counter market. New bond and stock issues typically are underwritten by securities houses. Only after the issues are sold by the underwriting houses and have become publicly held are they listed on an exchange. New companies may wait many years before their issues are listed. Hence, raising capital for new or old companies by the sale of new bond or stock issues depends more on effective action in the over-the-counter market than on the stock exchanges.

Actually, corporations today raise only a fraction of their corporate funds by sale of new securities issues. Here is a breakdown of their sources of funds from 1950 to 1960 inclusive:[2]

	Billions	Per cent
Internal sources:		
Retained profits	$ 88.0	20.2
Depreciation allowances	188.6	43.3
External sources:		
Net new security issues	64.2	14.7
Other external sources	95.0	21.8
Total	$435.8	100.0

[2] *Federal Reserve Bulletin*, April, 1961, p. 480, and Federal Reserve Board, Supplement No. 4, *Flow of Funds/Savings Estimates*, March 1, 1961.

It will be observed from this classification that 63 per cent of total funds came from internal sources alone. New securities issues provided only 15 per cent of total funds secured.

Our conclusions at this point, therefore, are: (1) the exchanges are not the primary market for new securities; (2) new security issues are underwritten in the over-the-counter market, as a rule, before being listed on any exchange; and (3) most of the new capital of corporations comes from internal sources and external sources other than the sale of new securities.

The organized exchanges, however, do make a real contribution to the financing of industry, although it is an indirect and secondary one. This is in the sale of rights of listed companies. Corporations may sell common stock and convertible bonds in either of two ways: (1) through the use of rights issued under a privileged subscription and (2) through sale in the over-the-counter market, at either public or private sale. A corporation listed on the Exchange frequently sells new stock or convertible bonds to its present stockholders on the basis of a privileged subscription. In this procedure, described in detail in Chapter 36, the stockholders are given rights permitting them to buy the new stock or bonds at attractive prices. These rights have an immediate and wide market on the Exchange. Many stockholders, in some cases over one-half, dispose of these rights by sale rather than by surrender to the corporation in the purchase of the new securities. Here the Exchange performs its service. By creating a continuous market for these rights during the period of the privileged subscription, the Exchange has enabled the company to market the new stock successfully. In case a stockholder does not wish to invest additional capital in his company, he can sell the rights to investors who do wish to do so. In this way the corporation secures new funds from the capital market. In this instance the Exchange, in a real sense, does aid corporations in their financing and enables them to secure additional new money on favorable terms. It is true that a given corporation, not listed, could issue rights and raise capital from its stockholders or others, but it is believed that this would be a more difficult operation than if the rights enjoyed a wide market on the Exchange.

Listed companies can sell their securities more readily than those that are not listed, either through underwriting syndicates or directly to stockholders; this facilitates new financing. The fact that a new security is to be listed improves its initial sale. The market prices of the listed company securities indicate trend of growth and earnings in such companies; this condition does enable the successful companies to raise capital more easily because of this publicity if they decide to raise additional money through the capital market. The listed stock, but not necessarily the listed bond, has a better and wider market than the unlisted issue. These gains are substantial; they cannot, however, be used to justify the broad assertion, occasionally found in books, that the exchanges furnish the primary market for new capital to industry.

Discounting Function. In earlier years it was generally believed by careful students of the stock market that stock price movements preceded business activity moves. The stock market was said to discount business conditions a number of months in advance. The term "discount" as used in this discussion means anticipation of change. The theory was that stock traders anticipating better business and higher earnings would buy stocks. When a decline in activity and profits was anticipated, traders would dispose of stocks. Their ability to do so resulted from their unusually well-informed position and knowledge of production, sales, and business conditions in general. It was assumed they were able to trade advantageously on this knowledge. Since many corporate "insiders" were in the market in these early years, weight was given to the view. Their knowledge of bookings or advance orders, rates of production, purchasing inquiries, and similar matters gave them invaluable background facts with which to speculate.

This notion about the ability of the stock market to forecast business conditions was stated many years ago by Huebner in these words: "Without exception every major business depression or boom in this country has been discounted by our security markets from six months to two years before the dull times or the prosperity became a reality."[3]

A number of studies have been made of the relationship between stock price changes and business conditions. Ayres, who examined twenty-five business cycles from 1829 to 1938, concluded that in the typical cycle the peak of stock prices was seven months in advance of the peak of business, and that the low of stock prices was five months in advance of the low in business.[4]

A study made by the Cleveland Trust Company covered the period from 1871 to 1953.[5] During this period there were thirty-nine cyclical turning points in business. The conclusion was that in twenty-nine of the thirty-nine cases, stock prices turned ahead of business; in two cases they turned in the same month, in four cases in a later month, and in four cases there was no satisfactory comparison. The average lead was found to be six months, but leads ran as high as twenty-one months and lags as much as three months.

[3] S. S. Huebner, *The Stock Market* (New York: Appleton-Century-Crofts, Inc., 1934), p. 39.
[4] L. P. Ayres, *Turning Points in Business Cycles* (New York: The Macmillan Co., 1940), p. 67.
[5] *The Cleveland Trust Bulletin*, April 16, 1954, p. 3.

Another very thorough investigation was made by Geoffrey H. Moore and his colleagues at the National Bureau of Economic Research.[6] In a study of twenty-six business cycles from 1899 to 1958, they found that the Dow-Jones industrial average of stock prices led the change in business activity in thirty-one out of fifty-two turns. The average lead was four and one-half months. This appears impressive. However, he also found that stock prices ran as much as twenty-one months ahead of the cycle change in one instance and as far behind as nine months in another instance. With this tremendous range of variation, the average lead of four and one-half months loses much of its significance as a reliable indicator of turning points in business conditions. The group did decide to retain stock price movement as one in a series of twenty-six measures of economic activity to be used to indicate business conditions.

However satisfactory stock prices may have been in discounting changes in business conditions in many years, they certainly have been less reliable on many other occasions. In 1929 the big break in stock prices came in late October. The Dow-Jones industrial average, however, reached its peak in September. It was already a laggard in predicting the depression. Construction contracts had reach their peak in June, 1928; wholesale prices, in July, 1929; and industrial production, in August, 1929. Only after a perceptible weakening of the economy took place did the stock market make its resounding crash in October. Only in signaling the severity of the depression did the market show real forecasting ability.

Since 1939 the market has been quite erratic in its discounting ability. Industrial production rose steadily from 1939 to 1942; in the same period, industrial stock prices fell consistently. Industrial production reached its war peak in December, 1943, and then fell until January, 1946; industrial stocks rose during this interval. The year 1946 has been called "the year of the depression that never came." In anticipation of this depression, stock prices broke sharply in August of that year and were down in 1947; industrial production, however, rose in both 1946 and 1947. Industrial production rose from 1949 to 1953; industrial stock prices also rose in that period. A small recession in production began in 1953 and continued into 1954; industrial stock prices, however, did a good job of discounting the subsequent recovery in production by reaching a trough and turning upward eleven months in advance of the index of industrial production. Out of these five movements in production, stock prices failed in three distinct instances to discount the trend of the business cycle, as measured by industrial production.

[6] Geoffrey H. Moore (ed.), *Business Cycle Indicators* (2 vols.; Princeton, N.J.: Princeton University Press, 1961), e.g., I, 56.

Anyone who seeks to forecast business conditions on the basis of stock market behavior is certain to have disappointments. Little reliance can be placed on the theory that stock prices alone anticipate changes in business conditions by four and one-half months. This is true of all series that are used to forecast business changes when taken individually. As two authorities on the business cycle once said, ". . . no sequence of average leads of time series in past cyclical revivals can tell what the exact sequence will be at the next revival."[7]

Other Functions. Four important functions of stock exchanges have been discussed in some detail above. Three other functions may be mentioned briefly. First, the exchanges provide accurate and continuous reports on sales and quotations, superior to those of any other type of market. This service is described in detail in Chapter 8. Second, they cause the release of much information on the listed companies, particularly in regard to financial conditions. This subject is treated more extensively in Chapter 7. Finally, the exchanges protect security owners through regulations designed to eliminate dishonest and irregular practices in the brokerage business.

[7] *Ibid.*

5

New York Stock Exchange—
Its History

A complete and authentic history of the New York Stock Exchange and Wall Street is yet to be written. Unfortunately, in the formative years of the Exchange no one ever seriously attempted to write a systematic, thorough, and unbiased account of its development. Few writers, in fact, were at all interested in the early financial history of the nation, in spite of the great importance of its financial institutions in promoting its growth. This brief report can outline only a few of the significant developments in this long and eventful chronology.

The First Market in Stocks. There is considerable doubt as to when the first securities market in New York began to function. Some dealings in securities were probably transacted as early as 1725. These operations grew out of an auction market in lower New York at the foot of Wall Street. The market dealt in commodities, such as wheat and tobacco, as well as securities; even slaves were bought and sold until 1788. Certainly the market for securities was of little importance.

The earliest mention of any definite market for securities in the newspapers is to be found in the *Diary, or Loudon's Register*, published in New York in March, 1792. A brief item on that date indicated that dealers in stock met each noon at 22 Wall Street; sales were conducted by a joint arrangement of auctioneers and dealers.[1] New York at that time boasted of one chartered bank, the Bank of New York; the city's population was only 35,000.

[1] Cited by F. L. Eames, *The New York Stock Exchange* (New York: Thomas G. Hall, 1894), p. 13.

Speculation in Revolutionary War Bonds. The securities market first achieved prominence when the federal government was established. Alexander Hamilton, one of the great financial minds of American history, was selected as the first Secretary of the Treasury. In his "Report" of January, 1790, he recommended that the newly created government fund all of the Revolutionary War bonds, those of both the Continental Congress and the thirteen colonies. The holders of these issues were to get new 6 and 3 per cent stock. Great speculation swept the country as bankers, brokers, governors, congressmen, and speculators scoured the nation to buy up the heavily depreciated bonds. Vast fortunes were made in the process.

Hamilton was able to fund the Continental bonds without great opposition, but met with stubborn resistance from Jefferson and others in his proposal to fund the colonial bonds. In a final Congressional battle he lacked one vote in the Senate and five in the House. Hamilton and Jefferson then made one of the most remarkable "deals" in American history.[2] Hamilton was to get his refunding bill; Jefferson was to obtain his wish that the national capital be moved—first to Philadelphia for ten years and then to the South. Great was the rejoicing in Wall Street.

Second only in importance to the speculation in war bonds was that in the stock of the First Bank of the United States. This bank, chartered in 1791, issued stock at 100. Immediately, great interest developed in its shares, not only among financiers and brokers but also among public officials. Within a year they had climbed to 195; the shrewd speculators then took their profits and the stock plummeted to 108 in one short month. Indignation ran high as the large profits of speculators and politicians became known.

The Buttonwood Tree Agreement. The first dealers in securities were not brokers so much as they were merchants and auctioneers. Trading in securities did not become a specialty of those men until speculation in government securities began in 1790. The commodity dealers and the securities brokers now began to separate; the latter took up trading under a buttonwood tree at 68 Wall Street. Eventually the brokers became tired of the monopoly of the auctioneers who sold the stocks, and sought to create an organization of their own. In March, 1792, they met secretly in Corre's Hotel to discuss the maneuver. On May 17, 1792, they drew up and approved in bold script the first document in the history of what was later to be the New York Stock Exchange. Its text was short, its intent unmistakable:

We the Subscribers, Brokers for the Purchase and Sale of Public Stock, do hereby solemnly promise and pledge ourselves to each other, that we will

[2] R. I. Warshow, *The Story of Wall Street* (New York: Greenberg, Publisher, Inc., 1929), p. 30.

not buy or sell from this day for any person whatsoever, any kind of Public Stock, at less than one quarter of one per cent Commission on the Specie value and that we will give preference to each other in our Negotiations. In Testimony whereof we have set our hands this 17th day of May at New York, 1792.[3]

In brief, the agreement had two provisions: (1) the brokers were to deal only with each other, thereby eliminating the auctioneers, and (2) the commissions were to be one quarter of one per cent.

The Period 1792–1817. Comparatively few records are available about this formative period. Although the Buttonwood Tree Agreement centralized the market, there was no great volume of trading other than in government stock. In 1793 the Tontine Coffee House was erected; it was the most elaborate structure in Wall Street and became the first indoor headquarters of the newly formed brokers' organization (Fig. 5–1). Actually, this structure was a merchants' exchange, and many kinds of business were conducted there, including that of brokerage, which was conducted in a room "high up under the eaves." On sunny days the brokers still met on the open pavement.

After speculation in the war bonds and in the stock of the First Bank died down, the business sank to a low level. The tactics of the speculators brought no little criticism upon the business, and public interest shifted to other commercial activities. Newspaper gave scant attention to securities prices and did not resume quotations until 1815. On March 10 of that year the *New York Commercial Advertiser* carried a complete list of twenty-four stocks.[4] Nearly all were government securities and bank stocks; only one manufacturing company graced the list. The small amount of trading at that time was confined largely to a few federal issues and the leading banks. There were few stocks except those issued to finance banks, insurance companies, canals, turnpikes, toll bridges, and water companies.

Brokers in that period were strictly brokers; they did not act as dealers. Hence, transactions in the market originated outside the small group of brokers.

The Indoor Exchange: 1817. A significant step toward a more formal organization was effected by the brokers in 1817. At that time there were eight firms and nineteen individuals engaged in the business. Business was improving as more and more corporations were organized in the country, and the nation increased in economic stature. Accordingly, it was decided that a change was in order. The New York brokers at that time were far behind their rival organization at Philadelphia. The latter group had been operating as an organized board of brokers since

---

[3] Eames, *op. cit.*, p. 14.
[4] Warshow, *op. cit.*, p. 59.

Fig. 5-1. Tontine Coffee House.

1790; it had a president, secretary, and a complete organization with rules. So, in early 1817 the New York group sent a delegate to visit the Philadelphia Exchange and return with a complete report. Immediately upon the return of this one-man delegation, the New York group formally organized its association in very much the same way as that at Philadelphia.[5]

The new organization adopted the name New York Stock and Exchange Board. A constitution was drawn up and officers were elected. Rules were established; one of them forebade "wash sales." Commissions which ranged from ¼ to ½ of one per cent were introduced. The group decided it was no longer proper to meet in the office of Samuel J. Beebe in the old Tontine Coffee House, so it rented a room for its exclusive use at 40 Wall Street at $200 per year with janitor service furnished.

Trading procedure from that period took on greater regularity than it had in the past. The president of the exchange called the stocks in order; there were about thirty on the list at the time. As each issue was called, the brokers made known their bids and offers. Business began about 11:30 A.M. and was usually completed by 1 P.M.. Discipline was maintained by fines. Contracts were settled by 2:15 of the day following the transaction, a practice continued for more than one hundred years.

From 1817 on, the Board became an exclusive organization. Members were voted in with great reluctance; three blackballs kept out an applicant, although there were many applications. In 1817 the initiation fee was the not exorbitant sum of $25; this was raised to $100 in 1827.[6]

The Period 1817 to the Civil War. In the years immediately following the formal organization of 1817, the Exchange Board moved a number of times seeking better quarters. Ten years later it was located in the Merchants' Exchange. Business, however, was still dull. It reached its all-time low of thirty-one shares on March 16, 1830; only two issues, whose total value was $3,470, were traded.

From this period on, trading on the Board improved steadily. The Mohawk and Hudson Railroad was the first railroad stock listed; trading started in August, 1830. Other important stocks were to follow. Millions of dollars' worth of stocks and bonds began to be issued for transportation companies and internal improvements. By 1838 $175 million in securities had been issued by railroads, banks, canals, and turnpikes; many of them found their way to the Exchange Board.[7]

A great fever of land speculation developed in the country in the mid-1830's. Throughout the nation everyone bought and sold land at

[5] J. K. Medbery, *Men and Mysteries of Wall Street* (Boston: Fields, Osgood & Co., 1870), p. 288.

[6] Eames, *op. cit.*, p. 85.

[7] Medbery, *op. cit.*, p. 292.

ever-increasing prices. Banks loaned huge sums on real estate; large quantities of credit poured in from Europe. Farmers neglected their crops in the wild craze. Speculation even reached the Exchange Board; a number of railroad and canal shares doubled and tripled in a few months between late 1834 and early 1835. At last the bubble burst; a crop failure of 1836 was followed by the collapse of land prices in the following year. Although the crisis was largely commercial, the financial district of New York was severely shaken. Many states repudiated their debts; bank failures were on every hand. Speculation again fell to low proportions.

The Exchange Board was burned out of its headquarters by the big fire of 1835. After various attempts to establish a permanent location, one of which was the temporary occupancy of a hayloft, it secured in 1842 a room in the new Merchants' Exchange Building, which was located on the present site of the National City Bank. At the same time it created the office of a paid president; the salary was to be $2,000 per year. Dues were also raised. In the 1840's telegraphic communications began; New York was greatly aided thereby in becoming a national securities market. It had long surpassed Philadelphia as the leading financial center.

The country and the Exchange recovered eventually from the panic of 1837. Nothing of great importance seems to have taken place in the history of the Exchange during the 1840's. By 1848 its membership had grown to seventy-five. Both morning and afternoon sessions were held. After hours much trading was done in the street in front of the Merchants' Exchange. Perhaps 5,000 shares were turned over daily.

By 1848 the Exchange was reporting its financial condition; it appeared to be in excellent shape. Receipts were $10,396 per year and expenditures only $9,317, which left a modest surplus of $1,079.

The volume of outstanding securities grew rapidly in the 1840's and early 1850's. It was estimated that in 1854 there were outstanding securities in the country in excess of $1,178 million. State issues accounted for $111 million alone. Perhaps 18 per cent of the grand total was owned by foreign investors.[8]

In the early 1850's money became more plentiful as wealth poured in from California. Speculation again was rife as the public flocked to the board rooms. So great was speculation that an "outside" board sprang up with even more brokers than the regular exchange. It leased quarters in the room below the Exchange Board, and constant communications were carried on between the two markets. Banks aided the speculative craze with a liberal hand. Brokers were known to deposit

---

[8] Secretary of Treasury, *Report on Foreign Holdings of American Securities,* 1854.

$1,500 in cash and then draw checks of $100,000 to $300,000 which were promptly certified. A popular magazine reported that the twelve months which ended June, 1853, had never been equaled in prosperity since the formation of the new nation.[9]

Suddenly the picture darkened. London began to sell American securities; banks called loans; deposits fell; the market crashed. In late 1853 it was said that Wall Street was as somber as a plague-stricken city and that brokers flitted in and out like uneasy ghosts. The Exchange almost ceased to exist. By the summer of 1855, however, prosperity was back again. Money was plentiful; crops were excellent; railway earnings were high; and speculation was again profitable. This pleasant situation was only of short duration; in 1857 the market declined abruptly. Erie stock fell from 64 to 18, and New York Central from 95 to 53. An irresponsible banking system had again created chaos in the nation's economic organization.

It is worth noting that the Exchange Board showed a marked strength in the crisis of 1857. Although its securities fell sharply, the decline was less than for unlisted ones, which had no market at all. The value of a seat became apparent to all brokers, and many applications were presented in 1858. The Board, however, was in no mood for new members. It had become, in great measure, an exclusive club, a situation of which the brokers were very proud. They wore silk hats and swallowtail coats during business hours. It was a genteel business as well as a profitable one. The entry of young men was frowned upon. To this end, initiation fees were raised to $1,000, a hard fact which kept many young men from joining the organization, even when they were able to overcome the hurdle of five blackballs for membership. As one broker of the period described it: "The old fellows were united together in a mutual admiration league, and fought the young men tooth and nail, contesting every inch of ground when a young man sought entrance to their sacred circle."[10]

Before the Civil War the call money market in New York had grown to extensive proportions. It enabled speculators to carry newly issued securities with bank credit and played no small part in keeping control of the railroads in the hands of American rather than foreign interests. Brokerage firms often advanced large sums to aid in the construction of railroads.

The volume of speculation showed a substantial increase in the late 1850's. In one month of 1856 trading reached one million shares; in one day of 1857 the volume was 71,000.

[9] Medbery, op. cit., p. 306.
[10] Henry Clews, Fifty Years in Wall Street (New York: Irving Publishing Co., 1908), p. 7.

Certain changes in the administration of the Exchange Board were made in 1856.[11] The use of a paid president was discontinued; the position was made honorary. It was not until after the reorganization of 1938 that a salary was again paid the head of the Exchange. Salaries, however, were paid to the first and second vice-presidents, who conducted the "calls" of securities. The income of the organization was now supplemented by annual dues of $50 per member.

During the period 1817–60 Wall Street knew a few great market operators, but not as many as in later years. An outstanding example was Jacob Little, one of the greatest of all "bear operators." In 1837 he founded his own firm of Little and Company. Always consistently bearish, he capitalized on the Panic of 1837. He made and lost four fortunes; from his last defeat he never recovered. Caught short 100,000 share of Erie stock in late 1856, he failed for $10 million. He had sold short too soon.

The Civil War. The Civil War witnessed a wave of speculation in the nation that had never before been equaled. Securities, gold, and commodities were all subject to unbelievable activity. Solid businessmen, brokers, lawyers, clergymen, society ladies, politicians—all were burned with the fever of speculation which continued from early morning to late hours of the night.

No less than four exchanges operated during the war. The New York Stock Exchange adopted its present name in 1863. In addition, there was an open air exchange, the forerunner of the present American Stock Exchange. It traded in the same stocks sold on the floor of the New York Stock Exchange and operated during those hours when the exchange was not in session. In 1862 the "Coal Hole" was established. This was in a basement at 23 William Street; it was operated by a shrewd individual who charged an admission fee for its use. Still another exchange was formed in the room next to the New York Stock Exchange; it traded on what news it could get from the leading exchange.

Trading in gold on the New York Stock Exchange began on the floor in 1861 as soon as the country refused to redeem its greenbacks in specie. Gold soon went to a premium and greenbacks sold at a discount. It was not long before trading in gold became so important that it overshadowed security trading. The Exchange authorities, mindful of this fact as well as the unpatriotic implications of such activity, banned the sale of gold; the activity was immediately transferred to other exchanges, notably the "Coal Hole" and later the Gold Exchange. Gilpin's news room at William Street and Exchange Place was also transformed into a gold market with a $25 a year admission fee. A vast amount of

[11] Eames, *op. cit.*, p. 37.

gold speculation took place in these two markets. In 1864 speculation became so rampant that still another group, the Gold Board, was organized. The "Gold Room" was established, and the major part of this gold trading activity left the "Coal Hole" and Gilpin's to center there.

Greenbacks heavily depreciated during the war and fluctuated with every news story of the war's progress. Gold sold at heavy premiums in terms of the inconvertible paper currency. News was carried to the gold exchanges with greater rapidity than the Associated Press could bring it to the newspapers. Gold first sold at a premium in April, 1862. As Confederate successes mounted, premiums advanced. On July 11, 1864, gold was selling at 285; greenbacks were worth 35 cents on the dollar.

The government made many fruitless attempts to stave off the steady depreciation of its currency. In February, 1863, Congress made it a penal offense to offer loans on bullion above par; the law was ineffective. In April, 1864, Secretary Chase attempted to sell gold at 165; the only effect was a sharp break in the market and a number of bankruptcies and the attempt was abandoned when the Treasury was unable to release a sufficient supply of gold. Congress passed the Gold Bill on June 21, 1864 which prohibited speculation in gold; gold rose from 210 to 250 and the act was repealed in two weeks. Even the successful termination of the war did not eliminate this curious speculative activity.

The Exchange suffered from two serious defects in the Civil War period: (1) its failure to provide a continuous market and (2) its lack of an effective administrative organization.

Black Friday. The most remarkable episode of the entire era of gold speculation developed in late 1869, four years after the close of the Civil War.[12] Jay Gould, called "the smartest man in Wall Street" by no less a personage than Commodore Vanderbilt, attempted to corner the entire gold market. The country was not yet back on a hard money basis; the government was not selling gold. Gould, with close relationships to leading political figures in Washington, including President Grant's son-in-law, was confident that the government would not sell gold. With his associate, Jim Fisk, he began to buy all the gold offered for sale in the Gold Room; it was then quoted at 130. Gould bought not only for his account but for that of Grant's son-in-law and the President's private secretary, although the latter refused the transaction. Confident that his scheme was politically secure, Gould accumulated through several firms contracts to deliever gold totaling $50 million. As there was only $20 million in gold on the market, more gold had been sold than could possibly be delivered on the future contracts. Grant's son-in-law, now

12 Clews, op. cit., p. 181.

thoroughly alarmed, withdrew from the deal, and this ended Gould's political ties with the government. In a short time the manipulator had accumulated $100 million in gold contracts. This had to be unloaded before the government would sell the precious metal. In order to do this he ordered his own associates, Jim Fisk and Albert Speyer, Fisk's chief broker, to buy gold. On Thursday, September 23, 1869, he was able to sell his entire $100 mililon in gold at the top of the market because of Fisk's support.

Friday, September 24, will always be known as "Black Friday." Fisk continued his buying as gold went to 145, 150, 155, 160, 161, 162. Then came from Washington the incredible news: the government was selling gold! Indescribable chaos took possession of trading as frenzied brokers in wild shouts sought to sell gold. Fisk and Speyer in futile attempts bid 160, 170, and 180 for gold; no one paid any attention to them as gold dropped to 140; as the gong sounded the close of the market, it stood at 135. Gould had failed to corner the market.

Thousands of failures resulted from "Black Friday." Gould's profits had been great, but Fisk and his two brokers, Belden and Speyer, were hopelessly involved. In a day when political corruption was a commonplace and justice a travesty, Gould devised a simple plan. Fisk, who had made no commitments on paper, repudiated all of his transactions. Belden and Speyer assumed all legal responsibility for them and went into bankruptcy. As a reward Gould pensioned the two brokers for life. Despite endless lawsuits the creditors could not and did not reach Gould. And thus ended one of the most bizarre manipulations in American history.

The Great Operators. During the period from 1860 to 1900, some of the greatest manipulations in the history of the stock market took place. Daniel Drew, Commodore Vanderbilt, Jim Fisk, Jay Gould, Sam Hallet, W. R. Travers, Leonard W. Jerome and his older brother, Addison, Anthony Morse, Jay Cooke, James R. Keene, Russell Sage—to mention only a few—were truly giants in their day. Each made great fortunes in securities; many of them died in bankruptcy. Giving no quarter to their opponents and asking none, they fought for fortune in the market with every weapon at their command. The only law they knew was the law of the jungle; their ethics, however unsavory they may appear today, were the ethics of their day. They played the hard game of business as the rules were known in that kaleidoscopic, but historic, epoch. Space prevents an adequate description of their many operations; a few are related briefly in Chapter 27.

The Exchange Expands. As the Civil War ended, the New York Stock Exchange began a period of rapid expansion. The West was opening up rapidly; railroads were spreading "like measles at a girls' boarding school," as Daniel Drew described it; manufacturing was achieving new records in mass production; and the securities market was growing apace. The vast development of the railroads was particularly important to the Stock Exchange, since those corporations were the chief issuers of securities in the trading market. About 70,000 miles of lines had been completed by 1873; their outstanding stocks and bonds totaled $3,780 million.

As the volume of trading on the Exchange improved, the system of "calls" was abandoned; this was about 1867. By 1871 the market was definitely operating on a continuous trading basis and the present auction method was in full operation.

New inventions greatly aided the mechanical efficiency of the Exchange. In 1867 the electric stock ticker facilitated the transmission of quotations and popularized trading on the Exchange. The telephone was installed in the Exchange in 1878 and linked the trading floor with the brokerage offices. An expansion of the telegraph system linked New York with brokerage offices in other cities. Seats were definitely declared salable in 1868; at that time they were worth $7,000 to $8,000.

In 1869 the Exchange made far-reaching changes in its organization; the 533 members of the Exchange joined with the 354 members of the Open Board of Brokers and the 173 members of the Government Bond Department. The Exchange then had 1,060 members. The number was limited; a membership or "seat" became salable personal property, and from that date a membership could be obtained only by an applicant's buying the seat from a retiring member.

At the same time the Exchange changed its form of administration. Until then policies of management were submitted to a vote of members. As this was no longer practical, a new constitution was adopted. The Exchange was to be managed by a Governing Committee with executive, legislative, and judicial powers. An elaborate committee system was set up, which continued to function until the reorganization of 1938. The Governing Committee of 28 members was subdivided into seven standing committees, which were responsible for such matters as admissions, stock list, commissions, arbitration, and finance. The president continued to serve without salary and was an active broker.

Membership was increased by 40 to 1,100 in 1879. The proceeds of the sale of the new memberships were used by the Exchange to expand its physical plant at Broad and Wall Street (Fig. 5–2). The number remained unchanged until 1929.

The Exchange introduced a number of much-needed regulations in 1869. Among them were certain listing rules. Listed companies were required to maintain both transfer agents and registrars as a safeguard

Fig. 5–2. New York Stock Exchange.

to prevent overissue of stocks; this was a prevalent practice in the easy-going days of Drew and Schuyler.

Trading in 1870. The character of trading in the post-Civil War period is well described by Medbery.[13] He relates that in 1870 trading on the Exchange was divided into two lists: a Regular List of 278 securities, which consisted of railroad stocks and bonds, city stocks, state bonds, and miscellaneous issues; and a Free List, which consisted of any issues that brokers desired to trade in. The trading in government

[13] Medbery, *op. cit.*, chaps. 2–5.

bonds was in a separate room; all other securities were sold in the Regular Room. Discipline was maintained by fines, for example, $5 for smoking a cigar, $10 for standing on a chair, $.50 for knocking off a man's hat, and $10 for throwing a paper dart. The call method was still used, the Regular List being handled first. Rules permitted cash, regular way, buyer's option, and seller's option deliveries; the first two types were used most. No sale could be made for less than 5 shares; 10 shares was the real unit. Stocks were quoted in the same fractional points as today.

Nearly all of the trading was for speculation; few bought stocks for investment. Bank credit was abundant; a broker could deposit $5,000 and have checks certified for as much as $200,000. Brokers carried stock on margin for customers at interest rates of 6 or 7 per cent; they allowed interest on margin deposited. Margins were very low; a good customer, properly introduced and financially responsible, could buy $1,000 in stock with a $50 margin. On active, speculative stocks, the banks would lend up to 80 to 90 per cent of selling value.

The Period 1870 to World War I. The post-Civil War expansion, which was particularly outstanding in railroads, came to an abrupt halt in 1873 as panic gripped the country. In several years improvement was again observable. From 1875 to 1879 about 51 million shares were traded on the New York Stock Exchange annually; by the next five years activity had doubled to 104 million per year.[14]

In 1873 the Exchange was forced to close down for the second time in its history; the first time was in 1835, when a fire forced the organization to cease operations for a week until it found new quarters. This time the cause was the failure of Jay Cooke and Company, promoters of the Northern Pacific Railroad. Panic gripped Wall Street as the Exchange remained closed for twelve days. Fifty-seven Exchange members and several important banks failed. Exchange business became depressed for several years.

Several noteworthy changes were made in this period in the operation of the New York Stock Exchange. In 1885 the Exchange provided for an Unlisted Department. This new department was created to permit greater trading in the ever-expanding number of industrials; it was to continue until 1910. Although railroad stocks were still the chief center of activity, the growth of giant trusts and combinations whetted the public's interest in these new industries. The Sherman Antitrust Act of 1890 had been passed to stem the flood of monopolies; it did little to curtail the growth of gigantic consolidations.

[14] H. P. Willis and J. I. Bogen, *Investment Banking* (rev. ed.; New York: Harper & Row, Publishers, 1936), p. 228.

The Exchange, after a number of informal and voluntary attempts, all of which ended in failure, established a successful clearing house in 1892. The new plan met with immediate success, but it was to be twenty-eight years before the present Stock Clearing Corporation was organized.

As the century drew to a close, the old manipulators were largely gone and a new group of financial leaders rose to power in Wall Street. These men were great railway magnates, bankers, and industrialists. They were builders rather than destroyers, even though their methods were often as ruthless as any employed by the early manipulators. Among them was J. Pierpont Morgan, a man of tremendous prestige in banking, railroads, and industrial combinations; his firm became the most powerful in Wall Street. Jacob H. Schiff of Kuhn, Loeb and Company was also a highly influential investment banker. Hill and Harriman were outstanding names in railroading. Rockefeller and his associates, Rogers, Pratt, and Flagler, held the controlling interest in the Standard Oil Trust. Andrew Carnegie and Charles Schwab were leaders in the steel industry. Many of these men, such as Rockefeller and Carnegie, never were in the stock market; others, such as Harriman, operated in it constantly. In this period the great investment banks dominated the securities markets more and more.

As the great industrial combinations rose to prominence, speculative activity took place in them. This first wave of speculation ended in the Panic of 1893. The depression of that year was one of the most severe in the nation's history. Railroads as well as industrials were hard hit. One-fourth of the railroads in the country were in bankruptcy courts, including such giants as the Union Pacific, Santa Fe, Northern Pacific, and Reading. The economic distress of the country was extreme. Those were "hard times" indeed; the term "depression" had not yet entered the popular jargon. The stock market was similarly stricken.

The second speculative wave in industrial combinations ran from 1897 to 1903. During that period J. P. Morgan, then at the peak of his power, organized the first billion dollar corporation, the United States Steel Corporation. Its stock, although entirely "water" at the time, became a dominant stock market leader at once, a position it has retained ever since. Many of the other consolidations, however, proved to be disappointments, and speculative interest after 1903 turned elsewhere.

The turn of the century saw a pronounced expansion in trading on the New York Stock Exchange. The annual stock volume, which had been only 57 million shares in 1896, rose to 265 million in 1901. The bond volume increased from $394 million to almost $1 billion in the same period. Huge amounts of new capital were authorized. In 1899 industrial corporations alone issued $2,244 million in new securities. New railroad issues totaled $107 million in the same year and increased to $527 million three years later.[15] Henry Clews estimated that $6 billion was the total capitalization of new combinations from 1897 to 1902.[16]

After the nation had decided unequivocally to go on the gold standard in 1900, the country began to enjoy a monetary inflation. Prices by 1907 were up 16 per cent from those of 1893. For ten years a continuous growth in production, corporation earnings, and dividends had taken place; and the market rose. In late 1906, however, signs of distress began to appear; new securities were not selling and the market weakened as big operators unloaded $800 million in securities. In March, 1907, panic broke out in Wall Street both on the Exchange and in banking. All leading stocks showed severe declines. Many leading trust companies came under suspicion; the Knickerbocker Trust Company closed its doors, and bank runs became general. Banks all over the country partially suspended specie payments. Call money rose to 125 per cent. The "rich man's panic" was short but severe.

The Exchange came under fire in two investigations before World War I. The first was the Hughes Committee investigation of 1909. Although highly critical of certain speculative practices, the committee did not press for legislation but recommended that the Exchange itself adopt a more vigorous program of self-regulation. The Pujo investigation in 1912, although authorized to study the stock market, was noted largely for its scrutiny of the so-called "money trust."

There were only 145 stocks and 162 bonds listed on the "Big Board" in 1869 when the Exchange was consolidated. By 1914 those had grown to 511 and 1,082, respectively. The market, however, was still a professional one when the war broke out in Europe, although many of the public were attracted during peak periods of activity. *The New York Times* in 1914 was carrying only two pages of financial news, and one column was sufficient for stock quotations. The *New York Herald Tribune* had only three persons in its whole financial department. About 150 million shares were listed on the Exchange contrasted with more than 6½ billion today. The typical stockholder of the newspaper cartoonist was the pudgy banker with the silk hat and striped trousers.

Corporations did not boast of vast stockholder lists before World War I. Much of the stock of the giant industrials was carried in "street names" for speculation. American Telephone and Telegraph had 8,000 stockholders in 1901, and United States Steel 14,000. Du Pont had not yet gone into industrial chemistry; it had only 2,800 stockholders as late as 1922. The vast Standard Oil empire was still closely held; Standard

15 *Ibid.*, p. 233.
16 Clews, *op. cit.*, p. 772.

Oil Company (New Jersey) reported only 8,300 stockholders in 1920. The public was not yet "in the market."

In 1910 a corporation that has been eclipsed only recently and briefly by A.T. & T. as a money-maker and seldom as a stock market leader was formed from twenty-four corporations, many of them worthless. It was General Motors, promoted by W. C. Durant, one of the greatest bull market operators since Commodore Vanderbilt. He lost control of the company to New York bankers in 1911, but ousted them from power in 1916. At that time the company had only 473 stockholders. By 1919 Durant had rolled up a very large fortune. In the following year the market fell and General Motors stock sagged to 12; Durant was bankrupt. In the 1920's he attempted to regain his position but his new automobile company was not a success. Re-entering the stock market, he produced another large fortune by 1929; again, market reverses destroyed his fortune and he died a comparatively poor man. His creation, General Motors, however, enjoyed brilliant industrial and financial management and went on to unprecedented growth and prosperity. Over a forty-year period it has been a market favorite.

World War I. The opening of World War I brought with it a great crisis. In the early summer of 1914 war clouds loomed ominously over Europe. Security selling by European interests developed rapidly, as attempts were made to convert values into gold in anticipation of needs at home. Stocks dropped about 20 points on July 31, when the London Stock Exchange closed down. A hasty meeting of leading bankers and Stock Exchange officials was called. When convincing evidence was presented of a new avalanche of selling orders from Europe, it was decided to shut the Exchange indefinitely. It closed the next morning and remained closed until December 12, 1914; this was the first such closing since the collapse of Jay Cooke and Company in 1873. Trading was resumed on a restricted basis but was not satisfactory for months. Eventually war orders poured in from Europe and prosperity began to stimulate industry. Speculation in some favored industries, known as "war brides," became pronounced; the market was again functioning in normal stride.

One important effect of the war was the great public participation in government bond buying. For the first time in the country's history the general populace became security conscious. The government, with every resource at its command, pushed the distribution of Liberty bonds. The taste for security ownership was stimulated; it developed with extreme rapidity in the next decade. Before the war it was estimated that there were only 200,000 security owners in the country; afterward there were 20 million, including those who owned government bonds.[17]

The New Era. The fabulous 1920's were called the "New Era" by some who had more imagination than foresight. The country witnessed a short but severe deflation in 1920 and 1921. There were great speculative losses in securities, commodities, and land. In several years, however, prosperity was again blanketing the nation as industry boomed. The world was at peace "for all time," it was hoped; factories were humming; prices were stable; the banking system was sound; the market was better and better. It was generally believed that depressions were a thing of the past and that the nation was on a permanent plateau of sustained and stable prosperity.

An unusual set of favorable circumstances paved the way for the market boom of the late 1920's. Our nation had emerged from the conflict the strongest and soundest nation in the world, with an incomparable productive system. We were now a great creditor nation and began to pour millions abroad; these great loans, which totaled $15 billion in a decade, sustained our foreign trade in no small measure. The government was friendly to big business and combinations grew on every hand—in banking, public utilities, automobiles, foods, motion pictures, petroleum, electrical equipment, etc. Promising new industries, such as radio and aviation, stimulated investment. Other industries, such as motion pictures, chemicals, automobiles, and electrical equipment, made remarkable progress. Investment bankers perfected the art of wide security distribution. Common stocks achieved wide popularity, not only those of well-established companies on the New York Stock Exchange, but also those of newly promoted corporations. The terms "holding company" and "investment trust" became magic terms. To further the boom, the Federal Reserve banks initiated an "easy money" policy in 1927.

Common stocks became "the thing" for both investment and speculation. The number of new stock issues floated in the capital market increased from 1,822 in 1921 to 6,417 in 1929. In the latter year 62 per cent of all new security issues were stocks, contrasted with only 15 per cent eight years earlier. The year 1929 saw the capital market absorb $5,924 million in new stock issues, contrasted with only $1,087 million three years before. Stock prices rose in the same remarkable degree. The market value of all listed stocks on the Exchange increased from $27.1 billion in early 1925 to $89.7 billion in September, 1929. *The New York Times* industrial average, which had reached a low of 66.24 in 1921, closed at 180.57 in 1925; after a short decline in 1927 it skyrocketed

---

[17] Willis and Bogen, *op. cit.*, p. 235.

to the all-time high of 469.49 on September 19, 1929, or seven times its 1921 low.

With all of this expansion the volume of trading on the Exchange grew rapidly as the public entered the market in greater and greater numbers. Never had brokers had so many customers; never had the trading floor witnessed such activity. From an annual volume of 171 million shares in 1921, trading rose to 450 million in 1925 and 1926, 920 million in 1928, and 1.1 billion in 1929. Brokers' loans were up to $8,549 million. Probably a million Americans were carrying 300 million shares on margin.

Then came the storm. On Wednesday, October 23, 1929, the market cracked. On a 6-million-share volume *The New York Times* industrial average dropped 31 points. On the next day the market dropped again as the ticker ran hours behind on a new record total of 12,895,000 shares. On October 28 the industrial average fell another 49 points, followed by 43 points on the 29th, when 16,400,000 shares changed hands. The New Era was over.

From 1929 to mid-1932 security values melted away as the country slid into its longest and worst depression. The Dow-Jones industrial average fell 89 per cent. The listed value of stocks on the Exchange slumped from $89.7 to $15.6 billion. United States Steel dropped from 262 to 21; American Telephone and Telegraph from 310 to 70; New York Central from 256 to 9; General Motors from 92 to 7; and Radio Corporation of America from 115 to 3. Seldom in all its turbulent history had gloom been so impenetrable in Wall Street. Grave troubles, however, were still ahead.

The Senate Investigation of 1933–34. The most exhaustive investigation ever made by the federal government of the securities market and the Exchange was that of the Committee on Banking and Currency of the Senate in 1933 and early 1934. Like many investigations of that day, it had two purposes: (1) to uncover real or alleged flaws and irregularities in our economic system and (2) to build up a strong political support by extensive publicity for the forthcoming legislation which was to follow the investigation.

The Pecora investigation, as it was often called because Ferdinand Pecora served as chief examiner for the committee, ran for seventeen months. It examined many of the most powerful figures in Wall Street: bank presidents, exchange officials, prominent brokers, investment bankers, and utility executives. When the investigation was over, twelve thousand pages of testimony, which filled twenty volumes, had been taken. Many irregularities, unethical practices, and often cases of outright fraud were uncovered by the inquiry, which was highly publicized by the press.

Four federal laws developed from the investigation: the Banking Act of 1933, the Securities Act of 1933, the Securities Exchange Act of 1934, and the Public Utility Holding Company Act of 1935. The Securities Exchange Act of 1934 subjected all stock exchanges to extensive government control for the first time. Temporarily, power to enforce the Act was given to the Federal Trade Commission. Shortly thereafter a new and powerful federal agency, the Securities and Exchange Commission, was established to enforce the Act. Its work is described in detail in Chapter 28.

The Exchange Reorganizes. Although the Securities and Exchange Act and the SEC compelled the New York Stock Exchange to make a number of changes in rules, for a while there was no significant change in its organization. As early as 1935 the chairman of the SEC had suggested to the Exchange administration that a reorganization was in order. A discussion of the proposal revealed divided reactions from Exchange members. Many of the commission firms believed some change was in order; the floor members, who owned most of the seats, opposed any such plan. A stalemate existed between the SEC and the Exchange until 1937, when the new chairman of the SEC, William O. Douglas, determined that a thorough reorganization of the Exchange was in order, whether it received a majority endorsement by Exchange members or not. In a very strong statement, dated November 23, 1937, Douglas stated in part:

Operating as private membership associations, exchanges have always administered their affairs in much the same manner as private clubs. For a business so vested with public interest, this traditional method has become archaic. The task of conducting the large exchanges (especially the New York Stock Exchange) has become too engrossing for those who must also run their own business. . . . Their management should not be in the hands of professional traders but in fact, as well as nominally, in charge of those who have a clearer public responsibility.[18]

The implications of the statement were clear. The Exchange must reorganize; there must be full-time, paid executives to run to Exchange; there must be public representation in Exchange affairs; the club method of operation was archaic and undemocratic. To this many of the Exchange members agreed; others, often labeled the "Old Guard" by the press, were strongly opposed.

After some reluctance the Governing Committee gave the President of the Exchange power to appoint the so-called Conway Committee, which was composed of five members of the Exchange and four prominent outside representatives and headed by a well-known manufacturer.

[18] *The New York Times,* November 24, 1937.

The actual writing of the report was largely the responsibility of a rising young member of the Exchange, William McC. Martin, Jr., who was thoroughly in favor of the reorganization plan; he had been named as secretary of the committee and was destined to be the first President of the reorganized Exchange. The committee was appointed on December 10, 1937, and made its report on January 27 of the following year. Specific recommendations were made for a thorough reorganization; among them were (1) a full-time, paid president; (2) an entirely new Board of Governors with representation for non-member brokers and out-of-town members; (3) public representation on the Board; and (4) a drastic revision of the committee system.

The committee report, which embodied most of Chairman Douglas' ideas on reorganization, was strongly praised by him as a sound step in the right direction. The great majority of the membership of the Exchange favored the recommendations of the report, but a few of the "Old Guard" counseled delay. Then a remarkable incident occurred. At 10:05 on March 8, 1938, the gong of the Exchange sounded and the president announced: "Richard Whitney and Company suspended . . . conduct inconsistent with just and equitable principles of trade." The leader of the "Old Guard" was not only bankrupt but guilty of dishonesty; his defalcations were extensive and could neither be concealed nor made good. The battle for reorganization was over. On March 17 the Governing Committee expelled Richard Whitney, former President of the Exchange; on the same day, by an overwhelming vote, it adopted the new plan of reorganization. The Whitney scandal was a bitter dose for the Exchange. Out of the reorganization fight, however, the Exchange emerged an organization with greater public responsibility than ever before and with rules which should make another Whitney scandal impossible. The new Board of Governors was voted into office in May, 1938. The first president, Mr. Martin, took office shortly afterward.

History Since 1939. Many chapters in this book cover the changes in the operation of the New York Stock Exchange since 1939 and the events that have affected its affairs. They will be only summarized at this point.

Despite the world-shaking events that developed in this period, the New York Stock Exchange has operated in an atmosphere that has been quiet compared with many of the turbulent episodes which colored its career in earlier years.

World War II broke out in the late summer of 1939. Hitler's legions stormed into Poland on September 1. *The New York Times* fifty-stock average gained a full point. On Sunday, September 3, England and France declared war on Germany. Monday was a holiday. On Tuesday the market rose sharply by 6 points. It continued to rise and by the end of the month there was an increase of another 7 points. Industrial stocks were especially bullish during September and climbed 25 points as traders dreamed of luscious war profits. A period of pessimism and doubt, however, engulfed the market in May, 1940 as the allies suffered heavy reverses. By April, 1942, industrial stocks were down by one-third from their best levels at the opening of the war. A bull market then began; it did not end until August, 1946, when fear of a phantom depression which never appeared unsettled the world of finance.

Stocks remained in the doldrums from late 1946 to 1949, and then began the longest bull market on record. Although the shock of the Korean War brought an immediate and drastic break in prices, the decline ran its course in two months. Recovery then became pronounced and the bull market re-emerged. There was a slight decline in early 1953 as a mild recession began. This was reversed in late 1953. The rise in *The New York Times* industrial average from September, 1953, to December, 1955, was 292 points, or 107 per cent, one of the most amazing bull markets on record. The only hesitancy in this rise took place in September, 1955, when the President of the United States suffered a heart attack. The ensuing break caused the widest one-day liquidation in points since 1929 and the greatest dollar loss in history. The market made a sharp recovery the following day and reached a new all-time high before the close of the year. These levels were maintained to mid-1957, when a second break in the market occurred. Between July and December of that year *The New York Times* average fell about 140 points, or 20 per cent, from its high point. Through 1958 and 1959 the market rose rapidly again; *The New York Times* average rose 200 points. A dip in 1960 was offset by a rise in 1961.

During the period of 1939 to 1962 there was a minimum of criticism of the Exchange and its operations as compared with earlier years. The regulations of the SEC and the Exchange on manipulation and irregular practices were effective in shielding the Exchange from the bitter criticism which was so common from 1929 to 1933. Few incidents of irregularity ever appeared in the press.

There were two major investigations of the stock market during the latter part of this period: the so-called "friendly investigation" of early 1955 and the broad study begun in 1961. The first was conducted by the Senate Committee on Banking and Currency and was known as the "Fulbright investigation" because the committee was headed by Senator Fulbright. The investigation was prompted by the uneasiness at Washington about the continued rise in stock prices and the fear that "another 1929" might be imminent.

The investigation began by the mailing of questionnaires to some 5,500 brokers, dealers, investment advisers, and others and to 113 economists. The study started on March 3 with the calling to the witness chair of many highly placed individuals in the field of finance and government. The investigation was at first concerned with the problem of whether stocks were too high in relation to earnings, dividends and future prospects. There was no unanimity of opinion. Naïve opinions were expressed by supposedly well-informed persons, such as the one that book values are a key factor in determining stock prices. This line of investigation ceased in a few days.

The examination of the market then proceeded to a study of the possibility that the country might be surging into a period of overoptimism and overspeculation. The views of one economist were so pessimistic in this regard that a sharp break in the market took place after his testimony. Whether or not this was actually the cause of the break was disputed; the President announced at the same time that he had asked Congress for a new Negotiation Act which would affect the profits of airplane companies. Subsequent testimony was very conflicting as to the credit situation, some viewing it with alarm and others with composure. Few found the market or credit situation at a dangerous level. There was no mention of possible manipulation.

During the investigation no one, not even the investigating committee, appeared eager to cause any disturbance of the market. Actual criticism of the operations of the Exchange was scarcely voiced during the investigation. In fact, the most bitter part of the investigation appeared when political leaders of one party accused those of the other that they were trying to wreck the inquiry. The investigation closed in late March. No new laws grew out of it, nor were any new regulations put into effect. The market and the public soon forgot the whole matter. The final report of the Committee made no drastic recommendations.

The second investigation has been an intensive inquiry by the SEC into the ways in which different operations are performed in the exchange market and by the brokerage community. Some recommendations for change of procedure, organization, and regulation are to be forthcoming, but at this writing no formal reports of findings have been released.

From 1939 to 1962 a number of internal changes were made in the operation of the Exchange. Commissions were raised substantially in 1953 and 1958 because of a rise of brokerage house operational costs. The Exchange during 1952 introduced the leased-wire system of operation of the ticker service. The age of automation struck the Quotation Department in 1952 when a system of tape recorders was installed to speed up the quotations on very active stocks.

Saturday closings became effective in 1952. The move was due in considerable measure to the use of the five-day week in other financial institutions in New York and the consequent employment problems. Partially offsetting this reduction in trading hours was an increase in the length of the trading day from 3:00 P.M. to 3:30 P.M., a move causing some unhappiness to the editors of evening newspapers.

A decade of low market volume brought several proposals to reduce the number of memberships. In 1952 the members approved a plan to purchase seats for permanent retirement at a specified maximum price. Improvement in market volume caused seat prices to rise above the figure chosen after only nine seats had been retired. Further action was postponed for an indefinite period.

Another step was the decision in 1953 to admit member corporations. This was a marked break with the traditional practice of admitting only individuals and partnerships. By 1961 seventy-eight corporations were members.

Early in 1954 member firms of the Exchange introduced a new technique for buying listed stocks. The Monthly Investment Plan, or MIP, provides a means for purchase of stocks in small amounts. Under the plan, an investor may make payments as small as $40 per quarter or as large as $1,000 per month to his broker. The amounts paid, after deduction of commissions, are invested in shares of stock of issues he chooses. A means for crediting his account with ownership of fractional shares is part of the plan. Every bit of his money is invested promptly. MIP is not an installment plan sale; the investor owns what he buys and is under no contractual obligation to make further payments. He can withdraw from MIP at any time he wishes to do so. Dividends on the shares he acquires are reinvested automatically in the same stock, thus increasing his investment more rapidly, or paid to him in cash.

In 1961 a decision to change the Exchange facilities was reached and the members voted to increase dues and other charges to create a building fund.

The Exchange in recent years has poured an immense amount of time, effort, and money into examining the security market, the stockholders of the country, and the public transactions of the Exchange. Outstanding among these were the investigations of the number and characteristics of stockholders of publicly owned corporations. The first such investigation was conducted for the Exchange by a well-known research organization. It was the first serious attempt ever made to determine the number of stockholders.[19] Succeeding studies were made by the Ex-

[19] Lewis H. Kimmel, *Share Ownership in the United States* (Washington, D.C.: The Brookings Institution, 1952).

change staff in 1956, 1959, and 1962, and the promise of continuing flows of information on this subject is real.[20]

Many surveys made by the Exchange in recent years have thrown light on such formerly obscure facts as the status and characteristics of individuals and institutions in the market and the characteristics of trading and investing transactions.

Today's management of the Exchange differs widely from that previous to 1939. Its management has changed from the old committee system to one resembling the modern corporation with a paid, professional staff in direct control. The public is now represented on the Board of Governors by three appointees of the President. Extensive changes have been made in its rules. The Exchange has opened its doors to the public for the first time, and hundreds of thousands of visitors now come to the Exchange yearly and observe its operations. An extensive campaign by a staff highly conscious of the importance of public relations in business has been conducted to educate the public about the functions of the Exchange, about investing on a sound basis, and about shareownership. The Exchange no longer considers itself an exclusive club, but rather an institution with a public responsibility; its operations are no longer concealed by an impenetrable screen of secrecy so characteristic many years ago. As J. Pierpont Morgan once observed, "The market will continue to fluctuate," but it is no longer dominated by the manipulative actions of pools and great operators as it once was. The stock market may be less colorful, but public protection is greater than ever before. The gains of bull markets and the losses of bear markets are ever-present, but fair practices are the order of the day.

---

[20] E.g., *Shareownership in America: 1959* (New York: New York Stock Exchange, 1960) and *1962 Census of Shareowners in America* (New York: New York Stock Exchange, 1962).

6

New York Stock Exchange—
Its Organization and
Membership

One of the most striking changes in the operation of the New York Stock Exchange in recent years has been the change in administration. This development followed the reorganization of 1938. A brief review of the management system in use before that date will indicate the contrast in the two organizational plans.

ORGANIZATIONAL FEATURES

Pre-1938 Organization. In 1869 the Exchange effected a consolidation with two lesser organizations: the Open Board of Brokers and the Government Bond Department. At that time the Exchange adopted a management pattern which was retained until 1938. It was based on the committee system. The Governing Committee was intrusted with complete powers of control over the affairs of the Exchange. It was selected from the membership by ballot, but was characterized by a rather slow turnover in its composition, so that a dominant faction was likely to retain control for some period of time. There were a number of standing committees or subcommittes, which were composed of members of the Governing Committee; for example, finance, admissions, stock list, arbitration, floor procedure, bonds. At one time there were thirteen such standing committees. At the head of the Exchange was the President, who served without pay; he was also a member of the Governing Committee and an active broker. The government of the Exchange was, therefore, vested entirely in the brokers and dealers.

This committee system of government and management was compared by some critics to that of a "private club," and did have some of the characteristics of such an association. The committee system of control was entirely changed by the reorganization of 1938; it was superseded by the present system, which resembles somewhat the organizational plan of the modern corporation which is owned by its shareholders (members), whose policies, subject to the provisions of the charter and bylaws (constitution and rules), are determined by a board of directors (governors), and which is managed by a paid staff of executive officers.

The Exchange as a Business Organization. The Exchange is neither a corporation nor a partnership, although it has some characteristics of both types of organization. It is an unincorporated association. It is like a corporation in that its existence is not affected by the death or withdrawal of any one member. It is similar to a partnership in that its members are subject to unlimited liability; the rights of ownership are not freely transferable; there is no stock issued; its powers flow from no statute; and new members must be personally acceptable to the existing membership.

In its early years the Exchange did not desire incorporation and, indeed, resisted any attempts to force incorporation, despite frequent agitation from the outside. This was based on the grounds that self-regulation was more desirable than government control; it felt that swifter administrative action over policies was possible; and it believed that this form of organization permitted greater disciplinary action over its membership.[1] It should also be pointed out, however, that since the Exchange was unincorporated in those years, it was able to transact its affairs and trading operations in whatever manner it pleased as long as it did not transgress the law. Under the Securities Exchange Act of 1934, Congress rejected the idea of complete self-regulation as being adequate for public protection and provided for registration of all exchanges that do an interstate business.

The Exchange may best be described as a "voluntary association."[2] This would seem to apply to any type of exchange, whether licensed or not, and in spite of the fact that it may resemble in some degree both a corporation and a partnership. This definition seems justified in view of the fact that the organization does not engage in business for itself; it does not attempt to make a profit from its operations; and it functions in

[1] J. E. Meeker, *The Work of the Stock Exchange* (New York: The Ronald Press Co., 1930), p. 463.

[2] C. H. Meyer, *The Law of Stockbrokers and Stock Exchanges* (New York: Baker, Voorhis & Co., Inc., 1931), p. 37.

order to create a convenient market place for its members in the transaction of their business.

A National Securities Exchange. The New York Stock Exchange is
now registered with the SEC, an agency of the federal government, as
a national securities exchange. This registration power is delegated to
the SEC by the Securities Exchange Act of 1934.[3] It is mandatory that
all exchanges operating in interstate and domestic commerce and through
the mails register under the Act. All securities exchanges in the country
must be so registered unless exempted by the SEC. An exchange must
file a registration statement with the Commission; it must agree to
comply with the Act and any regulations laid down under it; it must
file data on organization, rules of procedure, membership, constitution,
and bylaws; it must have rules that provide for the expulsion, suspension, or disciplining of members who violate the Act, its rules, or just
principles of trade. After an application for registration is filed, the
SEC is given thirty days in which to grant the registration or deny it.

Any exchange may make its own rules and bylaws as long as they
do not run counter to the Act. In other words, a registered exchange can
still conduct its affairs by a policy of self-regulation provided its rules
and practices are acceptable to the SEC and consistent with the purposes
of the Act.

THE BOARD OF GOVERNORS

Its Membership. The Board of Governors consists of thirty-three
members: (1) the Chairman; (2) the President; (3) thirteen members
from within the metropolitan area of New York, of whom not less than
seven shall be general partners of member firms or holders of voting
stock in member corporations having direct contact with the public and
of whom not less than ten shall spend a substantial portion of their time
on the floor of the Exchange; (4) six members or allied members from
within the metropolitan area of New York who shall be general partners
of member firms or holders of voting stock in member corporations having direct contact with the public, of whom five shall be allied members
and one a member of the Exchange; (5) nine members or allied members from outside the metropolitan area who shall be general partners
of member firms or holders of voting stock in member corporations having direct contact with the public, of whom not less than two shall be
members of the Exchange; and (6) three representatives of the public.

This rather complex composition of the Board is designed to insure
representation for the following groups: (1) brokers doing business with
the public; (2) brokers who work on the floor of the Exchange and those

[3] Securities Exchange Act of 1934, Sec. 6.

who do not; (3) regular members and allied members; (4) brokers whose place of business is in the metropolitan area and those whose place of business is outside the area; and (5) the general public.

A highly significant phase of the membership is that of the three public representatives. These men are not connected with the securities business; typically, they are important business executives. They represent an outside viewpoint; if active and well qualified, they are in a position to render a very useful service to the outside public. In earlier years the Governing Committee was criticized as being the controlling body of a "private club" concerned only with its own special interests. The admission of public representatives to the Board of Governors is a reform based on the realization that the Exchange is a truly public market.

Its Selection. The Board of Governors is selected by several methods. The President of the Exchange automatically becomes a member of the Board upon his appointment. The three public representatives are nominated by the President and approved by the Board; they serve one-year terms. The Chairman is elected by the membership and serves a one-year term. Twenty-eight members serve three-year terms with approximately one-third being elected each year. Candidates for the Board are placed in nomination before each spring election by a nominating committee of six members and three allied members, none of whom is on the Board of Governors. A new nominating committee is elected every year. Candidates for the Board also may be nominated by petition.

Its Functions. The Board of Governors meets every Thursday to transact the business of the Exchange (Fig. 6–1). The Board is the chief policy making body of the Exchange; it is responsible for over-all policy. Although the President prepares the estimates of income for the Exchange and makes recommendations as to expenditures, the Board makes the final decisions upon finances and the budget. It is responsible for the discipline of members and may impose such penalties as fines, suspension, and expulsion. The Board has the sole authority to approve the applications of new members, allied members, and other principals. In addition, it has final authority on the listing of new securities. One of its numerous duties is the allocation of stocks to trading posts on the floor of the Exchange. When a new security is being considered for allocation, specialists are permitted to apply for the right to act in the stock; the Board, after consideration of the qualifications of the applicants to make a market in the stock, will give it to the one best fitted.

The Board conducts its work largely as a body rather than through a number of highly specialized committees. In fact, it has no formal standing committees, which were characteristic of former years. There

Fig. 6–1. The Board of Governors of the New York Stock Exchange, 1961.

is an advisory committee of seven members, on which all Governors from New York serve in rotation, which brings before the Board matters of general importance. A subcommittee on admissions, composed of four floor members of the advisory committee, considers proposed members, allied members, and other principals, and makes recommendations to the Board. A subcommittee of Governors on the floor makes recommendations on location of stocks, assignment of stocks to specialists, and other floor matters. Special matters under discussion, such as commissions and trading hours, may be referred to *ad hoc* committees.

The Chairman of the Board. The Chairman of the Board is elected by the members of the Exchange and is eligible for re-election for two or more consecutive terms. He is a member of the Exchange. His principal duty is to preside over the meetings of the Board. He has the power to call special meetings of the Board upon request; he is an *ex-officio* member of all committees; he appoints committees that the Board has authorized to consider matters pertaining to the administration of the Exchange and Exchange policies concerning members and member organizations.

MANAGEMENT OF THE EXCHANGE

The President. The Exchange is managed by the President and the other executive officers of the organization. These men are full-time, paid executives, who function through a number of operating departments and subsidiary corporations. This is in marked contrast to the older system in which the powers of management were vested in the Governing Committee and the President, who was also a member of the Exchange.

Under the new Constitution the President has very great and extensive powers, similar to those wielded by the president of a large industrial corporation. He is selected by the Board and serves at its pleasure and his compensation is fixed by its members. The President not only sits on the Board but may call special meetings. He serves *ex officio* on all of its committees. He nominates the public representatives on the Board. In addition, he appoints all committees that consider public matters. Thus he has a very real voice on the Board.

The President has charge of all the executive officers and staff of the Exchange. In other words, subject to Board approval, he appoints all the other executive officers and employees, fixes their compensation, and determines their duties and responsibilities. They are responsible to him, and he may terminate their employment, subject to Board approval.

He has the duty of preparing the budget of the Exchange; its final approval is the responsibility of the Board. He also appoints the counsel of the Exchange.

During his term of office the President may not engage in any other business, nor may he be a member of the Exchange; if he is a member at the time of his appointment, he must dispose of such membership. Here, again, there is a radical departure from the earlier management of the Exchange, when the President was always a member, often a very prominent broker or trader on the floor and served without pay.

As chief executive of the Exchange and its official representative in all public matters, he becomes its principal spokesman. A heavy burden of the office is the making of speeches and appearances before governmental bodies to present the viewpoint of the Exchange and often that of the securities markets as well.

Internal Organization. Rather substantial reorganization changes have been made in the Exchange in recent years. The over-all control of the Exchange is, of course, vested in the Board of Governors. Beneath it in the organizational structure is the President.

Six executives report directly to the President. Three are line officers: the Executive Vice-president in charge of Operations, the Vice-president in charge of Administration and Finance, and the Vice-president in charge of Public Relations and Market Development. Three staff executives also report directly to the President: the Economist, the Special Assistant to the President, and the Assistant to the President responsible for consideration of Civic and Government Affairs (Fig. 6–2).

The largest of the organizational divisions is Operations. It includes six departments. The Floor Department has two sections: (1) the Floor Procedure section, which is concerned with the settlement of contracts, administration of floor rules, analysis of floor trading, investigation of the operations of specialists, regulation of odd-lot dealers, and answering questions on the floor about rules of the Exchange as they apply to trading; and (2) the Floor Operations section, which is concerned with the facilities and personnel necessary for the maintenance of efficient floor operations. This area of concern is described more fully in Chapters 10 through 15.

The Department of Member Firms is concerned with administration and enforcement of the rules and policies affecting member firms and their personnel. Compliance with the capital rules (see page 124) is one of the principal protections for other member firms and the public, enforced by a staff of twenty-eight skilled Exchange Examiners who visit all firms annually and review periodic questionnaires submitted by firms and their independent public accountants. Another section of the department exhaustively investigates the background of each candidate for registration as a representative of a member firm to the public. Other sections of the department review legal documents of member firms,

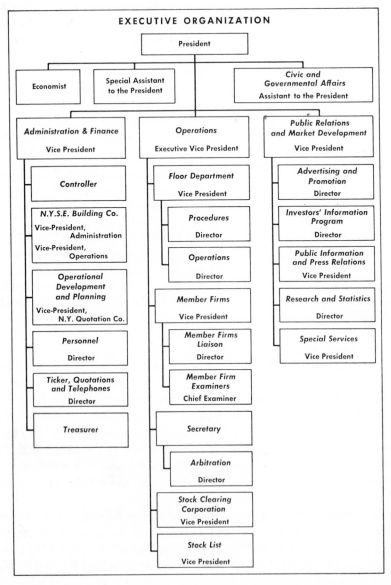

Fig. 6–2. Executive organization, New York Stock Exchange, 1962.

consider applications for extensions of margin credit under Regulation T, interpret margin rules, review wire connections with non-members, approve ticker applications, process applications for participation in secondary distributions and other special block marketing methods, interpret commission rules, register branch offices and enforce rules concerning offices, investigate conduct matters, and process inquiries and complaints from the public.

The Department of Member Firms Liaison coordinates Exchange relationships with member firms. It organizes regular visits to out-of-town firms by Exchange executives and is concerned with services in member firm operations and management. It exercises the Exchange's leadership function in improving training of registered representatives, operating employees, and managers. Approved courses for registered representative trainees have been organized in major cities, and a variety of educational conferences are conducted. The department also is responsible for preparation of the registered representative qualification examinations.

The Secretary of the Exchange also reports to the Executive Vice-president in charge of Operations. He and his Office provide various staff services for the Board of Governors, the Trustees of the Gratuity Fund, and certain committees; investigate and process applications for admission of Exchange members, allied members, and other principals (as described on page 118); administer the Exchange's arbitration facilities, which handle disputes between members and between the public and members; and supervise publication of the Exchange's official *Weekly Bulletin* and the *New York Stock Exchange Guide*. The latter is a three-volume, loose leaf service containing: (1) a directory of members, member firms, and listed securities, (2) the text of the Exchange's Constitution, Rules, and policies, and (3) information concerning securities laws and regulations. In this work the Secretary is assisted by an Assistant Secretary, an Arbitration Director, and a Manager of Admissions.

Two other departments of the Operations Division are the Department of Stock List and the Stock Clearing Corporation. The work of these departments is described in detail in Chapters 7 and 16.

The Division of Administration and Finance has charge of the Office of the Controller; the Department of Personnel; the Department of Operational Development and Planning; the Office of the Treasurer; the Department of Ticker, Quotations and Telephones; the New York Stock Exchange Building Corporation; the Newex Corporation; and the Newin Corporation.

The Division of Public Relations and Market Development has control over five departments: (1) Advertising and Sales Promotion, (2) Investors' Information Program, (3) Public Information and Press Relations, (4) Research and Statistics, and (5) Special Services.

Although the Exchange has long had a department for public relations and has conducted an extensive research program, the present organization goes far beyond any previous efforts made by the Exchange to build up its public relations. The Division now has a highly developed program designed to advertise the Exchange, its member firms, listed securities, its stock purchase plan, and Exchange activities. Extensive research is also done in the analysis of public and institutional transactions and the characteristics of stockholders, traders, and investors. A constant stream of publications and publicity calls attention to these activities. They are similar to activities now being undertaken by nearly all leading corporations in the nation, which have become acutely aware of the importance of sound public relations.

Subsidiary Corporations. Five subsidiary corporations aid in handling the affairs of the Exchange. The Stock Clearing Corporation is responsible for the clearing operations of the Exchange; its work is the subject of Chapter 16. The New York Quotation Company, which prior to 1958 operated the Exchange ticker-quotation system in downtown New York, is now an inactive corporation. The New York Stock Exchange Building Company owns and manages the Exchange Building. The Newex Corporation owns the land beneath the 20 Broad Street Building completed in 1956. The Newin Corporation carries $10 million insurance policies against losses to customers through fraud of employees, partners, or officers of members or member firms, which take effect if Exchange-required firm insurance and firm assets have been exhausted.

The Exchange and its subsidiaries employ about 1,600 people.

Finances. The consolidated balance sheet of the Exchange and its subsidiaries on December 31, 1961, carried assets of $39.0 million. Of this total $16.9 million represented investments in real estate, plant, and equipment, and $17.3 million was the value of U. S. Government securities owned by the Exchange. Gross revenues in 1961 totaled $23.9 million. The biggest revenue item was membership charges of $15.9 million, including $7.2 million from the 1 per cent charge on commissions, plus ticker service charges, quotation service charges, membership dues, clearing charges, charges for telephone spaces, and other floor charges and rents. The other major revenue source was $6.2 million from listing fees. Employee costs were the most important expenses of operating the Exchange. They amounted to more than half the total.

MEMBERSHIP

Number of Members. The number of members of the Exchange changes slowly. In 1869, after the consolidation of the Exchange with two other organizations, there was a combined total of 1,060 seats or memberships. Ten years later 40 more seats were sold at $13,000 each to finance a new building. The number of 1,100 then was stabilized until 1929, when an increase of 25 per cent was made during a period of great market activity. Members were given a "one-quarter right" per seat. The number of new seats, which was 275, brought the total up to 1,375. For a time during the depression of the 1930's, there was some discussion about reducing the number of seats; nothing was done about the matter.

In 1953 the Exchange began a program under which it can purchase and inactivate up to 75 memberships. Nine seats were retired under this plan in 1953 at a total cost of $366,000. This action reduced the total number to 1,366. No seats have been purchased since 1953 because the market value of memberships rose far above the maximum price authorized for the program. The authority for the program expired December 31, 1962. As an element in the program to build new Exchange facilities, the balance in the fund to carry out the membership retirement program was transferred to the building fund in 1962. It is unlikely that further seats will be retired.

Corporate Memberships. Throughout most of its history the Exchange permitted only individuals and partners in securities houses to become members of the Exchange. The unlimited liability aspect of single proprietorships and partnerships appealed to the financial community and therefore member corporations were not permitted. Reversal of this attitude was reflected in Exchange rules in 1953, when a policy permissive of incorporation was adopted. This allowed member firms to incorporate and also permitted non-member corporations to become members. Corporations so admitted to membership must be companies primarily in the securities business. It was hoped that the new policy would make memberships more attractive and enable firms to strengthen their capital positions more easily. In 1962, however, of 681 member organizations only 94 were incorporated. The proportion of member corporations has grown steadily, but tax and internal organization problems encountered on a changeover from partnership status have slowed the change.

Value of Seats. Seats on the Exchange have shown rather wide fluctuations in value over the years. Their value depends on the volume of market activity and the profits expected from seat ownership. Although seat prices vary from month to month and from sale to sale, a few figures are indicative of values. These are given in Table 6–1.

During 1929, before the increase in the number of seats, three memberships changed hands at $625,000 (equivalent to $500,000 after the 25 per cent seat dividend of that year). After the 1929 price decline the value of seats declined. In 1942 it reached a forty-five-year low of $17,000. Through 1961 there was a significant recovery and the value of a membership reached $225,000. This figure, however, was a bit less than the high price paid in 1933, at the lowest level of stock prices. The market drop in 1962 was accompanied by declining value placed on membership transfers.

Table 6–1. Membership Prices on the New York Stock Exchange, 1874–1962

Year	High	Low
1874	$ 5,000	$ 4,250
1900	47,500	37,500
1920	115,000	85,000
1927	305,000	170,000
1929*	625,000	550,000
1933	250,000	90,000
1939	70,000	51,000
1942	30,000	17,000
1950	54,000	46,000
1955	90,000	80,000
1960	162,000	135,000
1961	225,000	147,000
1962 (to mid-year)	205,000	115,000

* Before seat dividend of 1929.
Source: New York Stock Exchange, *Fact Book, 1962,* p. 36, and *Weekly Bulletin.*

Purchasers of Seats. From sixty to eighty seats may change hands in a year. The buyers of new memberships are, for the most part, already connected with the securities business. They may be former members, partners, or employees of Exchange organizations; they may be present partners or stockholders of members; they may be participants in non-member securities firms, which will become member organizations when the seat is purchased; they may have membership on another national stock exchange; perhaps a son in a family that has long been connected with the Exchange acquires a seat. Some candidates have had no previous connection with the securities business. In such a case they must arrange for appropriate supervision and training before acting as a broker or trader on the floor or doing business with the public.

Financing the Purchase of a Seat. There are a number of methods by which a candidate for membership may finance the expense of a new seat.[4] First, the applicant may buy a seat with his own money. This is the simplest of all means of financing and involves no problems of creditorship.

The second method is by a gift to the applicant, accompanied by a release from the donor; for example, a father may give a son the funds necessary to finance the purchase. In such a case the Exchange requires that the applicant file a release from the donor (the father, in our example) in evidence of the fact that the applicant is not required to make any payment to the donor.

Another method is through funds advanced by a subordinated loan. For example, the applicant may borrow part or all of the money from a creditor to finance the purchase. In such a case the applicant must file an approved "subordination agreement" with the Exchange; its purpose is to preclude the creditor from asserting any claim against the membership or the proceeds of its transfer and to insure that these proceeds will first be applied to claims given priority under the Constitution.

The subordination agreement is necessary because Article XI of the Constitution lays down a certain priority of claims against a membership, no matter how it was financed. The priority of claims against the proceeds of a transfer of membership are (1) sums due the Exchange, (2) sums due the Stock Clearing Corporation, (3) sums that the Board of Governors may allow other members for losses arising from transactions on the floor, (4) expenses incurred by the Exchange because of litigation arising from the disposition of proceeds, and (5) other claims under ordinary legal procedure. In other words, the Exchange and its members have a priority over all outside creditors when a seat is transferred, irrespective of the fact that an outside creditor may have advanced the funds to buy the seat. This practice is of long standing; it is well known to everyone in the securities business; it has been fully upheld by the courts.[5] The theory behind this priority system is that an exchange membership is not property that is freely alienable, but is subject to restrictions created at the time it is acquired.

The fourth method of financing a seat—increasingly common as seat prices have risen—is through a so-called "a-b-c agreement." By this method a firm advances the necessary funds to one of its partners who would become a member, releasing him from any obligation to repay the funds except under the terms of the agreement. Although the seat remains a personal franchise of the member, the risk of fluctuation in its value is shared by the other partners in proportion to their interests in the firm. An "a-b-c agreement" derives its name from the three options

---

[4] New York Stock Exchange, *Guide*, Rule 301.30 ff.

[5] *Belton v. Hatch*, 109 N.Y. 593.

provided for when the firm dissolves, the member dies or retires, or when something else occurs to terminate the agreement. The member (or his legal representative) then may (a) retain the membership and pay to the firm the amount necessary to purchase another membership, (b) sell his membership and pay the proceeds over to the partnership, or (c) transfer his membership for a nominal sum to a person designated by the firm and satisfactory for membership to the Board of Governors of the Exchange.

Procedure in Purchasing a Seat. An applicant for membership must be twenty-one years of age and a citizen of the United States, either by birth or naturalization. He will file with the Exchange at the time of application a complete statement about his business history and arrange for a physical examination. His application must be sponsored by two members or allied members of the Exchange of at least one year's standing who have known him long enough and sufficiently well to be able to give him an unqualified endorsement. Together with his sponsors, he must appear personally before the subcommittee on admissions. In addition, he must submit letters of recommendation from at least three responsible persons.

After his application has been received, it is posted by the Secretary for inspection by members and allied members of the Exchange. After a lapse of ten days, during which the Exchange staff supervises an investigation of his history, character, and financial responsibility, the subcommittee on admissions considers the application. If the subcommittee is satisfied with the applicant's qualifications, he is recommended for membership to the full Board. He must be approved by a two-thirds majority of the Governors present at a meeting of the Board.

At the time an individual applies for membership, he must arrange for the purchase of a seat. The Secretary of the Exchange, at all times, has a list of seats available for sale; these may be held by estates or by living members. Only the offering prices are disclosed; the identity of the holder is not revealed. If the lowest offering price is satisfactory, the applicant may purchase a seat at that price. If not, he is free to negotiate for a better price, by competitive bidding with other would-be members. This is the public "seat market." An applicant is also free to make a private arrangement to buy the seat of a member who has not offered it in the market. Under all circumstances, however, arrangements for transfer of the seat must be completed through the Secretary's Office and a sales price agreed upon privately by the buyer and seller must be considered reasonable by the Exchange.

Seat Expenses. The purchase and ownership of a seat represent substantial initial and continuing expenses. The highest cost, of course, is the price paid for membership. From 1950 to 1962 this ranged from $38,000 to $225,000. The initiation fee is $7,500. Dues run $1,500 per year and annual contributions to the membership retirement fund are $140. There is a 1 per cent charge on net commissions. Perhaps $400 per year goes to payments into the Gratuity Fund, from which benefits of $20,000 are paid to the families of deceased members.

Ownership of Seats. A small number of seats is held by estates. In mid-1961 the number was eight. As long as the estate pays the dues, there is no objection to its retention of the seat. Some may be held in the expectation of a better price; the estate may not be ready to sell; or it may be that a son expects to take over eventually.

The remainder of the seats are held by living members, most of whom reside in metropolitan New York. A few living members—thirty-four in mid-1961—have retired from business life and are inactive. The Exchange will not accept an application for membership from someone who does not plan to be active in the securities business, either on the Floor or in an office.

Most members are active and trade on the Floor, where from 700 to 900 may be in attendance on a given day, depending on market volume. There are six classes of activity for floor members: (1) commission broker, (2) bond broker, (3) specialist, (4) odd-lot dealer or broker, (5) floor broker, and (6) floor trader.

The number of members in each of these classes cannot be given precisely, since a member may shift from one function to another from time to time and for short intervals. For example, in a single day a floor member may function as a commission broker for a while, then as a floor trader, continue the commission business, change to floor broker and then floor trader again, and resume commission business. However, some approximations can be made, based on the member's primary activity in mid-1961.

The largest class of floor members is that of commission broker, of whom there were about 425 in mid-1961. Their primary function is the execution of orders received from the public by their offices. They act as agents, and their compensation consists of the commissions charged the non-member customers. Since they act on an agency basis, they take few risks.

The bond brokers engage primarily in brokerage activities, although at times some act as dealers. In mid-1961 there were 13 members in this category. Their operations are described in Chapter 15.

The specialists act both as brokers and as dealers. Their function is to make a market in the stocks in which they specialize. Because of the fact that they must be registered, exact figures are available as to their number. In 1961 there were 350 specialists, most of whom were members of specialist firms. Hence, about one member out of four is a specialist. Their work is described in Chapter 11.

Odd-lot dealers and brokers engage in the execution of odd-lot orders on the Floor. Although odd-lots are not actually sold on the Floor, the price of execution is determined there; it is based on sales or quotations in the round-lot market. Practically all the odd-lot business is carried on by two very large odd-lot firms. These firms had 22 members as full-time or limited partners and, in addition, employed 96 floor brokers as associate brokers in 1961. Odd-lot operations are described in Chapters 13 and 14.

Floor brokers—sometimes called "$2 brokers" because of a former way of figuring their commissions—are members who work for other members on a commission basis. They perform a useful function in aiding commission brokers and others to execute orders efficiently. Some member firms execute their orders exclusively through independent floor brokers instead of putting their own member on the Floor as a commission broker. In 1961 the number of floor brokers was 187. Their activity is discussed further in Chapter 10.

Floor traders are those members engaged primarily in trading for their own account; they do not execute orders on a commission basis when engaged in this capacity and have no dealings with the public. Although many members of the Exchange may do some floor trading from time to time, the term "floor trader" is usually used to describe the member who spends full time in this activity and depends on it for a livelihood. The number in small; about 30 in mid-1961. More detail on floor trading is supplied in Chapter 10.

The remaining living members of the Exchange—about 200 in number—were active off the Floor, in the office, dealing with customers, underwritings, and other phases of the securities business, as well as general management of firm affairs. The greater part of these members work outside the New York area.

Discipline of Members. Power to discipline members and allied members rests with the Board of Governors of the Exchange. The Board has delegated power to deal with minor offenses to the advisory committee and the Exchange staff, but reserves to itself consideration of major violations. Several kinds of disciplinary action may be taken: (1) censure, (2) fines, (3) suspension, and (4) expulsion. These measures may be combined; for example, a member may be fined and censured.

Conduct that indicates the need for disciplinary action might include such actions as bad conduct on the floor; violations of rules; violation of capital requirements; fraudulent acts; fictitious transactions in which there was no change in security ownership; failure to perform contracts; demoralization of the market; material misstatements; violation of the Constitution; violation of the Securities Exchange Act of 1934; dealing outside the Exchange that is not permitted by rules; failure to testify or produce records demanded by the Board; any act detrimental to the Exchange.

The severity of the offense dictates the type of discipline. In milder cases of misconduct fines up to $250 for each violation may be exacted by the Advisory Committee. The Board itself may impose fines of up to $5,000 per violation. These fines may be assessed against members or allied members. A more severe penalty would be suspension from the Exchange for a period of time, not longer than five years. The harshest penalty is outright expulsion, which terminates all rights and privileges of ownership.

Suspension or expulsion has been rare in the past generation. One instance that attracted attention a few years ago was a six-months suspension of an allied member for rebating commissions to a non-member securities house. A second, of three months, involved dealings in the government bond market in which the allied member exercised somewhat less than reasonable prudence in his relationships with his clients. In 1962 one-year suspensions were imposed on a member and on five allied members, and three other allied members associated with suspended members were censured. Two different firms were involved and the reasons were different, but the seriousness with which the Exchange viewed their misconduct is indicated by the penalties imposed. The members of one of these firms sold their assets and retired from business.

A member was expelled in 1956 when it was found that he had made a misstatement upon a material point in connection with his application for membership two years earlier. Another was expelled in 1960 when his firm failed owing to his misconduct.

Character of a Membership. In popular usage the term "seat" is used more frequently than the technical expression "membership," which is more exact and descriptive. The term "seat" is a carry-over from early days when members actually did occupy chairs on the Exchange floor; today the term is used to refer to the intangible rights and privileges of membership. When a membership is sold, there is nothing tangible transferred from the old to the new member. Actually, all that happens is that the old member retires from the Exchange for a consideration paid by an applicant; a vacancy is then said to exist. The applicant after approval is merely notified by a letter from the Secretary that he has

THIS IS TO CERTIFY THAT

OF THIS FIRM

IS A MEMBER OF THE

NEW YORK STOCK EXCHANGE

AN INSTITUTION WHOSE HISTORY DATES BACK TO 1792 AND
WHOSE RULES AND REGULATIONS HAVE BEEN FORMULATED
FOR THE PURPOSE OF MAINTAINING HIGH STANDARDS OF
HONOR AMONG ITS MEMBERS AND FOR PROMOTING AND
INCULCATING JUST AND EQUITABLE PRINCIPLES OF TRADE

SECRETARY   CHAIRMAN OF THE BOARD
THIS CERTIFICATE IS THE PROPERTY OF THE NEW YORK STOCK EXCHANGE

Fig. 6–3. Certificate, New York Stock Exchange.

been accepted by the Board for membership. His firm also receives a certificate indicative of this membership (Fig. 6–3).

Membership gives its possessor many rights and privileges. He may act as a broker or dealer on the floor; he may execute orders for others or for himself, this being the most valuable right. He may secure the services of other members in the execution of orders at commissions substantially less than those charged to non-members. The member also possesses a property right in the membership or its value.

A noted legal authority on stock exchange law has made this observation about memberships: "Although exchange membership is both a privilege and a property right, it is such only in a restricted and limited sense."[6] There are many ways in which a membership on the Exchange differs from the usual conception of property. It may not be owned by a partnership or corporation; it is subject to certain prior claims of the Exchange and its members over outside creditors; the purchase of a seat does not entitle the buyer to the privileges of membership unless the application for membership has been approved; the transfer of membership may be made only on such conditions as are determined by the Exchange; the rights of membership cannot be inherited; the Exchange by suspension or expulsion may deprive a member of his rights and privileges; the holder of a seat has no proprietary interest in the property of the Exchange upon withdrawing from it; and its tax status is often different from that of other forms of property.

Regulations of Members. Space limitations do not permit even a skeleton outline of the innumerable regulations which govern the actions of members. In addition to the Constitution of the Exchange, there are the bylaws and rules of the Stock Clearing Corporation and the rules of the Board of Governors. Finally, there are the Securities Exchange Act of 1934 and the numerous rules and interpretations of the SEC and the Federal Reserve Board that supplement the Act. All these regulations appear in large loose-leaf volumes issued by the Exchange known as its *Guide*. In addition, members are subject to numerous regulations of civil and criminal law. The most significant of the regulations will be presented in many of the remaining chapters of the book.

MEMBER FIRMS

Number. As of January 1, 1962, there were 681 member organizations. Of these, 587 were member firms and 94 were member corporations. These members had branches in 829 United States cities and 24 other countries. The total number of branches was 3,372. One corporate member had 145 branches; several organizations had in excess of 25 each.

6 Meyer, *op. cit.*, p. 78.

Partners. Member firm partnerships range in size from 2 partners to about 90 for one firm. The partners are of two classes: general partners and limited partners. Altogether in early 1961 there were 4,265 general partners of member firms (78 of whom were also limited partners) and 843 limited partners. The limited partners, once called special partners, have the same rights and limitations as in all limited partnerships.

Stockholders. In early 1961 member corporations had a total of 1,382 stockholders. Of these, 660 held voting stock; 126 held both voting and non-voting stock; and 596 held only non-voting stock. Generally speaking, a holder of voting stock is considered equivalent to a general partner of a firm, and a holder of non-voting stock is similar to a limited partner. The largest member corporation had 300 stockholders.

Exchange Memberships. In each member firm or corporation there must be at least one general partner or voting stockholder who is an Exchange member. The average organization includes one or two members. The highest number for any one organization is 13.

Allied Members. The Constitution of the Exchange provides for recognition of a relationship called "allied member." This development grew out of the reorganization of 1938. An allied member is a general partner or voting stockholder in a member organization who is not an Exchange member. The purpose of the classification is to bring such partners or stockholders under the disciplinary regulations of the Exchange in the same way as members. Before the present system was instituted, members were held responsible for the acts of non-member personnel of their firms; under the present plan allied members are held directly responsible for their own acts. Allied memberships are not bought or sold; they have no transfer value. They have no vote in Exchange elections, but they do have representation on the Board of Governors.

As in the case of Exchange membership, the Board of Governors must approve all new allied members, limited partners, and non-voting stockholders of member firms, and all holders of member corporation debentures or persons who make subordinated loans of cash or securities to member organizations. The history and character of these applicants are investigated as carefully as those of proposed members, although the admissions process is somewhat different in other details. As many as 800 applications of this type are considered in a year by the subcommittee on admissions and the Board of Governors.

Capital Requirements. Any member organization that carries customers' accounts must maintain a net capital of at least $50,000. The minimum net capital requirement for a member corporation is $60,000. In the computation of this capital the value of the seats possessed by partners or stockholders is not considered. Readily marketable securities are valued from 70 per cent of their market value for common stocks to 100 per cent for U. S. Government bonds having less than one year to maturity. The net capital at all times must be at least equal to one-twentieth (5 per cent) of the total liabilities of the organization. Included in these liabilities are the free credit balances of customers. Thus, a firm with liabilities to customers, banks, and member organizations of $2,000,000 would be required to have a minimum net capital of $100,000. The requirement has as its purpose the elimination of weak firms that attempt to transact a heavy volume of business without adequate protection to customers and other creditors.

Audits. The Exchange requires two types of questionnaire reports each year from member firms that carry customer accounts. One is based on an audit made by an outside, independent accounting firm—the member organization may choose the auditor, but the audit must be a surprise one. In addition, special financial questionnaires sent from the Exchange must be returned to the Department of Member Firms. These may be prepared by the organization's own staff or by an outside accounting firm. It is the expectation that the response to these questionnaires will detect financial weakness before it has developed far enough to cause a loss to the public.

That the present capital and audit requirements have served their purpose very well is indicated by the fact that there was but one organization insolvency in the period 1938 to 1962. The one failure resulted from the fraudulent use of customer securities by a partner of the firm. However, the Exchange took the unprecedented action of advancing to the firm's receiver more than $600,000 of its own funds so that bona fide customers of the firm would suffer no loss. Thereafter the Exchange arranged with insurance companies for a new type of stockbroker partnership bond covering partner's fraud and strengthened its rules on required member firm insurance coverage. This added protection to the public doing business with Exchange members was further supplemented by $10,000,000 surety policies taken out by the Exchange itself which are effective if the firm's insurance and asset coverage are exhausted by losses owing to fraud of employees, partners, or officers.

Registered Representatives. "Registered representative" is the term now used by the Exchange for any employee engaged in solicitation, handling, buying, selling, or trading in securities on behalf of his employer. Years ago such an individual was called a "customer's man," a term the securities business is seeking to replace with the newer term. Many abuses crept into the work of the customer's man during the 1920's, when his activities were not regulated. They included: (1) excessive solicitation of business, (2) insufficient training and experience, (3) "playing the market," (4) division of profits with customers, (5) distribution of stock being carried by pools, and (6) misrepresentation of facts about securities. The number of these abuses was so large that a thorough reform was in order.

In order to prevent such abuses all such employees must now be qualified by training and experience before being permitted to serve the public. They must also pass a comprehensive examination prescribed by the Exchange. Although Exchange rules are generally expressed in terms of conduct of members and member firms, registered representatives are also held personally accountable for proper personal conduct under all of the Rules. Several specific prohibitions have been included in the Registered Representatives Agreement: registered employees may not share in any profits of customers' accounts or guarantee a customer's debit balance; they may not engage in cash or margin transactions outside the Exchange jurisdiction; they may not receive or give any form of rebate in connection with transactions; they may not be paid any compensation for commissions or profits earned on any transaction in which they have a direct or indirect financial interest.

Member Organization Customers. There are no exact figures on the number of customers of member organizations. It is in the millions. One house alone has in excess of one-quarter million.

Member firms serve widely variant clienteles. At one extreme are the "wire houses" with numerous branches; the number of accounts with individual investors run into the tens of thousands, and they solicit both round-lot and odd-lot business. At the other extreme are those firms that do no public solicitation of business; they prefer large accounts, particularly of the institutional type. Some firms carry only their own accounts; others carry accounts introduced by other firms, and not only finance the accounts where they are of a margin character but also handle the securities and look after the bookkeeping details of such accounts; still others have their accounts cared for by other firms.

7

The Stock and Bond Lists

This chapter deals with the listing of stocks on the New York Stock Exchange, the requirements for listing made by the Exchange, and the value of listing to the owner of securities so listed.

THE LISTS

Stock List. The stock list is a roster of nearly all the major corporations of the United States. In early 1962 the list included 1,163 organizations. The familiar names of American Motors, Standard Oil Company (New Jersey), General Telephone and Electronics, Brunswick, Radio Corporation of America, United States Steel, General Motors, and American Telephone and Telegraph were among them. With very few exceptions apart from the banking and insurance industries, the stock list included all the concerns one readily identifies as significant in American industry.

The general significance of the companies on the stock list is indicated by the fact that in 1960 these corporations accounted for 30 per cent of the invested capital, 70 per cent of the net income, and 70 per cent of the dividends paid out of all United States corporations. These firms accounted also for 20 per cent of all civilian employment in the nation, their employment at that time being 14 million workers.

Bond List. Also in early 1962 the bond list included names of 486 organizations. Among them were 383 U.S. corporations, the governments of the state and city of New York, and the federal government. The par value of the list amounted to $113 billion, but the effective market on the Exchange was limited to about $30 billion par value. During the year 1961 the volume of transactions, mostly in bonds of U.S. corporations, was $1.6 billion.

LISTING AND REGISTRATION

Listing. A distinction should be made between listing and registration. Listing refers to the procedure by which a company applies and qualifies its stock for trading on the Exchange. Before its stock is approved for listing, a company must meet certain standards set by the New York Stock Exchange and must also agree to meet in subsequent years certain terms and stipulations for listed corporations.

Registration. Registration refers to the submission of certain information in prescribed order and content to the SEC under the provisions of the Securities Exchange Act of 1934 on a prescribed form for registration.[1] It does not imply approval by the SEC either of the company or of the securities.

THE VALUE OF LISTING

To Corporations. Corporations list their stocks for one or more of a variety of reasons. First, listing tends to make a security more marketable. The Exchange provides a ready, continuous market, thereby making the security more attractive to public investors. Next, listing tends to create lower financing costs when addition capital is raised in the future. Third, listing aids in the sale of rights.[2] Many stockholders, when they receive rights to buy new shares of an issue that they own, sell these rights rather than exercise them. If the stock is listed, there is a ready market for the rights, which helps to make the privileged subscription a success. Again, a company obtains a certain amount of publicity and advertising from having its securities listed. Consumers associate the company's product with its stock. Frequent sales on the Exchange keep the company's name before the public. In many cases, however, the brand name bears no relationship to the company name and the publicity value is non-existent. A fifth reason would be the desire to obtain more stockholders. Many corporations consider this one of their most important reasons. More stockholders tend to create more customers, improve public relations, aid future financing, diversify the company ownership, and advertise the organization. Finally, listing helps to determine fair prices for the company stock. It is believed that the auction market for the stock will give to it a fair value based on effective interaction of demand for and supply of the stock.

Not all large corporations—even when clearly eligible—desire to list their stocks and they find many reasons for this attitude. Inability to

---

[1] The work of this agency is discussed in Chapter 28.
[2] Discussion of rights is reserved to Chapter 36.

meet listing requirements would, of course, prevent a company from listing, even though it might desire to do so. Many companies, however, do not believe that the expense of listing is justified by the benefits received. Some managements dislike the required disclosure of financial affairs and other information imposed on all listed companies. In other cases, they dislike the regulations by the SEC of "insiders" (officers, directors, and large stockholders) in their securities transactions. Rules of the SEC, such as proxy requirements, that accompany Exchange requirements, also have been criticized. Finally, numerous companies believe that the market for their shares in the over-the-counter market is adequate for both the company and its stockholders.

To Investors. A number of advantages to investors have been or can be indicated. The Exchange provides a continuous market for stocks. Listing, therefore, provides greater liquidity, a continuous flow of transactions, close bid and asked prices, and quicker sales. This advantage is greater for listed stocks than listed bonds. In many cases, the over-the-counter market provides an excellent continuous market for bonds. Second, listing insures a high degree of publicity about corporate affairs. This publicity takes the form of data on the original application, of regular financial reports supplied to the Exchange and to stockholders, and of prompt publicity on dividends and other matters. Also, listing gives higher collateral value to such securities for loan purposes. Fourth, listing provides for fair and open price determination in an auction market where the broad forces of supply and demand meet. Again, listing usually gives to investors and traders lower buying and selling costs than are found in the off-board market. Finally, the Exchange releases continuous data on sales prices, as well as quotations. The over-the-counter market releases no figures, either on price or volume of actual sales.

A possible disadvantage of trading or investing in listed stocks is that such securities sell on a lower yield or at a higher price than if they were traded in the over-the-counter market. A second disadvantage is that the listed market is not consistently the best market for all kinds of transactions and issues.

LISTING PROCEDURE

Department of Stock List. At the present time the listing operations of the Exchange are carried on by the President and a full-time staff in the Department of Stock List. The Department is headed by a Director, who is a vice-president of the Exchange and has a staff of about fifty persons. The various corporations are dividend into industrial groups when examined for listing, these groups being assigned to listing representatives. These representatives handle all matters, including listing applications that come up in connection with the various companies assigned to them. Whenever necessary the Department calls upon the services of outside experts, such as accountants, lawyers, and engineers.

Preliminary Negotiations. Any formal application is preceded by informal discussions between the representatives of the company and the staff of the Department of Stock List. The purpose of the preliminary discussions is to discover any deficiencies in the company's record or bars to listing. If any are discovered, the proposed application can be quietly dropped and no harm is done to the company. Companies that are ineligible as of any specific date may in the course of time meet the requirements of the Exchange. In many cases the records of the company are reviewed from time to time. There is, therefore, no such thing as a permanent deferment of an application.

In the informal or preliminary review of an applying company, the Exchange is concerned principally with four sets of facts:

1. A description of the company's business, products, date of organization, and the market for its securities
2. Latest available financial statements together with annual reports for the past ten years
3. Distribution of the security under consideration
4. A copy of the charter and bylaws

A number of inquiries on possible listing are constantly before the Department of Stock List. During the preliminary discussions a majority of companies are advised that it would not be advisable to submit formal applications at that time. When no difficulties are evident in the informal discussion, the company proceeds with the formal application and registration statement.

Formal Application. If the preliminary negotiations have shown that there are no serious obstacles to listing, the company prepares a formal application which is to be considered on its merits. From that point on, contact is maintained between the company representative and the listing representative to whom the particular industry is assigned.

No prepared or blank forms of application are provided. The first draft is prepared in quadruplicate typewritten form, one copy of which carries the signature of a duly authorized executive officer. An application has two purposes: (1) to place formally before the Exchange the information essential to determine the suitability of the security for public trading on the Exchange; and (2) to provide the public with such information as may enable it to make a sound judgment as to the merits of the security.

The application is designed to give all the essential facts about the company's business, its organization, management and control, its financial condition and business, and its financial and accounting policies. Much data are included in the application, the order of content of which are set forth in an Exchange booklet entitled *Listing Procedure*. The following is an outline of principal data required:

1. Title	13. Stockholder Relations
2. Request for Listing	14. Dividend Record
3. Opinion of Counsel	15. Options, Warrants,
4. Status under Federal	Conversion Rights
and State Authorities	16. Litigation
5. History and Business	17. Business, Financial
6. Property Description	and Accounting Policies
7. Affiliated Companies	18. Financial Statements
8. Management	19. Listing Agreements
9. Capitalization	20. General Information
10. Funded Debt	21. Signature
11. Stock Provisions	22. Exhibits
12. Employees—Labor	
Relations	

In addition to the draft of the formal application, the company submits many supplementary and supporting documents, such as charter and bylaws, distribution schedule or form, certificates of transfer agent and registrar, prospectus under Securities Act of 1933, certified financial statements, listing agreements, and similar documents.

After the listing representative completes his examination of the application and accompanying documents and satisfies himself that the company meets the requirements of the Exchange, the application is scheduled for the next meeting of the department staff.

The staff meets every Tuesday; it includes the President of the Exchange or, in his absence, the Executive Vice-President, the director of the Department of Stock List, and the other executives of the department.

The staff, satisfied that the company and its securities meet the requirements of the Exchange, now submits the application to the Board of Governors, which meets every Thursday. On the basis of the staff studies and its own experience, the Board votes to approve or reject the application. In actual practice, the Board rarely finds it necessary to reject an application at this point.

The application having been approved, a certification is sent to the SEC to the effect that the Exchange has approved for listing the specified class or series of stock. Registration with the SEC becomes effective thirty days after the Commission receives the Exchange certification. The SEC may accelerate registration, that is, shorten the thirty-day waiting period. Trading in the securities on the floor of the Exchange begins when the registration is effective.

After an original listing application has been approved by the Board of Governors of the Exchange, a final copy is signed by an authorized company officer and the accounting firm certifying the financial statements. Six hundred and fifty copies of the application are printed at the applicant's expense for distribution to Exchange member firms, news and statistical services, and others who may request copies.

LISTING INFORMATION AND FORMS

Information on Policies and Financial Condition. A very important part of the formal application is the section on business, financial, and accounting policies. In this section the applicant must give a reasonably complete statement of leases, depreciation and depletion policies, amortization, commitments (such as for commodities), valuation of inventories, method of computing cost of goods sold, valuation of marketable securities, and consolidation.

Equally important in the application are the data on financial statements. Except for railroad companies, the statements are to be prepared by certified public accountants. A summarized statement of earnings for the past ten years is to be given and consolidated income statements for the past two fiscal years. Consolidated balance sheets are to be reasonably complete without being burdened with detail.

Distribution Form. One important document filed by the applying company is the stock distribution form. This shows the distribution of the stock in the company. There is one for each class or series of stock. This form shows the number of stockholders of each bracket size. For example, it shows how many own from 1 to 99 shares, how many from 100 to 300, how many from 301 to 500, and so on. The form also shows the holdings for the ten largest stockholders. These shares must be free for sale and must not be held under syndicate, agreement, or control. As indicated later under the discussion of listing policy, the Exchange is not interested in listing a company with a narrow distribution of stock. This form aids the Exchange in its examination of the breadth of distribution. A copy of the stock distribution form is reproduced in Figure 7–1.

Listing Agreements. An extremely important part of the listing policy of the Exchange is the requirement that the applying corporation sign a number of listing agreements.[3] These are the promises of performance by the corporation after the security is listed. Their purpose is to protect the security holders against any act that might be detrimental to their best interests. In general, the agreements require the corporation to

---

[3] For those who may wish to see exactly what the agreements are, a full copy of the Listing Agreement is appended to this chapter, beginning at p. 143.

. . . .
          Company   Issue

I. SIZE OF HOLDINGS

Number of Holders	Shares Held	Total Shares
. . . .	1 – 99	. . . .
. . . .	100 – 299	. . . .
. . . .	300 – 499	. . . .
. . . .	500 – 1000	. . . .
. . . .	1001 – up	. . . .
. . . .	Totals	. . . .

The ten largest holdings on the Record date were as follows:

1. . . . . Shares   4. . . . . Shares   8. . . . . Shares
2. . . . . "   5. . . . . "   9. . . . . "
3. . . . . "   6. . . . . "   10. . . . . "
                  7. . . . . "
                      Total   . . . .

II. GEOGRAPHICAL DISTRIBUTION

Holders	Shares	Holders	Shares	Holders	Shares
Ala.		Me.		Okla.	
Ariz.		Md.		Ore.	
Ark.		Mass.		Pa.	
Cal.		Mich.		R.I.	
Colo.		Minn.		S.C.	
Conn.		Miss.		S.D.	
Del.		Mo.		Tenn.	
D.C.		Mont.		Texas	
Fla.		Neb.		Utah	
Ga.		Nev.		Va.	
Idaho		N.H.		Vt.	
Ill.		N.J.		Wash.	
Ind.		N.M.		W. Va.	
Iowa		N.Y.		Wisc.	
Kan.		N.C.		Wyo.	
Ky.		N.D.		Canada	
La.		Ohio		Other	. . . .
			Totals	. . . .	

All stock is free for sale and is held under no syndicate, agreement or control.

                              Certified Correct

. . . .
      Transfer Agent

Fig. 7–1. Stock distribution form.

disclose information about its affairs and to perform certain acts to protect security holders. The evolution of these agreements will be taken
up later in this chapter. The company has no choice in the matter of
agreements; their acceptance is mandatory. The wording of the agreements has been carefully worked out and must be accepted verbatim by
the applying company.

There are two outstanding facts about the agreements. First, the
company agrees to disclose all significant details about its financial condition, such as changes in the character of the business, changes in its
capital setup, and changes in accounting policy. It promises to give
proper notice of all dividend actions and reports on earnings and financial condition. Second, the company promises to perform certain acts for
the best interests of the security holders, such as to have its books audited
by certified accountants and to maintain transfer agents and registrars.

The listing agreement also makes clear responsibilities of the issuer
for reporting to the Exchange. Listing implies the existence of a distribution of stock, in amount and over a geographical area, sufficient to permit
a national market to serve the shareowners and the corporation efficiently.
Hence, the issuer is required to report actions that reduce or increase the
stock outstanding, changes in asset structure that would affect financial
results from, or the nature of, corporate operations, and other actions that
would affect the stock market. More generally, the Exchange reserves
the right to ask for any information it requires.

OTHER LISTING REGULATIONS

Transfer Agent and Registrar. Significant among the agreements
signed by the applying company is an agreement to maintain a transfer
agent and registrar. The transfer agent or office must be maintained in
the Borough of Manhattan in the City of New York, where all the stock
of the company must be transferable and dividends and other disbursements shall be payable.

Similarly, the company must maintain a registry office or registrar for
its securities in lower Manhattan in the financial district. This must be
maintained at company expense. It must be an independent institution
and cannot be the same organization as the transfer agent.

Since the regulations applicable to the transfer agent and registrar
are discussed in Chapter 23, no further mention need be made of them
here.

Engraving and Text of Securities. Two further requirements of listed
securities should be given. In order to protect owners against counter-
feiting and duplication, strict regulations about the engraving of the
securities are made by the Exchange. All securities must be engraved

in a manner satisfactory to the Department of Stock List. Securities must be engraved with two steel plates and with the use of distinctive colors. Only a small number of engraving companies in the entire world have adequate facilities for the preparation of the actual certificates.

There are certain regulations in regard to the text printed on the face of the securities. They are for the purpose of giving investors at least the essential facts about the security. For example, on a stock certificate the following information is mandatory: par value, priority as to dividends and assets, voting power, and redemption. On bonds is given such information as conditions of issue, redemption, interest, principal, and tax features.

Listing Policy of the Exchange. In general, it can be said that the New York Stock Exchange is interested in listing only the larger and stronger corporations. It wants well-established companies and prefers that the newer and more speculative corporations serve an apprenticeship in the over-the-counter market, on the American Stock Exchange, or on one of the regional exchanges before applying for listing.

The present standards of eligibility for listing are both general and specific. Some standards are purposely couched in general language to permit flexibility. Requirements in this category cannot be measured by definite statistical or accounting standards. In other instances certain guides as to standards of size, earnings, and stock distribution are more exact in character.

Two general tests of eligibility for listing can be indicated:

1. *National interest in the company.* In this connection the Exchange considers the extent of national interest in the company and in its products or services. If this interest is broad, the market for the stock will be enhanced. Consideration is given, therefore, to the standing of the company, its stability, and the market for its products or services.

2. *Prospects of the company.* Here the Exchange is interested in whether or not a corporation is engaged in an expanding industry and whether or not it has good prospects of maintaining its position in the industry.

Three more specific standards are important. These are somewhat flexible and represent only minimum qualifications. These standards change with economic conditions. The Exchange considers them guides rather than precise mathematical formulas. These are the standards:

1. *Demonstrated earning power.* The minimum here is $1 million per year after all charges, including federal taxes. An exception is made for certain companies engaged in the business of supplying venture capital to small- or medium-sized businesses. They may list their shares when earning power is less than $1 million if stockholder equity is at least $16 million. Demonstrated or established earning power means net profits derived from normal operations of the business over a sufficient period of time to assure that it is firmly estab-

lished. Such earnings do not include income from non-recurrent sources. Thus, a company may report net profits of $1 million or more per year, but not meet the demonstrated earning-power test if these profits are less than $1 million after reduction by the amount of non-recurrent items.

2. *Substantial assets.* The test of substantial assets is a minimum of $10 million in net tangible assets or an aggregate market value of the common stock of that amount. Greater emphasis is placed upon the latter. The term "net tangible assets," as used in this connection, may be defined as the amount of the capital and surplus accounts of the company less intangible assets.

3. *Broad distribution of stock.* This requires that at least 500,000 shares of common stock should be outstanding (exclusive of concentrated or family holdings) among 1,500 or more holders of sizable amounts. Small holdings, of less than 100 shares, are discounted. Of course, the greater the number of shares outstanding and the greater the number of holders, the greater will be the potential market for the stock. Concentrated or family holdings in this situation include all shares controlled, directly or indirectly, by all officers and stockholders and members of their immediate families.

Listing Fees. The listing fees of the Exchange are a very important source of its operating income. In recent years income from this source has ranged from as low as $220,000 in 1946 to as high as $6.2 million in 1961.

At the end of 1961 there were 1,163 companies listed on the Exchange. Total stock listings included 1,145 common and 396 preferred issues, a total of 1,541 issues. The aggregate market value of the 7.1 billion shares was nearly $388 billion. The number of listed companies grows rather slowly. Nineteen new companies were listed in 1958, forty-one in 1959, and fifty-seven in 1960 and, again, in 1961.

Prior to 1939 the Exchange had a flat listing fee. It was paid once and for all time at the date the stock was listed. The Exchange derived no further income from the security. The result was a very unstable source of income, which depended on the number of new issues listed. The income was very high in such years as 1929 and 1937, when new stock financing was popular, but fell to low levels when such financing was at a minimum. Since the Exchange has very high overhead costs, it was decided in 1939 to work out a new and more stable form of listing fee. The new schedule is mandatory for all new listings, but does not apply to issues previously listed. The schedule has two parts: a basic initial fee and a continuing annual fee.

The basic initial fee provides for a charge of $100 per 10,000 shares, or fraction thereof, for the first 500,000 shares listed; $50 per 10,000 shares, or fraction thereof, for the next 1,500,000 shares; and $25 per 10,000 shares, or fraction thereof, for shares in excess of 2,000,000. The minimum fee is $2,000. The continuing annual fee is $100 per 100,000 shares, or fraction thereof, for the first 2,000,000 shares and $50 per 100,000 shares, or fraction thereof, in excess of 2,000,000. The minimum fee is $500 per year; for companies having more than one issue, the minimum is $250 per issue. This annual fee is payable for fifteen years after initial listing.

Let us take a moderate-sized company with 1,000,000 shares of common stock. Its initial fee would be $7,500. Its annual fee, paid for fifteen years, would be $1,000. At the end of the period the company would have paid into the Exchange a total of $22,500. Thereafter its fees would cease.

Listing fees for bonds differ in amounts from those for stock. There are also modifications of the basic fees for listings of stock, which arise from change or exchange of stock previously listed. In any case, the minimum initial fee on a stock listing is $250.

Delisting. There are two situations in which a listed security may be removed from the stock list or suspended from dealings. The first is the removal of the stock from the list or suspension of dealings by action of the Exchange.

The Exchange does not look with favor upon a company's request to remove its stock from the list once it has been listed. In the absence of special circumstances, the Exchange will not allow this to take place if the stock is eligible for continued listing, unless specific approval is given by the stockholders. The reason for this is that the Exchange believes that delisting is not in the best interest of the stockholders. Therefore, the Exchange will consider such a proposal only if it is approved by 66⅔ per cent of the outstanding shares and if 10 per cent of the individual shareholders fail to object. These are minimums.

Removal from the list or suspension of dealing by the Exchange is a more complex matter and may be done under a number of situations. First, the Exchange may receive authoritative advice that the security is without value. Next, the Exchange will cause a suspension of dealings and file a delisting application with the SEC if it believes that too small an amount, less than 100,000 shares exclusive of concentrated holdings, of securities is outstanding. Third, the Exchange will consider delisting if there is too limited a distribution of shares or if the size of the company becomes too small. The distribution of the stock among less than 300 holders is considered undesirable. Again, a decline of net tangible assets to less than $2 million or of the market value of the common stock to less than $1,000,000 would require the Exchange to consider delisting. Fifth, a decline of average net earnings for the past three years to less than $200,000 would be considered a cause for delisting. Thirty-eight common and six preferred issues were delisted in 1961, mostly as a result of limited size or distribution of the issue.

Sixth, the Exchange may suspend a company's securities from dealing and may apply for delisting to the SEC if the company, its transfer agent, or its registrar violates the agreements connected with listing. Seventh, the Exchange may suspend from listing any security for which registration is no longer effective under the Securities Exchange Act of 1934. Eighth, the Exchange will delist a security when it has been paid at maturity, redeemed, or retired. If there is redemption or retirement of only part of a class, issue, or series, the amount authorized for listing will, of course, be reduced accordingly.

It should be added at this point that the SEC also has its own rules of suspension of trading, withdrawal, and striking from listing and registration. These are discussed in Chapter 28.

Evolution of Listing Standards. The evolution of listing requirements of the New York Stock Exchange furnishes an interesting chapter in the history of American business practices and ethics. Directors of United States corporations in the early years of our national history shrouded the affairs of their organizations in an almost impenetrable cloak of secrecy. What they did, what they earned, how many assets they controlled, and similar matters were facts that they considered to be purely private affairs. To permit the public or their own stockholders to know even the barest details of their financial affairs was unthinkable, and this attitude changed slowly. It was the basis for an almost continuous struggle between the Exchange and the listed companies from 1869 to 1933.

The New York Stock Exchange consolidated in 1869 with the Open Board of Brokers and the Government Bond Department, and certain organizational features were developed that continued until its reorganization in 1938. A Committee on Stock List was established and certain rules were laid down which continued for many years. One set of rules related to various safeguards for security owners. They provided for transfer agents, registrars, engraving standards, and the printed text of certificates. There was no challenge to these requirements, which were certainly in the best interests of the corporation, the investing public, and the Exchange.

In 1869 the Exchange began the formulation of a policy on information on company financial condition. It was the hope or expectation that listed companies would supply with their listing application a statement of financial condition. In that early day such a policy was a dream, a Utopia, a case of wishful thinking. The mere suggestion was looked upon with horror by all right-thinking business managers. Corporations did not publish financial statements; they had no intention of doing so; and they believed that such information was no one's business but their own. They certainly had no policy of giving out such facts to anyone, including the Exchange.

A classic example of the attitude of corporations, prevalent shortly after the Civil War, as to the release of corporate information on affairs is cited by Shultz.[4] The letter was written to the New York Stock Exchange in 1866 by a railroad in answer to a request for a report on the company's affairs:

> The Delaware Lackawanna & Western R. R. Co. make no Reports and publish no statements,—and have not done anything of the kind for the last five years.
>
> A. C. ODELL
> Treasurer

It can be said that before 1900 little success was achieved by the Exchange in obtaining agreements by the companies to submit annual reports of condition. However, about that time applications began to be made to the Exchange that showed that the policy of making annual reports of condition was evident for some corporations and that the Committee on Stock List was "cautiously attempting to get industrial companies to agree to publish annual reports and include in them a balance sheet and income statement."[5] Utilities and railroads were very slow to accept such a policy. In fact, not a single railroad or public utility listing between 1900 and 1910 made an agreement to submit annual reports or, in fact, agreements of any sort.

It should be noted that up to 1910 the Exchange maintained an Unlisted Department, where most of the industrial stocks were traded. This department, of course, did not require listing; hence, no agreements were forthcoming. It was abolished on April 1, 1910, and most of the companies in that category applied for full listing. After 1910 slow but steady progress was made by the Exchange in securing agreements by companies to furnish reports on financial condition, to maintain transfer and registry offices in New York, not to speculate in the company's securities, to notify the Exchange about issuance of rights and subscriptions, and not to dispose of stock interests in subsidiaries without notice. The agreements were by no means uniform; the railroads were particularly slow to accept those designed to protect investors.

By 1928 the corporate attitude toward publicity on its financial affairs had shown a considerable change from earlier days. It was, therefore, decided by the Exchange to establish a new policy of corporate publicity. It urged that all annual financial reports be made from audits prepared

---

[4] B. E. Shultz, *The Securities Market* (New York: Harper & Row, Publishers, 1946), p. 9.
  [5] *Ibid.*, p. 17.

by independent certified public accountants. The Exchange could not force listed companies to do so, but it could urge them to do so. The policy, pursued over a five-year period, was largely successful and marked an important forward step in listing standards. By 1931, 83 per cent of all listed companies had accepted the policy. A few companies, however, were adamant in opposing it.

In April, 1932, the Exchange made the 1928 policy of independent audits mandatory for all new companies applying for listing. There were certain exceptions. The railroads were exempted, since they were already operating under a system of uniform accounting reports, prescribed by the Interstate Commerce Commission. It was impractical to insist on such a procedure in certain cases; for example, a government applying for listing of one of its bond issues or companies already listed.

In 1933 there occurred an important test of the listing standards of the Exchange. The Exchange decided to make a test case of one large industrial company which had been particularly hostile to the 1928 policy of complete financial reports of condition. The campaign to secure complete disclosure from the company began in 1930. The company, at that time, was a great financial mystery to the general public. It did publish a balance sheet and income account, but these were not satisfactory either to the Exchange or to investors. The company resented to an acute degree any suggestions that it should give complete disclosure on its affairs. The attitude of the company was stated in a letter to the Exchange in the following language: "The management of the Exchange is neither responsible to the company's stockholders in respect to information to be published regarding its affairs, nor in any position to determine what are the best interests of the stockholders in that regard."[6]

The Exchange, however, was equally firm in its attitude. It refused to accept the argument that disclosure would mean injury to the company or to its stockholders or that it would mean the revelation of trade secrets to competitor companies here or abroad. In a final showdown the company met the demands of the Exchange and the stock was retained on the stock list. Today that corporation is a model in supplying information on its affairs. Within a few months the new Securities and Exchange Commission made mandatory the submission of independently certified reports of financial condition for all companies registered on a national securities exchange. The SEC, a governmental body, completed overnight what the Exchange, a private institution, had been working toward for years.

[6] New York Stock Exchange, *Supplement to the Special Report of the Committee on Stock List,* April 26, 1933.

Another significant listing standard of the Exchange concerns the voting rights of stock. Since 1926 the Exchange has refused to list common stocks that do not carry voting rights. During the 1920's a decided trend in corporate financial policy was to issue classified common stock, the so-called Class A and Class B stock. The former, owned by the general public, carried no voting rights whatever. The latter, owned by the management and bankers, carried full voting power, often with little investment on their part. Thus the public, which furnished the capital of the company, was completely deprived of voting rights. This situation was believed by the Exchange to be against the best interests of the stockholders. The Committee on Stock List, wisely and with full courage, decided to list no further issues of this type. In recent years this type of stock has met with marked disfavor and has largely disappeared.

In more recent years the Exchange has acted to strengthen further the voting rights of common stockholders. It usually has refused to authorize listing of voting trust certificates, excepting cases where these certificates were issued as part of a reorganization of a company under court direction. The Exchange usually will not authorize listing for common stock that has restricted voting rights for any other reason, such as the existence of irrevocable proxies or concentration of voting power in one holding or several closely affiliated holdings. The Exchange urges listed companies to solicit proxies for all meetings of stockholders and will not list companies that do not agree to do so. They will consider delisting for a company that stops soliciting proxies. The common stock, Class A, of Cannon Mills was, in fact, delisted in 1961 because proxies were not solicited and the company refused to send forms to their stockholders.

Corporate depreciation policy became a major concern of the Committee on Stock List in 1938. Before that date the Exchange had contained in its listing agreements a section that required that the corporation give proper notice to the Exchange of any change in its depreciation policy. Such changes, if not properly publicized, were very apt to give substantial changes in corporate earnings, which might mislead stockholders. In 1938 the Exchange went further and stated that it did not desire to list companies unless their accounting policies were sound and logical and found common acceptance among engineers and accountants. It was a sound suggestion and one badly needed in many financial quarters at that time.

In 1940 the Committee on Stock List established a further policy in regard to preferred stocks. After that, the Exchange would not list any further issues of preferred stock unless the company gave at least the following minimum voting rights: (1) the right of the preferred stock, voting as a class, to elect not less than two directors after default of at least six quarterly dividends; (2) the affirmative approval of at least two-thirds of the preferred stock voting as a class, as a prerequisite to any charter or bylaw amendment altering materially any existing provision of such preferred stock. In a few cases these requirements must be modified somewhat because of the laws of the state of incorporation.

In recent years the Exchange has been particularly insistent upon correct principles of accounting for listed companies. If changes in accounting are to be made, they are to have sound justification and are to be publicized adequately to protect stockholders. This policy has been particularly evident since 1936.

Another recent policy of the Exchange has been its campaign to get all listed companies to prepare and release quarterly financial statements. In this it has attained a high degree of success. Although now mandatory for newly listed companies, the policy was not required in earlier years. Most of the companies listed in earlier years have now agreed to furnish quarterly reports, although such actions were required in original listing agreements. The Exchange has also pursued a vigorous policy of requiring companies to release promptly their reports on financial conditions.

The above examples indicate that the listing standards of the Exchange for over eighty years have followed a process of evolution. They were in advance of the publicity standards of corporate management throughout the period, and in some cases far in advance.

In looking back over the period 1869–1934, however, it is not difficult to see why the standards of the Exchange could progress no faster than they did. New ideas are accepted slowly, nowhere more so than in standards of conduct. The business corporation in a laissez-faire economy was always critical of any attempt at regulation. The Exchange knew of this attitude and was reluctant to press upon its customers (the listing companies) any reforms that were too unpalatable. There was competition from other exchanges with their lower fees and less rigid listing standards. Companies could be held only to agreements that they had signed, some of which had been entered into very many years before. If new and additional agreements were formulated by the Exchange, old listed companies could not be compelled to comply except by Exchange persuasion or if they applied for further listing of stock. The over-the-counter market was always available for any company that did not desire to list its stock. Too rigid a policy, if instituted too early, might have defeated its own purpose. Despite these obstacles to higher standards, which were very real, it might have been a wiser policy for the Exchange to have overcome them with even greater aggressiveness than it did display, not only in listing but in other Exchange practices. Congress under the New Deal apparently did not think that self-regulation had gone far enough in the security markets to protect the public and put into effect still stronger regulations.

145½-P-1-58.

NEW YORK STOCK EXCHANGE

LISTING AGREEMENT

Nothing in the following Agreement shall be so construed as to require the Issuer to do any acts in contravention of law or in violation of any rule or regulation of any public authority exercising jurisdiction over the Issuer.

.... (hereinafter called the "Corporation"), in consideration of the listing of the securities covered by this application, hereby agrees with the New York Stock Exchange (hereinafter called the "Exchange"), as follows:

I

1. The Corporation will promptly notify the Exchange of any change in the general character or nature of its business.

2. The Corporation will promptly notify the Exchange of any changes of officers or directors.

3. The Corporation will promptly notify the Exchange in the event that it or any company controlled by it shall dispose of any property or of any stock interest in any of its subsidiary or controlled companies, if such disposal will materially affect the financial position of the Corporation or the nature or extent of its operations.

4. The Corporation will promptly notify the Exchange of any change in, or removal of, collateral deposited under any mortgage or trust indenture, under which securities of the Corporation listed on the Exchange have been issued.

5. The Corporation will:

a. File with the Exchange four copies of all material mailed by the Corporation to its stockholders with respect to any amendment or proposed amendment to its Certificate of Incorporation.

b. File with the Exchange a copy of any amendment to its Certificate of Incorporation, or resolution of Directors in the nature of an amendment, certified by the Secretary of the state of incorporation, as soon as such amendment or resolution shall have been filed in the appropriate state office.

c. File with the Exchange a copy of any amendment to its By-Laws, certified by a duly authorized officer of the Corporation, as soon as such amendment shall have become effective.

6. The Corporation will disclose in its annual report to shareholders, for the year covered by the report. (1) the number of shares of its stock issuable under outstanding options at the beginning of the year; separate totals of changes in the number of shares of its stock under option resulting from issuance, exercise, expiration or cancellation of options; and the number of shares issuable under outstanding options at the close of the year, (2) the number of unoptioned shares available at the beginning and at the close of the year for the granting of options under an option plan, and (3) any changes in the exercise price of outstanding options, through cancellation and reissuance or otherwise, except price changes resulting from the normal operation of anti-dilution provisions of the options.

7. The Corporation will report to the Exhange, within ten days after the close of a fiscal quarter, in the event any previously issued shares of any stock of the Corporation listed on the Exchange have been reacquired or disposed of, directly or indirectly, for the account of the Corporation during such fiscal quarter, such report showing separate totals for acquisitions and dispositions and the number of shares of such stock so held by it at the end of such quarter.

8. The Corporation will promptly notify the Exchange of all facts relating to the purchase, direct or indirect, of any of its securities listed on the Exchange at a price in excess of the market price of such security prevailing on the Exhange at the time of such purchase.

9. The Corporation will not select any of its securities listed on the Exchange for redemption otherwise than by lot or pro rata, and will not set a redemption date earlier than fifteen days after the date corporate action is taken to authorize the redemption.

10. The Corporation will promptly notify the Exchange of any corporate action which will result in the redemption, cancellation or retirement, in whole or in part, of any of its securities listed on the Exchange, and will notify the Exchange as soon as the Corporation has notice of any other action which will result in any such redemption, cancellation or retirement.

11. The Corporation will promptly notify the Exchange of action taken to fix a stockholders' record date, or to close the transfer books, for any purpose, and will take such action at such time as will permit giving the Exchange at least ten days' notice in advance of such record date or closing of the books.

12. In case the securities to be listed are in temporary form, the Corporation agrees to order permanent engraved securities within thirty days after the date of listing.

13. The Corporation will furnish to the Exchange on demand such information concerning the Corporation as the Exchange may reasonably require.

14. The Corporation will not make any change in the form or nature of any of its securities listed on the Exchange, nor in the rights or privileges of the holders thereof, without having given twenty days' prior notice to the Exchange of the proposed change, and having made application for the listing of the securities as changed if the Exchange shall so require.

15. The Corporation will make available to the Exchange, upon request, the names of member firms of the Exchange which are registered owners of stock of the Corporation listed on the Exchange if at any time the need for such stock for loaning purposes on the Exchange should develop, and in addition, if found necessary, will use its best efforts with any known large holders to make reasonable amounts of such stock available for such purposes in accordance with the rules of the Exchange.

16. The Corporation will promptly notify the Exchange of any diminution in the supply of stock available for the market occasioned by deposit of stock under voting trust agreements or other deposit agreements, if knowledge of any such actual or proposed deposits should come to the official attention of the officers or directors of the Corporation.

17. The Corporation will make application to the Exchange for the listing of additional amounts of securities listed on the Exchange sufficiently prior to the issuance thereof to permit action in due course upon such application.

II

1. The Corporation will publish at least once a year and submit to its stockholders at least fifteen days in advance of the annual meeting of such stockholders

and not later than three months after the close of the last preceding fiscal year of the Corporation a balance sheet as of the end of such fiscal year, and a surplus and income statement for such fiscal year of the Corporation as a separate corporate entity and of each corporation in which it holds directly or indirectly a majority of the equity stock; or in lieu thereof, eliminating all intercompany transactions, a consolidated balance sheet of the Corporation and its subsidiaries as of the end of its last previous fiscal year, and a consolidated surplus statement and a consolidated income statement of the Corporation and its subsidiaries for such fiscal year. If any such consolidated statement shall exclude corporations a majority of whose equity stock is owned directly or indirectly by the Corporation: (a) the caption of, or a note to, such statement will show the degree of consolidation; (b) the consolidated income account will reflect, either in a footnote or otherwise, the parent company's proportion of the sum of, or difference between, current earnings or losses and the dividends of such unconsolidated subsidiaries for the period of the report; and (c) the consolidated balance sheet will reflect, either in a footnote or otherwise, the extent to which the equity of the parent company in such subsidiaries has been increased or diminished since the date of acquisition as a result of profits, losses and distributions.

Appropriate reserves, in accordance with good accounting practice, will be made against profits arising out of all transactions with unconsolidated subsidiaries in either parent company statements or consolidated statements.

Such statements will reflect the existence of any default in interest, cumulative dividend requirements, sinking fund or redemption fund requirements of the Corporation and of any controlled corporation, whether consolidated or unconsolidated.

2. All financial statements contained in annual reports of the Corporation to its stockholders will be audited by independent public accountants qualified under the laws of some state or country, and will be accompanied by a copy of the certificate made by them with respect to their audit of such statements showing the scope of such audit and the qualifications, if any, with respect thereto.

The Corporation will promptly notify the Exchange if it changes its independent public accountants regularly auditing the books and accounts of the Corporation.

3. All financial statements contained in annual reports of the Corporation to its stockholders shall be in the same form as the corresponding statements contained in the listing application in connection with which this Listing Agreement is made, and shall disclose any substantial items of unusual or nonrecurrent nature.

4. The Corporation will publish quarterly statements of earnings on the basis of the same degree of consolidation as in the annual report. Such statements will disclose any substantial items of unusual or non-recurrent nature and will show either net income before and after federal income taxes or net income and the amount of federal income taxes.

5. The Corporation will not make, nor will it permit any subsidiary directly or indirectly controlled by it to make, any substantial charges against capital surplus, without notifying the Exchange. If so requested by the Exchange, the Corporation will submit such charges to stockholders for approval or ratification.

6. The Corporation will not make any substantial change, nor will it permit any subsidiary directly or indirectly controlled by it to make any substantial change, in accounting methods, in policies as to depreciation and depletion or in bases of valuation of inventories or other assets, without notifying the Exchange and disclosing the effect of any such change in its next succeeding interim and annual report to its stockholders.

III

1. The Corporation will maintain in the Borough of Manhattan, City of New York, in accordance with the requirements of the Exchange:

a. An office or agency where the principal of and interest on all bonds of the Corporation listed on the Exchange shall be payable and where any such bonds which are registerable as to principal or interest may be registered.

b. An office or agency where

(1). All stock of the Corporation listed on the Exchange shall be transferable.

(2). Checks for dividends and other payments with respect to stock listed on the Exchange may be presented for immediate payment.

(3). Scrip issued to holders of a security listed on the Exchange and representing a fractional interest in a security listed on the Exchange will, during the period provided for consolidation thereof, be accepted for such purpose.

(4). A security listed on the Exchange which is convertible will be accepted for conversion.

If at any time the transfer office or agency for a security listed on the Exchange shall be located north of Chambers Street, the Corporation will arrange, at its own cost and expense, that its registrar's office, or some other suitable office satisfactory to the Exchange and south of Chambers Street, will receive and redeliver all securities there tendered for the purpose of transfer.

If the transfer books for a security of the Corporation listed on the Exchange should be closed permanently, the Corporation will continue to split up certificates for such security into certificates of smaller denominations in the same name so long as such security continues to be dealt in on the Exchange.

If checks for dividends or other payments with respect to stock listed on the Exchange are drawn on a bank located outside the City of New York, the Corporation will also make arrangements for payment of such checks at a bank, trust company or other agency located in the Borough of Manhattan, City of New York.

c. A registrar where stock of the Corporation listed on the Exchange shall be registerable. Such registrar shall be a bank or trust company not acting as transfer agent for the same security.

2. The Corporation will not appoint a transfer agent, registrar or fiscal agent of, nor a trustee under a mortgage or other instrument relating to, any security of the Corporation listed on the Exchange without prior notice to the Exchange, and the Corporation will not appoint a registrar for its stock listed on the Exchange unless such registrar, at the time of its appointment becoming effective, is qualified with the Exchange as a registrar for securities listed on the Exchange; nor will the Corporation select an officer or director of the Corporation as a trustee under a mortgage or other instrument relating to a security of the Corporation listed on the Exchange.

3. The Corporation will have on hand at all times a sufficient supply of certificates to meet the demands for transfer. If at any time the stock certificates of the Corporation do not recite the preferences of all classes of its stock, it will furnish to its stockholders, upon request and without charge, a printed copy of preferences of all classes of such stock.

4. The Corporation will publish immediately to the holders of any of its securities listed on the Exchange any action taken by the Corporation with respect to dividends or to the allotment of rights to subscribe or to any rights or benefits pertaining to the ownership of its securities listed on the Exchange; and will give prompt notice to the Exchange of any such action; and will afford the holders of its securities listed on the Exchange a proper period within which to record their interests and to exercise their

rights; and will issue all such rights or benefits in form approved by the Exchange and will make the same transferable, exercisable, payable and deliverable in the Borough of Manhattan in the City of New York.

5. The Corporation will solicit proxies for all meetings of stockholders.

6. The Corporation will issue new certificates for securities listed on the Exchange replacing lost ones forthwith upon notification of loss and receipt of proper indemnity. In the event of the issuance of any duplicate bond to replace a bond which has been alleged to be lost, stolen or destroyed and the subsequent appearance of the original bond in the hands of an innocent bondholder, either the original or the duplicate bond will be taken up and cancelled and the Corporation will deliver to such holder another bond theretofore issued and outstanding.

. . . .

By. . . . .

Date. . . . .

8

The Stock Ticker and Quotations

Those interested in current prices of stocks being sold on the New York Stock Exchange may keep abreast of them in two ways. First, they may follow the reports of actual sales on the stock ticker, on electronic memory and interrogation equipment or on the electric stock boards. Second, they may utilize the services of the Quotation Department of the Exchange, which supplies the latest quotations on request.

THE STOCK TICKER

Its Origin. The stock ticker was developed in 1867 by E. A. Calahan, an employee of the New York Stock Exchange.[1] The reason for its development was somewhat obscure; one authority believes that it was because of a demand by customers for a checkup on the skill and speed with which brokers executed orders on the floor of the Exchange.[2] Prior to the use of the ticker, the Exchange permitted visitors to the gallery, and speculators were given an opportunity to watch the brokers execute their orders. This was obviously an unsatisfactory method.

Another expedient was also tried before 1867. This was the interesting practice of "pad-shoving"; a number of messenger boys would collect sales figures from the Exchange and hurry from one brokerage house to another shouting the latest prices. The invention of the stock ticker

[1] J. E. Meeker, *The Work of the Stock Exchange* (New York: The Ronald Press Co., 1930), p. 596.
[2] *The Security Markets* (New York: Twentieth Century Fund, Inc., 1935), p. 251.

created technological unemployment for this group of harried individuals.

The first stock ticker was very slow and crude, and even the "pad-shovers" were able to view it with scorn. Its breakdowns were frequent and embarrassing. On one occasion the ticker on the Gold Exchange broke down. A youth of twenty-two, recently fired from his job as a railroad "news-butcher" because of his unorthodox habit of operating a home-made chemical laboratory in the baggage car, was making his living quarters temporarily in the boiler room of the Exchange. He was able to fix the ailing ticker and was promptly hired at $300 a month by the owner of the ticker service to manage the shop which made the stock tickers. In a short time this young mechanic increased the efficiency of the ticker and received the then princely sum of $40,000. He was Thomas A. Edison, later to become the greatest of American inventors.

Ticker Improvements. The first tickers were able to carry their load tolerably well, but were very crude by modern standards. They became totally inadequate to handle the four-million-share days of the late 1920's, although repeated efforts were made to increase efficiency and cut down on the material appearing on the tape.

A new ticker system was then developed with a maximum speed of 500 characters per minute, in contrast to the speed of 285 characters for the old machine. The new system was installed in late 1930, but unfortunately too late to handle the enormous markets of 1929, including those of the hectic days of October when the market crashed. An all-time record for the tape's being late was reported on October 24, 1929, when the tape ran four hours and eight minutes late. The volume on that day was a new record, until then, of 12,880,900 shares. Five days later, when the market broke all records with 16,388,700 shares sold, the ticker ran only one hour and thirty-one minutes behind. Even the new high-speed ticker, when installed, has not always been able to handle excessively active markets. In July, 1933, the ticker ran one-half hour behind on a day's volume of 9,573,000 shares. The present ticker system is geared to handle markets of probably four to five million shares per day if the volume is well distributed. Sudden bursts of selling, however, cause the ticker to run late. In May, 1962, it was over four and one-half hours late at one time.

The Ticker Mechanism. The stock ticker is a high speed printing telegraph. It was designed and geared to a constant printing speed of 500 characters per minute. In 1961 the Exchange experimented with a revision of the printer that would print 900–1200 characters per minute on a tape moving vertically rather than horizontally. Through the ticker standard in 1961 is fed continuously a paper tape three-fourths inches

Fig. 8–1. Reporter at post.

wide; about 800 feet are consumed for every 2 to 2½ million shares in sales. Sales begin to appear on the tape about one minute after the 10 o'clock opening and continue until the last sale of the day is reported.

How do sales get on the tape? The answer is complex. As soon as a sale is made on the floor, an employee of the Exchange, known as a "reporter," writes the price and volume on a small paper slip. The man in a dark suit with a badge on his lapel standing at the right of the post as shown in Figure 8–1 is a reporter noting details of trading in the crowd at that post. The slip will be given to a "carrier page," who goes to the end of the post and calls out the information on the slip. The carrier page then places the report in a small plastic container, often called a "widget," which is carried in a pneumatic tube to the ticker traffic room on the fifth floor of the Exchange building. The reports coming from the posts on the trading floor are divided among three control stations, each of which handles the load from six active posts. The reports are extracted from the containers and time-stamped by an employee and then placed on a moving belt. As they progress on the belt, another employee or operator, sitting at a machine resembling a typewriter, punches out the sales data on a tape (Fig. 8–2).

The tape from each of the three control stations is fed into a central control station, known as a reperforator. This machine automatically punches one sale from each of the three control stations in sequence, so that floor sales may be reported in order. In case the reports from one station become unusually heavy, an adjustment is made to keep the flow of reports in proper balance.

The control station or reperforator tape allows electrical impulses to be transmitted to the tickers which print tape in offices throughout the country. These impulses operate the ticker of the New York Stock Exchange and are sent to Western Union for distribution over the Exchange-leased wire network.

Ownership and Operation of Tickers. The Exchange maintains a monopoly control over the distribution of ticker service. The purpose is to assure uniform reports on transactions and also to prevent unauthorized users from obtaining the service. A number of years ago the Exchange barred all telegraph companies from the floor of the Exchange except the Commercial Telegram Company. This company was taken

Fig. 8–2. Transferring report to tape.

over by the Exchange and became the New York Stock Quotation Company. Western Union took over the other ticker company, the Gold and Stock Telegram Company, and absorbed its services.

At the present time, and ever since August, 1952, the ticker service has been operated under what is known as the leased-wire system. All users of ticker service, regardless of whether they are located in the financial district of New York, other parts of the country, or in foreign countries, sign ticker application agreements with the New York Stock Exchange. The Exchange, therefore, has complete control over the distribution of ticker service. The actual ownership of the tickers, however, is divided between the Exchange and Western Union. The Exchange owns, operates, and maintains all tickers in offices in the financial district of lower Manhattan south of Chambers Street. The Exchange leases from Western Union the tickers and circuit facilities for all other tickers that are located in 720 cities of the United States and Canada. Western Union owns and maintains these tickers, and Western Union either owns the circuit facilities or leases them from the American Telephone and Telegraph Company.

The present system differs from that prior to 1952, when Western Union leased ticker service directly to customers other than those in the financial district. The present arrangement has equalized charges among various customers, charges now being based on distances from New York. Thus, a substantial reduction in ticker rentals was achieved. By way of illustration, ticker rentals range from $65 in upper Manhattan to $130 per month on the Pacific Coast.

On January 2, 1962, there were 3,800 tickers in the leased-wire system, with the Exchange owning about one-third and Western Union the balance. Of these, 3,630 were stock tickers and 170 were bond tickers. The tickers were distributed among 674 cities in the United States and 46 cities in Canada. Approximately half of them were in the state of New York.

Legal Aspects of Ticker Service. The right to receive and to transmit ticker service has been the subject of much legal controversy in the past. In the following discussion the term "quotations," as used by the courts, refers to both quotations and prices at which sales are effected on the Exchange, rather than to the narrow meaning of bid and asked prices.

The New York Stock Exchange regulates the use of quotations in its constitution, which reads in part as follows:

> The Board of Governors . . . shall have supervision over all matters relating to the collection, dissemination and use of quotations and of reports of prices on the Exchange and shall have power to approve or disapprove any applica-

tion for ticker service to any non-member, or for wire, wireless, or other connection between any office of any member of the Exchange or member firms and any non-member, and may require the discontinuance of any such service or connection.[3]

Under this section the Board has the power to determine who shall receive and who shall transmit all quotations or reports of prices. Members of the Exchange are, of course, entitled to ticker service. Non-members who desire service must apply to the New York Stock Exchange for such service. For such applications the Exchange may require letters of recommendation from two members or member firms.

How have the courts treated these regulations of the Exchange? In the first place, it has been clearly held that quotations are the property of the exchange that originates them.[4] Since it owns the property, an exchange can secure protection from the courts for this property right.

Another problem arose as to whether an exchange or telegraph company could be compelled to give quotation service to a customer who did not have the approval of the exchange. Although courts in various states did not always agree, notably Illinois and New York, it was decided by the New York courts *In the Matter of Renville* that no party could compel either an exchange or the transmitting telegraph company to deliver quotations when such action was not approved by the exchange.[5] In this case the court held that the Exchange has an absolute right to give information on its quotations to whom it pleases and to give the information to the telegraph company upon condition that the telegraph company deliver such information to certain specified individuals and none other. This decision of the New York Appellate Division was upheld in 1925 by the United States Supreme Court.[6] The court laid down the rule that a telegraph company was a common carrier for hire and could not be compelled, and in fact was not even permitted, to deliver messages to others than those designated by the sender.

A further legal problem arose in early years: Could an exchange select one telegraph company to deliver quotations to the exclusion of others? This right was fully upheld in the case of *Commercial Telegram Co. v. Smith.*[7]

A final problem needs discussion. In case of erroneous reports on the ticker, is an exchange or telegraph company liable? The answer is: There

[3] New York Stock Exchange, Constitution, Art. III, Sec. 6.
[4] C. H. Meyer, *The Law of Stockbrokers and Stock Exchanges* (New York: Baker, Voorhis & Co., Inc., 1931), p. 50. A number of cases uphold this opinion, a leading one being *Moore v. N. Y. Stock Cotton Exchange,* 270 U. S. 593.
[5] *Ibid.,* p. 52; and *In re Renville,* 46 App. Div. (N. Y.) 37, 43, 44.
[6] *Ibid.,* p. 55; and *Moore v. New York Cotton Exchange,* 270 U. S. 593
[7] *Ibid.,* p. 58; and 47 Hun 494.

is no liability attached to such errors. In the case of *Jaillet v. Cashman* the court declared:

There is a moral obligation upon everyone to say nothing that is not true, but the law does not attempt to impose liability for a violation of that duty unless it constitutes a breach of contract obligation or trust, amounts to a deceit, libel, or slander.[8]

Hence, a customer who may lose money because of erroneous quotations has no claim for damages against either an exchange or a telegraph company that may have delivered the quotations.

THE TICKER TAPE

Difficulties in Reading the Tape. The ticker tape, although a very useful and, in fact, almost indispensable tool for the active trader and broker, has its limitations. In the first place, it is somewhat difficult to understand, since it is based on a code system. In the second place, it suffers from limited visibility. It accumulates in waste baskets, and only a few sales can be examined with ease and then only by a few persons.

Brokerage houses have attempted to overcome these two difficulties in several ways. The services of the Trans-Lux Movie Ticker Corporation have helped. This company has developed an ingenious device or "movie ticker," which is a projector operating much on the order of a motion picture projector. The tape for this projector is made of transparent film. When it is fed through the projector, the image is projected on a screen and can be seen at a considerable distance. Four New York Stock Exchange projectors for the stock tape and one for the bond tape operate on the main trading floor of the Exchange. Brokerage firms generally have Trans-Lux service in their rooms, where it becomes the center of attention throughout trading hours.

Because the projector does not solve all the problems of tape reading, stock boards have been developed. In the older and less well-equipped brokerage offices, the hand-operated stock board has played, and still plays, an important part in the operation of the customers' room. The operation of the board is simple. Essentially, it consists of a large blackboard divided into panels, each panel containing the name of a stock. The board may include as many of the stocks as the broker feels are necessary to the service of the customers. Beside the board is the regular stock ticker. As the tape is fed out, sections are torn off by the brokerage house employees, or "board boys," who hasten to chalk up the recent sales as reported on the tape. As fast as the panel on a particular stock becomes cluttered up with reports, the board boy erases the earlier data and continues with current prices.

[8] *Ibid.,* p. 59; and 115 Misc. 383, aff'd 202 App. Div. (N. Y.) 805.

The newer electric stock boards are leased to brokerage firms by the Teleregister Corporation. They are automatic in operation and carry prices on about 300 of the most active stock issues. On January 1, 1962, there were 663 such boards in the country. On these boards each stock has a separate panel. Each panel indicates the stock symbol, year's range, earnings, and five prices: previous close, open, high, low, and last. As fast as a new sale price is reported, it appears in the proper place on the panel.

A new approach to these problems was taken in 1960 with the introduction of Quotron, which is manufactured by Scantlin Electronics Corporation. As information is received on the ticker wire, it is stored electronically by the Quotron equipment. Desk-top printers are attached. The user may press a button to get a print-out on tape in the machine at his desk of the last sale for whatever stock is of interest. He may also get a scan of prices for the stock beginning with the last sale and adding all sales at approximately twenty-minute intervals since the opening of the market for that day. A separate wire may be attached to the equipment to provide quotations on 800 active stocks. Yet another wire may be used to provide quotations on active over-the-counter stocks. Variations of this concept have been introduced also by Teleregister Corporation with its "telequote" service and by Ultronic Systems Corporation with its SDP 4000. Further developments undoubtedly will be forthcoming.

Stock Abbreviations and Symbols. Each listed stock on the Exchange is given an abbreviation or symbol at the time it is entered for trading. These symbols run from one to three letters each. Since even the most experienced brokers and traders cannot identify all the symbols, it is necessary that they be carefully clasified in small booklets which are made available to brokers, employees, and customers.[9]

The selection of stock symbols has proceeded over a period of many years and has often been not too scientific. Many symbols adopted years ago are now held by stocks, although there is no justification for present possession. Some changes have been made, such as the change of A from Atchison to Anaconda. Little, however, has been done along this line.

Several objectives seem to be sought in assigning symbols to particular issues. First, a logical objective is to select a combination of letters readily associated with the company name, such as GM, GE, PA, and TWA. Such happy combinations, of course, are infrequent. The Exchange also attempts to avoid symbols used by other exchanges, so as not to confuse traders. Another objective is to make the symbol as short as

---

[9] The familiar red or green booklet of Francis Emory Fitch, Inc., is an example.

possible. Symbols leading to confusion in writing are avoided where possible.

There are, of course, twenty-six letters of the alphabet. In early 1961 four letters were not used: I, O, Q, and W. The letter Q is used for bankrupt companies. Hence, twenty-two companies enjoy the prestige of being identified by single letters. The symbol X for United States Steel is the best known of all. Other examples include C for Chrysler, J for Standard Oil Company (New Jersey), S for Sears, and T for American Telephone and Telegraph.

The two-letter combinations are in excess of 200 and the number of combinations has not yet been exhausted. Some of these that are better known include CN for New York Central, DD for du Pont, GE for General Electric, and GM for General Motors. All such selections are not so easily recognized by the layman. For example, few will associate XR with Crucible Steel Corporation or LT with the National Lead Company.

About 1,300 stocks are designated by three-letter symbols, and the tendency is to use this type of combination more and more. Many are obviously associated with their respective companies, apt examples being DOW, PET, RCA, and SUN.

For rapid identification all stocks are classified in two ways in the stock symbol books. In one classification all stocks are listed alphabetically, preceded by the symbol. In the second classification the stocks are arranged alphabetically according to symbols, followed by the stock thus identified.

Indicating Volume on the Tape. Since the great majority of sales on the floor of the Exchange are in 100-share lots, no volume needs to be indicated. Only the symbol and the price are reported; for example:

GE	X	C	DD
$55\frac{1}{4}$	51	$73\frac{1}{2}$	216

These sales are as follows:

> 100 shares of General Electric common at $55\frac{1}{4}$
> 100 shares of United States Steel common at 51
> 100 shares of Chrysler common at $73\frac{1}{2}$
> 100 shares of du Pont common at 216

All sales with a volume of 200 to 900 shares are printed with the volume in hundreds and the letter "s" dividing volume and prices; for example:

GM	S	CN
$2s41\frac{1}{2}$	$3s33\frac{1}{4}$	5s40

These sales are as follows:

> 200 shares of General Motors common at 41½
> 300 shares of Sears Roebuck common at 33¼
> 500 shares of New York Central common at 40

Sales of 1,000 shares or more are generally printed in full; for example:

PA	RCA	X
1000s23	5000s42¼	2000s53

These sales are as follows:

> 1,000 shares of Pennsylvania Railroad common at 23
> 5,000 shares of Radio Corporation common at 42½
> 2,000 shares of United States Steel common at 53

Preferred Stocks. All stock issues reported on the tape are common stocks unless otherwise indicated. Preferred stocks are identified by the abbreviation "Pr" after the stock symbol. In case there are two or more preferred stocks, the dividend rates are given. The rate is in Roman numerals if it appears on the top line, and in Arabic numerals if it appears on the bottom line; for example:

EK Pr	GM.V Pr	GM Pr
101	123	$3\frac{3}{4}$ 2s99¼

These sales are as follows:

> 100 shares of Eastman Kodak $3.60 preferred at 101
> 100 shares of General Motors 5% preferred at 123
> 200 shares of General Motors 3¾% preferred at 99¼

Ten-share unit stocks when reported on the tape are covered by a somewhat different set of rules than 100-share unit stocks. The volume is always given in full on the tape with "ss" instead of a single "s" separating the volume and price; for example, 40ss102. Ten-share unit stocks are described on page 168 and are specially designated in symbol books.

Late-Sale Reports or Delayed Prints. Some sales are not reported as they occur on the floor. Delayed prints may arise through error but usually result from the necessity for checking a point in trading procedure, such as a change in price of more than 2 points. The delayed character of the report is indicated by using the three letters SLD after the stock symbol; for example:

```
                TWA.SLD

                    24
```

This report indicates that 100 shares of Trans World Airlines, Inc., were sold at 24, that the sale was made on the floor sometime earlier, and this item is out of time sequence in the flow of information about the trading.

Errors. Very few errors ever get on the tape in spite of the tremendous volume of transactions carried daily. On an average day perhaps ten errors are made by the operators. Perhaps forty to fifty are made on the floor in reporting the sales. During a day with a 4.5 million share volume, this number of mistakes is minute when one finds that about 30,000 transactions have taken place in five and one-half hours.

As soon as errors and mistakes are discovered, the ticker operators indicate these on the tape. For example, let us suppose that an operator erroneously reports a price. The price was reported at 43; it should have been 44. The error would be corrected in this way:

```
        LAST. GM     WAS

                 43     44
```

Again, let us suppose that an error of volume was made. The sale was reported as 100 shares of American Telephone; it should have been 200 shares. The error would be corrected in this way:

```
        LAST. T       WAS

                 181      2s181
```

Third, let us suppose that an error in symbol took place. The sale was reported as 500 shares of General Motors; it should have been 500 shares of General Electric. The error would be corrected in this way:

```
        NO.GM          WAS. GE

             5s55            5s55
```

Next, let us suppose that a given sale was reported in error; there was no such sale. The error would be indicated in this way:

```
 LAST.  C  ERROR
       79
```

Fifth, let us suppose that a reported sale was canceled. The error would be indicated in this manner:

```
CANCEL. LAST. DOW
                58
```

Quotations on the Tape. Quotations do not generally appear on the tape. They are printed only under special circumstances. This is done by printing the bid and asked price after a sale or as a separate item. For example:

```
RCA
 5s48.B.47¾..0.48¼
```

This was a transaction of 500 shares of Radio Corporation common at 48, followed by a quotation of 47¾ bid, offered at 48¼.

Rights. Sales of stock rights are reported on the tape. The following is a sale of 5,000 rights of Continental Copper and Steel Industries, Inc., at $13/16$ of a point:

```
CCX.RT
  5000s13.16
```

Bankrupt Companies. Since 1946 the Exchange has been using a special symbol to indicate that a company is in bankruptcy. This symbol is the letter "Q" placed in front of the stock symbol; for example:

```
QV
  2⅛
```

This was a sale of 100 shares of New York, New Haven and Hartford common stock at 2⅛. It was the only issue in this category in 1962.

Late Tape. It is mechanically impossible for the tape to report sales at the same moment that they take place on the floor. The sales report must pass through several hands and be transmitted by pneumatic tube to the fifth floor of the Exchange. It must go through two control stations in proper sequence to other sales reports. This inevitable time lag ranges from thirty seconds to possibly as much as two minutes or more. Hence the report on the tape always lags behind the floor transaction, even when the tape is "up" or on time.

The amount of time that the ticker is late is indicated on the floor of the Exchange at all times by large clocks known as "tape delay indicators." The amount of delay is figured in the following manner. At each of the three control stations the time interval is measured between the point of time at which the report reaches the control station and the time the corresponding transaction is printed on the tape. The time lapses for the three stations are then averaged. Let us suppose that this figure is three minutes. The tape is then reported as being three minutes late.

Actually, the lag behind the transaction on the floor is somewhat greater, since the amount of time reported is in addition to the time taken for the information from the floor to be transmitted to the fifth floor by the tube carrier and then recorded by the operators there. Thus, if the normal information lag is one minute and the tape indicator shows the tape is three minutes late, then four minutes elapse from the time the sale was made on the floor until it is reported on the tape.

The Trans-Lux projector is slightly slower in displaying sales than is the regular stock ticker because there are several inches of tape between the point at which the transparent film tape passes the printing wheel in the stock ticker and the point at which the tape is projected.

Many traders in both round- and odd-lots seek to identify their own transactions as they appear on the tape. The inevitable time lag in reporting sales makes this operation a hazardous one in case several sales of the same stock are made at close intervals.

The stock ticker speed is set at 500 characters per minute. This means that about 85 separate sales can be reported in that time, since each sale requires about 6 characters to print. When the tape is late, the Exchange has adopted the practice of eliminating characters, thereby allowing the tape to "catch up."

The opening is the time at which delay is most likely to occur. At this time the last two volume digits of all transactions in 100-share unit stocks are deleted. Sales in a particular stock at the same price will be "bunched," that is, reported as a single series of volume figures with the price and without repetition of the stock symbol. Only the last price digit and fraction, if any, will be printed with the exception of prices ending in zero and the first report of price for an issue on that day. The printing of transactions in 10-share unit stocks with the exception of some common stocks dealt in at the active trading posts will be deferred. When volume conditions permit, these deletions will be made no longer and the words, DIGITS RESUMED, will be printed on the tape.

To illustrate the effect of these practices, let us observe three different ways of reporting stock transactions. First, assuming no deletions at all, a report of seven transactions might appear, as follows:

$$\begin{array}{cccccc} \text{X} & \text{PA} & \text{CN} & & \text{CCL} & \text{J} \\ \text{1000s53} & 25 & \text{5000s40} & & \text{20ss98} & \text{5s52}\tfrac{1}{2}\text{.2s.4s} \end{array}$$

If these were all first sales, the report would be as follows:

$$\begin{array}{cccc} \text{X} & \text{PA} & \text{CN} & \text{J} \\ \text{10s53} & 25 & \text{50s40} & \text{5s52}\tfrac{1}{2}\text{.2s.4s} \end{array}$$

If these were not first sales but the volume was still high during the opening, the report of these sales would be as follows:

$$\begin{array}{cccc} \text{X} & \text{PA} & \text{CN} & \text{J} \\ \text{10s3} & 5 & \text{50s40} & \text{5s2}\tfrac{1}{2}\text{.2s.4s} \end{array}$$

The printing of the transaction in CCL has been deferred for later reporting in both of the latter reports. The number of digits required for reporting has dropped from 47 in the first instance to 30 in the third, a drop of 37 per cent. In other words, 50 per cent more transactions could be reported in the same time with digits fully deleted.

After the opening, if it appears that the volume may cause the tape to become late, the words, DIGITS DELETED, will be printed and the changes in reporting used at the opening will be made until volume conditions permit resumption of standard reporting practices.

When this occurs, after the opening or after a late tape during the day, the printing of transactions in 10-share unit stocks which were deferred will be reported. The notice, THE FOLLOWING ARE DELAYED SALES, will precede the printing. When all deferred reports have been printed, the notice, END OF DELAYED SALES, will be printed.

Flash Printing. When the tape is five minutes or more behind schedule, traders become vitally interested in current prices, since sharp changes in prices are often being reported between sales. To keep the tape readers abreast of the market, the Exchange has evolved a system known as "flash printing." This consists of printing on the tape at two-minute intervals the last sale prices of a group of 5 stocks from a list of 30 carefully selected stocks.

As soon as the tape delay indicator shows that sales are running five minutes behind the normal time lag of the tape, an attendant in the ticker control room signals the floor for the latest prices on the list of flash stocks. These reports come up from the posts on the trading floor in red plastic containers via pneumatic tube.

In reporting flash stocks only the price is given, the volume being omitted. The sale is again reported in its regular order when its turn comes; the volume is indicated at that time. If a stock has not been sold since its previous turn on the flash list, it will be dropped for that time around. Flash printing ceases when the tape becomes less than five minutes late.

The tape appears this way when a flash report is printed:

FLASH.DD	IP	ED	GE	SN	END.FLASH
222	110$\frac{1}{4}$	48	55$\frac{1}{2}$	52	

The list of 30 stocks includes 24 regular members of the list and 6 stocks that were market leaders of the previous day. The 24 regular members of the list are those issues typically found in the popular market averages, such as du Pont, Consolidated Edison, General Electric, Chrysler, United States Steel, Anaconda, General Motors, Sears, Standard Oil Company (New Jersey), Radio Corporation of America, New York Central, and American Telephone and Telegraph.

QUOTATIONS AND THE QUOTATION DEPARTMENT

Nature of Quotations. The term "quotation" has a very precise and technical meaning in the market. It may be defined as the highest bid and lowest offer prevailing in the market at a given time for a given stock. A bid is an indication that a buyer is willing to pay a certain price. It is a buy order. An offer is an indication that a seller is willing to sell at a given price. It is, therefore, a sell order. Thus, a quotation is the highest price at which any buyer will buy and the lowest price at which any seller will sell.

Quotations are commonly called "quotes." They must be expressed in a definite order; namely, first the bid, and second the offer. The quotation may be expressed in a number of ways, but practice and usage have shortened the quotation to an irreducible minimum.

In quoting a certain stock, a broker may say, "63 bid, offered 63¼." This can be shortened to "63, 63¼." The most concise form and the one most likely to be used would be "63 to a ¼."

Another example may be given. A quotation of "22¼ bid, offered 22½," could be further reduced to "22¼, 22½." In its shortest and most favored form, it would be stated as "22¼, ½."

Whether the preposition "to" is necessary in expressing a "quote" depends on conditions. In the Quotation Department, where maximum clarity is demanded at all times, the operators are instructed to use the preposition; for example, "22¼ to ½." It is also standard practice to use the preposition where the bid has no fraction; for example, "147 to ¼."

It should be remembered that there are often many bids and offers in the market for a given stock. The only ones that are used in giving the quotation are the highest bid and lowest offer, as stated before. Quotations are constantly changing for the more active stocks, but may remain constant for a considerable time for the less active issues. There are several reasons why quotations are changed. Higher bids and lower offers may come into the market. Again, a sale may clear the market of all bids and offers at a given price. Finally, cancel orders may eliminate either bids or offers.

Quotations are valuable tools for the broker and customer in determining what action to take on orders and, in some instances, in which of several markets to trade. For this reason there is a continuous check on quotations before the execution of orders. The quotation is a close, if not exact, measure of the price at which the next sale will be executed. A man who buys a house or a pair of shoes wants to know the price before doing business. A broker or customer also wants to know the quotation on his stock before doing business. An intelligent customer should "check the market" through the quotation before placing a market order. He may not get the price indicated in the quotation, but the price will be fairly close to the quotation.

Kinds of Quotations. Two quotations are in common use. The first type is called a regular quotation or just a "quote." This is a bid and asked price only. Most quotations are in this form. All quotations issued by the Quotation Department must be of this type.

The second is the "quote and size" form of quotation. In this there is given not only the "quote" but also the size of the bid and offer. The party asking for the "quote" learns not only the best bid and offer price but also how many shares can be sold and bought at that price. It is permissible to ask how many shares are available in the market at the bid and asked price, but at no higher offering or lower bid price.

When a brokerage firm receives a request for a "quote and size," the quotation clerk in the New York home office of the firm calls the firm's telephone clerk on the floor of the Exchange. This clerk at once gets in touch with a floor partner of the firm. This partner then goes to the trading post where the particular stock is being sold and asks the specialist or specialists in the stock for the "quote and size." The specialist, after giving the usual quotation, will probably say that the size is "One hundred either way," an indication that both the bid and offer are for 100 shares only. He may also state a larger size; for example, "500, 1,000" to indicate that the bid is for 500 shares and the offer is for 1,000 shares.

This is a valuable piece of information for traders who may have large blocks of stock to accumulate or sell. It is obvious, of course, that every quotation without a size indication carries a size of at least 100 shares either way, since no round-lot orders may be executed for less than 100 shares in active stocks.

The Quotation Department. Regular quotations are handled through the Quotation Department of the Exchange. This department operates on two floors, the eighth and the fifteenth. The eighth floor contains the tape recorder system and the fifteenth the regular reporting room.

The operations of the regular reporting room will be described first, since that is the place from which quotations on the larger number of issues originate. This is a long, narrow room in which about seventy girls sit facing electric panel boards, somewhat similar to the teleregister electric boards in brokerage offices. In early 1962 this room handled quotations for 1,250 stocks. These stocks were divided into twenty groups, each group being identified by a code number. Each code number contains two digits running from 60 to 79. For example, Code 61 includes Sears, A. O. Smith, United Engineering, Ward Baking, and Commercial Solvents. The code numbers of the stocks are listed in the stock symbol books previously mentioned and on quotation code cards. The current quotations of these stocks are arranged on overhead electrically operated panels, which are clearly visible to the girls giving the quotations.

The regular reporting room is connected by telephones to the trading posts on the floor of the Exchange. Each operating posting has five lines and each trading post has three lines. By means of a plug-and-jack switchboard it is possible to connect a post to any operating posting position. The post quotation clerks constantly report to the Quotation Department all changes in the quotations of the stock at that post. They receive this information from the specialists dealing in the particular stock. As soon as a new quotation is given, the floor quotation clerk telephones it to the posting operator (Fig. 8–3). This employee, by pressing the proper keys, posts the new quotation in the corresponding electric panel.

The quotation girls are now ready to give the new quotations as soon as the next call comes in. These calls for quotations come from the various member firms who subscribe for the service. On January 1, 1962, there were 904 telephone quotation lines in operation. No one except a member of the Exchange with a private wire to the Quotation Department may receive quotations. Thus, the general investing public secure quotations through member firms which will gladly supply the quotation information.

The procedure of securing a quotation runs through the following channels. Customer A in Cleveland, for example, before buying Sears Roebuck would like the current quotation. Since the quotation service is with few exceptions available only in Metropolitan New York, the office in Cleveland contacts a New York office by private wire system, asking for the "quote." A quotation clerk in the New York office dials the Quotation Department on another private line. The code for Sears is 61, so he dials the number 61. The girl responds, "61." The clerk inquires, "Sears?" and the girl replies, "Sears, 33 to ¼." The conversation ends. The quotation clerk then sees that the quotation is transmitted back to Cleveland with all possible speed over the firm's private wire system.

Next, let us describe the tape recorder system installed recently by the Department. Service began on this system on April 20, 1953. A total of 300 of the most active stocks on the Exchange were selected and given code numbers of three digits each; for example: United States Steel, 411; General Motors, 524; and Radio Corporation, 352. Each of these 300 stocks has a tape recorder channel on the eighth floor. When a new quo-

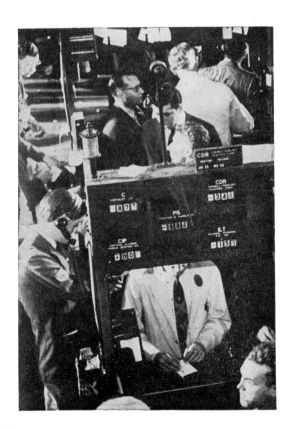

Fig. 8–3. Quotation clerk at phone.

tation is established on the floor the quotation clerk presses a key that connects the post telephone turret with the proper tape recorder. Next, he speaks the figures of the quotation and they are recorded on the magnetic tape of the recorder. The quotation is then ready for distribution to any subscriber.

Let us suppose that a broker wants to get a quotation on one of the 300 stocks; for example, United States Steel. He may dial number 411. The tape recorder will automatically respond, "X, 64 to ¼." Each quotation is continuously repeated at intervals of four seconds. The subscriber is cut off automatically after two complete quotations, thereby releasing the recorder for other dialed calls. Old quotations are automatically "erased" on the tape as the new ones are recorded. The benefit of the tape recording system to the trading public is a great speedup in the transmission of quotations. Thirty-seven telephone lines may be connected simultaneously to one tape recorder.

Quote wires are available in Chicago and in several Eastern seaboard cities south of New York. As noted above, the Exchange also transmits quotes on 800 issues on a system similar to the ticker system. The electrical impulses operate electronic memory and interrogation devices and provide quotations service to authorized users of these devices.

Number of Quotations. The number of quotations given by the entire Quotation Department is very large. During 1961 the daily average was 97,875. On May 29, 1962, a record 243,000 telephone queries were answered and hundreds more went unanswered because lines were busy.

The greatest demand for quotations comes, as a rule, during the first thirty minutes of trading. There is no reason, however, why quotations would not be useful at any time. They do have limitations. As rapidly as quotations are handled, a certain amount of time must elapse from the time the new quotation is given on the floor of the Exchange to the time the customer can obtain such information, place his order, and have it executed. During that interval several sales may have taken place on the trading floor and quotations may have changed as a consequence. Hence, quotations cannot guarantee firm prices to brokerage customers.

9

Kinds of Orders and Their Merits

A skilled investor, trader, or broker in the stock market may use only a few kinds of orders to buy and sell, but familiarity with all kinds is useful. He should know his rights and liabilities and the kinds of results to expect from different orders. He should understand how orders are processed in the market. Such knowledge is not only profitable but also helps to avoid much misunderstanding.

Classifications. There are many kinds of orders. These may be classified in various ways. The following classification is a convenient one:

    I. Size of Order
      A. Round-lot Order
      B. Odd-lot Order
   II. Type of Transaction
      A. Buy Order
      B. Sell Order
        1. Long
        2. Short
  III. Price Limits
      A. Market Order
      B. Limit or Limited Order
  IV. Time Limits
      A. Day Order
      B. Week Order
      C. Month Order
      D. Open or G.T.C. Order
   V. Special Types of Orders
      A. Stop Order

SIZE OF ORDERS

Round- and Odd-Lots. All trading in stocks on the floor of the New York Stock Exchange is divided into round- and odd-lots. The factor that differentiates the two is the so-called "unit of trading." A round-lot is one for the unit of trading or some multiple thereof. An odd-lot is one for less than the number of shares required for the unit of trading.

The floor of the Exchange has eighteen active trading posts. At these posts the unit of trading is 100 shares for nearly all issues. Approximately 1,350 active stocks are traded in at these active posts. Although 100-share transactions are the most common type, orders often run in larger sizes, such as 200, 300, 400, or 500 shares, and sometimes 1,000, 5,000, or more.

For the inactive stocks the unit of trading is 10 shares. These are usually preferred stocks which enjoy a relatively inactive volume of trading and most of them are handled at Post 30. Because of the high price and slower turnover, the Exchange permits a unit of trading of 10 shares.

An odd-lot for 100-share unit stocks is from 1 to 99 shares. For 10-share stocks the odd-lot is from 1 to 9 shares.

The Exchange can permit only the larger or round-lot orders to be traded on the floor. The extra work of executing thousands of small orders on the floor would place a great burden on the floor members and staff. Quotations would change in significance because many sales would represent only insignificant parts of the day's trading. The stock ticker, despite its mechanical efficiency, would be incapable of carrying reports on all sales during active markets, since approximately one-third of all orders placed by the general public are for odd-lots. The unit of trading is an inevitable requirement for orderly, rapid market operation.

The stock buyer must make an early decision whether to trade in round- or odd-lots. In most cases this is automatically decided in favor of odd-lots by the size of his investment or trading fund, since trading in 100-share lots of high-priced stocks runs into large figures. Purchase of 100 shares of an average-priced stock traded in 1961 would have involved a cash outlay of $4,075 plus commissions of some $39.38.

The odd-lot customer will find that his costs are somewhat higher than those of the round-lot customer. Detailed consideration is given to odd-lot costs in Chapter 14.

TYPE OF TRANSACTION

Buy and Sell Orders. No special discussion of buy and sell orders is necessary here except to point out that in all orders, except fully discretionary orders, the customer must decide whether he is buying or selling, and if he is selling, whether he is selling long or short.[1] If we assume that the trader is trading for purely speculative profits, buying orders are obviously placed in anticipation of a rise in stock prices, while selling orders are placed in anticipation of a decline in prices.

PRICE LIMITS

Market Orders. A market order is to be executed at the best possible price at the time the order reaches the floor.

Market orders usually are the most common of all orders and probably outnumber all other orders combined. They are more popular with larger traders, professional investors, brokers, and institutions than they are with the odd-lot public. They are also more common in the execution of selling orders than in buying orders, the reason apparently being that sellers want to sell quickly but buyers are less eager to buy at current prices. On some occasions during which there has been heavy selling in the market, 85 per cent of the orders have been market orders.

The greatest advantage of the market order is speed. The customer specifies no price in this type of order. He merely orders his broker to sell or buy quickly at the best possible price, regardless of what it may be. No other type of order can be executed so rapidly, often in a matter of several minutes after it is given the broker.

Limit or Limited Orders. The chief characteristic of a limit order is that the customer decides in advance on a price at which he desires to trade. He believes that his price is one that will be reached in the market in a reasonable time and that will be advantageous to him. He is willing to wait to do business until he has obtained his price, even at the risk that his order may not be executed either in the near future or at all.

In the execution of a limit order the broker is to execute it at the limit or better. A limit order to buy is executed at the limit or lower; a limit order to sell, at the limit or higher. If the broker can obtain a more favorable price for his customer than the one specified, he is required to do so.

For example, a customer wants to buy 100 shares of XYZ. The price has been fluctuating between 50 and 55. He places a limit order to buy at 51, although the current market price is 54. It is possible that within a

---

[1] Short selling is discussed at length in Chapter 12.

reasonable time the price will fall to 51 and his broker can secure the stock for him at that price. If the broker can purchase the stock at less than 51, he must do so, since the customer is entitled to the best possible price. Special rules apply to the execution of odd-lot limit orders, and these will be taken up in Chapter 13.

Let us take another example. A customer wishes to sell 100 XYZ. The market is 54. The limited order to sell is placed at 56. A soon as the market rises to 56, the broker will execute it at 56 or higher, if he can do so. In no case will the order be executed at less than 56.

The advantage of the limit order is that the customer has a chance to buy at less or to sell at more than the market price prevailing when he placed the order. He assumes that the market price will become more favorable in the future than it is at the time the order is placed. The word "chance" is important. There is also the chance that the order will not be executed at all. The customer, just mentioned, who wanted to buy at 51 may never get his order filled, since the price may not fall to that level. The customer who wanted to sell at 56 also may never get his order filled, since the stock may not rise that high during the time the order is in effect.

In a narrow, fluctuating market, when a stock is "making a line," it is often profitable to place limit orders. "Making a line," it should be explained, is a situation in which a stock moves within very narrow limits, usually three or four points up and down, over a period. If there is an upward trend or bull market, however, it is no time to be placing limit orders to buy. If there is a bear market, the investor should not place limit orders to sell. Bull markets, of course, are those that are showing strong gains; bear markets, the reverse, are those that are reporting heavy losses.

An obvious objection and disadvantage to limit orders is the danger of "missing the market." For example, in a bull market, if a buy order were to be placed several points below the current market price, it might never be filled because the market would continue upward. Similarly, in a falling market, if a sell order were to be placed above the current market price, the market might continue to fall and the order might never be executed. It is difficult to set a satisfactory limit. If the limit is very close to the current market price, the order has little advantage over a market order; if too far away, it may never be executed. Setting a satisfactory limit takes much more skill than is generally supposed. In a rising market, for example, just how far below the market is it safe to set a limit on a buy order?

Prices on limit orders have a definite relationship to market price. A limit order to buy usually is placed below the current market price, while a limit order to sell is placed above the market price.

A limit order never becomes a market order, even after the stock sells at the limit. The broker must always observe the limit and cannot execute the order, regardless of price, merely because the market has touched the limit price. This is a difference between the limit and the stop order, which will be described shortly.

How is a limit order to be executed if the broker cannot buy or sell at the limit at the time he receives the order on the floor? The broker, immediately upon receipt of the order on the floor, attempts to execute it at the limit or better. This often is not possible, although it may happen that the limit has been reached or passed by the time the order is on the floor if the limit is not too far away from the market price at the time it is entered. In the event that the order cannot be executed immediately, the broker places the order with a specialist, who enters it in his "book." The broker himself cannot stand by to handle one order; he has others to execute. It can, however, be left with the specialist in readiness for execution at the first possible opportunity. The broker is now freed to execute other orders that can be taken care of at once. The method of handling of such orders by the specialist is discussed in Chapter 11.

Limit orders are popular, but not quite as popular as market orders. Apparently less than half of all round- and odd-lot orders are limited.

TIME LIMITS

Day Orders. A day order is one that expires automatically at the end of the day entered, which is 3:30 P.M. All orders are considered as day orders unless otherwise specified by the customer. They are good for the day of entry only, or such portion of the day as remains after the order is entered. Market orders usually are day orders. Limit orders, however, may or may not be day orders.

The theory of the day order is that the customer believes that conditions, as of today, are such that either buying or selling is justified. Tomorrow the market may change, and other factors may indicate a different course of action.

Week Orders. These are orders that expire at the end of the calendar week, which is 3:30 P.M. on Friday. Specialists may not accept them on the floor of the Exchange. However, brokers may accept them if they care to do so. They are very rare. There is no particular advantage in placing them; the open order is preferable.

Month Orders. This is an order that expires at 3:30 P.M. on the last trading day of the month. Specialists may not accept them on the floor. Brokers may accept them and a few are placed. Again, there seems to be no particular advantage to them over open orders.

Open Orders. Open orders, also known as G.T.C. orders, are good until canceled. They remain in force until the customer explicitly orders them canceled or the broker fails to confirm them to the specialist on the check dates. This type of order is used when the customer believes that the action of the market is such that it will eventually give him his stock at his specified price. He is reasonably sure of his judgment and is in no hurry to have his order executed. He knows what he wants to pay or to receive and is willing to wait for an indefinite period.

Under earlier exchange practices such orders were carried for long periods without confirmation. This was very unsatisfactory for all parties concerned. Under present regulations members must confirm these orders with the specialists at regular intervals. If they are, the orders retain their priority on the books of the specialist. If they are not confirmed, they are canceled, must be re-entered, and thus lose their priority.

Confirmation is of two types. Since January, 1952, the Exchange has required brokers under Rule 123 to confirm these orders at six-month intervals and, specifically, on the last trading or business day of April and October. They will automatically expire unless they are confirmed or renewed with the specialist at that time. Brokers may, and usually do, ask their customers to confirm such orders at more frequent intervals, often once a month or quarterly.

Open orders to buy stock and open orders to sell stop are adjusted automatically when the stock goes "ex-dividend." A stock is considered to fall in price by the exact amount of the dividend on the date it goes ex-dividend. For example, if a stock is selling at 80 and pays a dividend quarterly of one dollar, it would be assumed to fall one dollar in price on the day it goes ex-dividend. Accordingly, limit buy or sell stop prices on all such open orders are reduced by the amount of the dividend on the day the stock goes ex-dividend, according to Rule 118. There is no such reduction of prices on open limit orders to sell or open stop orders to buy.

SPECIAL TYPES OF ORDERS

Stop Orders. A very important type of order is the so-called stop order or stop-loss order. There are two distinct types of stop orders. One is the stop order to sell, and the other is the stop order to buy. Either type is in the nature of a *suspended* market order; it goes into effect only if the stock touches or passes by a certain price. The fact that the market reaches or passes the specified stop price does not compel the broker to obtain execution at the exact stop price. It merely releases the order for execution as a market order at the best possible price thereafter obtainable.

A stop order to sell becomes a market order when the stock sells at or below the stop price.

A stop order to buy becomes a market order when the stock sells at or above the stop price.

The price used on a stop order bears a distinct relationship to current market price, which is exactly opposite to that on a limited order. A stop order to sell is placed at a price below the current market price. A stop order to buy is placed at a price above the current market price.

There are four well-established uses for stop orders. Two of these might be called protective:

1. Protection for the customer's existing profit on a long purchase
2. Protection for a short seller's existing profit on a short sale

Let us illustrate the first. A trader purchases a stock at 60. It rises to 70. On a 100-share trade he has made a paper profit of $1,000, disregarding expenses. He realizes that the market may reverse itself through either technical or fundamental conditions. He therefore gives his broker a stop order to sell at 69. If the reversal does occur and the price drops to 69 or less, the order immediately becomes a market order. The broker disposes of the stock at the best possible price. This may be exactly 69, or it may be above or below that figure. Let us suppose that the broker obtained 68½. The customer made a gross profit of 8½ points on his original purchase from which, of course, he had to pay commissions and taxes. If it had not been for the stop order, however, the stock might have fallen much below the stop price of 69 before an ordinary market order to sell could be placed and executed, and the trader's profit might have been further dissipated.

A similar situation arises in the protection of a profit on a short sale. A stop order to buy is placed above the market price. For example, a short seller sells a given stock at 80. His judgment is correct and the stock declines to 72. His gross profit is 8 points. To protect his paper profit against an adverse price change, he places a buy order above 72; for example, at 72½, and the broker "covers" for the short seller at the market price. Let us suppose that the order is executed at 72¾. The short seller makes a gross profit of 7¼ points.

Two other uses of the stop order may be called preventive:

1. Prevention or reduction of a loss on a long purchase
2. Prevention or reduction of a loss on a short sale

The first may be illustrated in this way. A customer purchases 100 shares of a stock at 30. His analysis of the issue leads him to believe that the price will rise in the near future. He realizes, however, that his judgment may be faulty. He therefore at once places a stop order to sell at a price below his purchase price; for example, at 29½. As yet he has made neither profit nor loss; he is merely acting to prevent a loss that might follow from an error in judgment and against a fall in price. If the price does go down, he is closed out at about 29½ with a gross loss of ½ point or thereabouts. It might have been more.

The second use involves a short sale. A short seller sells 100 shares at 110 in the belief that the market is going to decline. He then places a stop order to buy at 111, for example. If his judgment as to the market is wrong and the stock goes up, the broker covers at 111 or near that price. The trader acts to prevent the greater loss that might accrue in a rising market through a less rapid and effective way for placing a market order to buy.

There are two basic differences between stop orders and limited orders. First, they are placed on different sides of the market. The stop order to buy is placed above the market, and the limited order to buy usually is placed below the market. The reverse is true of orders to sell. Second, the limited order never becomes a market order when the limit is reached, while the stop order always does.

Stop orders have three inherent dangers or weaknesses. First, there is the danger that they will cause avoidable losses. The trader may place the order too close to the market. A temporary reversal of trend will "touch off" the order, and the market will then move as expected. In the meantime the trader must bear a needless expense of getting back into the market again. He should have placed his stop order farther away from the market. Of course, the farther away from the market the stop order is placed, the less the profit that can be salvaged or the greater the loss that will be incurred.

The second inherent limitation of the stop order is the fact that it may be executed at some distance away from the stop price. In a rapidly changing market the broker may not be able to execute at the stop price, but may have to execute at a price several points from it. There is no certainty of the exact price obtainable.

A third weakness is the possibility that accumulated stop orders will cause a sharp break in the price of the issue and the Exchange will suspend stop orders at the time and precisely under the conditions when the trader sought protection. In 1961 the American Stock Exchange ruled against acceptance of any straight stop orders—only limit stop orders could be accepted—and the New York Stock Exchange suspended temporarily such orders in particular issues; for example, Brunswick Corporation common.

Many uninformed stock traders overestimate the value of the stop order. It has its undeniable advantage, but it is no "sure-fire" profit-maker. If a stock is declining steadily, the order will merely sell the customer out of the market, with, perhaps, a small loss, but with a definite overhead cost. If the market is rising, the profit is made because of advancing stock prices and not because of stop orders. The profit comes from knowing when to sell in a rising market. If a speculator analyzes the market badly, all the stop orders in Wall Street will not bring him a penny's profit. They only limit losses.

The execution of stop orders by specialists and odd-lot dealers is a highly technical process which will be discussed in detail in Chapters 11 and 13, which deal with the work of these members of the Exchange.

Stop Limit Orders. Stop limit orders are used rarely. The trader who uses this type of order wants to obtain the advantage of the stop order, yet wants to be sure at what price his stock will be purchased or sold. He is not satisfied with the market price that results when a stop order becomes a market order. He seeks the advantages of both the stop order and the limit order.

A stop limit order to sell is effective as soon as there is a sale at the stop price or lower, and then it is executed, if possible, at the limit or higher.

An example will illustrate the rule. A customer own 100 shares of a stock selling at 74. He feels that the price may break, but is not sure. He has two ways to place his order. One is to specify a stop and limit figure, which is the same in both cases. He may state his order thus: "Sell 100 shares at 72, stop and limit." As soon as the stock falls to 72, the broker attempts to execute the order at 72 or higher, but in no case at less than 72. If the stock cannot be sold at 72 or better, there is no sale.

The order can be placed in another way. The order reads: "Sell 100 shares at 72 stop, limit 71." When the stock falls to 72, the broker immediately attempts to dispose of the 100 shares, but under no circumstances can he sell for less than 71. This has an advantage over the first method of stating the order, since in a falling market the order has more chance of execution under the stop price than at the stop price or higher.

A stop limit order to buy is executed as the reverse of a stop limit order to sell. As soon as there is a sale at the stop price or higher, the order is elected and executed, if possible, at the limit or lower. These orders may be used by short sellers, while the stop limit orders to sell ordinarily are used by owners of stock.

In spite of its apparent attraction, this type of order must be used with extreme caution. If the trend of the market is definitely downward, a speculator or investor must be realistic and act accordingly. It is no time to quibble over price. Delayed action increases the danger of a sharp loss. The best policy under such circumstances usually is to get out of the market completely. The stop order will do this more surely than the stop limit order.

Discretionary Orders. A discretionary order is one in which the customer grants the broker a certain amount of discretion in filling the order. The amount of discretion may be complete or it may be limited. It is assumed that the broker, using his knowledge of the market, can secure greater profits for the customer than the customer can for himself by relying on his own judgment.

Under a completely discretionary order, the broker or his representative would decide on the stock, the number of shares, whether the order should be buy or sell, the price, and the time of execution. A completely discretionary order is regulated by Rule 408 of the Exchange. The rule requires that such an order shall be approved and initialed by a general partner or voting shareholder of a member organization on the day the order is entered. In addition, the customer must give prior written authorization.

Under an order involving limited discretion, the broker or his representative has discretion only as to price and time of execution. Rule 408 does not apply to such orders.

Whether or not a customer should ever use a discretionary order is debatable. Of course, one should have considerable confidence in the broker; nevertheless, the wisdom of the action is open to question. Can a busy broker or his registered representatives with their many orders and customers give much individual attention to such orders? Is it not entirely possible that they will fill the order at the first opportunity, when the market looks fairly good, rather than wait an indefinite time in the hope that it may get better?

It is doubtful whether any broker really wants discretionary orders. His commission is the same for a discretionary order as it is for any other kind of order. If he gets a good price, he will probably get only a casual "thank you" from the customer. If the execution proves to be timed badly and the customer loses money, the customer is apt to blame the broker and may even sue him. It is human nature to credit one's self for all fortunate events and to shift the blame to others for one's misfortunes. Discretionary orders are no exception. Some brokers are so opposed to discretionary orders that they have standing rules prohibiting any employee from accepting them.

Probably the only people who should use discretionary orders are the ill, the very aged, or the individual on a prolonged vacation. In such cases it is perhaps advisable to place them with a trusted investment counselor. Customers sometimes give their bankers discretion in handling securities.

Discretionary orders were once used widely in manipulative operations. Pools would give such orders to specialists. The orders enabled the pool managers to use the services of specialists to insure the success of their operations. The specialist, by his intimate knowledge of the market, was able to buy and sell at the time that insured the greatest profit to the pool. Such actions are no longer permitted.

Immediate or Cancel Orders. These orders, often called "fill or kill orders," are rarely found. The rule for execution is that the order must be executed at once at the specified price or be canceled. A customer may want to sell a given stock that has a rather limited market. He is uncertain whether he can buy or sell at his limit. If he cannot obtain execution of the order, he wishes to withdraw it. For example, he may give an order to sell 500 shares of XYZ at 105, immediate or cancel. An attempt is made to dispose of the stock. If unsuccessful, the broker will cancel the order.

This order is restricted by Rules 61 and 79 of the Exchange, which forbid "all or none bids and offers" on the floor. For example, "all or none" orders may be accepted by brokers from customers, but they may not be bid or offered as such on the floor. Since a report on such an order includes quote and size to explain why the floor broker did not execute it, the order does provide a way to obtain information about the quotation itself.

Cancel Orders. These are orders, placed by customers, that cancel other orders previously given to the broker. They are of two types: the straight cancel order and the cancel former order.

The straight cancel order cancels a previous order; no other order replaces it. The customer has changed his mind and is no longer willing to buy or sell the stock under present conditions.

The cancel former order (CFO) also cancels a previous order but is replaced by a new order with some alteration in character. This alteration, as a rule, is a change in price. For example, a customer orders his broker to buy 100 shares at 36. He now cancels this order and reduces the limit to 35.

Other Orders for Odd-Lots Only. Chapter 14 describes a number of orders available to odd-lot customers only.

ILLUSTRATION OF ORDER FORMS

The following illustrations indicate the form used to send essential information about a customer's order to the trading floor of the New York Stock Exchange. Order forms for this purpose measure about three to four inches. They are filled out by telephone clerks when orders reach

Fig. 9–1. A round-lot market order.

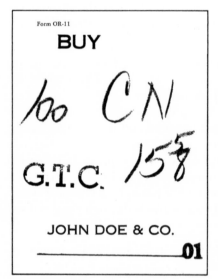

Fig. 9–2. A round-lot, limited, GTC order.

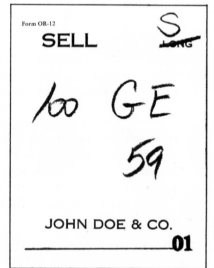

Fig. 9–3. A round-lot order to sell short.

the floor. Each firm has its own forms, which vary in details. Some firms differentiate between buying and selling forms by printing the former with black ink and the latter with red ink; others use the same form for both types of transactions. Some firms indicate in print on the form whether the sale is a long or short sale; others write in this notation.

Figure 9–1 is a round-lot order to buy 100 shares of United States Steel common stock at the market. It will be noted that no price is indicated.

Figure 9–2 is an example of a round-lot, limited, GTC order to buy 200 shares of New York Central common stock at 15⅝. It will be noted that on the day order no time limit is indicated, while on an open order there is a definite notation that the order is good until canceled.

Figure 9–3 is a round-lot, day order to sell short 100 shares of General Electric common stock at 59, limited.

10

Trading Floor Procedure and Mechanics

The trading floor of the New York Stock Exchange is the heart of the stock market. Onto it there flows constantly a stream of orders from all parts of the country. Upon it the forces of security investment and speculation are centered, as supply and demand balance themselves in creating market prices. The prices, so determined, have vast influences upon security values everywhere, both directly and indirectly, as well as immeasurable effects upon many broad fields of economic activity.

This chapter will deal with the chief trading procedures and regulations. In addition, it will discuss two important types of members: floor brokers, and floor traders. The operations of commission brokers, specialists, and odd-lot dealers will be taken up in other chapters of the book.

FLOOR MECHANICS

The Trading Floor. Stock sales on the Exchange are effected on two trading floors of unequal size and adjoining each other. The floor plans are shown in Figure 10–1. The main, or old, trading floor, on the right in the diagram, holds most of the trading activity. It measures 120 by 150 feet. There are twelve, U-shaped trading posts, numbered "1" through "12," on this floor. Adjoining the main floor is a smaller floor, extending along Wall Street. This floor was added to the Exchange at a date later than the main floor and is called the "garage." In this room there are six regular posts, numbered "13" through "18," and a counter (near the stairs on the Broad Street side) called Post 30. Most inactive, 10-share-unit issues are traded at Post 30. A special trading area was constructed in 1961 for handling issues in which extraordinary activity is temporarily present. This helps to reduce traffic congestion and interference with trading in other issues at the post where such an issue usually is assigned.

Telephone Booths. Extending around the edge of the trading floor in both rooms are telephone booths. Partitions extend out on the floor about 17 feet. There is a partition every 6 feet. On each side of a partition there is space for nearly a dozen telephones. Some booths are constructed for use of teletypewriters. Push buttons permit the telephone clerks to connect with as many as four different extensions, if necessary. The most important connection, of course, is that of the home office of the broker. About 1,800 telephone and teletypewriter wires are in service. The main use of the telephone is to transmit orders from the broker's office to the Exchange floor and to report back to the office the execution of such orders. Telephone clerks remain at their stations throughout trading hours, and are not permitted under any circumstances to step out on the trading floor (Fig. 10–2).

Active Trading Posts. As already indicated, there are now eighteen active trading posts. Until 1928 the trading stations actually resembled posts. They were tall affairs, circular in construction, and fixed to rounded bases with seats. In 1928 and 1929 the old posts were removed, and the much more practical posts now in use were installed. The present posts are horseshoe or U-shaped stations, occupying 100 square feet and standing 8 feet high (Fig. 10–3). A total of twelve or more clerks can work inside. A number of tubes connect the post with the telephone booths at the edge of the trading floor and with other areas, such as the stock ticker.

There is provision for 105 price indicators at posts in the main trading room and for 120 at posts in the garage. The number of stocks at each, however, is in the neighborhood of 75. Each stock is given a price indicator or dial for showing the last sale price. This indicator serves a very important function, especially in the making of short sales. At the opening of the market the indicators are set at 00.0 for all stocks. As soon as a sale is made for a stock, an employee of the Exchange posts the sale price, such as 24.5, meaning $24\frac{5}{8}$. The indicator also has a space for a plus or minus sign, showing whether the last sale was at a price above or below that of the previous different price. This is needed in the execution of short sales. All trading in a given stock takes place in front of the price indicator.

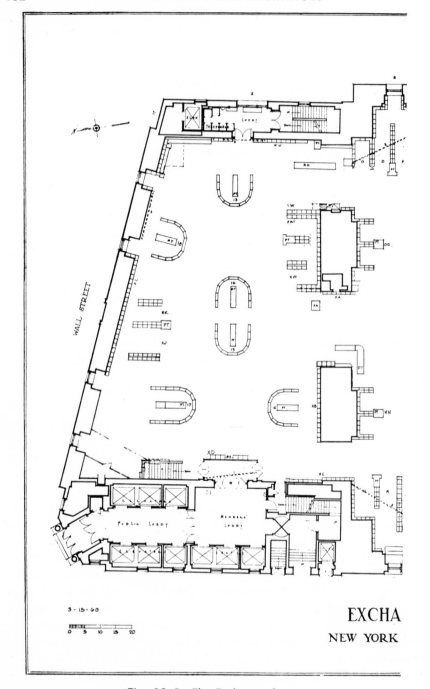

Fig. 10–1. The Exchange floor.

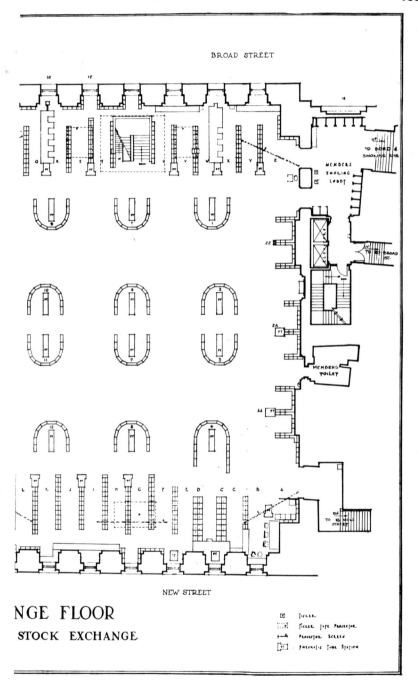

NGE FLOOR

STOCK EXCHANGE

Fig. 10–2. The telephone booths.

The group trading in a particular stock is called a "crowd." The group of men in the foreground of Figure 10–3 are a "crowd" that is trading, presumably, in one of the 7 stocks posted on the indicator board behind them. The indicator board shows that C (Chrysler) last sold at 87⅞ (some time ago) and this price was — (down) from the last previous different price. BAB (Babbitt) had not traded in that session when the picture was taken.

Distribution of Stocks. On January 2, 1962, there were 1,542 stock issues listed on the Exchange. Of these, 198 ten-share-unit stocks were assigned to Post 30. The balance, 1,344, was divided among the eighteen active posts. To the layman there seems to be no system or method by which stocks are distributed, since they follow no obvious pattern.

Post 2 is sometimes called the "steel post" since United States Steel common is traded there. To find United States Steel preferred, however, one must go to Post 5; for Bethlehem common, to Post 10; for Republic, to Post 16; and for Jones and Laughlin, to Post 4. For General Motors common one goes to Post 4; for Chrysler, to Post 2; for American Motors, to Post 10; and for Studebaker-Packard, to Post 7.

Despite the apparent confusion, there is a system. The Exchange purposely scatters the stocks of leading industries so that all the trading in stocks of a particular industry does not take place at one post. A heavy volume of trading in stocks of one industry, steel for example, does not thus create an unmanageable burden for any one post. The experienced members of the Exchange know the location of most stocks, but if in doubt they can readily refer to lists on the edge of the trading floor.

Fig. 10–3. Post 6.

The Tube System. Some 40 miles of aluminum tubing underlie the Exchange floor. This tubing operates at all times with 1½ pounds of air pressure to drive small plastic containers, often called "widgets," to their destinations. Each of the eighteen active posts is connected by tubes with each alternate telephone partition. The tubes operate in one direction only. Those running from the telephone partitions to the posts carry odd-lot orders to the associate brokers of the odd-lot firms and round-lot orders to specialists who work at each of these posts. The return tubes carry reports on the execution of such orders.

A separate set of tubes connects each post with the traffic department of the Exchange on the fifth floor. Through these tubes flow the reports of sales for the ticker tape.

Annunciator Boards. Each member of the Exchange has an identification number. There are two black annunciator boards facing each other from opposite walls in the main trading room, and a third board in the smaller room, or garage. Immense affairs, measuring 2,000 square feet each, they operate in unison. Each member is given an annunciator board position if he so desires; usually specialists and odd-lot dealers request no annunciator position since their location is always known. When no members are being paged, the entire board is black. When a telephone clerk wishes to contact a floor member of the Exchange, he pages the number by pushing an electric push button. A metal flap drops down and a number appears, such as 341. If broker 341 is urgently needed, the clerk may push the button several times, which causes a very audible clatter. Members refer to the board constantly to see whether any new orders need attention. As soon as a member sees that his number is being paged, he goes to the telephone clerk of his firm and picks up the order; if too rushed, he may send an employee of the Exchange.

EXECUTION OF ORDERS

The Double-Auction Market. All orders on the Exchange are transacted on the basis of a free, double auction. In every transaction stock is sold to the highest bidder and purchased from the lowest offerer. The Exchange fixes no prices, although this misconception of Exchange activity has been held at times by many persons. Prices are determined through a process of bidding and offering. Most bids and offers are made by the outside investing and trading public, although a substantial volume of buying and selling is done by members of the Exchange. In 1961, for example, members accounted for 22 per cent of the volume of shares purchased and sold on the Exchange. The public accounted for the balance.

PRIORITY OF BIDS AND OFFERS

The present rules on the priority of bids and offers may be divided into two classes: first, those covering bids and offers originating off the Exchange and, second, those initiated on the floor by floor traders. The first type will now be discussed.

Regulations on bids and offers cover about six pages in the New York Stock Exchange *Guide*. In the discussion that follows, only the chief principles of bidding and offering stock will be considered.

Highest Bid. Rule 71 of the Exchange states that the highest bid shall have precedence in all cases. For example, let us suppose that a broker bids 40 for a given stock; no other broker may bid for that stock at $39\frac{7}{8}$ or less.

Lowest Offer. Rule 71 also states that the lowest offer shall have precedence in all cases. For example, let us suppose that a broker wishes to offer stock at 50; no other broker may offer to sell the stock at more than 50.

Equal Bids. The problem of determining which broker is to buy stock becomes complicated when there are two or more bids at the same price. Since price is not involved, all bids being the same, priority must be determined by some other rule.

There are two methods of determining which broker is to buy. The first is that when bids are equal in price but enter the market at different times, the bid with time priority has precedence over later bids.

Rule 72 states that when a bid is clearly established as the first made at a particular price, the maker shall be entitled to priority and shall have precedence on the next sale at that price up to the number of shares specified in the bid. The term "first made at a particular price" means that the member clearly established his bid before any other member could do so. In this connection it should be noted: (a) a new auction starts with each new sale and (b) the priority of bids does not carry over from one auction to the next or from day to day.

In our first example, all bids and offers are at the same price:

Bids	Offers
A — 100 shares	X — 100 shares
B — 100 shares	

A made his bid first. He therefore gets the 100 shares, while B receives nothing. A had a time priority.

In our second example, A entered his bid first, followed by B, who in turn was followed in time by C. All bids and offers were made at the same price:

Bids	Offers
A — 100 shares	X — 200 shares
B — 100 shares	
C — 100 shares	

In this example, A secures 100 shares and B secures 100 shares. C obtains nothing since he was behind both A and B in time priority and bid for an amount equalling the excess after A's bid had been filled.

The second situation occurs when all bids are equal in price but at least one is for a larger number of shares than the others. No bid has time priority. Precedence here is determined by Rule 72, which may be stated, in substance, as follows:

On bids entered simultaneously, the larger ordinarily has priority with the following exception:

On bids entered simultaneously, each equal to or larger than the amount of stock offered at the bid price, the bidders toss a coin and the winner of the "match" purchases the entire amount of offered stock.

Simultaneous bids or offers usually come into existence when a transaction has occurred, some bids or offers in the market at that time remain unfilled, and bids or offers for these unfilled orders are re-entered in the new auction following this transaction. Under these conditions the bids and offers on the unfilled orders are considered simultaneously made. Similarly, since there is a new auction at the start of each trading session, bids or offers entered at the opening are all considered to have been simultaneously made.

Let us start with the simplest possible example. Two bids are entered simultaneously for 100 shares each. Only 100 shares are being offered:

Bids	Offers
A — 100 shares	X — 100 shares
B — 100 shares	

In this case, A and B match and the winner receives the 100 shares.

In our second example, there are three bidders wishing 100 shares each, but only 100 shares are being offered. All bids are entered simultaneously:

Bids	Offers
A — 100 shares	X — 100 shares
B — 100 shares	
C — 100 shares	

In this example, A, B, and C match and the winner receives the 100 shares being offered.

In our next example, there is the problem of unequal bids entered simultaneously:

Bids	Offers
A — 300 shares	X — 500 shares
B — 200 shares	
C — 100 shares	

No broker wishes to buy the entire 500 shares, but A has precedence, based on size. He receives 300 shares. There are now 200 shares left. B receives the entire amount since his bid was equal to or greater than the amount offered. C obtains nothing.

In our fourth example, 400 shares are being offered. There are three simultaneous bids:

Bids	Offers
A — 300 shares	X — 400 shares
B — 200 shares	
C — 100 shares	

On the basis of size A has precedence and receives 300 shares. One hundred shares are left. Both B and C can buy this stock since each has a bid equal to or greater than the amount offered. Accordingly, B and C match and the winner receives the stock.

In our fifth example, 300 shares are being offered:

Bids	Offers
A — 300 shares	X — 300 shares
B — 200 shares	
C — 100 shares	

Since only A has a bid equal to or greater than the amount of stock offered, he obtains all 300 shares.

In the next example, 200 shares are being offered:

Bids	Offers
A — 300 shares	X — 200 shares
B — 200 shares	
C — 100 shares	

A and B match since each has a bid equal to or greater than the amount offered. C receives nothing.

In our final example, only 100 shares are offered:

Bids	Offers
A — 300 shares	X — 100 shares
B — 200 shares	
C — 100 shares	

All three bids are equal to or greater than the amount offered. All three bidders must match and the winner receives the 100 shares.

Equal Offers. It is unnecessary to illustrate the manner in which equal offers are handled. The principles that govern equal bids apply to equal offers.

Stock Ahead. The phrase "stock ahead," which is often heard by customers, indicates that a customer's stock was not bought or sold on a particular sale, even though the transaction may have been made at the customer's limit price. "Stock ahead" means that the customer's order was not executed since other orders had a priority in the market on the basis of time entered.

Matched and Lost. This term also arises from the rules on floor procedure. As indicated in the discussion of equal bids, if there are two or more bids of equal or greater size than the offer, the brokers match to see which one gets the stock. A broker who loses such a match reports to his customer that he has "matched and lost." The same principle applies to offers. When a broker has "matched and won," he sends a report of execution but does not report the match.

All or None Bids and Offers. Under Rule 61 the Exchange does not permit the making of a bid or offer in which there is a specification that the bid or offer must be accepted for the entire amount of stock or no business will be done. For example, a broker cannot offer to sell 1,000 shares at 30 specifying that the buyer must take "all or none." The Exchange considers that all bids or offers for more than the unit of trading shall be considered to be for the amount thereof or any less number of units. For example, an order for 500 shares can be considered as five orders of 100 shares each. Hence, if 1,000 shares were to be offered, a buying broker, bidding for only 100 shares at 30, could effect a contract for 100 shares.

Customers may enter "all or none" orders with brokers, but bids and offers, except in bonds where the number specified is 50 or more, may not be made this way on the Exchange floor. The broker may endeavor to execute the "all or none" order if an opportunity presents itself without his making a bid or offer, but by selling on a bid or by taking an offer equal to or greater than his order.

BIDDING AND OFFERING STOCK

Buying and selling stock on the floor follows a rigid routine. Certain procedures must be adhered to in trading or the utmost confusion would result. Let us follow through the execution of a buy order for United States Steel common, placed by a customer.

Bidding on Stock. A broker receives his order from the home office to buy 100 shares of United States Steel common "at the market." The order may have come originally from an office, say in Chicago. He will go immediately to Post 2, where the stock is traded. Going to the "Steel crowd," he inquires about the market. It should be explained that a so-called "crowd" in any given stock may run from as many as two specialists and a number of other members to one lone specialist. As he inquires about the market in "Steel," he glances up at the indicator and sees that the last sale was made at 55. He knows, therefore, that the stock will sell at close to that price.

The broker asks for the quotation on the stock by using some such phrase as "What's Steel?" or "How's Steel?" So far, he has given no indication whether he wants to buy or sell. In response to his inquiry, he will receive the quotation from the specialists or one or more interested brokers or dealers. Let us say that the quotation is "55 to ¼." Our broker now knows that the best offer is 55¼, and it is doubtful, at the moment, that he can buy the stock for less. Nevertheless, he attempts to get a lower or better price. Since there is already a bid at 55, he would not make a bid at that price; hence, his bid will be 55⅛. It is given in the shortest possible phraseology, namely, "55⅛ for 100." What he really says in effect is, "I will bid 55⅛ for 100 shares of United States Steel common." This laborious statement is unnecessary. Everyone knows that he wants United States Steel common; otherwise he would not have inquired about it. It is certain that he is bidding on the stock since the price preceded the preposition "for," which is always used in bidding. Bidding always follows an ironclad rule: State the bid first, followed by the preposition "for," followed by the number of shares bid. If a selling broker wants to accept this bid, his response is "Sold."

Our broker has placed his bid ⅛ below the best offer; he has tried to get his customer a better price. It is possible that some other member may enter the "crowd" at this exact moment and sell our broker his stock at 55⅛. However, if this does not happen, our broker obtains no response to his bid of "55⅛ for 100." He must bid higher, and his new bid will be "¼ for 100." The member who has priority on the offer will make the sale; or members, on parity, if there is no priority, will "match."

As soon as the sale has been made, our broker and the other member of the Exchange verify each other's identity. This is done through badges worn by each member, which show the name, number, and firm represented. A member who executes a transaction for another may at this time "give up" the name of the member he is representing. In that case the further work of comparison and clearance on the contract becomes the responsibility of the member whose name is "given up."

No contract or paper changes hands at the time the transaction is completed. The only thing necessary is that each party to the transaction note the exact details of the deal. As soon as our broker has purchased his stock, he reports the transaction to the home office. The customer, in this case in Chicago, is then notified by a confirmation. The entire execution of the order may take only a few minutes.

As soon as the sale is completed, an employee of the Exchange, called a "reporter," writes out a sales slip which is sent to the ticker room. If there is a change in the price of the stock, he posts the price on the indicator and sets the dial to indicate whether the price was higher or lower than that of the last different price.

Offering Stock. The process of offering stock is identical with that of bidding on a stock, except that the phraseology is changed. The rule for offering stock is: State the number of shares first, followed by the preposition "at," followed by the price. For example, let us suppose that a broker with a market order wishes to offer 500 shares of General Motors at 45½. He would state his offer by saying, "500 at ½." The response of the buying broker or dealer would be "Take it." If possible, a selling broker would try to get a higher price for the stock than the prevailing bid; if not possible, he will lower his offer to the level of the current bid.

Execution of Other Orders. It is often not possible to execute orders with the same dispatch as the market order to buy that was just described. The type of order may not permit fast execution, or the broker may be too busy. In the case of limit and stop orders the broker is apt to turn the order over to a specialist, who will execute it when the market permits. If the broker is especially rushed, he may call in the services of a floor broker, who will execute it as his agent. In the case of odd-lot orders the broker does not get the order at all, since it is sent by the telephone clerk to the odd-lot dealer at the proper post.

POST 30

Description. Post 30 is located on the new trading floor, or garage, of the Exchange. It is not constructed as the other eighteen, but is a small counter-top filing cabinet with space behind it for two specialists and about a half-dozen employees to transact business. The chief equipment consists of the filing drawers, which are shown in Figure 10–4. In the photograph a specialist is checking the orders filed in one of the drawers.

The Stocks. The issues at Post 30 are inactive. For this reason a separate trading location with a concentration of issues is justified. For the most part the stocks are investment-grade securities. About 85 per cent are preferred stocks, the balance being common stocks. All price ranges

Fig. 10–4. Post 30.

are found at the post, a few stocks being priced in excess of $500. The spread between bid and asked prices is higher than for active stocks, with probably half of the stocks showing a spread of between 1 and 2 points. The number of stocks located at the post in early 1962 was 198.

These stocks are known as 10-share-unit stocks. In other words, the trading unit is 10 shares, not 100. Not all of the 10-share-unit stocks are traded at Post 30; 25 per cent of them are traded at the active posts.

Operations. The unit of trading, as indicated, is for 10 shares, orders from 1 to 9 shares being considered as odd-lots. The great majority of orders are G.T.C., or "good-till-canceled" orders. Perhaps one-fifth of them are day orders.

Most trading is done through the cabinets. Orders are filed in the trays in time and price sequence on special cards (Fig. 10–5). These colored cards indicate whether the order is a bid or an offer, the name of the broker placing the order, the name of the stock, the number of shares, and the time limit. Bids and offers so filed become binding as soon as accepted by other brokers. A bid or offer is accepted by the action of removing the card from the tray. Figure 10–5 illustrates a typical Post 30 bid card. It is a bid for 10 shares of XYZ preferred stock at 112 by a broker identified by the number 8.

There is some active bidding between specialists and other members of the Exchange, as there is at the active posts. The specialists make their own bids and offers if they feel in a position to make a closer market than exists on account of the cabinet bids and offers. They will at all times endeavor to make a market for a stock if no bids or offers are in the cabinets.

Post 30 trading goes on in a quiet way in contrast to much of the activity at the eighteen active posts. In its own way, however, the post serves in a useful capacity in making a market for the relatively high-priced, slow-moving investment stocks.

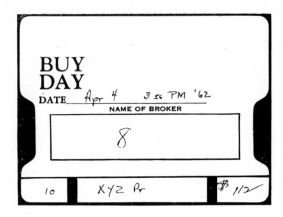

Fig. 10–5. A Post 30 bid.

PROCEDURE FOR LARGER BLOCKS

In contradistinction to trading in inactive issues at Post 30 is the problem associated with larger blocks of stock bid or offered. From time to time, individuals, institutions, or groups of investors in concert wish to buy or sell, not one or two hundred, but one or two thousand, or several thousand, shares of an issue. A market that is efficient for trading one or two round lots may not serve as well for an order involving ten or twenty. The Exchange has introduced three procedures designed to improve marketing for such blocks of stock. A market for very large blocks, either as primary or secondary offerings, exists over the counter (Chapter 24), but the procedures on the Exchange have increased the range of trading that may effectively be forwarded to the floor. The three procedures are the Specialist Block Purchase, or Sale; the Exchange Distribution, or Acquisition; and the Special Offering, or Bid.[1]

Specialist Block Purchase, or Sale. If an investor wishes to sell a substantial block (1,000 to 10,000 shares) of stock quickly, he may instruct his broker to obtain a specialist's block bid. The specialist in the issue, after considering his position, the current quotation in the market, and his estimate of what may be expected in the near future, usually will make a

---

[1] For more detail, see: the New York Stock Exchange *Guide,* Rules 107, 391, and 392, and *Marketing Methods for Your Block of Stock.*

bid. The bid will be somewhat below the bid then current in the regular auction market. The seller will pay a commission on his sale to his broker as usual. In practice, the over-all cost to the seller of a large block is equivalent to two to three times the normal commission rate paid on smaller orders in the same stock at that time. The specialist's bid must be reviewed by a Floor Governor of the Exchange before it becomes effective. The Floor Governor will consider the "depth" of the market in that stock, the relation of the specialist's bid to the current market quotation, and the reasonableness of the transaction in terms of the flow of stock through the Exchange. The transaction is not reported on the ticker; it is a private transaction. The specialist, presumably, will sell the stock in the normal course of his activity within a few days after buying the block. He will buy, of course, with the expectation that he can sell at a profit, but he has no guarantee of profit.

A specialist may also be willing to make a block offering to an investor seeking to obtain a substantial block of an issue. The costs, relative to the market for one or two round lots, would probably be nearly three times the commission on stock of that price. The specialist would sell from inventory or on the expectation that he would have the opportunity to cover the sale in the course of his ordinary activity in a few days.

Exchange Distribution, or Acquisition. For somewhat larger blocks (5,000 to 50,000 shares) another procedure often has usefulness. An Exchange Distribution is accomplished by obtaining sufficient buy orders from customers beforehand to permit a cross of the buy and sell orders on the floor in the usual auction market. Interest in buying is stimulated by offering the stock within the current quotation free of commission. The seller may pay a special commission to his broker to add to the incentive to obtain the buy orders. Success for the distribution depends on the ability of member firms to obtain these buy orders in sufficient quantity in a fairly short period of time.

An acquisition of a substantial block of stock of an issue may be accomplished by the obverse of this procedure.

An Exchange Distribution, or Acquisition, like the Specialist Block Bid, or Offer, must be approved by Exchange authorities before it is executed to assure conformance to trading practice. Notice of execution is given on the tape only after the orders have been obtained and they are crossed on the floor in the auction market.

Special Offering, or Bid. Still larger blocks (25,000 to 100,000 shares) of stock may be sold through the Special Offering procedure. In this instance, a price for the shares is predetermined, taking into account the current quotation in the auction market. For the buyer the price is net. He obtains stock at the offering price without paying the usual commission. He may also obtain stock at a price slightly below the best offer in the auction market at the time of the offering. Selling brokers are offered a special, incentive commission, perhaps two to two and one-half times the usual commission on a sale. The offering is published on the tape in the following way:

SP OFF   XYZ   COM
100   40   ½

The offering must remain open for at least fifteen minutes after this announcement, unless the announcement is made at least one hour before the offering becomes effective. When buy orders have been received on the floor, they are filled at the offering price until the entire block has been sold. A Special Offering must be approved by Exchange authorities before it is announced.

A Special Bid may be made by an investor seeking to acquire a large block of stock of an issue.

Extent of Use.[2] Since specialist block purchases and sales are private transactions, the volume of activity arising through this procedure is not made public. In 1960 there were 20 exchange distributions involving 450 thousand shares and $11 million. In that year there were three special offerings involving 72 thousand shares and $5 million. No exchange acquisitions or special bids were reported.

THE FLOOR BROKER

Operations. The floor broker often is a free-lance member of the Exchange, meaning that he does not ordinarily belong to a member firm. Typically, he owns his own seat and all commissions earned on transactions he executes are his own. It is difficult to give an exact figure on the number of floor brokers on the Exchange, since some members engage in this activity on a full-time basis while others engage in it only on a part-time basis.

The floor broker accepts orders from other brokers, who may, at a given moment, have on hand more orders than can be conveniently and efficiently handled. He therefore acts as an agent for other brokers. When he executes an order of this kind, he "gives up" the name of his principal rather than his own.

The floor broker renders a very useful service. He aids the commission firm during periods of peak loads. In addition, he permits many

[2] Based on data in the *Twenty-Seventh Annual Report of the SEC,* 1961, p. 66.

firms to operate with a smaller number of Exchange memberships since his services are always available.

Commissions. On stocks selling at $1 per share and above, the commission rate per share earned by the floor broker if he "gives up" another member's name when he executes a transaction for him is as follows:

Price per Share	Rate per Share in Cents
$ 1 and above but under $ 2	1.25
2 and above but under 5	1.40
5 and above but under 10	2.10
10 and above but under 20	3.10
20 and above but under 40	3.65
40 and above but under 100	3.85
100 and above but under 150	4.35
150 and above but under 200	4.50
200 and above	5.00

As an illustration of these commissions, let us suppose that a busy commission broker gives a floor broker an order to buy 100 shares at 50. The commission broker would collect a commission of $44 from the public customer. Out of this he would pay $3.85 to the floor broker for his services.

If the member does not "give up" the name of another but assumes responsibility for comparison and clearance of contracts himself, he earns commissions based on a different but similar schedule. The rates are approximately twice those shown above [New York Stock Exchange, *Constitution*, XV, 2(6)].

THE FLOOR TRADER

Nature of Operations. The floor trader, or, as he is sometimes called, the room trader, is usually a free-lance member of the Exchange. He has no contact with the public and he does no business for other members; as a floor trader, he trades strictly for himself. The floor trader is purely a speculator, since he has no commission duties.

This type of trader is free to roam around the trading floor in search of profitable opportunities to buy and sell. Operating as a rule for a quick profit, he is free to trade in any stock as he wishes. In the past he has tended to trade in market leaders; such activity has been criticized by the SEC.

Floor traders at times complete a "round-turn" in a stock during one day. By this practice they never are required to pay interest on a debit balance, since no money is borrowed overnight. By buying and selling in the same trading session, they are sometimes called "daylight traders."

Only members who are physically present on the trading floor can be called floor traders. The term is not applied to specialists and odd-lot dealers who may be dealing for their own accounts in the conduct of their particular business.

Kinds of Floor Traders. There are two kinds of flood traders. The first is the professional, full-time trader who makes a business of floor-trading and is interested in no other floor activity. The second is the part-time or occasional floor trader who trades at infrequent intervals and engages chiefly in some other activity, such as commission work, for his principal income. During free moments this part-time trader operates with the hope of making profits to increase his regular income. A floor trader may or may not belong to a member firm; most full-time traders do.

Number and Importance. A very great decline in the number and importance of full-time floor traders has taken place in the last half-century. In 1910 the number was estimated at 70; in 1929, 49; in 1933, 86; in 1950, 20; in 1961, 30, of whom but 2 or 3 were active.[3]

The importance of floor trading has shown a similar decline. Before World War I floor trading probably accounted for over 10 per cent of all round-lot transactions. In 1937 the percentage was down to 6.8 per cent. In 1960 floor trading accounted for 2.5 per cent of the total volume of shares purchased and sold on the Exchange.

Costs and Profits. An individual floor trader must own his seat and therefore pay annual dues of $1,500 to the Exchange. In addition, his contributions to the Gratuity Fund will amount to about another $400 per year. In early 1962 the cost of his own seat would have been $175,000. He must pay a clearing fee to a member of the Clearing Corporation. For stocks selling at $1 and above, these fees range from $0.75 to $3 per 100 shares on a "round-turn" if the purchase and sale are effected on the same business day. If not effected on the same day, they are computed at 1½ times these rates. He may pay some firm for office facilities. Hence, he is under a rather heavy expense, in spite of the fact that he need pay no commissions on orders that he himself executes. If he places an order with some other member for execution, he of course pays the commission required on such transactions.

Before World War I it was possible to trade on a very small price change, such as ⅛ or ¼ point, because the expenses of trades were low. At one time transfer taxes were only $0.02 per 100 shares. Today transfer taxes range from 1 to 12 cents per share, or $1.04 to $12.00 on a 100-share sale. Clearing fees are also higher than formerly. On a single transaction with a gross gain of ⅛ point, a trader can still obtain some net contribution to his office, investment, and living expenses.

On a series of trades, some resulting in gains and others in losses, however, trading on such narrow price changes is not profitable. Let

[3] Furnished author by the Exchange.

us illustrate the situation by an example. Assume that a floor trader has the average good fortune to gain on 60 per cent of his trades. On three trades of five he gains; on two, he loses. Assume also that the gains or losses are ¼ point in each instance and that all trades are "daylight trades." He completes them within the trading day and carries no inventory overnight. The stock in which this illustrative trading takes place is priced around $50 per share.

Gross gain, ¼ point on three trades		$75.00
Offset by:		
Gross loss, ¼ point on two trades	$50.00	
Transfer taxes on sales	30.00	
Clearing fees	15.00	
SEC fees	.50	92.50
Net outcome—a loss of		$20.50

If he were able to make three out of four trades advantageously—a fine result—he would have a net gain of $13.60 in his contribution to the office, investment, and living expenses. If he had the same average number of successful trades but gained or lost ½ point on each, five trades would contribute $4.50 to coverage of these other expenses. In either of these latter cases the figures for gain are so small that few men would wish to limit themselves to these results as measures of daily income. The amount of funds used as a practical matter would be much greater than the $5,000 indicated in the illustrative case, and the amount at risk in this floor trading operation would be sufficient to establish a small business in another industry.

Floor traders, as was indicated earlier, have declined in number and importance in recent years. Higher transfer taxes and clearing fees have played some part in this. Federal and state income taxes have also been important. Another factor has been stricter regulations, which will be discussed in detail shortly.

Functions and Services. Four economic functions have been ascribed to the floor trader:

1. The floor trader aids in maintaining a continuous market. By his constant buying and selling he creates a better and more continuous market. He becomes a buyer upon price declines and a seller upon advances. This continuous activity creates a much-needed liquidity in the market, which may become thin during times when the public is not trading.
2. He creates a closer market. If bid and asked prices result in a wide spread on a stock, the floor trader, expecting an opportunity for profit, will narrow the spread by buying above the present bid and selling under the existing offer.
3. He stabilizes prices. When stocks are low, judged by fundamental conditions, they are purchased; when too high, they are sold. Low prices

create buying activity by presenting profit opportunities; high prices bring on selling when they get out of line with real values.

4. He renders conspicuous services to the market during periods of stress, such as when there is a great volume of buying or selling on balance from orders originating off the Exchange floor, either in the United States or from abroad.[4]

Criticisms. Although little concern has been expressed in recent years, it is doubtful that any other type of activity on the Exchange has been subject to so much debate as floor trading. The controversy reached a peak in 1945 when the SEC released its *Report on Floor Trading*. The following adverse criticisms were included:

1. The floor trader has a tendency to concentrate on stocks where great activity is already present. The liquidity thus created is superfluous. Floor trading fails to create narrower spreads to the extent that it concentrates on market leaders.
2. The exercise of the broker and dealer functions by the floor trader may react to the disadvantage of members and customers, whose orders may not be executed with the best efforts of the trader.
3. The floor trader has marked advantages over the public in trading because of the following circumstances: lower trading costs; up-to-the-minute and precise knowledge of trading developments; a better chance of getting orders executed than the public, because of his physical presence on the floor; ability to act jointly with other members to raise and lower the price of a security; and greater ease in executing short sales, since he can seize existing opportunities to short sell, as they occur.
4. Floor trading creates market acceleration in that the trader tends to ride up and down with the market in a majority of cases, rather than to trade against the trend.[5]

Recent checks on floor trading, the fact that the investment needed virtually removes the opportunity for casual activity, and the forms of regulation now in effect appear to show strengthened positive and reduced negative contributions from floor trading.

Regulations. The *Report on Floor Trading* included a recommendation by the SEC staff for prohibition of this form of activity on the Exchange.[6] By August, 1945, it was forecast by the press that severe restrictions would be placed on floor trading. To forestall these restrictions, on August 27 of that year the officials of the New York Stock Exchange offered to adopt a set of their own rules of self-policing. The

---

[4] For an elaboration of these arguments, see: J. E. Meeker, *The Work of the Stock Exchange* (New York: The Ronald Press Co., 1930), p. 204; and the press statement of Emil Schram in *The New York Times*, May 16, 1945.

[5] Condensed from the SEC *Report to the Commission by the Trading and Exchange Division on Floor Trading*, released January 15, 1945, pp. 3–11.

[6] *Ibid.*, p. 44.

SEC agreed to give the Exchange regulations a fair trial, and the plan to restrict floor trading by the SEC was tabled. The rules adopted in 1945 were quite restrictive and have been modified somewhat in recent years.

The present regulations on floor trading are embodied in Rules 108, 109, and 110 of the Exchange. A floor trader buying stock cannot have time priority over an off-floor order except under certain circumstances. He cannot, for example, have time priority on bids at a higher price than the last sale, or on what the brokers call a "plus tick." He may, however, retain priority on a bid at a lower price than the last sale, or what is called a "minus tick." Let us illustrate these regulations. Suppose that the last sale was at 50 and the new quotation is 49¾ to 50. A floor trader can bid 49⅞ for 100 shares, his action narrowing the spread in the market. He can retain this priority over a public bid at 49⅞ because if a sale occurred at 49⅞ it would be a "minus tick," in other words, lower than the last sale. However, if the market were quoted, for example, 50 to ¼ following the sale at 50, the trader could not enter a bid of 50⅛ and retain priority over a subsequent public bid at that price.

The floor trader cannot have parity with an off-floor order. The fact that his bid or offer is equal to an off-floor order does not allow him to match for the stock. The off-floor bid or offer comes first.

A floor trader making a bid or offer does not have precedence based on size over an off-floor bid or offer. As was noted earlier, the larger bid or offer ordinarily has precedence. In this case, however, the floor trader has no such advantage.

In these three instances the floor trader obtains no trading advantage over off-floor customers merely because he is operating on the floor. In the case, however, of a floor trader selling stock to create or increase a "short" position, he may retain priority over an off-floor order, although he cannot have parity with or precedence based on size over such an order.

The above regulations apply to active bids and offers made by a trader in the crowd. He may, however, give an order to a specialist and it will have all the privileges of an off-floor order except that it may not have the privilege of a "stop." A specialist is not permitted to "stop" stock" for a floor trader.[7]

A further provision of these rules is that a floor trader cannot acquire "long" stock by pairing off with a sell order entered before the opening unless all off-floor bids at that price are filled. Here, again, the floor trader may not take advantage of his position to secure precedence over an off-floor customer.

[7] This action of a specialist is described in the next chapter, p. 209.

Present rules prevent floor traders from having great influence on the market. The rules prevent floor traders from buying stock, either individually or in a group, where such action, either intentionally or unintentionally, tends to dominate the market. They must not make purchases except in a reasonable, orderly, and inconspicuous manner. To avoid violation of this rule, the Exchange requires each floor trader to post a card giving details of restricted purchases immediately upon execution. This card is placed in a special clip at the price indicator for the particular stock traded. Traders—as a group, not individually—after purchasing limited amounts of stock in a given issue, may not trade further for fifteen minutes. Thus, the actions of one or two traders affect all and the opportunity for concentrated purchasing is substantially eliminated.

There are certain exceptions to the rules just described. In general, the rules do not apply to odd-lot dealers, specialists, arbitragers, to transactions to make an orderly market, and to transactions to offset other transactions made in error.

These rules appear, in general, to have reduced the possibility for conflict between service to the public and the self-interest of traders on the floor without preventing floor trading. The rules give opportunity for the advantageous functions of floor trading to aid in the maintenance of orderly marketing while suppressing the types of action criticized some decades ago. There has been little comment in recent years, although, in effect, a continuing study is carried on by the Exchange in the routine checking of floor trader reports and compliance with the rules.

11

The Work of the Specialist

A specialist is a member of the Exchange who engages in the buying and selling of one or more specific issues of stock on the floor. His work is central to the maintenance of a free, continuous market in the issues in which he acts as speciailst. About one out of four members of the Exchange is a specialist. In recent years the total number has been close to 350.

A specialist may act as a broker or as a dealer in a transaction. In his capacity as broker he executes orders for other brokers on a commission. In his capacity as a dealer he acts for his own account, profit, and risk. In this latter capacity he buys from the public when it offers stock for sale but other public bids for purchase are not available, and sells to the public when it bids but other public offers to sell are not available at or near the price of the last transaction. In other words, he maintains markets by purchasing stock at a higher price than anyone else is willing to pay at the time, and by selling stock at a lower price than anyone else is willing to take at the time. The customers of the specialist are other members of the Exchange; as a specialist, he does not transact business directly with the public.

NATURE AND IMPORTANCE OF WORK

Origin. The origin of the specialist is somewhat obscure. Tradition has it that a certain Mr. Boyd, about 1875, suffered a broken leg. Upon returning to the floor, he conducted his trading while seated in a chair. Because of his limited mobility he confined his operations to Western Union stock, a very popular issue at the time. This plan proved so successful that he continued this practice, even after he became well again. The specialist's function, however, grew rather slowly and it was not until about 1910 that it became of much importance. During World War I it fully justified its expectations and proved of great value in handling the active war stocks of that period.

Number of Specialists. On January 2, 1962, there were 352 specialists on the floor of the Exchange, including those operating at Post 30. A member of the Exchange who wishes to act as a specialist notifies the Exchange of his intention and, subject to its approval, registers for that function. The work is carried on by individual members, who may be, in turn, members of specialist firms. About 90 per cent of the specialists are members of specialist units, which are joint ventures of individuals, firms, or both.

Distribution of Work. There is at least one specialist for each stock issue listed on the Exchange. On January 2, 1962, there were 1,542 listed issues. A total of 198 of these were traded at Post 30 by two specialists. The balance, 1,344, was divided among the eighteen other posts on the floor. There was competition between specialist units in 54 of the active issues; there was one specialist book in 1,290 issues.

For the 54 issues with competition there are two specialist units competing for business. No issue at present has more than two competing specialist books.

The number of issues handled by an individual specialist unit depends on the activity of the market in the issues. The average specialist unit handles about 12 stocks. One firm with nine partners has a total of 55 issues, while another unit handles 1. Averages are not very meaningful in a market with such a range of activity for individual issues, but the "average" specialist is responsible for 3 or 4 stocks.

Importance of Work. A specialist is willing and required to quote a stock and to buy or sell the stock, either for his book or for his own account. He is a leading figure on the floor. As a rule, no one is eager to trade in stocks in which there is a poor market. Because a specialist's commission income depends on his ability to maintain a good market for the stocks in which he is specializing, it is in his self-interest to maintain as continuous and close a market as possible.

During 1961, specialists accounted for 15.3 per cent of all reported volume of purchases and sales on the Exchange and 14.7 per cent of actual volume. This volume is based on the number of shares that specialists accounted for as dealers for their own account. Actually, they were much more important than this, since the figures just indicated did not include transactions in which they acted as brokers. These brokerage transactions were much more than 15 per cent. One investigation, conducted some years ago, concluded that specialists accounted for about half the volume of sales on either a dealer or broker basis.[1] That estimate is still a reasonable one in today's markets. In any case, the specialist is a key figure in the market.

Capital Requirements. Specialists are selected by the Board of Governors of the Exchange on the basis of experience, ability as dealers, and capital. Since 1953 a regular specialist at an active post has been required to have sufficient capital to assume a position of 400 shares of each 100-share unit stock and 100 shares of each 10-share unit stock for which he is registered. In addition, he must own a seat, which, as before indicated, was selling for about $175,000 in early 1962. A regular specialist at Post 30 must have at all times net liquid assets of $50,000.

Commissions. As already indicated, the specialist operates both as a dealer and as a broker, his operations shifting back and forth between these two functions. When he acts as a dealer, he buys and sells for his own account and risk, and, of course, secures no commissions. However, when he operates as a broker, he charges the commissions fixed by the Exchange for this work.

The commissions vary with the price of the stock. These were the commissions in effect in 1962 on stocks selling at $1 per share and above:

Price per Share	Rate per Share in Cents
$ 1 and above but under $ 2	1.25
2 and above but under 5	1.40
5 and above but under 10	2.10
10 and above but under 20	3.10
20 and above but under 40	3.65
40 and above but under 100	3.85
100 and above but under 150	4.35
150 and above but under 200	4.50
200 and above	5.00

An example will show how the commissions are handled. Let us suppose that Commission Broker A asks Specialist B to execute a limit order to sell 100 shares of XYZ at 50. The order is duly executed by B. Broker A collects a commission of $44 from his public customer. Out of this he pays $3.85 to the specialist for his services. A rough guess suggests that a specialist's commissions on a day with 4.5 million volume would be $175 to $200. These, of course, provide revenues with which to meet office, investment, and living expenses and are not a measure of "take home" pay. It is of interest, however, to compare this guess with that made for the gains to be achieved by floor trading (p. 199).

---

[1] *The Security Markets* (New York: Twentieth Century Fund, Inc., 1935), p. 425.

THE SPECIALIST'S BOOK

Nature of Book. The chief tool of the specialist is his book. It is a ring binder with pages about 4 to 11 inches and is prepared to meet his own special needs. The pages are ruled and are usually printed with fractional stock points at regular intervals to permit easy insertion of orders. The left-hand page holds the bids or buy orders with the lowest bids at the top of the page, while the right-hand page contains the offers or sell orders with the highest offers at the bottom. If the orders are not too numerous, two pages will contain all the orders at a given full point, for example, all orders from 60 to 60⅞. In active markets, such as 1929, it is sometimes necessary to have several books to contain the orders for a given stock. The orders are entered in the book by the specialist according to price and in the sequence in which they are received by him at the post. He notes the number of shares, putting down 1 for 100 shares, 2 for 200, etc. He also notes the name of the member placing the order and the time limit, such as G.T.C. Stop orders are so indicated. When orders are executed by a specialist, they are executed in the sequence in which the names were recorded in his book at the price. This is the sequence in which he received the orders from brokers on the floor.

For purposes of illustration, Figure 11–1 shows two pages of a specialist's book, employing hypothetical firm names. Orders from twenty-eight members or firms are indicated in the illustration. There are thirteen buy orders, eleven sell orders, and four stop orders. Open orders are identified by crosses and day orders by short dashes. Let us now examine how these orders would be handled.

Handling a Buy Order. Let us suppose that Broker A comes to Post 2 where the specialist is handling XYZ. Broker A would first ask for the quotation on the stock. The specialist can quote from his book and will, therefore, reply, "45¼ to ½." This represents the highest bid and lowest offer in his book. At that time the specialist does not know whether Broker A wants to buy or sell, or is merely asking for information.

Broker A, however, has a buy order for 100 shares. Noting that the quotation is 45¼ to ½, he will not expect to pay less than 45½, but he must attempt to get as good a price for his customer as possible, so he bids 45⅜ for 100. If no other member of the "crowd" is willing to do business at this price, Broker A will raise his bid to 45½. The specialist immediately calls out "Sold!" He then allocates the sale to the first order on his book at that price. It was entered by Smith & Green. The specialist "gives up" the name, "Smith & Green," to Broker A and sends a report of the execution to Smith & Green. Moyer has now moved into the first

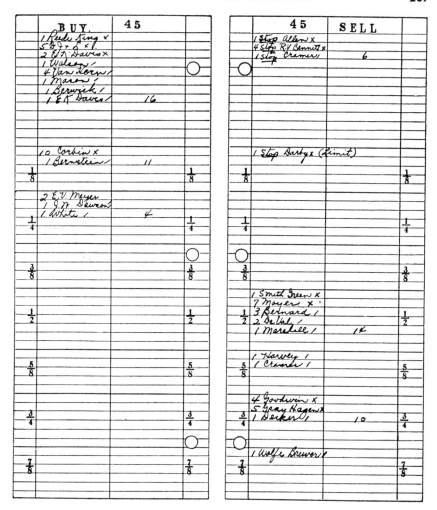

Fig. 11–1. Two pages from a specialist's book.

position at 45½ on the book of the specialist, and if the specialist sells additional stock at that price, Moyer will be the first to receive a report of the execution.

Figure 11–2 has illustrations of two aspects of this process. At the left, a specialist is consulting his book, which he holds in hand, perhaps to quote but more probably to enter an order. At the right, the specialist, his back turned to the post where his book rests on the counter, notes a transaction on his report pad, or "stubs." The information will be conveyed later to the party he represented in the transaction. The size of the crowd in this photograph suggests that other trading is taking place.

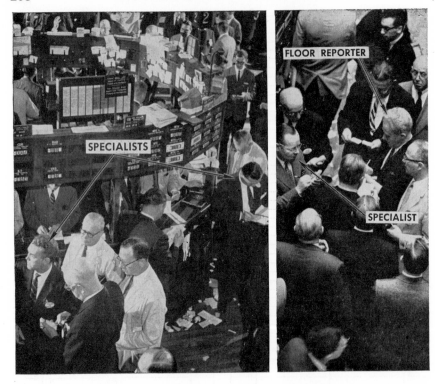

Fig. 11–2. Specialists on the Exchange floor.

Handling a Sell Order. Let us suppose also that Broker B comes to the post and wishes to sell 300 shares. After inquiring as to the quotation, Broker B begins to offer the stock at a price higher than the best bid on the specialist's book in the hope that he may obtain a higher price for the customer. Since the best bid at the moment is 45¼, there is not much sense in making more than two offers. Accordingly, Broker B offers 300 shares at 45⅜. Receiving no acceptance, he lowers his offer to 45¼. The specialist calls, "Take it!" or "Take them!" The specialist now notifies E. V. Meyer, the ranking bidder, that 200 shares were bought at 45¼. The other 100 shares goes to J. W. Dawson, next in priority. The names of these members are "given up" to Broker B when the transaction takes place.

Handling a Stop Order. A stop order to sell is one that becomes a market order when the stock sells at or below the stop price. The reverse is true of a stop order to buy. On our book being illustrated, the specialist has Darby's stop order to sell 100 shares at 45⅛. In order not to complicate matters, let us assume that the buying and selling orders just discussed were never put into effect and the book contains all of the original orders.

Let us assume that trading in the stock becomes active and that the specialist has bought for his book 500 shares. This cleared all the buy orders at 45¼ and 100 shares at 45⅛. Since there has now been a sale at 45⅛, it is possible to execute the stop order of Darby; it has now become a market order. The specialist now offers the stock at 45¼, to see whether he can get a better price. If this is not forthcoming, he proceeds to cross an order for 100 shares between Darby and Corbin and so notifies both brokers.

Stopping Stock. Stopping stock is a practice by which a specialist or another member on the floor guarantees purchase or sale of a specified number of shares of a given issue at a given price. This amount of stock is reserved for another broker but not earmarked for any particular account. The stop may be given for the specialist's, or member's, own account. At no cost to the broker asking the favor, the specialist or member, by his "stop," gives that other broker a definite reservation.

Let us suppose that a broker comes to the specialist's post with an order to buy 100 shares "at the market." In our hypothetical book the best price that the broker could expect at the moment would be 45½. The broker, desiring to get his customer as good a price as possible, would like to buy it for less than 45½, but at the same time he does not want to "miss the market" and pay more than that price. So he requests the specialist, or another member in the crowd, to stop 100 shares at 45½. It is possible that in the next few minutes stock may be offered on the floor at less than 45½. If the broker could buy 100 shares at 45⅜, he would do so and then say, "The stop is off."

However, if our broker cannot buy the stock at 45⅜ and a transaction takes place in the crowd at 45½, this immediately puts into operation the buy order of the broker. The specialist or member who granted the stop now sells the stock and so informs the customer's broker by some phrase, such as "You are elected," that indicates the broker has bought the stock at 45½.

The amount of stock that a specialist will stop for a public order at a given price depends not only upon the amount of stock at a given price he has on his book, but also on the size and number of orders and what is reasonable. He will not stop any part of the biggest order on his book at a given price. In the hypothetical book under consideration, the specialist would probably be willing to stop 200 shares on the buy side and 700 on the sell side.

The practice of "stopping stock" allows an active floor broker an opportunity to obtain the best price possible for his customers. A broker with several orders to execute has assurance that the price on the order for which stock was stopped will be the best in the market at the moment if a transaction occurs while he is handling another order and before he returns to try to get a still better price a few minutes later. This privilege is not similarly available to members themselves. Stock offered may be stopped for them at the offer price and stock bid for may be stopped at the bid price, but not the reverse. A member's order may not go ahead of public orders.

Opening the Market. The most difficult period of the day for the specialist is usually at the opening of the market. At that time many orders have piled up, some at the market, some limited, and some stop orders. It is his duty to open the market at a price that will permit all market orders to be executed, and yet at a price as close to the previous day's close as possible, so that the market may be as orderly as the situation permits. He does this by considering all orders and establishing as fair a price as possible. He must make adjustments for cancellations and other changes and enter the orders that he received before the opening. This situation may permit him to arrive at an equilibrium price between buyers and sellers. It may, however, be necessary for him to obtain buyers when sellers predominate, or the reverse may be true. In many cases it may be necessary for him to supply stock or buy stock for his own account in order to equalize the volume of buying and selling.

In the first fifteen minutes of the day many stocks open in large blocks, often from 1,000 to 5,000 shares. These large openings represent the consolidation of numerous small orders put together by the specialists. At times the work of consolidation of small orders becomes arduous. A recent instance was reported in the *Wall Street Journal* for August 31 and September 1, 1961, and in *Business Week*, September 3, 1961. On August 30, 1961, the market in TelAutograph Corporation common stock was opened very late in the day with matching of orders transferring 80,000 shares. The total number of buy orders at one time prior to this opening totaled 180,000 shares. There had been no transactions at all on the preceding day because the buy and sell orders could not be matched at prices at all close to the market. On August 31, 1961, the market for Comptometer Corporation common stock opened about mid-day with transfer of 65,000 shares. Markets in both issues had been disrupted by public reaction to news about equipment presumed to be significant in telephonic communication.

The services of the specialist under trying circumstances are well illustrated also by action in the market of Monday, September 26, 1955, on the frenzied first day of business following President Eisenhower's heart attack on September 24. At the opening of the market on that day all specialists were carrying a total inventory of 1,651,000 shares, valued at nearly $50 million on the previous Friday. Because of the great liquidation at the opening on September 26, it was necessary for the specialists as a group to buy another 1,099,000 shares at a cost of $49.1 million to help stabilize the market. During the day purchases by specialists accounted for 23 per cent of all purchases. At the close of the day specialists held 2,246,524 shares with a market value of $73.4 million. A similar performance took place on May 29, 1962, but at this writing (1962) the details are not available.

Spread on Listed Stocks. In order to maintain an orderly market in stocks, specialists attempt to keep spreads in quotations and the size of variations between sales reasonable. The difference between the bid and ask price should not be too great. For the active stock the spread in the quotation is usually very small. In perhaps 86 per cent of the cases the variation between sales is ¼ point or less. For the less active stocks the spread is apt to run from ⅝ to a full point.

FUNCTIONS OF THE SPECIALIST

Services as Broker. There has, from time to time, been considerable criticism leveled at the specialist and his work. The defense of the specialist may be based on two counts: first, his services to the market as a broker and, second, his services as a dealer in making an orderly market.

As a broker the specialist serves in somewhat the same capacity as a floor broker. In this function he executes limit, stop, and market orders for other members of the Exchange. If we assume that he performs these duties rapidly and efficiently, he serves a very useful purpose. His work saves time for other members, thus permitting them to operate more effectively for their customers and with a smaller investment in floor memberships. It seems questionable whether a more efficient system of handling limit and stop orders could be devised. He also serves a useful function in maintaining an orderly market at the opening, as well as at other times.

Services as Dealer. The function of the specialist when acting as a dealer is to maintain an orderly market in the stock in which he specializes. The Board of Governors of the Exchange has defined the function as follows (Rule 104):

> The function of a member acting as a regular specialist on the floor of the Exchange, includes, in addition to the effective execution of commission orders entrusted to him, the maintenance, in so far as reasonably practicable, of a fair and orderly market on the Exchange in the stocks in which he is so acting.

The interpretation of this requirement, backed by numerous rules, is that the specialist should maintain a continuous market with price continuity and close bid and asked prices, and minimize the effect of temporary disparity between public supply and demand. To the extent that the specialist does maintain a better, more stable, and orderly market, he is performing a useful function. The criticisms of the specialist that have been made in the past have stemmed from the belief that in his capacity as a dealer he did not always perform his duties faithfully. The numerous rules that now restrict the specialist are a result of the belief that the specialist will not adequately perform his dealer function without proper regulation. The rules come from both the Exchange and the SEC.

CRITICISMS OF THE SPECIALIST

Over a period of years a considerable volume of criticism has been directed at the specialist. Some developed out of the Congressional investigation of the exchanges in 1933 and 1934; some grew out of studies made by private research foundations; and some came from the SEC.

The present regulations of the specialist can be understood only in the light of the criticisms that have been made of him and his operations in the past. These regulations were introduced in order to prevent or correct practices that would be injurious to the best interests of the market.

The SEC, in evaluating the activities of specialists, arrived at the following conclusions:

(1) The specialist enjoys competitive advantages over the general public similar to those of other members on the floor; in addition, by virtue of the great volume of trading in which he participates and by virtue of his exclusive access to the information contained in his book, he enjoys the advantage of special knowledge of the market for securities which he handles.

(2) The specialist has exceptional opportunities to engage in manipulative activity, by reason of his exclusive information concerning the existence of bids below and offerings above the market. Since the enactment of the Securities Exchange Act of 1934, however, the Commission has little evidence of such manipulative activity by specialists.

(3) Specialists, during the period under review, traded against the daily trend more often than with it, and thus, on the whole, did not tend to accentuate price trends but contributed to the continuity and orderliness of the market. However, it should be observed that, insofar as they traded with their books, rather than with others, they tended to augment the spread between bid and asked prices and thus to diminish the continuity of the market.

(4) During the period studied, specialists traded in moderately active and inactive stocks in relatively greater proportion than in active stocks.

(5) In the capacity of broker, the specialist renders a useful service in the execution of limited and stop-loss orders.

(6) Although it is argued that brokerage activity of the specialists renders him particularly liable to loss from errors, for which he must find compensation in trading, the evidence is inconclusive to justify giving any weight to this contention.

(7) The specialist has an important incentive to maintain an orderly market.[2]

The above conclusions are in part critical and in part commendatory. The SEC stressed the advantages of the specialist arising from his exclusive access to information on the market and his exceptional opportunities to engage in manipulation. It will be noted that the Commission concluded also that the specialist, when acting as a dealer, did tend to trade against the trend of the market, and that he performed a useful function in the execution of limited and stop-loss orders.

When the Securities Exchange Act of 1934 was first put into operation, there arose considerable discussion among economists generally and among the members and staff of the SEC as to the desirability of the segregation of members of the Exchange. By segregation is meant the separation of all member activities into brokerage and trading. No member could function both as a broker and as a dealer or trader. He must permanently confine himself to one or the other activity. This segregation would even have applied to the specialist, that member being permitted to do only brokerage and no trading. There was apparently a division of opinion among the members and staff of the SEC, and the Commission never formally went on record in favor of segregation. The original report of the Trading and Exchange Division of the Commission favored segregation; this recommendation was not accepted by the Commission; the final report did not recommend segregation.

The possibility that the specialist could use his intimate knowledge of the market to trade for his own advantage was examined in detail by the Twentieth Century Fund in its investigation. Its conclusions were these:

It is not argued here that specialist and other floor members do, as a rule, trade with the market as revealed to them through their brokerage business. The evidence presented in Section 2 above is not sufficiently detailed to answer this question either in the affirmative or negative. Nor is it argued that, as a rule, specialists' personal trading has an undesirable market effect. The point being stressed is the fundamental conflict in interest between the specialist's brokerage business and his own trading. It may be possible but certainly extremely difficult for him to trade without prejudice to the best interests of his customers. That this is true is witnessed by the fact that during the past six years every case of expulsion or suspension of the specialists has involved indiscretion on the part of the specialist in handling his customers' business while trading for himself.

[2] *Report on the Feasibility and Advisability of the Complete Segregation of the Functions of Dealer and Broker*, June 20, 1936, p. 41.

In view of the fact that a large part of the specialists' profits is derived from their trading function, it is expecting too much to ask that their trading be given secondary place at all times.[3]

The Fund report, therefore, doubted whether specialists could carry on jointly the activities of both dealer and broker without injury to the market. For this reason the Fund made the following recommendation:

It is desirable to center the work of brokerage specializing as well as general brokerage in firms of brokers. These specializing brokers and general brokers would not be permitted to have any interest either directly or indirectly in any trading account.[4]

This was a recommendation of complete segregation of the activities of specialists. They would be permitted no trading whatever for their own accounts.

The above criticisms and those of others in the past may be summarized: (1) the specialist is in a position to take advantage of his knowledge of the market; (2) he has the opportunity to manipulate the market; (3) there may be a conflict between his trading and brokerage activities that would cause him to neglect the latter; (4) there is the possibility of fraud or indiscretion in executing orders with himself. They were under consideration again by the SEC in 1962.

Because of these four possibilities, the SEC and the New York Stock Exchange have issued a number of rules in recent years designed to give greater protection to customers and to restrict specialists' activities to those necessary for a well-regulated and orderly market.

REGULATIONS UNDER THE SECURITIES EXCHANGE ACT

Maintaining an Orderly Market. The Securities Exchange Act requires that the SEC make such rules and regulations as may be reasonably necessary to permit the specialist to maintain a fair and orderly market. It will be noted here that the intention of Congress was to limit the specialist's function to maintaining an orderly market rather than to trading for his own profit.

Disclosure. A specialist may not disclose the contents of his book to any person other than an official of the Exchange, an authorized visitor to the floor, or a specialist who may be acting for such specialist. The SEC, however, may require disclosure when necessary in the public interest. There is, of course, little doubt that at times a specialist's book contains information that might be very useful to a few speculators. It

[3] *The Security Markets*, p. 439.
[4] *Ibid.*, p. 440.

is not considered disclosure of the book for the specialist to state the number of shares involved in the best bid and offer. However, he is not compelled to do so if he believes such action would be inadvisable.

Discretionary Orders. Specialists may execute only market or limited price orders. In other words, the specialist must be instructed as to the issue, the type of order, the total amount, and whether purchase or sale. There can be no discretion given the specialist in these matters. Rules permit, however, a certain amount of brokerage judgment on such things as whether the specialist should stop stock, bid for or offer the full amount of the order, and bid at or below or offer at or above the price of the order.

Discretionary orders are subject to abuse and blanket discretionary orders are now prohibited. A violation of this prohibition was a factor in disciplinary action against a specialist firm on the American Stock Exchange in 1961.

Segregation. The SEC in 1934, three decades ago, was ordered by Congress to make a study of segregation of broker and dealer functions on the Exchange and report its findings. The report was duly made, but it contained no formal recommendation for action concerning segregation.

Manipulation. Any form of manipulation of security prices by a specialist is made unlawful by Sections 9 and 10 of the Act. This prohibition also applies to all other members of the Exchange. It should also be noted that manipulation is prohibited by the Constitution of the Exchange and by its rules.

REGULATIONS OF THE STOCK EXCHANGE

A body of rules was drawn up originally in 1938, and amended from time to time, by the New York Stock Exchange in regard to specialists. The purpose has been to assure efficient and honest service by the specialist for his customers at all times.

Registration. Under Rule 103 all specialists must register with the Exchange. This permits the Exchange to check on the activities of members acting in this capacity. No specialist activity is possible without registration.

Trading for Orderly Market. Probably the most important rule of the Exchange is Rule 104, which states that no specialist shall buy or sell for his own account, or for one in which he is interested, unless such dealings are reasonably necessary to maintain a fair and orderly market. The rule is similar to Section 11 of the Securities Exchange Act and has as its purpose the prevention of excessive trading for profits. In principle, the rule is very clear. In practice, the determination of what constitutes trading to maintain a fair and orderly market becomes complex. There can be no exact answer. The rule does not prevent a specialist from trading for profit; he may also incur a loss in such activity. It is not practical to believe that a specialist would engage in trading without the objective of making a profit. The rule, however, seeks to prevent excessive and unreasonable trading for a specialist's own account to the possible disadvantage of the investing public served by the market.

Pools and Options. Rule 105 provides that no specialist or his organization or a participant in that organization shall have any direct or indirect interest in any pool dealing or trading in the stock in which the specialist is registered, nor shall these parties directly or indirectly hold, acquire, grant, or have an interest in any option in the stock in which the specialist is registered. As will be noted in Chapter 27 on manipulation, options played an important part at one time in the manipulation of security prices by pools.

Quotations for Own Account. A specialist may quote a stock for his own account and not from his book, in order to maintain closer prices and incur proper price continuity.

At what price may the specialist quote a stock for his own account? He may and should quote the stock either when he has no bids or when he has no offers on his book. When he has bids and offers on his book, he may quote the stock, but he may not compete with his book. He may bid and offer for his own account within the bids and offers on his book in order to improve the market. However, he cannot buy at or below the price of any order on his book to buy unless he has executed the orders of his customers at these prices, nor can he sell at or above the price of an order on his book to sell until he has executed the orders of his customers at these prices. For example, let us suppose that the quotation from the book is 25 to 25½. He could offer the stock under 25½, such as ⅜, ¼, or ⅛. He could bid for stock at 25⅛, ¼, or ⅜. In none of these examples does he compete with bids and offers on his book. He is merely making a better and closer market.

In the illustration just given, if the last sale were 25⅜, the specialist would not be allowed to bid 25½, since regulations prohibit him from buying above the price of the last sale in the same session, except as noted below.

Deals for Own Account. A specialist may deal for his own account only if the transactions are necessary for the market, to render his position adequate for immediate or anticipated needs of the market or to cover a short sale.

Except for transactions reasonably necessary to render his position adequate for his needs, he is not permitted to purchase shares at a price above the last sale in the same session.

Again, he is not permitted, unless it is necessary to render his position adequate to meet the needs of the market, to purchase all or substantially all the stock offered on the book at a price equal to the last sale when the stock so offered represents all or substantially all the stock offered in the market. For example, let us suppose that the last sale of XYZ was 25 and the specialist had 1,500 shares in his book at that price on limited orders. He could not clear his book, except as noted, of these 1,500 shares for his own account, since this would leave the market with no offers at 25.

Similarly, with the same exception, the specialist may not supply all, or substantially all, the stock bid on his book where the stock so bid represents all, or substantially all, the stock bid in the market. Such a trade would clear the market of all available bids at that price.

The specialist is forbidden to buy for his own account when he has an unexecuted market order to buy; he is also forbidden to sell for his own account when he has an unexecuted market order to sell. To permit him to do this would mean that he would be competing with his own customers and would not be performing his duties as an agent in the interest of his customers.

While on the floor he is also forbidden to buy stock for his own account at or below a price at which he has a limited order to buy. For example, let us suppose that the quotation is 25 to 25½ from the book. He could not buy for his own account at 25 or less since this would be in direct competition with his own book. In 1953 an exception to this rule concerned only with off-board trading was put into effect. The specialist unit with prior approval of a floor governor may purchase off the floor a block of one of the stocks in which he is registered, without executing purchase orders on his book, at prices at or above the per-share price paid by the specialist for such stock. In other words, if the Exchange believes that the regular market on the Exchange floor cannot within a reasonable time and at reasonable price or prices absorb a given block of stock, the purchase of this stock off the floor is permitted if this purchase will aid the specialist in maintaining a fair and orderly market.

Finally, a specialist may not sell stock for his own account, except in similar manner as a block off the floor, at or above a price at which he has a limit order to sell. To do so would be competing with his customer.

Crossing Orders. If a specialist has a buy order for 100 shares at 40 from Customer A and another order to sell at 40 from Customer B, he might cross the orders by selling B's stock to A at 40.

Two rules govern such action. One rule requires that when a specialist has an order to buy and an order to sell the same security, he must publicly offer the security at the minimum variation higher than his bid. Since nearly all stocks sell above $1 per share, the minimum variation in practice means $1/8$ point. In our example, the specialist would first offer the stock publicly at $40\frac{1}{8}$. If there was no sale, he could then cross orders and collect the usual commission from Broker A and Broker B.

A second rule prevents the specialist from trading for his own account whenever it is possible to cross orders.

There are several reasons for these rules. One is to assure the customer the best possible price; another, to make the transaction publicly in the open market; a third, to protect the rights of the bidders and offerers in the "crowd" of that stock; and a final reason is to prevent the specialist from crossing orders merely to get the double commission which would result.

Crossing for Own Account. "Crossing for own account" is a phrase used to describe a transaction in which the specialist sells his own stock to the book or buys from the book for his own account. Let us suppose that a specialist has a bid of 30 for 100 shares of stock on his book. By selling his own stock for 30 to the book, he would be crossing for his own account.

There are three restrictions on such activity. First, the specialist must offer the stock at $1/8$ higher than his bid before crossing. Second, the price must be justified by the market. Third, the broker who originally gave the order to the specialist must accept the trade after proper notification. When crossing orders for his own account, the specialist receives no commission.

Stopping Stock. A specialist is prevented from stopping stock on his own book or in the book of a competing specialist for his own account. Such an action would give him an undue preference over orders of his customers. The specialist may give the privilege to others, but he may not accept it for himself. When a specialist desires to buy or sell stock for his own account, he must bid for or offer it in the open market.

12

Short Selling

Short selling is a practice of particular importance to specialists, odd-lot dealers, and others at the heart of the market. It is a trading device used by some, but not many, members of the general public. Like floor trading, short selling is a form of action in the markets that has been subject to criticism. It is proposed in this chapter to examine the procedures and regulations pertinent to the technique and assess briefly its history and importance.

HISTORY AND IMPORTANCE

Early History. Short selling in the stock market is the practice of selling stock, delivery of which is to be effected by borrowing shares for the delivery. It has been a practice in the markets since their earliest days. Records show that the Dutch tried to forbid it as early as 1610. Although the London Stock Exchange was not formally organized until 1773, the use of short selling had already become so prominent in the unorganized market that, as early as 1733, anti-short-sale legislation was introduced in Parliament.[1]

A study of the history of American securities markets will show that short selling attained a major importance early in the development of the New York Stock Exchange. Jacob Little, often called the first great manipulator on the Exchange, operated from 1835 to 1857; he was a heavy and consistent short seller. In the early 1860's short selling became a major speculative tool of such great traders as Drew, Vanderbilt, Fisk, and Gould. One of the most spectacular displays of short selling was reported in 1901, when the famous struggle of the Hill-Morgan and

---

[1] J. E. Meeker, *The Work of the Stock Exchange* (New York: The Ronald Press Co., 1930), p. 607.

Harriman-Kuhn, Loeb interests for the control of the Northern Pacific resulted in great advances in the price of that stock.

The influence of short selling was recognized during World War I, when members were required to report secretly to the Exchange such sales in order to prevent "bear raiding" by irresponsible speculators or enemy agents.

1929 and After. There are no accurate figures on the amount of short selling in the 1925–29 bull market, as data were not being tabulated at that time. No figures show what the short interest was in October, 1929, just before the break. However, a president of the Exchange, in testifying before the House Committee on the Judiciary, stated: "At that time the short position was relatively small, and when the panic started, there were comparatively few persons who had sold short at higher levels and were ready and willing to buy stocks."[2]

On November 12, 1929, three weeks after the crash, the Exchange gathered figures on the short interest. The short interest, it should be mentioned, means the number of shares carried in short accounts of brokers. About 1,692,000 shares were in the short interest on that date. No more figures are available until May 25, 1931, when short selling was heavy. By then, the short interest had risen to 5.6 million shares. The highest figure ever reported was 6.8 million shares in 1962.

It is generally recognized that short selling was heavy in 1931. The exact ratio of short selling to total trading is not known for that year, but it was estimated to be less than 5 per cent by the president of the Exchange.[3]

Present Importance. The present volume of short selling is easily obtainable from the reports of the SEC, published monthly. During 1961 short selling on the New York Stock Exchange could be broken down into the following:[4]

Short Sellers	Per Cent of Total
Specialists	63.9
Other members	19.0
Non-members or public	17.1
	100.0

Of a total of 1,064 million shares transferred through the Exchange in 1961, 44 million, or 4 per cent, represented short sales. This per-

[2] J. A. Ross, *Speculation, Stock Prices, and Industrial Fluctuations* (New York: The Ronald Press Co., 1938), p. 200.

[3] R. E. Whitney in public address on "Short Selling and Liquidation," December 15, 1931; quoted in Ross, *op. cit.*, p. 265.

[4] SEC, *Statistical Bulletin*, February, 1962.

centage is not far out of line with activity in recent years. For example, in a fifty-two-month period from July, 1945, to October, 1949, the percentage was 3.4 per cent. As a general statement, it can be said that short selling since World War II has ranged from 3 to 5 per cent of total sales on the Exchange.

Another way to relate short selling to market activity is to examine the ratio of the short interest, that is, the total number of shares that have been sold short and still have not been covered by a purchase at a given date to the total number of shares in listed issues. For the years 1931 through 1962 this ratio is shown in Figure 12–1. In recent years the ratio has fluctuated between 0.05 and 0.12 per cent.

A third way to measure the importance of short selling is to compute the ratio of the short interest to daily volume on the Exchange. In 1961 this ratio was as low as 74 per cent and as high as 95 per cent of an average day's volume. In other years it was over 150 per cent at times. In slightly different words, the short interest was large enough to have an effect on a given day's volume if a substantial part of the short interest was covered on that day, but the sustained influence of a short interest that did not exceed one and one-half day's volume was not likely to be significant.

TECHNIQUE

Meaning of Short Sale. A short sale has been precisely defined by the SEC under Rule 3B–3 in this language: "The term 'short sale' means any sale of a security which the seller does not own or any sale which is consummated by the delivery of a security borrowed by, or for the account of, the seller.

A similar definition is given by the New York Stock Exchange. Its significance is that it covers two possibilities: (1) a sale of a security that the seller does not own; and (2) a sale effected by the delivery of a security borrowed by, or for the account of, the seller. These would appear to be two definitions of the same thing, which they certainly are not. In one case, the seller must borrow the stock because he does not own it; in the second, the seller may own the stock, but prefers to sell it short. These latter transactions are called "sales against the box" in that the seller has the securities in his safety deposit box or account and can actually deliver them at the time of sale but chooses not to.

At one time the "box short sale" was not considered to be a genuine short sale. Such sales were often made by important stockholders, executive officers, or directors in order to protect themselves against the loss of stock values; yet they did not desire to divest themselves of ownership of particular shares, either because of position, prestige, or need for control.

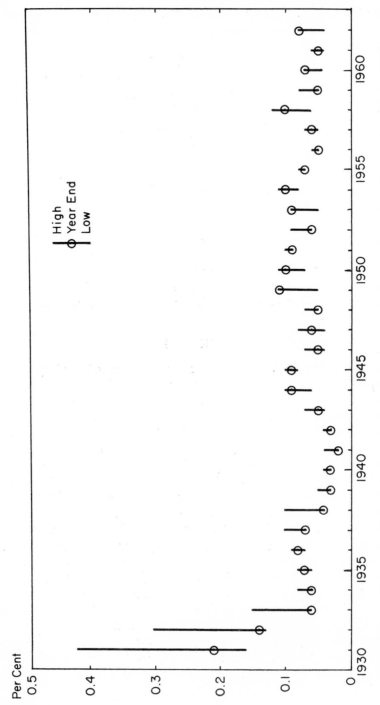

Fig. 12–1. Shares short as a per cent of shares listed. (Source: New York Stock Exchange, *Fact Book, 1962.*)

Reasons for the Short Sale. The short sale may be made by a speculator in anticipation of a price decline in a stock. In his opinion, the stock may be nearing the end of a substantial rise or be on the downgrade. The important thing is that the trader believes that in the near future the stock will decline enough to permit him to cover at a profit after all expenses are deducted. This is the so-called speculative short sale, which is probably the usual public conception of this type of transaction.

There are a number of technical short sales, which may or may not have anything to do with speculation in anticipation of a price decline. Many of these are made regardless of the possibilities of a price decline in the stock sold short. They will be described in detail later in the chapter.

Tax selling in recent years has accounted for a substantial amount of short selling. Before 1951 the short sale could be used to stretch short-term capital gains into long-term ones; this is no longer possible because of changes in the tax law. It is still possible, however, to carry a short-term capital gain over from one year into the next year.

Borrowing Stock. The short sale is possible because a trader can borrow stock from a lender and then made a delivery of it. The stock is never that of the short seller. The first problem of the short seller, therefore, is to borrow the stock from someone who is willing to lend it.

The customer's broker always obtains the stock. The broker himself may have the stock to lend to the short seller. In view of the large number of issues being sold short, it is doubtful whether this is a common occurrence. In many cases the broker will be able to borrow the stock from some of his other customers who have told the broker of their willingness to lend stock. The broker will have a list of such customers.

A third source of stock is other brokerage firms. Contact with these other firms is made through the cashier's department, which contacts other such departments. It is well-known in the financial district what firms make a policy of lending stocks. These may be very large firms, but occasionally rather small firms do an extensive lending business. The reason why the cashier of one firm borrows from the cashier of another firm may be no more substantial than that the two cashiers are mutually acquainted.

At one time practically all stock was loaned by way of the "loan crowd" operating at the "money desk" on the floor of the New York Stock Exchange. Stock is no longer loaned in this manner. Financial institutions, such as investment funds, formerly loaned some stock, as well as banks. There is none loaned this way today.

Reasons for Lending Stock. Today, there is usually only one motive for lending stock. This is to obtain a loan on stock without the payment of interest, since the loans are "flat loans" without compensation to either party.

Years ago lenders of stock were often able to obtain premiums on loans, some of which ran to handsome amounts, as will be described shortly. This is seldom possible now.

In practice, stock loans actually benefit the lending broker more than the owner of the stock. If stocks are in cash accounts and fully paid for or are in general accounts where the equity is in excess of the minimum initial margin required, the lender of the stock may use the cash deposit for the purpose of holding or carrying securities if the deposit is properly margined.[5]

However, when the stock is in a restricted margin account, the customer has no use of the money received for the stock loan. The loan of stock in this instance provides a way for the broker to finance the customer's debit balance without paying interest to a bank. The customer still pays interest to the broker at the regular rate. Thus the broker can reduce his costs by lending customers' stock.

The normal procedure for bookkeeping is to continue to show the customer's account "long" the stock and to show a credit for stock loaned in the brokerage firm's "stock borrowed and loaned" account.

Margins on Loaned Stock.[6] Strict margins are now effective on all stock loans. The amount of margin required depends upon the use made by the lender of the cash deposit received.

Let us assume that the broker has turned over to the lending customer the cash proceeds from a stock loan. Such a case might be where the customer owned stock in a cash account fully paid for. If the lender of the stock in this case intends to use the cash deposit for the purpose of trading in securities, the loan comes under Regulation T of the Federal Reserve Board. This means that the customer may use the cash deposit only to the amount of the current loan value on stock. In early 1962 the loan value under Regulation T was 30 per cent. This would mean that the lender could use only 30 per cent of the cash deposited to protect the stock loan. For example, Mr. A loans 100 shares of XYZ to Mr. B. Mr. A is protected by a cash deposit of $5,000 when he loans the stock, but he can use only $1,500 for trading or speculation in stocks.

If the cash deposit is not to be used for purposes covered by Regulation T, the Reserve Board imposes no requirement. The Exchange, how-

---

[5] Margin requirements and trading are discussed in Chapter 21.
[6] See footnote 5.

ever, does have a requirement. The Exchange will not permit a member firm to pay more than 75 per cent of the market value of the stock to the lender of the stock, nor permit the lender to use more than that amount. This is to insure that the lender of the stock will return the cash deposit when the stock loan is terminated.

Lending Terms. Historically, stock has been loaned under three kinds of terms: (1) at a rate, (2) flat, and (3) at a premium.

When stock was loaned at a rate, as it was frequently before 1930, the lender of the stock received a cash deposit exactly equal to the market value of the stock. On this cash deposit the lender of the stock paid interest at slightly less than the going call loan rate. The lender of the stock had the full advantage of ownership of the stock on loan and the additional advantage of cash to use for his own purposes. If he desired to trade in securities, he could employ all cash over the amount then required as a margin. The lender of stock, then, was willing to pay interest on the cash made available to him by the short seller. This was common procedure many years ago. Changes in attitudes toward both trading and margins and changed call loan rates have altered the conditions. No stock has been loaned this way in recent years.

When stock is loaned flat, no compensation passes either way between the lender and the borrower. The lender receives no compensation in the way of premiums, while the borrower receives no interest on the cash deposit received. Nearly all stock loans today are made this way.

When stock is loaned at a premium, the borrower must pay to the lender a charge based on the number of shares and the number of days during which the loan was in effect. In such situations the stock is in demand for short selling, and the lender can take a profitable advantage of this to demand, not only a 100 per cent cash deposit as a protection, but also a daily fee for the use of the stock. This is a very attractive situation to the lender if the premiums are high.

The premium is not interest and is not figured on a percentage basis. It is figured as so many cents or dollars per day for the life of the loan. In earlier years the premium was calculated on a fractional point basis. For example, a given stock might have been loaned at $\frac{1}{8}$ point per share per day. In some cases it might have been loaned at a full point or more for short periods, such as when there was danger of a corner. (Corners are discussed in Chapter 27.)

Under Rule 157 of the Exchange the premiums must now be based on a certain number of dollars per 100 shares. The premiums may be quoted only at the following rates: 1, 2, 3, 6, 10, 15, and 20; higher rates must be in multiples of $10. Let us suppose that a trader borrows 100 shares at a dollar premium for forty-five days; he would pay 45 times $1, or $45 in all, since the premium is a daily rate.

Premiums have varied greatly in the past. Probably the all-time record was made in 1927, when for a short period the stock of the Wheeling and Lake Erie Railroad was loaned at $7 per share, or $700 per round lot, per day.[7] Several companies at that time were trying to buy control. Brisk bidding forced the price up beyond reasonable limits; this resulted in extensive short selling. In August, 1918, General Motors stock commanded a premium of 1½ points per day for a time. During one week of January, 1932, United States Steel common was loaned at ½ point per day. Such situations, however, are unusual. In 1931 and 1932, when a considerable number of stocks were being loaned at a premium, the average premium on such stocks was probably about $3 per 100 shares per day; on several occasions the average exceeded $5; at one time it was almost $12.

Stock lending at a premium has been infrequent the last few years. For example, in 1955 only one stock was loaned in this way. This was for 100 shares of a well-known chemical stock, which was loaned for about ten days at a premium of $1 per day. Again, in 1958 stock of a sugar company loaned for three days at a $1 premium.

Protection to the Lender. As has already been indicated, the short seller must protect the lender of the stock by depositing an amount of cash equal to the market value of the stock. Where does this money come from? It comes from the proceeds of the sale of the borrowed stock. After the stock is sold, it is delivered to the purchaser through the Stock Clearing Corporation on the day it is paid for. The proceeds are then used by the broker to protect the stock loan.

Mark to the Market. It is a practice in short selling for the loan to be secured at all times by approximately 100 per cent of the market value of the stock. If the stock moves up, more cash must be deposited with the lender by the short seller; if it declines, the lender must return cash. Thus, full protection is always present regardless of the fluctuations in the price of the stock.

In order to be certain that the cash deposit is no more or no less than required, a notice is used by either lender or borrower. This formal notice is called a "mark to the market." An example is given in Figure 16–6. If the stock goes down, the broker representing the short seller sends a mark to the market to the lender's broker; it demands that cash be returned. If the stock goes up, the lender's broker sends the notice for more cash to be deposited. This demand is sent either directly or

[7] J. E. Meeker, *Short Selling* (New York: Harper & Row, Publishers, 1932), p. 198.

through the offices of the Stock Clearing Corporation. The money must be paid directly or cleared through the Corporation on the same day; there is no four-day delivery rule.

In case either party fails to comply with Rule 165 of the Exchange for marking to the market, the other party can close the contract. This is done by giving notice to the offending party. After a short time lapse the contract may be closed the same day by an officer or employee of the Exchange who is authorized to do so. The right to close the account protects both parties to the stock loan against irresponsibility.

Cancellation of Loan. A stock loan resembles a call loan in that either party may terminate the transaction by notice. Rule 160 of the Exchange, in describing the proper notice required, states:

Unless otherwise agreed, notice for the return of loans of securities shall be given before 3:45, and such return shall be made on the fourth business day following the day on which such notice is given.

Short Covering. The phrase "short covering" or "to cover" is given to the act of buying in the stock that has been short sold. The shares so purchased are then returned after notice to the lender, together with any dividends or premium that may be necessary.

Dividends on Stock. The problem often arises: What happens to dividends declared to stockholders of record during the time a short sale is in effect? The answer is that the dividends go to the lender of the stock. When the stock is returned, the short seller also returns any cash or stock dividends that were payable during the period of the sale. The lender would have received the dividends if he had not loaned the stock; it is logical that he be reimbursed for them. Such an action on the part of the short seller usually creates no hardship since stock drops in market price an amount approximating the dividend at the time it goes ex-dividend; he may "cover" at a lower price than if the stock had not gone ex-dividend.

Expenses. The short seller, in making his sale and short-covering, will pay the usual buying and selling commissions. At the time he makes the sale, he will also pay the regular federal and New York transfer taxes, as well as the SEC fee.

An old expression in Wall Street is: "The bull pays interest, but the bear does not." This is true, of course, since the margin buyer pays interest on his debit balance, whereas the short seller borrows no funds, hence pays no interest. However, if a short sale is marked to the market and a debit balance is created in the seller's account, he will incur interest expense. The short seller must, of course, pay the lender any dividends on the stock during the period of the loan. In actual practice, this may be no expense at all, since, as noted above, the stock usually falls by the amount of the dividend when it goes ex-dividend, and can thus be purchased at a lower price than prevailed before it went ex-dividend. Even if, later, the price rises and the sale is completed at a loss, the loss presumably is less than it would have been had no dividend been paid.

Example of Expenses and Profits. In order to show the expenses and profits from a short sale, a transaction will be traced through. Let us assume that Mr. A., anticipating a decline in the price of stock XYZ, has decided to sell short. The stock is selling at 45. He sells 100 shares at that price and covers in thirty days at 40, after a decline in the price of 11 per cent. The stock was borrowed flat.

Short sale: 100 shares at 45		$4,500.00
Selling expenses:		
Commission	$41.50	
Federal transfer tax	1.80	
New York transfer tax	4.00	
SEC fee	.09	47.39
Net proceeds		$4,452.61
Add margin (assume 70 per cent)		3,116.83
Total credits to account		$7,569.44
Covering purchase: 100 shares at 40	$4,000.00	
Commission	39.00	4,039.00
New credit balance		$3,530.44
Deduct margin deposit		3,116.83
Net gain on transaction		$ 413.61

Mr. A, successfully forecasting the trend of the market, makes a net gain of $413.61, or about 13 per cent on his original investment of $3,117.

KINDS OF SHORT SALES

The following classification is commonly found and serves as a basis for discussion:

A. Speculative sales
B. Hedges
C. Technical sales
   1. Against the box
     a. For tax purposes
     b. For hedging purposes
     c. For future deliveries
   2. For arbitrage purposes
     a. Between different markets
     b. Between equivalent securities
   3. By security dealers and brokers
     a. By specialists
     b. By odd-lot dealers
     c. By investment bankers

Speculative Short Sales. The popular idea of the short sale is the speculative short sale; the seller owns no stock but borrows it and sells. His expectation is that the stock can be sold at a higher price than that used to cover or close the transaction. The initial impact of the speculative short sale is to increase the supply of stock offered for sale and thereby slow price change down. On the other hand, the effect of covering is to support or raise the price. The speculative short seller has one purpose only, namely, to sell at one price and to cover at a lower price for a trading profit. In this he may or may not be successful.

The Hedging Short Sale. In this type of sale the short seller fears that there will be a decline in the market or in business conditions. Being a security holder, he does not want to take a loss on his portfolio. He would, therefore, hedge against the anticipated decline by selling stock short, presumably market leaders, which lend themselves well to this purpose. He is not selling against the box, an operation to be described shortly, since he does not own the stock being sold. If his forecast is correct, his hedging operations will tend to protect him against losses due to the drop in the security market or in business activity. How much activity of this sort takes place is not known; it may be very small.

Technical Short Sales. These short sales include all those in which the short seller either own the securities sold or will come into possession of them shortly. In earlier years such transactions were not even considered as short sales. Rulings of the SEC, however, have placed them in the short sale category.

Short Sales Against the Box. The "box" used in this connection means the safe deposit box or account of the short seller. He actually possesses the security being short sold. He makes delivery, however, by borrowing stock rather than delivering the stock that he owns. He may cover either by using his own stock or by buying stock in the market. There are three important examples of short selling against the box.

The first type is short selling for tax purposes. Prior to the changes in the Revenue Acts of 1950 and 1951, it was possible to obtain substantial tax reductions by selling securities short that had been purchased long for a price rise. Once a profit has been made on the transaction, the buyer would sell the stock short. The purpose was to stretch a short-term capital gain into a long-term capital gain, thereby securing the benefit of the reduced tax rate on long-term capital gains. Once the six-month period had passed, the speculator could cover his short sale by delivering the stock he had bought long. Substantial tax savings were thus effected. This is no longer possible.

The present tax law, however, does give the taxpayer an advantage. He can use the short sale to carry over a profit from one year to the next.

For example, in November of a given year a trader buys 100 shares of XYZ at 40. In December the stock is selling at 50. He wants to retain his $1,000 profit but does not want to report it as taxable income that year. Accordingly, he sells 100 shares short at 50 in December. In January he instructs his broker to deliver the long stock to the lender of the stock. His long and short position are both closed out. He now reports his $1,000 profit for the current year instead of in the previous year. Exactly how much of this is done is not known; there appears to be a considerable amount near the end of the year.

A short sale may also be made against the box for hedging purposes. A stockholder possesses a considerable block of stock and fears a market decline. Not certain of his judgment, however, he prefers to hedge rather than to make an outright sale. He, therefore, hedges by short selling the amount of stock owned. If the stock falls, his gain on the short sale exactly offsets the loss on his long stock, disregarding taxes and commission. If it goes up, his gain on his long stock offsets his loss on the short sale. He has successfully hedged. This type of short selling in earlier years was often done by corporate "insiders" who did not want to sell outright stock that might represent a substantial controlling interest in the company. They, therefore, did secretly what they dared not do openly. Today "insiders" may not sell the stock of listed companies short.

Occasionally, a stockholder may sell stock short that he cannot deliver immediately. For example, he may be on vacation and his stock is not immediately accessible. He sells short and then covers with the stock in his box.

Sales for Arbitrage Purposes. Two types of arbitrage transactions are possible. The first is between different markets. A stock may be sold in two markets, for example, New York and Los Angeles. A professional trader, seeing an opportunity to sell in New York at a higher price than that in Los Angeles, would make a short sale in New York and a purchase in Los Angeles. The short sale would be necessary because stock could not be delivered regular way in such an operation. A stock selling on several exchanges tends to have nearly the same price on each exchange; hence, there is little opportunity for profitable arbitrage of this type.

Arbitrage between equivalent securities takes place when it is profitable to buy, say, a convertible bond, convert into common stock, and sell the stock for an over-all profit after commissions and taxes. Professional traders are quick to take advantage of such opportunities. These may occur at the time a new convertible issue comes onto the market. Such arbitrage may for a time reach immense proportions. For example, in 1955 when American Telephone and Telegraph was marketing its record issue of debentures, the short interest in the stock totaled 258,000 shares at the end of the subscription period. This represented a money value of nearly $46 million. In a situation like this the arbitrageur buys the rights, subscribes to the new debentures, using the debentures as a hedge against the short sale if the price runs up. There is usually a small profit in the conversion. In an opportunity does not arise to reverse the positions in a short time, the arbitrageur generally goes through with the conversion.

Sales by Security Dealers. Three classes of dealers and brokers might use the short sale. Specialists need to use this type of tranaction in order to make an orderly market in the stock in which they specialize. As noted previously, these Exchange members account for 64 per cent of all reported short sales in 1961.

Odd-lot dealers and brokers do a considerable amount of short selling. Their combined short interest may range from 50,000 to 100,000 shares. Such sales are not reported in the monthly statistics of the short interest.

Investment bankers bringing out new security issues or holding substantial inventories might find it advantageous on occasion to sell short. Such short sales would protect them against inventory losses in case of a market decline.

REGULATION

Criticisms and Defenses. Short selling has been the subject of many studies. The idea of selling short, of selling something not owned, is outside the experience of people used to ordinary retail and manufacturing practices. It is easy to find analogies in common experience—such as accepting prepayment on an order to deliver manufactured goods—but these are not usually thought to be the same kind of operation. Thus it is easy to criticize the practice.

Opportunities for abuse are evident too. If a number of traders made short sales in substantial volume of a given stock, their action obviously would increase the supply of that stock on the market. It might increase the supply significantly. If at the same time the price of the stock was falling because a tendency for supply to exceed demand at given prices already existed, the action of short sellers would accelerate the price decline. Similarly, if traders who had made short sales covered their transactions by purchasing in a rising market, their action would accelerate the rise. In these instances short selling would reinforce both booms and recessions. It would draw criticism.

In contrast, of course, if traders sold short when prices were rising (in anticipation of a turn down) and covered their sales by purchasing when prices were falling (in anticipation of a turn up), their actions would add to the stability of the market. It will be observed that the regulations imposed on short selling as described below are designed to make this kind of action more likely.

Most significant to an evaluation of the usefulness of short selling in the market is the preponderant use of the technique by professionals for technical reasons. With the arguments for the technical short sale there is little quarrel. These, in summary, are: (1) it enables owners of securities to sell with a minimum of risk and delay when it is not possible to effect immediate delivery; (2) it permits both individual and institutional security holders to avoid the risk of price fluctuations; (3) it aids in the operations of odd-lot dealers; (4) it facilitates the work of specialists; and (5) it makes arbitraging possible in (a) different markets, (b) rights, and (c) convertible securities.

Present Criticism. There is less criticism today of short selling than at any time in many years. In fact, little comment on it—pro or con—appears in the press. The Senate investigation of the market in 1955 did not concern itself with short selling at any time, and the final report makes no mention of this aspect of speculative activity. The regular monthly reports on the short interest continue to appear in the press, but few are able to attach any significance to them.

Rules Prior to 1931. Before 1931 the New York Stock Exchange had three rules on short selling. The substance of their content was that no short sale should be made that would demoralize the market. In other words, members were not to effect such sales for their own account or for customers if such transactions created a disorderly market. The rules were not definite in application, however well intentioned they may have been. They did not result in effective control of short selling.

The 1931 Rule. In 1931 the Exchange made a rule that required all sales to be marked as "Long" or "Short." The purpose was to enable the Exchange to detect the amount and source of short selling; it was a publicity regulation. In no way did it deter the rights of speculators to sell short.

The 1935 Rule. Although the rule of 1931 did not actually restrict short selling, it became a practice of brokers not to allow short selling at a price lower than that of the last sale; such an operation was considered to "demoralize the market." Under this unofficial code a short sale could never be made at a given price until a long sale had been made at that price or below. Hence the brokers, by interpretation of the 1931 rule, made some attempt to prevent excessive selling on a declining market. At the suggestion of the SEC, the practice was officially incorporated as a rule of the Exchange in this language: "No member shall use any facility of the Exchange to effect on the Exchange a short sale of any security in the unit of trading at a price below the last 'regular way' sale price of such security on the Exchange."[8]

Although this rule tended to eliminate a succession of short sales at continuously declining prices, it did not entirely prevent excessive short selling.

The Securities Exchange Act. The Securities Exchange Act of 1934 neither abolished short selling nor made any specific regulation about it, in spite of a rather considerable body of lawmakers who would have liked to eliminate or severely restrict it.

Only three references were made to the short sale. First, Section 7 gives the Federal Reserve Board the power to fix margins on such transactions. Second, Section 10, in relation to the use of manipulative and deceptive devices, states that it is unlawful on a national securities exchange to effect a short sale in contravention of such rules and regulations as the SEC may prescribe as necessary and appropriate in the public interest or for the protection of investors. Third, Section 16 forbids short selling by directors, officers, and principal stockholders of stock of the companies in which they have this position. The Act, therefore, gave the SEC complete power to eliminate or regulate such transactions in whatever way it saw fit.

Under powers given by the Act, the SEC has formulated Rules 10A–1 and 10A–2, which now govern short selling on any national securities exchange.

The 1938 Rule. The first regulation of short selling by the SEC was introduced on February 8, 1938, after the Commission had examined the market decline of 1937, when a substantial amount of short selling took place in certain market leaders. Regulation was through Rules 10A–1 and 10A–2. Both are essentially the same today as when written in 1938 except for the provision that states when a short sale can be made. We are concerned at this point only with that part of Rule 10A–1 that stated: "No person shall . . . effect a short sale of any security at or below the price at which the last sale thereof, regular way, was effected on such exchange."

This rule meant that no short sale could be made at or below the price of the last sale; that is, all sales must be made at least $\frac{1}{8}$ point above the last sale. As long as the market continued down, no short sale could be made.

The result of this rule was that the short interest dropped sharply and short selling was almost wiped out. For a time a loophole existed; the SEC rule had exempted odd-lots. As a result, short selling through

---

[8] Chapter xiv of the Rules of the Governing Committee (1935).

odd-lots rapidly increased. The Exchange closed the loophole by putting both round- and odd-lots on the same basis (Rule 435). The SEC admitted that its rule was impractical, but did not change it.

In time the Committee on Floor Procedure of the Exchange worked out a proposed change in the rule and presented it to the SEC. After an investigation it was quickly adopted. The amendment became effective on March 20, 1939.

Other Sections of 1938 Rule. The 1938 rule has several other provisions worthy of note. No sale may be executed unless it is marked "Long" or "Short." This is, of course, merely a continuation of the 1931 rule established many years ago by the Exchange.

No sale shall be marked "Long" unless the security to be delivered after the sale is actually carried in the account of the customer or is owned by the customer and will be delivered as soon as is possible without undue inconvenience and expense. If available securities are not to be delivered on the sale, it is a "sale against the box" and must be marked "short."

Certain short sales are exempt from the "up-tick" rule; they include: (1) any sale if the person owns the security and intends to deliver it as soon as is possible without undue inconvenience and expense; (2) any order to sell that is marked "Long"; (3) any sale of an odd-lot; (4) any sale by an odd-lot dealer; (5) any sale for an arbitrage transaction, either between international or domestic markets, or between equivalent securities.

The 1939 Rule. The regulations of the SEC on short selling as amended in 1939 have been changed only in minor detail since that year.

Section (a) of Rule 10A–1 is so vital to the understanding of present regulations on short selling that it is quoted in part:

> No person shall, for his own account or for the account of any other person, effect on a national securities exchange a short sale of any security (1) below the price at which the last sale thereof, regular way, was effected on such exchange, or (2) at such price unless such price is above the next preceding different price at which a sale of such security, regular way, was effected on such exchange.

It is always possible to sell short at a higher price than that of the last sale. Hence, if a stock last sold at 50, one can sell short at 50⅛. Under the 1938 rule this was the only type of short sale allowed.

No short sale may be made below the price of the last sale, regardless of the trend of the market. This eliminates "hammering of the market" when it is on the decline.

One may sell short at the price of the last sale under only one condition; namely, such price is above the next preceding different price.

A few examples on page 236 may clear up what seems to be a complex rule.

As long as prices are stable and the last change in price is upward, an endless number of short sales may be made at the same price.

A minor part of Section (a) should be mentioned at this point. In case a stock goes ex-dividend, all sale prices prior to the "ex" date are reduced by the amount of the dividend. For example, a stock may be sold short at 50. The company declares a dividend of $1 per share; after the stock goes ex-dividend, the stock may be sold short at 49.

Brokers and customers who are familiar with the operations of the short selling rule have a special terminology in place of the very legalistic expression "at such price unless such price is above the next preceding different price." They use the phrases "plus tick," "minus tick," or "zero plus tick." A "plus tick" takes place when a given sale is made at a higher price than the previous transaction. Dials at each post on the trading floor indicate the price of the last sale of each stock. Plus and minus signs indicate whether the figure represents a "plus tick" or a "minus tick." The plus sign on the indicator dial for Colgate-Palmolive as shown in Figure 12–2 illustrates this feature. For another example,

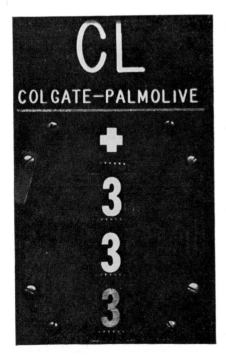 

Fig. 12–2. Indicator dials, showing "plus ticks" and "minus ticks."

let us take two sales: 40, 40⅛. This is a "plus tick" since 40⅛ is obviously higher than 40. One may always sell short at the price of a "plus tick," that is, 40⅛ in the example just cited.

Round-Lot Sale		May Sale Be Made?	Short Sale Possible at	Explanation
Number	Price			
1.	40	—	—	—
2.	39	No	39⅛	Last change in price was downward
3.	39	No	39⅛	Last change in price was downward
4.	39¼	Yes	39¼	Last change in price was upward
5.	39¼	Yes	39¼	Last change in price was upward
6.	38½	No	38⅝	Last change in price was downward
7.	38¼	No	38⅜	Last change in price was downward
8.	38¾	Yes	38¾	Last change in price was upward
9.	38⅞	Yes	38⅞	Last change in price was upward
10.	38⅞	Yes	38⅞	Last change in price was upward

A "minus tick" takes place when a sale is made at a price lower than that of the previous sale. For example, let us take three sales: 35, 34⅞, and 34¾. Both the second and third sales are "minus tick" in sequence. A short sale may not be made on a "minus tick." The indicator dial for Cudahy Packing shown in Figure 12–2 illustrates the way a "minus tick" is shown on the floor. Of course, a short sale may be made after a "minus tick" if it can be made against a bid at least ⅛ higher than that which produced the "minus tick."

A "zero plus tick" takes place when a given sale is at the same price as that of the previous sale, but the last change in price was upward. To illustrate, let us take three sales: 50, 50¼, and 50¼. There was no change in price between the second and third sales; this was the "zero." However, 50¼ was above the sale at 50, giving us our "plus." The third sale was level with the second sale, but above the first sale. A short sale can always be made on a "zero plus tick."

THE SHORT SELLERS

Short sellers are primarily professional traders, usually members of the Exchange. As indicated, in 1961, 83 per cent of all short selling was done by members of the Exchange and only 17 per cent by the trading public.

Various studies in earlier years indicated that much short selling was done by relatively few individuals. For example, the SEC, in a study of short selling in five market leaders from September 7 to 25, 1937, reported that most of the selling was done by eleven members of the Exchange. One member was the leading short seller in three stocks and two other floor traders were leading short sellers in two stocks. Five floor traders accounted for 24 per cent of the short selling in one stock and almost as much in two others. These eleven members accounted for 60 per cent of all the short selling in these five stocks.[9]

The odd-lot public in general is unfamiliar with short selling and afraid to use it. Typically an on-balance buyer of stocks, it distrusts short selling. During 1961 only ½ of 1 per cent of all sales by the odd-lot public were short sales.

[9] SEC, Release No. 1548, October 18, 1937.

13

The Execution of
Odd-Lot Orders

The odd-lot business is complex. Discussion of the subject is divided here into two chapters. The present one will deal only with the pricing of odd-lot orders on the New York Stock Exchange. The following chapter will describe operations of odd-lot dealers, methods of handling orders on the floor, and some characteristics of the odd-lot public.

ODD-LOT ORDERS

Size of the Order. An odd-lot order is one for less than the round-lot unit of trading. The New York Stock Exchange has ruled that in active issues the smallest order that can be executed in the auction market is 100 shares. Such a sale is the unit of trading and any sale for less than 100 shares (that is, 1–99) becomes an odd-lot order. At Post 30, where most of the inactive stocks are traded (198 in 1962), the unit of trading is 10 shares. In such issues any order of from 1 to 9 shares is an odd-lot order. Seventy 10-share-unit issues are traded at posts other than Post 30; for these also an odd-lot is an amount from 1 to 9 shares.

Odd-Lot Differentials. The odd-lot dealers charge a differential on each order that they execute. In nearly all transactions, on shares selling at less than $40 per share, the differential is ⅛ point or 12½¢ per share, and on shares selling at $40 or more, the differential is ¼ point or 25¢ per share.

To this general rule as to differentials there are several exceptions significant on occasion. Two of these, the ½-point and 1-point rules, will be considered in some detail later (p. 245). Three others are as follows:

1. The differential charged on execution of an order for stock priced at $ 1/8 (12 1/2¢) or less is as nearly half the effective price as practicable. For example:

If the Effective Round-Lot Sale Price Is	The Odd-Lot Differential Is
$5/32	$3/32 on sale, or 1/8 on purchase
4/32 (i.e., 1/8)	1/16
2/32 (i.e., 1/16)	1/32
1/32	1/64

2. The differential charged for odd-lots in the inactive, 10-share-unit issues has more classifications by price and is larger than that on active issues.

If the Effective Round-Lot Sale Price Is	The Odd Lot Differential Is
$25 or less	$1/4
25 1/8 to 74 3/4	3/8
74 7/8	1/2
75	5/8
75 1/8 or more	3/4

3. A differential of $ 1/8 is charged on shares that have been called for redemption if dealings in them are at variations of price of $ 1/32 rather than the customary minimum variation of $ 1/8.

The appropriate differential, in any case, is added to the effective price on buy orders and subtracted from the effective price on sell orders. The differential is not a commission, since the dealer is acting for his own account and not as an agent. As far as the odd-lot public customer is concerned, however, it certainly does represent a cost of buying or selling in odd-lots.

Method of Execution. Briefly, an odd-lot order is executed by being sent to the floor of the Exchange where an odd-lot dealer holds it until a round-lot sale puts the order into effect (Note dealer at post, Fig. 13–1). The round-lot sale may be the very next sale, as in the case of a market order, or it may not, as in the case of a limit or stop order. After an effective round-lot sale has taken place, the odd-lot dealer determines the price of execution, which is the price the odd-lot customer will pay in the case of a purchase or receive in the case of a sale. On buy orders the differential is added to the round-lot price. On sell orders the differential is subtracted from the round-lot price. Thus, the public customer is paying slightly more for his stock when buying in odd-lots and receives slightly less when selling. In executing these orders, the odd-lot dealer is acting for his own account as a dealer, and not as an agent of the customer.

Fig. 13–1. Odd-lot dealer at Post 12.

Placing Odd-Lot Orders. The customer who wishes to buy or sell stock in odd-lots places his order with a commission broker, exactly as would a round-lot customer. He does not deal directly at any time with an odd-lot house. His commission firm sends the order to the Exchange floor, where it is transmitted to one of the odd-lot dealers, who executes it in the manner just described.

Kinds of Orders. The odd-lot customer may place any type of order that a round-lot customer may. In addition, he has the choice of a number of methods of execution, some of which are not used in the round-lot market. On a time basis, he may have his orders handled in any of the following ways:

    I. Day Order
    II. Open or G.T.C. Order
    III. Week Order
    IV. Month Order

The same rules apply to the above orders as apply in the round-lot market.[1]

The odd-lot customer also has a choice of a number of kinds of orders. They may be listed as follows:

    I. Market Order
    II. Limit or Limited Order
    III. Stop Order
    IV. Short Sale Order
    V. Special Types of Orders
        A. Stop Limited
        B. Cash
        C. Seller's Option
        D. Buy on Offer or Sell on Bid
        E. Basis Price
        F. On Close
        G. With or Without Sale
        H. Immediate or Cancel
        I. Scale
        J. Alternative
        K. Contingent
        L. Special Instruction

MARKET ORDERS

Terminology. In the execution of odd-lot orders two terms must be borne constantly in mind:

Effective sale: this is the round-lot sale, which effects or puts into operation the odd-lot order. The price of execution is based on the price

[1] See Chapter 9 (p. 171) for a discussion of these orders.

of this sale. In other words, the odd-lot dealer waits for the proper round-lot sale on the floor; he then uses the price of this round-lot sale to fix the price at which he executes the odd-lot order.

Price of execution: this is the price at which the odd-lot order is executed. The customer pays this price on a purchase and receives this price on a sale.

Nature of Market Orders. A market order is always executed at the price prevailing when the order reaches the post. The customer has stated no price at which he will trade, but has merely ordered his stock to be purchased or sold as soon as possible. In a market order the very next round-lot sale on the floor after the receipt of the odd-lot order by the odd-lot dealer at the post becomes the effective sale. The only exception to this rule is in the case of the market order to sell short; then the rule for selling short must apply. The effective sale is not necessarily the next sale that appears on the ticker tape.

Buy Orders. The rule is: *The order is executed on the very next round-lot sale by adding the differential to the price of that sale.*

For example, a customer enters an order to buy 20 shares of a stock at the market. The next round-lot sale after the order reaches the post is 22½. The effective sale is 22½ and the price of execution is 22⅝. The differential in this case is ⅛ point.

Again, a customer enters an order to buy 50 shares of a stock at the market. The next round-lot sale after the order reaches the post is 60½. The effective sale is 60½ and the price of execution is 60¾. The differential is ¼ point.

Sell Orders. The rule is: *The order is executed on the very next round-lot sale by deducting the differential from the price of that sale.*

For example, as illustrated by the order slip in Figure 13–2, a customer enters a market order to sell long 25 shares of General Motors Corporation common stock. The very next round-lot sale is 45, which is the effective sale. The price of the odd-lot is 44¾. The differential, subtracted from the effective sale price on a sell order, is ¼ point.

Again, a customer enters a market order to sell long 10 shares. The very next round-lot sale is 22⅜, which is the effective sale. The price of execution is 22¼. The differential is ⅛ point.

LIMIT ORDERS

Nature of Limit Orders. In all limit or limited orders (the names are interchangeable), whether round- or odd-lot, the customer demands that the stock be bought or sold at a specified price or at a price that is better. In the case of a buy order, the price must be at the limit or lower;

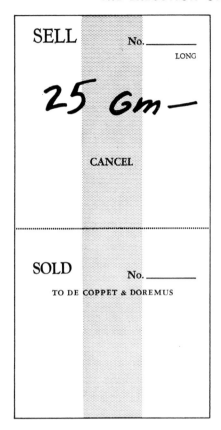

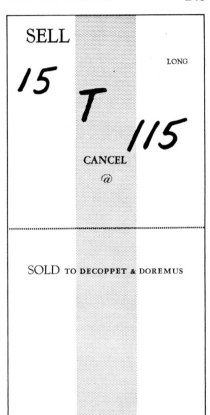

Fig. 13–2. An odd-lot market order to sell long.

Fig. 13–3. An odd-lot, limited, day order to sell long.

in the case of the sell order, the price must be at the limit or higher. This limit complicates execution of the odd-lot order, since the customer wants his limit while the odd-lot dealer must also make his differential. Hence, the effective sale must be such that the customer not only gets his limit or better, but also the odd-lot dealer gets his differential. On a buy order the effective sale must be under the limit, and on a sell order the effective sale must be above the limit. The usual differential on limit orders is ⅛ or ¼ point, but under certain conditions it may be as much as ½ to 1 point.

Usual Method of Execution. The rule is: *The limit order is ordinarily executed at its limit.*

This rule governs the execution of limit orders with the five exceptions to be noted shortly. The customer ordinarily gets his limit price. This procedure may give the odd-lot dealer a differential of ⅛, ¼, or even more in some cases.

The following are examples of limit orders to buy, executed by the usual method:

1. The customer enters an order to buy 25 shares at 30. Round-lot sales then take place in this order and at these prices: 30¼, 30⅛, 30, 29⅞. The effective sale is 29⅞; the price of execution is 30. The odd-lot dealer adds his ⅛ point differential to 29⅞, which makes the price of execution the customer's limit.

2. The customer enters an order to buy 50 shares at 65. Round-lot sales then take place in this order and at these prices: 65⅛, 65, 64¾, 64⅝. The effective price is 64¾; the price of execution 65, the customer's limit. The effective price is the first price below 65 by the amount of the differential or more.

The following are examples of limit orders to sell, executed in the usual way:

1. The customer enters an order to sell long 10 shares at 36. Round-lot sales then take place in this order and at these prices: 35¾, 35⅞, 36, 36⅛. The effective sale is 36⅛; the price of execution is 36, the customer's limit.

2. The customer enters an order, as illustrated by the order slip in Figure 13–3, to sell 15 shares of American Telephone and Telegraph Company (T) common stock at $115. Round-lot sales then take place in this order and at these prices: 114, 114½, 115, 115¼. The effective price is 115¼; the price of execution, 115, the customer's limit. The odd-lot dealer deducts his ¼ point differential from 115¼ and gives the customer his limit.

On Very Next Sale. The first exception to the rule that limit orders are ordinarily executed at their limits is the one based on the very next sale.

The rule is: *If the very next round-lot sale entitles a better price, the order is executed at the usual differential.*

The very next sale is, of course, the first sale of the stock after the odd-lot order has reached the odd-lot dealer. If this sale is effective and more than the amount of the differential from the limit, the order is executed as a market order.

For example, a customer enters a limit order to buy 25 shares at 30. The very next round-lot sale is 29, which becomes the effective sale. The price of execution is 29⅛. The customer receives a better price than his limit because of this exception.

Again, a customer wishes to sell 10 shares at 75. The very next sale is 75¾, which becomes the effective sale. The price of execution is 75½. The exception gave the customer a better price than he anticipated.

On an Opening Sale. A second exception is governed by the opening sale, which means the first sale in a given trading session. This exception is an adaptation of the "On very next sale" rule which takes into account a technical market rule. Open orders are re-entered daily. They reach the market, in this sense, at the opening. The opening sale, therefore, is the very next sale after this entry of the order. Similarly, for day orders reaching the odd-lot dealer before there is an opening sale in the issue, the opening sale is the very next sale.

The rule: *If the opening sale entitles a better price, the order is executed at the usual differential.*

For example, a customer enters an open order to buy 50 shares at 45. The opening sale is 44½, which is the effective sale. The order is executed at 44¾. The exception gives the customer a better price by ¼ point than he expects.

Again, the customer enters an open order to sell 10 shares at 60. The opening sale is 61, which is the effective sale. The price of execution is 60¾, which is the opening price less the differential.

Buy Orders at a Limit of 40⅛. The odd-lot dealer executes buy orders with a limit of 40⅛ as though the limit were 40. An effective sale of 39⅞, or less, sets off the order. The odd-lot customer pays no more than 40, rather than 40⅛, and obtains an unexpected benefit.

One-Half Point Rule. The fourth exception to the usual rule for executing odd-lot limit orders is based on the ½-point rule.

The rule is: *If the effective round-lot sale is less than 40, the order is filled at its limit unless the effective sale is more than ½ point away from the limit. In the latter case the order is executed at a ½-point differential.*

Under this rule the customer is entitled to a better price for a stock selling at less than 40 if the effective sale is more than ½ point away from the limit.

For example, the customer enters an order to buy 50 shares at 36. Round-lot sales then take place in this order and at these prices: 38, 37, 36, 35. The effective sale is 35, or more than ½ point away from the limit. The price of execution is 35½, which the odd-lot dealer obtains by adding the ½-point differential to the price of the effective sale.

Again, the customer enters an order to sell 25 shares at 20. Round-lot sales then take place in this order and at these prices: 19½, 20¾, 21, 20. The effective sale is 20¾. The order is executed at 20¼; the odd-lot dealer deducts the ½-point differential from the price of the effective sale.

One-Point Rule. The fifth and final exception to the usual rule for executing limit orders is the 1-point rule.

The rule: *If the effective round-lot sale is 40 or more, the order is filled at its limit unless the effective sale is more than 1 point away from the limit. In the latter case the order is executed at a 1-point differential except that for a sell order the price of execution in no case is less than 39⅜.*

This rule gives the customer a better price than his limit for stocks selling at 40 or more, provided the effective sale is more than 1 point away from the limit.

For example, the customer enters an order to buy 10 shares at 148. Round-lot sales then take place in this order and at these prices: $148\frac{1}{2}$, $146\frac{1}{2}$, 146. The effective sale, which is $146\frac{1}{2}$, is more than 1 point away from the limit of 148. The price of execution is $147\frac{1}{2}$, which is the effective sale price plus a 1-point differential to the odd-lot dealer.

Again, the customer enters an odd-lot order to sell 25 shares at 80. Round-lot sales then take place in this order and at these prices: $79\frac{3}{4}$, 80, $81\frac{1}{4}$, 82. The effective sale is $81\frac{1}{4}$, and the price of execution is $80\frac{1}{4}$.

The exception to the 1-point rule should be explained briefly. On odd-lot *sell* orders only in cases where the effective round-lot sale is 40, $40\frac{1}{8}$, or $40\frac{1}{4}$, the 1-point differential is not charged in full and the order is executed at $39\frac{3}{8}$ or at its limit, whichever is higher.

The limit price specified in a buy limit order is reduced by the odd-lot dealer on ex-dividend or ex-rights dates excepting the prices on orders entered on the first day of a month. This action is equivalent to the adjustment made on orders in the round-lot market.

STOP ORDERS

Stop Orders to Sell Long. The rule is: *As soon as there is a round-lot operative sale at the stop price or lower, the order is executed at the usual differential below this price.*

Stop orders to sell are used when the price of a stock is believed to be in danger of falling and the customer wishes to sell if it reaches a specific price, regardless of the price then obtainable. In the execution of odd-lot stop orders, the customer gets the effective sale price, minus the customary differential. There are no exceptions like those for limit orders; the odd-lot dealer charges his regular differential, usually $\frac{1}{8}$ or $\frac{1}{4}$ point, and no more.

For example, a customer places a stop order, as illustrated by the order slip in Figure 13–4, to sell 25 shares of Radio Corporation of America (RCA) common stock at 55 stop. The next four round-lot sales are 56, $55\frac{1}{2}$, 55, $54\frac{1}{4}$. The effective round-lot sale is the first sale at 55; the price of execution is $54\frac{3}{4}$.

Stop Orders to Buy. The rule is: *As soon as there is a round-lot sale at the stop price or higher, the order is executed at the usual differential above this price.*

As an example a customer places a stop order to buy 50 shares at 30. The next four round-lot sales are $29\frac{1}{2}$, $29\frac{7}{8}$, 30, $30\frac{1}{4}$. The effective round-lot sale is 30; the price of execution is $30\frac{1}{8}$.

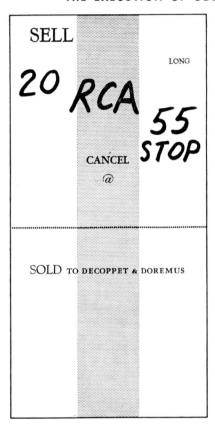

Fig. 13—4. An odd-lot, stop order to sell long.

Again, a customer places a stop order to buy 10 shares at 75. The next four round-lot sales are 74, 74¾, 75½, 76. The effective round-lot sale is 75½; the price of execution is 75¾.

The stop price specified on a sell stop order is reduced by the odd-lot dealer on ex-divided or ex-rights dates excepting prices on orders entered on the first day of a month. This action is equivalent to that on orders in the round-lot market.

ORDERS TO SELL SHORT

Short Selling Rule. Orders to sell odd-lots short are complex in execution because of the present rules that limit short selling. These rules, established in 1938 and 1939 by the SEC, limited the right to sell short on a declining market.[2] Rule 435 of the Exchange now governs the execution of odd-lot orders. It is stated in part, as follows:

No member, member organization, partner or stockholder therein shall effect on the Exchange any short sale of a stock in an amount less than the unit

[2] See Chapter 12 for a detailed analysis of short selling operations.

of trading, unless such sale is based upon a sale, in the unit of trading, the price of which (A) is higher than the price of the last "regular way" sale on the Exchange of such stock in the unit of trading, or (B) is the same as the price of such last sale and such price was higher than the last different price of a "regular way" sale on the Exchange of such stock in the unit of trading.

The rule may be restated, in simplified form, as follows:

A short sale may always be made at a price higher than that of the last sale. It may be made also at the same price as the last sale, if the last preceding change in price was upward.

The application of the rule is simpler than the wording of the text would seem to indicate. A round-lot sale is effective for the odd-lot short sale only if it is higher than the last different round-lot price. The last different price may have been on the previous sale, or it may have been a number of sales before. The only thing necessary is that the effective sale must have been made at a price higher than that of the last different price.

Let us assume a series of ten different round-lot sales and indicate for each sale whether it is effective for an odd-lot short sale.

1. 25
2. 25¼—effective since above last different price
3. 25¼—effective since above last different price
4. 25—not effective since below last different price
5. 24½—not effective since below last different price
6. 24½—not effective since below last different price
7. 24¾—effective since above last different price
8. 24⅞—effective since above last different price
9. 24⅞—effective since above last different price
10. 24¾—not effective since below last different price

The time factor is important in determining the effective sale. It is not necessary for the sale at the last different price to take place in the same trading session. It may take place a day or a week before. It may also take place either before or after the time that the odd-lot order is entered. The effective sale, of course, must take place after the order is entered, but the sale at the last different price may take place either before or after the order is entered.

Market orders for odd-lot short sales are executed according to the following principle: *The order is executed at the usual differential below the first round-lot sale that is higher than the last different price.*

For the sequence of ten round-lot sales just discussed, execution of an odd-lot sale could take place after five of the last nine sales:

Round-Lot Sale	Odd-Lot Short Sale Can Be Executed at
1. 25	—
2. 25¼	25⅛
3. 25¼	25⅛
4. 25	—
5. 24½	—
6. 24½	—
7. 24¾	24⅝
8. 24⅞	24¾
9. 24⅞	24¾
10. 24¾	—

Stop or limit orders to sell short may be affected by still more factors. A stop order becomes a market order when the stop price is reached or passed. The rule above then applies. Let us suppose that an order is placed to sell short at 43 stop. In the round-lot market, transactions at 43½ and 43 then occur in that order. The stop order becomes a market order when the sale at 43 is made. Thereafter, however, the prices may change substantially before a short sale may be executed, and the direction of change may be different. Two examples serve to illustrate this point. After the round-lot sale at 43, suppose a sequence of sales in the round-lot market is as follows: 42¾, 42½, 42½, 42¼, 42, 42⅛. The last price is the first on which execution may be made. The odd-lot is sold at 41⅞. In contrast, suppose the sequence of prices in the round-lot market following the sale at 43 to be 43, 43¼. The odd-lot stop order for a short sale can be executed on the 43¼ price; the sale would be made at 43. If the first sale in the round-lot market after an odd-lot stop order to sell short reaches the floor is at a price both at or below the stop price and above the last different price in the round-lot market, the order can be executed immediately on that sale.

An odd-lot limit order to sell short would be executed on the first price in the round-lot market that was both above the limit by the amount of the applicable differential and above the last different price in the round-lot market. If the very next sale permits execution, the usual differential applies. If one or more round-lot sales are made at less than a differential above the limit after the odd-lot order reaches the floor, the ½- or 1-point rules for differentials, described above, apply.

In both instances, stop sell and buy and limit prices would be reduced on ex-dividend or ex-rights dates, as noted above.

SPECIAL TYPES OF ORDERS

Stop Limited Orders. In this type of order the customer specifies both a stop price and a limit price. Both prices must be considered by the dealer in executing the order. The order has, in addition to the stop price, a designated limit above which, if it is a buy order, it may not be filled, and below which, if it is a sell order, it may not be filled.

For example, a customer places an order to sell 25 shares at 50 stop, limit 49. The following round-lot sales take place: 50½, 49½, 49, 48¾. The order is filled at 49¼. The effective round-lot sale is 49½. After substracting the ¼-point differential, the customer receives 49¼, which is above his limit.

Cash Trades. These orders are similar to round-lot sales for "cash." A sale for "cash" means that the stock is delivered the same day as sold instead of the usual four-day delivery. This type of order permits the odd-lot customer to trade on a "cash" basis the same as the round-lot customer. The order is filled either on a round-lot transaction or on the quotation at the usual differential. The odd-lot dealer will make a cash trade if he is able to do so. For example, on a buy order for cash, the dealer will fill it if he has the required stock on hand or can procure it.

Seller's Option. These orders contrast with cash sales. The seller desires to delay delivery of the stock beyond the four-day, "regular-way" period. The odd-lot dealer will fill such an order with delivery delayed to a point to be chosen by the seller between the fourth and thirtieth day. Execution is at the same differential from the effective sale as for regular way. If the stock involved is loaning at a premium, however, a charge to cover the loan premium may be added.[3] If delay beyond thirty days is desired, the price will be reached by mutual agreement rather than arbitrary rule.

Buy on Offer or Sell on Bid. One difficulty encountered with odd-lot orders is that they are not to be executed until there is a round-lot sale of the particular stock. In a slow market this may result in a considerable delay in the execution of the order. A method of avoiding such a handicap is for the customer to specify that the stock be bought on the offer or sold on the bid. This is sometimes known as an order "without waiting."

Such orders are executed on the basis of the prevailing quotation on the stock. An order to buy is executed by adding the differential to the offer. For example, the quotation is 66 to ¼. An order to buy 25 shares on the offer would be executed at 66½, which is the offer plus the ¼-point differential.

Again, let us suppose that the customer places an order to sell 10 shares on the bid. The quotation is 25½ to ⅝. The order is executed at 25⅜, which is the bid minus the ⅛-differential.

Basis Price. An odd-lot customer may specify that his order is to be executed at the basis price, sometimes called the basis market. This is a

---

[3] The loan of stock is discussed in Chapter 12, p. 223.

special type of execution the purpose of which is to permit the execution of odd-lot orders in relatively inactive stocks traded at the eighteen active posts. There is not much activity in orders at the basis price, one or two stocks a day being typical. The number seldom exceeds six stocks.

At the close of the market the odd-lot dealers get together and establish basis prices for 100-share-unit stocks in which there have been no sales during the day, and where the bid and offer are 2 or more points away. On this basis price the dealers will execute orders at the usual differential. Orders must have been received by the odd-lot dealers at least a half-hour prior to the close. Market, limited, and stop orders may be filled at the basis price, but not orders to sell short. The basis prices, established by the odd-lot dealers, are printed on the ticker tape after the close.

As an example, let us suppose that stock XYZ has not been sold during the day and the closing quotation is 110 to 112. A basis price of 111 will be a logical one. Buy orders would then be executed at 111¼ and sell orders at 110¾.

On Close. An order may be placed for execution on the closing quotation in the regular market. It will be executed at the applicable differential away from the closing bid on sale or the asking price on purchase orders. A limit order may be marked "or on close." If it is not executed at its limit prior to the close, it will then be executed on the closing bid or offer without reference to the limit price. "On close" orders will not be executed on the last sale price; they are executed on the closing quotation only.

With or Without Sale Orders. These orders are frequently called "W.O.W." orders. These are limited orders that specify this method of execution. The order is executed either on the quotation or on the round-lot sale, whichever is first effective. If it is filled on the quotation, the differential is subtracted from the bid in the case of a sale or added to the offer in the case of a purchase. If the order is filled on the basis of a round-lot sale, the rules for limited orders apply.

Immediate or Cancel Orders. These are limited orders to be executed at once on the basis of the current quotation or to be cancelled. If the round-lot quotation does not permit immediate execution, the dealer will cancel the order, report the quotation, and tell the customer of the cancellation.

For example, a customer places an immediate or cancel order to buy 25 shares at 50. The quotation is 49¾ to 50. The order cannot be executed and so it is cancelled. If the dealer were to have added ¼ point to the offer of 50, the price of execution would have been 50¼, which was higher than the customer wanted to pay. Round-lot sales are not used in the execution of these orders.

Scale Orders. This is an uncommon type of order. It is an order to buy or sell two or more lots of the same stock at designated price variations. For example, a customer might have 200 shares of stock XYZ. He could give an order to sell 50 shares at 80, 50 shares at 81, 50 shares at 82, and 50 shares at 83. Again, a customer might place a scale order to buy 25 shares at 30, 25 shares at 29½, 25 shares at 29, and 25 shares at 28½.

Stop orders can be used in the same way. Orders to sell short are governed by the rules on short sales of odd-lots.

Alternative Orders. A customer may elect to enter a group of orders with the limitation that execution of any one of the orders results in immediate cancellation of the others. The group may include limited orders in two or more issues; e.g., orders to buy XYZ with a limit at 25 or to buy ABC with a limit at 23. If the price action of either stock leads to execution of one of the orders, the other is cancelled. Another use of the alternative order establishes a range; e.g., orders may be placed simultaneously for the sale of XYZ at 33 limit or at 29 stop. If the price rises to 33⅛, the limit order will be executed and the stop order will be cancelled. If the price drops to 29, the stop order will be executed and the limit order cancelled.

Contingent Orders. Somewhat similarly, a customer may elect to have one order executed *if and only if* another is. For example, an order might instruct the broker to buy XYZ when an order to sell ABC can be executed also but at a price 2 points higher. For another example, buy XYZ and then enter a limit order to sell the same number of shares at a price 2 points above the purchase price.

In accepting either an alternative order or a contingent order, the odd-lot dealer agrees to make every effort to execute it satisfactorily but does not assume responsibility for or guarantee exact execution.

Orders with Special Instructions. Customers may enter orders with special instructions. The following are four examples. All are to buy or sell a given number of shares under certain conditions.

> "On opening sale only"
> "On second sale"
> "Good until ——— o'clock"
> "To be entered at ——— o'clock"

If the order cannot be executed under the terms stated, it is cancelled. For example, it may not be possible to execute a limited order at 40 on opening sale only.

ODD-LOTS ON OTHER EXCHANGES

On exchanges in the United States other than the New York Stock Exchange, the specialists in individual stock issues make an odd-lot market. Orders for stock of issues listed on such an exchange, for which the exchange provides the primary market, are executed in the same way as described above: the specialist fills all odd-lot orders accepted by him at prices a designated differential away from the first effective sale in the round-lot market. Most of the special pricing devices described above may also be used. Differentials are generally identical with those charged by odd-lot dealers on the New York Stock Exchange.

Orders for stock of issues listed on the New York or American Stock Exchanges and also traded on a regional exchange are handled in slightly different fashion. The specialist executes such orders a differential away from the first effective sale price reported on the ticker tape for the New York market three minutes or more after he received the order on the floor of his exchange. The "three minute" rule recognizes the average delays in (1) transmission of an order from the region of origin to New York and then to the floor of the exchange, (2) execution on the floor, and (3) the process of putting the report of round-lot transactions on the ticker tape. Three minutes is an estimate of the average time these steps might take; it is not a precise measure of time for any individual transaction. It provides a useful working rule. In general, execution on a regional exchange under this rule will yield the same price to the public customer that transmission to New York would have obtained. Some advantage may accrue to odd-lot sellers through avoidance of the New York State transfer tax.

The New York Stock Exchange has several times considered permitting the odd-lot firms to effect executions in their offices, using the same sort of procedure. This would relieve some congestion on the floor. Because averages are not facts and many variables affect transmission, execution, and reporting, however, the Exchange has concluded that the odd-lot customer is benefited by execution on the floor of the Exchange itself. This, they believe, is particularly significant in times of rapidly changing prices and rapid turnover of shares.

14

Odd-Lot Dealers and the Odd-Lot Public

This chapter would appear to combine two entirely distinct subjects, since odd-lot dealers and the odd-lot public at no time have a direct contract with each other. All relationships between the two are negotiated by the commission firms which serve the public. On the other hand, the operations of both the dealers and the public are so intertwined in the market that one cannot be explained without constant reference to the other. When the public buys, the odd-lot dealer must sell; when the public sells, the odd-lot dealer must buy. There is thus a very logical reason for considering the two subjects as merely parts of one broad topic.

DEVELOPMENT OF THE ODD-LOT BUSINESS

Early History. Before the Civil War trading on the New York Stock Exchange was conducted on a "call" basis. The presiding officers of the Exchange, during trading hours, would call out the names of stocks. These would be bought and sold on the basis of bids and offers.

The first real trading in odd-lots after establishment of round-lot practices was apparently on a negotiated basis between the buying and selling broker. This gave way to a method of trading on the basis of bid and offer which gave the market a great breadth, although it still failed to meet the needs of the odd-lot public. The third and final step in developing the business was to execute sales on the basis of market prices as reported on the stock ticker, which was introduced in 1867. The first firm to operate in odd-lots began about 1871 on an over-the-counter basis. Three years later the firm of Jacquelin and De Coppet Brothers started to make a market in odd-lots on the floor of the Exchange. When the practice of doing business on a bid and offer basis was abandoned for the procedure of basing the price of execution on the next sale in the round-lot market, subject to a standardized differential charge, the odd-lot business increased rapidly in popularity.

A number of firm names appeared and disappeared in the history of the business. From 1917 to 1941 there were three large firms. In the latter year two firms combined to make the present firm of Carlisle and Jacquelin. The other firm, De Coppet and Doremus, has been operating continuously under the name since 1891.

Present System. The present odd-lot business on the New York Stock Exchange is handled by three distinct groups of dealers. In the active market, which comprises Posts 1 to 18, there are the two big odd-lot firms mentioned—De Coppet and Doremus, and Carlisle and Jacquelin. In recent years these two firms have done over 99 per cent of the business at the active posts. In addition to these two firms, there are two specialists who do a small amount of business. One handles odd-lots in about 55 stocks, the other in about 10. The odd-lot business at Post 30 is handled by two specialists who operate at that location and who handle both round- and odd-lots.[1]

Importance of the Odd-Lot Business. The odd-lot business forms a highly important part of the stock market. The ratio of total odd-lot purchases and sales to total round-lot purchases and sales for selected years is shown in Table 14–1.

Over a period of four decades, the ratio of odd-lot trading to round-lot trading has ranged from a low of 9.0 per cent in 1958 to a high of 16.1 per cent in 1937. In the ten-year period, 1952–1961, the ratio has averaged 10.2 per cent. In summary, in recent years for every 100 shares sold in the round-lot market there have been about 10 shares sold in the odd-lot market.

Several explanations have been offered as to why the odd-lot volume is not quite as important on a relative basis as it was a number of years ago. One is that the rise of mutual funds has diverted investment funds into that type of purchase and away from odd-lots. Another is that stock splits have enabled investors to buy round-lots instead of odd-lots because of reduced prices. The third explanation is that the odd-lot business on smaller exchanges has increased at the expense of the New York Stock Exchange. There are no adequate figures to prove or disprove this theory.

[1] The positions of the posts on the floor are shown in Figure 10–1.

Table 14–1. Ratio of Odd-Lot Business to the Round-Lot Market on the New York Stock Exchange, Selected Years

Year	Ratio of Odd-Lot Purchases and Sales to Round-Lot Purchases and Sales
1961	10.1%
1960	10.9
1959	10.8
1958	9.0
1957	10.9
1956	10.6
1954	9.2
1952	11.0
1950	9.3
1946	13.8
1937	16.1
1932	15.1
1929	13.2
1925	11.4
1920	14.3

Source: New York Stock Exchange, *Fact Book, 1962*

For those who wish to compare the odd-lot volume of sales on the Exchange with the round-lot sales, it should be always be remembered that the round-lot volume should be doubled before calculation of the ratio. In the round-lot market only sales are reported; yet, obviously, for every sale there is also a purchase. In the odd-lot market, purchases and sales are reported separately. Thus, total purchases and sales in one market should be compared only with total purchases and sales in the other market.

The Odd-Lot Specialists. Since the remainder of the chapter is devoted to the operations of the two large odd-lot firms, mention is made at this point of the two odd-lot specialists in the active market. As indicated before, one handles 55 stocks and the other about 10 on an odd-lot basis. They are specialists in 100-share-unit stocks as well. They furnish only limited competition to the two big firms.

OPERATION OF THE ODD-LOT FIRMS

Dealer Basis. An outstanding characteristic of the odd-lot system is that the odd-lot firms operate solely on a dealer and never on a commission basis. In other words, they always buy the stock offered to them by the commission firms with which they deal and sell to the commission houses the stock from their own inventories. They receive no commission; they add a differential to the round-lot price. They are constantly delivering stock to commission firms and receiving stock and must carry the risk of such operations.

The odd-lot dealer's compensation, as just indicated, comes from the differential, which is ⅛ point for stock selling under $40 per share and ¼ point for those selling at $40 or more usually.[2] As was explained in the previous chapter, for market orders to buy, these differentials are added to the round-lot effective price, and for selling orders they are subtracted from the round-lot effective price. For example, on a purchase of 25 shares of XYZ on a market order, the customer would pay 50¼ if the effective sale in the round-lot market were 50. Again, on a sale of 10 shares on a market order, the customer would receive only 29⅞ if the effective sale in the round-lot market were 30.

These differentials are the only source of income from public trading for the odd-lot dealer. They are not profits. The dealer must carry the risk of inventory gains or losses and cover the costs of his operations as well. The differential is a pricing mechanism.

An odd-lot dealer may purchase stock from an odd-lot public customer at 50. Whether he can liquidate it in the round-lot market or to another odd-lot public customer at 50¼ is another matter. He may or he may not. In some cases he may take an actual loss; in others he may make more than than the ¼ point. Similarly, when an odd-lot dealer sells stock to a customer at 25⅛, he has no assurance that he can buy the stock in the round-lot market at 25. Hence, the differentials are revenues contributing to, but not in themselves assurance of, profitable operation.

Customers. The only customer that the two odd-lot firms have are those commission firms that channel odd-lot business to them. In 1961 there were about 215 such firms. These 215 firms also represented about 350 other commission firms that did not clear directly with the two odd-lot houses.

The firms that clear odd-lot orders directly through the two odd-lot firms divide their business between the two houses in different ways. There is vigorous and continuous competition between the two houses. It is seen in the extent and variety of services offered and the quality of service rendered by each. This competition has benefited the member firms and their customers in the odd-lot market. Some firms are permanent customers of one or the other house and do not shift their business; these are in the minority. Most firms rotate business between the two odd-lot houses. A common procedure is to deal with one firm for six months and with the other for the next six months. Other procedures

[2] Some exceptions to this general statement about odd-lot differentials were given in Chapter 13, pp. 238–9.

are used. The clearing members see different means for benefit from the competition between the odd-lot houses.

Office Procedure. The office personnel of each firm is chiefly occupied with the routine work of processing some 12,500 orders which may be received per day, answering calls from commission firms, making adjustments, clearing stocks, recording ticker reports, and doing the usual accounting work of a large security house.

Each firm must conduct its own clearing operations. In the round-lot market the clearing firms offset purchases against sales of stock and deliver or receive balances through the Stock Clearing Corporation. In the odd-lot business each of the two firms must be its own clearing house and determine net balances to be delivered to and received from each of the clearing members.

The so-called "order department" plays an important part in the operation of the odd-lot firm. The department is somewhat misnamed since it does not handle orders. Its function is to handle many thousands of calls per day from commission firms, who may request information on particular orders, ask for adjustments, want reports on sales, or ask for the latest data on ticker prices.

The firms operate the largest Teleregister boards in the security business. These electric quotation boards carry ticker reports for all stocks at the eighteen active posts. This means that the boards carry nearly 1,344 stocks, the total number in which the two firms make a market. In addition, prices for several "when issued" stocks and rights are displayed. There is competition between the two firms in every stock at present, although this was not always true in the past, when certain stocks were "syndicated" or divided between the two houses.

The odd-lot dealers keep elaborate records of all stock sales reported by the ticker in order to answer the large number of inquiries on orders. In order to handle the work effectively, a so-called "deleted tape" is used. The principal of the deleted tape is to divide the sales reports coming from the floor of the Exchange by posts. A firm employee will scan a tape showing transactions at six posts only and will record whatever sales data are required for the 70 or more stocks at each post assigned to him. The deleted tape is fed out of a ticker which reports from six posts. The tape is time-stamped each minute.

The purpose of the time stamp is to enable the firm to check the time at which particular round-lot sales appear on the tape. These effective sales govern the price at which the odd-lot orders are executed. In case of a check on the execution of any order, the deleted tape record is useful in determining at what time and at what price the effective round-lot sale took place. It would appear that this is an exact check, but it is not, as everyone connected with the odd-lot business well knows. The tape is stamped every sixty-seconds; it does not indicate the particular time at which sales took place within the minute. If several sales of a given stock took place within the minute, it would be difficult to determine the exact sale that made effective the odd-lot order. Finally, the tape could not indicate with any high degree of accuracy just when the round-lot sale actually took place on the floor. As explained in Chapter 8, the tape is always from thirty seconds to several minutes behind floor transaction, even when it is "up" or on time. The time stamp may indicate that the effective sale appeared on the tape between 10:41 and 10:42. Actually, it may have taken place on the floor anywhere between 10:39 and 10:41. If a number of sales took place between 10:39 and 10:42, it would be very difficult in many cases to identify the effective sale. Time-stamping can be very accurate in terms of the time a sale is reported and yet provide no more than an approximation for the time of execution.

Regular Firm Members. The two odd-lot houses have two types of stock exchange members: partners and associate brokers. In 1962 one firm had twenty-six partners of whom eleven had seats on the Exchange. The other firm had twenty-two partners of whom eleven had seats on the Exchange. Most of the members with seats work full time on the floor of the Exchange as supervising partners. They advise the associate brokers of major decisions, aid the firm in keeping within its lines, keep the home office advised of the market, and relieve associate brokers if necessary. They may or may not make major decisions as to the size of the investment in stocks held by the firm. As a general rule, they do not execute odd-lot orders as a regular part of their work.

Associate Brokers. Each firm has a large number of associate brokers. These are floor brokers, who work on a permanent arrangement with the firm. Many of them have been with the firm for years. They own their own seats but work exclusively for the odd-lot firm with which they are affiliated. They receive commissions on all odd-lot orders they execute but have no financial interest in the profit or loss of the odd-lot firm. The associate brokers are agents for the firms.

The number varies from time to time. In 1950 the number averaged forty-two per firm; in 1962 it was forty-nine. Two brokers customarily are assigned to each active post. If there is great activity at a particular post, three might be assigned. Some of the brokers or partners travel from post to post to aid in execution of orders where the business is particularly active at the moment.

The associate broker performs a very useful service for the odd-lot firm. He executes the orders of the firm as its representative. The odd-lot house does not need as heavy an investment in seats as would be necessary if it were required to own enough seats to transact all of its business on the floor. It may finance the purchase of seats by associate brokers in order to service orders properly.

Associate brokers are paid a commission on each order that they execute for the firm. The rate is 1⅛ cents for each share selling at less than $10 and 2¼ cents for each share selling at $10 or more.

An associate broker has three important functions. First, he fixes the price of execution for all orders on the order slips transmitted to him by the commission houses. Second, he effects the execution of round-lot orders necessary for inventory control. Whenever the firm has received on balance too much stock, he liquidates the excess; if the firm is short stock on balance, he buys. Third, he keeps the firm within its "basis" or "line" (page 262); in other words, he keeps the inventory of stock under control.

Order Execution. The steps in processing an odd-lot order are shown in the diagram of Figure 14–1. In the next two paragraphs numbers in parentheses refer to the numbers on that diagram.

Odd-lot orders to buy or sell (1) originally come from the odd-lot public and are received (2) by the various commission firms in their offices. The order is then wired (3) to the firm's order room in New York; transmission is usually by teletype. An order clerk then calls (5) the commission firm's telephone clerk on the floor of the Exchange. The telephone clerk is located on the edge of the trading floor in a booth. The order is written on a slip and inserted in a plastic carrier or cylinder to be transmitted (6) by pneumatic tube to the particular trading post where the stock is handled.

A post tube attendant takes the order when it reaches the post, time-stamps it, and puts it on a clip (8) reserved for the associate broker of the firm who will fill it. The associate broker then removes the slip and waits for the effective round-lot sale. This may be the very next sale in the case of market orders, or it may be a later sale in the case of limit, stop, and short sale orders. As soon as the effective sale takes place, the broker notes (9) the price of execution and writes out a report for the commission firm. The report is again time-stamped and sent back (10–11) by the same means as it was transmitted; namely, the tube system. The telephone clerk then calls back (12) to the New York office and reports execution. The New York office relays (13–17) the information on the order to the office of origination and, thence, to the customer.

The original order slips after execution are sent back to the offices of the odd-lot firms. They are carefully segregated by posts and inserted in small bags; these are picked up at regular periods, varying from thirty to sixty minutes, by messenger who carry them from the Stock Exchange

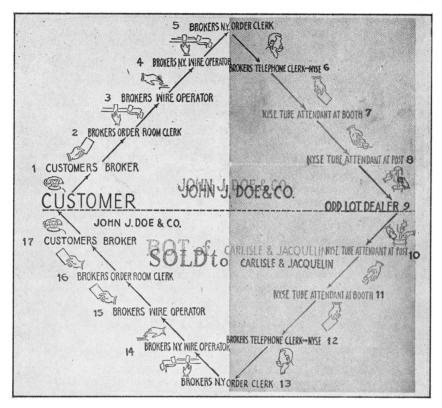

Fig. 14–1. Steps in handling an odd-lot order.

Source: Carlisle & Jacquelin

to the offices of the odd-lot firm. The orders then undergo immediate processing, which continues until the last order of the day is out of the way.

Problem of Fraud. The odd-lot customer may sometimes ask the question, "Are my orders honestly executed?" This question arises from the fact that the dealer fixes the price of the order on the basis of an effective round-lot sale. May not the dealer try to increase his usual ⅛-point differential by choosing only the most favorable effective sales; e.g., the high ones on buy orders and the low ones on sell orders? May not the dealer deliberately put down on the order slip a price unfavorable to the customer in order to increase the profit to the odd-lot firm?

The question, of course, is a fair one since the possibility of fraud exists in all kinds of business, and the security market is no exception. However, fraud as a factor in the execution of odd-lot orders probably can be disregarded entirely. Errors arise in the execution of such orders, and a number of adjustments are made daily between the commission firms and the odd-lot houses, but there has been no evidence of fraud.

The customers of an odd-lot house are commission firms that clear odd-lots with it. Suspicion that a particular odd-lot house was attempting fraud in the execution of orders would result quickly in the switching of business to the other firm. Even with the most meticulous handling of orders, many customers question price and there are continuous checks on the activities and accuracy of execution of an odd-lot firm.

An odd-lot order goes through a great many hands from the time it is entered until it is completed. That a considerable amount of checking does take place is indicated by the fact that an order room of an odd-lot firm may receive 12,000 to 25,000 requests a day for information; several hundred of these result in claims and requests for adjustment.

New York Stock Exchange and the SEC also maintains staffs for the purpose of investigating fraud in the relations between customers and brokers and dealers. Their function is to investigate such relations, not only on the complaint of customers, but on their own initiative.

BASIS AND INVENTORY

Terminology. Each firm establishes what is usually called a "basis" or "line" for each issue of stock it deals in. This is the limit that the firm sets on the long or short position it will accept in a given stock issue before making a round-lot sale or purchase in the market.

The firm's "inventory" or "position" is the actual amount of shares in a given issue that the firm is long or short at a particular moment.

Basis or Line. An odd-lot house is constantly receiving stock from commission firms and also delivering stock to them. There is an ebb and flow. For a while a firm may receive much stock on balance as the odd-lot public sells a particular stock. The flow may then reverse itself; the odd-lot house must deliver on balance as the public begins to buy more than it sells. Since the public at times is buying on balance and at other times selling on balance, it is evident that, to some extent at least, the flow of stock into and out of an odd-lot firm would tend to equalize itself.

The question now arises: How much stock is it safe and practical for a firm to go long or short before making a round-lot sale or purchase in the market? Should it accumulate 50, 100, 1,000, or 10,000 shares before it begins selling? If the pubic is buying on balance, how many shares short should the firm allow itself to become before it begins buying in the round-lot market? The answer is the basis or line.

Each odd-lot firm makes a market in each of the approximately 1,344 stocks traded in at the eighteen active posts. This means that each firm must determine a basis or line for each of these stocks at all times. The basis is expressed in terms of a position, long or short, the firm will take if necessary. It may be expressed as "two-two," meaning that the firm will go 200 shares long or short in that stock. It may be "five-five," indicating that 500 shares either way is the maximum number of shares allowed. A "one-one" basis, of course, means 100 shares either way. Sometimes this is called a "zero basis" in that the firm attempts to keep its inventory at the lowest possible amount at all times.

The determination of the basis or line requires the highest management skill in the firm. Errors can be very expensive and may result in significant losses on the inventory. The factors that determine the basis are complex. The market is the dominant factor at all times. A very active stock in which the public is constantly buying and selling a large number of shares will require a larger basis than one with very little activity. Hence, volume is always a primary consideration. It is expensive to carry a large inventory in high-priced issues. Volatility is important. A very erratic issue, subject to extreme price fluctuations, will receive a small basis because of the inherent danger of large inventories. The trend of the market has some weight, although not so much as might be supposed. A firm naturally would not care to be caught with a heavy inventory in a rapidly declining market; yet if the odd-lot public were buying heavily, as is often the case in such markets, the firm would need to be able to supply the stock.

The question may be asked: Do firms tend to broaden or shorten lines because of a rising or falling market? The answer is: Yes. The purpose is not to make speculative profits but to protect the firm against heavy losses. The lines may be changed as often as daily if there is a sharp rise or decline in the market. During a rising market there is a tendency to accumulate stock and increase the size of lines. If the market is falling, however, the firm tends to hold down lines to a minimum to avoid an excessive inventory or position.

Who determines the basis for an odd-lot firm? The primary responsibility rests with certain partners who are given this job by the firm. They may operate in the home office or they may work on the Exchange floor. It is perhaps the heaviest responsibility in the management of the odd-lot firm.

Let us suppose that the basis for a given stock is "one-one." It is evident in this case that the firm is anxious to hold down its inventory in that stock to the lowest possible limit. Hence, it does not want to go long or short more than 100 shares at any one time. Let us assume that during a given day a firm is buying stock on balance from the odd-lot public. During the day the inventory rises to 25, 50, 65, 85, 105, 125 shares. At what point under a "one-one" line would the firm have sold

100 shares in the round-lot market? No precise answer is possible. A decision might be made to sell at 65, 85, 105, or even 125 shares. Unless the market were very strong, however, there would probably be little delay once the inventory reached 100 shares.

In case of a line of more than "one-one," the situation is similar. Let us imagine that on a given stock the basis is "five-five." In this instance the firm would probably take no action unless the inventory was close to 500 shares either long or short. For example, suppose that the firm had accumulated a long inventory of 525 shares. Since this is more than the theoretical limit of 500 shares, the associate broker would immediately sell 100 shares in the round-lot market to get the inventory back within the line. He would not accumulate more stock unless a regular partner so decided. It should be observed here that the asociate member does not sell all the long inventory, but only enough to get back into the correct basis. After selling 100 shares the firm is only 425 shares long, and no further round-lot purchases or sales are necessary until the "five-five" line is again exceeded.

Examples of Lines. As already indicated, lines are carried for each of the 1,344 active stocks. The largest line carried today by one house is "five-five." Only such favorites of the odd-lot public as American Telephone and Telegraph, General Motors, Standard Oil Company (New Jersey), General Electric, Radio Corporation of America, du Pont, United States Steel, New York Central, and similar issues come in this category. Forty to 50 stocks usually fall into this classification. There are no "four-four" lines; just why, no one seems to know. The "three-three" lines include stocks somewhat less popular with the odd-lot public than those in the "five-five" lines. The number may range from as low as 30 to as high as 100. In the "two-two" lines the number carried by this firm may range from 200 to 250. All other stocks fall in the "one-one" lines.

The other firm has dropped fixed bases. They have a policy of keeping small positions rigidly and continuously supervised by the floor partners of the firm. Supervision extends not only to the aggregate money invested in the market as a whole but to individual issues. The amounts they are willing to commit are subject to change and are reviewed daily by the members of the firm's Floor Committee.

A striking change in the odd-lot management policy over the years is observed in the size of lines. In the 1920's a firm might carry lines as large as 1,000 to 3,000 shares. Such wide limits are no longer in use.

Inventories and Positions. An inventory or position is carried for each stock except at those unusual times when a firm may have no long or short position. On General Motors a firm may be short 225 shares; on General Electric it may be long 40 shares; on Radio Corporation of

America it may be long 455 shares; on American Telephone and Telegraph it may be short 85 shares at any given time.

Added together, these inventories of 1,344 stocks run into immense figures. A firm might have a gross long position of 50,000 shares in certain stocks at the same time that it has a gross short position of 35,000 shares in other stocks. Its net long position in this instance would be 15,000 shares. As a rule, firms are more likely to have net long positions than to have net short positions. The average net long position is usually less than 50,000 shares.

The present-day policy of the odd-lot firms is to keep far smaller positions than in the boom days of the 1920's or in the depression of the 1930's. At one time in the 1930's one firm had an inventory of 20,000 shares of United States Steel common. Even as late as 1937 inventories of 3,000 to 5,000 shares in a single market leader were not uncommon. In July, 1929, the combined net positions of the three firms in operation at that time reached 500,000 shares.[3]

Reasons for Inventories. Two reasons dictate the use of inventories in excess of 100 shares, which is the smallest round-lot order that can be executed at the eighteen active posts except for the few 10-share-unit stocks. In the first place, the ebb and flow of public buying and selling tends to cancel out. For a while the public buys on balance; then it reverses itself and sells. The odd-lot house tends to go short as the public buys and long as the public sells. To a large extent, purchases and sales do balance each other; this makes use of the round-lot market unnecessary. Hardy, in an extensive study based on the operations of the odd-lot market from 1920 to 1938, believed that only 20 per cent of the purchases and sales of the firms had to be offset by sales and purchases in the round-lot market.[4] The percentage today is higher, probably ranging between 30 and 35 per cent.

The second reason for the use of inventory is that it is cheaper for the odd-lot firm to sell purchased stock back to the odd-lot public than to the round-lot market or vice versa. On 100 shares sold out of inventory to the odd-lot public, the odd-lot dealer pays no transfer taxes. He pays no clearing fee to the Stock Clearing Corporation. The floor brokerage commission for selling the 100 shares is saved. This might average $3.85. Hence, it is less expensive to sell to the odd-lot public than to the round-lot market. The additional costs would have to come out of the odd-lot dealer's differential. The odd-lot dealer, of course, has his expenses in dealing with the odd-lot public, but they are less than if he were to deal more extensively in the round-lot market.

[3] C. O. Hardy, *Odd-Lot Trading on the New York Stock Exchange* (Washington, D.C.: The Brookings Institution, 1939), p. 77.
[4] *Ibid.*, p. 30.

Inventory Risk. It is apparent that in carrying a large inventory an odd-lot dealer must take a substantial risk because of market fluctuation. Inventory risk, however, is an assumed and calculated risk, which must be taken by such firms if they are to stay in business and compete for orders. It can be reduced by keeping minimum lines, which is done in the big majority of issues, but it cannot be eliminated.

The odd-lot firms do not speculate on the trend of the market in the strict sense of the word, but they do tend to allow inventories to expand somewhat in a rising market and to contract in a falling market. Nevertheless, inventories usually are kept as low as feasible for service of the buying and selling needs of the odd-lot public.

It has never been any more possible to determine how much profit or loss in odd-lot firm operations is attributable to price differentials and to inventory appreciation or depreciation separately than it is for any other kind of trading business.[5] The price differential is not a realized profit; it is merely a pricing device. If a firm were to buy 100 shares from four customers at 50 and sell 100 later in the round-lot market at 50½, what then is the measure of firm profit?

Effect on Market. Do the inventories of the odd-lot houses have an effect on the market? In the past the question has been the subject of much controversy. Simpson and Ballinger, in an extensive study of the subject some years ago, were critical of the inventory policies of the odd-lot firms. Their conclusion was that "odd-lot dealers tend to trade with the market and therefore widen the amplitude of price fluctuations in the same manner, though to a much smaller extent, than do floor traders."[6] Hardy, later studying the problem, not only criticized their technique but arrived at his own conclusion that in the markets of 1928–31 "the influence of the changes in dealer inventories on the month-to-month changes of price must have been very trivial."[7] Certainly the figures for recent years support Hardy.

Present-day inventories carried by the two odd-lot houses are so small relatively that they cannot have much effect on market changes. Let us assume that the two firms on a given day have a net long position of 100,000 shares. On a typical day's trading of 4 million shares, this entire position could be liquidated in eight minutes. Even if this highly unlikely operation were to take place, the effect on a day's trading would be small.

[5] *Ibid.*, p. 54.
[6] Kemper Simpson and Willis J. Ballinger, *The Feasibility and Advisability of the Complete Separation of the Functions of Dealer and Broker* (mimeographed report), SEC, 1936.
[7] Hardy, *op. cit.*, p. 79.

THE ODD-LOT PUBLIC

Volume of Orders. The odd-lot business is of substantial significance to commission firms on the New York Stock Exchange. In an extensive study of the odd-lot public in 1953, the Exchange found that the odd-lot customers of commission firms accounted for 33 per cent of all orders placed with these firms.[8] These orders represented 8 per cent of the shares purchased and 12 per cent of the money value of such purchases. The number of purchase orders was in excess of 1,331,000. Including sales, the number of transactions was undoubtedly in excess of 2 million.

Size of Orders. The odd-lot public buys and sells all sized lots from 1 share on up. There are many orders for 1, 2, 3, 4, and 5 shares. The average in 1960 was 25.4 shares. There are rather marked preferences for such round figures as 10-, 20-, and 50-share lots. In 1960 the average order was $1,235, the average price per stock being $48.65.

Type of Stocks. The general opinion of dealers in the odd-lot business is that the odd-lot public deals in very much the same stocks as does the round-lot customer, and for about the same reasons. The opinion, once held, that the odd-lot public particularly favored the low-priced stock does not seem to have been prevalent in recent years. In fact, there is evidence that the odd-lot public buys stocks as high-priced as or higher-priced than does the round-lot customer. It has also shown a distinct preference for investment grade securities. Certain stocks are nearly always "one way short," meaning that the public, as a rule, is buying for investment more shares than it liquidates. Such a stock is International Business Machines Corporation common stock, which has an enormous odd-lot market; it is larger than its round-lot market.

The most popular stocks with odd-lot investors are the highly popular "blue chips," such as are found in the better-known industrial averages. These stocks are usually near the top of the list of institutional favorites. The "five-five" lines, just discussed, are invariably composed of high-grade investment issues, which are equally popular with round-lot buyers and financial institutions.

Type of Orders. A majority of odd-lot orders are buy orders. The customers typically buy on balance, meaning that they buy more stock than they sell. This fact may reflect accumulation of stock in odd-lots and subsequent sales by the owners of round-lots and the effect of stock splits or dividends that turn odd-lot quantities into round-lot quantities by their occurrence. Day orders exceed G.T.C. or open orders by a wide margin. Ten to 15 per cent of the total is a reasonable estimate of the

[8] *The Exchange,* February, 1954, p. 1.

latter. Market orders are more popular than limit orders. The latter probably range from 20 to 40 per cent of total orders, with 50 per cent as the absolute maximum. Although there are many other kinds of odd-lot orders available, such as stop orders, buying and selling on the bid and offer, on the opening, stop and limit, with or without sale, immediate or cancel, and the basis market, there seems to be little use made of them. Stop orders tend to become important in periods of market correction.

Margin Buying and Short Selling. Neither margin buying nor short selling are as popular with the odd-lot customer as with the round-lot customer. Short selling is a practice little used by the odd-lot public.

Customers with low incomes do little margin buying. In an analysis of public transactions in September, 1961, the New York Stock Exchange found that customers with incomes of less than $5,000 did 80 per cent of their buying for cash and 20 per cent on margin.[9] For all public individual transactions the ratios were 68 and 32 per cent. Odd-lot buying is often done by buyers in income groups of $5,000 or more.

Length of Transactions. The odd-lot customer appears to have changed his buying and selling habits over a period of time. Hardy, in examining the period from 1920 to 1939, concluded that 80 per cent of the volume handled by the odd-lot houses came from customers who turned over their stock within a month.[10] The New York Stock Exchange, however, in 1955 found that only 13 per cent of the small investors turned over their stock within a month, while 31 per cent did so from one to six months and 56 per cent carried the stock for more than six months.[11] This would seem to indicate that today's small customer is becoming less of a trader and more of an investor than was formerly the case. The very small odd-lot customer is somewhat less likely to be a short-term trader than the average trader. As just indicated, his percentage of stock turned over within a month was 13 per cent; that for all public individual customers is about 18 per cent.

On-Balance Buying. The odd-lot public typically buys on balance. This is clearly shown by Table 14–2, which tabulates the purchases and sales data for the odd-lot market by decades since 1920 and the years 1960 and 1961. It will be noted that in each of the periods the public bought more stock in odd-lots than it sold. The average for the four decades was 8 per cent. For the entire period, 42 years, the public bought on balance 185 million more shares in odd-lots than it sold.

---

[9] New York Stock Exchange, *Eleventh Public Transaction Study, September 13, 1961,* pp. 3, 5, 9.

[10] Hardy, *op. cit.,* p. 65.

[11] New York Stock Exchange, *Stock Market Activity—A Study of Public Transactions in the Nation's Market Place on June 8 and June 15, 1955,* p. 4.

Table 14–2. Purchases and Sales of Odd-Lot Customers Made Through Odd-Lot Dealers on the New York Stock Exchange, 1920–61

| | Millions of Shares | | | Ratio of |
Period	Purchases by Odd-Lot Public	Sales by Odd-Lot Public	Net Balances	Purchases to Sales
1920–29	612	579	33	106%
1930–39	693	651	42	106
1940–49	323	295	28	109
1950–59	595	522	73	114
1960	87	78	9	111
1961	107	107	0	100
42 years	2,417	2,232	185	108%

Source: New York Stock Exchange, *Fact Book, 1962.*

Although the average annual balance of purchases over sales was 4½ million shares, this was little more than one day's trading in 1961.

An examination of Table 14–3 will throw some light on the investing and trading habits of the odd-lot public. It will be noticed that the public bought more shares than it sold in 33 years out of the 42. How well timed was this buying? Does it confirm the commonplace saying in Wall Street that used to be heard so often, "The public is always wrong!" There is no question but that the odd-lot public makes many mistakes in its buying if the action is tested on a year-to-year basis. In 1929 it bought on balance 15,486,000 shares. This was the year of the big crash. In November, 1929, shortly after the October decline, the odd-lot public was accumulating 50 per cent more shares than it was selling. It ended up the year with many more shares than it started with—certainly no great indication of trading skill.

During 1930 and 1931 stock prices were deteriorating steadily in value, yet the odd-lot public was buying heavily on balance. In fact, during 1931, when there seemed to be no support for prices and short selling reached an all-time high, the odd-lot public bought more shares on balance than at any time in history. This represented the zenith in bad judgment.

In 1937 there was a very sharp liquidation in the stock market, yet on-balance buying was very high, being 11.8 million shares. During that year *The New York Times* 50-stock average dropped nearly 51 points.

Prices fell in both 1940 and 1941. In the former year the public bought on balance and in the latter it sold. The year 1942 was a wonderful year to buy stocks, since it was the beginning of the 1942 to 1946 bull market. The public, however, sold on balance in that year. It

Table 14–3. Net On-Balance Buying and On-Balance Selling of the Odd-Lot Public on the New York Stock Exchange, 1920–60

Year	Thousands of Shares		Change in *New York Times* 50-Stock Average	
	Bought by Public	Sold by Public	Plus	Minus
1920	5,122			21.73
1921	4,252		.54	
1922	1,697		18.03	
1923	1,664			2.38
1924		772	22.57	
1925		749	30.74	
1926	801		44.50	
1927	1,747		42.43	
1928	3,158		48.56	
1929	15,463			24.12
1930	13,352			61.60
1931	15,487			72.45
1932	4,102			16.74
1933		134	30.05	
1934		1,078		.95
1935		4,384	26.34	
1936	338		23.81	
1937	11,834			50.76
1938	1,396		22.51	
1939	1,367		1.49	
1940	1,483			16.18
1941		1,287		15.69
1942		199	4.17	
1943	2,306		10.18	
1944	2,010		13.93	
1945	5,855		27.77	
1946	10,707			14.57
1947	3,225			1.25
1948	3,147			3.67
1949	622		19.09	
1950	708		24.85	
1951	7,433		17.59	
1952	6,298		19.89	
1953	3,478			17.48
1954		633	93.23	
1955	8,378		61.01	
1956	14,296		1.92	
1957	14,933			67.37
1958	3,668		98.55	
1959	14,191		47.13	
1960	9,257			68.56
1961		543	59.25	

Sources: New York Stock Exchange, *Fact Book, 1962; The New York Times.*

showed good judgment in buying in 1943, 1944, and 1945. In 1946, however, when stocks reached a peak and then collapsed, the public bought very heavily on balance.

One of the best years since World War II to buy stocks was in 1949, which was the year the bull market began. However, the public bought fewer shares on balance than in any postwar year. The year 1951 was not a particularly good year to buy stocks, since stocks had reached a plateau after a sharp 1949–51 climb, yet there was a heavy odd-lot buying movement.

Few years since the end of World War II were as favorable to buying stocks as 1953. Stocks declined during the first three quarters of the year and then began a very sharp ascension, amounting to more than 100 per cent in two years. The public bought fewer shares on balance than in the preceding years.

The year 1957 was not too good a year to buy stocks, since it was the culmination of a price rise that began in 1949 and was momentarily reversed in 1953. Yet, in 1957 the public came into the market and purchased nearly 15 million more shares than it sold. It followed this action by reducing the balance of purchases in 1958, the year of greatest price rise in forty years. It bought in the market decline of 1960 and sold in the rise of 1961.

The odd-lot public by the year-to-year test shows very bad timing in many cases when it sells on balance. It sold on balance during 1924 and 1925 as the 1929 bull market gathered increasing volume. The years 1934 and 1935 were excellent years to buy stocks, since stock prices doubled from 1934 to late 1936, yet the public sold on balance in both 1934 and 1935. The year 1941 was a good year to sell stocks and the odd-lot public did so. But certainly the year 1942 was no time for liquidation, which is exactly what the odd-lot public did. The year 1954 was an extremely unfortunate year to sell stocks on balance and yet there was a heavy liquidation in that year as *The New York Times* 50-stock average rose over 93-points. Premature profit-taking seems a common habit of the odd-lot public. However, one is less sure of the sales made in 1961 and the short selling done in May, 1962.

In short, from these examples and a further examination of Table 14–3, one can draw certain conclusions about the activities of the odd-lot public:

1. The odd-lot public tended to buy heavily on balance near the close of a bull market.
2. It bought heavily on balance after the close of a bull market as stock prices deteriorated.
3. It showed no marked skill in buying on balance at the bottom of a stock cycle.

4. It frequently sold on balance in the early months of a bull market.
5. It engaged in premature profit-taking.

These conclusions would seem to point to the notion that "The public is always wrong!" It buys stock of high quality, but its timing is poor. On the other hand, little is known about how long an odd-lot buyer holds stock. The year-to-year test may mislead. Buying stock in 1931 and selling stock in 1961 may appear unwise when judged by the very near future in these years. It seems less so if stock bought in 1931 was sold in 1961.

Can one use the activities of the odd-lot public as a trading system? Some stock market experts place considerable reliance upon these activities.[12] Others such as Hardy, however, have stated their belief that the correlation between the market and the direction of odd-lot trading has little or no forecasting value.[13]

[12] Garfield A. Drew, *New Methods for Profit in the Stock Market* (Boston: The Metcalf Press, 1954), p. 193.

[13] Hardy, *op. cit.*, p. 62. See also: Marvin L. Krasnansky, "A Look at the Odd-lot Investor," *The Exchange*, XXII (February, 1961), 7–9.

15

The Bond Crowd

Although this book deals primarily with the market for stocks, a brief description of the bond market on the Exchange should be included. This market is an integrated part of the work of the Exchange.

Importance. As of January 2, 1962, there were 1,186 bond issues listed on the New York Stock Exchange. These were grouped in the following manner:

Free Bonds:		
Rails	9	
Industrials	88	97
Cabinet bonds		
Domestic corporations:		
Rails	262	
Industrials	530	792
U. S. Government issues		32
Interntional Bank issues		14
State and city issues		14
Foreign:		
Government, state, and city issues	209	
Corporation issues	28	237
Total issues		1,186

As will be observed, the issues are divided into two main groups, the free bonds and the cabinet bonds. All trading in these issues takes place in the bond trading room, which is off the stock trading floor. In Figure 10–1, page 183, the entrance to this trading room is shown at the upper-right corner. The room itself is shown in Figure 15–1. Its main features are the trading cabinets and telephone booths.

At one time there were a number of so-called "bond crowds" carry‑ing on activity in distinct groups of issues. Today that distinction has

Fig. 15-1. The bond trading room.

largely disappeared. Trading is now carried on in free bonds and cabinet bonds.

Over a long period there has been a substantial decline in the number of bond issues listed on the Exchange. The highest total ever reported was for November 1, 1930, when 1,615 issues were listed. The number fell rather steadily from that date until it reached a low of 888 as of November 1, 1946. Since that time there has been an expansion of the list.

To use January 1 totals only, the highest volume of par and market values listed on the Exchange was on January 1, 1946, when these figures were $138 billion and $143 billion, respectively. The great increase in the debt of the federal government during World War II was responsible, of course. Table 15–1 shows the trend of listing over a thirty-six year period.

Table 15–1. Bond Issues Listed on the New York Stock Exchange, January 1 of Selected Years (values in millions of dollars)

Year	Number of Issues	Par Values	Market Values
1962	1,186	$113.4	$104.6
1961	1,191	116.1	108.3
1960	1,180	120.5	105.4
1955	1,014	106.4	106.5
1950	915	125.4	128.5
1945	1,063	111.1	112.6
1940	1,395	54.1	49.9
1935	1,540	44.8	40.7
1930	1,543	49.1	46.9
1925	1,332	35.5	33.6

Source: New York Stock Exchange, *Fact Book, 1962*, p. 39.

Bond sales have been in considerably lower volume in the last quarter of a century than they were during the 1920's. The volume of $1,636 million reported in 1961 was higher than in any recent year, but was still low compared with that of years ago. At no time from 1918 to 1945 did volume fall this low. During the 1920's an annual volume of close to $3 billion was the rule. The peak year, 1922, showed a volume of $4,133 million.

The daily volume of bond sales shows considerable variation. The high record was on September 6, 1939, at the opening of World War II, when $83.1 million were turned over in five hours. Daily volume during 1961 averaged $6.5 million and ranged from as low as $4.5 million to as high as $10.1 million. The change in yearly bond volume since 1920 is indicated in Table 15–2.

Table 15–2. Bond Sales on the New York Stock Exchange, Selected Years (in millions of dollars)

Year	Reported Bond Volume In Par Values
1961	$1,636
1960	1,346
1955	1,046
1950	1,112
1945	2,262
1940	1,669
1935	3,339
1930	2,720
1925	3,427
1920	3,868

Source: New York Stock Exchange, *Fact Book, 1962,* p. 46.

About 90 per cent of the bond volume on the Exchange in recent years has been concentrated in railroad and other domestic corporate issues, as indicated in Table 15–3. It will be observed from this table that

Table 15–3. Bond Sales on the New York Stock Exchange by Groups, 1957–61 (in millions of dollars of par value)

Group	1957	1958	1959	1960	1961
Railroad, utility and industrial	$1,031	$1,314	$1,517	$1,271	$1,566
Foreign governments	59	68	69	76	70
International Bank	*	*	*	*	*
United States government	*	*	*	*	*
Total	$1,082	$1,382	$1,586	$1,346	$1,636

* Less than ½ million.
Source: *Bank and Quotation Record,* February, 1962.

in 1961, 96 per cent of the bonds were in railroad and other corporate issues, such as industrials and utilities, and 5 per cent in obligations of foreign governments. Most popular among the corporate issues were convertibles. The amount of trading in obligations of the International Bank was small in these years, generally, and non-existent in 1960. Trading in obligations of the United States was very small. During 1961 the total was only $2,000. This would be much less than the average single sale on the over-the-counter market. Because of this fact the large par value figure of listed United States securities is deceptive. The list is inflated by these bonds, which have practically no market on the Exchange.

Some indication of the most frequently traded issues is found in an examination of the 5 most active issues in 1961. Activity in these bonds accounted for $142 million, or about one-twelfth of total bond volume. The issues were as follows:

	Millions
Am. Mch. Cv 4¼s 1981	$ 34
Avco Mf. Cv 5s 1979	29
Brunswick Cv 4½s 1981	29
Kayser Roth Cv 5½s 1980	25
N.Y., N.H. & H. 4s 2007	25
Total	$142

Nine-Bond Rule. Although the totals for listing and trading on the Exchange are substantial, there is concentration of trading in a relatively small number of issues. Daily volume on some days is small in total. Customers' orders might not be executed as effectively in this market as in another. To preserve the fundamental policy of membership use of Exchange trading facilities and still permit the members to give their customers the best possible service, compromise is needed. For many bond issues an efficient over-the-counter market exists. The Exchange has recognized this in the nine-bond rule (Rule 396). Under this rule, orders for ten or more bonds may be executed in the over-the-counter market by members of the Exchange. They need not seek to trade on the Exchange. Orders for nine or fewer bonds, however, are to be sent to the floor for execution. Bids and offers are to be maintained on the floor for at least one hour before execution is sought in another market. If within this time any part of an order can be filled, it shall be. Only the remainder, then, is referred to the alternative marketplace.

Commissions. The minimum commissions, with exceptions noted below, depend on the price of the bond and whether the charge is to a member or non-member. The rates are shown in Table 15–4. The exceptions relate mostly to United States government bonds, bonds of Puerto Rico and the Philippines, bonds of the International Bank, bonds due within six months to five years, and bonds maturing or called for redemption within six months. Rates on these are to be determined by mutual agreement, unless the Exchange sets special rates, as indicated for some in Table 15–4, on any or all of the issues.

For example, as shown in Table 15–4, the commission to a non-member for one bond with a $1,000 par value and selling at 102 would be $2.50. If the non-member were to sell five bonds of this issue, the commission would be five times $2.50, or $12.50. Members deal with each other on lower commissions, of course, than the rates charged non-members.

Table 15–4. Commission Rates on Bonds on the New York Stock Exchange (per $1,000 of principal)

Rates Charged	On Orders for Bonds Selling at			Special Rates on Bonds
	Less than $10	$10 and Above but Under $100	$100 or more	Maturing in 6 Mos. to 5 Yrs.
Non-members and allied members, including joint accounts	$0.75	$1.25	$2.50	$1.25
Members when a principal is not given up	0.50	0.62½	1.25	0.62½
Members when a principal is given up	0.25	0.37½	0.75	0.37½

Source: New York Stock Exchange *Constitution,* Article XV and *Rule* 377.

Free Bonds. The term "free bonds" includes those bonds of American railroads and industrials which enjoy an active market. The term "free crowd" was formerly applied to brokers who dealt in these bonds.

There are, as already indicated, 9 domestic rail issues and 88 domestic industrial issues in this group. There is little difference in the activity between these two classes of bonds. A few years ago there was great activity in reorganized rail issues. This is largely a thing of the past.

Trading is carried on through active, audible bids and offers. The brokers employ a brass ring inserted in the floor; it is eight-sided and is approximately 4 by 6 feet in size. It is clearly visible in Figure 15–1. Whenever a broker wishes to buy or sell free bonds, he goes into the ring and in a loud voice expresses his bid or offer. The order in which an offer is made must be followed strictly, as in the stock market: the number of bonds, the name of the issue, and the price. If the offer is too high, it may be lowered fractionally until some buyer is willing to take them. The response of the buying broker is "Take them."

If a broker wishes to buy a bond, his bid would be expressed in a manner different from that of an offer: the price, the number of bonds, and the name of the bond. A selling broker, ready to do business at that price, would respond "Sold."

It is possible to cross orders in the free crowd in accordance with Rule 76 of the Exchange. If a member has two such orders that can be crossed, he must enter the ring and announce at least twice, in a very audible tone of voice, the full name of the security to be crossed and indicate his intention of crossing the orders. He must offer such security at a price that is higher than his bid by the minimum variation permitted in such security before making a transaction with himself.

Fig. 15–2. Bond quotation card.

Quotation cards are maintained by Exchange clerks; the cards carry practically all bids and offers, as well as current quotations; they also indicate the name of the broker or firm making the bid or offer. A quotation card is shown in the hands of a clerk in Figure 15–2. He is informing a broker on the floor of a bid or offer inscribed thereon.

Cabinet Bonds. All listed bonds other than the 97 free bonds are traded as cabinet bonds. This category on January 1, 1962, included 1,089 issues, two-thirds of which were those of domestic corporations. Other issues included those of the United States government; the International Bank; New York State and cities; foreign governments, states, and cities; and foreign corporations.

Fig. 15–3. Cabinet files in bond trading room.

Trading takes place by using metal filing cabinets, colloquially known as "cans." These cabinets might be described as metal, loose-leaf notebooks. They are clearly observable in the areas around the floor ring in Figure 15–1 and are shown in more detail in Figure 15–3. Each of the files contain orders for bonds of an issue. Each security is given two panels, one for bids and one for offers. The bids for a particular bond are printed in black and filed in order of price and time. Offers are printed in red. There is no precedence on the basis of size.

The bids and offers are written out on standard cards about 3 by 4 inches. Each card has a place for the date of the order, the name of the broker, name of bond, number of bonds, and price. Various colors identify time limits, such as white for day, blue for week, salmon for month, and yellow for G.T.C. By far the biggest number of cards is the G.T.C. order; few week or month orders are used. The cards, filled out, are inserted usually by employees of the Exchange, rarely by brokers. At the execution of the orders, the cards are removed from the cabinets.

Orders are carefully filed in order of their receipt at indicated prices. Bids are filed on the left side of a panel with the highest bids at the top; offers are filed on the right side with the lowest offer on top and graded down. Sales must take place on the basis of time priority. Once the order is filed, it becomes a binding bid or offer until it is removed from the cabinet.

A sample order card, illustrating a bid for ten bonds of XYZ 4s of 1965 at 102½, is given in Figure 15–4.

Fig. 15–4. A bid in the cabinet.

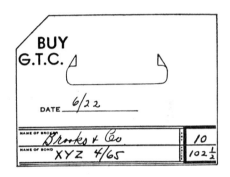

Here is an illustration of the way execution of orders takes place in the cabinet crowd. An order comes to the floor to buy ten bonds of XYZ, just indicated. An employee of the member firm will fill out the proper yellow card and it is then filed in the cabinet for this bond on the bid side of the panel. Some time later another order comes to the floor to sell ten bonds at 102½. The broker responsible for the offer, noticing that the cabinet contains a bid for his bonds at 102½, takes the bid card from the cabinet and steps into the trading ring. He now states in a loud voice his offer to sell ten bonds. If no other broker is willing to buy the bonds at a higher price, the two brokers complete the trade by confirming price and exchanging names.

It should be emphasized that once a member has filed a bid or offer it becomes a binding obligation unless that member withdraws it. If another member removes a card and informs the member who caused it to be inserted or his representative, the bid or offer cannot be withdrawn; the transaction must be consummated.

In order to cancel an order in a cabinet, the card must be physically removed. If the price limit is changed on the order, the date must also be changed at the same time, since the priority of time is affected.

A broker in this crowd may cross orders by following the regulations laid down in Rule 85. He is permitted to do so, provided that the bid or offer that he has accepted has been filed a reasonable time.

16

Delivery and Clearing

Sale of stock is completed by a transfer of title to the buyer at the time he makes payment. As a step to this end, a delivery of stock from the seller's broker to the buyer's broker usually is required. At this time, too, payment by the buyer's broker is made. For New York Stock Exchange transactions delivery is a physical conveyance of stock certificates from one member to another. It is a physical delivery of certificates to an ultimate buyer in a broader sense. The movement of certificates between buyers and sellers can be reduced by a clearing operation. In this operation the total purchases and sales by a member in an issue in a day are matched against one another; only net balances of the stock need then be conveyed to others. Similarly, net balances of cash can be computed and the amounts of payments reduced to these balances. Efficient completion of Exchange transactions requires formality in delivery procedures and is expedited by formality in clearance procedures. In this chapter the discussion will center on rules for delivery and clearing as well as the nature of the clearing process.

DELIVERY

Delivery Time. With the exception of deliveries on "cash" contracts, the time of day by which delivery must be made on each of the several kinds of exchange contracts is noon. A delivery is made if by this time the certificates are at the offices of the Stock Clearing Corporation or the offices of the buying broker. The Stock Clearing Corporation may advance or extend the time under unusual circumstances. The delivery dates are established for the different types of exchange contract by Rules 64–68 of the Exchange.

Cash Contracts. This is the form of contract calling for the most immediate delivery. If a transaction is made for cash at or before 2 P.M., delivery is due before 2:30 P.M. the same day. On transactions made after 2:00 P.M., delivery is due within thirty minutes.

Cash contracts are requested only in emergencies or because of a technical problem in the market. They arise when someone is in urgent need to sell a security or obtain possession of one. Although they occur infrequently, cash contracts may be made for any type of stock or bond. The nature of the contract must be specified clearly in the order, which then is rushed through with all possible speed.

Reasons for the need for speed are, of course, various. Three recurrent technical reasons are the expiration of tax years, rights privileges, and conversion privileges. Cash contracts may be used to register capital losses in the last few days of a tax year. Such contracts may be used also to acquire rights to purchase shares of stock on the last day of the period in which this privilege is offered. Trading in rights of the American Telephone and Telegraph Company common stock, issued in 1961, was suspended on April 14, the last day of the subscription period. Trading on a cash basis took place that day. Similarly, only cash contracts are permitted in convertible securities called for redemption during the last three days that the conversion privilege is in force. The expiration of a conversion privilege may be contractual and, if so, cash trading takes place only on the last day; but the issuer usually calls convertible securities. The $2.98 cumulative, convertible preferred stock of General Precision Equipment Corporation was called for redemption on July 21, 1961. Cash trading in that stock began on July 18 and continued on July 19 and 20.

Regular Way Contracts. This is the standard contract. In the absence of a specific agreement or order to the contrary, this is the contract made on the floor. In practice, nearly all contracts are of this type.

Regular way contracts, with exceptions noted below, intend fourth-day delivery. As the name implies, delivery on these contracts is to be effected by noon on the fourth business day following the day of the transaction. Thus, contracts made on Monday call for delivery on Friday; those made on Wednesday, for the Tuesday of the next week. Saturdays and Sundays are not business days. Nor are holidays. If a holiday fell on a Monday, contracts made the previous Wednesday would call for delivery on the following Wednesday. Adjustment is automatic.

In the market for United States government bonds, regular way delivery is first day. Bonds under such contracts are to be delivered on the next business day by noon. This "next-day" delivery is used also during the last few days of the subscription period for transactions in rights. Next-day delivery starts on the fourth business day preceding the day of expiration of the subscription privilege. This, of course, is the first day on which fourth-day delivery would fail to place rights in the hands of buyers within the subscription period. On the last day of the period, cash contracts are used. Thus, next-day delivery is a feature on regular way contracts for three days in this situation. The number of next-day contracts cleared in 1960 through the Stock Clearing Corporation was 4,155 or $\frac{8}{100}$ of 1 per cent of the total number of contracts cleared. In 1959 the number was 17,457, or $\frac{29}{100}$ of 1 per cent. Next-day delivery is not greatly used.

Odd-lots in the 10-share-unit issues are deliverable on the fourteenth day on regular way contracts. The seller may elect to deliver earlier, but not earlier than the fourth day after the transaction.

Another exception is found, again, in the bond market. Bonds, other than convertible bonds, may be sold for delayed delivery on regular way contracts. If the seller so specifies in closing the transaction on the floor, he may extend the delivery period from the fourth to the seventh calendar day following the day of the transaction. On this "regular way-delayed delivery" contract, he may deliver on the fourth or fifth day, at his option. Such a contract is used by a seller unable to meet the deadline of the regular way contract. It is entered into at the option of the seller. A buyer must accept delayed delivery terms unless he has specified "regular way" when making his bid.

Seller's Option. This form of contract allows the longest delay of deliveries. It permits the seller, at his option, to make delivery up to sixty days from the day of the sale or contract. A seller's option is permitted in all types of securities. For government bonds delivery may not be less than two business days nor more than sixty calendar days. For stocks and convertible bonds it may not be less than five business days nor more than sixty calendar days. For other bonds, it may not be less than eight nor more than sixty calendar days.

Under this delivery contract the seller may make delivery before the end of sixty calendar days by giving notice of his intent to deliver on the next business day. This notice can be given at any time on or after the day when delivery would have been made on a regular way basis. In these deliveries written contracts must be signed and exchanged not later than the second business day following the transactions.

THE NATURE OF THE CLEARING PROCESS

Meaning of Clearing. The clearance process is one whereby sales of securities are offset by purchases and only resulting net balances of shares are delivered or received through a clearing house. In addition, the resulting money transfers among security firms are offset and settled.

Briefly, there are six steps involved in the clearing settlement:

1. A comparison of contracts between buying and selling firms to check their accuracy
2. A summarization for each firm of total sales to and purchases from all other clearing firms
3. A determination for each firm of net balances of stock to be delivered to or received from other clearing firms
4. A determination of the settlement price at which net balances of securities are to be settled
5. Actual delivery of net balances of stock and payment thereof
6. Settlement by each firm with the clearing house of the differences between settlement prices and actual contract prices

Each of these steps will be discussed below under the description of the work of the departments of the clearing house.

Need for Clearance. An overwhelming need for the clearing of securities and resulting money balances has been present in the operation of the stock market since its early years. With several hundred commission firms constantly buying from and selling to each other for their customers, a non-cleared system would mean that for each purchase or sale a separate comparison and confirmation would have to be effected between the parties; all securities would have to be delivered and received; and payment for each would have to be made. Literally thousands of such sales take place between these many firms each day. With the use of a clearing system, it is unnecessary to deliver *all* securities sold to other firms; only net balances need be delivered through the Clearing Corporation. In addition, it is possible for each firm to settle its payments with all other firms with but a single check for all transactions, instead of having literally thousands of checks to pay for or receive payment for individual transactions.

The advantages and economies of the clearance, while obviously great, are somewhat difficult to measure. Perhaps a few key statistics will convey some idea of the magnitude of the over-all operation on the New York Stock Exchange and the resulting benefits to clearing members.

During the year 1960 over 5.4 million contract items representing more than 790 million shares were entered into the daily clearances conducted by the Clearance Department. By means of the balance and allotment technique, it was possible to reduce this to 2.4 million balance orders covering 563 million shares. Thus the number of items was reduced by 55 per cent and the number of shares for delivery between members was reduced by almost 30 per cent.

Also in the year 1960, 4 million security deliveries were made among clearing members and non-member banks through the Central Delivery Department of the Clearing Corporation.

In the Settlement Department deliveries valued at $48 billion were accomplished with a net cash settlement of $7½ billion. Thus, about 85 per cent of the funds otherwise necessary to effect this amount of business was obviated. Since these settlements were made with many fewer checks than would have been necessary if delivery had been direct, the reduction in the need for such checks is obviously much greater than the 85 per cent reduction in the amount of funds.

Similar figures have been characteristic of the process for many years. Meeker indicates that 97.8 per cent of the checks and 81.7 per cent of the total value of contracts was obviated in 1929, the most active year in terms of dollar volume in Exchange history.[1]

Principles of Clearance. The actual operation and technique of clearance are, perhaps, the most complex of all stock exchange operations. A few examples, however, will indicate the nature of the clearing process.

Let us suppose, first, that Firm A sells 1,000 shares of General Motors in a given day to other clearing firms and buys 1,100 shares. The clearing house will order that 100 shares, the net balance, be delivered to Firm A. The firm can take the other 1,000 shares from its own selling customers and deliver them to its buying customers. In the end, every selling customer of the firm will have sold his stock and delivered it, and every buying customer will have received delivery of his stock.

Again, let us suppose that Firm A sells 100 shares to Firm B, and Firm B sells 100 shares to Firm C. Through the clearing process Firm A will be directed to deliver 100 shares to Firm C. Firm B has been relieved of the need for receiving 100 shares from Firm A and for delivering 100 shares to Firm C. Firm A had to deliver 100 shares in any case, and Firm C had to receive 100 shares in any case. The clearing process simply did away with an unnecessary action by Firm B. All purchases and sales were accomplished by the one delivery.

As a third example, assume that Firm A sells 100 shares to Firm B, while Firm B sells 200 shares to Firm C. Firm A will be asked to deliver 100 shares to Firm C and Firm B will do so also. Firm B does not need to receive 100 shares; the other actions were necessary in any case.

These examples illustrate the fundamental principles in clearance of securities. The problem of money settlement is somewhat different.

The Settlement Price. A uniform delivery price, established by the clearing house, is used in the settlement of money payments. This settle-

---

[1] J. E. Meeker, *The Work of the Stock Exchange* (New York: The Ronald Press Co., 1930), p. 646.

ment price is determined each day for each issue traded by dropping any fraction from the closing price. Thus, if an issue traded with a closing price of 51⅝, the settlement price would be 51.

To indicate the use for such a price, let us go back to our first two illustrations and suppose that the stock being cleared is in the range of $60 per share. On the particular day of this transaction, the clearing house fixes a price of 60 for settling all transactions as of that day. In our first example, Firm A has sold 1,000 shares and bought 1,100 shares, making a net balance of 100 shares. When these 100 shares are delivered to Firm A by some other firm under clearing house orders, what should be the price at which Firm A should settle? Obviously, the delivering firm would not likely be the actual seller of 100 shares to Firm A; hence, no contract price could be used to settle for the 100 shares. Here the settlement price comes into operation. The clearing house orders Firm A to pay 60, or $6,000, for the 100 shares net balance when the clearing house computes the clearance cash adjustment.

This price of 60 may or may not correspond with the actual contract prices of Firm A's sales to other firms or with the prices at which stock was bought from other firms; hence, a further adjustment must be made. Let us suppose that the average contract price at which Firm A sold the 1,000 shares was 59, and the average price at which it bought the 1,100 shares was 61. The money now involved is:

Clearance Statement—Firm A	at Clearing Corp.	
	Debit	Credit
Purchase of 1,100 shares at 61	$67,100	
Sale of 1,000 shares at 59		$59,000
Balance to receive: 100 shares at 60		6,000
	67,100	65,000
Debit balance (clearance cash adjustment)		2,100
	$67,100	$67,100

It is evident, therefore, that Firm A has purchased $8,100 more in stock than it has sold, and it owes other firms this amount. On settlement day it was charged $6,000 by the clearing house for the receipt of the 100 shares, as the following figures indicate:

Settlement Statement—Firm A		
	Debit	Credit
Clearance adjustment	$2,100	
Received on balance order	6,000	
Check in payment		$8,100
	$8,100	$8,100

It will be seen that the $2,100 is the difference between the amounts due, computed on the basis of contract prices and the amount computed on the basis of the settlement price. All transactions have now been cleared to everyone's satisfaction, with the clearing house acting as an intermediary. Firm A has sold 1,000 shares for its customers and has obtained from all sources 1,100 shares to deliver to its buying customers. It has sold $59,000 in stock and bought $67,100. The difference of $8,100 is represented by a check for $8,100 payable to the Stock Clearing Corporation.

HISTORY OF STOCK CLEARANCE

Early Attempts at Clearance. The first attempt at stock clearance, anywhere in the world, was apparently at Frankfurt am Main, Germany, in 1867.[2] This experiment was followed by similar plans in most of the leading exchanges of the Continent. In the United States the first successful system was that of the Philadelphia Stock Exchange, which began clearing in 1870. The New York Stock Exchange was not able to introduce a successful clearing plan until 1892. It is interesting to note that the clearing operation for banks was introduced in New York thirty-nine years before that for the stock market.

Repeated attempts were made in New York to establish an informal clearing system before any measure of success was obtained. In 1868 some members of the Exchange organized a voluntary system on a fee basis. It soon collapsed for want of support. Another attempt was made five years later, only to suffer the same fate; these were followed by equally futile plans in 1877, 1879, and 1880.

The delay in establishing a sound clearing system was due to two causes. The early plans were voluntary, and many members were reluctant to enter them because their merits were as yet unproved. Also, it was sheer horror for brokers to consider the effects of the plan upon the secrecy that shrouded transactions in the market at that time. It was feared that the system would reveal business secrets to the clerks in the clearing house to the detriment of the clearing firms. The horror just mentioned was, of course, no monopoly of brokers. A love of secrecy was characteristic of all business operations. Corporations would not reveal their financial status to banks, the public, their customers, the press, their stockholders, or to the Exchange. The stock market, however, paid a heavy price for this gospel of business secrecy.

Since there was no clearing system, it was necessary for each firm, before 1892, to handle all transactions on a cash basis, settling each transaction with a separate payment. This posed a perplexing problem. When a firm delivered 100 shares of stock, it expected payment at the time of delivery by messenger. In many cases the buying firm had in-

---

[2] B. E. Shultz, *The Securities Market* (New York: Harper & Row, Publishers, 1946), p. 281.

sufficient funds to meet all such payments. Of course, once the buying firm secured title to the stock, it could pledge the stock at the bank for enough money to meet the entire amount due; but it could not pledge the stock until it secured title, and it could not secure title until it paid for the stock.

This seeming impasse was broken by two expedients, neither of which pleased the bankers of that day.[3] First, the purchasing broker could secure temporary funds by overcertification of his check. In this process the bank certified the check for more than the broker's balance. The check became, in effect, an unsecured loan, which neither the bank nor the government looked upon with approval. Another method was for the bank to give the broker a "morning loan." This was a loan for a few hours, which was to be secured as soon as the broker received possession of the collateral. In both cases the banks were extending vast amounts of credit to brokers, often without sufficient credit standing. In the end, the bankers threatened to curtail this excessive credit and a clearing system became imperative.

The Clearing House of 1892. The New York Stock Exchange put into operation its first successful clearing system in May, 1892, exactly 100 years after its first formal organization with the famous "Buttonwood Tree Agreement."[4] The system was, at first, strongly opposed by the most conservative members of the Exchange, but its value was soon apparent to all. The new system was compulsory, but involved only 4 railroad stocks. On the first day's clearing, the system obviated $7 million in certified checks and operated with only one error. Opposition, because of the secrecy factor and the possibly extra clerical expense, died down as the system revealed its inherent advantages.

The Clearing House was not a corporation but an informal organization, managed by a committee of five members of the Exchange, appointed by the Board of Governors. In 1920 this informal plan was superseded by the present Stock Clearing Corporation.

THE STOCK CLEARING CORPORATION

The Charter. The clearing of issued and when issued or when distributed round-lots of stocks, rights, and warrants listed on the Exchange is now handled by the Stock Clearing Corporation. It is a wholly owned subsidiary, capitalized at $500,000 and controlled by five directors, including the Chairman and Vice-chairman of the Board of Governors of the New York Stock Exchange and the President and two executive

[3] S. S. Huebner, *The Stock Market* (New York: Appleton-Century-Crofts, Inc., 1934), p. 236.
[4] Meeker, *op. cit.*, p. 637.

officers of the Exchange. These directors appoint the administrative officers of the Corporation.

Clearing Members. The clearing members of the Stock Clearing Corporation consist of those members or member organizations of the Exchange who have applied for membership, have been approved, and have contributed to the Clearing Fund. They are, largely, commission firms that can make extensive use of the clearance system. In 1961 there were 246 such members.

Non-Member Banks. Some large commercial banks and trust companies in New York that are members of the New York Clearing House Association utilize services of the Stock Clearing Corporation. In 1961 eleven such institutions were doing so.

Non-Members. Some other securities houses that are not, or cannot qualify as, members of the Exchange have entered into special agreements with the Clearing Corporation and are permitted a limited use of certain of the facilities of the Corporation. There were sixteen firms in this category in 1961.

The Clearing Fund. Each clearing member must contribute to the Clearing Fund. The amount of the contribution is based on the dollar volume of settlements effected for the clearing member as computed by a complex formula. The minimum contribution is $10,000, with some larger members contributing upwards of $400,000.

The Fund in 1961 was about $8 million. Nearly 60 per cent of the Fund was held by the Clearing Corporation and was invested in United States government securities. The remainder was represented by receivables on clearing members. These receivables were fully secured by United States government and high-quality municipal obligations deposited with the Stock Clearing Corporation. The purpose of the Fund is to protect the Corporation against any losses resulting from the default of a clearing member. In the event of such a default with resultant loss, the loss is first borne by the contribution of the said clearing member. Any excess is charged against the surplus of the Corporation to the extent that this is possible. If the surplus is insufficient, the additional losses are made good from the Clearing Fund and charged pro rata to the members at the time of the transaction that resulted in the loss. All liabilities of the Stock Clearing Corporation are guaranteed by the Clearing Fund. In brief, the Fund is set up to protect the Corporation, members of the Exchange, and the customers of the Exchange against any losses that might grow out of the clearing operation.

Cleared Securities. At the present time all listed stocks, rights, and warrants are cleared. No bonds, however, are cleared.

Clearing Charges. The Stock Clearing Corporation has a complex system of charges based on the amount of service received by members. The charges are made on a cost basis so that the Clearing Corporation may obtain a return of 6 per cent on its capital. Any excess above this return is lessened by reducing the charges to the members. In 1960 total charges were $1.4 million.

Assets and Personnel. At the close of 1961 the assets of the Clearing Corporation were $2.3 million, excluding $8.0 million in special funds. The offices and clearing facilities of the company are at 18 Broad Street in the main Stock Exchange Building. The full-time payroll consists of approximately 120 persons.

THE STOCK CLEARING CORPORATION DEPARTMENTS

List of Departments. The Stock Clearing Corporation is organized into six departments. They are as follows:

1. Distributing Department
2. Central Receiving Department
3. Clearance Department
4. Central Delivery Department
5. Settlement Department
6. Direct Clearance Department

As noted before, the complexity of operation of the clearance system is great. This description can only outline the actual operations. Automatic business machines and magnetic tape computers are now fully in use to carry out the variety and number of steps in accounting and data processing. Involved in the clearance process are some forty forms for the use of the Corporation and the clearing members. Space limitations permit illustration of only a few of the most essential.

Distributing Department. The Distributing Department is the post office of the Corporation. Each of the members and non-members is assigned a locked box. Into this box any material can be placed for distribution, such as tickets, checks, papers, and documents incidental to the ordinary course of business. One very important form, the deliver exchange ticket, must not, under any circumstances, be placed in such boxes, but must be delivered to the Central Receiving Department. The Corporation assumes no responsibility for the form or content of material placed in the boxes nor for any improper removal of the contents of the boxes. Clearing firms and others using the boxes are required to send authorized messengers to this department at frequent intervals to collect material. In this department, as in all others, armed guards at all times prevent the entrance of unauthorized parties.

Central Receiving Department. The Central Receiving Department is charged with the responsibility of handling exchange tickets. On the business day following transactions, every clearing member must report to this department all sell transactions involving a cleared security. These reports are made separately for each transaction on special forms called deliver exchange tickets. Data for about 60 per cent of all transactions were submitted on punched tabulating cards in 1961. The ticket indicates the settlement date of the transaction, the clearing number of the delivering firm, the clearing number of the receiving firm, the official symbol of the security, the number of shares, and the contract value. These tickets or cards are delivered not later than 1:00 P.M. A specimen of a handwritten ticket, involving a hypothetical transaction of 100 shares of XYZ common stock, sold by Jones and Company to (641) Smith and Company, is given in Figure 16–1.

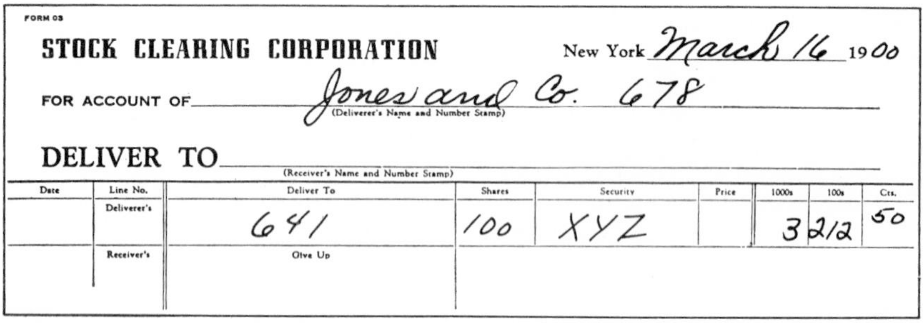
FORM 03

STOCK CLEARING CORPORATION New York March 16 19 00

FOR ACCOUNT OF Jones and Co. 678
(Deliverer's Name and Number Stamp)

DELIVER TO
(Receiver's Name and Number Stamp)

Date	Line No.	Deliver To	Shares	Security	Price	1000s	100s	Cts.
	Deliverer's	641	100	XYZ		3	212	50
	Receiver's	Give Up						

Fig. 16–1. A deliver exchange ticket.

At the same time, the clearing member makes another report to the Corporation, summarizing the total number of shares and the total contract value of all transactions covered by all the deliver exchange tickets. This report gives a summary of "sale" contracts to be included in the clearance operation. It is illustrated in Figure 16–2.

Tabulating cards are keypunched from all summaries and tickets. These sales data are then processed by high-speed data processing equipment through a number of programs that establish the validity of the summary totals, the clearing numbers, and the stock symbols. The reasonableness of the indicated contract value is also reviewed to see that the contract price as calculated (it need not be shown on the exchange ticket) falls within the particular security's price range on the trading date. Any discrepancies thus detected are resolved immediately with the clearing member.

With the information now at hand from the entire list of over 240 clearing members, the Corporation is ready to prepare its contract lists.

STOCK CLEARING CORPORATION

CLEARANCE DEPARTMENT

SUMMARY COVERING ALL TRANSACTIONS
TO BE INCLUDED IN CLEARANCE OPERATION OF_____ *March 16.00*

SETTLEMENT DATE

*PURCHASES		SALES	
TOTAL NO. OF SHARES	TOTAL CONTRACT VALUE	TOTAL NO. OF SHARES	TOTAL CONTRACT VALUE
		1000	*41,000.*

* PURCHASE TOTALS TO BE INCLUDED FOR SPECIAL CLEARANCES ONLY.

TO BE FORWARDED TO STOCK CLEARING CORPORATION BY EACH CLEARING MEMBER. IN ACCORDANCE WITH ITS RULES. IN THE EVENT NO TRANSACTIONS ARE TO BE INCLUDED. STATE "NONE" IN THE APPROPRIATE SPACE OR SPACES.

087–12–55

JONES & CO.   678

NAME AND NUMBER OF CLEARING MEMBER

Fig. 16–2. A summary of sale contracts.

For each clearing member two lists are prepared. One shows the purchases and the other the sales of the clearing member for the preceding business day. In other words, the Corporation has made its own list, based on the deliver exchange tickets, of all the business that each member has transacted on that particular date. These contract lists are prepared during the afternoon and are ready for distribution in the boxes of the Distributing Department by 6:00 P.M. the same day. Many firms pick up their lists shortly after; the balance do so shortly after 8:00 A.M. the next day.

These lists are immediately checked. Any errors are reported at once by telephone by both the buying and selling members to members on the opposite side of the transaction. If any error is found, the selling clearing member who has made the error on the deliver exchange ticket notifies the Clearing Corporation and the receiving member at once by sending two copies of a correction notice to the Corporation. The Corporation makes the appropriate adjustment in the file of contracts and forwards a copy of the correction notice to the receiving member.

If a receiving member does not receive in due time the correction notice just described, the receiving member is permitted to delete the error from its contract list; it forwards two copies of a deletion notice to the Clearing Corporation between 12:30 P.M. and 1:30 P.M. The Corporation forwards a copy of the deletion notice to the delivering member and removes the contract from the file. The Corporation then issues supplementary contract lists that show the details of all adjustments as well as an adjusted final total of shares and money. A written confirmation of these contracts is executed and forwarded to the Corporation by each clearing member.

Clearance Department. The Clearance Department has several important functions. The first is to establish settlement prices for each day. The nature of the settlement price was discussed earlier in this chapter. This price is indicated on the deliver balance order, and the amount shown is the extension of that price times the number of shares on the deliver balance order.

The second function of the Clearance Department is to determine for each clearing member its debit or credit clearance cash adjustment for the day. This balance is the difference between the amounts computed on the basis of contract prices and the amounts computed on the basis of settlement prices. The Corporation charges or credits the clearing member with this balance on the day of settlement; the Settlement Department, to be described later, is the department responsible for the final part of the operation.

For purposes of simple illustration, let us suppose that Jones and Company sold 1,000 shares of XYZ stock at an average contract price of 41 and bought 800 shares at 40. No other stocks need be considered. The firm, therefore, had a net balance of 200 shares to deliver. The settlement price was 40. The settlement would work out this way:

Sale of 1,000 shares at 41	$41,000
Purchase of 800 shares at 40	32,000
Difference based on contract prices	9,000
Delivery of 200 shares at settlement price of 40	8,000
Credit balance due from Clearing Corporation	$ 1,000

The clearance and settlement statement used by the Corporation in computing the net money balances just described is illustrated in Figure 16–3.

A third function of the Clearance Department is to prepare the so-called deliver balance orders and receive balance orders. On the basis of the information that the department now has at hand, it computes for each clearing member the net balances of shares to deliver and receive. A separate deliver balance order and receive balance order is made out for each security to be delivered. The deliver balance order indicates the settlement date, the identity of the delivering and receiving firm, the security, the number of shares, the settlement price, and the settlement amount. A reproduction of this form, which would be used to order the delivery of 200 shares of XYZ common just described, is given in Figure 16–4.

SETTLEMENT DATE			CLEARING MEMBER		STOCK CLEARING CORPORATION
MO.	DAY	YR.	NAME	NO.	8 BROAD ST. — NEW YORK

CLEARANCE STATEMENT

	AMOUNT	
	DEBIT	CREDIT

	SHARES	
	PURCHASED	SOLD
TOTAL CONTRACTS: PURCHASES (DR) SALES (CR)		
	DELIVER	RECEIVE
TOTAL BALANCE ORDERS: DELIVER (DR) RECEIVE (CR)		

DO NOT INCLUDE THE ABOVE IN TOTALS.

SETTLEMENT STATEMENT	DEBIT	CREDIT
CASH ITEMS:		
02 CLEARANCE ADJUSTMENT		
03 MEMBER TO MEMBER AND NON-MEMBER BANK		
05 NON-MEMBER BANK TO MEMBER		X X X X X X X X X X X
60 FEDERAL TAX		X X X X X X X X X X X
61 N.Y. STATE TAX		X X X X X X X X X X X
71 MARKS TO MARKET (ESCROW)		
78 MARKS TO MARKET (SPECIAL) (WHEN APPROPRIATE TAKE CREDIT FOR BONDS DEPOSITED)		
SUB TOTALS		
97 SUSPENSE		
98 DRAFT (DR) CHECK (CR)		
TOTAL		

AUTHORIZED SIGNATURE

FORM 086

THE EGRY REGISTER COMPANY

Fig. 16–3. The clearance and settlement statement.

A receive balance order containing the same information is also sent to the receiving clearing member to be used as a check against deliveries. It is not illustrated because of space limitations.

The deliver and receive balance orders are sent to the clearing members together with the settlement statement indicating the totals of each as debits and credits on the morning of the day preceding settlement date.

Central Delivery Department. The Central Delivery Department handles the actual stock certificates or other securities that are to be delivered and received on the basis of deliver balance orders sent out by the Clearance Department. On the settlement date, currently the fourth full business day after the date of the transaction, the delivering clearing members send the required securities by messenger to the Corporation delivery entrance, where they are tossed down the receiving chute. Securities other than cleared securities may also be delivered through this department.

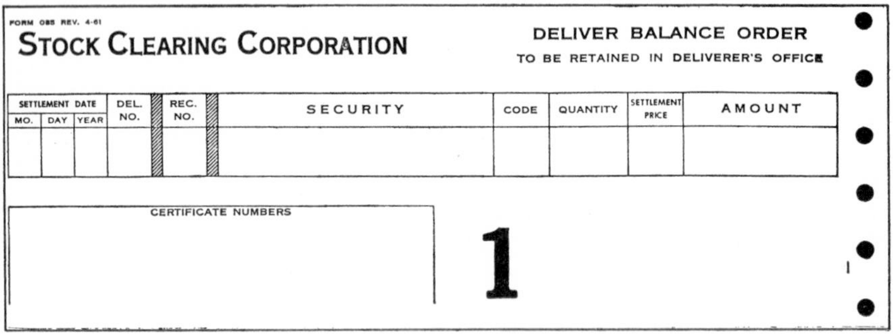
FORM OBS REV. 4-61

STOCK CLEARING CORPORATION

DELIVER BALANCE ORDER

TO BE RETAINED IN DELIVERER'S OFFICE

SETTLEMENT DATE			DEL. NO.	REC. NO.	SECURITY	CODE	QUANTITY	SETTLEMENT PRICE	AMOUNT
MO.	DAY	YEAR							

CERTIFICATE NUMBERS

1

Fig. 16–4. A deliver balance order.

The securities come to the Central Delivery Department in large manila envelopes which bear only the clearing number of the receiving firm and contain only securities with corresponding balance orders or tickets. The envelopes are accompanied by a credit list in duplicate. This lists each of the envelopes delivered, indicates the number of the clearing member to whom the envelope is addressed, and the total money value of the securities in the envelope. In case more than one item is contained in the envelope, an adding machine slip must be enclosed. This shows the total money value of the items in the envelope. Final delivery time in 12:00 noon.

The Central Delivery Department checks the envelopes against the credit lists to see that all envelopes have been received. Duplicate lists are then stamped and returned to delivering members. A sample credit list is shown in Figure 16–5.

The Central Delivery Department next sorts the envelopes and makes them available to receiving members at the department windows. These envelopes are picked up as soon as available, with final pickup shortly after noon. In the whole operation the department at no time examines the contents of the envelopes or verifies the amount of money on the credit lists. This is the responsibility of the delivering and receiving

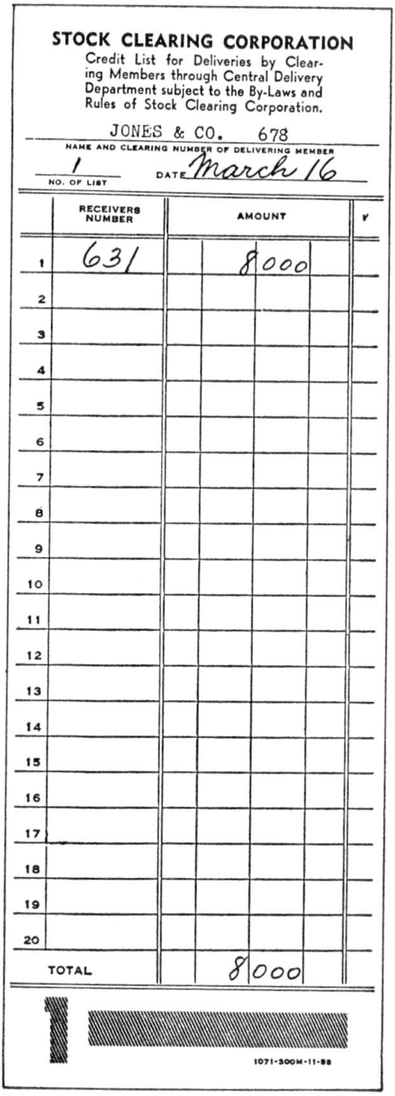

STOCK CLEARING CORPORATION			

Credit List for Deliveries by Clearing Members through Central Delivery Department subject to the By-Laws and Rules of Stock Clearing Corporation.

JONES & CO.   678
NAME AND CLEARING NUMBER OF DELIVERING MEMBER

_1_   DATE _March 16_
NO. OF LIST

	RECEIVERS NUMBER	AMOUNT	V
1	631	8 000	
2			
3			
4			
5			
6			
7			
8			
9			
10			
11			
12			
13			
14			
15			
16			
17			
18			
19			
20			
TOTAL		8 000	

1071-300M-11-88

Fig. 16–5. A credit list.

members. Securities other than cleared securities, as noted, may also be delivered in this way.

In case a receiving member finds an irregularity in any item, it is permitted to return the item at once through the Central Delivery Department. The original delivering member must accept the returned item if it is returned in accordance with the rules of the Corporation.

The above description involves only clearing members. Where non-member banks and non-members are also involved, the procedure varies somewhat.

Settlement Department. The Settlement Department is charged with the responsibility of settling money payments among the Corporation, the clearing members, and the non-member banks. On each delivery date each clearing member is required to return the settlement statement to the Corporation. This form has now been completed according to the actual receipts and deliveries. These entries are verified by the Corporation, and a determination is made of the amount due.

If, at the end of the day, a firm or bank finds that it has a balance due the Corporation, it delivers a check to the Corporation for the amount payable. These checks, if $5,000 or over, are certified unless drawn by a bank. On the other hand, if the firm or bank finds that the Corporation owes a balance, it sends the Corporation a draft for the amount due. The Corporation then endorses the draft for payment.

Direct Clearing Department. Since 1955 the Corporation has operated a sixth department, known as the Direct Clearing Department. In 1961 there were 47 direct clearing members, 29 being out-of-town members with the balance made up primarily of individual floor traders and specialists in New York.

In the case of out-of-town members, purchases and sales are effected on the floor of the Exchange through their New York office or by a New York correspondent for the account of the out-of-town member and are handled directly between the office of the out-of-town member and the Direct Clearing Department. In general, the out-of-town clearing member maintains a bank account in New York, ships his securities to the Direct Clearing Department for subsequent delivery through the Corporation, and receives purchased securities directly from the Corporation through this department. Payment and receipt of funds are made by and received for his account by this department acting under a power of attorney.

The Direct Clearing Department handled 53 million shares and $1.9 billion dollars in values of shares for these members in 1960.

OTHER FUNCTIONS OF THE STOCK CLEARING CORPORATION

Marking to the Market. According to Exchange rules, a party to an exchange contract who is partially unsecured because of a change in the market value of the stock subject to the contract may demand that the contract be "marked to the market."

A "cash" mark to the market generally takes place in connection with a stock loan made, most likely, as the result of a short sale or an open exchange contract (a fail to receive or deliver). For example, at the time stock is borrowed to deliver on a short sale, the borrower normally deposits with the lender an amount of money equal to the market value. For the lender this is 100 per cent protection in the form of cash. If the market value of the stock rises, the lender has the right to demand that the borrower deposit more cash; and if the market value falls, there may be a return of cash. Thus the contract is "marked to the market."

To accomplish a cash "mark," the payee issues a charge ticket to the payor. This notification is inserted in a delivery envelope addressed to the payor which is then sent through the Central Delivery Department in the same manner as security deliveries. From the entry on the Credit List, the Corporation charges the daily settlement account of the payor and credits the account of the payee.

Let us suppose that Smith and Company borrowed 100 shares of XYZ common stock when it was selling at 29. At that time Smith and Company would deposit $2,900 with Jones and Company, the lender. If the market value of the stock rose to 33, for example, Jones and Company could mark the contract to the market value of 33 by sending a charge ticket for the difference of $400 (Fig. 16–6) through the Central Delivery Department.

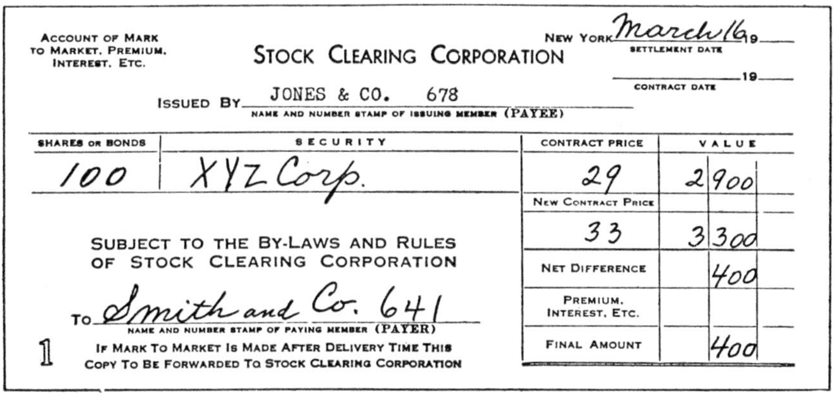
ACCOUNT OF MARK TO MARKET, PREMIUM, INTEREST, ETC.

STOCK CLEARING CORPORATION

NEW YORK March 16 19__ SETTLEMENT DATE

19__ CONTRACT DATE

ISSUED BY JONES & CO. 678
NAME AND NUMBER STAMP OF ISSUING MEMBER (PAYEE)

SHARES OR BONDS	SECURITY	CONTRACT PRICE	VALUE
100	XYZ Corp.	29	2900
		NEW CONTRACT PRICE	
		33	3300
		NET DIFFERENCE	400
		PREMIUM, INTEREST, ETC.	
		FINAL AMOUNT	400

SUBJECT TO THE BY-LAWS AND RULES OF STOCK CLEARING CORPORATION

TO Smith and Co. 641
NAME AND NUMBER STAMP OF PAYING MEMBER (PAYER)

1 IF MARK TO MARKET IS MADE AFTER DELIVERY TIME THIS COPY TO BE FORWARDED TO STOCK CLEARING CORPORATION

Fig. 16–6. A charge ticket for mark to the market.

An "escrow" mark to the market is used principally in conjunction with "when issued" or "when distributed" contracts. Individual "when issued" or "when distributed" contracts (usually for unlisted securities) that are not entered in the daily "When Issued or When Distributed" Clearance may be marked by the unsecured party by charging the settlement account of the party on whom the demand is made. The money so charged is then held by the Corporation in a special bank account in favor of the party who made the demand. When either the contract is closed, i.e., consummated, or there has been a change in the market value reducing the amount of the deposit necessary, the deposit or part of it is returned to the depositor.

"When issued" or "when distributed" contracts that have been entered into the daily "When Issued or When Distributed" Clearance conducted by the Corporation may be subject to a procedure that closely resembles an "escrow" type of mark to the market. At the discretion of the Corporation, each firm's contracts entered in the Clearance may be adjusted to a new delivery price. Firms having a debit cash balance as the result of such adjustment deposit with the Corporation cash to be held in a special escrow account for the protection of firms having a credit cash balance. The Corporation may permit all or part of a firm's debit cash balance to be evidenced by an open account indebtedness secured by unmatured bearer bonds that qualify under the Corporation's rules.

In the course of normal business "escrow" marks to the market are not frequent. However, in 1960 escrow funds and bonds deposited with the Corporation in connection with the clearance of Studebaker-Packard "when issued" contracts reached $17.8 million. This amount was simply returned to the depositing members in January, 1961, when security balance orders were issued covering the definitive, "issued" shares.

Clearing House Comparison Service. In 1961 the Corporation permanently established the Clearing House Comparison Service to provide clearing members with the mechanism for effecting the comparison and confirmation of transactions that were not compared through the regular clearance operation. Both buyer and seller may submit exchange tickets, of the kind illustrated in Figure 16–1, for "ex-clearance" trades on the afternoon of the day preceding the established settlement date. The Corporation matches the tickets and, on the following morning, issues to the members contract lists and security orders extended at contract price for those items that compared. Any ticket that is uncompared is returned to the member who originally submitted it.

Handling Transfer Taxes. Another important function of the Stock Clearing Corporation is the collection and payment of security transfer taxes on all cleared securities. It also acts as a receiving agent for transfer taxes on other security transactions in which a tax liability is incurred. The Corporation debits the settlement account of each clearing member with the amount of the tax liability as reported by the member. Certain non-clearing members have executed an agreement with the Corporation under which taxes are reported and paid by check through the Corporation to the tax authorities. In 1960, $69 million was collected and paid by the Corporation in transfer taxes.

Settlement of Commissions. Another duty of the Corporation is the settlement of floor commissions between members. Many members of the Exchange employ other members on the floor to help in handling transactions, such as specialists and floor brokers. The Corporation has set up a system by which the payment of such commissions may be made through its facilities. This settlement is made once a month and is included in the clearing member's statement.

Non-clearing members entitled to such commissions receive checks drawn to their order.

17

American Stock Exchange

The American Stock Exchange is the second largest stock exchange as measured by share or dollar volume of transactions in the United States. It is also the second largest exchange in dollar value of transactions in Canadian securities on the North American continent. In 1961 transactions on this exchange accounted for 11 per cent of the dollar volume and 26 per cent of the share volume on all national securities exchanges in the United States.[1] Although its volume is small compared to the New York Stock Exchange, it is greater than that of all other United States exchanges combined.

History. This exchange, like many other leading exchanges of the world, began as an outdoor or "curb market." It actually operated in the street for many years and was generally considered, during that early period, to be one of the most colorful spectacles in New York. The exact time of its origin is not too well documented. It is believed to have had its beginning before the Civil War, probably after the gold rush of 1849.[2] There is some evidence that it was dominated in its early years by marine auctioneers, who left the less lucrative business of cargo selling to deal in securities. However, it became a fully functioning market only when brokers dealing in unlisted securities began to do active trading in such stocks and bonds.

The first trading on the Curb was at Wall and Hanover Streets. It continued from 8 A.M. until sundown and made Wall Street almost useless for traffic. During the Civil War the market operated on William Street, where its activities caused less disruption to business. The highly

---

[1] Computed from data in the SEC *Statistical Bulletin,* February, 1962.
[2] *The New York Curb Exchange,* a historical brochure issued by the Exchange in 1946.

disorganized character of the market took somewhat more tangible form in 1873, when E. E. Mendels, sometimes referred to as "the Father of the Curb Exchange," effected a personal agreement under which he and other brokers dealt in unlisted securities.[3]

By the 1890's the Curb Exchange had developed a very heavy volume of trading. Moving from the narrow confines of William Street, it centered its activities in Broad Street, just below the offices of J. P. Morgan and Company. Here its operations overflowed into Wall Street and caused still further difficulties. Gradually it was pushed southward from Wall Street, but remained in Broad Street from 1900 until 1921, when it was moved indoors. Exchange business increased steadily in volume and importance during that period, particularly in World War I, when speculation, stimulated by war production, was rife in industrials.

The operation of the Curb Exchange in the period before it was moved indoors was in a highly fluid state. Brokers, traders, and clerks were jammed together in a noisy milling mass. Other brokers and telephone clerks leaned out of office windows; a constant interchange of signals, whistles, and shouts passed to and from the windows and the street. As an identification brokers wore headgear of different colors to distinguish themselves from each other and to the clerks. A complex system of hand signals for the transmission of orders and information was developed; this is a technique still used in the indoor market. Since signals were not uniform, it was often a qualification of a good clerk that he be able to steal the signals of competing firms. Since the market had no membership requirements, it was said that any one could be a broker if he "had a weatherproof body and a strong pair of lungs."

In spite of the hectic character of the market, it transacted a substantial volume of trading and made a market for many securities that were not handled in the already fully organized New York Stock Exchange. Although it was not supervised, it was still a market in which unwritten trading customs and practices were followed faithfully. As an indication of its importance, it handled, during the year 1915, $60,748,000 in bonds, $8,976,000 in oil stock, $41,158,000 in mining stock, and $20,074,000 in other industrial issues.[4]

Gradually the market took on a semblance of organization. In 1908 E. E. Mendels in cooperation with a number of brokers in the market, formed the New York Curb Agency. A listed department was established, which permitted corporations to list their issues for a nominal fee. The chief function of the organization was publicity and the protection of brokers and customers against irregular practices. By 1911 the organiza-

---

[3] *History of the New York Curb*, a pamphlet published in 1916 by the brokerage firm of Jones and Baker, New York.

[4] Jones and Baker, *op. cit.*, p. 9.

tion had become still more formalized as the New York Curb Market Association with offices, rules, membership, trading hours, and records. Many of the regulations adopted at that time were similar to those of the New York Stock Exchange. Memberships were limited to 500, with annual dues set at $250. Securities of qualified corporations were admitted to listing privileges, although most of the trading remained on an unlisted basis.

The Association eventually was moved indoors in 1921 into a new building. As its needs expanded, the building underwent extensive enlargement and was completed in its present form in 1931.

The name was changed in 1921 to the New York Curb Market and again in 1929 to the New York Curb Exchange. The most recent alteration of title came in 1953, when the exchange became known as the American Stock Exchange, a name believed to be more descriptive of its importance as a national and international securities market.

The rules and practices of the American Stock Exchange are so similar to those of the New York Stock Exchange that separate discussion in detail would be repetitive of the preceding chapters. Emphasis here is placed on small differences, where they exist, and on facts descriptive of the Exchange as an entity.

Organization.[5] The American Stock Exchange is an association. It has a Board of Governors, elected by the membership. Its executives are salaried officials, subject to appointment and control by the Board of Governors. Subsidiary corporations own its real estate and its clearing operations. At the end of 1960 its physical plant and equipment were valued at $9 million, and operating expense in that year was $4 million.

The Board of Governors consists of thirty-two members, divided into four classes; these represent regular members of the Exchange, associate members or non-member partners, the general public, the Chairman of the Board, and the President of the Exchange. A significant aspect of the Board membership is that the public is represented by three men not in the securities business. The Board is the over-all policy making body of the Exchange. Salaried executives carry out these policies laid down by it as they would in a corporation. An advisory committee, comprised of seven or more Governors, appointed by the Chairman for four month terms, consults with and advises the President and the other officers and employees of the Exchange on the administration and interpretation of the provisions of the Constitution, the rules of the Exchange, and the policies promulgated by the Board.

Executive operations are handled through five divisions, each in charge of a vice-president: administration, securities, transactions, floor

[5] Based on the *Constitution* of the American Stock Exchange, effective September 4, 1962.

supervision, and public relations. The division of administration has charge of the records of receipts and disbursements. The division of securities handles the listing and delisting of securities, rules on deliveries, dividends, and the validity of due bills. The division of transactions has many responsibilities, including floor transactions and practices, floor investigations, specialists, members and member firms, member employees, capital requirements, margins, commissions, quotations, tickers and communications. The division of floor supervision has responsibility for the mechanical operation of the trading floor. The public relations division provides to the press all important statistics concerning the operation of the Exchange.

All operations of the Exchange are governed by the Constitution and Rules.

Regular Members. The American Exchange has three classes of members: regular members, allied members, and associate members. Full privileges of membership are accorded only to regular members: chief of which is the privilege of trading on the floor. There are 499 of these seats.

An individual to be admitted to regular membership must be an American citizen at least twenty-one years of age. He must appear personally before, and his application must be approved by, a subcommittee of the Board of Governors on admissions. His application must be approved also on referral from the admissions committee by a two-thirds majority of the Governors in meeting. There are a few special cases in which a minimum majority of nineteen of the thirty-two governors is required.

Each member must acquire a seat at the time of admission. Seats have varied in price over the years from as high as $254,000 in 1929 to as low as $650 in 1952. In 1961 the sales price was as high as $80,000. In early 1962 the range of sales prices was from $65,000 to $40,000. Upon the death of a member, the seat may be sold by the heirs at whatever price is obtainable and, of course, a member has this right to sell during his lifetime. If a member becomes bankrupt, there is a definite priority of claims against the seat: (1) the Exchange and its affiliates, (2) member contracts, and (3) creditor claims under ordinary legal procedure.

In addition to purchasing a seat at the time of admission, a member must pay an initiation fee, based on the latest sale price of a seat. This fee may range from as low as $1,000 to as high as $2,500. Annual dues in 1961 were $500. The Constitution places a maximum of $800 on them.

The capital requirements vary with the type of member. For an individual the capital requirement is $10,000 plus cost of seat and initiation fee. For a partnership or corporation the requirement is $25,000 if it does not deal directly with the public or $50,000 if it does.

The Board of Governors may discipline any member for such practices as fraud, fictitious transactions, market demoralization, misstatements, or violations of the rules of the Exchange and the Securities Exchange Act. Three penalties are possible and depend upon the seriousness of the offense: fines up to $5,000, suspension, and expulsion.

A great majority of the regular members belong to firms that have membership on the New York Stock Exchange.

Associate Memberships. The Constitution provides for an unlimited number of associate memberships. In 1962 there were 410 such memberships, 80 being held by corporations.

Admissions to membership are subject to approval by the Committee on Admissions and the Board of Governors; no personal appearance, however, is necessary. The purpose of membership is to obtain lower commissions on issues traded in on the Exchange. Thus, a commission firm without a regular seat on the Exchange may, nevertheless, execute orders on it by transmitting them through regular members. The savings on commissions are substantial. For example, the commission per 100 shares to a regular member on a "give-up" on a $60 stock is $5.65; to an associate member, whose transaction is affected by the floor member, it is $7.40. In contrast, the commission to a non-member customer would be $45.00. A "give-up" is a transaction in which one member "gives up" the name of another for clearance of the order; it is not for his own account.

The associate member does not buy a seat. He does, however, pay an initiation fee, which is roughly 10 per cent of the market value of a seat. He pays the same annual dues as regular members.

Associate memberships are not salable or transferable, except that if the member is a firm partner or executive officer of a corporation, such membership may be transferred to another firm partner or executive officer in the case of death or retirement.

No associate member may trade on the floor; he does, however, have other privileges of membership and participates in control of the Exchange through representation on the Board of Governors.

Allied Members. The conditions and responsibilities for allied membership are so similar to those for the New York Stock Exchange that repetition is needless (see page 124). However, allied membership on the American Stock Exchange is a privilege granted on application, rather than a necessary condition of general partnership or voting stock ownership in a member organization.

Commissions. Commissions to non-members, i.e., the public, are identical to those charged on the New York Stock Exchange transactions. Four typical commissions on non-member orders are given below to illustrate the commission schedule on round-lot orders:

Price of Stock	Commission
$10	$17
20	27
40	39
60	45

Floor Members. Of the 499 regular members of the American Stock Exchange, 325 are active on the floor. The rest of the members transact their business through floor members; this is true of the associate members as well. There are three classes of floor members: specialists, commission brokers, and floor traders.

The specialists are by far the most numerous type of member, about 160 being in this class.[6] The average specialist on the American Stock Exchange handles about 5 stocks; some handle as many as 20.

A certain amount of competition exists among the specialists. For most of the stocks there is only one specialist. There is competition in about 60 stocks. The largest number of specialists competing in any one stock is four. Examples of such stocks are Pacific Petroleum, Remington Arms, North Canadian Oil, and Israel American Oil.

The specialists have varied methods of handling orders. Some use a specialist's book, as on the New York Stock Exchange. More often, bids and offers are filed on cards easily available for inspection; they may be filed in "pigeonholes" in the post. Specialist try to make a market in all stocks that they handle. The average spread is $\frac{1}{4}$ to $\frac{3}{8}$ point; on very active stocks the spread is $\frac{1}{8}$ point.

All specialists deal in odd-lots. There is no odd-lot dealer system as on the New York Stock Exchange. The differentials are usually $\frac{1}{8}$ or $\frac{1}{4}$ point on issues traded in round-lots of 100. In these issues the $\frac{1}{4}$-point differential is charged on stocks priced at $40 or more. On issues traded in round-lots of 10, the differential is $\frac{1}{2}$ point. On issues traded in round-lots of 25 or 50 and on American Depository Receipts (or other evidences of foreign issues), the differential is $\frac{1}{4}$ point. Stocks selling under $0.50 carry a differential of $\frac{1}{16}$ point.

There are 140 commission brokers. They buy and sell on a commission basis for their own organizations or for other brokers. In no way do

---

[6] Chapter 11 describes the work of specialists. A highly critical report of specialist activity on the American Exchange was issued by the staff of the Division of Trading and Exchanges of the SEC on January 3, 1962. See SEC *Staff Report on Organization, Management, and Regulation of Conduct of Members of the American Stock Exchange* (Washington, D.C.: Securities and Exchange Commission, 1962). The Exchange underwent a substantial reorganization later in 1962.

they take a risk, nor do they make a profit except from the regular commissions charged.

About twenty-five members operate exclusively as floor traders. These buy and sell for their own account exclusively. Their operations take advantage of favorable buying and selling opportunities on the floor. Typically, they trade on fast turnover and at small margins of profit. Some specialists and commission brokers also do a certain amount of floor trading on occasion.

Floor Mechanics. The trading floor of the American Stock Exchange differs somewhat in mechanics from that of the New York Stock Exchange. It is about 150 feet in length and nearly as wide. On two sides of the floor are tiers of telephone booths. At these booths the telephone clerks, one to three per broker, sit facing their respective brokers on the floor. This high visibility permits a constant interchange of signals between brokers and clerks on orders, prices of execution, quotations, and size of bids and offers. All signals are executed with one hand. This signal system, a carry-over from the outdoor market, is still popular because of its speed and efficiency. Each clerk is connected by telephone with the home office.

Twenty-one trading posts are in operation on the floor. They are open octagons, which serve as chest-high counters for the work of brokers and clerks. Several clerks stand inside each post and help the specialists with their work. The brokers operate on the outside of the post. Each post is equipped with numerous compartments or "pigeonholes," called "coops," for filing orders and records. Time clocks, telephones, and pneumatic tubes complete the equipment of each post. Each of the twenty-one posts carries about 40 stocks.

Bond trading takes place at one of the posts. There is only a small amount of bond activity today.

There are two immense annunciator boards on the walls to carry broker numbers. Brokers may be called by these boards; in practice, they are little used. Nearly all communications between brokers and clerks are effected by voice and hand signals.

The American Stock Exchange operates its ticker service under what is known as the leased-wire system. In other words, all ticker service is handled by the Exchange. Western Union handles the physical operations of the tickers and leases the tickers to the Exchange. The main ticker control station is located on the trading floor. To it are fed constantly the sales reports from each post. The ticker tape, similar in principle to that of the New York Stock Exchange, carries both stock and bond prices. Large Trans-Lux screens carry magnified images of the tape at all times, not only of the American tape but also of the New

York Stock Exchange tape. Over 2,210 tickers furnish service to 425 cities and 43 states.

The operations of the trading floor are supplemented by the Quotation Department. This department furnishes, at all times, the latest quotations on stocks. Over 23 million quotations were supplied in 1961.

Orders reach the floor from 3,000 member offices in the United States and 138 in foreign countries.

Listed Securities. The American Stock Exchange trades in two types of securities: listed and unlisted. Listed securities are those in which the issuing company has formally applied for listing privileges. It has paid the required listing fee, furnished the necessary information about its business, and entered into certain agreements with the Exchange, such as maintaining a transfer agent and registrar.

Listing requirements follow somewhat the same lines as those of the New York Stock Exchange, but are not as rigid. The listing application furnishes the American Stock Exchange with the essential facts about the company's history, business, products, capitalization, management, and financial condition. In cases where the company has already filed a prospectus with the SEC under the Securities Act of 1933, the listing procedure is simplified. Since all securities fully listed on a national securities exchange must also be registered with the SEC, there is considerable similarity on all exchanges in the information filed by companies applying for listing.

The American Stock Exchange is not so insistent on a company's being long established and "seasoned" before it may be listed as is the New York Stock Exchange. Some companies, still in the developmental stage and without established earning power, are listed on occasion. In such cases the American Stock Exchange is more concerned that the company be soundly financed and have good future prospects than with its present size and operating results.

As a rule of thumb, the Exchange has set standards for listing as follows: $1 million in net assets (or net worth); 200,000 shares outstanding in the hands of public shareowners; at least 750 such shareowners, of whom 500 at least shall own one or more round-lot quantities; a market value for outstanding stock equaling at least $2 million in total and $1 million for the shares in the ownership of public shareholders; and $150,000 of net income in the year preceding listing and an average of at least $100,000 of net income for the three preceding years. Some exceptions are made for organizations, such as SBIC's, that more than adequately meet the other requirements but do not meet the requirement as to net income.

Although the listed company must maintain transfer agent and registrar facilities, such facilities need not, as required by the New York Stock Exchange, be separate organizations nor have offices in New York City.

Listing procedure covers five steps: (1) a preliminary talk between the applying company and the Exchange; (2) a formal application; (3) the printing of the application; (4) an investigation by a committee of the Board of Governors; and (5) a final approval by the full Board of Governors.

Listing costs on stock are lower than on the New York Stock Exchange. The original listing fee is 1 cent per share on the first 250,000 shares and ¼ cent per share on the remainder listed, up to a maximum of $5,000. No minimum fee is stated, but the listing standards imply a minimum of about $2,500. When additional shares are listed at a later date, an additional fee of 1 cent per share is charged on the total thus listed in any one subsequent application, with a minimum fee of $100 and a maximum fee of $2,500. Some other special cases are referred to in the listing regulations of the Exchange.

An annual charge of $250 is made on all listed issues.

An examination of stocks newly listed in 1960 and 1961 gives an indication of the type of stocks being listed currently. Over one hundred stock issues were listed in each of these years for the first time. These represented some companies still in the developmental stage, without established records; companies newly incorporated but considered by the Exchange to be adequately financed and properly managed; and companies with substantial records but heretofore without broad public markets for their stocks.

The listing requirements of the American Stock Exchange may be compared with those of the New York Stock Exchange in three ways: (1) they are less rigid and exacting; (2) they permit younger and less strongly established companies to list; and (3) they are less expensive. These factors tend to make the American a market for small business.

Unlisted Trading. About 20 per cent of the stocks traded on the American Stock Exchange are unlisted securities. For these issues the issuer corporation or government did not apply for listing. A specialist requested, and was granted, approval to make a market on the Exchange. The practice of trading unlisted issues on the Exchange began early in the century. Congress reviewed this situation in 1934 and the SEC in 1936, and both concluded that persons who had purchased stocks in this unlisted market on the Exchange had done so on the assumption that they were receiving the benefits of an auction market and such a market should not be denied them.

The Securities Exchange Act now permits three types of unlisted trading: (1) in securities thus traded prior to March 1, 1934; (2) in securities listed and registered on some other exchange; and (3) in those in which there are registration statements and periodic reports filed under the Securities Act of 1933. The first type refers mostly to issues thus traded in 1934 on the then New York Curb Exchange; the second type relates to securities listed on the New York and other stock exchanges, but admitted to unlisted trading on yet other exchanges; the third type has seldom been used by the SEC.

In cases where an exchange admitted stocks to unlisted trading prior to 1934, the trading may be continued. Investors, however, are not protected by the proxy rules of the SEC, "insider trading" regulations, or financial reporting requirements.

Both the Securities Exchange Act itself and its administration by the SEC have prevented an extension of unlisted trading for stocks traded on one exchange only. As a matter of fact, such unlisted trading is being contracted rather than extended. Securities that already have the status may continue in it, but if any material change takes place in the security, it is dropped. A company may alter the security's title, maturity, interest rate, par value, or amount outstanding or authorized, and it can continue trading unlisted. However, if the security is so altered that it is not substantially equivalent to the security already admitted to unlisted trading, it must be dropped by the exchange or be listed. The result has been a steady and substantial decline since 1937 in the number of securities trading unlisted on one exchange only. For example, if a bond issue or preferred stock is retired, it is automatically dropped. If a new issue replaces it, such issue does not trade unlisted. As a result, the number of unlisted issues traded on the American Stock Exchange has declined steadily in recent years. On December 31, 1944, some 461 issues were traded under this condition. By December 31, 1961, the number had fallen to 197. Unlisted bond issues traded on the Exchange dropped in number from 140 to 28 over the same period.

A stock listed on the New York, American or any other national stock exchange may be admitted to unlisted trading on other exchanges upon application by such exchanges to the SEC and its approval. Since this form of unlisted trading is more significant to exchanges other than the two major New York exchanges, it will be discussed further in the next chapter.

At one time unlisted trading on the American Stock Exchange accounted for 67 per cent of all stock volume and nearly 100 per cent of all bond volume. More recently it has been less significant. In 1961 it accounted for less than 11 per cent of stock volume and 15 per cent of bond volume on the Exchange. Table 17–1 provides some data on the relative importance of listed and unlisted issues on the Exchange in 1961.

Table 17–1. Relative Importance of Listed and Unlisted Issues on the American Stock Exchange, December 31, 1961 (Dollar and Share figures in millions)

Type of Security	Listed Issues	Unlisted Issues
Stocks:		
Number of issues	797	204
Number of shares	1,309	493
Market value	$16,365	$16,647
Bonds:		
Number of issues	45	28
Amount outstanding (par value)	$807	$367
Market value	$752	$335

Source: American Stock Exchange.

Type of Stocks. The securities sold on the American Stock Exchange show great variation. They range from many as old and as well established as any on the New York Stock Exchange down to new and highly speculative issues. On a third of the stocks, dividends have been paid from 10 to over 100 years, while some stocks are so new that no dividends have ever been paid.

The American Stock Exchange is a testing ground for many younger corporations. Many of these eventually graduate to the New York Stock Exchange. Such important companies as General Motors, du Pont, Montgomery Ward, Kresge, Kennecott Copper, Goodyear, Radio Corporation of America, Cities Service, Aluminum Corporation, and nearly all the Standard Oil companies were at one time listed on the Exchange.

The 5 most active stocks traded in 1961 were, in order: Cabol Enterprises, Ltd.; Seaboard World Airlines, Inc.; Webb & Knapp, Inc.; Occidental Petroleum Corporation; and Technicolor, Inc.

Foreign Securities. The Exchange is the nation's leading market in foreign securities. The trading in Canadian oil and mining stocks have at times been especially important. Many British securities are also traded. In 1960 and 1961, 14 per cent of all trading on the Exchange was accounted for by transactions in Canadian securities, and 4 per cent by trading in other foreign security issues.

The American Stock Exchange originated and uses an effective system for trading in European securities, which has been adopted by others. The Exchange trades in American Depository Receipts (ADR's). These certificates are issued by New York banks and trust companies against the deposit of the original foreign shares with the foreign branches of the American bank. When foreign shares are deposited abroad, the equivalent American depository receipts are issued in New York upon the cabled advice from the foreign depository. When these stocks are sold on the Exchange, an exchange is made of depository receipts, not of the actual stock certificates. This eliminates the actual shipment of stock certificates between New York and Europe and greatly expedites the arbitrage in securities traded on foreign securities exchanges.

18

Regional and Local Stock Exchanges

More than a hundred stock exchanges at one time or another have been in operation in the United States.[1] In 1929 there were thirty. Several of the smaller ones stopped doing business in the 1930's, when public interest in securities was restrained and when registration with the SEC became a source of business cost. Other exchanges merged. One new exchange, the National Stock Exchange, was formed in 1961 and began operations in 1962.

In 1961, in addition to the New York and American Stock Exchanges, fourteen regional or local exchanges had stock transactions on them. They accounted for about 7 per cent of the dollar volume and 10 per cent of the share volume in the United States. The figures for 1961 are shown in Table 18–1.

The amount of activity, the lists of issues traded, and the forms of operation varied greatly among these exchanges. These regional and local exchanges, however, provide services for their memberships; they add to the market for stocks the customer accounts of their members and member organizations; they increase clearing facilities; and they provide primary markets for some stock issues.

ORGANIZATION

The Securities Exchange Act of 1934 forbids transactions on an exchange not registered or specifically exempted from registration with the SEC. Registration is accomplished by filing a registration statement and

---

[1] *Eighteenth Annual Report of the SEC,* 1952, p. 37.

Table 18-1. Volume of Sales of Stock on Active Regional and Local Exchanges, 1961

Exchange	Market Value	Share Volume	Per Cent of U. S. Total Market Value	Volume
Midwest	$1,761,745,759	43,790,470	2.76	2.18
Pacific Coast	1,275,104,186	70,639,165	2.00	3.51
Philadelphia-Baltimore .	663,319,743	16,002,728	1.04	.80
Boston	318,519,634	6,268,720	.50	.31
Detroit	240,532,401	6,532,761	.38	.33
Cincinnati	46,539,670	894,299	.07	.04
Pittsburgh	35,400,234	1,025,768	.06	.05
Honolulu*	25,361,003	889,231	.04	.04
Spokane	4,814,961	8,010,874	.01	.40
Salt Lake City	3,048,824	19,572,905	**	.97
San Francisco Mining .	2,893,541	20,128,636	**	1.00
Richmond*	686,016	16,281	**	**
Wheeling*	325,345	6,749	**	**
Colorado Springs*	80,205	312,832	**	.02
Total	$4,378,376,522	194,091,919	6.86	9.65

* An exempt exchange.   ** Less than 0.005 per cent.
Source: SEC, *Statistical Bulletin,* February, 1962, p. 10.

supplying a number of specified documents. Among the latter are copies of the constitution and rules under which the exchange will operate. The SEC may determine that an exchange is exempt from registration because the volume of busines transacted on it is small. In 1962 exchanges in the United States were classified registered or exempt as follows:

Registered:

American Stock Exchange
Boston Stock Exchange
Chicago Board of Trade
Cincinnati Stock Exchange
Detroit Stock Exchange
Midwest Stock Exchange
National Stock Exchange

New York Stock Exchange
Pacific Coast Stock Exchange
Philadelphia-Baltimore Stock Exchange
Pittsburgh Stock Exchange
Salt Lake City Stock Exchange
San Francisco Mining Exchange
Spokane Stock Exchange

Exempt:

Colorado Springs Stock Exchange
Honolulu Stock Exchange

Richmond Stock Exchange
Wheeling Stock Exchange

In Table 18-1 it may be observed that the Honolulu exchange was somewhat more active than three of the registered exchanges, on which there were stock transactions in 1961, as measured by the dollar volume of business transacted, but the share volumes on these registered exchanges greatly exceeded that on the Honolulu exchange. In this sense the four exempt exchanges are clearly those doing the least volume of business among the active exchanges.

Two registered exchanges were inactive in 1961. Inactivity on these two exchanges came from different causes. The Chicago Board of Trade was at one time an active exchange but trading in stocks dwindled. The last transaction on the Chicago Board, as a stock exchange, was in 1953. The National Stock Exchange, in contrast, was inactive because it had not yet become ready to handle trading. Trading in a very limited number of issues began early in 1962. This new exchange sought specifically for itself a niche in trading in issues of new enterprises.

Mergers. The decline in the number of active exchanges from thirty in 1929 to sixteen in 1962 resulted in part from withdrawal of organizations from the market. It resulted also, however, from mergers of organizations and consolidation of exchange facilities. These came in response to the need of the member firms for both a sufficient trading area and efficient service. Profitable operation in the fragmented market prior to merger was not possible. Three mergers are significant.

The Philadelphia-Baltimore Stock Exchange, as the name indicates, was formed, in 1949, by merger of exchanges in these cities. The Washington (D.C.) Stock Exchange merged with them in 1953 and now operates as a branch.

The Midwest Stock Exchange was formed also in 1949. After talks among representatives of a substantial number of the then existing exchanges, the members of four exchanges entered on this merger. The exchanges of Chicago, Cleveland, St. Louis, and Minneapolis-St. Paul were included. The New Orleans exchange joined them in 1960.

On the West Coast, the exchanges of Los Angeles and San Francisco merged in 1956 to form the Pacific Coast Exchange. Trading floors were retained in both cities but staff and services are centralized.

In a decade, then, ten exchanges combined to form three. These three are the most important in terms of dollar volume of trading of the regional and local exchanges.

Membership. The regional and local exchanges have organizations very similar to that of the New York Stock Exchange. A limited number of memberships in an association are available. The memberships may be transferred. Membership entitles the holder to privileges in trading on the floor and in dealing with other members. A board of governors is elected by the members. The board, in turn, exercises the powers of the members in the day-to-day activities of the exchange. It appoints officers and staff personnel. Like the earlier rather than the present organization of the New York Stock Exchange, standing committees of the membership are responsible for floor procedures, listing, and other fundamental operations.

Regulation. The Securities Exchange Act of 1934 is concerned with trading activities on all exchanges. The constitution and rules of each regional or local exchange must be filed with the SEC and must conform to basic requirements of the Act and the agency. To some extent requirements may be less restrictive than those the New York Stock Exchange has chosen to adopt and, thus, the quality of regulation of trading on the regional and local exchanges may be said to be less. The pervasive nature of the requirements in the Act and of the SEC, however, leave distinction on this point somewhat lacking in significance. Uniformity of regulation is more remarkable than departure from it.

Trading Procedures. Some differences in trading procedures are to be found among these exchanges. The Detroit exchange has no specialists; members on the floor bid or offer in any issue as they choose or as they execute customer orders. Places, or posts, at which issues are assigned for trading do exist, but individual members do not carry specialist responsibilities for maintaining an orderly market in assigned issues. The Pacific Coast Stock Exchange has a schedule of discounted commissions on orders originated by non-members but sent to the floor of that exchange for execution. This represents an effort to bring onto the floor transactions that would otherwise be executed over-the-counter in issues traded on this exchange. The Wheeling exchange, one of the exempt exchanges, has a membership extending to all brokers doing business in the city. There is no trading floor as such. Orders are telephoned to the Executive Secretary, who matches bids and offers in his file. The parallel with cabinet trading at Post 30 on the New York Stock Exchange is close. The existence of these procedural differences, however, is notable because most of the trading procedures follow those described in previous chapters on the New York Stock Exchange procedures.

The *commission schedules* for stocks traded in competition with the New York exchanges usually are identical with those set by those exchanges and charged by their members. On issues traded only locally, a second commission schedule may apply. One reason, at several of the exchanges, is the very low price of shares in such issues. The stocks listed exclusively on regional and local exchanges often are priced at $1 per share or less. Prices of 5 to 10 cents per share are common. Such stocks usually are traded in round- (or board-) lots of 500 or 1,000 shares and price changes are made in cents rather than the larger fractions of the dollar common to the pricing conventions used for higher-priced shares. As noted above, the Pacific Coast exchange has a preferential commission arrangement for some non-member firms that place orders on this exchange. The Boston exchange has a split-commission arrangement with Canadian brokers.

Odd-lots are traded on the floor of each active regional exchange. Those exchanges that have specialists require them to make a market for odd-lot orders. Indeed, the odd-lot business is substantially more important than round-lot business on several exchanges. This is given a form of recognition on the Philadelphia-Baltimore exchange by the assignment of issues for trading to Odd-lot Dealers, rather than specialists. These Odd-lot Dealers are expected to act as specialists on such round-lot orders as may reach the floor. The emphasis on the odd-lot business, however, is clear.

The odd-lot differential charge is usually identical to that set for similar transactions on the New York exchanges.

THE STOCK LISTS

The lists of stock traded on the regional and local exchanges are not as large as those of the major New York exchanges. The larger regional exchanges list 500 to 600 issues. The smaller ones list less than 100. In 1961, 634 issues were traded on the Philadelphia-Baltimore exchange and 11 at Colorado Springs.

On the larger regional exchanges the number of issues listed for trading is no indication of the number of regional issues. By far the greater proportion of trading on these exchanges is done in competition with the major New York exchanges. The American and New York Stock Exchanges have no duplications with each other in their lists. They have deliberately avoided competition in individual issues. Regional exchanges, however, trade many of the issues listed on one or the other of the New York exchanges. They seek those with markets in which public interest is high.

The list on a regional exchange can be divided into three parts: the regional issues, for which the exchange provides a primary market; issues traded, for technical reasons explained below, unlisted; and the dually listed issues. Competition with the New York exchanges arises in the last two categories.

One indication of the extent of such competitive trading may be seen in the data of Table 18–2. The total number of issues traded on one or more exchanges in the United States in 1961 was 3,042. The sum total of the items on the lists of all these exchanges was 5,501. The difference between these two figures, 2,459, is the number of items on some lists duplicating items on at least one other list. For example, the common stock of Kennecott Copper Corporation was listed on the New York and Boston exchanges and traded unlisted on the Cincinnati, Detroit, Mid-

Table 18–2. Stock Issues Admitted to Trading on Exchanges, June 30, 1961

Classification	Number of Issues		
	Unduplicated	Duplications	Total
On registered exchanges:			
Registered issues	2,748	867	3,615
Temporarily exempted issues	12	12	24
Unlisted trading permitted	197	1,545	1,742
Total on registered exchanges	2,957	2,424	5,381
On exempt exchanges:			
Listed for trading	70	31	101
Unlisted trading permitted	15	4	19
Total	3,042	2,459	5,501

Source: *Twenty-Seventh Annual Report of the SEC,* 1961, p. 217.

west, Philadelphia-Baltimore, Pacific Coast, and Pittsburgh exchanges. This issue, then, represents one unduplicated registered issue, one duplication of a registered issue, and six duplications as an item where unlisted trading is permitted as shown by the figures in Table 18–2.

Duplication is greater for unlisted trading than for dual-listing. The number of instances of the former is 1,549; of the latter, 898. These figures do not provide information on the volume of trading in these issues, but the substantial numbers for which competitive trading is possible suggests that trading volume would be significant.

Unlisted Trading. The practice of trading in unlisted issues on the American Stock Exchange was discussed in the preceding chapter. Under the Securities Exchange Act of 1934, exchanges were permitted to continue to trade in unlisted issues that were being traded at the time the Act became effective. Nearly all such issues were on the American exchange, but a few were similarly traded on other exchanges. In 1961 the total traded under this provision of the Act was 212 issues, of which 174 were on the American exchange list. The number of these issues declines each year as companies merge, or go out of business, or replace old issues with new.

However, unlisted trading in issues fully registered on at least one exchange is permitted on other exchanges, and far more of the trading in unlisted issues arises in this way. The Kennecott common stock referred to above was listed on two and traded unlisted on six exchanges.

The practice of unlisted trading in such issues apparently began on the Boston exchange in the 1920's and was adopted on the Philadelphia exchange in the same decade. It became more widely spread in the 1930's. In those years regional exchanges were trying to maintain a sufficient volume of trading to justify continued existence. They turned quite naturally to trading those issues that traded in large volume on the New York and American Stock Exchanges. The SEC has held that the extension of unlisted trading privileges is needed for preservation of a system of competitive stock markets. Applications for this privilege continue to be made and permission to trade is granted. In 1961 about sixty additional applications were granted.

The significance of trading in unlisted issues for individual exchanges ranges from great to negligible. In 1960 the proportion of share volume generated by transactions in unlisted issues was 77 per cent on the Boston exchange, 72 per cent on Philadelphia-Baltimore, 64 per cent on Cincinnati, 55 per cent on Pittsburgh, 47 per cent on Detroit, 32 per cent on Midwest, and 21 per cent on the Pacific Coast exchange. Dollar volume percentages would be higher for each of these exchanges because the prices of shares traded unlisted are usually high relative to prices of regional issues.

Exchanges only slightly affected by unlisted trading are Spokane, Salt Lake City, and San Francisco Mining. The last of these has no issues in this category. The other two have only a small number, representing only a small fraction of their total lists.

The significance of trading in unlisted issues to the total market for them on the exchanges is much less obvious than suggested by the percentages for individual exchanges. In 1960 the total volume of trading in unlisted stock issues (other than the ones on the American exchange) was 45 million shares, which is somewhat less than 3 per cent of total share volume in that year.

The New York Stock Exchange at one time opposed the practice of having its listed stock traded unlisted on other exchanges. In 1940 the exchange adopted a rule that prohibited its members from trading in such issues on other exchanges. The rule did not go into effect, however, because the SEC expressed disapproval of the restriction and approval of multiple markets.

Dual Registration. Trading in issues registered on more than one exchange provides another area of competitive trading. Dual registration may arise when an issue is listed first on a regional exchange and subsequently on one of the New York exchanges. An instance is Sundstrand Corporation common stock, which was listed first on the Midwest and some years later on the New York Stock Exchange. It is now traded on both exchanges.

Regional exchanges may also seek dual registrations. Some are obtained after an original listing on one of the major exchanges. Listing is both a source of some income for the exchange and a clear basis for competitive trading in the issue. For active stocks the competitive trading may increase the total market for issues by bringing into it the customer accounts of firms that are members of regional exchanges but are not members of the New York exchanges. It may also provide additional financial capacity for the specialist function and for the maintenance of orderly, active markets in such issues.

In the example of Kennecott common stock referred to above, listing on the New York and Boston exchanges was cited. American Telephone and Telegraph common stock is listed on the Boston, Midwest, New York, Pittsburgh, and Pacific Coast exchanges.

Regional Listings. A third class of stocks traded on the regional and local exchanges are those listed on and only on one of these exchanges. The specialized exchanges at Spokane, Salt Lake City, and San Francisco are concerned almost entirely with regional issues. Their lists are confined for the most part to stocks of companies in the extractive industries, which are, again, for the most part speculative. They do a large volume of trading in very low-priced shares. The figures in Table 18–1 indicate average prices in 1961 of $0.60, $0.16, and $0.14, respectively. Activity on these exchanges and these lists is affected greatly by investor and speculator interest in metal and petroleum stocks.

All the regional exchanges, however, are in competition with the over-the-counter market for some issues. Listing on a regional exchange may be a means to provide an efficient, well-publicized market for a small issue. The existence of an organized market is significant for broadening the interest in the issue and the number of shareholders. Many investors are not willing to buy issues traded over the counter. They prefer knowledge of current transactions as reported in the daily newspapers and the flow of information from the company required of companies with registered issues.

At times the direct interest in selling an issue, which is more characteristic of dealers in the over-the-counter market than of brokers using exchanges facilities, is important for getting investors interested in owning shares. Most stock issues are distributed first through the over-the-counter market and secondary trading in the issues starts in that market. Company managements may prefer limited trading in the issue and limited publicity about corporate affairs, which are characteristic of the over-the-counter market, and may not seek listing.

Once interest has developed in an issue and a fairly broad stockholder distribution does exist, the organized trading, clearing, and information facilities of an exchange benefit shareholders. For some, the mere registration of securities and the consequent opportunity to use those owned as security for collateral loans may be significant. In the periods of high volume of activity in the stock markets of 1960 and 1961, the efficiencies of the organized exchanges and their members in handling transactions for investors were observable.

The extent to which regional and local issues find markets and are traded on regional and local exchanges is, however, in total not great. The last publication of data on competitive trading for the larger exchanges covered trading in the year 1948.[2] It showed the following proportions of competitive trading:

	Per Cent Competitive
*Exchange**	*with New York Exchanges*
Philadelphia	98.5
Boston	93.0
Detroit	90.6
Chicago	88.0
Los Angeles	82.9
Pittsburgh	82.6

* Note these are exchanges in operation before the mergers of 1949 and 1956.

Obviously, at that time the amount of trading in non-competitive, regional issues for which these exchanges were primary markets was a small element in total volume. The importance of competitive trading, and the relative unimportance of purely regional trading, on the larger regional exchanges apparently has changed very little since the figures above were published.

In 1960 on the Pacific Coast Stock Exchange, for example, the trading list included 573 issues. Of these, 320 were registered on the exchange, 3 were temporarily exempt at year end, and 250 were traded in the unlisted category. Of the registered issues, 16 per cent, or 50 issues, were listed only on the Pacific Coast Exchange; the remainder were dual listings. Of the unlisted issues, 9 were traded only on this exchange; the remainder were listed and traded on one or more other exchanges. Of the total list, 10 per cent were exclusively regional issues. Trading in these contributed about 40 per cent of the share volume but only 8 per cent of the dollar volume of trading on the exchange in that year. In contrast, 92 per cent of the dollar volume of trading was done in issues traded competitively. Since the membership earns income in ratio to dollar volume of trading, the relative insignificance of regional listings is clear.

Viewing the same facts in another way, we may also say that the competitive trading in issues on the New York exchanges is important for the continued existence of regional exchanges on which markets for regional issues may develop.

[2] *Eighteenth Annual Report of the SEC*, 1952, p. 37.

THREE REGIONAL EXCHANGES

The data of Table 18–1 show that three regional exchanges are clearly more active than the others. Each contributes more than 1 per cent of the total dollar volume of transactions, measured in market value, on the organized exchanges. Each also has characteristics that help describe the nature of the regional markets.

Midwest Stock Exchange. This exchange, as was noted above, is the result of merger of four exchanges in late 1949 and subsequent merger with a fifth exchange in 1960. The exchanges of Chicago, St. Louis, Minneapolis-St. Paul, Cleveland, and New Orleans combined facilities and membership in the Midwest exchange. The Detroit, Cincinnati, and Pittsburgh exchanges were invited to join but have not done so. As the biggest of the regional exchanges, this one started with 407 issues listed for trading. Seats were limited to 400. Initial sales of seats were made at $2,500. During 1961 there were 522 issues available for trading, the volume reached new highs, and the price of a seat reached $16,000. The Exchange membership operated 1,937 offices in 561 cities in 49 states. Obviously, in some senses, this is a national, rather than regional, organization, but the concentration of offices is still in the Midwest.

The Exchange has a single trading floor, which is located in Chicago. Branch offices are set up in Cleveland and St. Louis. Members in these cities telephone instructions to these offices for transmittal by teletype directly to the floor. Other out-of-town brokerage houses are on direct wires to the floor.

The move to merge and consolidate facilities took place for several reasons: (1) the members expected to reduce overhead costs by eliminating separate trading facilities; (2) the number of regional and local issues consolidated on one exchange was expected to grow and the breadth of the market for each was expected to increase; (3) the larger market was expected to attract new listings and trading opportunities and more orders for the whole list; and (4) competition with the New York markets was expected to become more effective. Each of these expectations has been met to some extent. The Exchange has gained volume and listings, although it has not gained relative to the New York exchanges.

The Midwest has introduced a number of innovations. The administration of the Exchange has recognized quite clearly that a small exchange can succeed only by providing services more effectively or more widely than its larger competitors. The Midwest was first to accept the incorporation of member firms. They have a plan for unrestricted trading in inactive issues, which permits members to deal in these issues both off and on the Exchange. Clearing by mail through a Chicago office increased the efficiency of clearance for the widely distributed membership. The Exchange was the first to offer member firms a complete, central accounting service.

Pacific Coast Stock Exchange. Share volume on the Pacific Coast exchange has been greater than that on the Midwest. In 1961 the Exchange provided a market for 578 issues. The dollar volume of trading was $1,275 million, 2 per cent of the total on all exchanges. The share volume, however, was over 3 per cent of the total.

A substantial number of issues traded on this exchange are low priced. The average price per share of issues traded only on the Pacific Coast exchange in 1960 was approximately $4. Contrasts in volume and price are often great. The three volume leaders in February, 1961, among the issues priced under $5 were Nordon, Idaho Maryland Industries, and Aeco Corporation. The share volumes for that month were 900,000, 278,000, and 218,000, respectively. Among issues priced at $5 or more per share, the volume leaders of that month were Occidental Petroleum, Friden, and General Electric. Trading in these issues created volumes of 96,000, 92,000, and 71,000, respectively. Earlier in the chapter it was noted that 10 per cent of the issues accounted for 40 per cent of the share volume but only 8 per cent of the dollar volume of trading in 1960.

Under the terms of the merger in 1956, two divisions, Los Angeles and San Francisco, were established where separate exchanges had existed. Each division was given 80 memberships. Voting powers were written to provide for equivalence in the governance of the affairs of the Exchange. The Chairman of the Board of Governors is selected in alternate years from one division and by the membership of that division. The officers and staff operate as a single administrative unit.

A special aspect of operation on the Pacific Coast Stock Exchange is the provision for "preferred" commission rates. Approved non-member firms, that pay $100 annually for the privilege, are eligible to transact business through the Exchange at a rate 25 per cent below the general non-member commission schedule. This preference is an inducement for non-member organizations to transact business in listed issues on this exchange rather than over-the-counter or on another exchange.

Philadelphia-Baltimore Stock Exchange. This exchange resulted from merger of two of the oldest stock exchanges in the United States. The Philadelphia exchange was organized in 1790, two years before the New York Stock Exchange, and its organization for trading provided a model for the exchanges formed later. The present exchange was enlarged in 1953 by the merger of the Washington, D.C., Stock Exchange. The combined memberships provided the third largest dollar volume of activity among the regional exchanges in 1961.

A special feature of this exchange is the explicit recognition of the importance of odd-lot orders for activity on the regional exchanges. The Exchange appoints Odd-lot Dealers, rather than specialists, in issues. Nearly all the trading on this exchange is in issues with a primary market in New York.

19

Foreign Stock Markets

Opportunities for profitable use of funds in foreign investment have stimulated the flow of funds from the United States to all parts of the world in the post-war period. Some of the flow is directed into plant and equipment by corporate managements establishing foreign subsidiaries, or adding to them. Some, however, represents "portfolio," rather than "direct," investment—the purchase of the securities of foreign companies for investment rather than control in foreign locales. The procedures leading to decisions by investors to purchase such securities are not greatly different from those leading to decision to purchase domestic securities, but an aspect that deserves attention is difference in the stock markets in the countries where the primary markets for such stocks are made.

This chapter is a brief note on stock markets in different parts of the world. A simple count of exchanges about which some record had been made in the library of the New York Stock Exchange in the summer of 1960 indicated that one hundred and twenty stock exchanges were in operation in foreign cities at that time. A full description of so large a number of exchanges is far beyond the scope of this book. This chapter is limited to description of a few characteristics of markets in other places, with emphasis on some of the kinds of differences that might affect the decisions of American investors.

A partial escape from some of the risks of investment in foreign securities is offered American investors through purchase of American Depository Receipts (ADR's), or foreign shares listed on U. S. exchanges. The market value on December 31, 1960, of all shares and certificates representing foreign stocks on U. S. exchanges was about $11 billion, of which $10 billion was in Canadian stocks. The number of issues involved were listed as follows: 145 on the American, 25 on the New York, and 3 on other stock exchanges. Trading in foreign stocks declined somewhat in the late 1950's in the United States.

ADR's were described briefly in Chapter 17 (page 312). In general, ADR's or listings permit ownership interest in foreign companies with pricing and transfer conventions of American stock markets. It is not, nevertheless, appropriate to assume that price, at least, is free of the effects of pricing practices on the primary markets for these securities. The rapidity and efficiency of international arbitrage usually makes the American investor in ADR's or foreign shares fully as susceptible to price swings in the primary market as direct ownership would.

CANADIAN EXCHANGES

An area of great interest to American investors is Canada. Five stock exchanges provide markets for Canadian issues. In recent years American investors have shown a great deal of interest in some of the issues for which these exchanges are primary markets.

As in the United States, two exchanges have a much greater significance in terms of trading volume than the others. Where about 93 per cent of the money value of all U. S. stock sales is registered in transactions on the New York and American stock exchanges, about 98 per cent of Canadian exchange dollar volume is registered on the Toronto and Montreal-Canadian exchanges. The Toronto exchange alone accounts for 63 per cent. The exchanges of Vancouver, Calgary, and Winnipeg have small fractions of the total for the country.

The Toronto Exchange. More than 1,100 issues are listed for trading on the Toronto Stock Exchange. Nearly all of them are traded in any one month. The total volume of trading reached a high in 1955, when about 1½ billion shares were transferred. In 1960 and 1961 volume was about ½ billion shares.

This exchange, like the Detroit exchange in the United States, does not have specialists for individual issues. A place on the floor for trading a particular issue is designated by the Exchange. A trader wishing to buy or sell that issue goes to the designated part of the floor and shouts his interest. Other traders attracted by his shout, gather to state their bids or offers. The best price at which the trade can be made is determined from the information then available.

Trading may be done for the account of a firm rather than a public customer. To the extent that a member firm trades regularly in an issue, it is to some degree performing the specialist function without the specialist responsibility. It is probably fair to say that variation of price for issues of comparable investment quality is higher on the Toronto

Stock Exchange than on the New York exchanges because of the absence of the specialist function in the Canadian market.[1]

EUROPEAN STOCK EXCHANGES

One very interesting summary of the stock exchange organization of Western Europe lists sixty-three exchanges, excluding those in Spain.[2] It indicates also that one exchange in Belgium has four trading centers and another in England has twenty-two. The total thus might be eighty-seven. All important urban centers have trading facilities.

On the continent control of the stock exchange organizations lies generally in the hands of the state. A board of brokers is appointed by public authority and it, in turn, appoints or admits to membership the persons qualified to transact securities business. This board, or a sub-committee, is responsible for establishing and inspecting trading procedures. A supranational association, the Fédération Internationale des Bourses de Valeurs, has been formed to provide clearance of information and an approach to common standards for trading procedure and for taxation of transactions in the Common Market and neighboring countries. In general, only those issues accepted for listing are traded on the European exchanges.

The London Stock Exchange. An exchange of special interest for investors throughout the world is the London Stock Exchange. Trading in a very large list of securities from widely distributed areas is a feature. It lists and trades in more than six times the number of issues listed on the New York Stock Exchange. The number of members is three times that of the New York counterpart.

The trading practice of the London exchange is unique. Broker and dealer functions are distinctly separate. Members may act as brokers or as dealers (jobbers), but not as both. Brokers transact business with jobbers; the latter may transact business with other jobbers as well as with brokers but do not transact business with public customers. Unlike the handling of orders on American exchanges, public orders are executed in every instance by a purchase from or a sale to a dealer. The broker acts as an agent for his customer in locating the best price for his customer.

Dealers are competitive. Brokers check prices with several dealers in a given issue. Dealers are not required to make a market in any issue. They may bid without offering, offer without bidding, or bid and offer

---

[1] For more comparisons, see: James E. Walter and J. Peter Williamson, "Organized Securities Exchanges in Canada," *The Journal of Finance*, V (September, 1960), 307–24.

[2] *Indici e Dati Relativi ad Investimenti in Titoli Quotati Nelle Borse Italiane (1948–1960)* (Milan: Mediobanca, 1960).

at different prices (differing by the "jobber's turn"). They are not confined to trading in assigned issues but may trade those issues in which they have an interest.

The floor of the Exchange is divided into areas. Trading in issues of similar industrial characteristic—motors, oils, foreign industrials—are assigned to floor areas for trading. Dealers usually confine their trading to a few issues of similar kind. Those dealing in motors congregate in the area assigned for trading of motors stocks. Brokers go to that area to obtain price information, to bid or offer securities, and to execute orders for their customers. Commission charges average about $1\frac{1}{4}$ per cent on the money value of transactions. The brokers gain from commissions; the dealers gain from the spread in prices. The dealers in the issues find their opportunities for business in the areas assigned for transactions in the stocks they have chosen to do business in.

Neither the amount nor the price of a transaction need be reported. There are no data on volume of shares traded comparable to those reported on the ticker in the United States. Share prices are low in comparison with American prices; prices of less than $10 per share are common. Such prices, or course, arise from traditional notions about size of transaction and in no way reflect quality. Quoted prices provide the basis for publication of information about price movements.

OTHER STOCK EXCHANGES

About as many more exchanges are in operation in other parts of the world, outside the area of Communist domination. As industry develops in Asia, Africa, and Latin America, the exchange of stock becomes a matter of commercial importance. The flow of available funds into business enterprise also becomes a matter of national importance, which is facilitated by development of stock exchanges. The larger urban communities, acting as centers for finance, establish facilities for stock trading. The range of activity may be from a select, small list of recognized companies to a form of trading, similar to the cabinet trading at Post 30 on the New York Stock Exchange, through which all transactions of any kind in local stocks are effected through stock exchange facilities. Where trading is limited to a list, call markets are not uncommon. The idea of trading in unlisted issues on the exchange floor is accepted in several places but, more often, a specific list is maintained and does include those issues most likely to be actively traded. Many of the exchanges are modeled on those of the United States. On these, floor procedures and clearing practices are similar and relationships between brokers and their customers have parallels.

The Japanese Stock Markets. The stock markets of Japan are in many respects a post-war institution. The history of stock trading in that country extends into the last century, but the changes in market procedures and securities laws in the period 1945–49, were of such magnitude that a new business may be said to have emerged. The influence was American. Trading procedures are markedly similar to those of the New York Stock Exchange, and securities laws are markedly similar to the securities acts of the United States.

In 1960 nine stock exchanges were in operation. They were at Tokyo, Osaka, Nagoya, Kyoto, Kobe, Hiroshima, Fukuoka, Niigata, and Sapporo. The exchange at Toyko clearly dominated stock volume. Two-thirds of the transactions were made on that exchange. Trading on these exchanges is characterized by very large volumes of share transfers at low prices. In 1960 the share volume was 43 billion and average share price was 217 yen (about 60 cents). On one day in Tokyo 250 million shares were traded. Trading in approximately 300 other issues was done on an unlisted basis. Some issues traded in units of 1,000 shares but lots of 500 or 100 were usual. The trading commissions and procedures on these exchanges are generally like those described in earlier chapters dealing with American exchanges.

The Japanese practices do permit, however, the crossing of orders in brokerage offices. The transaction is called "Bai-kai." Price on such transactions is based on prices established on the exchange floor and commissions on the transaction are identical to those charged on floor transactions.

In 1961 the "Second Market" was opened, with trading in Tokyo, Osaka, and Nagoya. This market replaces for practical purposes the over-the-counter market in Japan.

The major Japanese securities houses have begun actively to seek American business. Several have opened offices in the United States and have undertaken publication of some excellent statements about the capital markets in Japan as a means of informing American investors of opportunities for investment in that country.[3] The flow of information from these firms to investors in the United States is fairly clearly a benefit to those investors seeking to place funds abroad. The distribution of Japanese investment company shares has also been considered. The aggressive securities houses of Japan may find a niche in the American market before other foreign firms do.

SPECIAL RISKS

The American investor seeking to place funds abroad should see clearly the presence of some risks different from those found when in-

---

[3] For example, *Handbook for Investment in Japanese Stocks* (Tokyo: The Nikko Securities Co., Ltd., 1961).

vestments are made locally. A brief cataloging shows four areas for consideration: (1) risks arising from the separate, individual political and economic policies of the nation in which an investment is made; (2) changes in the price of the money of foreign nations; (3) differences in the amounts and kinds of information available for investment decision; and (4) factors affecting the ways in which prices are established in the primary stock markets for the issues in which investments are made. Briefly and in the most general terms, these are factors the American investor should consider.

National Unity. The American investor must accept risks related to the national concerns of a foreign country in which he commits funds. The domestic policies of that country may lead to taxation, restrictions on rights to add or remove funds, and direct intervention in decisions as to how to operate and what products to make. These policies may contemplate nationalization of some or all of the productive facilities of the nation. Without presently concerning ourselves with questions of right or wrong, we can see that the separate concerns of a foreign nation may lead to policies and actions different from those an American investor would expect at home. The mere concept of national unity, then, defines an area of risk for alien investors. It may, at times, be risk of great profit rather than loss. Investment incentives, for example, are greater in some countries than they are in the United States. In any event, however, the American investor has an additional risk.

Money Rates. International relationships are adjusted in part by changing rates of exchange for money. A dollar invested in Venezuela in 1958 bought $3\frac{1}{3}$ bolivars worth of securities. In 1961 identical securities at identical bolivar prices in Venezuela had a value of $0.73. A change in the rate of exchange had depreciated the investment of an American by one-third. This kind of investment risk is not a factor in domestic investment.

Availability of Information. The kinds and quality of information about securities characteristic of registered issues in the United States are not available for foreign securities. Even the comparative lack of information on over-the-counter issues in this country is a less severe block for effective security analysis than the mixture of lack of information and misinformation found abroad. The dependability of accounting standards in this country is a significant factor for investment decision. The American investor placing funds abroad must expect to have little or no information for analysis and considerably less assurance about the meaning of such data as he does obtain. The investor is likely to find that he cannot know whether an active market for an issue exists, what prices are in fact current, what the real balance sheet and income record of companies is, and what his own liability as a stockholder may be.

This latter point is one that few American investors consider. In the United States, assessable stock, which has the feature of liability for the stockholder, is very unusual. Not so abroad. Stock is issued subject to assessment in most foreign countries. For example, the common stock of Banco Union (40%) in Venezuela has been distributed on payment of 40 per cent of its par value. The holder may be called on at any time for payment of the remaining 60 per cent of par value. His obligation to the creditors of the company is real and may be significant. Over a number of years assessments on the stockholders will bring the payments to par. Fully paid stock does exist. In general, the stock of companies that have been in business for many years is fully paid up. On such stock the stockholder is not subject to assessment. The frequency of assessable stock, however, makes attention to this subject one necesary for investment decision. To accept liability in a situation where dependability of information about the company and the market is suspect must require at least some second thought.

Market Breadth. The effectiveness of price determination in stock markets also affects the investment results for shareholders. In the earlier sections of this chapter some differences among stock exchanges were described. These, generally, had procedures and breadth of trading likely to provide effective price determination. However, the ability of a market to absorb a substantial volume of transactions in a brief period of time is not characteristic of many around the world. The likelihood of price manipulation is quite high on some. The breadth of shareowner-ship is not as great in most countries as it is in the United States.[4] As a corrolary, concentration of ownership is often a factor. The decisions of a few important shareholders have a definite effect on the prices of issues in which they are interested. There is not the publicity nor the regulatory restraint in other countries that investors in this country expect. Again, however, this is a consideration for investment analysis and not a bar to investment by informed investors.

---

[4] For information on public participation in stock ownership in fifty-five nations, see: New York Stock Exchange, *Individual Shareownership Around the World,* May, 1962.

III

WORK OF
THE SECURITIES HOUSES

20

The Customer and His Broker

Over a long period of time there has developed a vast body of law, customs, and regulations that protect the rights and define the duties of both customers and brokers. The purpose of this chapter is to describe the main business and legal relationships that exist between these parties. The reader who is interested in the more technical aspects of the customer-broker relationship is referred to a standard legal treatise on the subject.[1]

OPENING AN ACCOUNT

Procedure. In general, the responsible individual who wishes to open up a new account with a brokerage firm will find that such an operation can be accomplished quickly and with a minimum of inconvenience. It is no more difficult than the opening of a new account with a bank.

It should be realized that a broker cannot accept an irresponsible party for an account. The New York Stock Exchange requires that members and member firms handle transactions for customers only after obtaining information on the essential facts about each customer (Rule 405).

The procedure and forms used in opening up a new account vary from firm to firm. Those used as illustrations in this chapter represent standard procedure in large firms.

Customers become clients of a brokerage firm in various ways. Some are "walk-ins" who come to firm offices, introduce themselves, and ask

---

[1] For example: C. H. Meyer, *The Law of Stockbrokers and Stock Exchanges* (New York: Baker, Voorhis & Co., Inc., 1931) and *Supplement* (1936). Also: W. H. Black, *The Law of Stock Exchanges, Stockbrokers and Customers* (New York: Edward Thompson Co., 1940).

to open up an account. Others are introduced by present customers of the firm, a procedure highly favored by member firms, but by no means necessary. Some are obtained through the direct selling effort of registered representatives.

The first step in opening an account is to fill out a signature card, an example of which is shown in Figure 20–1. The amount of information on this card varies from firm to firm, but usually spaces are indicated for name, address, telephone number, employer, age, citizenship, and one or more references. The signature of the customer is, of course, highly important.

SMITH, BARNEY & CO.	*REFERENCE SIGNATURE*

New York - Philadelphia - Chicago - Boston - Albany - Allentown
Cleveland - Hartford - Milwaukee - Minneapolis - San Francisco

Please check the data below when signing this card.

S I G N A T U R E

NAME (MR. MRS.* MISS)........................
LAST NAME   FIRST NAME

HOME ADDRESS........................
☐ CHECK IF NOTICES ARE TO BE SENT HERE

BUSINESS ADDRESS........................
☐ CHECK IF NOTICES ARE TO BE SENT HERE

OCCUPATION AND TITLE........................ FIRM........................

*HUSBAND'S OCCUPATION AND TITLE........................FIRM........................

BANK........................AGE: OVER 21 ☐   CITIZEN OF........................

ORDERS MAY SOMETIMES BE TRANSMITTED BY........................

ADDRESS........................

Date........................   Registered Representative........................

V.P.   Rev. Sept. 1959

Fig. 20–1. A signature card for a new account.

Frequently, a second card is also used for new account information. This card is necessary if the signature card does not provide a means for obtaining all information desired. Figure 20–2 is an example of a new account information form. This form contains a number of items necessary for correct handling of the account, such as: designation as a cash, margin, or commodity account; credit information; instructions on notices and statements; account number; and signatures.

Credit references are always required. A bank reference is usual and at least one other reference frequently is requested. A business associate, friend, or firm customer serves this purpose.

CODE 21 R 12/59 PTD. IN U.S.A. **NEW ACCOUNT INFORMATION**

STENCIL HERE

ORIGINAL

☐ NEW ACCOUNT
☐ TRANSFER OF ACCT. FROM (OFCE) ______

ACCT. NO. ______

TYPE OF ACCT.	
CASH	☐
MARGIN	☐
COMMODITY	☐
CUSTODIAN	☐

DATE OPENED ______

BUSINESS PHONE ______

RESIDENCE PHONE ______

A. E. No. ______

IF CLIENT IS A MARRIED WOMAN, SHOW HUSBAND'S NAME, EMPLOYER AND OCCUPATION

FULL NAME MISS MRS. MR. ______

IF MRS., SPECIFY GIVEN NAME (PLEASE PRINT)

MAILING ADDRESS ______ STREET ______ CITY ______ ZONE ______ STATE

FIRM NAME ______ BUSINESS ______ POSITION

HUSBAND'S NAME ______ BUSINESS ______ POSITION

IF CLIENT HAS ANOTHER ACCT. WITH US, SPECIFY ☐ CUSTODIAN ☐ CASH ☐ MARGIN ☐ COMMODITY ☐ S. S. A.

IF ACCT. TRANSFERRED, SPECIFY OLD ACCT. NOS. IF KNOWN ______

MAIL DUPLICATE:

NOTICES ONLY ☐ NAME ______ (PLEASE PRINT)

STATEMENTS ONLY ☐ ADDRESS ______ (INCLUDE POSTAL ZONE NUMBER)

NOTICES AND STATEMENTS ☐

U. S. CITIZEN ☐

HOW LONG HAVE YOU KNOWN CLIENT? ______ IS CLIENT OVER 21? YES ☐ NO ☐

OTHER ☐ ______

BANK OR BROKER REFERENCE

OTHER COMMENTS

NET WORTH ETC.

SIGNATURE OF EMPLOYEE (OPENING ACCOUNT) | APPROVED (OFFICE MANAGER) | ACCEPTED BY (AUTHORIZED OFFICER)

Fig. 20–2. A new account information form.

Although new accounts do come to a brokerage firm on the customer's own initiative, many result from solicitation by firm partners and registered representatives, a part of whose duties is to bring new business to the firm.

Types of Account. Eight different kinds of account are recognized in the securities business. There are variants within the basic types, too. Briefly defined, the eight kinds are:

General accounts. These are more popularly known as "margin" accounts since this is the type commonly established by customers intending to use credit in their transactions.

Cash accounts—all transactions for cash. A cash transaction does not restrict the customer to payment before purchase but does imply payment very shortly thereafter. This point is discussed further below.

Subscriptions accounts. Since different margin rules apply to the purchase and carrying of securities acquired through exercise of rights during a subscription period, segregation of such transactions from a general account in a special subscriptions account may be arranged.

Arbitrage accounts. Arbitraging may be defined roughly as executing a sale order in one market and a buy order at or about the same time in another market to take advantage of a price disparity in the same or convertible securities in the two markets. Again, difference in margin rules leads to use of this kind of account.

Commodity accounts. Trading in commodities takes place in different markets and under different regulations. A special account for this activity facilitates both bookkeeping and regulation.

Specialists accounts. The unique nature of specialist activity is recognized by handling specialists accounts separately.

Omnibus accounts. For some purposes accounts will be established for execution of orders of a number of persons all of whom are customers of a securities house that, in turn, is placing these orders through a correspondent house.

Miscellaneous "memorandum" accounts. Special activities that one securities house might perform for other securities houses or members of stock exchanges are handled through miscellaneous accounts. In addition, collection or exchange of securities, transactions in foreign exchange, and "non-purpose" credit arrangements may be recorded for any customer in such accounts.

Although each of these types of account has significance in its appropriate use, the types of greatest use are the cash and general accounts. These are described in more detail below, together with a description of some of the variations that may be useful in particular instances.

Cash Accounts. The cash account is the simplest form of account. All transactions are made for cash. No credit purchases or short sales are permitted and no loans on securities in the account are made. This account serves for the outright purchase or sale of securities.

The customer who opens a cash account may do business immediately. He may not be required to deposit the full amount of cash necessary to make the initial purchase, although the full amount is expected within seven days, as a limit, and, more usually, within four days. This procedure is followed for subsequent transactions. When purchases are made, it may not be required that the full cash balance be in the hands of the broker at the time of purchase.

Once an account has been opened, it is customary to assign it to an employee of the firm who will handle the account. Various titles are given to the employees who handle customer accounts. Firms have different and definite preferences on this point. Usual titles are: registered representative, account executive, customer's man, and securities salesman. After assignment all transactions of the customer usually are handled by the designated person.

General Accounts. General, or "margin," accounts provide for more complex transactions than do cash accounts. Such an account contemplates the broker's extension of credit to the customer when securities are purchased on margin. On a short sale the broker is expected also to borrow securities for the customer and accept responsibility for their return. Cash purchases may be made if desired.

In addition to the regular signature card, indicated in Figure 20–1, the customer must sign another form, which is usually called a Margin Agreement, Customer's Agreement, or Standard Customer's Agreement. Figure 20–3 provides an example. This agreement, to be discussed more fully later, permits the broker to pledge the customer's securities at a bank and to sell them when margin requirements necessitate such action.

Joint Accounts. It is possible for two or more individuals, such as a husband and wife or two business associates, to open an account in which they hold joint interests. There are two types of joint account. The first goes by two names: (1) tenancy by entireties and (2) joint tenancy with right of survivorship. Only a husband and wife may use the first tenancy. Although there is a slight legal distinction between the two, they are alike in that the ownership of securities and cash in the account passes to the survivor in the event that either of the tenants dies. This is a logical tenancy for husband and wife under certain conditions. It is well for a stockholder to consult a lawyer or broker in the state of residence as to which type of tenancy is recommended.

FORM G4

GLORE, FORGAN & CO.

135 South La Salle Street, Chicago 3, Illinois

ACCOUNT NUMBER ....

SOCIAL SECURITY NUMBER ....

Dear Sirs:

This is to confirm my understanding and agreement relating to my account now open or about to be opened with you.

It is understood and agreed that any securities (this term as used herein to include puts, calls, commodities and contracts for or in relation to commodities) at any time held by you for me, (either individually or jointly with others), whether through delivery, purchase or otherwise, and whether carried in one or more accounts, are pledged as collateral security for any and all claims and demands that you now or may hereafter have against me, until paid in full. You are hereby authorized to hypothecate, rehypothecate the same, for my account or for your account, in your general loans or otherwise as you may see fit, either separately or together with securities belonging to others, and for more than your claim against me, and otherwise to use, transfer or deliver the same, and without obligation to retain in possession or control securities of like character and amount. You may deliver or return to me an equal quantity of each security of like tenor and amount, and need not deliver or return the specific securities pledged or held by you. In the case of the sale of any securities by you for my account, I authorize you to borrow any security necessary to make delivery thereof and I hereby agree to be responsible for any loss which you may sustain thereby, or any loss which you may sustain by reason of your inability to borrow the security sold. I further agree that I am to pay to you on demand, the whole or any part of my indebtedness to you as the same may be at any time, and to furnish you, on demand, such additional margin or security as you may from time to time require. In default of compliance with any such demand for payment or security, or if at any time you should in your discretion believe that the condition of my account with you warrants such action, I hereby authorize you, without prior or further demand, tender or notice to me, and without advertisement, to sell, for my account, any securities then held by you for me, as above, or to purchase for my account any security of which I may be short or which I may have failed to deliver to you, on any exchange or market, or at public or private sale, at your option, without liability for subsequent difference in value, whenever such sale or purchase is deemed necessary by you for your protection; any excess or deficiency to be paid or received, as the case may be, on demand. It is understood that a prior tender, demand, or notice shall not be considered a waiver of your right to sell or buy any securities at any time as above provided. At any sale you may be the purchaser.

All transactions heretofore or hereafter between us are subject to the rules and customs of the New York Stock Exchange and its Clearing House, except that, if any transaction shall have taken place on an exchange other than the New York Stock Exchange, it shall be subject to the rules of such exchange and of its clearing house, to the extent that such rules shall be different from the rules prevailing on the New York Stock Exchange.

This agreement shall not be subject to modification or revocation except in writing signed by me and you, such modification or revocation to affect only transactions thereafter entered into between us.

Yours very truly,

(Name)...............

(Date)...............

I hereby re-affirm the consent heretofore given by me to you authorizing you to lend (either separately or with other securities) to yourselves as brokers or to others, any securities which you may be carrying for my account or under my control on margin. This authorization shall apply to any and all accounts (including joint accounts with others) carried by you for me or under my control, and shall remain in force until revoked by me by written notice received by you.

Witness:...............

Accepted and Recorded:...............

Signature ....

Fig. 20—3. A margin agreement.

The second type of joint account is known as tenancy in common. In this, the survivor secures no additional interest in the account. If A and B enter into such an account and A dies, the heirs of A receive A's share of the securities and cash in the account at the time of his death. None of that share goes to B by virtue of the joint tenancy.

Joint accounts require signature of an additional agreement by the tenants.

Discretionary Accounts. Some brokers permit customers to open an account with the understanding that the broker may make transactions for that account at his discretion. Other brokers refuse such accounts entirely. In a discretionary account the broker is given the power in the execution of orders to decide with the approval of a general partner or voting stockholder of his organization on timing and price, and perhaps even the selection of issues and size of order. Such accounts are not generally recommended. They lend themselves to abuse or, at least, to the accusation of abuse. In recent years several instances in which member firms have been disciplined have arisen from handling of discretionary accounts. Nevertheless, in some circumstances, the customer's interests may be served better by giving his broker the power to act when necessary.

Discretionary orders were discussed in Chapter 9.

Accounts of Minors. Strict rules govern the acceptance of certain accounts that are said to have "disabilities," particularly where margin transactions are involved. Brokers will not accept an account, either cash or margin, of a person under twenty-one years of age. This rule is based on the well-known legal principle that a contract made by a minor is voidable at his election. If the contract is voided by the minor, the broker cannot recover any advances, losses, commissions, or interest that may arise after the contract is closed. The minor can successfully void his contract by the defense that he was under twenty-one, even in cases where he has fraudulently asserted that he was of age.[2]

Although brokers will accept no accounts of minors, it is possible for a parent to buy securities for his own account and then transfer them to the minor when he reaches the age of twenty-one. All states have enacted statutes that make possible the outright gift of securities to a child by registering them in the name of an adult as "custodian" for the child. Laws in the several states differ somewhat, but usually the custodian has the right to sell the stock originally given, reinvest the proceeds in stock or other securities, collect dividends, and generally manage the investment for the child until the child becomes twenty-one years of age.

---

[2] Meyer, *op. cit.*, p. 496; Black, *op. cit.*, p. 177.

Other Accounts with Disabilities. There are other accounts involving "disabilities" which require special handling by the broker. An employee of the New York Stock Exchange or a member firm may not make cash or margin transactions without the consent of his employer. Employees of banks, trust companies, insurance companies, and other firms or companies dealing in securities cannot have margin accounts without the express permission of the employer. This rule (407) was made by the New York Stock Exchange to prevent secret speculation by employees of financial institutions who may have access to large sums of money or securities.

In the event of a customer's decease, the broker cannot continue to buy and sell for the account; however, outstanding commitments may be continued.[3] It is the usual practice of brokers to protect themselves at the time of the death of a customer by an express agreement that permits the broker to close out the account without notice.

HANDLING THE ACCOUNT

Placing Orders. Once an account has been properly opened, an order may be placed by any means convenient to the customer, such as telephone, mail, wire, or personal contact. In actual practice, most orders come to brokers' offices over the telephone, 80 per cent being a reasonable estimate of their importance.

When an order is received by the registered representative, he fills out an order blank at once. These blanks differ in form from firm to firm, but all are designed to tabulate essential information about the order. An example is given in Figure 20–4. It was placed by Mr. (Joseph) Karns, whose account number is 795–517. It is being handled by account executive No. 50. The order is a limited order to buy 100 shares of Chrysler common at 64. The broker is to hold the securities in his office. Since there is no time limit specified, it is a day order.

Certain legal interpretations can be made of this order. The purchase or sale is at the customer's risk. It is to be executed in the usual or customary market. Regular way delivery is implied. The customer is responsible for the proper identification of the stock, which is always considered to be common stock unless otherwise specified. If the order is a limit order, as it is in this case, the broker must obtain the limit or better. Unless a time limit is specified, the order is considered a day order.

Office Procedures. Without attempting detailed examination of the multiplicity of activities that take place after the order is received, an

---

[3] *Hess v. Rau*, N. Y. 359.

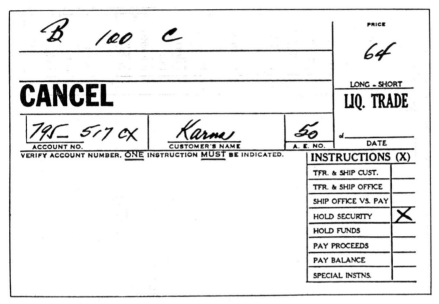

Fig. 20–4. An order form.

effort to indicate their scope and nature is made in the presentation of Figure 20–5 and the accompanying notes.[4] In general, of course, the order is forwarded to the floor of the Exchange for execution. Meanwhile the "back office" is at work on the job of recording the facts in the customer's and firm's records, checking the accuracy of executions and

[4] Notes describing steps numbered in Figure 20–5:
1. Executed order ticket received in P. & S. from order room.
2. Figuration clerk adds to ticket:
    a. Blotter Code (denotes where trade was made; i.e., on an exchange or over-the-counter)
    b. Sales credit (if applicable)
    c. Taxes and interest (if applicable for IBM use)
3. Stock ticket clerk:
    a. Sorts tickets by blotter code
    b. Splits ticket into original and duplicate
3a. Duplicate ticket temporarily filed in pigeonhole.
3b. Stock ticket clerk matches floor broker's report with duplicate ticket and staples them together.
3c. Figuration clerk figures floor broker's commission from duplicate ticket and floor broker's report.
3d. Figuration clerk files duplicate ticket.
4. Original ticket sent to IBM room via tubes.
5. IBM clerk sorts tickets by office from which order originated.
6. Customer's IBM name, address, and account number card matched with original ticket and removed from customer's IBM card file.
7. IBM security card (i.e., name of security bought or sold) matched with original ticket and removed from file.

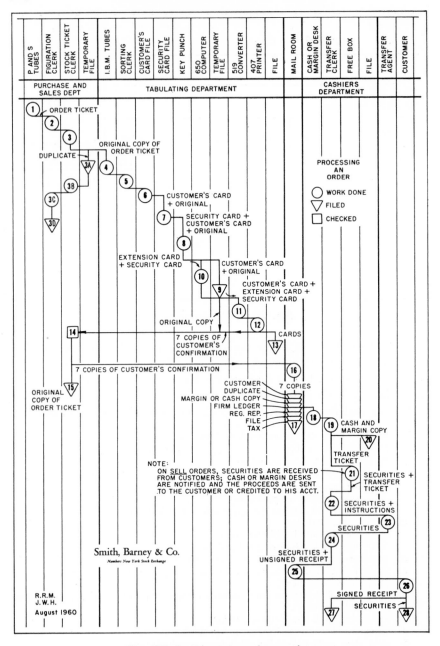

Fig. 20–5. Processing of an order.

the conformance to regulations, and preparing reports for the customer and registered representative.

8. Key punch operator punches IBM extension card (third IBM card involved) to show:
   a. Number of shares bought or sold
   b. Blotter code
   c. Price of security
9. Original ticket and customer's IBM card are temporarily filed.
10. 650 computer records on IBM cards:
    a. Principal
    b. Commission
    c. Taxes (where applicable)
    d. Net money
11. 519 Converter:
    a. Customer's card, security card and extension card matched and fed into converter
    b. Converter transfers information from extension card to security card
    c. Converter checks for errors in account number and registered representative's number
12. 407 Printer prints customer's confirmation consisting of seven copies.
13. The three IBM cards are filed for use in printing blotter.
14. Original ticket and customer's confirmation are checked for errors.
15. Original ticket filed.
16. Mail clerk splits customer's confirmation into its seven copies.
17. Mail clerk distributes the seven copies as follows:
    a. Original—mailed to customer
    b. Duplicate—sent to person or institution other than customer who is to receive confirmation of the transaction
    c. Cash and margin copy sent to cash or margin desk
    d. Firm ledger copy sent to accountant for recording non-agency transactions
    e. Registered representative's copy mailed to registered representative
    f. File copy sent to accounting clerk for recording of salesman's commission
    g. Tax copy sent to cage for confirmation of daily transfer tax charges
18. Cash or margin desk clerk receives cash or margin copy:
    a. Records money and security involved on customer's account card
    b. Sends cash and margin copy of customer's confirmation to transfer clerk when payment is received for security purchase
19. Transfer clerk fills out a transfer ticket and sends it to the free box.
20. Cash and margin copy filed.
21. Free box—Security certificates are issued against transfer ticket for change to customer's name and returned to transfer clerk. (N.B.: on sell order, when securities are received from customer, the cash or margin desk is notified and the proceeds of the sale are sent to the customer or credited to his account.)
22. Transfer clerk staples instruction copy of transfer ticket to securities to be changed to customer's name and sends them to transfer agent (a bank).
23. Transfer agent receives instruction ticket and security certificates. He registers customer as new owner and returns the certificates in customer's name.
24. Transfer clerk checks certificates for accuracy of information and sends receipt copy of transfer ticket with security certificates to mail room.
25. Mail clerk sends certificates and receipt copy of transfer ticket to customer.
26. Customer receives certificates and receipt. He signs and returns receipt slip.
27. Transfer clerk receives signed receipt and files it.
28. Customer stores stock for safekeeping.

Confirmations. A confirmation, or "confirm" as it is often called, is a report by a broker to his customer on how an order has been executed. A typical confirmation indicates all or most of the following facts about the order:

1. Settlement date
2. Number of shares
3. Name of security
4. Market where transaction was executed
5. Price
6. Amount of money value
7. Transfer taxes
8. Interest
9. Commissions
10. Postage
11. Net amount due customer or broker
12. Trade date

Let us trace a typical transaction. As indicated by Figure 20–4, our hypothetical customer, Mr. Joseph Karns, placed a 100-share, limit order to buy Chrysler common at 64. This was duly executed by his broker on June 25 at the limit. The settlement date for the transaction is four days later on June 29. His commissions came to $45.40. The net amount due was $6,445.40.

Confirmations are mailed out by brokerage firms as soon as the purchase and sales department can process the transaction, often the same day. A sample confirmation is shown in Figure 20–6. In addition to the mailed confirmation, firms will confirm the transaction by telephone to the customer when it seems advisable to do so. Confirmations are issued for both purchases and sales. Confirmation forms differ in detail among member firms.

The legal interpretation of confirmations is important. It is a practice of brokers to add as footnotes a number of conditions on which the accounts of the broker are carried, such as the right of the broker to close the account without notice where necessary to protect the broker; the right to rehypothecate; and other conditions. Whether or not this confirmation with a statement of conditions constitutes a contract is a case for a jury to decide in case of a dispute.[5] Certainly the first confirmation received by the customer, after opening an account, cannot be considered a contract. Later confirmations may or may not be considered as contracts, since the customer then knows on what conditions the broker handles accounts. In any case, the broker is likely to have the customer sign a customer's margin agreement embodying the same conditions as stated on the face or reverse side of the confirmation, before allowing him to use the margin account.

[5] Meyer, *op. cit.*, p. 440.

SMITH, BARNEY & CO.

NEW YORK
20 Broad Street, New York 5, N. Y.
529 Fifth Avenue, New York 17, N. Y.

PHILADELPHIA
Philadelphia National Bank Bldg.
Broad & Chestnut Streets, Philadelphia 7, Pa.

CHICAGO
39 S. La Salle Street
Chicago 3, Ill.

ALBANY • ALLENTOWN • BOSTON • CLEVELAND • HARTFORD • MILWAUKEE • MINNEAPOLIS • SAN FRANCISCO

YOU BOUGHT

MR JOHN DOE
900 42ND STREET
NEW YORK 27 N Y

ACCOUNT NO.	T	RR
6-09-500		200

TYPE OF ACCOUNT

1-CASH
2-MARGIN
3-SHORT
4-BOND ACCOUNT
5-SPECIAL SUBSCRIPTION
6-WHEN ISSUED—CASH
7-WHEN ISSUED—MARGIN
8-OTHER

Sample

WE HAVE MADE THE FOLLOWING TRANSACTION SUBJECT TO THE TERMS AND CONDITIONS SET FORTH ON THE REVERSE SIDE. WE HAVE ACTED **AS YOUR AGENT** FOR YOUR ACCOUNT AND RISK UNLESS OTHERWISE STATED IN CODE BELOW.

QUANTITY	SECURITY	PRICE	CODE
100	INTERNATL BUSINESS MACHINES CORP	550	1

PRINCIPAL AMOUNT	INTEREST OR TAX		POSTAGE	COMMISSION		TOTAL COST
55.000.00				125 00		55,125.00

TRADE DATE	SETTLEMENT DATE
8/30/60	9/06/60

THE TOTAL COST SHOWN IS DUE AND PAYABLE ON THE SETTLEMENT DATE INDICATED

CODE

1. NEW YORK STOCK EXCHANGE
2. AMERICAN STOCK EXCHANGE
3. OTHER EXCHANGE (NAME ON REQUEST)
4. OVER THE COUNTER
5. AS AGENT FOR THE SELLER WE HAVE SOLD TO YOU
6. AS AGENT FOR THE SELLER WE HAVE SOLD THROUGH YOU
7. AS PRINCIPAL AND FOR OUR OWN ACCOUNT WE HAVE SOLD TO YOU.
8. WE HAVE ACTED AS AGENT FOR BOTH BUYER AND SELLER IN THIS TRANSACTION AND HAVE CHARGED LIKE COMMISSIONS

Fig. 20–6. A confirmation.

Monthly Statements. It is the general practice of most member firms of the New York Stock Exchange to issue monthly statements (Fig. 20–7) to all customers with active accounts. These are prepared at the close of a given month and usually reach the customer on or about the first of the next month. Some firms now stagger these statements so that they do not all fall at the end of the month.

The customer's statement is an itemization of all transactions affecting the account in the past month. The typical statement lists the number of shares bought or sold, the price, and the debit or credit to the account resulting from the transaction. Any amount paid or received is noted, together with dividends credited. A final column indicates the

B NAME ADDRESS

MO. DAY YR. 08 30 62 STATEMENT DATE

IN ACCOUNT WITH
GLORE, FORGAN & CO.
45 WALL STREET NEW YORK 5 — 135 SO. LA SALLE STREET CHICAGO 3

PLEASE REFER TO 28 4591 31 ACCOUNT NUMBER — 20

TYPE OF ACCOUNT: 1. CASH 2. MARGIN 3. SHORT 4. CLEARANCE 5. NON-PURPOSE LOAN 6. SPECIAL SUBSCRIPTION 7. WHEN AS AND IF ISSUED AND RECEIVED BY US

INSTEAD OF ISSUING SEPARATE STATEMENTS, ALL YOUR ACCOUNTS ARE LISTED BELOW. EACH TYPE OF ACCOUNT IS INDICATED IN THIS COLUMN

DATE	SHARES OR PAR VALUE OF BONDS: BOUGHT RECEIVED OR LONG	SOLD DELIVERED OR SHORT	DESCRIPTION	PRICE OR EXPLANATION*	DEBIT	CREDIT	BALANCE DEBIT UNLESS MARKED "CR"	TYPE	BLOT. CODE
			BAL FWD JUL 26 1962			6045 93		1	
AUG 01			A/C		150 00			1	20
AUG 01			CURRENCY					1	20
AUG 13		100	KNAPE & VOGT MNFG CO	DEL				1	53
AUG 15	210		INTERSTATE FIRE &CAS	REC				1	43
AUG 29		102	INTERSTATE FIRE &CAS	21⅝		2204 87		1	60
							8100 80CR*		
	204		INTERSTATE FIRE &CAS	BAL				1	
	200		KNAPE & VOGT MNFG CO	BAL				1	
			BAL FWD JUL 26 1962		1295 63			2	
AUG 13			CHECK		500 00			2	20
AUG 15		210	INTERSTATE FIRE. &CAS	DEL				2	50
AUG 17		100	HURLETRON	6¾		660 97		2	30
AUG 20		100	HARCOURT BRACE WORLD	24¾		2438 57		2	10
AUG 20		100	MEAD JOHNSON MJ	21		2067 11		2	20

E. & O. E. KINDLY PRESERVE THIS STATEMENT AS IT WILL BE VALUABLE IN MAKING UP YOUR NEXT INCOME TAX RETURN. * SEE REVERSE SIDE

Fig. 20–7. A monthly statement.

MO. DAY YR.
8 30 62
STATEMENT DATE

2

IN ACCOUNT WITH
GLORE, FORGAN & CO.
45 WALL STREET
NEW YORK 5
135 SO. LA SALLE STREET
CHICAGO 3

PLEASE REFER TO
28 4591 31
ACCOUNT NUMBER

TYPE OF ACCOUNT
1. CASH 3. SHORT 5. NON-PURPOSE LOAN
2. MARGIN 4. CLEARANCE 6. SPECIAL SUBSCRIPTION
7. WHEN AS AND IF ISSUED AND RECEIVED BY US

INSTEAD OF ISSUING SEPARATE STATEMENTS, ALL YOUR ACCOUNTS ARE LISTED BELOW. EACH TYPE OF ACCOUNT IS INDICATED IN THIS COLUMN

DATE	SHARES OR PAR VALUE OF BONDS: BOUGHT RECEIVED OR LONG	SHARES OR PAR VALUE OF BONDS: SOLD DELIVERED OR SHORT	DESCRIPTION	PRICE OR EXPLANATION*	DEBIT	CREDIT	BALANCE DEBIT UNLESS MARKED "CR"	TYPE	BLOT. CODE
AUG 20		20	MEAD JOHNSON MJ	20 7/8		407 35		2	20
AUG 20		50	MARSH&MCLENNAN INC	37		1825 78		2	30
AUG 24			INT THRU AUG 20 1962		5 65			2	
							5598 50 CR*		
	200		ATLANTIC IMPROVEMENT	BAL				2	
	30		BANCO HISPANO AMER	BAL				2	
	361		WTS 1ST COLNY LF INS	BAL				2	
	200		HERFF JONES CO	BAL				2	
	300		HURLETRON	BAL				2	
	1875		INS SECURITY INC	BAL				2	
	200		JAGUAR CARS LTD A	BAL				2	
	30		NORTHWSTRN NATL INS	BAL				2	

E. & O. E. KINDLY PRESERVE THIS STATEMENT AS IT WILL BE VALUABLE IN MAKING UP YOUR NEXT INCOME TAX RETURN. * SEE REVERSE SIDE

Fig. 20–7 (*Cont.*). A monthly statement.

debit or credit balance at the end of the month. The trade and settle-ment dates are indicated, the settlement date being four full business days later than the former date. A so-called "bring-down" may be added to indicate the "securities position" at the end of the month.

The example of a monthly statement shown in Figure 20–7 is for the month ending August 30, 1962. This customer has both a cash account, which is shown first in the statement, and a general account. A (credit) balance of $6,045.93 is shown for the beginning of the month. This is the amount of cash the customer was holding on deposit with his broker at that time. On August 1, he withdrew $150 in currency, as the debit to the account shows. On August 13, 100 shares of Knape and Vogt were delivered from the account, presumably to him. On August 15, 210 shares of Interstate Fire and Casualty stock were transferred to the cash account from the general account and on August 29, 102 shares of this stock were sold for $21⅝ per share. The net proceeds from the sale, $2,204.87, were credited to the account. The credit balance at the end of the month was $8,100.80.

At the end of the month, 204 shares of Interstate and 200 shares of Knape were held for the customer in this account by his broker. This is shown in the list immediately under the report of account activity for the month. This list is the "bring-down."

The margin account had a debit balance of $1,295.63 at the beginning of the month. This debit balance reflects a loan by the broker to his cus-tomer. The loan was increased by $500 on August 13, when a check for this amount was sent out. Several sales were recorded. On August 24, interest on the loan was debited ($5.65). The net result was an ending credit balance in the account of $5,598.50. The loan was fully paid off.

The bring-down shows items in 8 different issues held by the broker for his customer in this account. One of the issues was warrants for First Colony Life Insurance stock.

No dividends or rights were received during the month. If they had been received, debits to the appropriate account would be shown.

Significant court decisions have grown out of customers' statements. Once the statement has been given to the customer and expressly or by implication accepted by him, it becomes an account stated and is, there-fore, binding on him except for fraud or mistake. The customer needs to make no active or formal acceptance, since his mere silence implies consent. Hence, a customer who finds an error on his statement should immediately call this fact to the attention of his broker. The customer is allowed a reasonable time after receiving the statement to voice an objection to it. What constitutes a reasonable time is a question for a jury to decide.

Cash Balances. Brokers do not require any minimum amount of cash to be carried as a cash balance. Customers do not receive interest on any free credit balances left with brokerage firms. There is no general rule as to how much cash should be in a cash account at the time of purchase of securities. This varies from firm to firm, but it is not a usual practice to require the full cost of a purchase at the time the order is placed.

In margin accounts the New York Stock Exchange requires that an initial margin of $1,000 is necessary before a margin transaction can be executed. This $1,000 may be in cash or in securities the loan value of which is $1,000.

Dividends. A customer is entitled to all dividends on stock owned or purchased. These will be mailed out to him or deposited in his account upon his orders. If the stock has been purchased on the margin and is being held in the broker's name, commonly called "a street name," the customer is still entitled to the dividends. If the account is restricted, as described in Chapter 21, the dividends may be withdrawn in thirty-five days. The customer is also entitled to all stock rights on his stock, even though it may be carried in the broker's name.

Voting Rights. Voting rights to pledged stock depend on the various state statutes and court decisions. Although a customer who carries stock on margin is considered to be the true owner of the stock, he does not have the stock in his name, since it has been hypothecated and is in a "street name." Corporations grant voting rights to stockholders of record; hence, the voting proxy would go to the "street name." In New York it is possible for the customer if his interests are prejudiced, to go to a court of equity and restrain the broker from voting his stock. New York Stock Exchange rules prohibit a member from voting customer's stock in contests without specific, prior instructions from them. The problem of voting rights is not one that causes the average customer much concern. He does not particularly care who votes the stock and is usually quite agreeable to having the broker sign and return the voting proxy.

Lien on Securities. A broker has a lien on securities of a customer for all commissions, interest, and advances that may be due. In order to enforce the lien, the broker may withhold delivery or, if necessary, he may secure payment by sale of the stock. The lien applies to securities owned outright or carried on margin. If the broker is to enforce the lien, he should not surrender the securities to the customer until he receives payment for all charges due. As a pledgee the broker also has a lien against dividends paid on pledged stock.

Commissions. Brokers are entitled to commissions for all transactions for which the Exchange has established charges. These minimum commissions are fixed by the Board of Governors of the New York Stock Exchange and are treated in full in Chapter 22. The broker, of course, has a right to charge commissions on other than Exchange security transactions.

Multiple Accounts. There is no reason why a customer may not have two or more accounts with the same broker. Many have both margin accounts and cash accounts. The latter often serve a useful purpose when the margin account is restricted or when the customer wishes to deal in unlisted securities. If, however, a customer has more than one general account, the firm must consider them as one account in meeting federal margin requirements.

Interest on Debit Balances. When a customer carries stock on margin, he must borrow from his broker the difference between the cost of the securities and his margin. This loan, or debit balance as it is called, carries an interest or service charge. This is true whether the broker uses his own funds, those of his other customers with free credit balances, or the proceeds of a bank loan.

It should be remembered that the rates on call money, as quoted in the newspapers, are what might be called wholesale rates. They are rates charged by banks upon large loans to brokers, usually in units of $100,000 or more. The customer cannot expect and does not get his loan at these very low rates. The customer's rate is the call money rate, plus a service charge added by the broker.

The amount of the service charge that the broker may add to the call money rate has been a matter of much interest and discussion. The broker defends the charge as a proper one in that it defrays the cost of a service to the customer, namely, securing funds to help the customer buy on margin. This charge is fixed by the brokers and the New York Stock Exchange. In mid-1962 the call rate in New York was 4½ per cent. To this was added a service charge of ½ per cent for large accounts and 1 per cent for small accounts. This brought the rates, therefore, to 5 and 5½ per cent on customer accounts. The rates in smaller cities of the country were somewhat higher and ran from 5 to 6 per cent in many localities.

In fixing an interest rate to be charged any customer, the broker usually takes into consideration many factors, including size of the debit balance, type of securities carried, competitive conditions, and the general activity of the account. There are no hard-and-fast rules. Interest on debit balances is computed monthly and reported to the customer on his regular monthly statement. Since this interest accumulates from month to month, it means that the customer will pay interest on this accumulated interest which is a part of his debit balance. He can avoid this compound interest charge by paying by check each month the accumulated interest for the preceding month.

EXECUTION OF ORDERS

Broker as an Agent. A customer must employ a broker as his agent before any question of agency arises. This broker is free to reject this relationship, but once the order is placed and accepted, the broker becomes the agent of the customer and must carry out his orders according to instructions.

Due Care and Skill. A broker is required to use due care and skill in executing orders. If he fails to do so, he will be liable for any resulting losses.[6] In the case of *Warwick v. Addicks*, it was held that due care and skill consisted of that which was typical of good businessmen in the same business and community.[7] In other words, the broker is expected to execute orders with the same care and skill that is common in the brokerage business.

Following Instructions. A broker must follow carefully the instructions of the customer or he will be liable for damages. The broker, however, cannot be held liable for failure to execute an order if the failure was not his fault; i.e., inability to buy or sell a stock at a limit price because of market conditions. The broker must conform to the customer's instructions and cannot deviate from them even if the customer would not be injured by the deviation. If instructions are not followed, the customer may repudiate the transaction and hold the broker liable for damages.[8] Rules governing the execution of particular types of orders are discussed in detail in Chapter 9.

Executing of Orders in Part. The broker, under certain conditions, is permitted to execute an order in part according to the rules of the New York Stock Exchange. In the case of round-lot orders for multiples of 100 shares, it is permissible for the broker to sell or purchase 100 shares or any multiple thereof. For example, if a customer has 500 shares to sell at 50, the broker may be able to sell only 200 shares. The customer must accept the transaction, even though 300 shares are unsold. To take another example, a customer places an order to buy 1,000 shares and the broker can buy only 500 shares. In this case the customer must again accept the transaction. This operation is based on Rule 61 of the Exchange, which states: "All bids and offers for more than one trading

[6] Meyer, *op. cit.,* p. 265; Black, *op. cit.,* p. 76.

[7] 35 Del. 43, 157 Atl. 205.

[8] Black, *op. cit.,* p. 77.

unit shall be considered to be for the amount thereof or any lesser number of units." However, a customer who places a round-lot order for 100 shares cannot be required to accept delivery for only 50 shares, since this would mean that the broker has changed the order from a round-lot to an odd-lot, which was not the intention of the customer at all.

Cancellation of Orders. A customer has the right, at all times, to cancel an order. His cancellation, of course, must reach the broker before the execution of the original order.[9] A discussion of cancel orders is given in Chapter 9.

Market of Execution. A broker must execute an order in the customary, usual market for the security.[10] If the stock were listed on the New York Stock Exchange and customarily sold there, that would be the customary market. If the stock were an over-the-counter security, that would be the customary market.

The New York Stock Exchange has ruled (394) that members and member firms must handle all transactions in listed stocks, either as broker or dealer, on the floor of the Exchange and cannot effect such transactions off the floor without permission from the Exchange.

In respect to bonds the situation is somewhat different. Orders for large blocks of bonds may be executed off the floor. The so-called "nine bond" rule states that every order for the purchase or sale of bonds shall be sent to the floor for execution with four exceptions. The exceptions are: (1) where the order calls for ten bonds or more; (2) where a better price may be obtained elsewhere; (3) where the customer directs that the particular order shall not be executed on the floor; and (4) where the order calls for securities of the United States government and its possessions, municipalities, and those to be redeemed within twelve months.

Execution of Orders in Broker's Name. It is customary for brokers to execute all orders without divulging the names of principals. Since brokers on the floor of the Exchange hold each other responsible for delivery of securities and payment therefor, rather than the actual customers, there is no reason for the names of customers to be divulged.

Broker and Dealer in Same Transaction. Strict rules and numerous court decisions prevent a broker from acting as a broker and dealer in the same transaction. For example, a broker cannot accept an order to sell 100 shares, charge the usual commission, and buy the stock himself, even with the consent of the customer. He would be making a double compensation: first, the broker's commission, and second, the dealer's profit; this would be a complete violation of the law of agency. There is, how-

---

[9] *Sibbald v. Bethlehem Iron Company*, 83 N. Y. 378.
[10] Meyer, *op. cit.*, p. 274.

ever, no reason why a brokerage firm may not act as a broker in one transaction for a customer, such as buying stock on the floor of the Exchange, and act in another transaction in the over-the-counter market as a dealer. These are separate transactions, it should be noted, and not the same transaction. The problem of a member acting as a broker and dealer in the same transasction becomes particularly important in the work of specialists. This subject was examined in detail in Chapter 11.

Secret Profits. A broker may not make a secret profit in a transaction at the expense of a customer. An example of such a transaction would be where a customer placed an order to sell 100 shares at 25. The broker would execute the order at 26 and pocket the difference of 1 point per share, or $100. A customer may bring an action to recover such a profit. This violation of fair practices also might result in the expulsion of a member from the Exchange.

Crossing Orders. Brokers receive many orders to buy and sell the same stock the same day. It would be entirely possible for the broker to cross many of these orders in his own office were it not for strict rules (76, 85, 91) and repeated court decisions to the contrary.[11] For example, let us suppose that Customer A gives an order to sell 100 XYZ at 50 and Customer B gives an order to buy 100 XYZ at 50. The broker might then cross the two orders and avoid the trouble of buying and selling the stock on the floor, but he would have failed to determine whether he could obtain a higher price for A or a lower price for B in the auction market.

The New York Stock Exchange prohibits the crossing of stock orders in brokerage offices. An order to buy or sell must go to the trading floor to be executed at the most favorable price to the customer. The crossing of orders on the floor is a common practice of the specialist and may be done by the commission broker, but it must be done according to a precise rule. When the specialist or any other member has both a bid and a sell order with the same price limit, he may cross them on the trading floor, but he must first publicly enter the bid and offer in the market at a ⅛ spread. In this way the customer is assured of the best possible price.

LEGAL RELATIONSHIPS IN GENERAL

Principal and Agent. The law of agency weighs heavily in the interpretation of the customer-broker relationship. In the typical transaction the customer is acting as a principal and the broker as his agent. In this relationship the broker must act in the best interests of the customer and

---

[11] Meyer, *op. cit.*, p. 287.

receives therefrom the customary commission. This is the sole compensation of the broker, since he is taking none of the risks of ownership but is merely acting as an intermediary between the customer and a third party to the transaction.

Debtor and Creditor. The debtor-creditor relationship becomes important in the margin transaction. In this, the customer borrows from the broker the amount of the so-called debit balance in order to purchase the securities. The debit balance is the net amount owed to the broker. Whether the broker advances his own money or funds secured from a commercial bank is immaterial. The broker is still the creditor and the customer the debtor. Under such conditions the prevailing laws on debtors and creditors apply to the transaction.

Pledgor and Pledgee. Another relationship arises when stock is pledged or hypothecated for a loan during a margin transaction. The term "hypothecation" is generally used in such transactions and needs to be defined. It is an act whereby securities are deposited or pledged as collateral for a loan, either with a bank or with a broker. The term "rehypothecation" is also used. In this case the securities are repledged (pledged a second time). For example, a customer pledges 100 shares of stock with his broker for $2,000. This is an act of hypothecation. If the broker were then to repledge the stock with his bank for a loan of $2,000, this would be an act of rehypothecation.

The problem of pledged stock becomes extremely important in the margin transaction, since the courts have built up a great body of opinion as to the rights involved in the selling of such pledged collateral. These rights will be discussed in full later in this chapter.

Fiduciary Relationship. The fiduciary relationship is said to exist between the broker and his customer. This is a "faith relationship." The customer has intrusted his money or securities with the broker because of his faith in the honesty, judgment, and responsibility of the broker. The broker accepts the obligation—legal, ethical, and moral—to serve the best interests of his customer. In a sense the broker becomes a quasi-trustee of the customer's affairs.

HYPOTHECATION OF SECURITIES

Nature of Hypothecation. Hypothecation was defined above as an act in which securities are deposited or pledged as security for a loan. A customer commits the act of hypothecation when he buys stock on the margin and pledges the purchased stock to pay for it. Rehypothecation goes one step further. It takes place when the broker repledges the collateral with a bank to secure a broker's loan. He is taking the securities of the customer and repledging them so that he may secure accommodation at a commercial bank. In these two acts a number of legal problems arise. They concern the rights of the customer or pledgor, the broker or pledgee, and the bank or broker's pledgee.

Right of Customer to Secure Accommodation. Once a broker has accepted a margin account, it becomes the duty of the broker to advance the customer accommodation. He must advance funds to the customer to purchase and carry the securities to the amount that is the difference between the cost of the securities and the required margin set by the broker.[12] This accommodation continues until the account is properly closed, either by the customer or by the broker acting within his rights.

Securities in Broker's Name. Securities which have been hypothecated may be carried in the name of the customer, of the broker, or of one of his nominees.[13] In practice, the broker carries stock in his own name rather than in the name of the customer. This simplifies procedure in case the broker wishes to rehypothecate the stock or to sell it. The customer, of course, has the right to pay off his indebtedness to the broker and demand that the broker transfer the stock to the customer's name.

Ownership of Margined Securities. The legal problem involving the question of who owns the securities in the hands of the broker is a troublesome one for customers in the margin transaction. In such cases the stock technically is not in the name of a customer but in a broker's or so-called "street name." If the customer were to own the stock outright, no problem would ordinarily arise, since the stock certificate would be in the name of the customer. When stock is bought on margin, however, it is not the practice to transfer it to the name of the customer. It is registered in the name of the broker so that it may be easily sold or hypothecated. If the stock is carried thus, the question may be asked, "Who owns the stock, the customer or the broker?" The answer is that the customer owns the stock. It was held in the case of *Hobart v. Vanden Bosch* that the title to stock belongs to the customer as soon as it has been purchased, even though the broker has not delivered the certificate.[14] Regardless of the legal technicalities of the name shown on the stock certificate, the customer owns the stock. He has the responsibility for its purchase and sale; he takes the risks of ownership; he assumes any profits or losses; and he is entitled to its dividends and voting rights.[15]

---

[12] *Markham v. Jaudon*, 21 N. Y. 235.
[13] Meyer, *op. cit.*, p. 317.
[14] 256 Mich. 686, 240 N. W. 1.
[15] Meyer, *op. cit.*, p. 258.

Substitution of Collateral. A broker has the right to substitute collateral that has been hypothecated by a customer.[16] In other words, if a customer were to buy 200 shares of General Motors on margin, the broker would not be required to keep the identical stock certificate throughout the life of the pledge. Since one stock certificate is identical with any other, it is immaterial whether the broker keeps any particular certificate; certificates are not property, but merely evidences of it. In the case just mentioned, the broker would be legally permitted, if the need arose, to substitute two certificates of 100 shares each for the original certificate of 200 shares. The broker, however, must at all times keep in his possession, or under his control and available for delivery, stock of a like kind and amount.

Right to Rehypothecate Securities. The broker is within his rights in rehypothecating a customer's securities. This right has been upheld in numerous cases.[17] Many brokers must regularly obtain brokers' loans to handle the large amount of credit necessary for margin accounts. In recent years nearly all brokers with large numbers of margin accounts were making brokers' loans.

The broker, by law and by agreement with the customer, is perfectly within his rights in rehypothecating the customers' securities in order to secure a broker's loan. The following clause in a margin agreement of a large brokerage firm is typical of such agreements:

All securities, now or hereafter held by us, or carried by us in any account for you (either individually or jointly with others), or deposited to secure the same, may from time to time and without notice to you, be carried in our general loans, and may be pledged, repledged, hypothecated or rehypothecated.

Rehypothecation for an Excessive Amount. A very important problem arises in rehypothecation: May the broker rehypothecate securities for more than the amount of the customer's indebtedness, or, to put it in another way, for an excessive amount? For example, if a customer were to borrow $1,000 on 100 shares worth $5,000, could the broker rehypothecate them for $1,500?

Years ago this rehypothecation was permitted, provided the broker had permission in the customer's margin agreement. Today it cannot be done. The broker may not borrow more than the indebtedness of the customer, any agreement to the contrary notwithstanding.

Rule 402 of the New York Stock Exchange prohibits a member firm or corporation pledging securities for more than "is fair and reasonable in view of the indebtedness of said customer to said member organization."

16 *Gorman v. Littlefield*, 229 U. S. 19.
17 *Leishing v. Van Buren*, 193 App. Div. (N. Y.) 296.

The SEC acts under even more precise language. Its enabling act states that no member of a national securities exchange shall hypothecate any securities carried for the account of any customer under any circumstances "for a sum in excess of the aggregate indebtedness of such customers in respect of such securities."[18]

Hypothecation of Fully Paid Securities. A somewhat different problem of hypothecation arises when a customer owns securities that are fully paid for and that the broker pledges at a bank for a broker's loan. May the broker do this? The answer is: If the broker has no agreement that permits this, he is guilty of conversion.[19] If a customer has purchased securities on the margin and then paid his indebtedness to the broker, the broker must immediately withdraw the securities from the possession of the repledgee or lending bank; otherwise he commits conversion, even though the original pledging was perfectly legal.

If a customer wishes to give his consent to the hypothecation of specific fully paid securities, there is, of course, no reason why he may not make such an agreement and permit the broker to do so.

Rights of the Broker's Pledgee. The next problem concerns the rights of the broker's pledgee or the repledgee. The broker has pledged the stock of a customer with a bank. What are the rights of the bank? The answer is: If the lending bank becomes a bona fide holder for value, it has a claim to the securities superior to that of the customer.[20] It is given this right by numerous court decisions and by the Uniform Stock Transfer Act. The right is an extremely strong one provided, of course, that the stock certificate has been properly endorsed with a valid assignment. This right prevails even though the securities may have been pledged for an excessive amount, the broker may have no right of pledging, or the securities may actually have been obtained from the customer by fraud or theft.

Commingling Securities. A broker has a right to commingle securities and pledge them *en bloc.* Commingling may be defined as an operation in which a broker takes the stock certificates of a number of customers and pledges them as security for a single or general loan. The need for this operation arises from the fact that brokers' loans are made in large units, usually $100,000 or some multiple thereof, as already indicated. In order to protect adequately such a loan, it may be necessary for the broker to pledge the certificates of a number of customers. Hence, the practice of pledging *en bloc.* The problem involves the rights of the customer; in case the broker has pledged the certificates for an excessive

---

[18] Section 8 (c) of the Securities Exchange Act of 1934.
[19] Penal Code of N. Y., Sec. 956.
[20] Black, *op. cit.,* p. 580.

amount and is unable to pay off his broker's loan, a loss over and above the amount of his indebtedness to the broker may fall on the customer. For example, a customer may owe his broker $1,000. If his stock were pledged for an excessive amount, the broker were to fail, and the bank were to sell the stock, the customer might take a loss considerably in excess of his $1,000 indebtedness.

It is, therefore, a matter of concern to the customer whether or not the broker may commingle stocks. There have been many cases on the subject, some of which were conflicting. In general, it may be stated that commingling without the customer's consent is illegal[21] and the Stock Exchange has its own rule (402) on commingling.

To enable the broker to commingle securities of customers, there has been inserted in the customer's margin agreement a phrase that specifically permits this practice (Fig. 20–3, page 340). This eliminates any legal dispute.

SALE OF HYPOTHECATED COLLATERAL

The Problem. The chief problem involved in the sale of hypothecated collateral is the right of the broker to sell stock carried on margin without giving notice to the customer of such action. The desire of the broker to sell pledged stock arises when the stock declines in value, and the account becomes undermargined. The broker, fearing that his advance to the customer is not sufficiently protected, sells the collateral before it declines further. The question, therefore, is: May the broker sell collateral carried on margin without proper notice?

Need for Adequate Margin. The rule that a broker is entitled to adequate margin has long been upheld by the courts and demanded by the New York Stock Exchange, which sets minimum margin requirements for member firms. The broker has been allowed by the courts to require a margin that is adequate to protect him against loss.[22] If we assume that a broker decides that a given account is not properly margined, may he sell the stock without notice? The courts have had much to say about this matter.

Sale of Collateral Without Notice. The courts have interpreted hypothecation as being a pledging of property. The customer is the pledgor, and the broker the pledgee. In the absence of agreements to the contrary, the broker may not sell the pledged property without giving a reasonable notice of the time and place of sale of such property. The courts have held that before such property may be sold, the broker must demand additional margin, and if such margin is not forthcoming, he

---

21 *Thompson v. Carpenter,* 17 App. Div. (N. Y.) 329.
22 *Small v. Housman,* 208 N. Y. 115.

must give notice of sale. Hence, in the absence of prior agreement, both a demand for margin and a notice of sale are necessary.[23]

The notice of sale may be given by the usual practice, such as mail, telephone, telegraph, or person-to-person contact, but the actual demand for margin and notice of sale must reach the attention of the customer.

The Customer's Margin Agreement. Without going further into the legal technicalities of the right of the customer to a demand for additional margin and notice of sale, it is evident that in the absence of an agreement to the contrary, the broker is extremely limited in his right to sell pledged collateral. To avoid the consequences of this situation, the brokers have evolved, and for many years have used, what is generally known as a "margin agreement," or "standard customer's agreement" (Fig. 20–3, page 340). This agreement, which varies among firms in exact legal terminology but not in principle, permits the broker to sell pledged collateral whenever he deems it necessary for his protection. Such a sale may be on any market, without notice of sale and without demand for additional margin. In other words, the broker has protected himself against the ruling that a demand for margin must be made and proper notice given before pledged securities may be sold. This is the general practice of all brokerage firms carrying margin accounts. In order to hold the goodwill of customers, however, brokers do not, in practice, sell pledged collateral without notice. It is not good business. Nevertheless, if circumstances necessitate the sale of margined collateral, because of market conditions, the broker possesses the legal right to do so. In earlier days, when margins were very small, sometimes as low as 10 per cent, the danger of the undermargined stock was great. Today, with the relatively high margin requirements, the chances of a broker selling undermargined collateral without notice are small. A customer, willing and able to put up more margin, will have that opportunity.

Sale by Broker's Pledgee. The banker or broker's pledgee has a clear right to sell pledged securities in the manner allowed by law or agreement with the broker in order to enforce his claims against the broker. In such an action the banker does not incur any liability to the customer, who is the true owner of the stock or to the broker, who repledged the stock.[24] This right of sale, in practice, is given to the banker under the loan agreement between the broker and the lending bank. The agreement permits the bank to sell the collateral without giving notice either to the broker or to the customer.

---

[23] For a full discussion of the subject, see: Meyer, *op. cit.*, pp. 369–91; *Small v. Housman,* 220 N. Y. 504; *Markham v. Jaudon,* 41 N. Y. 235; *Thompson v. Baily,* 220 N. Y. 471; *Villet v. Whiting,* 120 N. Y. 402.

[24] *Rothschild v. Allen,* 90 App. Div. (N. Y.) 233.

In summary, therefore, the customer, in opening a margin account, waives his rights by agreement, so that he cannot demand a notice for more margin or for notice of sale. His broker in turn waives such notices from the banker, who acts as repledgee. Hence, either the broker or the banker may sell the customer's stock without notice.

CLOSING THE ACCOUNT

Rights in General. The legal relationships in a brokerage account involve the rights of debtor and creditor as well as those of principal and agent, as has been stated previously. The law of agency is that an agency may be terminated at the will of either party if it has no fixed term.[25] Similarly, a pledge may be terminated by either party upon demand and proper performance by the party asking the termination.

Right of Customer to Close Account. The customer has a legal right to close any account, long or short, upon proper notice and a full settlement of all obligations involved in the transaction. In the case of the long account the customer may either order the stock sold or pay any amount due the broker, and require delivery of the stock to himself or any designated person. In a short account he may either deposit the securities borrowed or have the broker repurchase them in the market and settle the account.

Right of Broker to Close Account. The broker has an equal right to close an account upon proper notice. In the case of a long account it can be terminated, regardless of whether there is adequate margin or not, and with or without cause.[26] In the case of a short account the situation in somewhat different; the short sale involves both the sale of stock and the repurchase of it at a later date, when the customer "covers." The broker need not carry such an account indefinitely, but he must carry it a reasonable time if adequately margined. After he has done so, he may close the account upon proper notice. If the account becomes undermargined, he may close it at any time after he has given proper notice, demanded additional margin, and received none.[27]

Death of Customer. When a customer dies, it is the practice of the broker to cancel all open orders and to mark the account with the date of decease of the customer. The typical customer's agreement gives the broker the right to close the account immediately. Such an agreement gives the broker the right to sell all securities that he is carrying for the customer, to buy all securities of which the account may be short, and

---

25 Black, *op. cit.*, p. 223.
26 Meyer, *op. cit.*, p. 361.
27 Black, *op. cit.*, p. 556.

to close out any commitment that has been made on behalf of the customer. Such acts protect the broker against any changes in the market prices of securities in the account from the date of the death of the customer to the date on which he turns the assets over to the estate.

After the death of the customer, the broker no longer has authority to execute orders placed before death.[28] The broker, however, must continue to protect the securities.

Bankruptcy of Customer. A broker is permitted to close an account of a bankrupt customer. There is nothing that prevents this action in the bankruptcy statutes. He is, however, not compelled to do so and may continue to carry the account if he so desires.[29]

---

[28] *Lewis v. Commissioner of Banks,* 286 Mass. 570.
[29] Meyer, *op. cit., 1936 Supplement,* p. 203.

21

Margin Trading[1]

Technically, there are two kinds of margin trading: margin buying and short selling. In each case the customer deposits margin. For the most part margin trading consists of buying on margin; only a small part of the total trading of customers on the margin is short selling. The procedures for short selling were discussed in Chapter 12; the margin practices are discussed here.

NATURE AND IMPORTANCE

Margins. The term "margin" is used quite freely in speculative circles. It has two different meanings. Generally speaking, it refers to a sum of money deposited with a broker to protect an account in securities against any unfavorable changes in the prices of those securities. It has two purposes: (1) to prevent the customer from overtrading or buying excessively in view of his trading fund and (2) to protect the creditor against unsound security loans. Usually a purchase is under consideration, but margins are also used in short selling.

A margin, however, is not a constant sum of money deposited in a brokerage account. If a customer bought 100 shares of stock at 50 on a 70 per cent margin and the stock price fell to 40, the customer's margin would no longer be the $3,500 deposited, but $2,500, the equity in the account. Margin is the equity.

There are, therefore, two ways to measure margins: as a number of dollars and as a proportion of equity. A *dollar margin* represents so many dollars or so many points. For example, a customer puts up a dollar

[1] For a definitive, comprehensive study, see: Jules I. Bogen and Herman E. Krooss, *Security Credit: Its Economic Role and Regulation* (Englewood Cliffs, N.J.: Prentice-Hall, Inc., 1960).

margin of $1,000 to buy 100 shares at 20; he has a point margin of 10 points per share.

An *equity margin* is one that expresses the relationship between a customer's equity in the account and the value of the collateral. For example, in 1961 the Federal Reserve Board permitted a loan value of only 30 per cent on registered, non-exempt stocks, thus requiring the customer to have a margin or equity of 70 per cent at the time of purchase. If the stock were to decline in value, the margin or equity might fall, for example, to 50 or 60 per cent.

In summary, a margin may mean either a definite sum of money or a proportion of equity in an account.

Importance of Margin Accounts. In 1929 there was more margin trading than in any other year in the history of the nation. In that year there were 1,550,000 customers doing business with all exchanges in the country.[2] The New York Stock Exchange accounted for 1,372,000, or 90 per cent, of the total. Approximately 600,000, or 40 per cent, of the total were margin customers. By 1933 the number of customers on all exchanges had fallen to 1,028,000, with the ratio of margin customers to total customers remaining about the same. Margin trading in the next seventeen years declined in relative importance, but showed a marked increase after 1946, as the following figures will indicate. These are the number of margin accounts handled by members of the New York Stock Exchange over a period of time.[3]

> December 31, 1939—257,000
> December 31, 1946— 56,000
> December 31, 1949—123,000
> December 31, 1955—278,000
> May 28, 1962—387,000

The New York Stock Exchange in recent years has made a number of studies of margin trading. In a study of public transactions of individuals for September, 1961, it found that margin transactions accounted for 32 per cent of these public transactions, while cash transactions accounted for 68 per cent.[4] Over several years about one-third of all transactions of individuals have been on a margin basis and two-thirds on a cash basis.

Another way to place the importance of margin trading in perspective is illustrated in Figure 21–1. Margin transactions involve borrowing by

[2] Kemper Simpson, *The Margin Trader* (New York: Harper & Row, Publishers, 1939), p. 9.
[3] Data furnished by the Exchange.
[4] *Tenth Public Transaction Study, September 13, 1961* (New York: New York Stock Exchange, 1961), pp. 3, 8.

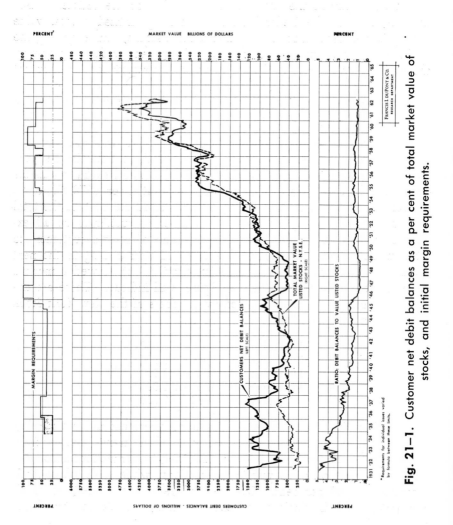

Fig. 21–1. Customer net debit balances as a per cent of total market value of stocks, and initial margin requirements.

customers. Their borrowing is measured by the "debit balances" to their accounts and loans from banks or others. This term, "debit balance," is explained more fully below, but for the moment we may accept the idea that the sum of customer debit balances is the total amount they are borrowing to purchase and carry securities through credit advanced by their brokers. The ratio of this total to the total market value of listed stocks on the New York Stock Exchange is shown in Figure 21–1.

Length of Margin Transactions. How long is the typical transaction of a margin trader? How soon does he liquidate his stock? Some light has been thrown on this matter by study of public transactions by the New York Stock Exchange on several days of the decade ending in 1961.[5] In this period it was found that 18 to 25 per cent of the margin transactions of public individuals were liquidated within thirty days, 27 to 37 per cent in from one to six months, and 40 to 53 per cent in more than six months. It appears that public margin trading is not for speculative reasons. However, one must not attempt to generalize too much on whether transactions of more than six months were made for speculative or investment purposes. Many speculators carry transactions over the six-month period to take advantage of the capital gains tax law. How many margin buyers eventually pay for their purchases in full and then retain their stock over long, investment periods is unknown.

Income of Margin Traders. Recent studies of the Exchange make it possible to classify margin traders by income status. The analysis of public transactions just discussed above reported that about 2 per cent of the transactions were effected by individuals with an income of less than $5,000; 16 per cent by individuals with incomes of $5,000 or more, but less than $10,000; 46 per cent by individuals with incomes of $10,000 or more, but less than $25,000; and 36 per cent by individuals with incomes of $25,000 or more. Margin trading is done mostly by individuals with substantial incomes, the income bracket of $10,000 to $25,000 being the most important one.

Location of Margin Trading. The exact domicile of the margin trader is not clear. New York is undoubtedly the leading center of margin trading. Simpson in his studies concluded that margin traders tend to concentrate in the large cities, where brokerage houses offer office and ticker facilities.[6] Some of the smaller exchanges, in reporting to the Committee on Banking and Currency indicate that very little margin trading takes place on their exchanges.

[5] *Ibid.*, p. 10.
[6] Simpson, *loc. cit.*

ADVANTAGE AND DISADVANTAGES OF MARGIN TRADING

Advantage. Margin trading has a great advantage. With a given sum of money the trader may buy more shares than if he trades on a cash basis. This creates the possibility of increasing the rate of profit on his trading fund. With a 50 per cent margin, for example, the customer can buy twice as many shares as he could with a cash transaction, the only additional expense being commissions, taxes, and interest on his debit balance. These expenses are largely offset by the cash dividends received on the stock. With a 20 per cent margin, which was common in the 1920's, the customer could buy five times as many shares as on a cash basis. With the 10 per cent margin, prevalent before World War I, the number of shares was increased ten times. With margins of 70 per cent, as existed in 1961, the buying power, of course, was relatively lower.

The following tabulation indicates the relative profits of cash and margin buying at various ratios. In each example it is assumed that the customer is buying a $50 stock. Commissions and taxes are ignored.

	Rise in Points		
	5	10	20
Cash account profit	10%	20%	40%
Margin account profit:			
10% margin	100	200	400
20% margin	50	100	200
50% margin	20	40	80
70% margin	15	29	57
90% margin	11	22	44

Danger. Margin trading, however, has certain inherent dangers and disadvantages not present in cash transactions. There is a substantial risk which balances the profit possibilities. When the stock falls in value, the equity of the customer is wiped out faster than in the cash account. For example, in 1929, when a 20 per cent margin was common, a 20 per cent fall in the value of a stock would have wiped out the equity of the customer and left him in debt for commissions, interest, and taxes, whereas only 20 per cent of his equity would have been wiped out in a cash transaction.

Margin buying in earlier days was done on the basis of narrow margins, and the danger of overtrading was a real one. Overtrading may be defined as carrying more stock than is justified by a customer's financial resources. In case of an unexpected margin call, the small, over-extended customer would be unable to meet the call and be wiped out by the sale of the stock. He would be forced to take a loss which his meager bank account could ill afford to absorb.

To prevent overtrading by small speculators, the New York Stock Exchange has issued a regulation that prevents a customer from opening a margin account where he cannot furnish an initial margin of at least $1,000 or 25 per cent of the market value of the first trade, whichever is greater.

THE CUSTOMER'S ACCOUNT

Importance. A thorough understanding of a customer's account is of great importance in margin transactions, since all margin computations are based on the debit balance. Certain transactions increase the debit balance, while others reduce it or create a credit balance.

Debits and Credits to an Account. All the following transactions result in debits to a customer's account:

1. Cost of securities bought, including commission and taxes, if any
2. Interest charged on debit balance
3. Withdrawal of cash

All these transactions result in credits:

1. Net proceeds from sale of securities (sale price less taxes and commission)
2. Deposits of cash
3. Dividends and interest received from securities

The reader may refer to Chapter 20 for an illustration of a typical customer's statement.

The Debit Balance. A basic element in the computation of all margins is the debit balance. This is the net amount owed to the broker. He lends the customer this amount and charges him interest on it. The debit balance is the difference between the total debits to the account and the total credits.

A significant thing about the debit balance is that it does not change in an account until another of the six transactions described above is effected. A rise or fall in the value of the stock held on margin has no effect on the debit balance. For example, a customer buys 100 shares at 50, putting up $3,500 as margin. His debit balance is $1,500, excluding commissions. If the stock were to rise to 60, his equity or margin would increase to $4,500, but his debit balance would remain at $1,500. If the stock were to fall to 40, the margin would be only $2,500, but the debit balance would still be $1,500.

Equity. The equity in an account is equally important in understanding margins. By equity is meant the value of collateral minus the debit balance. This is the net amount which a customer owns or holds in the account after paying all commissions and taxes, and interest on the debit balance. It may be expressed by the following formula:

$$\text{Equity} = \text{Value of Collateral} - \text{Debit Balance}$$

The equity in an account rises or falls every time the collateral rises or falls in price. A stock bought at 50 with a 70 per cent margin shows an equity of $3,500 at that price. At 65 the equity is $5,000, while at 15 the equity is wiped out entirely.

COMPUTING MARGINS

Point Margins. The earliest form of computation was the point margin. So many points per share were put up, such as 1, 5, 20, or 50, representing $1, $5, $20, and $50, respectively. Such a system was simple and easy for the customer to understand. Its defect was that there was no possibility of establishing a uniform margin requirement. A 2-point margin might be considered adequate for a $10 stock but certainly not for a $50 stock. Use of this type of statement of margin for stocks had declined greatly by the 1930's, but it retains usefulness and is heard in bond trading.

Percentage Margins. Margins today are computed as percentages, although the New York Stock Exchange does require a minimum initial margin or equity of $1,000 or 25 per cent, whichever is greater. Two types of percentage margin have been used. One was based on the debit balance; it was important before 1934, but is no longer used. The other is the margin based on the equity in the account and the value of the collateral; it is in universal use today.

Present Margin Formula. The present margin formula for finding a margin may be expressed in two ways, both giving the same results:

$$\text{Margin} = \frac{\text{Value of Collateral} - \text{Debit Balance}}{\text{Value of Collateral}}$$

or

$$\text{Margin} = \frac{\text{Equity}}{\text{Value of Collateral}}$$

Those who prefer an algebraic statement will find the following useful:

$$M = \frac{V - D}{V} \times 100$$

or

$$M = \frac{E}{V} \times 100$$

where M = margin per cent
V = value of collateral
D = debit balance
E = equity = $V - D$

Examples of Changing Margins. Suppose that a customer bought 100 shares of XYZ at 50 putting up a 70 per cent margin. His margin would be $3,500 and his debit balance $1,500. His margin is computed this way:

$$\text{Margin} = \frac{5,000 - 1,500}{5,000} \times 100 = 70$$

Now, let us suppose that the stock rises to 60. The margin will rise to 75 per cent, as the following figures will show:

$$\text{Margin} = \frac{6,000 - 1,500}{6,000} \times 100 = 75$$

Now, let us supose that the stock falls to 40. The margin will now be only 62.5 per cent:

$$\text{Margin} = \frac{4,000 - 1,500}{4,000} \times 100 = 62\tfrac{1}{2}$$

Margins on Short Sales. There are a number of ways by which brokers compute the margin on a short sale. All give the same results. Generally speaking, the margin on a short sale is more difficult to grasp than that on a margin purchase. One fundamental fact to remember is that the margin declines as the stock rises in value and increases as the stock falls in value. This is the reverse of the margin purchase.

Three things are necessary to know at all times: (1) the net proceeds of the short sale, (2) the initial margin, and (3) the current market value of the stock.

The following is a workable formula:

$$\text{Margin} = \frac{\text{Net Proceeds of Sale plus Initial Margin}}{\text{Market Value of Stock}} \text{ minus } 1.00 \times 100$$

Those who prefer an algebraic statement here also may use the following:

$$M = \left(\frac{N + I}{V} - 1\right) \times 100$$

where M = margin per cent
  N = net proceeds of sale
  I = initial margin deposited
  V = value of stock

Let us suppose that Mr. A. sells 100 XYZ at 100 putting up a 70 per cent margin. For simplicity, let us assume that the net proceeds are $10,000. The margin will, of course, be 70 per cent, as these figures will indicate:

$$\text{Margin} = \left(\frac{10,000 + 7,000}{10,000} - 1\right) \times 100 = 70$$

The stock falls to 85. The new margin will be 100 per cent as the following figures will indicate:

$$\text{Margin} = \left(\frac{10{,}000 + 7{,}000}{8{,}500} - 1 \right) \times 100 = 100$$

The stock rises to 125. The new margin is 36 per cent, as the following figures will indicate:

$$\text{Margin} = \left(\frac{10{,}000 + 7{,}000}{12{,}500} - 1 \right) \times 100 = 36$$

The stock rises to 131. The new margin is 30 per cent. This is a very significant example in that 30 per cent is the minimum maintenance requirement of the Exchange. A further increase in price would lead to a call for more margin, if one had not already been issued.

$$\text{Margin} = \left(\frac{10{,}000 + 7{,}000}{13{,}100} - 1 \right) \times 100 = 30$$

Valuing Securities. Computation of percentage margin is affected by the value placed on the securities involved: the collateral, in the case of a purchase; the borrowed stock, in the case of a short sale. For this purpose current market prices are used. Two rules govern the choice of figure, however. This choice is expressed by the Federal Reserve Board in Regulation T, Section 3 (c) (4), as follows:

> For the *current market value* of a security throughout the day of its purchase or sale, the creditor (broker) shall use its total cost or net proceeds of its sale, as the case may be, and at any other time shall use the closing sale price of the security on the preceding business day as shown by any regularly published reporting or quotation service. In the absence of any such closing sale price, the creditor may use any reasonable estimate of the market value of such security as of the close of business on such preceding business day.

In other words, on the day of the transaction the broker uses the actual cost or proceeds net of commissions and taxes, if any, as the current market value. On succeeding days the collateral is valued at the closing price of the previous business day. This is the ordinary situation. There is no reason, however, why a broker in a period of sharp market change cannot and should not use the current market value as indicated by the ticker tape. He has the right to do so under Rule 431 of the Exchange. Margin calls are often based on current prices during periods of heavy liquidation of stocks and may be based on such prices in rapidly rising markets if short sales exist.

HISTORY OF MARGIN REQUIREMENTS

Before 1914. There were no uniform rules in the early years of the New York Stock Exchange. Each broker made his own requirements, which were based on the point system, as already indicated. The margins were low. Based on the present system, they were probably 10 per cent on the average. Antwerp, an early authority on the stock market and a governor of the New York Stock Exchange, writing in 1914, stated that margins were 10 points for middle-grade, speculative securities, 20 points on higher-priced, erratic securities, and 5 points on very low-priced shares that move slowly.[7] It is interesting to note that the *Report of the Hughes Commission* on the stock market recommended 20 per cent margins as early as 1909.[8] Although Antwerp favored the recommendation of the commission for adequate margins as a general principle, his reaction to the suggestion of 20 per cent margins was negative. Said he: "An insistence by the broker on a 20 per cent margin would be silly and would merely drive the business elsewhere or prevent it altogether."[9]

Margins in 1929. By 1929 margins had probably reached a level of 20 to 25 per cent of the value of the collateral, although some firms allowed customers to trade on smaller margins. They were based on the debit balance. The New York Stock Exchange itself had no specific rule on margins, allowing each firm to set its own requirements. It did, however, insist in its constitution that margins should be adequate and that carrying an account without proper and adequate margins was to be condemned in that it was not in the best interests and welfare of the Exchange.[10]

Uniform Margins in 1933. In 1933 the New York Stock Exchange established the first system of uniform requirements. It provided that there should be a margin of 50 per cent of the debit balance on all accounts with a debit balance under $5,000 and one of 30 per cent of the debit balance for those with a debit balance of $5,000 or more. Translated into present margin terms, the margin was 33 per cent for small accounts and 23 per cent for large accounts. Although this meant an increase in the requirements for small accounts, it was not substantially higher than the standards prevailing in 1929 for large accounts.

Federal Reserve Margins. The Securities Exchange Act of 1934 gave the Federal Reserve Board the power to control margins by regulating

---

[7] W. C. Antwerp, *The Stock Exchange from Within* (Garden City, N.Y.: Doubleday & Co., Inc., 1914), p. 51.

[8] *Ibid.*, p. 415.

[9] *Ibid.*, p. 58.

[10] *Constitution* (1929), chap. xii.

the maximum amount of credit that could be extended on registered securities. Since that agency was responsible for the credit structure of the banking system, it was deemed by Congress to be the proper authority for such regulations. Another agency, the SEC, was delegated power to control all other activities of the securities markets. Under the Act the Board has issued a regulation, supplemented by rulings, known as Regulation T, which controls the extension and maintenance of credit to customers by brokers, dealers, and members of national securities exchanges. Regulation U, also issued by the Board, regulates loans by banks for the purpose of purchasing and carrying stocks registered on national securities exchanges.

The Federal Reserve has set minimum initial requirements and does not prevent either exchanges or member firms from making other and higher requirements. Hence, a customer may be subjected to as many as three different margin requirements in his account. To make the situation even more complex, different rules have been set up for many different transactions in the restricted account, thus making margin trading probably the most complicated of all security transactions.

The Board under the Act received broad powers to publish regulations appropriate in view of the extension and accommodation of credit to commerce and industry and to prevent excessive use of credit to finance security transactions. It was authorized to set margins by any reasonable method. In practice, it has always used the percentage system, based on the total cost of securities at the time of purchase. The Board changed the percentage required sixteen times in the period 1934 to 1962. The rate was as low as 30 per cent in 1937, a requirement which stayed in force eight years. The maximum rate, 100 per cent, was effective in 1946 and 1947, when there was concern over a runaway market. Since then, rates varying from 50 to 90 per cent have been imposed, as shown at the top of Figure 21–1. In 1962 a 50 per cent margin requirement was in effect.

Changes are made in the Federal Reserve margin whenever the Board believes that conditions justify them. Increases may be made because of a belief that excessive credit is going into the market. Similarly, decreases may be put into effect when it is believed that these conditions no longer prevail or are receding.

The effects of changing margin requirements on the market show much variation. In perhaps one-third of the cases, a change in the requirements had no perceptible effect on prices over long or short periods. Where there has been a change, it varied from an abrupt, short-lived reaction to one whose effects were observable for four or five months.

Bogen and Krooss, after studying the effects of change in margin requirements over this period, concluded that increases generally slowed but did not reverse rising price movements while decreases generally slackened or reversed declining price movements. They concluded also that changed margin requirements did affect the amount of customer borrowing in the way expected, which after all is the stated purpose for margin regulation. The changes may have affected volume and the tendency for traders to deal more frequently in low-priced stocks, but the evidence over these years was not conclusive.[11]

CLASSIFICATION OF SECURITIES

Registered Securities. Registered securities are subject to provisions of Regulation T of the Federal Reserve Board. There are two types of registered securities. The first consists of those securities that have gone through formal listing and registration on a national securities exchange. The second class consists of those that have been given unlisted trading privileges on an exchange and are, therefore, subject to this regulation. All corporate issues traded on the New York Stock Exchange and the other organized exchanges would, therefore, be considered as registered, non-exempt securities.

Exempt Securities. These securities are not subject to the provisions of Regulation T. Chief among them are the securities of the United States government, state and local bonds, and bonds of the International Bank for Reconstruction and Development. They receive favored treatment in the matter of margins. Regulation T makes no margin requirements, and those of the New York Stock Exchange are very low.

Minimum margin requirements, established by the New York Stock Exchange under Rule 431, for all United States government obligations issued or guaranteed as to principal and interest are 5 per cent. Some brokerage firms, however, may demand higher margins, such as 10 per cent. This 5 per cent requirement is based on the principal or par value and not the market value. It is effective both for initial and maintenance requirements.

Other exempt securities carry a margin of 15 per cent of the principal amount or 25 per cent of the market value, whichever is lower; the Exchange, however, may grant a lower minimum on a particular issue upon application to the Department of Member Firms.

Unregistered Securities. These are not registered on any national securities exchange. They are, of course, not listed. Typical examples are stocks and bonds dealt in on the over-the-counter market. They have no collateral value under Regulation T, which does not allow the extension of credit in a general account on unregistered securities. Unreg-

[11] Bogen and Krooss, *op. cit.*, pp. 114–27.

istered securities must be bought on a strictly cash basis. They may, however, be sold short on a margin basis.

INITIAL MARGIN REQUIREMENTS

Two Kinds of Margin Requirements. Under present rules there are two distinct margin requirements. The first type is called the initial margin requirement and applies only to the day of the transaction. The second type is called the maintenance requirement; it applies to the account after the day of the transaction.

Both the New York Stock Exchange and the Federal Reserve Board have initial margin requirements.

Exchange Requirements. Effective February 13, 1956, the New York Stock Exchange established the following initial margin requirement in Rule 431.

For the purpose of effecting new securities transactions and commitments, the margin deposit shall be an amount equivalent to the requirements of paragraph (b) [discussed on page 377 as "maintenance margin requirements"] of this Rule, with a minimum equity in the account of at least $1,000 except that cash need not be deposited in excess of the cost of any security purchased. The foregoing minimum equity and cost of purchase provisions shall not apply to "when distributed" securities in cash accounts and the exercise of rights to subscribe.

In other words, no member firm may accept an account with a margin or equity of less than $1,000. The minimum prior to February 13, 1956, was $500.

Securities Deposited as Margin. It is generally known that securities may be deposited as margin in lieu of cash. What is not understood, however, is the amount of securities that must be deposited to equal a given amount of cash margin. The following figures may be helpful. They show how much cash or securities must be deposited to buy $1,000 in securities at various initial margin requirements of the Federal Reserve Board.

Margin Requirement	Cash Margin	Equivalent in Securities
50%	$500	$1,000
60	600	1,500
70	700	2,333
80	800	4,000
90	900	9,000

Stated in another way, a customer under a 50 per cent margin may buy securities equal to 100 per cent of the value of securities deposited; under a 60 per cent margin, 67 per cent; and under a 70 per cent margin, 43 per cent.

Federal Reserve Requirements. The Federal Reserve Board has changed initial requirements many times, as already indicated. Both the Board and the Exchange require that margin be deposited as promptly as possible, and, in any event, before the end of four business days following the transaction. Many customers believe that the margin must be deposited at the time of the transaction. This is not a general practice for well-established accounts. If the customer does not have sufficient margin in his account, he is allowed four days in which to deposit it.

Example of Initial Margin. Let us suppose that a customer wishes to buy 50 shares of XYZ at 24. These would be the computations:

Cost: 50 shares at 24	$1,200.00
Commission	17.00
Total costs	$1,217.00
Margin deposit (70% assumed)	851.90
Exchange minimum requirement	$1,000.00

Although the Federal Reserve requirement would have been satisfied with a cash deposit or equity in the account of $851.90, this amount is less than the $1,000 requirement of the Exchange. Hence, the customer would have had to have deposited an additional $148.10 in cash or securities loan values.

MAINTENANCE MARGIN REQUIREMENTS

Exchange Requirements. Rule 431 of the New York Stock Exchange requires that a margin must be maintained in an account with a minimum of 25 per cent of the market value of all securities "long" in the account. On short sales the maintenance margin is $2.50 per share or 100 per cent of market value on stock priced under $5.00, and it is $5.00 per share or 30 per cent on higher-priced issues of stocks or on bonds. There is no reason why a broker may not demand a higher margin, and some do. Some firms even maintain dollar minimums as well, especially for low-priced stocks. The $1,000 equity requirement need not be maintained but new purchases or short sales are prohibited if it is not.

Under the 25 per cent maintenance and a 70 per cent initial margin requirement, a broker may allow the price of stock to decline 60 per cent before he asks for more margin. Let us suppose that a customer bought 100 shares at 100 and put up a 70 per cent margin. The stock price then fell to 40. The margin would be down to 25 per cent, as the following figures will show:

$$\text{Margin} = \frac{4,000 - 3,000}{4,000} \times 100 = 25$$

It will be noted in this example that the customer's original equity of $7,000 dropped to $1,000.

Under the 25 per cent maintenance requirement, if the initial rate is 90 per cent, a drop in price of purchased stock equaling 87 per cent might take place before there was a margin call. If the initial rate were 50 per cent, a drop of one-third would lead to a margin call.

Margin Calls. Margins are watched daily at brokerage houses, particularly in those accounts in which the need for more margin is becoming apparent. This is no great task today with high initial margins, but was a hectic occupation in bull markets like 1929, when margins were no more than 10 or 20 per cent. When the margin gets too low in the opinion of the broker, he sends out a margin call for more cash or securities. This notice may be sent by telephone, telegraph, or letter.

In practice, brokers give reasonable notice for a margin call, which means not more than four business days may be used to meet the call. The Exchange makes no specific time limit for meeting a call, using only the word "reasonable." In the brokerage business "reasonable" is usually defined as four days. Although a broker would be perfectly within his legal rights to demand a margin deposit within a shorter time, he will always attempt to give a reasonable notice under normal conditions.

Federal Reserve Requirements. There is no maintenance requirement by the Federal Reserve Board provided no activity takes place in the account. Activity brings the account into the restricted status, shortly to be discussed.

UNDERMARGINED ACCOUNTS

Meaning. The term "undermargined account" has a very technical meaning and is not to be confused with the term "restricted account," defined below. It applies only to the maintenance requirements of the Exchange. As already indicated, the margin must not be less than 25 per cent on "long" stock or, usually, 30 per cent on "short" stock. When it is below this percentage, the account is said to be "undermargined." There is no dollar minimum used to measure whether or not an account is undermargined.

Transactions in Undermargined Accounts. It is possible to purchase securities for an account that is undermargined, but the broker must issue a margin call at the time of the transaction. For example, the equity in the account might fall until the margin was only 22 per cent. At that precise moment the customer might wish to buy more stock. He could do this if he were to deposit enough margin to buy the new stock and to bring the undermargined stock up to a reasonable level.

Additional Margin Required. The problem here is how much additional margin must be required if a margin were to fall to 25 per cent or less. There is no Exchange rule. The prevailing practice of brokers is to ask that enough margin be deposited to bring the margin up to around 33 to 35 per cent.

RESTRICTED ACCOUNTS

Meaning. Accounts that have less than the prevailing initial margin required by Regulation T of the Federal Reserve Board are "restricted." If the Federal Reserve Board initial margin requirement were 50 per cent, an account would be said to be restricted if the margin were under that figure. Hence, whether or not an account is restricted depends on the initial margin requirement. There is no objection by the Board to an account being restricted but the regulations apply to new transactions in the account.

Account Sales. A customer may sell stock from a restricted account and withdraw an amount equal to the difference between the market price and the retention requirement on the securities sold. In 1962 the retention requirement defined by the Federal Reserve Board in Regulation T was 50 per cent of market price for registered, non-exempt securities and was the maximum loan value for exempt securities. The Exchange requires that the account shall not become undermargined by any such withdrawal.

To illustrate, suppose a customer purchased XYZ at 50. The price of the issue dropped to 40 and the margin dropped to 62½ per cent. If the initial margin requirement then was 70 per cent, the account would be restricted. However, a sale of stock at 40 could be made and one-half, i.e., 50 per cent, of the proceeds withdrawn on the day of sale. If 100 shares were sold, ignoring commissions and taxes, $2,000 could be withdrawn from the account.

Security Withdrawals. Unregistered securities, against which no loan may be made under the provisions of Regulation T and the Securities Exchange Act of 1934, may be withdrawn from a restricted account provided the Exchange maintenance margin requirements are met after the withdrawal.

Registered securities or exempt securities, however, may be withdrawn only under one of four conditions, or a combination of them:

1. The customer may pay up his entire debit balance leaving no loan outstanding against the account.
2. He may substitute on the same day registered or exempt securities with at least the same retention requirement value as those withdrawn.

3. He may deposit cash on the same day equal in amount to the current retention requirement on the securities withdrawn. If the withdrawal is for sale of the item, this option is identical to that described in the preceding section on "account sales."
4. He may deposit cash to bring the account to full initial margin requirement.

Of the four alternatives the customer should, of course, choose the one most favorable to him. In any case, the account must not be allowed to go below the minimum maintenance requirements of the Exchange after such action.

Dividend Withdrawals. A customer may withdraw interest or cash dividends received in a restricted account within thirty-five days after they have been deposited in the account provided that they have not been used within this period to margin new purchases. Furthermore, the account must meet the maintenance requirement of the Exchange after withdrawal. Such a withdrawal means that cash dividends and interest receive special treatment in the restricted account.

A customer may withdraw stock dividends if they do not exceed 10 per cent of the market value of the stock itself. Dividends classified as "arrearages" may not be withdrawn. By arrearages is meant accumulated preferred dividends which are sometimes paid at the time a company emerges from reorganization or from a period of financial difficulties. Such instances are rare.

Account Purchases. A customer may purchase securities for a restricted account. He need not bring the account up to the full initial margin requirement. The only regulation is that he must deposit the full, initial margin on the value of securities purchased. The old securities still may be margined for less than the current initial per cent, but the net effect of the transaction is to raise the average margin.

Substitutions. Regulations permit a customer to make substitutions or "switches" in the restricted account without a deposit of additional margin. Such substitutions must be made on the same day. For example, a customer may want to sell $1,000 of one stock and simultaneously purchase $1,000 of another. It will be observed that the account is in exactly the same condition after the substitution as it was before. If the customer were to buy more securities than he sold, he would have to put up the initial margin on the excess amount. For example, the customer sells $1,000 in stock and buys $1,200. If the initial rate were set at 70 per cent, he would then deposit an additional margin of $140. This "switching" permits a considerable amount of activity in an account without the necessity of bringing it up to the full initial requirement.

Transfer of Accounts. It is possible to transfer a restricted account from one broker to another. It may not, however, be transferred from a bank to a broker until it has been brought up to the full initial requirement.

Special Accounts. Regulation T governs, for the most part, the management of the general account, the typical account in which a customer conducts margin purchases and short sales. This regulation, however, permits a customer to open and use any number of special accounts in addition to the general accounts. Brief definitions of the seven special types were given on page 338. The purpose of the special accounts is not to evade the limitations placed upon a restricted account, and it is not to be used for that purpose. Such an account, however, will permit a customer to handle certain transactions even though the general account may be restricted.

For example, a customer who may have a restricted general account is permitted to use a special cash account. This account is entirely distinct from the general account. The fact that the general account is restricted has no effect on transactions in the special account, provided that such transactions are bona fide cash transactions.

A customer may purchase any securities for cash through this account. He must pay promptly in cash for the securities and must not contemplate selling the securities before making such a payment. In case he does not make full cash payment within seven full business days, the broker must cancel or liquidate the transaction or the unsettled portion thereof. If conditions warrant, additional time may be requested in lieu of liquidation on the seventh day at the discretion of the broker. There is also a ninety-day restriction if the customer sells stock he has bought before making full cash payment.

22

Figuring Commissions
and Taxes

COMMISSIONS

All investors and speculators who buy and sell securities listed on the
New York Stock Exchange pay the commissions established by the
Board of Governors of the Exchange. These commissions are mandatory
on both purchases and sales. The commission schedules are somewhat
complex, or at least appear so, on first inspection. Commission tables
have, therefore, been prepared which indicate commission on both round-
lots and odd-lots for orders of many sizes.[1]

Since security buyers can always obtain information on commissions
from their brokers, it would seem unnecessary to know the formula by
which commissions are computed. This is an unsound concept. The
intelligent stock buyer should be able to compute his own commissions,
just as a taxpayer should be able to compute his own income taxes, or
the automobile buyer to figure the costs of buying his car on the installment plan, or the home owner to determine the costs of financing a new
home. It is simply good business practice.

History of Commission Schedules. When the New York Stock Exchange began as a curb market in 1792, one of its first decisions was to
establish a uniform schedule of commissions. This schedule was based
on a money-involved method of computation. The rates were ¼ of 1

---

[1] A good example of a commission schedule is found in the booklet: *Stocks, New
York Stock Exchange: Ticker Symbols, Code Numbers, Par Values, Post Locations,
Minimum Commission Rates*, published by Francis Emory Fitch, Inc., at regular
intervals.

per cent of the money involved in the order.[2] Thus, on an order of 10 shares of stock selling at $100, the commission would be $2.50. This system lasted until 1840.

Commission rates were changed a number of times prior to the establishment of the current schedule. Until 1947 the Exchange used a schedule based on cents per share. On November 3, 1947, the Exchange reverted to its original plan of computing commissions on a money-involved basis. The 1947 schedule was revised in 1953, 1958, and 1959. Under the current schedule the average commission is estimated to be about 1 per cent of the money involved in a typical round-lot order.

Commission Schedule (in force in 1962). This is the present schedule of non-member minimum commissions on stocks, rights, and warrants traded in 100-share and 10-share units:

On stocks selling at $1.00 per share and above, commissions shall be based upon the amount of money involved in a single transaction and shall be not less than the rates hereinafter specified:

1. On each single transaction, not exceeding 100 shares, in a unit of trading; a combination of units of trading; or a combination of a unit or units of trading plus an odd-lot:

Commission

2% on the first $400 of money involved, plus
1% on the next $2,000, plus
½% on the next $2,600, plus
1⁄10% on amounts over $5,000, plus $3.00

2. On odd-lots the same rates, less $2.00
3. Notwithstanding the foregoing:
   a. When the amount involved in a transaction is less than $100, the minimum commission shall be as mutually agreed;
   b. When the amount involved in a transaction is $100 or more, the minimum commission shall not exceed $1.50 per share or $75 per single transaction, but in any event shall not be less than $6 per single transaction.[3]

Examples of Commissions on Round-Lots. The following examples will show how commissions are computed on specific orders:

1. *A round-lot buying order involving a money value between $100 and $400.* The order is for 100 shares purchased at $3.

100 shares at $3	$300.00	
2% of money value		$6.00
Plus		3.00
Commission		$9.00

[2] Birl E. Shultz, *The Securities Market and How It Works* (New York: Harper & Row, Publishers, 1946), pp. 222–3.
[3] New York Stock Exchange, *Constitution,* Art. XV.

2. *A round-lot selling order involving a money value between $400 and $2,400.* The order is for 100 shares sold at $20.

100 shares at $20	$2,000.00	
2% on the first $400		$ 8.00
1% on the next $1,600		16.00
Plus		3.00
Commission		$27.00

3. *A round-lot selling order involving a money value between $2,400 and $5,000.* The order is for 100 shares sold at $40.

100 shares at $40	$4,000.00	
2% on the first $400		$ 8.00
1% on the next $2,000		20.00
½% on the next $1,600		8.00
Plus		3.00
Commission		$39.00

The commission on this order is less than 1 per cent on the money involved. A round-lot sold at 38 carries a $38, or 1 per cent, commission. The ratio drops on sales of higher-priced shares.

4. *A round-lot buying order involving a money value in excess of $5,000.* The order is for 100 shares purchased at $75.

100 shares at $75	$7,500.00	
2% on the first $400		$ 8.00
1% on the next $2,000		20.00
½% on the next $2,600		13.00
$\frac{1}{10}$% on the next $2,500		2.50
Plus		3.00
Commission		$46.50

5. *A round-lot buying order for more than 100 shares.* The order is for 300 shares purchased at $75 per share, the same price used in example 4. The commission on 100 shares at that price is $46.50, as was just indicated. For 300 shares the commission is three times that amount, or $139.50. This principle is very important; on orders for more than 100 shares, the commission on 100 is computed first, and then this figure is multiplied by the number of 100-share, or round-lot, units involved in the order. Each round-lot transaction is a single transaction for the purpose of computing commissions.

6. *A round-lot selling order with $6 minimum commission.* The order is for 100 shares sold at $1 per share.

100 shares at $1	$100.00	
2% on money value		$2.00
Plus		3.00
Computed commission		$5.00
Minimum commission		$6.00

In this example the computed commission of $5 is less than the minimum commission for any $100 transaction, i.e., $6.

7. *A round-lot selling order with a $75 maximum.* The order is for 100 shares sold at $375.

100 shares at $375	$37,500.00	
2% on the first $400		$ 8.00
1% on the next $2,000		20.00
½% on the next $2,600		13.00
1/10% on the next $32,500		32.50
Plus		3.00
Computed commission		$76.50
Maximum commission		$75.00

The effect of the $75 maximum commission is that all stocks selling at $360 or more in round-lots of 100 are subject to the maximum. No broker need charge a commission exceeding $75 per round-lot of 100 shares but he may charge more. On very high-priced shares, such as Superior Oil and IBM, some elect to do so.

Examples of Commissions on Odd-Lots. The following examples will show how commissions are computed on specific orders (note that the overhead charge is $3 — $2, or $1):

1. *An odd-lot order to buy 25 shares at $10.*

25 shares at $10	$250.00	
2% on the $250		$5.00
Plus		1.00
Commission		$6.00

In this instance the computed and minimum commissions are equal.

2. *An odd-lot selling order for 40 shares sold at $70.*

40 shares at $70	$2,800.00	
2% on the first $400		$ 8.00
1% on the next $2,000		20.00
½% on the next $400		2.00
Plus		1.00
Commission		$31.00

3. *An odd-lot buying order with a $6 minimum commission.* The order is for 20 shares purchased at $6.

20 shares at $6	$120.00	
2% on the $120		$2.40
Plus		1.00
Computed commission		$3.40
Minimum commission		$6.00

It should be noted in connection with the $6 minimum that all odd-lot orders involving $100 to $250, inclusive, carry a $6 minimum commission. Others, such as a 2-share order for IBM, involving $1,000 dollars, also would carry the $6 minimum charge and is held to it by the rule that the maximum charge per share is $1.50. The latter rule is in abeyance if it would yield a charge under $6 on an order amounting to $100 or more.

4. *An odd-lot selling order involving the $1.50 per share maximum.* The order is for 10 shares sold at $120.

10 shares at $120 .... $1,200.00	
2% on the first $400	$ 8.00
1% on the next $800	8.00
Plus	1.00
Computed commission	$17.00
Maximum commission of $1.50 per share	$15.00

Comparative Commissions on Round- and Odd-Lots. The question often asked is: Are commissions lower on round-lots than on odd-lots? The answer is usually clear. Odd-lot customers almost always pay higher commissions per share than round-lot customers. There are two reasons: first, many orders are subject to the $6 minimum; and second, rates are higher on orders with low money value than on those with high money value. An exception occurs for odd-lots in large amounts, e.g., 99 shares. The general case is illustrated in Table 22–1.

Table 22–1. Comparative Commissions on Some Round- and Odd-Lot Orders

Price of Share	100-Share Order Commission		10-Share Order Commission	
	Total	Per Share	Total	Per Share
$ 10.00	$17.00	$0.17	$ 6.00	$0.60
25.00	31.50	0.31½	6.00	0.60
50.00	39.00	0.39	10.00	1.00
100.00	49.00	0.49	15.00	1.50
200.00	59.00	0.59	15.00	1.50
500.00	75.00	0.75	15.00	1.50

However, on an order for 99 shares executed at $100 per share, the commission would be $46.90. The cost per share in this case would be $0.47½, or slightly less than the $0.49 of a round-lot order.

The odd-lot customer, however, is subject to another expense which increases the cost of an odd-lot. This is the odd-lot differential, usually ⅛ to ¼ point, charged by the odd-lot dealer. Fairly substantial savings in costs per share, therefore, can be effected if the investor or trader can deal in round-lots rather than in odd-lots.

NEW YORK STATE TRANSFER TAXES

Background. Prior to 1932 the state of New York levied a transfer tax on stocks at $0.02 a share. In 1932 the rate was raised to $0.04 for each $100 par value or fraction thereof, and $0.04 per share for each no-par share. In the following year the law was changed somewhat, and stocks that were selling at $20 or more were taxed at $0.04 per share, regardless of par or no-par status. Those selling under $20 were taxed at $0.03.

The state was greatly in need of revenue in 1932, and the new tax law brought in about $32 million per year.[4] In later years the revenue declined as the volume of trading fell off, and in 1941 the yield was less than $12 million. The yield in 1959 and 1960 was $50 and $64 million, respectively.

Present Schedule. The present rates are as follows and apply to all stock transfers, regardless of whether the stock has par value or no-par value. The tax levied on the transaction is paid by the selling customer.

Selling Price of Stock	Tax per Share
Less than $5	$.01
$5 but less than $10	.02
$10 but less than $20	.03
$20 or more	.04

The computation of New York transfer taxes is very simple. For example, a customer sells 500 shares of a stock at 15. The tax is 500 × $0.03, or $15. Another customer sells 100 shares of a stock at 65. The tax is 100 × $0.04, or $4. Transfers not involving a sale are taxed at $0.02 per share.

FEDERAL TRANSFER TAXES

Background. The federal transfer tax on stocks has had a checkered career, beginning with the Civil War, when a small tax of $\frac{1}{20}$ of 1 per cent was levied on the par value of stocks and bonds. The tax was short lived and was not followed by another tax until 1898, when a tax of $0.02 per $100 of par value was passed. This tax survived only four years. From 1902 to 1914 there was no tax. In 1914 another law was enacted, and it stayed on the books only two years, the rate being $0.02. Again, in 1917 the tax was revived with the rate again $0.02; it has remained on the books at that rate or more until the present time. In 1932 the rates were raised to $0.04 per 100 of par value for stocks selling at less than $20 and to $0.05 for stocks selling at $20 or more. These rates later were raised to $0.05 and $0.06.

Present Schedule. The rate structure of the Federal transfer tax was changed radically, beginning January 1, 1959. A rate based on the dollar

[4] Birl E. Shultz, *The Securities Market* (New York: Harper & Row, Publishers, 1942), p. 223.

amount involved in a transaction was substituted for the par value basis of the earlier legislation. The transfer tax became $0.04 per $100, or major fraction thereof, in the actual total price of securities sold or otherwise transferred. A "major fraction" is an amount in excess of $50; a transaction for $450 would be considered as four hundreds for this purpose, but a transaction for $450.01 would be five hundreds for this purpose.

Maximum tax per share and minimum amount of tax per transaction both were included in the legislation. The tax per share may not exceed 8 cents; on shares selling at $200 or more the tax does not increase as the size of transaction does but is limited to $0.08 per share included in the transaction. The minimum tax per transaction is $0.04. Even on transactions involving less than $50, therefore, a tax of $0.04 is imposed.

There is no double taxation of odd-lots, as there was in earlier years. An odd-lot seller pays the tax but an odd-lot buyer does not.

SEC Fees. In addition to the federal and state transfer taxes, there is a small transfer fee assessed by the SEC. The rate is 1 cent for each $500 in value or fraction thereof on all security sales on a registered exchange. The fee is not collected on purchases. It is collected by the exchange and goes into the general fund of the United States Treasury. An exchange is charged this fee for the privilege of doing business as a national securities exchange. In practice, it is shifted to selling customers. No member firm is permitted to absorb the fees, according to the rules of the New York Stock Exchange.

Although small as related to the individual order, these fees are large in the aggregate. In recent periods of high activity they have run in excess of $800,000 per year on the New York Stock Exchange alone.

THE COSTS OF TRADING

The New York Stock Exchange has estimated that about 9 to 16 per cent of all transactions by public individuals are liquidated within thirty days and another 19 to 29 per cent within six months. This brings up the problem: What are the overhead costs of a "round-turn" in the market? How large a gross profit must a trader make in order to come out even in a speculative transaction? An example will throw some light on the matter. Let us suppose that a trader is buying and selling a typical common stock in the buying range of $40 per share. He carries out four "round-turns" of 100 shares each in less than six months. He makes a 2-point profit on three of the transactions and loses the same amount on the fourth one. This would be excellent performance. How would he come out in his trading?

Funds committed		$4,000.00
Gross profit on three trades		$ 600.00
Costs:		
Loss on one trade	$200.00	
Commissions	312.00	
Transfer taxes	22.40	
SEC fees	.32	534.72
Net gain from trading		$ 66.28

From the foregoing example it will be observed that an average trader will need a gross profit of about 2 points on his successful transactions to come out even on his trading. This would be a 5 per cent profit on a $40 stock.

23

Stock Transfer

Stock transfer refers to a process by which a record of the transfer of title to stock from one owner to another is made. Change of ownership may arise owing to sale, gift, hypothecation, or other acts. There may be delay between the date of delivery of the stock and the date of transfer on the corporate records. There usually is. The requirements and convenience of the transferee or the receiving broker influence the timing.

Stock delivery was discussed in Chapter 16. Attention here is directed to the separate, distinct operation of transfer. Some of the details are stated, for convenience of description, in terms of rules and practices affecting member organizations of the New York Stock Exchange but most statements apply equally to all transfers.

TECHNIQUE OF STOCK TRANSFER

There are two aspects to the transfer of title to stock. First, the transfer is accomplished by delivery of properly endorsed certificates. Second the transfer is recorded on the books of the issuing corporation. Until the latter step has been taken, the new owner is unknown to the corporation. When it has been taken, the new owner will receive a certificate evidencing his interest, dividend, or other distributions made by the issuer and notice of stockholder meetings at which questions affecting his interest are raised.

Both steps may be taken within a short time of each other, perhaps a day or two. On occasion, certificates are delivered after the transfer has been recorded on the corporate books. However, the record of transfer may be delayed days, weeks, or even years without invalidation of the title if properly endorsed securities have been delivered.

Assignment Form. Proper endorsement involves use of an assignment form. On the back of every stock certificate there is printed a form, commonly known as an "Assignment and Power of Attorney." This form is illustrated in Figure 23–1. When a stock certificate with the assignment properly executed is delivered, with intent to pass title, title passes from the named owner of the certificate to the new owner, or transferee, regardless of the fact that the transfer has not yet been recorded on the books of the issuer or its transfer agent.

As shown in Figure 23–1, the assignment has spaces for the name of the new owner, or transferee, the number of shares and the class of stock, the name of an attorney, the date, the signature of a witness, and the signature of the owner. Not all of these spaces need be filled to effect a transfer of title. Of greatest significance is proper signature by the named owner.

Name of Owner. Each stock certificate should carry on its face the exact name of the rightful owner. Accuracy is important. It is not necessary for status or sex to be shown by such abbreviations as "Mr.," "Mrs.," or "Miss," but the name of the owner should be shown correctly. If a

---

𝕱𝖔𝖗 𝖁𝖆𝖑𝖚𝖊 𝕽𝖊𝖈𝖊𝖎𝖛𝖊𝖉,..

hereby sell, assign and transfer unto..

....(....................) Shares of the

....Capital Stock represented by the within

certificate and do hereby irrevocably constitute and appoint.....................

....attorney to transfer said stock

on the books of the within named Company with full power of sub-

stitution in the premises.

Dated.....................................

....

IN PRESENCE OF

....

Fig. 23–1. An assignment and power of attorney.

buyer, or transferee, of stock receives from a transfer agent a certificate on which the name is the wrong one or, if right, is misspelled, he should have the error corrected promptly. The correction is made by sending the certificate back to the transfer agent, who will issue a new certificate. Under no circumstances should anyone attempt to alter the owner's name on the certificate.

Joint names may be used. A husband and wife, for example, may have a joint account with their broker and carry the stocks that they own in their joint name with right of survivorship thinking they will save taxes. They may find they have incurred unnecessary taxes. If the husband paid for the security but had it registered in the joint name, he may have to pay a gift tax. If the wife dies, the tax authorities will seek to tax the shares as part of her estate. A joint name may be useful, but one should not be adopted without consulting a lawyer.

There are three ways in which joint ownership of stock may be indicated on the certificate:[1]

> JAMES W. SMITH & MARY K. SMITH JT TEN WROS
> JAMES W. SMITH & MARY K. SMITH TEN ENT
> JAMES W. SMITH & MARY K. SMITH TEN COM

The first indicates joint tenancy with right of survivorship. Several persons may be included among the joint tenants. In some states this form of tenancy is not recognized. Where it is, probate proceedings usually are not necessary for transfer of title to the survivor. This is the form of tenancy referred to in the illustration above.

The second way of showing joint ownership indicates tenancy by the entireties. This type of tenancy is restricted to husband and wife. The right of survivorship is implicit in this tenancy.

The third way of stating joint ownership indicates tenancy in common. Two or more persons may hold stock under this tenancy. If there is joint ownership and it is not clear from the inscription on the certificate that one of the other two tenancies is intended, tenancy in common is usually assumed. Each tenant has an undivided interest in the securities and there is no right of survivorship. The fractional interest of the tenant is part of his estate.

Transfer of a certificate held in joint name requires endorsement by both or all of the joint owners, or executor, administrator, or guardian, if applicable. Dividend checks and other distributions will be made out to the joint owners and must be endorsed jointly unless an order has been given by one or more of them to make such distributions to one

---

[1] These are illustrated in *Forms of Registration for Corporate Stock,* published by The Chase Manhattan Bank, 1961.

owner. A mother and son, for example, might hold stock jointly, but the son might authorize the payment of dividends to the mother alone.

State laws differ on joint ownership. Stockholders are advised to consult their lawyers before deciding on a form of joint ownership.

Street names are used on many stock certificates. The term "street name" means that the stock is in the name of a broker or brokerage firm, or nominee. The courts have defined a street name as "the name of a person other than the owner, which is inserted for convenience of rapid handling."[2] Such certificates may pass through many hands before being transferred on the corporate records. Instances exist where this situation continued for years. However, prompt transfer is usual.

It is a practice of brokers to transfer all stock, even stock that customers have left with them for sale, to their name at the time they receive it. This action has as its purpose ease of delivery. If the stock already is in a street name, the transfer need not be recorded. Dividends or other distributions can be obtained by filing a claim against the owner whose name does appear on the certificate. However, ease of record-keeping and clarity with respect to ownership usually lead, even in this case, to a transfer to the name of the firm itself. Endorsement of stock in street name is, of course, easy for the firm.

Endorsement. Proper signature by the owner in the proper place in the assignment form is essential for sale. The signature must be genuine and must agree with the name shown on the face of the certificate.

An owner may endorse an incorrectly identified certificate, such as one on which the name is misspelled or one that was made out before the owner's name changed (by marriage, for example), by writing the incorrect name as well as the correct name and noting that they are both names for the same individual. For example, the certificate may be endorsed "Marth K. Smith (as on the face), Mary K. Smith, one and the same person." It is clearly better, however, if the name on the face of the certificate and that in the signature correspond in every particular. There should be no alteration or enlargement or change whatever, except for such obvious words as "and" for "&" and "Company" for "Co.," which may be written either way. If a certificate has "Charles J. Brown" on its face, the endorsement should be identical and not "C. J. Brown." This is a matter of good business practice to assure proper identification of the stockholder.

Endorsement of a certificate by a married woman in Texas may require the written consent of her husband. A form is available for this purpose.

---

[2] *Barthelmess v. Cavalier,* 2 Cal. App. 2d 477.

Endorsement in blank is accomplished when the certificate carries only the signature of the owner. No transferee is named. If the name of a transferee is added, either with or without indication of an attorney, the certificate is said to be specially endorsed.

Once a stock certificate has been properly endorsed in blank by the rightful owner, it becomes for all extents and purposes a negotiable instrument. It may then be transferred from person to person by delivery, like any other form of negotiable instrument. This is true even though it is not witnessed and contains no mention of attorney. The quality of negotiability is highly important to the owner, since any bona fide holder for value, who may obtain possession of the certificate, has a valid claim to the stock. He can demand that title to it be recorded in his name, as will be shown later. The signature on the assignment is effective for transfer of title.

Guaranty of Signature. It is a well-established principle of law that a corporation or its transfer agent must recognize the transfer of stock on proper authority. This means that the signature on the assignment is genuine, the signer was the appropriate person to sign, and the signer had the legal capacity to sign. If, for example, the signature was forged, the corporation or its transfer agent may be liable to the rightful owner if the stock has been transferred to a bona fide transferee. No corporation or transfer agent cares to record a transfer and issue a new certificate unless proper signature has been obtained.

How can the corporation or its transfer agent or a purchaser be assured that the signature is genuine? The answer is found in the guaranty of the signature. A signature guarantor warrants that the signature is genuine and that the signer was the appropriate person and had the legal capacity to sign. Rule 209 of the New York Stock Exchange exempts registered securities of the United States government and those in the name of a member or member organization from a requirement for guarantee of the signature on the assignment. The signatures on other securities, however, must be guaranteed by a member or member organization or by a commercial bank or trust company.

The guarantor will add his guaranty below the name of the endorser, or owner. A duly authorized employee of a member organization or a bank or trust company may sign his name to make the guaranty. Transfer agents keep a record of all persons authorized or empowered to guarantee signatures.

Witness. Although a space is provided on the assignment form for the signature of a witness to the endorsement, it has not been the practice for a number of years to require such a witness. Since all stock transfers are made only on the guaranty of an authorized person or organization (unless the transfer agent is satisfied of the genuineness of signature by other means), the use of a witness has become superfluous.

Attorney. The use of a power of attorney is an evolution in stock transfer practice. Years ago, when stock was to be transferred, it was expected that the actual owner would go to the offices of the corporation and with his own hand authorize the transfer of the stock to a new owner. This proved to be impractical. Instead, owners found it expedient to have an agent, or attorney, who was authorized to make the transfer. The appointment of an attorney is not always necessary, because stock certificates endorsed in blank transfer without it.

An attorney may be designated on the assignment if there is danger that certificates might be lost or stolen—as, for example, when shipped by mail. A brokerage firm may then be designated as attorney. Since the broker also may find it awkward to actually present the certificate for transfer, upon transfer or delivery, he will fill out a "Power of Substitution" in blank. This permits "good delivery." The power of substitution is illustrated in Figure 23–2. The signature on this also should be guaranteed.

5-5-33 CONTINENTAL ILLINOIS NATIONAL BANK
       AND TRUST COMPANY OF CHICAGO

To be attached to Certificate Number.......... *for* ....*shares of*

.... *stock of* .... *Company.*

.... *hereby irrevocably constitute and appoint* ....

....

substitute to transfer the within named stock under foregoing Power or Attorney, with like power of substitution.

Date..........................

Signed........................

Witness...........................

....

Fig. 23–2. A power of substitution.

Usually, certificates are delivered to other firms or to the transfer agent with the space for an attorney's name left blank. The actual attorney then is the employee in the office of the transfer agent, who physically performs the operations involved in canceling the old certificate and issuing the new one.

Transferee. The transferee is the new owner of the security to whom title is transferred. When a new certificate is issued, the name of the transferee is inserted on the face of the certificate. Transferees may be one or more individuals, a corporation, a nominee for some institution, a trustee, an agent, a brokerage firm.

Naming a transferee is not necessary for transfer of title. Title passes by delivery of a properly endorsed certificate. The usual reasons for naming a transferee is to have the stock records show the transfer and thus permit the new owner to have a certificate evidencing his interest, to receive dividends and other distributions from the corporation, and to receive notice of meetings directly. Naming a transferee also makes a certificate non-negotiable.

Stock Powers or Detached Assignments. An assignment may be made on a form separate from that on the stock certificate. Such a separate form is called, variously, a stock power, a detached assignment, or an assignment separate from the certificate. The phrasing of this form, which closely resembles that on the back of a stock certificate, is identical with that on the certificate, except that the words, "Assignment Separate from Certificate," are printed at the top and a space is added to the form to provide for identification of the stock certificate or certificates covered by the assignment.

When properly executed and delivered with a certificate or any number of certificates identified on the form, a stock power serves to transfer title as fully as does endorsement on a certificate itself. The New York Stock Exchange (Rule 195) requires that there be a stock power for each certificate to be transferred, but for other transfers a single power may be used to cover a number of certificates. Obviously, it provides simplification where several certificates are forwarded for transfer; repetitive signature of certificates becomes unnecessary. Stock powers may be used also to prevent loss of securities values in the mails. Although certificates may be sent by registered mail, properly insured, it is possible to obtain greater protection by sending certificates at one time in one package and a stock power separately. The danger that both mailings will be lost or fall into the hands of a dishonest person is small. This practice is most useful in shipment of certificates overseas. Similar protection could be obtained by naming the addressee attorney for the transfer.

A stock power may be useful in conjunction with hypothecation of securities. Although many banks actually transfer deposited securities to their own name, some will accept a stock power and the certificates and forego transfer. When the loan is paid, the clean certificates are returned. The need for transfer and then retransfer is obviated.

Cremation of Certificates. The question sometimes is asked: What happens to canceled stock certificates? This depends on instructions given the transfer agent by the corporation and on legal technicalities. Some corporations save certificates for four years for stamp tax purposes and then cremate the certificates after having recorded them on microfilm. Others extend the period to seven years. Yet others retain them for very long periods. One New York transfer agent reported it was storing certificates canceled as far back as 1911.

OTHER TRANSFER REGULATIONS

Transfer Agents. One of the agreements signed by all companies applying for listing on the New York Stock Exchange is that the corporation will maintain a transfer office or have a transfer agent in the financial district of New York. The agent may have his principal place of business out of the district but there must be transfer facilities within the district. The agent must be approved by the Exchange and may be either the company itself or a commercial bank or trust company. Most issuers appoint a bank or trust company as transfer agent because they have specialized and efficient departments established for carrying out this function.

All companies with stock listed on the New York Stock Exchange, as just indicated, must have stock transfer facilities in New York to assure maximum speed of transfer. They may also maintain additional facilities in other cities, such as Los Angeles, Chicago, or Boston. The Midwest Stock Exchange, for example, has urged companies to establish transfer agencies in that area to save time and postage, to minimize the amount of funds tied up, to facilitate trading on that exchange free of New York State transfer taxes, and to encourage a greater market for dually listed or unlisted issues traded in competition with the New York exchanges.

The procedure in a transfer agent's office may be described briefly. When a certificate is taken to the transfer agent's office by a messenger, it should be properly endorsed; the signature should be guaranteed; the name of the transferee and his address should be clear; and stamp taxes, if any, should be paid. If an attorney was named in the assignment, a power of substitution properly executed should accompany the certificate. At the transfer agent's window, a receipt is given for the certificate.

After determining that the certificate and the other documents, if any, are in order in all respects, the agent issues a new certificate or certificates for the same number of shares represented by the old certificate, which is then canceled. An appropriate record is made of the transaction. The old and new certificates then go to the registrar.

Registrar. Each company with stock listed on the New York Stock Exchange must maintain a registrar. The registrar, for New York Stock Exchange stocks, must be a bank or trust company and cannot be the same one that is serving as transfer agent for the corporation. This restraint is not imposed by other stock exchanges.

The work of the registrar, while potentially important, is routine. It is concerned solely with assuring that the new number of shares issued exactly equals the number canceled, or, if the new shares are being issued for the first time, that the total outstanding is within the authorization granted the corporation to issue stock. The purpose is prevention of dilution of the equity of the stockholders through over-issuance of stock; this did occur years ago and resulted in the present requirement for a corporation to have a registrar.

After registration the stock certificates usually go back to the transfer agent. The canceled certificates are filed for later destruction. A messenger from the broker picks up the new certificates and surrenders his receipt for the old ones.

Endorsers with Disabilities. Certain owners of stock have legal disabilities that make transfers of stock by them subject to special rules. Stock owned by a corporation, for example, will be transferred only if proper documents are filed by the endorser with the transfer agent to show the authority for the endorsement. Signature guarantee would also be provided. This is to prevent corporate officials from making transfers without proper authority to do so. Certain other owners have similar disabilities, and assignments must be supported by proper documents to show that the endorser is an appropriate person and is legally capable of signing.

Simplification legislation has been enacted in thirty-five states and the District of Columbia in recent years to deal with the special problems of fiduciary transfers. American courts have placed a special duty on issuers and transfer agents to check fiduciary transfers to make sure the fiduciary (trustee, guardian, executor, administrator, receiver) was not exceeding his power. The onus was on the transfer agent. As a result, transfer agents required the filing of all legal documents necessary to fully support the legal capacity of the fiduciary to give instruction for transfer. This documentation requirement became more and more complex and expensive and caused unnecessary delays in transfers. The situation became more difficult as the number of small shareholders increased. In 1957 legislation was drafted by a group of prominent lawyers expert in transfer law which went a long way toward alleviation of the situation. The bill they drafted is known as the Uniform Act for Simplification of Fiduciary Transfers. It enables such transfers to be completed on the basis of a certificate of appointment (dated within sixty days) by a proper court official and eliminates the need for all other legal documents. Similar provisions were incorporated in the Uniform Commercial Code, adopted (in 1962) in twelve states (see page 400).

Bond Transfers. Bonds may be issued in coupon form as bearer bonds, as coupon bonds registered as to principal, or as fully registered bonds.

Bearer bonds are coupon bonds payable to bearer or bonds registered as to principal and endorsed in blank. Title passes by delivery. Most bonds are of the former type because of tradition, ease of negotiation, and simplicity of transfer. Since title passes by delivery, there is no need for the formality of transfer on the books of the bond registrar (i.e., for bonds, transfer agent). This characteristic increases the danger of loss by theft. It is difficult to recover such a security if it is lost. Provisions are made in the bond indenture for duplication of lost or destroyed bonds; the usual ones are the filing of an affidavit describing the circumstances and the procuring of a surety bond sufficient to indemnify the company and the trustees for the bond issue in case the bond reappears. These problems together with the simplification of bookkeeping and collection procedures obtained with fully registered bonds have led to some increase in popularity of the latter.

Most coupon bonds may be *registered as to principal only* by having the name of the owner inserted in the registration panel on the reverse of the bond by the bond registrar. Such bonds are non-negotiable. The owner must endorse the bond in blank or direct its transfer to a new owner on the books of the bond registrar.

Fully registered bonds are registered as to principal and interest. They carry no coupons. Interest and principal payments are made by check to the owner, whose name is recorded on the registry book of the trustee for the bond issue. When a transfer is made, the bond must be endorsed and forwarded to the trustee for transfer, the old bond is canceled and a new bond, registered in the name of the transferee, is issued.

Lost and Destroyed Certificates. Many securities are lost or destroyed each year. They may disappear in the mail, in homes, or in offices. They may be accidentally destroyed or misplaced. A fire may consume them or a thief may make off with them. They may be gone forever or only for a while. No one can be certain that lost certificates will not reappear in the market. Even in cases of a sinking ship or fire, there is no assurance that a reported loss did not come from a dishonest person. In such circumstances it is necessary for the transfer agent and the corporation to protect themselves against the possibility of reappearance of securities presumably lost or destroyed. As mentioned briefly before, the usual form of protection is the surety bond.

If the owner of a lost or destroyed certificate notifies the issuer in a reasonable period of time, upon provision of satisfactory proof of such loss or destruction and upon giving a bond of sufficient surety, he may be issued a new certificate. A bond of sufficient surety is one adequate to protect the corporation or any person injured by the issue of the new certificate from any liability or expense that it or they may incur by reason of the original certificate's remaining outstanding.

The actual procedure for obtaining a new certificate varies from state to state, but the usual procedure may be summarized in this way. First, the issuer (and transfer agent) must be notified. The agent proceeds to place a "stop order" against the certificate record. Under certain conditions it is possible to stop transfers in this way, but if the certificate is in the hands of an innocent, bona fide holder for value, the rights of the new holder must be protected. Second, the original owner files an affidavit with the issuer, setting forth the facts about the loss. Third, a surety bond is posted with the issuer to protect it against the possibility that the certificate may turn up later in the hands of an innocent, bona fide purchaser for value. Such a bond will be issued by a reputable surety company. Usually the bond runs in perpetuity and without limitation on amount. The surety company providing such a bond will be held responsible for all time in case the stock certificate reappears. If it does, the surety company may be required to buy in an equivalent number of shares, regardless of market value.

The surety company would attempt to recover the cost of the stock from the original owner if the old certificate did reappear in the hands of a bona fide purchaser for value. If it does not recover the cost, it still is liable for payment to the corporation or any other injured party. The premium on a perpetual bond is about 4 per cent, or less, of the market value of the stock at the time the bond is written. This premium is paid once only. On the perpetual bond the protection runs forever; no statue of limitations protects the surety company against the possibility that a certificate might reappear.

UNIFORM COMMERCIAL CODE, ARTICLE 8

A bold effort to modernize the law dealing with sales of goods, tangible and intangible, with documents of title, and with secured transactions has crystalized in the Uniform Commercial Code. In 1962 this

Code had been enacted into law in twelve states. The principal commercial states were among them. Article 8 of the Code applies to transactions in investment securities.[3] A basic consideration is protection of the rights to title of bona fide purchasers of securities for value without notice of any adverse claim at the time of purchase or before. The notion of negotiability is adapted to problems of securities transactions, including the formal problems of transfer and registration. A purchaser is afforded protections against claims by the issuer or by third parties.

If a purchaser acquires a security for value, without any notice of adverse claims, and it is properly endorsed by the appropriate persons (if the security is registered as stock is), he can have title and can have a certificate registered in his name. This right is his even if the issuer may subsequently claim that there were faults in transactions prior to delivery unless: (1) the security is counterfeit; (2) the signature of the issuer is forged; or (3) the issue was illegal or unconstitutional. He also has clear title even though another person may show that the delivery was wrongful provided the certificate was properly endorsed and no notice of adverse claim was given at or before the time of the purchase transaction. The effect is to protect buyers against loss of their rights due to faults in relationship between or among persons of which he had no knowledge and which were not present in the transaction to which he was a party.

The Code makes clear that a person transferring a security warrants that his transfer is effective and right, the security is genuine, and that he knows of no impairment of the validity of the security as a claim of the issuer. It also makes clear that a signature guarantor warrants that the signature is genuine, that the signer is an appropriate person to endorse the certificate, and that the signer had the legal capacity to sign. The issuer, or his transfer agent, in issuing a new certificate to the purchaser warrants that the security is genuine and in proper form, it is issued under proper authorization, and that it is within the limits authorized for the issue. The transferee, in presenting a certificate for cancellation and for issue of a new certificate in his name, warrants that he has no knowledge of any unauthorized signature in the necessary endorsement. Obviously, if each person in this sequence acts to make his warranty good, stock transfer is effectively accomplished.

[3] Prior to passage of the Uniform Commercial Code, two statutes, the Uniform Negotiable Instruments Act and the Uniform Stock Transfer Act, together with the body of common law, were significant for transfer of title to stock in the states that did adopt the Code. They remain significant in other states. The fundamental characteristics of the law under them, however, is not greatly different from that to be described here.

The comments in this section are based primarily on a *Summary of the Uniform Commercial Code for Illinois,* published by the Continental Illinois National Bank and Trust Company, November, 1961.

24

The Over-the-Counter
Markets

The over-the-counter, or OTC, markets, in which securities houses act independently as brokers and dealers, are far more important in total dollar volume of business than all of the organized securities markets together. This volume, however, is much more significant in the bond than in the stock market. Dollar volume of stock sales is probably about half that on the organized exchanges.

The OTC markets serve three functions: (1) making a market for securities already outstanding; (2) distribution of new issues of securities; and (3) secondary distributions of large blocks of outstanding securities for which liquidation is desired by individuals, estates, or financial institutions. This chapter is concerned mostly with the first of these functions. The other two are discussed in Chapter 25.

ACTIVITIES

The over-the-counter markets may be defined as those broad markets for securities that exist outside the organized exchanges. They are sometimes called the "off-board" markets. They have been identified also as the "over-the-telephone" markets because so much business is conducted by negotiation through that medium. Sometimes they have been designated as the market for unlisted securities; but this is not accurate, for a considerable volume of trading in unlisted securities takes place on the American Stock Exchange and other exchanges and a very substantial volume of trading in listed issues, particularly United States government bonds, takes place OTC.

Organization. These markets are not organized in the sense that the national securities exchanges are. There is no building or central market place where brokers and dealers transact business. Dealers trade directly with each other, with brokers and customers, largely through the media of telephone, telegraph, and teletypewriter. There is one association in these markets, the National Association of Securities Dealers, Inc. (NASD), but it is not an organization providing rules and regulations for trading in the same sense that one of the organized exchanges provides for its membership. It does, however, provide general rules and regulations for the activities of its members. These markets involve securities houses scattered throughout the United States and some foreign cities.

The term "over-the-counter" is old. It originated as a designation in the early days of the colonies, when securities actually were traded over the counters of the various dealers in face-to-face transactions, as one might buy a savings bond at a bank today. Although the term is no longer accurate, none better has supplanted it and it continues to serve a useful function.

Number of Issues. Careful estimates made some years ago indicated that probably 80,000 to 90,000 different corporate and governmental issues could be traded in these markets.[1] The maximum number actually traded was estimated to be 40,000, with some 15,500 issues traded in a three-month period. These figures apparently remained reasonably descriptive of 1961.

Despite the large potential number and even the large number of issues traded at least once in a year, there is a high degree of concentration in certain issues. In a typical day's trading the Wharton study found trading in 3,000 issues was an active day. Of these, 73 per cent were corporate stock issues; 10 per cent, corporate bond issues; and 17 per cent, government bond issues of all types. Trading in these issues accounted for about 25,000 transactions in the day. Of these, 80 per cent were transactions in corporate stock, and 10 per cent each were transactions in corporate and in government bonds. The dollar volume of trading has increased in recent years. Absence of data makes precision of measurement difficult, but Merrill, Lynch, Pierce, Fenner and Smith, Inc., reported their OTC business in 1961 to be thirty times that of 1949.[2]

---

[1] Substantial parts of this chapter are based on: Irwin Friend, G. Wright Hoffman, Willis J. Winn, Morris Hamburg, and Stanley Schor, *The Over-the-Counter Securities Markets* (New York: McGraw-Hill Book Co., Inc., 1958). To avoid repetitive reference, acknowledgment of debt to these authors is made here. It is referred to as "the Wharton study" in some places.

[2] *Wall Street Journal*, April 26, 1962.

Business transacted through stock exchanges increased six-fold in this period. The ratios of volume may have shifted more toward stock transactions but the evidence suggests that no shift of substantial amount has occurred. It is probably still fair to indicate that three-quarters to four-fifths of the daily activity in the OTC markets is business in stock trading.

Size of Transactions. Wide variation in the size of transactions is evident in these markets. Huge quantities of U. S. government securities trade in single transactions. Perhaps more than 90 per cent of these transactions are handled in amounts of $100,000 or more. Yet, sales in these issues may be $1,000 in amount. In state and municipal bond issues, 80 per cent of the transactions are $50,000, or more. The transactions in stocks, of course, usually are in much smaller amounts.

Competition with Organized Exchanges. OTC markets are very real competitors with the organized exchanges. Perhaps 25 per cent of all OTC transactions are in securities listed on exchanges. Although the issues of U. S. government bonds, notes, and certificates are all listed on the New York Stock Exchange, the OTC market in bonds accounts for nearly 100 per cent of the trading in these issues. OTC resales of listed corporate bonds are much greater in amount than those on the exchanges where they are listed. Resales of listed preferred stocks are about one-half the volume of those on the exchanges. The volume of trading in listed common stocks, however, is probably less than one-tenth that on the exchanges.

Share of the Entire Securities Business. The Wharton study estimates indicated that the OTC markets accounted for the major portion of all securities resales in the United States. The relative shares of the OTC and organized exchange markets are shown in Table 24–1. It will be noted that the OTC markets for two months in 1949 accounted for almost nine-tenths of the securities resales in the United States. The shares in bonds were very large. It is in the area of resales of stock that the dominance of the organized markets is clear. Although volume of activity has increased over the years, these ratios probably are still reasonably descriptive of market shares.

The SEC estimated the aggregate market value on December 31, 1960, for the 4,000 issues of stock held by three hundred or more stockholders and traded only over the counter was $69 billion.[3] This was about 20 per cent of the aggregate of the market values of stock traded on organized exchanges at that time.

[3] *Twenty-Seventh Annual Report of the SEC,* 1961, p. 58.

Table 24–1. Gross Value of Security Resales in the United States, September–November, 1949

Type of Security	Total Resales (millions)	Percentage Share	
		OTC Markets	Organized Exchanges
U. S. government	$24,444	100.0	0.0
State and municipal	1,056	100.0	0.0
Corporate bond	949	82.4	17.6
Corporate stock	4,877	33.5	66.6
All resales	$31,327	89.1	10.9

Source: Irwin Friend *et al.*, *The Over-the-Counter Securities Markets* (New York: McGraw-Hill Book Co., Inc., 1958), p. 116. Subtotals may not add to totals because of rounding.

SECURITIES TRADED

Trading over the counter takes place by negotiation. By this is meant that prices are fixed by traders bargaining directly with each other. On occasion, considerable haggling may occur, but in the active markets dealers state their bids and offers and traders either take them or leave them. In the sale of some securities, this technique is useful and perhaps necessary to establishment of prices.

High-Grade Securities. Many of the securities handled in the OTC markets are definitely of high grade. Some are the best investment issues in the world. The markets handle nearly all the U. S. government issues. The same is true of state and municipal bonds. Many of the best listed issues are sold here—both bonds and stocks. The market in stocks of banks, insurance companies, and investment companies is centered here. Choice issues such as railroad equipment obligations are sold exclusively in these markets. Such securities, for the most part, might well be sold on the organized exchanges. Others are actually listed on these exchanges but find a less active market there than in the OTC markets.

Narrow-Market Securities. A great many issues are traded in the OTC markets because they are not suited to the specifications of the auction markets found on the large exchanges. Their only possible sale is through highly specialized negotiations. There are literally thousands of issues in this classification. They usually have one or more of the following characteristics:

1. Distribution is narrow.
2. Capitalization is small or the amount of the issue is small.
3. The issuer is unknown.

 4. The security is unseasoned.
 5. The security is very high priced.
 6. Buyers and sellers desire secrecy.
 7. The security has serial maturities.
 8. Few bids and offers are available.
 9. There is a lack of investment or speculative interest.
10. Buyers and sellers wish to trade upon a "net basis."
11. The security is issued by a financial institution.
12. The security is issued on real estate.
13. Large blocks are held by estates, individuals, or institutions.
14. The security is regional in interest.
15. The company simply doesn't want listing.

CUSTOMERS IN THE MARKET

There are probably nearly five million customers who deal at one time or another in these markets.[4] They include financial institutions, individuals, and broker-dealers. The financial institutions include commercial banks, trust companies, savings banks, investment companies, and similar institutions. Of the so-called "public customers" (excluding broker-dealers) the financial institutions are by far the most important. They probably still account for about 83 per cent of the dollar volume of public transactions and 30 per cent of their number as in 1949. The commercial banks are particularly important in dealing in government bonds of all types as well as in corporate bonds. Such institutions as insurance companies deal heavily in preferred stocks as well as in corporate bonds.

Large numbers of individuals deal in OTC securities. Their activity probably accounts for more than two-thirds of the transactions. At the same time, the dollar volume of their activity is probably less than one-quarter of the total for the market.

Broker-dealers trade among themselves. Their activity probably represents a third to a half of the activity in corporate securities.

THE BROKER-DEALERS

Number. As a maximum estimate, about 8,000 broker-dealers are engaged in OTC business in the United States. About 5,500 are registered with the SEC, which means that they use the mails and instrumentalities of interstate commerce to effect transactions. The rest do business exclusively intrastate or exclusively in exempt securities, principally U. S.

---

[4] Based on *1962 Census of Shareowners in America* (New York: New York Stock Exchange, 1962), p. 4. This reports 2.6 million owners of over-the-counter issues and 2.2 million owners of investment company shares only.

government issues. The bulk of the OTC business is handled by the 4,600 broker-dealers who are members of the NASD.[5]

Making a Market. A dealer who "makes a market" or "has a market" in a security is expected to maintain firm bid prices and offering prices in the security. He stands ready both to buy and sell at his quoted prices in amounts at least equal to the recognized trading unit in the security. Making a market can refer to an isolated instance in which a dealer provides firm bids and offers for a short period of time but it usually implies continuing activity.

Concentration of Business. As in many other lines of American business, there is a high degree of concentration of OTC business with a few securities houses. Some four hundred firms, mostly with offices in New York City, account for nine-tenths of the business. They are large houses; the usual capital account exceeds $5 million. Their chief interest is in the bond market. They assume a high amount of risk in their two chief activities, which are underwriting new security issues and sponsoring markets for selected OTC issues. Both these activities necessitate holding temporary investments subject to the risks of market fluctuation. The names of the houses are prominently displayed in the list of underwriters in the top-grade new securities issues. The majority hold membership on the New York Stock Exchange.

The Small Broker-Dealers. At the bottom of the broker-dealer pyramid are the small broker-dealers. Their capital is often in the range of $40,000 to $50,000. As a whole, they are more interested in stocks than in bonds. They do not make markets for securities, as a rule, but rely on the big broker-dealers for this service. The usual policy is to hold down risks to the lowest possible level.

Specialization. Firms vary greatly in the amount of specialization in their business. Some deal only with other broker-dealers and financial institutions. These are the professional traders. Others are retail houses and deal with the general public. Some engage in both types of activity. Some firms handle all kinds of securities, while some specialize in bank stocks, insurance stocks, equipment trust obligations, or real estate securities.

Types of Dealers. The broker-dealers fall into about six main classifications. One type is the OTC house; its primary function is trading in the OTC issues. Typically, it does not belong to an exchange. It usually does little business in government bonds; in some cases, however, it may do a substantial amount.

[5] *Twenty-Seventh Annual Report of the SEC,* 1961, pp. 74–86.

A second type is the investment banking house. It engages heavily in the underwriting of new issues of stocks and bonds. To diversify its business, however, it may do a substantial amount of business in listed and OTC securities.

A third type is the dealer bank. This term applies to a commercial bank or trust company that seeks to make a market for federal obligations and state and municipal bonds. It does not act as a dealer in other types of securities because of banking legislation enacted in 1935.

A fourth type is the municipal bond house. This highly specialized type of firm concentrates on municipal issues, in the capacity of both underwriting and making markets for them. It does not, as a rule, engage in buying and selling corporation securities.

Another type is the government bond house. Its specialty is the obligations of the federal government, its agencies, and instrumentalities.

A final type is the stock exchange member house. It has memberships on one or more of the organized exchanges where it may do a large commission business. A separate department is organized to carry on trading in the OTC markets. Some of the largest broker-dealers are in this class.

Organization and Income. Three forms of organization are found among the 5,500 registered broker-dealer houses. About 33 per cent are organized as sole proprietorships, while 23 per cent are partnerships. About 44 per cent are corporations. Many firms belong to the New York and other stock exchanges.

Approximately 70 per cent of the gross income of the OTC houses comes from OTC business and 30 per cent from exchange business. Profits and commissions on securities transactions in the OTC markets accounts for the largest share of the OTC income. Other income is earned in this market in the forms of investment banking and underwriting fees, interest and dividends on securities owned, management fees, and non-security income, such as profits and commissions on commodity trading operations.

Charges. OTC transactions are effected on a "net," or "dealer," basis and on a commission basis. If the house handling a customer's order usually handles trades for him on a commission basis, it probably would do so OTC. In some instances houses permit registered representatives to decide whether to use a net basis or a commission charge in dealing with their customers. The customer will be informed of the basis, and told the amount of commission, to be charged, if that basis is chosen. For houses that are members of the organized stock exchanges, commissions usually are the same as those charged on exchange transactions. There is, however, no fixed schedule of commissions for OTC business.

When a "net," or "dealer," basis is used, the difference between the price paid for the security and the price at which it is sold to the customer, i.e., the spread, is significant. There is no specific schedule of dealer spreads accepted as reasonable. The Maloney Act prohibits the NASD from adopting such a schedule and the whole concept of negotiation is opposed to it. The business naturally has resisted any attempts at standardization of charges even at a maximum level. A guide, the 5 per cent rule, referred to below, does have the effect of indicating a maximum.

Inventories. One of the big problems in the management of a broker-dealer firm is the handling of its security inventories. In the language of the trade this is known as "positioning." When a firm is holding selected securities as an inventory, it is said to keep a position in them. This may be done either to make or sponsor a market for the securities in question or to conduct trading operations.

To hold a position is a risky operation. It is not done on a large scale or for long periods by many firms. In fact, positions are small in most firms, and these firms are usually only the largest in the business. About 20 per cent of the firms carry heavy inventories; 60 per cent have less than half of their assets in positions; 20 per cent never carry inventories. Small houses generally lack the capital, personnel, skill, and desire to take substantial positions.

The very large firms typically are the ones that carry positions. Ten per cent of firms in the business carry 90 per cent of the inventories. They are willing to assume the risks; they have the capital and personnel; and they wish to sponsor certain issues. Their positions are principally in bonds, probably 90 per cent of their commitments being in this class because of customer interests, greater safety, legal restrictions, and type of specialization desired by the firm. When small firms carry inventories, they are more likely to be in stocks because of the preferences of customers, who are usually individuals, and because of higher returns.

The character of a position depends on the type of security held. In U. S. government securities the dealer position varied in 1961 from $2.0 to $3.8 billion, about one to two day's supply.[6] The inventories are low in relation to volume of sales because of the ready market for them and the availability of quantities. Inventories for state and municipal issues tend to be high in relation to sales because of narrower markets. The positions taken in corporate securities usually fall between these extremes. The aggregate position in these latter two classes, however, is not nearly as great as that taken in U. S. government issues. An estimate for 1959 shows positions totalling $540 million in corporate securities, $250 million

[6] *Federal Reserve Bulletin,* February, 1962, p. 204.

in municipals, and $1,820 million in U. S. government bonds (Table 26–1, page 434).

Positions are typically held for only short periods. In U. S. government securities positions are held about a day. The majority of positions in state and municipal securities, foreign securities, and corporate stocks are also held less than a day. Corporate bonds are held for longer periods. Few securities are carried for longer than a week. Perhaps 33 per cent of corporate bonds, 21 per cent of state and municipal bonds, and 16 per cent of preferred stock fall in this class. These long positions occur when a firm is making a market for a given issue, when a new issue is being underwritten, or when idle capital is being invested. Needless to say, the longer a position is held the greater the possibility of loss.

Legal Relationship with Customers. The term "broker-dealer" indicates that firms act in both capacities at various times. Predominantly, the firm acts as a dealer rather than as a broker. This is true in every type of security transaction. About 96 per cent of all federal, state, and local bonds are handled this way, 72 per cent of all common stock, and 60 per cent of all corporate bonds and preferred stock. The customer involved has a bearing on whether a firm acts as a broker or dealer. In transactions with commercial banks, for example, 95 per cent of the business is handled on a dealer basis, whereas in the case of transactions with individuals only 60 per cent is so handled. It is also true that the larger the transaction, the more apt it is to be handled on a dealer basis.

Office Operations. The heart of the OTC office is the trading room. Here shirt-sleeved traders sit at long tables connected with a vast network of telephones. Each trader operates independently. From 10:00 A.M. until about 4:30 P.M. these traders are continuously contacting other houses in the market as they check the market and close their deals. To the outsider the shouting and seeming confusion in the trading room give the impression of unorganized bedlam. A somewhat similar impression, of course, is received by the casual visitor to the New York Stock Exchange. Trading rooms are connected with those of other houses by a vast network of private wires for telephone and teletype service. A leading house has thousands of miles of private wire and hundreds of private telephone lines and teletype machines. An efficient house can ordinarily receive an order, carefully check the market, and notify a customer of the execution within a few minutes.

Clearing, Delivery, and Transfer. OTC houses, of course, have no central clearing organization such as the Stock Clearing Corporation of the New York Stock Exchange, although a clearing house for OTC markets in New York is under consideration. Clearing methods in practice depend on whether or not the transaction is local or out of town. The usual method for local transactions in New York is for the selling house to deliver the securities by a messenger who picks up the buyer's check. This is usually done by 12:30 P.M. of the fourth full business day after the sale was made. In out-of-town transactions two methods are used. The selling house may send the securities by registered mail directly to the buying organization, which remits by check, using New York funds. The seller, however, may draw a draft on the buyer and use a bank in the city of either the seller or the buyer to collect the proper amount before delivering the securities.[7]

Securities sold in the OTC market are usually sold with regular way delivery, which means on the fourth full business day. They may, however, be sold with delayed delivery, which means on or before the seventh day. If delivery is by seller's option, delivery may be after the seventh day with a one-day notice required. Cash and "when issued" deliveries are also possible. If a selling house is unable to make delivery and the buying house insists upon it, the seller may be required to borrow the security; if this is not possible, the buyer is permitted to purchase the security in the open market at the going price. This is known as "buying in."

Government Bond Dealers. Because the government bond market forms such an important segment of the OTC business, it seems desirable to give special attention to the dealers in this field. This market has long been dominated by only a few houses. There were only two at the beginning of World War I. At the present time there are about twenty, four or five of which are outstanding. Many other banks and firms, of course, play some part in the government bond market, which is largely centered in New York.

Government bond dealers can be divided into two main groups: the bank dealers and the non-bank traders. Large commercial banks and trust companies in the market maintain government bond departments devoted exclusively to the buying and selling of Treasury securities for their own account and for their customers

Non-bank dealers are divided into two classes. The first group specializes in government bonds exclusively. The second type is the OTC firm that deals in government bonds through one department of its organization but engages in other forms of OTC business as well, such as underwriting, sponsoring securities, and similar activities.

Government bond dealers trade in very large blocks, the usual trading block being $1 million. In handling this large market, they serve a num-

---

[7] J. C. Loeser, *The Over-the-Counter Securities Market* (New York: National Quotation Bureau, Inc., 1940), p. 17.

ber of useful functions, such as providing and creating markets, doing market and portfolio analysis, acting as agent for the Federal Reserve banks, and serving as advisers to the federal monetary authorities.[8]

QUOTATIONS AND PRICES

Price Data. No prices are ever given for the OTC market, as they are for the organized exchanges. The only information available to the general public is that on the bid and asked quotations, carried in leading financial pages. To the public this is a decided disadvantage of trading in the OTC market.

Newspaper Quotations. The leading financial pages of the nation's newspapers regularly carry information on quotations in the OTC markets. Some carry as many as 300 to 400 quotations per day. The publications usually gather these data from the NASD, which has committees throughout the country composed of men in the business who supervise the quotes published and the selection of issues for quotation. The published bid and asked prices will represent, typically, an average based on quotations from three or four firms. The quotations represent the so-called "outside" or "retail" market, to be described shortly. They are indications of the range of prices for an issue which the public might expect to pay or receive in the market.

National Quotation Bureau Quotations. The chief source of information on quotations in the "inside" or "wholesale market" is a Wall Street organization known as the National Quotation Bureau, Inc. This forty-year-old organization gathers quotations on about 7,000 stock issues and 2,000 bond issues each day. During a year perhaps 25,000 different stock issues and 5,000 bond isuses will be quoted.

Each afternoon this organization gathers the bid and asked prices, with the names, telephone, and teletype numbers of the firms wishing to trade in them. Price sheets are then mimeographed rapidly for distribution. A set of bond quotations is prepared in one distinctive color and a set of stock quotations in another. These reports are immediately mailed. This overnight service reaches nearly 3,000 subscribers by the next morning. These subscribers do nearly all of the resale security business in the nation. The bids and offers contained in these reports are not so much firm bids and offers as they are declarations of intent to do business at approximately the quotations indicated. Actually, they amount to advertisements by firms making markets in particular issues. The public seldom sees these reports, and even if it did, could not do business net at the prices shown.

---

[8] Marcus Nadler, Sipa Heller, and Samuel S. Shipman, *The Money Market and Its Institutions* (New York: The Ronald Press Co., 1955), p. 122.

Broker-Dealer Quotations. As in the organized exchange markets, the wire houses are prepared to obtain quotations for customers. Thousands of quotations are provided daily and the scope of price information for the public investor is widened substantially through this medium.

The Outside or Retail Market. The general public trades with most houses in the OTC markets on the basis of quotations generally known as "outside" or "retail market." On low-priced stocks, such as those selling at less than $20, the spread between the bid and asked price may run about 10 per cent. On higher-priced stocks the spread tends to decline on a percentage basis to a low of 5 or 6 per cent. It is believed that, in practice, the public often gets slightly better prices than are indicated by published quotations. The following examples, reported in 1962, indicate spreads at various price levels:

Stock	Bid	Ask
Artmetal	7	7⅛
Standard Screw	21	23
Beneficial Corp.	23½	26¼
International Textbook	44	48¼
Hanna Manufacturing Corp.	85	90¾
American National Bank, Chicago	525	560

The Inside or Wholesale Market. This is the market in which the dealer-brokers trade with each other and in which major houses trade for their customers on a commission basis. The quotations found in the daily reports of the National Quotation Bureau are typical. In these the spread between bid and asked prices is closer than in the outside market. Spreads are greater for unlisted securities than for listed ones. For unlisted common stocks the spread in the inside market runs about 2 per cent on low-priced stocks and 1 per cent on high-priced ones.

Customer Costs. As just indicated, it is evident that the public customer, as in any other business, pays more for his securities than does the broker-dealer in trading with other broker-dealers. The gross profit margin obtained by the broker-dealer when trading with the public varies with the type of security. The University of Pennsylvania study found these to be the typical costs in 1949:

Common stock	3.0%
Preferred stock	1.7
Corporate bonds	0.7
State and municipal bonds	0.6
U. S. Government bonds	0.05

Customer costs, or the gross spreads of dealers, tend to be higher on small stock issues and on small trades.

Generally speaking, it costs the customer more to trade in OTC stocks than in listed stocks. As just indicated, typical costs of trading in common stock in the OTC markets were about 3 per cent. If it were assumed that these percentages for 1949 still prevailed in 1962, there would have been a substantial differential in favor of listed stocks. In the latter year a commission charge of 1 per cent was made on the New York Stock Exchange for 100 shares of a stock selling at $38. If the price were $50, the commission would be only $44, or 0.9 per cent.

In large "block" transactions, however, the OTC markets can and do handle securities on a very low cost basis. This is particularly true of U. S. government obligations, in which the OTC markets have obtained a practical monopoly.

Handling a Customer Transaction. An example of a transaction between a broker-dealer and an individual customer, who shall be known as Brown, illustrates how sales are made in this market. Brown wishes to purchase 100 shares of Dixie Steel, an OTC stock. Accordingly, he telephones Jones and Company, a local OTC firm. This firm is not itself making a market in Dixie Steel.

A registered representative at Jones and Company, R. R., on receipt of the inquiry tells Brown that he will check the market and call back shortly. A trader with Jones and Company now checks the market by calling four or five houses that are sponsoring this stock. All give the trader quotations from the inside market; none knows whether the Jones houses wishes to buy or sell. These are the quotations received by the Jones trader:

Dealer	Quotation
A	19 to 19½
B	19 to 19⅜
C	18⅞ to 19½
D	19 to 19⅝

The trader informs R. R., who now knows that the stock can be purchased on the inside market at about 19⅜ or 19½. R. R. then calls Brown and offers to sell him 100 shares at 20. Brown accepts. R. R. checks with the trader, who calls back to Dealer B and again asks, "What is your market in Dixie Steel?" Dealer B responds, "19 to 19⅜," which is unchanged from his earlier quotation. The trader says, "I will buy 100 at 19⅜." Dealer B replies, "I have sold you 100 at 19⅜." R. R. then confirms the purchase at 20, net, to Brown. The transaction is now complete. Jones and Company purchase the stock from Dealer B at 19⅜ and resell it to Brown at 20, thereby making a gross profit of ⅝ of a point.

In this transaction the sale could have been made to Brown on a brokerage basis. Jones and Company could have purchased the stock for him at 19⅜ and delivered it to him at that price plus a commission. Major securities houses dealing with the public and in all securities markets usually do execute orders for their customers on a commission basis. If the New York Stock Exchange commission schedule were used, Brown would be charged $1,937.50 plus $26.38.

One further point needs to be mentioned. It should be stressed that when the trader at Jones and Company was checking the market, he was not getting firm quotations. They were good only "over the wire," which means while the conversation was going on. Jones and Company accepted the risk of calling back later and finding the quotation changed. In the example given, the quotation happened to be unchanged. It is not a practice of broker-dealers to give firm quotations to each other except "over the wire," although they may give them for short periods to public customers.

NATIONAL ASSOCIATION OF SECURITIES DEALERS

History. The National Association of Securities Dealers, Inc., has its roots in the early days of the New Deal and the NRA codes. The investment bankers in 1933, as did leaders in many other industries, formed an industry code of fair competition. When the NRA was declared unconstitutional in 1935, the association continued its code of practices under the title of Investment Bankers Conference Committee; the group changed its name in 1936 to Investment Bankers Conference, Inc. By 1938 Congress had amended the Securities Exchange Act of 1934 by adding Section 15A, commonly known as the Maloney Act.

The Maloney Act. This amendment to the 1934 Act is very long and covers some eight pages of fine print. In summary, it permits OTC associations to organize, for purposes of self-regulation, as registered membership associations with the SEC. To date there has been only one association so organized, the NASD.

An association is permitted to set up rules designed to prevent fraudulent and manipulative acts and practices, to prevent unreasonable profits and commissions, and to protect investors and the public interest. The section provides, furthermore, that the association may discipline its members by expulsion, fine, censure, or any other penalty for violation of rules. An association has the power to restrict its membership if in the opinion of the SEC such restrictions appear in the public interest. An association may also provide in its rules that no member shall deal with any other non-member broker or dealer except at the same prices or commissions and on the same terms as are accorded by the member to the general public.

Its Organization. In 1961 the NASD had more than 4,600 registered members, an all-time high and an increase of about 1,900 in the past ten years. Registered representatives numbered 94,000. These included all individuals, partners, officers, traders, and other employees who do business directly with the public.

The NASD is controlled by a central body, known as the Board of Governors; it is assisted by committee organizations in the thirteen districts of the association. An important part of the organization is the district business conduct committee; there is one for each district. Its function is to enforce the rules of fair practice which have been set up by the Association.

Rules for Fair Conduct. The NASD has drawn up a considerable body of rules designed to maintain high standards of business conduct, and a violation of these rules subjects the dealer or broker to disciplinary measures. There are twenty-eight of these rules; a few of the important ones will be mentioned to indicate their nature.

Charges for services performed shall be reasonable and not unfairly discriminatory between customers. If a member buys and sells for his own account, he shall buy or sell at a price that is fair, taking into consideration all conditions, including the market situation, the expense involved, and the fact that he is entitled to a profit. No quotations shall be made unless the dealer intends to do business at such prices. No payments shall be made to anyone to influence market prices, other than paid advertising. Customers must be informed whether a member is acting as a dealer or broker in a transaction. No manipulative, deceptive, or fraudulent device shall be used to effect a purchase or sale. Members shall be ready to disclose their financial condition to bona fide customers upon request.

Particularly important is the rule that no member shall deal with any non-member broker or dealer except at the same prices or commissions and on the same terms as those accorded the general public. In other words, brokers and dealers not in the NASD must pay retail prices, the same as the public does. Price concessions are permitted only among NASD members. This rule makes the privilege of membership a valuable one, since a non-member can buy only at prices available to the general public.

Uniform Practice Code. In addition to the rules of fair practice, the NASD has prepared an elaborate uniform practice code with some sixty sections. It is designed to codify and bring about a standardization of practices similar to that long in use on the organized exchanges. It covers deliveries, confirmations, assignments, computation of interest, transfers, and reclamations.

Discipline. A very important part of the work of the NASD is the disciplining of members for violation of its rules of fair conduct. In this capacity it usually acts as complainant, prosecutor, judge, and jury, as it is permitted and expected to do under the Maloney Act. A complaint in writing may be made by another member of the NASD, the NASD itself, or a person outside the NASD. The accused is given an opportunity to answer the complaint and may ask for a hearing at which he may be represented by counsel. After the investigation is made by the business conduct committee, a decision is made. If the complaint is unjustified, the proceedings are dismissed. If disciplinary action is necessary, it may take the form of censure, fine, suspension, or expulsion. From a decision of the committee, the accused has recourse to an appeal to the Board of Governors of the NASD, the SEC, and finally the courts.

The extreme penalty of expulsion is more severe than might appear at first inspection. An expelled member cannot receive the price concessions, which may be given only to members. He may not engage in underwriting, obtain securities at prices less than those charged to the general public, or participate in the distributions of investment company shares underwritten by members. Since the leading dealers in the OTC market, for the most part, are also members of the NASD, the opportunities of an expelled member to carry on his business are restricted. Furthermore, his status as a registered representative is terminated, and he may not be reinstated without clearing his record with the NASD and the SEC; this lessens his chances of further employment in the securities business.

In connection with the matter of discipline, it could be noted that the NASD has power to inspect members' books and records. These inspections may be made directly or by questionnaire. They are made at frequent intervals and take place whether or not there is cause to believe that any violations of the rules of fair practice have taken place. The association in this way may be able to find violations of its rules without waiting for complaints to be filed.

The severity of disciplinary measures varies with the seriousness of the offense. In some cases only censuring takes place. In more serious cases suspension may run from one week to as long as two years. Fines may be large. In 1959–60 fines ranged from $20 to $25,000. Expulsion, of course, is the severest penalty. The SEC has power to review all NASD disciplinary actions, either on application by the aggrieved party or upon the Commission's own motion.

The Problem of Markups. The problem of how much profit a broker-dealer in the OTC market should make has always been a controversial one. The NASD in its code of fair practices does not state any definite figures as to what is considered a reasonable markup, but merely states that profits shall be fair and reasonable in view of all relevant circumstances. In 1943 it made a study of the matter through a questionnaire to determine markups actually being made. Following this survey, the Board of Governors of the NASD made the announcement, but not a ruling, that markups in excess of 5 per cent would be looked upon with disfavor unless justified by circumstances. Many members of the Association did not favor such a rigid policy, nor did they want it incorporated formally into the rules of fair practice. The Maloney Act, furthermore, prohibits the adoption of a rigid schedule of markups, and the whole concept of a negotiated market stands as a limitation to such a practice. The NASD has, however, continued to express strongly the belief that most transactions should be effected at a markup of 5 per cent or less. More generally, it has said that some of the factors members should take into consideration in determining the fairness of a markup are: the type of security involved; its availability in the market; price; the amount of money involved in the transaction; the extent of disclosure of commission or markup information prior to a transaction; the prevailing pattern of markups in the firm; and the nature of the member's business. The basic test is adherence to the first rule of fair practice: "A member, in the conduct of his business, shall observe high standards of commercial honor and just and equitable principles of trade."[9]

Registered Representatives. As already indicated, a registered representative is any partner, officer, or employee of a broker-dealer organization who does business directly with the public. Registration requires satisfactory completion of a qualifying examination and the filing of an application with the NASD. On the application an owner, partner, or voting stockholder of a member organization must certify that the applicant is of good character and repute and is qualified by experience or will be qualified by training to perform his duties and accept his responsibilities as a registered representative. An individual who has engaged in unethical practices in the securities business by violation of the rules of fair practice may not be registered; and he may not secure employment with a registered broker or dealer until clearance has been given by the NASD and the SEC.

Registration, therefore, subjects all such persons to the same rules, regulations, and disciplinary powers as those of registered brokers and dealers in the NASD. Hence, the NASD may discipline such individuals by censure, fine, suspension, or expulsion in the same manner as it may discipline firms.

[9] NASD, *Manual*, March, 1961, pp. D–5, G–1 to G–6.

25

The Investment Banking
Function

The distribution of new securities issues and large blocks of outstanding securities is another function of securities houses. It is a part of investment banking, which includes also the underwriting of securities distributions and advisory functions. The distribution of securities issues is, however, clearly the most important aspect of investment banking and the one most significant in the general economy. The amounts of funds raised by businesses and governments in any year in the United States are substantial. Figures for some recent years are shown in Table 25–1.

Table 25–1. Proceeds from Cash Sales of New Securities and Secondary Distributions of Outstanding Securities in the United States, 1955–61 (in millions of dollars)

Year		New Securities			Secondary Distributions of Stock
	Total	Non-corporate	Corporate		
			Bonds	Stock	
1955	$26,772	$16,532	$7,420	$2,820	$345
1956	22,405	11,467	8,002	2,937	521
1957	30,571	17,687	9,957	2,927	339
1958	34,443	22,885	9,653	1,905	362
1959	31,074	21,326	7,190	2,558	822
1960	27,541	17,387	8,081	2,073	425
1961	35,494	22,347	9,425	3,722	927

Sources: SEC, *Statistical Bulletin*, February, 1962, pp. 3–4; *Twenty-Seventh Annual Report of the SEC*, 1961, pp. 206–7, 221.

419

The total for all issues sold for cash in each of the recent five years in the table has been close to $30 billion, which represents about 2½ to 3 per cent of all outstanding credit and equity instruments for the United States. The secondary distributions of outstanding securities were high in 1959 and 1961, as shown in the table and equalled about one-fourth to one-third of the sales of new issues of stock. The amounts of new money obtained by non-corporate issues, primarily governments, were twice as great as the amounts obtained by corporate issues. We shall not be concerned further with special characteristics of such distributions; these figures, however, give some perspective on the scope of the whole function. The amounts of corporate bond issues have been three to four times as great as the amounts of corporate stock issues. The latter are the distributions of principal interest for discussion in this chapter, but, in fact, there are more similarities than differences in the procedures for distribution of the two types of corporate securities.

ROLES FOR INVESTMENT BANKERS

Securities houses may undertake investment banking as one among several functions in the securities business or may specialize in this one function. Most houses allocate only a fraction of effort to it. When engaged in investment banking, however, a securities house may have any one or a combination of roles. The house may act as investor, as underwriter, as distributor, or as advisor.

The Investment Role. In its generic sense, as the term "banking" implies, investment banking was a process of collecting sums of money from investors and investment of the funds in obligations of business or government. The claims of investors were on the securities house and the securities house held claims on securities issuers. This kind of activity has not been of great significance in the United States. However, the role is played to some extent today when the partnership or corporate accounts of securities houses are invested in stocks and bonds held for an investment return. In general, an active investment banking house can employ its funds more profitably in other ways, but occasionally it is advantageous to take a position in an issue with a view to gains from long-term appreciation of market price or from the income to be earned on the securities.

The Underwriting Role. "Underwriting" is a term associated with insurance. It means that a guarantee or assurance of some specific minimum result from an undertaking has been given by the underwriters. In the securities business underwriting is the provision of a guarantee or assurance that a specific, minimum amount of money will be received by a securities issuer if a distribution of securities is made. When the distribution has been made, if the proceeds are less than the amount guaranteed, the underwriters are obligated to make up the difference. In practice, underwriting is a part of the distribution process itself, but it can be a separate activity. Later in this chapter, in the description of "stand-by" procedures, a way in which underwriting does appear as a separate role in securities distribution will be observed.

The Distributor's Role. The most important and frequent role for investment bankers is distribution of securities issues. They provide the marketing organization for a high proportion of the distributions in this country. They act as middlemen in arranging distributions in other cases. Distributions of new securities issues or secondary distribution of outstanding securities may be made by public offering or private placement. The principal distinction is found in the number of investors offered an opportunity to invest in an issue. If the number is large, the offering is public; if the number is small, a private placement is made. The relative amounts of public and private distributions of corporate issues in recent years are shown in Table 25–2. The data indicate that public offerings are more than half the total; that private offerings of bonds are much greater in amount than private offerings of stock; and that private offerings of stock, when compared to the totals for new issues shown in Table 25–1, are a small proportion of stock offerings. The investment banking role usually differs in these two types of offerings.

Table 25–2. Public and Private Offerings of New Corporate Securities in the United States, 1955–61 (in millions of dollars)

Year	Total	Public	Private Bonds	Private Stock
1955	$10,240	$6,763	$3,301	$176
1956	10,939	7,053	3,777	109
1957	12,884	8,959	3,839	86
1958	11,558	8,068	3,320	170
1959	9,748	5,993	3,632	122
1960	10,154	6,657	3,275	221
1961	13,147	8,149	4,720	279

Sources: SEC *Statistical Bulletin,* February, 1962, pp. 3–4; *Twenty-Seventh Annual Report of the SEC,* 1961, p. 236.

A *private* placement involves the direct sale of an issue by the issuer to one or a few investors. Sale of a bond issue to an insurance company or, for example, to an insurance company and a commercial bank would be typical. The investment banking house, if involved, would probably act as a middleman to bring buyer and seller together. The house would arrange for the sale but would commit none of its own funds. Compensation would be for skill and speed in placing the issue at a fair price.

A *public* offering in which the facilities of investment banking are used would require the investment banking houses usually to assume risk and commit funds to affect the distribution of securities to a large number of widely separated individuals, each willing or able to buy only a relatively small part of the issue. As one might expect, public distributions of securities range widely in complexity and risk. A description of a typical process of such distribution will be given in more detail in paragraphs below. In brief, however, the process of public distribution ordinarily requires that investment bankers purchase the issue at a specified price, arrange with a larger group of securities houses for sale of the securities to individual investors at a somewhat higher price, and maintenance of a market for the issue after its distribution.

The Advisory Role. Businessmen seeking information about the means for financing their enterprises turn quite naturally to investment banking houses for advice about capital markets. Corporate officials who do not have experience with the sale of securities need to gain understanding of the opportunities and limitations for them. The boards of directors of many companies include an investment banker for the advice he can give on current financial questions. The variety of services the investment banker can supply in his advisory function defies simple description. Suffice it to say that the role is one often assigned. It quite usually begins when an offering of securities is first considered by a corporation and continues after a distribution has been made.

A PUBLIC DISTRIBUTION

The very brief description of a public distribution given above indicates that there are a number of different jobs to be done by an investment banker. The principal activities may be classified as follows: origination, purchase, sale, financing, and maintaining a market. The process gives rise to costs and risk.

Origination. The first step toward distribution of a new issue of securities may be taken by the issuer or an investment banker. In any event, someone must start preliminary discussions. If a tentative decision to sell securities is reached, more detailed study begins. Accountants, engineers, lawyers—all play their parts in determining the state of the business of the issuer and the appropriateness of selling securities. The different kinds of securities that might be sold are discussed and the most useful selected for further study. The amounts to be issued are determined from considerations involving the issuer's plans and the current state of the market for new issues. Preparation for registration of the issue with the SEC and for informing investors is made. In total, the fundamental questions about what kinds and amounts of securities to issue, how to sell them, and when to make the distribution are answered in this preliminary period.

Purchase Syndicate. The distribution of an issue of substantial size usually is made by a group of investment banking houses rather than one house acting alone. The banking houses are more likely to prosper with limited participation in each of a large number of issues than with full risk in a few. In general, therefore, the banking houses prefer to accept some, but not all, risk associated with any one issue. The originating house usually asks other houses to join with it in forming a purchase syndicate under the management of the originator.

The purchase syndicate is formed to buy the issue at a specified price on a specified date. The agreement to buy all of the issue under these conditions is an underwriting of the distribution. On the specified date the issuer receives the predetermined amount of money for the securities issued. The risk to the issuer is made minimal by the purchase. On occasion, the date for payment to the issuer is different from the date on which distribution of the issue begins. The agreement of the purchase syndicate remains an assurance or guarantee to the issuer of the specified proceeds from the issue during that interval.

When the syndicate buys the issue, it obtains the funds in the first instance from the individual accounts of its members and from borrowings by them at their commercial banks. The issue serves as collateral for loans at the banks. A high proportion, upwards of 90 per cent, of the purchase price can be borrowed on most issues. The amount of money supplied by the securities houses from their own accounts is relatively small. In time, of course, the houses expect to obtain from sale of the issue sufficient funds to repay the loans, recover their own funds, meet expenses, and earn a return on the transactions. In many instances issues "go out the window." They are sold immediately. Funds are tied up in the distribution process only a few hours or days. Only occasionally, and then often unfortunately, are funds tied up more than a week. Such an occurence arises when there is a "sticky issue" and the sale to investors does not proceed as planned and losses are likely to follow.

If the purchase syndicate agrees to pay a specified price for an issue and then finds that it cannot resell the securities at expected prices to investors, the losses they sustain are absorbed by their own accounts. Losses can be substantial. In the bull market of the 1950's and early 1960's, they were not frequent. Nevertheless, the members of a purchase syndicate accept risk of loss. This risk may be shared or separate for the members. The latter is more common. With separated liability for payment, a security house assumes responsibility only for the purchase of that part of the issue it accepts when the syndicate is formed. If this liability were shared a house might be obliged to pay for a larger part of the issue if one or more syndicate members failed to meet obligations in full. This risk can be avoided by drawing an agreement in which the separateness of liability is made explicit. The risk of loss from a failure to market the issue as planned is shared in ratio to purchase commitments.

The Selling Group. The advantage of rapid sale of an issue as a means for reducing risk should be clear. In general, a purchase syndicate adds to its ability to make a rapid sale by bringing additional securities houses into a selling group. This increases the number of investors that can be reached by the investment bankers.

The purchase syndicate manager may prepare a statement of the basic characteristics of an issue with which to inform potential selling group members about it. Such a statement is required later in the distribution to the public, and is discussed in the next section. The preliminary, or "red herring," prospectus duplicates the required prospectus excepting for information about price. The name "red herring" comes from the requirement that the preliminary nature of the prospectus be stated clearly in red-inked type on the cover. This prospectus will contain sufficient information for potential selling group members to determine their degree of interest in the proposed issue and to decide for how large a fraction to subscribe.

The selling group may include all of the members of the purchase syndicate, and usually does. If a member of a purchase syndicate does not become a member of the selling group, he takes on the role of underwriter only. Since some profit is to be obtained from the selling function, most purchase syndicate members also sell. The additional securities houses do not, usually, accept the same risk as members of the purchase syndicate. They agree to sell a part of the issue to their customers. If they sell the amount agreed on, they are compensated for their selling effort. If they do not, they may be penalized for not meeting agreed goals but they do not become obligated to the issuer to pay for the amount of the issue unsold. That responsibility remains with the purchase syndicate members.

Disclosure. Under the Securities Act of 1933, issuers and underwriters are required to disclose to potential purchasers sufficient information for an informed investor to use in making a decision about investment value of the new issue. The issuer must prepare a registration statement to be filed with the SEC. An offering may take place twenty days after the filing of the registration statement unless the SEC acts to delay it and requests amendment of the statement. In practice, offerings were delayed, on the average, about fifty-five days in 1960 and 1961. Much of the delay arose from the large number of statements filed relative to the availability of staff of the SEC.

A part of the registration statement is the prospectus, which later will be reproduced in quantity for delivery to potential investors. This prospectus must be in the hands of an investor before a sale is made to him. The information to be provided includes the business and financial history of the issuer over a period of years, management personnel and holders of large blocks of securities, intended uses for proceeds from the sale, and such other facts as might affect an investment decision. It is an offense to make false or misleading statements or to omit stating information of material importance.

Some issues are exempt from registration under the Securities Act. These include issues of governments, of companies whose activities are regulated by other governmental agencies, and certain special classes. The latter are defined by regulations and obtain exemption only on application and demonstration of conformance to the conditions for exemption. The conditions most frequently affecting registration are: (1) offers limited to a small number of investors, (2) intrastate offerings, and (3) offers of only a small amount (less than $300,000) of securities. This last group, exempted under the SEC's Regulation A, is largest. The numbers of issues qualifying is large relative to all issues registered. In fiscal 1960 there were 1,049 applications for exemption under this regulation and 1,628 registrations of non-exempt securities. The figures for 1961 were 1,057 and 1,830, respectively. The dollar amounts in total however, are small. Issues registered for cash sale in fiscal 1960 aggregated $10,908 million while issues exempt under Regulation A aggregated only $225 million, about 2 per cent of those registered. The figures for 1961 were $14,115 and $240 million, respectively. A large number of small issues qualify. Under the exemption some of the costs of flotation of a new issue are avoided. In particular, a less elaborate offering circular may be used. Exemption does not relieve the issuer or underwriters of liability for damages, however, if fraud is an element in the sale of the securities.

The purpose of the disclosure law is prevention of the sale of securities at prices substantially different from investment value. The SEC does not pass judgment on investment value; it makes an effort to assure that enough pertinent information is made available to investors for them to pass such judgments. Some reliance is placed in establishing standards for disclosure on the dissemination of investment advice from those most able to make sound judgments—investment counsellors, investment services, trustees, and the registered representatives of the securities houses

—to those investors less well qualified. The disclosure law does not of itself prevent the marketing of issues of questionable value; it provides for an opportunity for investors to decide investment merits before purchase.

The careful preparation of the material required in compliance with the disclosure law is one of the activities of investment banking.

Pricing. The most delicate and significant activity for investment banking is decision on the price at which securities will be offered to investors. The price must be one the investors will pay for all of the securities. If it is higher, the issue will be sold only at a loss to the purchase syndicate. If it is lower, the issuer may have cause to doubt the ability and, perhaps, the honesty of the securities houses involved. Too high a price leads to losses; too low a price may lead to loss of reputation. A succession of losses or even one substantial loss may make further operation in this business impossible. The securities houses have a small margin of investment in issues financed largely by bank loans. Losses small in proportion to the full price of the issue are large in terms of the houses' accounts. Reputation, on the other hand, is a necessary element for continued business. The financial community is sensitive to reputation. Action that is destructive of this intangible has great cost for the future of a firm in this business.

The price put on an issue is reached by considering those paid by investors for issues that appear to be comparable. The investment banker must decide what issues on the market are most similar to that he is about to distribute. The pricing of these issues provides a base for determining the offering price of the new issue. In general, that price will be set slightly below a figure that is expected in the market.

There have been instances in which prices apparently were set much below expected market prices and "windfall" gains accrued to the purchase syndicate, or closely related persons. The difficulty of precise determination ahead of time of the price the market will place on an issue, especially the first publicly offered by a new enterprise, certainly leads to some errors of pricing. Deliberate mispricing, however, is not likely to occur often. Pricing is too significant both to the issuer and investor.

When an offering price has been placed on the issue, prices to the participants in the distribution can be established. The participants incur costs in the distribution and expect to obtain some profit from it. The prices to participants are discounts from the offering price. Such discounts are large enough to cover costs and provide profit if the distribution goes as planned. Three prices are common: (1) a price for members of the selling group, (2) a price to members of the purchase syndicate, who carry more responsibility than members of the selling group, and

(3) a price to the syndicate manager, who carries yet more functions. Discounts to selling group members often are ¼ or ½ point. Discounts to purchase syndicate members may be 1 or 2 points. A further discount of ½ to 1 point may be granted the syndicate manager. Issues requiring a lot of selling effort might have even larger discounts for the participants. Some very large issues of high-quality bonds would be sold on smaller margins.

Costs. The discounts from public offering price are costs to the issuer. Further costs are incurred in making an issue ready for the market. Investigations, audits, printing of certificates, registration fees, and other preliminary actions give rise to cost. The ratio of cost to price varies inversely with the size of an issue and is affected by the kind of market in which it is sold. The over-all costs to the issuer of a small stock issue, under $1 million, may amount to 25 or 30 per cent of the offering price. On bond issues in the same size class, costs of 7 to 10 per cent are common. The proportion of cost to offering price on large industrial stock issues, for $20 million or more, is about 5 per cent. Large bond issues may be marketed with costs equaling 1 to 1½ per cent of the issuing price. The average costs for all registered corporate issues offered for cash in 1960 were 4.9 per cent of gross proceeds. The figure for 1961 was 4.4 per cent.

Subsequent Market. As soon as distribution of securities has begun, the secondary market for the issue becomes important. During the first few days of the offering, the investment banking syndicate may stabilize price in the market. Present regulations of the SEC permit this if full, prior disclosure of intent to stabilize is made. The purpose of stabilizing price is facilitation of distribution. If prices tend to rise, the securities can be offered more rapidly. If prices tend to fall, the supply in the secondary market may be reacquired by the syndicate and reoffered. Some securities in a public distribution will be bought by individuals who cannot or do not hold them. If the number is small, the shares they sell can be reacquired in the secondary market without great risk. If the offering price itself is too high, however, the flow back into the secondary market may absorb rapidly the capacity of the syndicate to repurchase. In the ultimate instance, of course, the sellers would find themselves in the ridiculous position of reacquiring all shares offered. Factors that affect the general willingness of the market to accept the new issue at the offering price cannot be offset by stabilizing activity. Bad pricing will lead to losses. The natural return of a small fraction of shares through the secondary market can be absorbed, however, and the shares resold to investors willing and able to hold them.

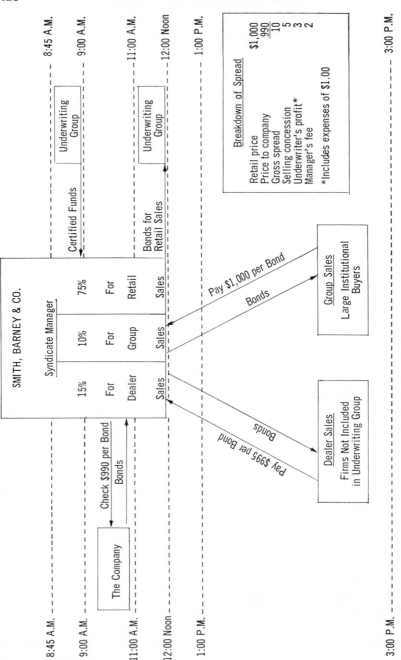

Fig. 25–1. A syndicate closing.

Stabilizing activity is confined, usually, to a few days after initial offering of an issue, but responsibility for interest in the secondary market for the issue is a continuing factor. Most investment bankers consider it a part of their function to maintain a secondary market, if none already exists. They stand ready to buy or sell in the market and to facilitate transfers of securities among investors. An over-the-counter market for the issue comes into being.

An Illustration. To illustrate the fundamental elements of the distribution process, a chart (Fig. 25–1), provided by one of the principal investment banking houses is reproduced. It illustrates the sale of a new issue of bonds but represents equally well the steps in distribution of stock.

In this example, the members of the purchase syndicate deliver funds to the syndicate manager at 8:45 A.M. of the closing day. Shortly thereafter the manager delivers $990.00 per bond to the issuer and receives the bonds. The proportion to be sold by the members of the purchase syndicate, 75 per cent, is allocated to them. Fifteen per cent is allocated to dealer sales and the remaining 10 per cent to group sales. At the close of the day, 3:00 P.M., the results of the sales are reported.

The delivery price of bonds for dealer sales is $995.00 per bond. It is $1,000.00 per bond for group sales. If all sales are made in ratio to the allocations, gross profits of $5 will be obtained from the dealer sales and $10 from the group sales. From these figures, $1 is subtracted for expenses incurred in the distribution, $2 is subtracted as a fee for the manager, and $0.50 is subtracted as tax on the transfers. The net profit is distributed by the manager, in approximately four weeks, to the members of the purchase syndicate in ratio to their participation.

Dealers Sales			*Group Sales*			*Retail Sales*		
Gross		$10.00	Gross		$10.00	Gross		$10.00
Less:			Less:			Less:		
Selling conc.	$5.00		Expenses	$1.00		Expenses	$1.00	
Expenses	1.00		Mgt. fee	2.00		Mgt. fee	2.00	
Mgt. fee	2.00		Tax	.50		Tax	.50	
Tax	.50							
		8.50			3.50			3.50
Net profit		$ 1.50	Net profit		$ 6.50	Net profit		$ 6.50

Meanwhile the members of the purchase syndicate have sold bonds allocated to them. They receive these bonds at the purchase price, absorb expenses and taxes, and profit from their own selling activity.

OTHER DISTRIBUTION PROCEDURES

The underwriting and distributing procedure described above is used for a large proportion of new issues, especially, of bonds. In general, it is not used if the marketing of an issue is so assured that the issuer will not pay for underwriting or if the marketing is so risky that no invest-ment banker will underwrite it. In either case, other distribution pro-cedures may be used. In still other cases, entirely different channels for distribution which do not use investment banking facilities may be chosen.

Three kinds of procedure are sufficiently common to deserve descrip-tion here: "best efforts," "all or none," and "stand-by."

Best Efforts. Securities houses may agree to use their best efforts to secure distribution of an issue of securities without entering into an underwriting agreement. They agree to try to sell the issue but do not give a guarantee of success. As they sell units of the issue, they turn the proceeds, less compensation for the selling effort, over to the issuer. The full risk of success or failure in raising a given amount of funds rests with the issuer. This type of arrangement is desired by companies issuing very high-quality securities when they have no fear of declining prices in the markets or no pressing need for a given amount of funds. It is used also by issuers who cannot obtain underwriting but need funds.

All or None. A more sophisticated variant of the best efforts agree-ment includes the all-or-none agreement. Under this arrangement units of the issue are sold by a marketing organization on a best efforts basis but no sales are final unless the entire issue is sold. Customers agree to accept securities at the issue price but do not take delivery or pay for them until all of the issue has been placed. This arrangement has a definite advantage for the investors. A company seeking funds through sale of securities usually has a definite need for an amount sufficient to carry out a plan of action. Receipt of less than that amount would not permit accomplishment of objectives. The investors that had bought securities would be disappointed by the result. Under the all-or-none agreement, no investor need pay for the securities unless the necessary amount has been sold. Each is protected against the possibility that the market will not supply enough funds. They are not protected, of course, against inadequacy in the original estimates of the amount needed or of the gains to be had by carrying out the planned activity.

Stand-by. Each of the distribution processes described above has made use of the facilities of the investment banking houses. Other chan-nels for distribution may be used. Securities may be sold to customers, to employees, to suppliers, to financial institutions. A channel often used in the distribution of stock or convertible issues is one direct to stock-holders. This may be accomplished by issuing subscription warrants to stockholders entitling them to buy a proportion of the new issue equal to the proportion their stockholdings bear to the total outstanding. These warrants permit the stockholder to buy a part of the new issue at a favorable price. If all these warrants are used in purchasing the securities offered, the whole issue will be distributed. The details of rights offerings and valuation of subscription warrants are discussed in Chapter 35.

If such a channel is chosen, however, the issuer also may choose to have the distribution underwritten. Should the stockholders decide not to exercise all the warrants, part of the issue would remain unsold and some part of the amount of funds desired would be missing. An underwriting agreement would require the underwriters to buy the remainder of the issue and supply the funds. The agreement used is a stand-by agreement. The investment bankers, for a fee, agree to stand by while the distribution is made. If at the end of a designated period some part of the issue is unsold, the bankers agree to buy it at a predetermined price. This purchase completes the distribution as far as the issuer is concerned. The investment bankers may hold the purchased securities for investment or make a further distribution through their own organizations. The stand-by agreement is an instance of underwriting as a separate function for investment bankers.

Secondary Distributions. The need for a formal distribution process and, perhaps, underwriting is not confined to the sale of new issues. Large blocks of outstanding securities are marketed on occasion. The principal stockholder or stockholders of a closely held company may decide to market some or all of their holdings. Investors who have accumulated large blocks of stock, as investment companies have, may wish to liquidate them in order to invest in other securities. Settlement of estates may require sale of concentrated holdings of securities. The figures in Table 25–1 show that substantial offerings of outstanding securities do occur.

The stock exchanges have created means for handling quite large transactions. Exchange distributions and specialist block purchases (see page 194) are effective for many sales. Very large blocks of securities, however, need the broad distribution found only through the investment banking facilities of securities houses. The procedures for distribution of outstanding securities are the same as those for new issues. Since, however, the stocks or bonds involved are already outstanding, the term "secondary distribution" describes the operation.

26

Broker's Loans

This chapter is concerned with the supply of funds to securities houses.[1] Following a description of several characteristics of broker's loans, an examination will be made of the market for the principal kind of loan, the call loan. A third section will deal with regulation.

NATURE OF BROKER'S LOANS

Broker's loans are, by definition, loans made by banks and others to brokers and dealers in the securities markets. There are a number of ways to view the volume of such loans. They may be classified by the market in which they are used. Loans are secured by government obligations, on the one hand, and by other collateral, mostly stocks, on the other. Loans are related to the provision of credit by brokers and dealers to their customers, to the firms' purchases of bonds and stock for inventory and for member accounts, and to the firms' investment banking activities in the market for new issues of bonds and stock. The needs for funds by brokers relate mostly to the demands by their customers for credit in margin accounts. The brokers have funds available from the net credit balances of some customers and from capital accounts of the firms, but the total often is less than the demand for credit by margin buyers and short sellers. The balance is supplied by loans from banks and others to the brokers. Dealers require funds to carry inventories as part of their function of making markets in the issues they trade. Specialists and odd-lot houses are among the important dealers in the exchange markets, but many other houses make markets over the counter in issues

[1] For more detail on broker's loans and security credit in general, see: Jules I. Bogen and Herman E. Krooss, *Security Credit: Its Role and Regulation* (Englewood Cliffs, N.J.: Prentice-Hall, Inc., 1960).

traded in those markets. They have capital funds available, but the size of inventories may require that additional funds be obtained by borrowing. Investment bankers are engaged in distribution of new issues or large blocks of outstanding securities. While the distribution process is in progress, funds are needed to carry the securities. Again, capital funds are available, but a successful investment banking house distributes issues aggregating substantially more than its capital accounts and seeks funds by borrowing from banks and others. As we have observed often in previous chapters, a securities house may be broker, dealer, and investment banker, and find need for funds for all of the reasons indicated above. In addition, the funds of partners or stockholders may be invested. The amounts of securities carried in these portfolios may exceed the accounts of the members of the organizations, and borrowing is necessary to carry out this investment operation as well. The clearing and delivery of securities may be another source of need for funds; customers may be paid for securities sold although actual delivery is delayed and funds are not received from buying brokers until the delivery is made.

A Distinction. Broker's loans must be distinguished from loans by brokers to their customers. The latter loans arise from trading on margin, and it is easy to associate the term "broker's loan" with these loans that they make. The term, however, is used to refer to borrowing by brokers and dealers from banks and others.

Amount of Broker Borrowing. At the end of 1961, in addition to the credit balances of customers, broker-dealers were borrowing $5.1 billion from banks. At that time, customer net credit balances were $1.2 billion, and loans by banks to individuals other than brokers and dealers for the purchase and carrying of securities equalled $2.1 billion. The total credit extended for securities trading, therefore, was at that time $8.4 billion, of which 75 per cent was extended through brokers and dealers. These relationships are shown both more clearly and in more detail in data supplied to Bogen and Krooss by the research department of the New York Stock Exchange. The data have been adapted for Table 26–1. In these data loans by banks directly to investors are included, as noted.

Customer margin accounts ($4,870 million, 46.5 per cent) and inventories ($2,690 million, 25.9 per cent) provided the major kinds of employment for the $10,380 million supplied by the various sources. Among the sources the $4,240 million of loans to brokers and dealers, 40.8 per cent, was the largest. Inspection of the sources shows that borrowing is the only source readily variable at the option of management of the securities houses.

Different Measures of Broker's Loans. The $4,240 million shown for broker's loans in Table 26–1 includes loans to brokers and dealers from

Table 26–1. Securities Credit and Capital Funds, June 30, 1959
(in millions of dollars)

Employment		Source	
Cash balances	$ 680	Customers' net credit	
General accounts:		balances	$ 1,760
Brokers' customers	3,140	Bank loans direct to	
Banks' customers	1,730	investors	1,940
Special accounts:		Loans to broker-dealers	
Subscription accounts	80	from:	
U. S. Government bonds	400	Domestic banks $2,320	
Cash purchases in process	630	Foreign bank	
Underwriting and firm positions:		agencies 850	
Corporate securities:		Other lenders 1,070	4,240
As specialists .... $ 60		Firm credit balances	160
As odd-lot dealers 20		"Housekeeping"*	940
Other 540		Capital accounts	1,340
Municipal bonds ... 250			
U. S. Government			
bonds 1,820	2,690		
"Housekeeping"*	680		
Total	$10,380	Total	$10,380

* Includes balances of securities on loan or borrowed, securities house balances, securities with delivery pending, and all other balances.
Source: Adapted from: Jules I. Bogen and Herman E. Krooss, *Security Credit: Its Role and Regulation* (Englewood Cliffs, N.J.; Prentice-Hall, Inc., 1960), Table I, p. 22.

domestic banks, agencies of foreign banks, and other lenders. This figure is related to, but different from, a measure of loans published by the New York Stock Exchange as "member borrowings." It is different also from the series on loans by all commercial banks to brokers and dealers, which is published by the Federal Reserve Board.

Member borrowings includes, in addition to loans from banks and others, loans from one security house to another. It is limited, however, to borrowings by members of the New York Stock Exchange and is not, therefore, a comprehensive measure of broker's borrowings. The Federal Reserve Board series is comprehensive as far as loans by domestic banks are concerned but includes neither foreign bank loans nor loans from others than banks. No single series provides a complete measure. The "member borrowing" series covers the longest period of time and has been reasonably consistent in its definitions over that period.

Changes in Amounts of Broker's Loans over Time. Differing conditions in the securities markets and in the practices of investors affect the demand for broker's loans. The picture provided in Figure 26–1 reflects the great increase in borrowing by the member firms of the New York

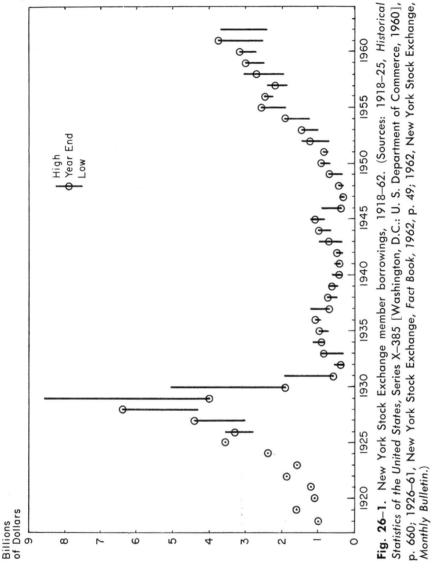

Fig. 26-1. New York Stock Exchange member borrowings, 1918–62. (Sources: 1918–25, *Historical Statistics of the United States*, Series X–385 [Washington, D.C.: U. S. Department of Commerce, 1960], p. 660; 1926–61, New York Stock Exchange, *Fact Book, 1962*, p. 49; 1962, New York Stock Exchange, *Monthly Bulletin.*)

Stock Exchange during the 1920's. Following the precipitous decline in borrowing accompanying the decline in market prices and public interest in the stock market of the early 1930's, the amount of borrowing remained fairly level until the beginning of the 1950–61 bull market. In this market, in which stock prices reached much higher figures than they did in 1929, the amount of member borrowing increased but remained far below its earlier peak.

An expansion of broker's loans is to be expected during a period of rising stock prices. Margin trading during such a period would increase, and this leads to borrowing by broker-dealers. More specifically, as pointed out by Haney, Logan, and Gavens in their exhaustive study of the subject,[2] broker's loans will increase or tend to increase under the following circumstances:

1. Increased number of margin buyers
2. Increased number of shares bought on margin
3. Increased average price of shares bought on margin
   (a) because of rising market prices or
   (b) because of a shift in trading to higher-priced issues
4. Decreased net credit balances of customers or decreased capital and other resources of securities houses

The periods of the 1920's and 1950's were characterized by the increases referred to in this list. In the 1950's net credit balances rose somewhat, but not enough to offset the increased margin trading. The ratio of borrowing to total market value of securities outstanding reached nowhere near the same figures in the 1950's, however, that it reached in the 1920's. While the amount of broker's loans rose in the 1950's, this ratio to market value stayed low throughout the boom.

Kinds of Loans. Several different kinds of loans are made by banks and others to brokers and dealers. Banks make "day loans." These are unsecured loans repayable before the end of the day on which granted and are used by securities houses to pick up securities and pay off other loans. Since they do not affect the lending bank's reserve position, an interest charge of only 1 or 2 per cent is made. So-called "overnight loans" are secured and carry the regular call loan rate. A large volume of loans secured by U. S. government bonds is made to government bond dealers. Low margins and low interest rates are characteristic. Loans are made to underwriters when new securities are being distributed. Margins of 10 per cent are common but the call loan rate is charged on these loans. Repurchase agreements, under which securities are purchased, often by corporate treasurers, on an agreement that the seller will repurchase at a price slightly below the price paid by the investor,

[2] L. H. Haney, L. S. Logan, and H. S. Gavens, *Brokers' Loans* (New York: Harper & Row, Publishers, 1932), p. 18 .

have become common. The principal loan arrangement, however, is the call loan. These loans are repayable on demand at the option of either borrower or lender.

THE CALL LOAN MARKET

As recently as 1950 many brokerage houses, perhaps one-fourth, were able to finance their needs without recourse to borrowing. By the mid-1950's, however, the pressure for customer credit had led all leading brokerage firms to borrow. Firm capital plus customers' net credit balances were no longer sufficient to meet the needs of margin customers. This remained true in the early 1960's. Reference back to Table 26–1 will show that, on June 30, 1959, borrowing by brokers provided 41 per cent of the funds employed in the purchasing and carrying of securities.

Sources of Loans. The chief source of call money is now, as it has been for years, New York banks and trust companies. However, in recent years, considerable amounts of funds have been coming from other cities in the United States, from corporate lending, and from abroad, primarily from Canada.

Banks usually lend to firms maintaining accounts with them. In recent years large brokerage firms have carried accounts with several banks, perhaps a dozen, to obtain adequate accommodation.

Out-of-town banks may make loans in participation with New York banks, or their New York correspondents may place funds for them. They also lend directly to securities houses.

Loans from "others," including non-financial concerns, decreased significantly in the 1930's but became both significant in amount and a matter of concern to the regulatory authorities in the late 1950's and early 1960's. Non-regulated lenders were sources of funds for large investment and trading operations.

Interest Rates. A characteristic of call money rates in earlier years was extreme volatility. These figures give some indication of variations in call rates over a long period:

Year	High	Low
1899	186%	Unknown
1919	30	3¼%
1925	6	3
1929	20	4½
1931	4	1
1935	1	1¼
1936–45	1	1
1946–50	1½	1
1951–55	4½	1½
1956–60	5½	3½
1961–62	4½	4½

Years ago interest rates on call loans changed daily, and even hourly. The market for these funds centered at the money desk of the New York Stock Exchange. They were the most sensitive of interest rates. Changes in banking practices, among other things, have changed this. There is no longer a money desk at the Exchange. Call loan rates have changed infrequently and by small amounts in recent years. The call loan is a substantially less important factor in the money market.

Types of Call Loans. Call money loans are of two types today. In the first type the broker will make a series of individual loans. The denomination will be $100,000 or some multiple thereof, such as $700,000. A bank might make ten such loans in providing a broker with $1 million. Each loan is a separate entity and has its own collateral. It may be paid off as a unit without disturbing any of the other loans made at the same bank. This is an old process still followed to some extent.

The other, newer type is the "accordion" loan. It has become increasingly prominent in the last few decades. A large firm wishing to borrow $10 million, instead of making a number of small loans for $100,000 or $200,000, would make one loan for $10 million and deposit adequate collateral. If it wished to repay part of the loan, say $2 million, it would merely contract the total to $8 million and leave the collateral with the bank. If it wished to expand the loan, it would merely increase the size of the one loan, putting up more collateral if necessary. This type of loan benefits both the broker and the bank in that only one loan has to be serviced instead of a number of smaller loans.

Renewals. Practically all call loans are renewed daily. There are no precise figures to indicate what percentage of loans are renewed each day. Actually, such a figure would be very difficult to compute. For example, if a $10 million accordion loan is contracted to $8 million on a given day, would the renewal percentage be 100?

It has been rare for a lending bank to refuse to renew a call loan. The initiative on renewal is usually left to the broker. In late 1955 one New York bank called a loan; it was the first such incident in two years. The few loans called recently have been called because of a need for funds by the lending banks rather than because of any lack of adequate security.

Margins. The margins now required on call loans vary. Regulation U of the Federal Reserve Board, which governs the extension of credit by banks to brokers and dealers, makes a distinction between loans to brokers and dealers for their own account and loans based on customers' collateral. The initial margin requirement on loans to brokers and dealers for their own account on non-exempt securities was 70 per cent in 1961.

Such loans are governed by the same rules as those for customers of the brokerage houses. The maintenance requirement of the New York Stock Exchange on them is 25 per cent.

For loans to brokers on the security of customers' collateral, the banks are allowed to set their own initial margins. In recent years these margins have been 33 per cent. In other words, the brokers, using their customers' collateral, could borrow up to 67 per cent of the value of deposited collateral. When making such loans, the brokers are required to inform the lending banks whether the loan is for firm account or on customers' collateral. The usual maintenance requirement on these customers' loans is also 25 per cent. As long as the borrowing broker maintains the 25 per cent margin, no additional collateral is required. In practice, brokers usually keep a margin in excess of 25 per cent, say 30 per cent, to avoid the possibility of margin calls.

Diversity of Collateral. There are no hard-and-fast rules about the diversity of collateral today. The banks like diversity, however, especially on larger loans, where no more than 10 per cent of the collateral should be of one stock.

Loan Agreements. Call loans are made by the use of the "loan agreement." Instead of signing a promissory note every time a loan is made, a broker may borrow under the terms of a continuing agreement, a copy of which is filed with every bank at which he expects to do business. This is a blanket agreement, covering all future loans to the broker by the bank. It states the terms on which the bank will lend on call. No interest rate is set, it is fixed at the time each loan is taken out or renewed. These agreements are legal masterpieces, often over 1,500 words in length. Once the agreement is signed, the broker needs only to deposit with the bank an appropriate loan envelope which contains the hypothecated collateral and is signed by a member of the brokerage firm, when obtaining accommodation. After examination of the collateral in the envelope, the bank automatically grants the requested loan, provided, of course, that the bank's requirements are met; they always are.

FEDERAL REGULATION OF SPECULATIVE CREDIT

Securities Exchange Act of 1934. In the early years of the New Deal, both the administrative and legislative branches of the federal government, backed by popular opinion, were strongly in favor of government regulation of the stock exchanges and the brokerage business. After extensive hearings the Securities Exchange Act was passed and became effective June 6, 1934.

Section 7 of the Act gave to the Federal Reserve Board complete power to "prevent the excessive use of credit for the purchase and carrying of securities." It prescribed initial margins and gave the Board power to fix other margins in the future. Subsequently, the Board issued many such regulations. Those governing the extension of credit by brokers have been issued under the so-called Regulation T. They have already been examined in detail in Chapter 21.

Section 8 placed restrictions on borrowing by exchange members, brokers, and dealers on all national securities. The power to determine such regulations was also intrusted to the Federal Reserve Board. Subsequently, the Board issued a number of regulations under the title of Regulation U, which will be discussed shortly.

The essential features of Section 8 will be examined here briefly. Brokers and dealers on national securities exchanges may not borrow in the ordinary course of their business except from member banks of the Federal Reserve System or from non-member banks that file agreements with the Federal Reserve Board to comply with provisions of the Act. The purpose of this clause is to prevent the repetition of the situation in 1929, when vast quantities of non-banking funds were thrown into the market without responsibility and without control by banking authorities. The Board is given power to issue regulations on any loans to be made by brokers and dealers subject to the Act. Brokers are not permitted to incur an indebtedness to all persons, including customers, in excess of 2000 per cent (20 times) their net capital. This is to prevent an overextension of credit to customers.

Certain other provisions also are included to restrict the power of brokers to rehypothecate customer collateral. No commingling of such collateral is allowed without written consent of the customer or with securities of any person other than a bona fide customer. Securities also may not be hypothecated for a sum in excess of the aggregated indebtedness of such customers unless written permission is given by the customers. Finally, the securities of customers may not be loaned without written consent.

Regulation U. Section 1 provides that no bank shall make a collateral loan for the purpose of purchasing and carrying stock registered on a national securities exchange in an amount exceeding the maximum loan value of the collateral, as prescribed by the Board from time to time. In other words, brokers and dealers, subject to exceptions to be noted shortly, may borrow from banks only on such margins as are determined by the Board. All indebtedness is considered as a single loan for purposes of regulation. The section also goes on in detail with regulations about restricted accounts. No withdrawals of collateral are permitted if such action would increase the deficiency. But a loan may be increased by depositing additional collateral that has a maximum value at least equal to the amount of the increase. The terms on which withdrawals and substitutions may be made are also indicated.

The significant thing about this section is that it places under Federal Reserve control all collateral loans made by banks to brokers and dealers for their own or firm account. Board margin requirements control such loans exactly as they do loans by brokers to customers.

Section 2 contains the important exception to the general rule stated in Section 1: No margin requirements are made for loans to brokers and dealers on customers' collateral. In other words, when a broker obtains a broker's loan secured by collateral carried for the account of one or more customers, the bank, and not the Federal Reserve Board, sets the margin. Hence, there is presented the interesting situation in which a broker may secure a loan subject, in 1961, to a 70 per cent margin if it is for the broker's own or firm account, but one with only a 33 per cent margin if the loan is based on customer collateral.

The section also contains other exceptions to the general rule. No margins are required for loans by banks to any bank, to any dealer to aid in the distribution of securities to customers not through an exchange, or to brokers or dealers to meet emergencies; for loans that are temporary advances to finance the purchase or sale of securities; or for loans that are loans against securities in transit, or day, arbitrage, or odd-lot dealer loans.

From time to time the Board issues supplements to Regulation U which fix the maximum loan value of stock. The one effective in 1961 set it at 30 per cent; i.e., margins were set at 70 per cent of the current market value. The percentage of margin was reduced to 50 in 1962.

Thus, through the Exchange Act and Regulations T and U, the federal government has now assumed an extensive control over both margins and brokers' loans.

Other Federal Regulations. Congress, through amendments to the Federal Reserve Act and the passage of the Banking Act of 1933, has further restricted the call money market and the extension of brokers' loans. By federal regulation, no banks may pay interest on demand deposits. In early years much call money flowed into New York to obtain the interest from demand deposits. This money now goes to the Federal Reserve banks, since there is no return either way and the Reserve banks have certain advantages as depositories. Banks no longer are allowed to count as legal reserves the money on deposit in banks other than Federal Reserve banks; this has stopped much of the flow of funds to the great

New York banks, which at one time were correspondents for nearly all of the interior banks.

The Federal Reserve Board has the power to limit collateral loans made by member banks; it did not have this power to any great extent in 1929. It may even remove officers of such banks as may be engaged in unsound lending. If the Board considered that a given bank was lending an excessive amount of money in the call loan market and the bank refused to comply with requests for a reduction, the Board could remove the responsible officers. This would prevent any such anomalous situation as prevailed at one time in the 1929 bull market when the Board was attempting to reduce member bank credit and certain banks more or less openly defied such requests.

IV

REGULATION

27

Manipulation in the
Old Market

One of the most colorful, and yet most criticized, aspects of the old stock market was the manipulation of security prices. Because of it the operations of the stock exchanges and brokerage firms came in for much criticism during the Senate investigation of 1933–34. The present Securities Exchange Act of 1934 is due in no small part to such activities.

Present-day markets show little trace of the old manipulative practices; hence, this chapter is largely one of historical interest. An understanding of the reasons for many of the regulations of the Exchange Act, the SEC, and the exchanges, however, is not possible without a rather broad knowledge of conditions that prevailed in the market as it operated in earlier years.

The activities to be described reflect little credit upon the men who engaged in them, who profited as a result, and who tolerated them, nor upon the public that saw little harm in them and hoped to share in some of their easy, but unethical, gains. This chapter is, in a sense, a commentary upon business and social ethics in the past; it is not particularly flattering.

Lest one be too hasty in condemning the securities market and the speculators who engaged in manipulation in the market, it is well to consider that ethics in all social activities during the same period of seventy-five years were of an equally low state; for example, the insurance scandals, bootlegging, land grabbing, timber thieving, the baseball scandals, the political spoils system, the Teapot Dome scandal, war profiteering, draft dodging, patent medicine frauds, sales of impure foods, corrupt political machines, misleading advertising, child labor exploitation, sweat shop manufacturing, unfair trade practices of the trusts, and bribery of legislators—to mention only a few examples that come readily to mind.

As one views the subject of manipulation in the securities market, the significant thing is not that it existed in the past, but that present regulations have almost eliminated it. It is senseless to condemn an industry because of unethical activities in its development; the important thing is how well does it function in the public interest in the present.

CHARACTERISTICS OF MANIPULATION

Its Nature. Manipulation is an artificial control of security prices; it is an attempt to force securities to sell at prices either above or below those that would exist as a result of the normal operations of supply and demand. The manipulator hopes to profit by creating fictitious prices at the expense of the general trading public.

Purposes. Manipulation has three possible objectives. The first is to raise the price; the manipulator then unloads on the buyer. This is the most common type. The second purpose may be to stabilize the price. The net result is usually that the security sells at a better price than it would if it were allowed to seek its own level. This is often done in the underwriting of new securities; it is an accepted practice which is permitted by the SEC provided the public is fully informed that such operations are contemplated. It is probably the least condemned of all manipulative practices. The third objective is to force prices down; this type of manipulation is rarely found except in the activities of the so-called "bear raiders" who hope to obtain short selling profits in this way.

Classification. Manipulative activities are difficult to classify in that there are so many different forms and so many diverse devices by which they can be carried on. For purposes of simplicity, the discussion which follows will consider the subject under three main heads: wash sales, corners, and pool operations. The first is least important; the second was largely a nineteenth-century activity; the third was typical of the market of the 1920's and included almost every device used in the manipulator's handbook.

WASH SALES

Little need be said of the wash sale, which was one of the earliest forms of manipulation. It was a fake sale; no real change in ownership took place. There was no one meaning of the term, since several methods could be used to obtain the same result. One of the earliest devices was for two brokers to simulate a sale on an exchange; a price was agreed upon, an offer or bid was accepted, yet no stock or money changed hands. Another device was for a speculator to place a matched order with two brokers; he sold a given amount of stock through one broker and bought it through another. Although more subtle and secretive than the first method, no real change in ownership took place. A third method was for a trader to sell a given block of stock and have a friend or accomplice purchase it. The accomplice was then indemnified for his expenses and the stock was retrieved. A fourth method was for a man to execute a wash sale to his wife, often to establish a tax loss. Some highly placed individuals did this in the past. Income tax officials took a dim view of this evasion procedure.

Wash sales have as their primary purpose the establishment of a fictitious price, either to create a profit opportunity or to establish a loss, generally for tax purposes. They have been illegal for many years; the stock exchanges have long barred them. In later years manipulators were able to obtain essentially the same results in some cases by matched orders placed by different individuals so as to conceal the identity of the operation. As these have always been minor manipulative activities, no further consideration will be given to them.

CORNERS

Nature. A corner is a speculative situation in which the ownership of outstanding shares becomes so concentrated that short sellers are unable to secure stock except from this owner group. It grows out of a price rise in a stock, whether natural or manipulated. As the stock rises in value, it is short sold by speculators who feel that it is too high and is certain to decline. They borrow the stock to short sell; it is often loaned by the controlling group. Eventually they attempt to cover by buying back the stock which they have sold short. Since the controlling group is the only one that has any stock to sell, the short sellers are forced to settle with them at whatever price the group dictates. At this point the short sellers are "cornered."

Corners were very frequent in the early years of the New York Stock Exchange. In fact, they were so common and so profitable in the nineteenth century that Henry Clews, a noted financier and chronicler of Wall Street, observed in the post-Civil War period that "all large fortunes are made by corners."[1]

In many cases they were deliberately engineered as "traps" for unsuspecting speculators, who were often great operators. Such situations

[1] Henry Clews, *Fifty Years in Wall Street* (New York: Irving Publishing Co., 1908), p. 101.

have been labeled as manipulative corners. Examples have been the Harlem Railroad corner of 1863, the "Erie raids," the Stutz corner of 1920, and the Piggly Wiggly corner of 1923. In these instances the manipulators freely loaned stock to the short sellers. As the price rose, short sellers continued to sell while the manipulators purchased all stock offered on the market. The stock was reloaned for more short selling. Eventually more stock would often be on loan than was actually outstanding. When this situation had continued to a point where the short sellers sought to cover either as a precautionary measure or in desperation, the manipulators called the stock loans. The corner was complete and the short sellers had no recourse but to settle.

Other corners have sometimes been called natural corners in that they were a result of speculative activities not connected with manipulation. In such cases several controlling groups may have attempted to purchase control of a given company. As the stock was bid up for control, short sellers, without realizing the background of the situation, would sell. In the end they were cornered as before, since only the controlling group had stock to sell. The classic example of this situation was the famous Northern Pacific corner of 1901.

Some of the most colorful episodes of Wall Street history are those of the corners executed by the great stock market operators of an earlier day. A few examples will be cited.

The First Harlem Railroad Corner. The two Harlem Railroad corners involved principally two men. The first was Commodore Cornelius Vanderbilt, whose early fortune was made in the steamship business; he turned to railroads in the early 1860's as a greater opportunity. The second was Daniel Drew, a deeply religious man on Sunday and as ruthless a businessman as ever operated in Wall Street.

In 1862 Vanderbilt purchased stock in the Harlem Railroad in New York City for $8 a share.[2] By the time he had control, it had reached 50. He then proceeded to extend the road to lower Manhattan. Drew also bought some shares but was not content with his modest profit. The stock had now reached 100. At this point Drew conspired with Boss Tweed and the members of the Common Council to repeal the Harlem Railroad franchise; at the same time all heavily short sold the railroad stock. It was driven down to 72 but refused to go further as Vanderbilt purchased every possible share at that point. The short sellers then realized that something had gone wrong. It had indeed, since they had short sold 137,000 shares, or 27,000 shares more than were outstanding.

[2] R. I. Warshow, *The Story of Wall Street* (New York: Greenberg, Publisher, Inc., 1929), p. 91.

Vanderbilt then jumped the price back to 179, at which price Drew, Tweed, and the members of the Common Council were forced to settle.

The Second Harlem Railroad Corner. The second corner involved Vanderbilt, Drew, and the members of the New York State Legislature. Vanderbilt, now determined to get a charter from the state government, went directly to the legislature. Drew, by instigating a favorable report by the legislature, forced the price up to 150 from 75 in a few days. At this point Drew and the chief members of the legislature heavily short sold the road's stock. The legislature now defeated the petition for a charter by a heavy vote. In two days the stock fell 50 points and then began to rise rapidly. There was no stock to be obtained for short covering. Once again, more stock had been short sold than could be covered. Up and up went the price, and Vanderbilt began to corner the speculators. At 285 he finally settled with the short sellers. Drew paid Vanderbilt $500,000 in a private settlement.

The Erie Raids. In its early years the Erie Railroad was one of the great roads of the nation. It was also the victim of some of the worst stock manipulations in the history of American railroading.[3] These manipulations are commonly known as the "Erie raids." There were a number of them; two are typical. The market operators who engaged in these raids were principally Vanderbilt, Drew, Fisk, and Gould.

Jim Fisk began his business career as a dry goods peddler in Vermont. Later he became a partner in a large dry goods firm in Boston. During the Civil War his highly unorthodox methods of securing army blanket orders were so unsavory to his partners that he was given some $60,000 in cash to withdraw from the firm. He next joined forces with Drew and Gould.

Jay Gould was one of the shrewdest market operators who ever speculated in Wall Street. He married a wholesale grocer's daughter in his early twenties and was given control of a small, bankrupt railroad—its stocks were worthless. In a short time he reorganized the road and sold it at a handsome profit. His next venture was the purchase and sale of a road connecting Pittsburgh and Cleveland at another high return. He was still only twenty-five years of age.

After the Erie Railroad passed into receivership in 1859, it received a loan of $1,500,000 from Drew on the condition that he be made a director. By 1868 it had accumulated a surplus of $16 million and had become a valuable piece of property. At that time Vanderbilt, flushed with his successes with the consolidated New York Central, determined to wrest control of the Erie Railroad from Drew and his two associates,

---

[3] Warshow, *op. cit.*, p. 109; Clews, *op. cit.*, p. 137.

Gould and Fisk. He bought heavily of the stock as Drew and his associates sold at steadily advancing prices. Not only did he buy all of the
outstanding stock, but he also bought an additional 50,000 shares; he felt
certain that, again, Drew was cornered.

This time Drew avoided a repetition of the disastrous Harlem Railroad corners. At a secret, midnight meeting, the board of directors issued
$10 million in convertible bonds. Through a wash sale to Drew, these
were converted into 100,000 shares of common stock. Vanderbilt was
now confronted with 100,000 new shares thrown on the market in a few
days. He bought every share at a cost of $7 million. Now he had 100,000
shares he dared not sell and which no one would buy; his money was
tied up completely. In desperation he turned to a friendly judge who
vowed to have the triumvirate in jail by nightfall. In order to avoid
arrest, the three members of the executive committee of the Erie Railroad now rushed with their money and account books to the shores of
New Jersey; with them they carried $4 million in greenbacks.

The situation was now a stalemate. Drew, Fisk, and Gould were safe
in New Jersey with their money, but they could not return to their
homes. Vanderbilt had lost his $7 million; he was unable to borrow at
the banks; his resources were badly strained. A compromise was agreed
upon: Drew and his two associates were to keep their $7 million but
were to repay Vanderbilt that sum out of the Erie Railroad treasury.
This was done and that ill-fated railway was left a weakened hulk.

Drew was required by the agreement to leave the management of the
Erie Railroad to Gould. He was now a wealthy man with a fortune of
$13 million. His retirement, however, left him an unhappy man. Eventu-
ally he came back into the market like the proverbial moth attracted to
the scorching light.

Again, Drew became associated with Gould and Fisk in another "Erie
raid." It was decided that the scene would be set with a created panic.
The men suddenly withdrew $14 million in cash from their banks, which
severely restricted the credit situation; call money rose to 160 per cent.
All three men were to short sell Erie stock. For a while the pool was a
success and Erie stock fell 30 points. Drew now became timid and withdrew from the joint operation as Gould and Fisk planned to continue the
raid with a new campaign. In a short time Drew regretted his timidity
as the market weakened; he began to short sell on his own account.
Since they knew of his operations, Gould and Fisk now determined to
break Drew. As he short sold, they reversed their operations and bought
every share thrown on the market. Soon Drew found himself 70,000
shares short; he could not cover since Gould and Fisk controlled the
entire floating supply of the stock. Drew was cornered by his erstwhile

associates; he had no legal recourse; he had not a friend in Wall Street; his losses were staggering.

From then on Drew was a beaten man. In several successive operations his entire fortune melted away. In a few years, he died a poor man; his total assets were less than $1,000. Wall Street smiled with relief; "Uncle Daniel" was gone. A fitting epitaph on his tombstone would have been a jingle, which he once composed:

> He who sells what isn't his'n,
> Must buy it back or go to prison.

From the Erie raids Jay Gould emerged stronger than ever. His most publicized corner was not in stocks but in gold. On October 4, 1869, he attempted the audacious feat of cornering the gold market. On that "Black Friday" he met his worst defeat. Always wily to the last, he made Jim Fisk bear the brunt of the losses; Fisk's firm went down in complete ruin.

The Northern Pacific Corner. The great Northern Pacific corner took place in 1901; it was perhaps the most remarkable corner ever to occur in Wall Street.[4] It grew out of an attempt of two financial giants to acquire control of one small railroad, the Chicago, Burlington and Quincy, commonly known as the Burlington. The two opposing contestants were James J. Hill of the Northern Pacific and Edward H. Harriman of the Union Pacific. Behind Hill was J. P. Morgan and Company; behind Harriman was Kuhn, Loeb and Company. Hill wanted the Burlington to prevent the encroachment of the Union Pacific in his territory; the road would also provide him with a much-needed Chicago terminus. Harriman wanted the road because it paralleled his own Union Pacific and, as such, was a potential competitor.

Both parties started to buy up the Burlington stock at about the same time. At first the Harriman syndicate attempted to buy the stock in the open market. This resulted in failure when the Hill group negotiated with the majority stockholders of the road and bought control at $200 per share. The Harriman interests now took a very bold step. As someone described it, they "bought the cow to get the calf." Their operation was to secure control of the Burlington by buying the Northern Pacific. Without a single share to start with, Kuhn, Loeb and Company bought a clear majority of all the stock in two months. Although they had a majority of all the stock, they did not have a majority of the common stock alone.

Morgan, however, was not disposed to accept defeat. On his orders 150,000 shares of common stock were purchased on the Exchange; as

---

[4] Warshow, *op. cit.*, p. 242.

they were bought, the stock rose from 112 to 150. Morgan was now in a position to exercise a very unusual clause in the charter of the Northern Pacific. This clause permitted the board of directors, at its option, to retire, on any January 1, the preferred stock. Controlled by Morgan, the board immediately made this decision in order to eliminate the influence of the other group.

In the meantime the great struggle had created a very large volume of short selling. In a short while more stock had been borrowed and short sold than was outstanding; the shorts, in desperation, found that no stock could be purchased for covering; an unintentional corner had been created. The stock soared to 170, 225, 280, 300, 650, 700, and then one sale was reported at 1,000. Call money went to 70 per cent. The market crashed as speculators dumped conservative issues on the market to raise cash. Near the close of the market on May 9, the two great banking interests made a truce; they announced that they would lend their stock to the short sellers. The market quickly subsided to normal and call money fell to 3 per cent; the greatest volume on record up to that day was reported by the Exchange, a total of 3,200,000 shares. On the following day the shorts were allowed to settle at $150 per share and the corner was ended.

The struggle between the two financial interests was terminated with a compromise. Morgan did not retire the Northern Pacific's preferred stock; Harriman did not attempt to control the Burlington. Instead, the stock of all the roads were taken over by a new holding company, known as the Northern Securities Company, and each interest was given equal representation. The greatest financial battle in Wall Street was over.

The Stutz Corner. Only two important corners took place on the New York Stock Exchange after World War I: the Stutz corner in 1920 and the Piggly Wiggly Stores corner of 1923.[5] In the Stutz corner the operation involved the stock of Stutz Motors, producer of that popular young man's medium of fast transportation, "the Stutz Bearcat." The company had 100,000 shares of capital stock: Allan A. Ryan, of the Stock Exchange firm of Allan A. Ryan and Company, engineered a manipulative corner in the stock. As it rose to great heights, much short selling took place. Ryan and his associates accumulated contracts which totaled 110,000 shares, or 10,000 more than were outstanding. Seeking to take advantage of his fortunate position, Ryan agreed to settle with the "shorts" at prices varying from $500 to $1,000. The Exchange, alarmed at the situation, suspended dealings in the stock. The contracts immediately became the subject of extensive litigation; the short sellers declared

---

[5] J. E. Meeker, *The Work of the Stock Exchange* (New York: The Ronald Press Co., 1930), p. 604.

that the whole operation was illegal. Subsequently the stock fell to 20. Allan Ryan and his firm were ruined; heavy losses were accepted by several banks that had backed the venture.

The Piggly Wiggly Corner. In 1923 Clarence Saunders, president of Piggly Wiggly Stores, attempted to corner the market in his own company.[6] For a time he was able to corner the entire floating supply of the stock. He offered to settle with the short sellers at prices varying from $100 to $1,000. The Exchange, however, suspended delivery requirements on the stock. As soon as stock held out of town could be rushed to New York, the corner was broken rapidly and Saunders received all of the stock due him. In the meantime the stock was stricken from the list.

POOL OPERATIONS

Nature of the Pool. A pool is a temporary association of two or more individuals to act jointly in a security operation of a manipulative character. There is no inherent reason why manipulation should be carried on through the use of pools; many such manipulations have been carried on with great financial success by single operators, such as Drew, Little, Vanderbilt, Gould, and Keene. During the 1920's, however, the pool developed a high degree of popularity. The possibility of combining capital, trading skill, experience, and corporate connections into one co-operative venture appeared so attractive that it became the typical organization procedure of the manipulators of that era.

There was no particular size of the pool of the 1920's and early 1930's. The Radio pool, one of the largest, had about 70 members; the first Fox pool had 32, and the second, 42. The profitable alcohol pool of 1933 had only eight participants.

Pool Contracts. A pool contract was typically used in pool operation. It may have ranged from a simple, verbal agreement of several men to trade actively in one security through a joint account to a very long and complex contract which described every aspect of the rights and liabilities of the members. In the more formal contracts, the pool was usually known as a syndicate. The contract named the manager and his compensation; it indicated the capital contribution of each member; it stated the time limit and the manner in which profits and losses were to be divided; it noted any option agreements. Letters were usually sent to participants; these were countersigned and returned to the pool organizers.

Management. Successful pool operations necessitated skillful, experienced managers. These may have been traders with a past record of deft

[6] *Ibid.*, p. 605.

handling of such operations; they may have been corporate executives; often they were brokers and dealers. Members of exchanges were frequently asked to be managers; their knowledge of the market and their skill in executing orders were invaluable. Through them discretionary orders could be placed for execution at the best possible time.

Managers shared in the profits of the pool, both as participants and as paid managers. A compensation of 10 per cent of the net profits was often a manager's compensation; no losses were shared. The manager if a broker also received the regular commissions for execution of orders.

Stocks. Many of the most prominent stocks on the New York Stock Exchange and the New York Curb (now American) Exchange were subjected to syndicate, pool, or joint account operations. In 1929, 107 stock issues of the larger exchange were manipulated one or more times by pools in which members of the Exchange were interested.[7] Although no attempt was made in that year to manipulate General Motors or United States Steel, such illustrious names as American Tobacco, Chrysler, Curtiss-Wright, Goodrich, Montgomery Ward, National Cash Register, Packard, Radio Corporation of America, Standard Oil of California, Studebaker, and Union Carbide appeared on the list of manipulated issues. After 1929 the number of manipulated stocks declined rapidly; in 1930 it was only 35 issues; in 1931, 6; in 1932, 2; in 1933, 23. These figures include only operations in which Exchange members participated. There are no definite figures on the total number of stocks manipulated. Less activity took place on the New York Curb Exchange in these years. For example, in 1929 there were 27 on that exchange that were manipulated by pools in which members participated.

Pool Profits. Successful manipulation was not without compensation. In a few cases the profits of pools have been publicized. One of the most profitable was the Sinclair Consolidated Oil pool in 1929; its profit from purchasing and trading syndicate operations was $12,618,000.[8] The spectacular operations of the Radio pool of 1929 netted the participants $4,900,000. Those of the American Commercial Alcohol pool yielded $210,000. The first Fox pool made a profit of $433,000; the second netted $1,938,000. Four participants of the Kolster Radio Pool divided $1,341,000 among them.

Insider Collusion. It was a rather common practice during the 1920's to invite important directors and executive officers of corporations into the pools. As a matter of fact, many of such so-called "insiders" often were instrumental in getting the pools organized in the first place. This collusion worked to the mutual benefit of the pool and the "insiders." It

---

[7] *Stock Exchange Practices,* Senate Report No. 1455, 73d Cong., 2d sess., p. 32.
[8] *Ibid.,* p. 63.

was collusion of the most obvious sort; the pool and the "insiders" profited at the expense of the public stockholders.

Collusion benefited the pool in three ways: (1) it enabled the pool to secure options from the company; (2) it guaranteed a friendly attitude toward the pool by the company's management; and (3) it yielded invaluable information to the pool managers. The use of options will be discussed fully later on; the other two advantages will be mentioned briefly.

By collusion the pool was assured of a friendly attitude. The "insiders," since they profited by the pool operations, cooperated in every way. They did not release unfavorable information about the company or the pool operations; they did not attack the pool nor give anyone else any opportunity to do so.

The pool also had the advantage of inside information. This could be obtained at will but withheld from the public and the stockholders. It could be properly interpreted; it was entirely adequate. In addition, the pool could release the information on corporate affairs at times when the most benefit to the pool activities would result. Such advantages were exploited to the full. There were many ways to disseminate information favorable to the stock; the pools neglected none of them, as will be pointed out later.

Insider collusion was not uncommon in pool operations of the 1920's. In one pool the wife of the top executive of the company received a substantial share of the profits with no personal capital commitment. In another, substantial participation was reported for the chairman of the board, the president, the chairman of the executive committee, and several directors and principal stockholders. In another operation among the participants were the president, the chairman of the executive committee, the treasurer, the counsel, several directors and vice-presidents. In another the president of the company received 25 per cent of the net profits.

That such collusion was the grossest breach of the fiduciary relationship is beyond dispute. It did, however, exist; and in certain circles it was considered a strictly legitimate activity.

Specialist Collusion. Another form of collusion involved specialists. The services of such members often proved valuable to the managers of the pools. Their knowledge of the market was first hand; this could be used to great advantage in timing pool operations. In numerous cases the manager of the syndicate would give discretionary orders to the specialist who was handling the account on the floor. By using his best judgment, he could conduct the pool's buying and selling operations so as to make the greatest possible profit for the pool.

That specialists benefited from such operations was clearly indicated by the Senate investigation of stock exchange practices. For example, in one of the Fox pools two specialists, who were vested with discretionary orders to execute on the exchange floor, received $42,000 as participants, plus a check of $10,000 from the manager in "appreciation for the work done in running an orderly market."[9]

Trading Pools. Two types of pools were present in the 1920's. One was known as a trading pool. It did not acquire its stock through options but bought it in the open market. The managers of these pools had to buy the stock in the open market at the most favorable price possible. There would, of course, be no purpose in running up the price of the stock unless the pool was able to unload it on the market at the new, high price. Several methods were used to purchase the stock. The first was to depress the price of the stock by short selling or dissemination of unfavorable publicity about the issue, thus forcing it down to prices advantageous to the pool. A second method was to stabilize the price; its failure to rise with the rest of the market made the stock unpopular. As owners shifted to other issues, the pool quietly acquired substantial blocks of it. The third method was to buy it at advancing prices, an expensive method at best. In trading pools the managers employed various devices, such as "shake-outs," to discourage public ownership until the pool had accumulated a sufficient supply of stock to justify price increases or "markups."

The famous Radio pool of 1929 was an example of a trading pool in which the manager used no options. Its operations will be described in more detail later on.

Option Pools. The option pool was one that acquired much, if not all, of its stock at fixed prices agreed upon before the pool started operations. These options were acquired from the corporation itself, large stockholders, directors, officers, banks, and speculators. The use of calls was often a device for acquiring stock. Once the option was acquired, the manager could exercise it at the stated price at any time during its life.

These options had various maturities. Some ran only three or four weeks; nearly half ran as long as one year. In one reported instance it ran for twenty-five years.

The options did not have to be exercised unless the price was favorable. In other words, if the option permitted the manager to acquire the stock at $50, it would not be exercised unless the price could be forced above this $50 limit. In a successful pool it was often raised substantially above the option price.

[9] *Ibid.*, p. 48.

Option pools were very common in the 1920's; a majority of them seem to have been conducted in that way. The Senate Committee found a record of 286 options involving 17,380,000 shares over the period 1929–33.[10]

The reasons for the popularity of the option pool were not hard to discover. The managers were assured a definite supply of stock at no financial risk; the makers of the options were often able to unload large amounts of undigested stock at attractive prices, and if calls were written, they received the usual premiums of $137.50 per 100 shares for thirty-day options. There were many option pools on record; e.g., Sinclair Consolidated Oil, American Commercial Alcohol, Goodyear Tire, Fox Theaters, Remington Rand, Curtiss-Wright, National Cash Register, Park and Tilford, National Steel, Crosley Radio, Canada Dry, Colgate-Palmolive-Peet, North American Aviation, Standard Brands, Republic Iron and Steel.

In many cases pool managers were able to secure, at no cost to the syndicates, options given by the corporation. These options involved authorized, but unissued, stock. Sometimes the options involved as much as 20 to 25 per cent of the outstanding stock. The reason the pool could obtain this option without expense was that many "insiders" profited from the pool operation; these directors and top executive officers were participants in the pool.

Several examples will indicate how an option pool operated. In the Sinclair Consolidated Oil pool, the managers received from the company an option to buy 1,130,000 shares at 30; this was about 20 per cent of all authorized stock.[11] At the time the negotiations over the option began, the stock was selling at 28. However, on the day the agreement was actually signed, the stock opened at 32 and closed at 35¾. On the next day it sold as high as 37¼ and closed at 36¾. The syndicate acquired the entire 1,130,000 shares at no risk to itself; these were disposed of at substantial profits in the market. In addition, the syndicate acquired 634,000 shares in the market and disposed of them at a gross profit of $465,000. It also sold short an additional 200,000 shares at a profit of $2 million.

In early 1933 there was great speculation in the so-called "repeal stocks." To take advantage of this situation, the American Commercial Alcohol pool was formed. It was given an option to buy 25,000 shares of that company's stock at $18 per share.[12] On the day that the directors actually authorized the issuance of the new stock, the price range of the stock was 30⅞ to 33½. The stock sold as high as 89⅞ within two months

10 *Ibid.*, p. 45.
11 *Ibid.*, p. 63.
12 *Ibid.*, p. 55.

after the option was given. Officers, directors, and principal stockholders made heavy profits from the pool's operations.

Publicity. Adequate publicity was an invaluable tool in the operations of a pool. Its purpose was to attract the general public into the stock and to keep it there until the pool had unloaded its holdings. Operations of the pool were carefully timed with news releases about earnings, dividends, new orders, stock splits, and favorable company developments. Even reports right at the time that the pool was operating were found beneficial to the price of the stock being manipulated. There were many ways to obtain publicity.

Tips and rumors were a profitable field of publicity. Such rumors, planted in receptive ears, found wide circulation. They flew from board room to board room, from trader to trader. Many eventually found their way over the ticker service and into financial news columns. Often there was no way to confirm or refute them. Why were they so often believed? Part of the answer, no doubt, was in the large extent of gullibility of the market in that period. On the other hand, many correct facts about corporate affairs first appeared as rumors and "news leaks." Not many persons were able to distinguish between actual fact and fabricated rumor.

Many brokerage firms were not above the practice of sponsoring stocks in which they were interested as pool participants or managers. These subtle references were often used to encourage speculators to purchase the pool stock. The method was the market letter issued by the firm. Seemingly objective analyses of the particular stock were used to attract outsiders.

Paid publicity experts were also highly effective in establishing public interest in the stock. One of these gentlemen made no less than $500,000 in three years; his compensation came from cash payments, stock options, and calls. One of his most effective devices was a short radio program entitled "The Friendly Economist." Presented each night at 10 o'clock, it reviewed the day's market and was judiciously interlaced with subtle comments about the profit possibilities of the pool stocks being sponsored. This particular expert was said to have conducted publicity for as many as 250 pools in three years, often as many as 30 at a time.[13] There were many instances of such paid publicity revealed by the Senate investigation of 1933–34.

Much of the pool publicity eventually found its way into newspapers. Glowing stories about company prospects often found ready acceptance in financial columns. These stories contained not only statements of fact but also forecasts of brilliant prospects. During the peak of activities in

[13] *Ibid.,* p. 44.

the Radio pool, a New York paper played up a story about how the company was planning to extend activity abroad, how its business was expanding, how many developments were pending, etc. In another paper a subsidized columnist reported that Radio was a wonder stock and making history every day; he stated that those who had sold it at 100 were buying it back, and the latest rumor was that it was going to 200 very soon. It did go to 109 and then the pool unloaded. It fell back to 80 within a month. This particular writer was found to have been given a guaranteed account at a brokerage firm; his profits in eight months were $20,000.

"Ticker support" was another publicity device. This consisted of getting on the stock exchange tape and the news ticker a constant stream of publicity. On the stock ticker this was done by repeated sales to attract attention; on the news ticker it was obtained by a succession of news stories about the corporation. The method was subtle but effective, since a great many traders in that day were "tape readers" and speculated almost entirely on the basis of the ticker tape action and reports.

Artificial Market Activity. A final device of the pool was artificial market activity. This consisted of a heavy "churning" of the stock in the market; it was bought and sold by the pool in heavy volume. If the public participated, the operation was easy; if not, the pool members bought and sold to each other. The principal objective was to step up the volume of sales.

Its purpose was obvious to all familiar with pool operations. The public must be attracted to the stock; few things attract speculators more quickly than a rising volume. The public's attitude became whetted in anticipation of "something big going on." It rushed in to buy before it was "too late." As the stock rose under increased activity, the public entered the market in ever increasing numbers; this was exactly the purpose of the operation.

Artificial market activity was accomplished in two different ways: (1) through matched orders and (2) without matched orders. In the former method the pool placed identical orders with two different brokers; e.g., one to buy 10,000 shares at 60 and one to sell 10,000 shares at 60. It was not a wash sale in the technical sense of the term because the 10,000 shares actually did change hands and two parties were involved. It had, however, the same net effect since both parties were members of the same pool. Such activities were hard to detect since orders were placed with different brokers and identification of the orders with pool memberships was carefully concealed. Matched orders were in violation of state law and the rules of the New York Stock Exchange; hence, they were only infrequently used.

The same effect as the matched order could be obtained without its actual use. The pool would buy and sell many thousands of shares in different orders of varying sizes. For a while it would sell on balance; then it would reverse its operations and buy on balance. Orders would vary in size from 5,000 to 25,000; they were placed with different brokers by different individuals. Such actions made detection difficult. As a matter of fact, there were no rules against such activities by the New York Stock Exchange. It was considered a perfectly legitimate activity.

The immense amount of artificial market activity which often accompanied the activity of large pools was often difficult for those outside the market to believe. Perhaps the classic example of this was the Radio pool of 1929. This pool began on March 12. In five days it bought 988,400 and sold 1,176,300 shares; during that time the stock rose from 93 to 109.[14] At the end of these five days, the pool was short 187,900 shares; this proved highly profitable since the stock dropped to 80 by the end of the month. As already indicated, the operations of the pool were very successful; the syndicate netted $4,900,000.

During the peak activity of the Sinclair Consolidated Oil pool of 1928, it was operated through a purchase and a trading syndicate. On one day alone, November 5, the two syndicates sold 101,000 shares and purchased 62,000 shares.[15] Similar activity was found in the operations of many other pools of the late 1920's.

Steps in a Pool Operation. Now that all of the devices of pool activity have been examined, it would be well to trace through the steps of a typical pool operation as it was practiced in the heyday of such activities.

The first step was to select an auspicious time for the operation. This would be one in which the market was in a position to make a substantial advance. The company's position would be suitable for good publicity, because of the fine earnings, attractive trade reports, increased dividends, or new developments.

The second was the accumulation of a supply of stock. As already indicated, this was obtained either by trading in the market or by options. Once this was assured, the pool was ready to begin extensive operations.

The next step was to create activity in the stock. This was done through artificial market activity; the pool was always careful to effect a change in beneficial ownership on each transaction. As this activity increased, the public became attracted to the stock.

The next operation was to create favorable interest in the stock through a steady flow of glowing publicity. Increased activity plus favor-

---

[14] *The Security Markets* (New York: Twentieth Century Fund, Inc., 1935), p. 479.
[15] *Stock Exchange Practices,* p. 65.

able reports made the stock a speculative favorite. Its price would then rise steadily, often precipitously.

The final step was distribution. The pool with its heavy accumulation of stock would seek to unload at advantageous prices. This required the highest skill that the manager could command. The problem was to distribute the stock without breaking the market. Stock would be sold on days when the market was strong and purchased when it was weak. Finally, the manager would find a day on which the market was especially strong; all of the remaining stock would be dumped on the market; in addition, he would short sell the issue heavily. Not long afterward the market, shorn of its artificial pool support, would collapse. The pool was a success for the participants; a disaster for the outsiders.

Present Regulations. Restrictive rules now make difficult, if not impossible, the pool operations of the 1920's. These rules have been formulated both by the exchanges and the SEC. The Securities Exchange Act of 1934 forbids manipulations in any form on national securities exchanges. Pool operations must be reported. No member of an exchange may participate in pool operations; he may not manage a pool; he cannot advance credit to one. Members may not execute orders for the purpose of creating an artificial appearance of activity in a security. Specialists may not execute discretionary orders. The market activities of corporate directors, executive officers, and principal stockholders are sharply curtailed. These and numerous other regulations are designed to curtail manipulative operations, which formed so much a part of the old market.

28

Securities Exchange Act

The present chapter will indicate the background for the Securities Exchange Act of 1934, the principal provisions of the Act, and the work of the Securities and Exchange Commission. Regulation in the stock market also comes from other sources. Forty-eight of the fifty states have adopted laws affecting securities transactions. Forty-four of these include: antifraud provisions, under which an agency of the state may act to protect the citizens in cases involving misrepresentation; required registration for securities dealers and salesmen; and registration of stock issues before sale within the state. The rules of the exchanges and other organizations in the market are significant also. Most importantly, however, the stock market requires of participants in it the highest standards of personal integrity. This requirement is imposed on traders on an exchange floor, the personnel of securities houses, and on customers. That there are failures on the part of some to hold such standards is evident, but it would be a mistake to suppose that the present institutions of the stock market could exist unless the overwhelming proportion of people associated with them did in fact hold to high standards.

BACKGROUND TO FEDERAL REGULATION

Federal Regulation Before 1933. The United States government did little in the way of regulating the stock market prior to 1933. Security dealers, of course, could not use the mails to defraud. This section of the postal laws applied to all types of business. Little use seems to have been made of postal laws in regulating the stock exchanges.

It might be said, therefore, that the stock exchanges before 1933 were regulated by their own rules and by state criminal and civil law. The statutes of New York and the court decisions of that state that related to the stock market were particularly important, since the two leading stock exchanges of the nation were located there. Control of such markets was not considered as being within the jurisdiction of the United States government.

Gold Speculation Act of 1864. A brief venture in federal regulation of speculation took place in 1864. At that time the nation was off the gold standard and the United States notes or "greenbacks" were fluctuating at various fractions of face value; as a result, gold was selling at substantial premiums in terms of paper currency. Much speculation took place in currency, and gold was bought and sold on the Exchange by brokers and dealers. Considerable bitterness developed in Congress over this situation; it was popularly believed that the federal currency was selling at a discount because of the speculation which was being carried on. The Gold Speculation Act of 1864 was passed, therefore, to forbid this practice; this promptly stopped speculation in the "Gold Room." To the amazement of Congress, however, the price of $100 in gold bullion in terms of paper currency immediately jumped from $200 to $300.[1] The law was repealed in fifteen days; it was something less than a complete success.

The Hughes Commission Report of 1909. An investigation of the stock market that received wide attention at the time took place in 1909. Charles Evans Hughes, then Governor of New York and later Chief Justice of the United States, appointed a commission to investigate security and commodity speculation. The commission was headed by Horace White, a noted authority on money and banking. Its report dealt extensively with the operation of the New York Stock Exchange.[2] The commission, while critical of a number of practices of the Exchange, believed that correction could be attained better by self-regulation than by any other method. It did not favor incorporation of the Exchange as a satisfactory solution of its criticisms. There was no suggestion in the report that federal control was either desirable or necessary. No investigation of equal importance by a public body was made of the stock market for another twenty years.

The Pujo Money Trust Inquiry of 1912. Although the 62d Congress authorized a committee to investigate Wall Street, the investigation centered largely in the concentration of economic control by a system of interlocking directorates of banks and corporations. Any investigation

---

[1] W. C. Antwerp, *The Stock Exchange from Within* (Garden City, N.Y.: Doubleday & Co., 1914), p. 251.

[2] New York State, *Report of Governor Hughes' Committee on Speculation in Securities and Commodities,* June 7, 1909.

of the stock exchanges that may have been made received little or no public attention.

The Market Decline of 1929–33. Two events of great importance serve as a background for the Securities Exchange Act of 1934. The first was the public clamor which developed from the precipitous drop in stock prices from 1929 to 1933. In that period declines in industrial stock prices of 89 per cent were registered by the Dow-Jones average and 87 per cent by that of *The New York Times*. The sharp declines, with resultant losses to thousands of small speculators and investors, brought about a great outcry for investigation and control of the securities markets. The pleas fell upon receptive political ears. Such a program of investigation and control would have been "good politics" in 1933 without regard to its economic merits.

The Senate Investigation of 1933–34. During the 72d and 73d sessions of Congress, the Senate Committee on Banking and Currency made a very thorough investigation of manipulation in the securities markets, as already indicated in Chapter 6. Out of this investigation came the Securities Exchange Act of 1934.

SECURITIES EXCHANGE ACT OF 1934

Purposes and Objectives. The Securities Exchange Act was passed for the broad purposes of regulating the securities exchanges and the over-the-counter market and preventing inequitable and unfair practices in such markets.[3] Specifically, it may be said to have these objectives: (1) to set up machinery to regulate these markets; (2) to limit the amount of speculative credit; (3) to regulate unfair practices of dealers and brokers in both the organized and unorganized securities markets; and (4) to insure that the general public receives adequate information about securities traded in such markets and that so-called "insiders," i.e., directors, officers, and large stockholders, do not benefit from an unfair use of such information. It was hoped that the attainment of these objectives would enable the markets to perform their expected functions more satisfactorily.

The SEC. The Act created a new federal body, the Securities and Exchange Commission.[4] It was to have five members, who were to be appointed by the President; each was to serve for a term of five years. The Commission was given very far-reaching powers to enforce the Act. Its headquarters were established in Washington, although during World War II the Commission was located temporarily in Philadelphia. It was

[3] Sec. 2.
[4] Sec. 4.

charged with enforcement of all sections of the Act except those dealing with control of speculative credit; these were given to the Board of Governors of the Federal Reserve System.

Exempted Securities. Securities exempted from provisions of the Act include: (1) direct obligations of the federal government; (2) those issued or guaranteed by corporations in which the United States government has a direct or indirect interest; (3) direct or guaranteed obligations of the states and their political subdivisions; and (4) any other securities that the SEC may deem necessary to exempt, such as unregistered securities and those of an intrastate character.[5]

Unregistered Exchanges. The SEC is permitted to exempt organized stock exchanges from registration.[6] These are small, local exchanges that have a very limited volume of transactions; registration is not considered necessary to protect the public interest in such cases. Four such exchanges have been given this status in recent years: Colorado Springs, Honolulu, Richmond, and Wheeling.

Registered Exchanges. Any exchange that operates in interstate or foreign commerce and through the mails must register with the SEC.[7] Under the procedure of registration, an exchange must file a registration statement as well as data on its organization, constitution, bylaws, rules of procedure, and membership. Registration will not be granted unless the exchange has adequate rules for the disciplining of members. The Commission may grant an application for registration or deny it. There is nothing in the Act that prevents an exchange from making and enforcing any rule or regulation it may deem proper; such rules, however, cannot be inconsistent with the Act, with regulations laid down under the Act, and with the statutes of the state in which the exchange is located. All of the larger exchanges are now registered under the Act; their number was fourteen in 1961.

A registered exchange pays an annual registration fee to the SEC. It is equal to 1/500 of 1 per cent of the aggregate dollar amount of sales of non-exempt securities.

Margin Requirements. The power to determine margin requirements is delegated to the Board of Governors of the Federal Reserve System, or the Federal Reserve Board, as it is commonly called.[8] Investigation and enforcement of the regulations, however, are in the hands of the SEC. Although the Act established initial margin requirements, the Board has changed these regulations a number of times since 1934. These

[5] Sec. 3 (12).
[6] Sec. 5.
[7] Sec. 6.
[8] Secs. 7 and 8.

regulations are popularly called Regulations T and U; they were examined in detail in Chapter 21. The purpose of such regulations is to prevent the excessive use of credit for purchasing and carrying securities.

The Act not only governs the amount of credit that may be extended for the purpose of buying and carrying securities, but also places severe restrictions on the source of such credit. In general, the Act seeks to prevent such credit from being extended by others than member banks of the Federal Reserve System, by non-member banks signing agreements with the Board, and by brokers and dealers under such rules as may be laid down by the Board. The most obvious source of credit affected by the Act is the loans of "others" or non-banking lenders, such as corporations, which were so important yet unstable in their lending operations in the 1929 market.

In addition, the Act prohibits a broker and dealer from permitting his aggregate indebtedness to exceed 2000 per cent of his net capital (exclusive of fixed assets and exchange membership).

Manipulation. A very important part of the Act deals with manipulation, which Congress found to be a real evil in the markets prior to the passage of the Act.[9] The prohibition against manipulation applies, not only to brokers and dealers, but to any person who uses the mails or the facilities of any national securities exchange.

Certain types of manipulation are definitely barred: (1) wash sales, (2) matched orders, (3) artificial market activity, (4) circulation of manipulative information for a remuneration, and (5) making false and misleading statements about securities.

In addition, the Act lists certain practices that, while not forbidden, are brought under control by the Act. They include: (1) pegging or price stabilization; (2) puts, calls, spreads, and straddles; (3) short sales; and (4) stop orders. In addition, the SEC is given power to make rules about any other manipulative or deceptive device in the public interest.

In summary, therefore, the Act defines and prohibits certain practices; it provides regulation for others, which are specifically identified; finally, it gives the SEC power to make other regulations in the public interest.

Segregation. A member of an exchange may operate in a transaction in either one of two capacities: as a broker or as a dealer. In the former he acts as an agent for a principal; in the latter he acts on his own behalf and for his own risk. On no occasion may a member act in both capacities in the same transaction; this has been a rule of law and the exchanges for years. Segregation would confine each member in all transactions he made to one or the other of the two activities; he could not engage alternately in one and then the other.

[9] Secs. 9 and 10.

The Act does not require segregation nor does it demand that the SEC effect segregation.[10] The SEC may make such rules as it believes in the public interest. For example, it may regulate or prohibit floor trading; it may make rules to prevent excessive trading by members of an exchange either on or off the floor. In addition, it may require the registration of odd-lot dealers and specialists and make rules to govern their activities. The section that deals with specialists is specific in stating a number of regulations about these members: (1) they should restrict activities to making a fair and orderly market; (2) they must disclose their books only under certain conditions; (3) they may accept only limited price and market orders when acting as brokers.

The Commission was also charged with the responsibility of studying the feasibility and advisability of complete segregation of the functions of dealer and broker. This report was made and duly presented to Congress.[11] The SEC has not seen fit to take any segregation measures.

Registration. No member of a registered exchange may effect a transaction on such an exchange except in registered securities; the only exceptions are exempt securities and those given unlisted trading privileges.

To register a security on a national securities exchange, the issuing company must file an extensive application with the exchange and with the SEC. This application contains a great amount of information about the company and its financial affairs. These are the principal items required:[12]

1. Organization, financial structure, and nature of the business
2. Terms, position, rights, and privileges of the different classes of securities outstanding
3. The terms on which their securities are to be, and during the preceding three years have been, offered to the public or otherwise
4. The directors, officers, and underwriters, and each security holder of the issuer; their remuneration and their interests in the securities of, and their material contracts with, the issuer
5. Remuneration to others than directors and officers exceeding $20,000 per year
6. Bonus and profit-sharing arrangements
7. Management and service contracts
8. Options existing or to be created in respect of their securities
9. Balance sheets for not more than three preceding fiscal years, certified, if required by the rules of the Commission, by independent public accountants
10. Profit and loss statements for not more than the three preceding fiscal years, certified, if required by the rules of the Commission, by independent public accountants

10 Sec. 11.
11 See Chapter 10.
12 Sec. 12.

11. Any further financial statements required by the Commission
12. Copies of articles of incorporation, bylaws, trust indentures, underwriting agreements, etc., as the Commission may require

It will thus be seen that the Act requires a great body of information for the protection of investors. It is similar to that required for listing on the New York Stock Exchange; in fact, the same information is now used for both listing and registration.

The process of registration consists of the issuer's filing with both the exchange and the SEC a registration statement conforming to the rules of the Commission, and the certification by the exchange to the Commission that it has received a registration statement and has approved the particular securities for listing and registration. Registration becomes automatically effective thirty days after the receipt by the Commission of the exchange's certification; it may, however, become effective within a shorter period by order of the SEC.

Information on Remuneration. It was noted among the requirements for registration that the issuer must divulge salaries and other payments to all directors, officers, and other employees in excess of $20,000 per year. The purpose of this requirement is to allow investors and stockholders to determine whether a company is paying unreasonable salaries and fees. In the past, certain corporations were notorious in paying exorbitant salaries to so-called "insiders" at the same time that they were paying few or no dividends. Information on remuneration would enable an alert body of stockholders to protect its best interests in case such an event should arise.

Periodic Reports on Registered Securities. Issuers of registered securities must file periodic reports each year to keep the information in the registration statements reasonably up to date. Of particular interest to investors is the requirement about annual financial statements. The periodic reports, as well as the original registration statements submitted by issuers, are available for public inspection at the offices of the Commission and the regional offices and are widely used by financial services, publishers of securities manuals, and advisory services; thus, their information is widely disseminated.

"Insider" Holdings of Stock. An important section of the Act pertains to the reporting of holdings in equity securities by so-called "insiders."[13] An "insider" is a director, executive officer, or a stockholder who owns 10 per cent or more of any class of stock. The names of these parties are filed with the Commission at the time of registration, as already noted. In addition, anyone who attains this status after registration of the security

13 Sec. 16.

must file his holdings of stock within ten days. If there is any change in such ownership in a given month, the "insider" must file a report within ten days after the close of the calendar month; this report indicates this ownership at the close of the month and such changes as have occurred during the month.

The purpose of this regulation is to enable the SEC and stockholders of the company to watch the actions of such holders, who may speculate in their own stocks to make profits on the basis of insider information. Such information is given out through public releases of the SEC.

Short-Term Profits of "Insiders." A further provision of the Act limits the right of "insiders" to speculate in the stock of their own companies.[14] Any profit from the purchase or sale of the stock realized within a period of six months can be recaptured for the company. A suit to recover this profit may be brought either by the issuing corporation or by a stockholder on behalf of the company.

The purpose of this provision is to prevent such individuals from speculating in the stocks of their companies on the basis of an unfair use of confidential information. It does not, however, prevent speculation for a period longer than six months. For example, a top executive in an important automobile company in 1935 purchased 6,000 shares of his company's stock at 44 and sold it a year later at 77; he thus realized a gross profit of about $200,000.[15]

Some criticism is made of this section of the Act in that it may discourage the ownership of stocks by the top management. It is possible that some evasion of the Act is possible in that there would be nothing to prevent an executive of one steel company, who felt optimistic about the prospects of the entire steel industry, from buying the stock of another steel company. This is true of course, but the profit opportunities are not so certain and the abuses of confidential information are not so flagrant as they formerly were. Certainly, the provision is an advance in business ethics over conditions prevailing before World War I, when it was a common practice of corporate boards of directors to declare or pass dividends at board meetings and then run to the nearest telephone to order brokers to buy or sell the stock before the information was released to the general public.

The taking of short-term profits was, at one time, a very common practice. A prominent newspaper interviewed a number of corporate directors in 1915; 90 per cent of them stated that they speculated in the stocks of their own companies and that they considered this to be a legitimate compensation for their services.[16]

[14] Sec. 16.
[15] *Thirteenth Annual Report of the SEC*, 1947, p. 40.
[16] *New York Times Annalist*, 1915, VI, p. 65.

The SEC reports a number of cases which have come to its attention where companies have recovered short-term profits; these are often returned voluntarily by "insiders" because of the filing of reports.[17]

Short Selling by "Insiders." A provision similar to that on short-term profits is the one on short selling by "insiders." These individuals may not sell a stock of the issuer (1) that they do not own or (2) if owning the security they do not deliver it against such a sale within twenty days thereafter, or do not deposit it in the mails within five days. It will be seen that this provision covers not only the speculative short sale in which the seller must borrow the stocks; it also covers the sale "against the box" in which the seller owns the stock but is making a short sale as a hedge against a drop in the price of securities owned.

The purpose of this section is also to prevent the "insider" from taking an unfair advantage of confidential information. The practice at one time was very common, particularly during periods of severe market declines.

Proxy Regulations. The Act also provides that the SEC shall make regulations about the issue of proxies by registered issuers.[18] When solicitations for proxies, consents, or other authorizations from holders of registered securities are made, the security holder must be supplied with a reasonable amount of information so that he may make an informed judgment on the merits of the proposal when he votes. The information must be complete and accurate. A copy of the proxy, consent, and authorization must be filed with the Commission for review before solicitation is possible.

Termination of Registration. The SEC is given the power to deny registration to a security, to suspend the effective date, to suspend registration, or to withdraw it from registration if it finds that the issuer has failed to comply with the Act or any regulations made under it.[19] The Commission would prefer that the exchange take this action itself, but it holds this weapon in reserve in case action is not taken to protect the interests of the public. The power has been used sparingly. In the year ending June 30, 1960, the SEC reported four instances and, in 1961, one instance of withdrawal of registration from securities traded on a national stock exchange.[20]

Registration and Listing. Now that the chief aspects of registration under the Act have been stated, it may be well to make some comparisons between registration and listing. It may be supposed that listing and

[17] *Thirteenth Annual Report of the SEC*, 1947, p. 41.

[18] Sec. 16.

[19] Sec. 19.

[20] *Twenty-Sixth Annual Report of the SEC*, 1960, pp. 74–79; *Twenty-Seventh Annual Report of the SEC*, 1961, p. 62.

registration represent a duplication of the activities of the work of the stock list department and the SEC. In some cases this is true, since much of the information required at the time of listing is also required at registration and, as a matter of fact, the same information is used for both operations.

The listing standards of an exchange, such as the New York Stock Exchange, however, still play an important part in determining the desirability of securities for listing. The Exchange must decide whether there is a listed market for a given stock. It is free to make, and has initiated, a number of excellent listing policies in recent years, such as those on depreciation, accounting standards, and voting rights of stock. While listing standards are not so vital to public protection as they once were because of registration requirements, they still have a real function in protecting the public and making a free market. This is particularly true when additional shares of a registered issue are sold. No new registration statement is required, but new listing information must be filed and thus becomes available.

Investors in listed securities have more information about these issues than ever before. Such a condition is highly desirable; it is up to the public to use the information wisely. Neither the exchanges nor the SEC can or does guarantee any security. The buyer must take the responsibility for purchase and ownership. The public would seem to have been given reasonable protection.

Unlisted Trading. The Act permits the Commission to make rules and regulations that admit securities to unlisted trading privileges in spite of the section that permits trading on national securities exchanges only in registered and exempt securities. Although three conditions permit such trading, in practice the only two types of securities now admitted to such privileges are (1) those admitted to unlisted trading privileges prior to March 1, 1934, and (2) those already listed on another exchange. In 1961 there were 212 common and preferred stocks given trading privileges on all exchanges under the first condition; these were registered on no exchange.[21] Under the second condition, a great many more were given unlisted trading privileges on certain exchanges but were registered on some other exchange, usually the New York Stock Exchange. The primary market for these stocks was in New York, but the regional exchanges were attempting to build up markets for them through unlisted trading privileges granted by the SEC.

The third condition under which unlisted trading privileges could be granted was in the case of securities covered by the Securities Act of 1933. Almost no privileges have been granted under this condition.

[21] *Twenty-Seventh Annual Report of the SEC*, 1961, p. 63.

Over-the-Counter Markets. The Act as originally passed in 1934 did not make specific regulations about the over-the-counter market; it merely gave the SEC power to make such rules and regulations as it saw fit.[22] In 1936 the Act was amended to provide for the registration of all brokers and dealers who do business in this market. In 1960 there were 5,288 brokers and dealers so registered. This registration consists of filing with the SEC an application that contains such information as is considered desirable by the Commission.

In its regulations of brokers and dealers in this market, the SEC has the power to deny registration, to revoke registration, and suspend or expel from membership in the National Association of Securities Dealers (NASD). During the fiscal year ending June 30, 1960, some 106 such proceedings were instituted. The SEC also has the power to make examinations of the books and records of registered brokers and dealers, who are required to file financial reports each calendar year. An important regulation is that no broker or dealer may permit his aggregate indebtedness to exceed twenty times his net capital.

Section 15A, or the Maloney Act, as it is sometimes called, was introduced as an amendment to the Act in 1938, together with several sections which deal with manipulation and other fraudulent and deceptive practices in the market. The Maloney Act provides for self-regulation by associations of brokers and dealers. To date, only the NASD has been organized; this organization is examined in Chapter 24. The SEC is given the right of supervision over the activities of the NASD. It reviews disciplinary action by that organization on its own motion or on application by any aggrieved person.

Enforcement of the Act. Enforcement of the Exchange Act and its rules is obtainable in a number of ways. Criminal penalties include fines up to $10,000 and imprisonment up to two years for individuals and fines up to $500,000 for exchanges.

Civil suits by injured parties are permitted under the Act; these suits may be brought only in federal courts. Thus, injured individuals become part of the enforcement machinery of the law.

The Commission itself has many actions which it may take to enforce the Act and the rules under it.[23] This is a list of methods available:

1. Withdrawal or suspension of an exchange from registration
2. Expulsion or suspension of a member or officer of an exchange, or an allied member
3. Suspension of trading in a particular security

[22] Sec. 32.
[23] Secs. 3, 17, 19, 21, and 22.

4. Request exchanges to make changes in organization or to prescribe rules for trading. In the event an exchange refuses, the SEC has broad powers to make such changes and rules in its own right.
5. Require exchanges and their members to keep such books and records as may be necessary; to examine such books and records; and to require reports when necessary
6. Make investigations and conduct hearings to assist in the enforcement of the Act
7. Prevent violations of the Act by injunctions
8. Compel compliance with the Act by writs of mandamus

In summary, the Act permits a very extensive amount of self-regulation in securities markets; the markets and exchanges may make their own rules and regulations so long as they are not inconsistent with the Act and the regulations of the SEC. In the last analysis, the SEC possesses the well-known "iron hand within the velvet glove" which it can use as a last resort.

It is worth noting that civil injunctions and criminal prosecutions may be used against anyone who engages in securities transactions, whether or not he is in the securities business. Administrative measures by the SEC, however, may be directed only against exchanges, registered associations, and registered brokers and dealers.

THE SEC AND ITS WORK

Much of the work of the SEC has already been discussed in this and in preceding chapters of this book. Only a brief summary, therefore, will be given at this point.

Staff. The SEC consists of five appointive members. Assisting it is a staff of 1,000 lawyers, accountants, engineers, security analysts, examiners, and clerical and administrative employees. The Commission maintains its headquarters at Washington, D.C. To facilitate its work, it has set up ten regional offices; the largest of these is in New York.

The work of the Commission has been subdivided into a number of operating divisions. The one that is primarily responsible for administering the Act of 1934 is the Trading and Exchange Division. This is further broken down into subdivisions on exchange trading, exchange regulations, research and statistics, and over-the-counter regulations. The legal and registration divisions also aid in enforcing the Act.

Administered Acts. Only part of the activities of the Commission are concerned with the Securities Exchange Act of 1934. Other acts include the Securities Act of 1933, the Public Utility Holding Company Act of 1935, the Investment Company Act of 1940, and the Investment Advisers Act of 1940. Certain duties are also delegated to it in connection with Chapter X of the National Bankruptcy Act.

Investigations. A final word needs to be said about the investigative work of the Commission. One type of investigation starts with "tape watching." The Commission has ticker service from the New York Stock Exchange and the American Stock Exchange. In addition, it receives the Dow-Jones financial news ticker service. In the New York office, for example, one man at all times watches these services. Any irregularity in trading activity on either of the exchange tapes is noted as soon as possible. Let us suppose, for example, that a very inactive stock suddenly takes on great activity and shows unusual price changes. An explanation is sought at once. If the explanation is legitimate, such as a change in the company's financial standing, earnings, dividends, or orders that explains the activity, the matter is dismissed. If, however, it appears that manipulation may be present and that news reports do not give any clue as to the activity, then an investigation starts. It may not stop until the staff has discussed the matter with brokers, customers, and officers of the corporation. Any action taken will depend on whether a violation of the Securities Exchange Act and its accompanying rules has taken place. It may be necessary to watch a particular security from two weeks to three months. The Commission is concerned at no time with prices or volume as such; it is concerned only when dealers, brokers, customers, or security issues may be violating the law.

The SEC conducts many kinds of investigations to determine violations of rules and practices. These may start on its own initiative, either on routine checks or because of evidences of violation; they may come from inquiries or complaints by customers, brokers, or dealers; inspection of broker and dealer records may bring irregularities to light. Investigations for the most part are conducted privately. Facts are brought out by informal inquiries and the examination of witnesses, books, and records. If necessary, the Commission has power to take more formal steps and may apply to a federal court for aid.

The regional offices are primarily responsible for the investigative and enforcement work of the Commission. Investigations of unusual market activity are kept confidential as much as possible since publicity may affect the market as well as the individuals concerned. Two forms of investigation of such activity may be used: (1) the "flying quiz" and (2) the formal investigation. In the "flying quiz" a quiet but speedy investigation is made to determine unusual market behavior. If the facts discovered warrant it, a formal investigation is ordered; material may be subpoenaed and testimony may be taken under oath; many records may be searched over a considerable period before the investigation is over. If the "flying quiz" is effective, the formal investigation may never be necessary.

INVESTOR RESPONSIBILITY

In a statement of its work, the SEC points to the need for investor responsibility in the stock market. The comment reads: "It should be understood that the securities laws were designed to facilitate informed investment analyses and prudent and discriminating investment decisions *by the investing public,* and that it is the investor and *not* the Commission who must make the ultimate judgment of the worth of securities offered for sale."[24]

24 *The Work of the Securities and Exchange Commission,* April 1, 1958, p. v.

V

INVESTING PRACTICES
AND
SPECIAL INSTRUMENTS

29

Stock Price Averages
and Indexes

This and the next several chapters are concerned with factors affecting investment opportunities and results. Often of major importance is price increase or decline, and the present chapter discusses the usual ways in which price movements for the stock market as a whole are measured. The next is concerned with relationships between stock prices and changes in economic activity. The third discusses selection of investments for a portfolio. Subsequent chapters are descriptive of different plans and techniques that some investors have used to aid their decisions on timing of purchases and sales and of different special instruments that may be helpful under certain conditions for investment operations.

The daily newspapers and investment services publish a number of stock price averages and indexes. The New York Stock Exchanges also publishes a stock price profile, which shows stock price changes in a different and meaningful way. As Figure 29-1 indicates, price movements over the years have been wide, but a general, continuing upward trend has been characteristic.

STOCK PRICE AVERAGES

There are a number of well-known stock price averages. Certain characteristics are common to all.

Common Characteristics. These averages are all based on what is considered to be a representative list of issues. The list may number from 15 or 20 upward. Usually, the full list is divided into at least two subdivisions: the industrials and the rails. Separate averages of the prices

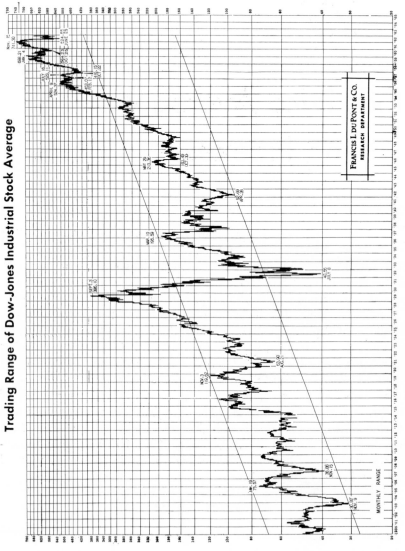

Fig. 29–1. The Dow-Jones industrial average.

of stocks in these subdivisions are computed and published. A third group, public utilities, is added to the more complex averages. If there is no public utilities group, per se, one or more outstanding utility issues is added to the industrial classification. The usual method of computation is to add the daily prices of the issues and divide by some sort of divisor. The typical average is unweighted in the sense that the importance of the company in the market or in the economy is not considered. The averages are weighted, however, in that the higher-priced stocks have more effect than the lower-priced ones. Stock price averages always show closing prices for the day, at least. They also show, as a rule, the high and low for the day. At least one average, the Dow-Jones average, is computed hourly. Many of the services publishing stock price averages have booklets that show the averages in detail as far back as they have been computed.

Problems after Original Computation. Unfortunately for the editors of the averages, these devices constantly present problems of compilation. There are three main problems, and each service has developed routine methods of dealing with them. The first is making substitutions; the second, changing the size of the list; and the third, adjusting for stock splits.

Making Substitutions. It is occasionally necessary for a service to drop one stock and add another. The dropped issue may have declined in importance. Again, it may have disappeared in a merger or consolidation. Sometimes it may become subject to such unusual influences that it is no longer considered a representative issue. Two possibilities present themselves to the editor of the average. One would be to select another stock in the same industry that sells at about the same price. If one selling at the exact price is not obtainable (the usual situation), the difference between the prices of the old and new issues could be adjusted for by adding to, or subtracting from, the average a certain number of dollars. This is not a very sound statistical procedure, but works satisfactorily for rough accuracy. A second method would be to adjust the divisor as described below.

It is not usually necessary to make many substitutions. From 1950 to 1955, inclusive, there was no change in the Dow-Jones industrial average and only two changes in the rail average. From 1956 to 1961 five substitutions were made in the industrial and one more in the rail averages. The dropping of Northern Pacific from the rail average in 1952 is illustrative of such substitutions. In that year oil was discovered in the Williston basin in which the road had substantial land holdings. The stock became so erratic in behavior that it was dropped and a more stable issue was added to the list.

Changing the Size of the List. This situation would arise if it were desired to increase an average from, say, 25 to 30 stocks, or the reverse. The average for the new list must be made equal to the average of the old list at some point of time if a continuing series is to be published. This could be done either by recomputing the old average over its entire period to conform to the average of the new list or by using a divisor that makes the new average identical to the old at the moment of change in the list. Fortunately for the editors of the averages, this situation seldom arises. For example, the Dow-Jones industrial and rail averages have remained constant in number since 1928 and the public utility average since 1938.

Adjusting for Stock Splits. An ever-recurring problem is that of adjusting the average for stock splits. These occur with great frequency in periods of bull markets. For example, in 1955 no less than 72 common stocks on the New York Stock Exchange were split two for one or better. The splitting of a stock presents a serious problem. Let us suppose that a stock selling at $250 is split five for one as was Eastman Kodak a few years ago. In this case $200 is immediately subtracted from the total. If it were a 25-stock average, this would mean a drop of $8 per stock. The average would then show a sharp decline, which would not be appropriate. There are three possible methods of adjustment.

First, another stock could be substituted. This was formerly done in some averages, but was difficult to do, since stocks in the same industry and at the same price level are hard to find. If the stock were an important one, this method would be severely criticized.

A second method would be to use a multiplier. If the stock were split five for one, the new price would be multiplied by five. If it were split two for one, the new price would be multiplied by two. This is an acceptable method of operation.

A third possibility is to change the divisor so that the level of the average remains unchanged. This method is used by the editor of the Dow-Jones averages. The divisor is merely a figure, which, when divided into the new aggregate of prices, will give the same level on the new basis as that reported on the old basis on the day before the new divisor was put into use. A simple example will illustrate this method. Let us suppose that we have an average of only three stocks:

Stock	Price
A	20
B	25
C	45

$$3\overline{)90}$$
$$30$$

Stock C is now split three for one; its price falls to 15. The aggregate of the three stocks is now 60, which divided by 3 would give 20. Obviously, no editor could allow this average to fall from 30 to 20. At this point the divisor is changed. Its formula is:

$$\text{Divisor} = \frac{\text{New price aggregate}}{\text{Old average price}}$$

If we solve with this formula, we get:

$$\text{Divisor} = \frac{60}{30} = 2$$

Applying the new divisor of two to the new price aggregate, we get:

$$\frac{60}{2} = 30$$

The average is now restored to 30 and the level is unaffected by the three-for-one split.

In 1962 the Dow-Jones industrial average was employing a divisor of 2.988, the rail average was using one of 5.34, and the utility average had one of 6.55. The entire 65-stock average had a divisor of 15.46. The theory behind the changes of divisor as used by this service is that no one stock should be counted more than once. This theory necessitates the use of the divisor change and rejects the alternate theory that multiplication by the amount of the split is a suitable adjustment.

The Dow-Jones Averages. These are probably the best known of all of the averages. For this reason, and because their characteristics are for the most part common to other popular averages, they will be discussed in somewhat more detail below. These averages were developed by Charles Dow, founder of the Dow-Jones Company, publisher of the *Wall Street Journal*. He developed the theory of the average. His first list went back as far as 1884 and consisted of only 11 stocks.[1] As will be observed, it was almost entirely a rail average, railroad shares being the leading stocks at that time:

Chicago & North Western	New York Central
Delaware, Lackawanna &	Northern Pacific Preferred
Western	Pacific Mail
Lake Shore	St. Paul
Louisville & Nashville	Union Pacific
Missouri Pacific	Western Union

[1] *The Dow-Jones Averages* (New York: Barron's, 1931), p. 5.

The original average of 11 stocks was converted into a 20-stock rail average in 1897. This number has been retained to the present. The use of the constant divisor was introduced in 1928. The rail average in late 1961 consisted of these stocks:

Atchison	Illinois Central
Atlantic Coast Line	Kansas City Southern
Baltimore & Ohio	Louisville & Nashville
Canadian Pacific	New York Central
Chesapeake & Ohio	New York, Chicago &
Chicago & North Western	St. Louis
Chicago, Rock Island &	Norfolk & Western
Pacific	Pennsylvania
Delaware & Hudson	Southern Pacific
Erie-Lackawanna	Southern Railway
Great Northern	Union Pacific

The first Dow-Jones list of industrials consisted of 12 stocks and goes back as far as 1897. In 1916 a number of changes were made and the list was increased to 20. Prior to 1928 the company used the policy of frequent substitutions and also the multiplication method to adjust for stock splits. In that year it was decided to adopt the constant divisor method, which has been used ever since. In the same period the list was increased to 30 stocks. A number of changes in the stocks have been made since 1928, but the size of the list has remained the same. The list in December, 1961, included the following stocks:

Allied Chemical	International Nickel
Aluminum Company	International Paper
American Can	Johns-Manville
American Tel. & Tel.	Owens-Illinois Glass
American Tobacco	Proctor and Gamble
Anaconda	Sears Roebuck
Bethlehem Steel	Standard Oil of Calif.
Chrysler	Standard Oil (N.J.)
Du Pont	Swift & Company
Eastman Kodak	Texaco
General Electric	Union Carbide
General Foods	United Aircraft
General Motors	United States Steel
Goodyear	Westinghouse Electric
International Harvester	Woolworth

The first utility average was introduced in 1929, when a list of 18 stocks was compiled. This was increased to 20, but in 1938 was reduced to the present level of 15:

American Electric Power	Niagara Mohawk Power
Cleveland Electric Illum.	Pacific Gas & Electric
Columbia Gas System	Panhandle E. P. & L.
Commonwealth Edison	Peoples Gas
Consolidated Edison	Philadelphia Electric
Consol. Natural Gas	Pub. Ser. E. & Gas
Detroit Edison	Southern Cal. Edison
Houston Light & Power	

The Dow-Jones averages are quite popular among investors. Several reasons account for this popularity. They are the oldest of the averages, running back more than half a century, as indicated. They are the best known and enjoy a very wide press distribution. Finally, they enjoy a special advantage not possessed by any other averages. This special advantage gives them a certain respect, which greatly contributes to their use. The advantage is that they are used for the interpretation of the famous Dow theory. However sound the theory may be is a matter of personal judgment. The important thing is that many devoted followers of this theory feel that no other averages, however good, can be used in the interpretation of this theory. It might also be noted that the Dow-Jones industrial average is used extensively in the construction of formula trading plans, which are described in detail in Chapter 33.

A number of adverse criticisms have been and can be made of the Dow-Jones averages. Six will be mentioned here.

The first is the use of American Telephone and Telegraph stock in the industrial average. This is usually classified as a utility; its high price tends to give it substantial weight in the average; and its relative stability of price has at times made for a dubious stability in the average. This stock was part of the utility average in 1931 and was then transferred to the industrial average.

A second criticism is that the Dow-Jones averages do not include large enough samples of stock. This is particularly true of the industrial average. Many question whether only 30 industrial issues are representative of the vast list of stocks in that classification.

Another criticism is that the industrial average is made up entirely of what might be called "blue chips," or high-grade and high-priced stocks. As such, it is not a representative list. No low-priced issues of less than top-grade are used. This is a definite weakness when one realizes that low-priced issues often show a different trend from that of "blue chips."

The inflated character of the averages is another limitation. The industrial average was above the 700 level in the latter part of 1961. Not a single stock in the average was near that price. The average stock in the average was selling at slightly above 72. As a result, slight percentage changes in the industrial average result in unrealistic movements in the average on a point basis. This was illustrated in the "Eisenhower break" of September, 1955. The industrial average fell 32 points on Monday, September 26. This sounds large. It was, however, a drop of only about 6 per cent and took the average back to the level at which it was on August 15, just six weeks earlier. Similarly, the 35 point drop in the average on May 28, 1962, was only a 6 per cent drop. A simple way to deflate the industrial average is to divide it by ten; this will give a better picture of how stocks really are and how significant is the day-to-day change in points.

Professional statisticians find many technical weaknesses in the Dow-Jones averages. These apply to all averages. Two are noteworthy at this point. One is the lack of weighting. The higher priced a stock is, the more weight it carries in the average. This is true regardless of how important the company may be or how many shares it has outstanding. A small company with high-priced stock is much more important than a giant company with low-priced stock. For example, in 1961 Woolworth had twice the influence of Standard Oil Company (New Jersey) in the Dow-Jones industrial average. Du Pont stock carried more weight in that year than did United States Steel, General Motors, General Electric, and Westinghouse Electric combined. Eastman Kodak carried almost twice as much weight as General Motors, the greatest industrial corporation in the country. A sound statistical formula for measuring stock prices should weight each stock on the basis of its relative importance in terms of aggregate market value or volume of trading or other means for measuring its significance in the market. This the Dow-Jones averages fail to do.

A final criticism is that the averages are subject to unfortunate influences because of stock splits. Every time a stock is split, its influence drops in direct ratio to the split. When Eastman Kodak split its stock five for one and two for one, its influence declined by 90 per cent. In recent years United States Steel split its stock three for one and two for one. As a result, its influence fell 83 per cent. A similar situation was true for General Motors. This characteristic of computation of the average tends to reduce the effect of gains by the more successful companies. They tend to split their stocks more frequently. Over a period, therefore, the average fails to rise as fast as it might otherwise. A comparison over the full period shown in Figure 29–2 between the Standard and Poor's index and the Dow-Jones industrial average reflects this characteristic.

The New York Times Averages. These well-known averages possess many of the same characteristics, advantages, and weaknesses of the

Dow-Jones averages. Hence, their discussion will be limited. They consist of an industrial average of 25 high-grade issues, including one public utility, American Telephone and Telegraph Company, and a rail average of 25 leading railroad stocks. The averages, as published, consist of three simple, arithmetic averages of high, low, and closing prices. The averages go back as far as 1911.

The problem of stock splits is handled differently from the Dow-Jones method. In earlier years the method of substitution was used. In 1925 it was decided to change to the multiplier system. Each time a stock is split, the new price is multiplied by the amount of the split. This policy leads to rather large multipliers. For example, du Pont prices are multiplied by fourteen and International Harvester prices by twelve.

The failure to weight the prices in this average by some fair measure of market importance often leads to certain stocks having a disproportionate influence on the industrial average. For example, several years ago Firestone had five times as much influence on the index as General Motors, and du Pont had seven times as much influence as Standard Oil Company (New Jersey).

These averages are sensitive indicators of stock prices and often move more rapidly in the stock cycle than do indexes covering more issues. They represent a good sampling of high-grade industrials and rails.

The *New York Herald Tribune* Averages. These averages are now available in published form as far back as 1925, although the computation of the averages themselves dates back to 1923. These averages are somewhat more comprehensive than the two averages just described. The list is divided into 70 industrials and 30 rails, a total of 100 issues. The 70 industrials are again broken down into the following subgroups:

15 manufacturing issues
10 oil issues
 8 public utilities
 6 steels
 7 coppers
 4 equipments
 5 stores
10 motors
 5 food stocks
―――
70 industrials

The 30 rail issues are also broken down into 20 Grade A rails and 10 Grade B issues. The ratings A and B are assigned by the editor. The paper also has a separate average for 10 aircraft stocks.

The problem of stock splits usually is taken care of in these averages by the method of substitution. Immediately after a substitution becomes necessary, the item is dropped and the remaining stocks in a group are weighted to maintain the average; a substitution is then made as soon as a satisfactory substitute issue can be found. Because of the large number of issues in the averages, the effect of substitutions is believed to be less damaging to the average than it would be if there were a smaller number of components.

The averages are recorded in terms of high, low, and closing daily prices; the computations usually are made by simple, arithmetic averages. In other words, the aggregates of each group are divided by the number of different issues involved.

The advantage of the *Herald Tribune* averages over the Dow-Jones and *The New York Times* averages is that they give a considerably wider sampling of the list of New York Stock Exchange stocks. As already indicated, there are nine separate subgroups of industrials and two subgroups of rails. An investor can, therefore, follow each subgroup with greater facility than with the other two averages. These averages however, suffer from the same statistical weaknesses as were noted for the Dow-Jones averages.

The Associated Press Averages. The Associated Press also compiles and releases its own 60-stock averages which are widely distributed. These are broken down into 30 industrials, 15 rails, and 15 public utilities. These averages bear a close resemblance to the averages of the Dow-Jones Company.

The Moody Averages. The Moody Service prepares an extensive stock average; it is based on 125 industrials, 25 public utilities, 25 railroads, 15 banks, and 10 insurance issues; the total is 200 stocks. The service also compiles yields and dividends per share for these issues. These are the most comprehensive of the stock averages in general use.

Choice of an Average. The choice of an average by the market trader is perhaps not as great a problem as it might appear to be. In daily fluctuations the averages go up and down together more than 90 per cent of the time. A comparison of the larger movements of stock price levels as measured by the averages discussed above is shown in Figure 29–2. The great similarity is apparent. Often the same day marked the beginning of a move for all four measures. None showed any particular superiority in anticipating these turning points in stock price cycles.

STOCK PRICE INDEXES

Common Characteristics. Stock price indexes are more refined methods of measuring changes in the level of stock prices than are the averages. All use base periods, which vary from index to index, such as 1926, 1935–

COMPARISON OF LEADING STOCK MARKET AVERAGES

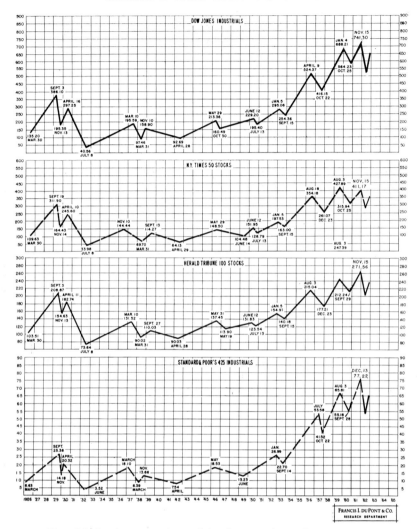

Fig. 29–2. A comparison of leading stock market averages.

39, 1939, and 1940. They are weighted by various methods, a common method being the number of shares outstanding for each stock multiplied by the price per share of the stock. The number of stocks used is invariably large, sometimes running into as much as 500 or more issues. Precise, statistical formulas are used to eliminate the statistical weaknesses present in averages. As a result, the indexes are extremely useful in measuring changes in the entire market. Often the indexes are broken down into a large number of stock groups, which give a more representative picture of what various industries are doing.

Despite their advantages traders find certain objections to them. There is a popular belief that certain averages, despite thier limitations, are more sensitive than the indexes with their larger stock lists. As a rule, the indexes are not given as wide publicity as are the averages. Excepting Standard and Poor's, most of the indexes are computed on a weekly basis, which is too infrequent for many traders. For these reasons the average is still more popular than the index. The statistician may prefer the index, but the market operator clings to his average.

Standard and Poor's Indexes. Prior to 1957 this service used two indexes, a daily and a weekly index. In 1957 the service scrapped these indexes for a modern index of 500 stocks, calculated hourly by a high-speed electronic computer. It is based on 425 industrials, 25 railroads, and 50 utilities. The base period, computed as an average of the years 1941–43, is given a value of 10. The index is carefully weighted according to the importance of the various stocks used. The 500 stocks represent the prices of shares comprising from 90 to 95 per cent of the value of New York Stock Exchange common stock issues held by the investors. Because of its careful weighting, wide sampling, and almost instantaneous calculation, the index justifies a very high rating and fairly extensive use.

SEC Index. The Securities and Exchange Commission introduced a stock index in 1951 which is now widely distributed. It now uses 1957–59 as a base period of 100 and is composed of 300 stocks. The index is broken down into five main classifications: manufacturing; transportation; utilities; trade, finance and service; and mining. The index is well constructed.

Merrill Lynch Index. The brokerage firm of Merrill Lynch, Pierce, Fenner and Smith publishes the index with the largest sampling of stocks. It includes 540 stocks broken down into 112 classifications. The base period is 1940. Computations are made on both arithmetic and geometric scales.

Comparison of Indexes and Averages. As has been indicated, there is a belief that averages are more sensitive to market changes than are indexes. The comparison of the measures shown in Figure 29–2, however, provides little basis for distinction. For short periods any average or index appears adequate to reflect market moves. For longer periods the better constructed indexes warrant greater consideration.

Bond Averages. For those interested in changes in bond prices, there are a number of well-constructed averages. Dow-Jones prepares a 40-bond average, subdivided into 10 first- and 10 second-grade rail issues,

10 public utilities, and 10 industrial bonds. In addition, it has an average for income rail bonds. The Associated Press publishes averages for 20 rails, 10 industrials, 10 utilities, and 10 foreign bonds. *The New York Times* prepares a 40-bond average; its subgroups are 20 rails, 10 industrials, and 10 utilities. The *Herald Tribune* has a 30-bond average; its subgroups are 10 first-grade rails, 5 second-grade rails, 10 industrials, and 5 utilities. The Standard and Poor's Corporation publishes a high-grade average of 11 industrial, utility, and railroad bonds and one of 12 medium-grade bonds; in addition, it has a 15-bond municipal average. Moody's Service also has very complete bond averages, based upon different ratings.

30

Stock Prices and Levels of Economic Activity

Perhaps the most difficult aspect of the stock market is understanding the many factors and conditions that affect stock prices. There is no easy road to fathoming how and why they move, nor is there any set of rules that can be used to obtain quick and certain profits in the market. The movements of prices, however, are often more significant to investors than the dividend income received from their stocks.

The multiplicity of factors or conditions that affect the market may be classified in two categories. First, there are fundamental conditions that develop outside the market. These are the underlying or basic causes of price changes which in the long run dominate the market. Second, there are the so-called "technical" factors or conditions that operate entirely within the market over short periods. They also affect stock prices, no matter what the long-run or fundamental conditions may be.

These two sets of conditions sometimes work together and sometimes in opposition. Thus, a given market may be fundamentally strong but technically weak, or the reverse. Again, both sets of conditions may be strong or weak at the same time. The student of the market will do well to distinguish between the two elements of market determination at all times.

This chapter will examine so-called fundamental factors and conditions outside of the stock market that many consider important in influencing stock price movements. As will be seen later, many of these fundamental factors have much less direct influence on the market than is generally supposed.

Chapter 34 will deal with a technical analysis of the market, which means a study of the internal factors or conditions of the market which are believed to influence stock price movements. Both fundamental and technical analyses are difficult and each has its limitations.

TWO THEORIES OF STOCK PRICES

The Conventional Theory of Stock Prices. For many years there has been a fundamental, orthodox, and conventional theory to explain the movement of stock prices. Reduced to the simplest phraseology, it can be stated in this way: *The basic cause of stock price movement is the anticipation of change in corporate earnings.*

The expected result, according to conventional theory, of all changes in fundamental conditions is that they will affect the earnings of corporations, either individually or as a group. These changes in earnings will, in turn, affect dividends. The belief is that earnings constitute the most important single factor in determining stock prices. The shrewd trader or investor, therefore, must properly evaluate all fundamental conditions as they affect future earnings. By buying and selling in advance of changes in fundamental conditions, traders and investors are said to "discount" changes in earnings before they occur. To wait until actual changes in earnings take place is too slow for maximum profits.

The theory considers dividends as an important factor but gives them secondary consideration. It is the belief that dividends must follow earnings and will change as earnings change.

In summary, any condition or situation that indicates a change in earnings of a particular company or of a specific industry, or of many companies, or of the entire economy will affect stock prices, which will move in advance of actual changes in earnings and dividends.

This is the classic theory or explanation of stock price movements. They move in advance of changes in business and in advance of changes in earning power.

The Confidence Theory of Stock Prices. This theory of stock price movements is even less formalized than the conventional theory. In fact, a formal statement of the theory is not a part of the literature of the stock market. In some men's opinion, however, the theory justifies at least equal emphasis with the conventional, or orthodox, theory. In view of many recent developments in the market, a good case can be built up to give it precedence as the dominant explanation of stock price movements.

The theory may be formalized in these terms: *The basic factor in the movement of stock prices is the rise and fall of trader and investor confidence in the future of stock prices, earnings, and dividends.*

This theory would seem to be but a variation of the theme of the conventional theory, namely, that stock prices depend upon earnings. Actually, it is fundamentally different in that it explains stock prices on the basis of market psychology rather than on statistical fundamentals. Its value is that it can be used to explain many vagaries of stock price movements not explained through conventional theory.

The confidence theory does not accept the precise principles of the conventional theory. The latter theory assumes that fundamental conditions are cold, objective facts about earnings, dividends, levels of interest rates, prices changes, production, sales, gross national product, political developments, and similar factors. The theory is based on the premise that decisions on buying and selling are made on the basis of well-developed rules and standards, such as that stocks should sell at certain price-earnings ratios or that stocks should carry certain yields as compared to bond yields. The trained statistician and investment expect would, therefore, be ideally situated to forecast the market because of his skilled knowledge of, and handling of, economic data. When fundamental conditions were favorable, stock prices should move upward in accordance with well-discounted changes in earnings and dividends. When conditions turned unfavorable, stock prices would move downward in accordance with scientific discounting of these changes.

To this mechanistic theory of the market, the followers of the confidence theory cannot subscribe. They believe that the market does not respond to statistics and economic data with any high degree of exactness. They believe that the market's indifference to both good and bad news is often incredible. They are aware that measurements of stock price levels, such as price-earnings ratios and yields, change constantly; sometimes they are very high, sometimes very low, but seldom unchanging. Finally, they know that a very old axiom is still very true: "The market can do anything."

According to the confidence theory, if a sufficient number of traders and investors become optimistic about fundamental conditions, or about prospects for an individual company, they will buy stocks. If they become overoptimistic, they will buy stocks until prices reach unwarranted levels, as measured by normal levels of prices, earnings, and dividends. On the opposite side, when they become pessimistic they will sell, regardless of basic, fundamental conditions. If their pessimism becomes excessive, they will dump stocks on the market until they fall to entirely unrealistic levels as measured by normal standards. In this theory the buyers and sellers are extremists, whose moods range from extreme optimism to exaggerated pessimism. Like the fabled southern judge, they are often in error but never in doubt.

The confidence theory can be used to explain many bull and bear markets that appear inexplicable by the conventional theory. It can explain a bear market in the face of pronounced strength in economic conditions. It can explain a bull market in the face of unfavorable economic developments. It can explain falling stock prices during a period of rising earnings, or the reverse.

Although many examples can be used to illustrate the movement of stock prices according to the confidence theory, few are better than the bear market of 1946. At that time fundamental conditions were very strong; gross national product was rising; price controls had been abandoned and both retail and wholesale prices were increasing; corporate dividends and earnings were improving. Then the speculative public became pessimistic. It was convinced that a post-war depression was in order as it had been so many times in the past. Stocks were sold and the market broke badly in August and September. It did not recover its 1946 level until 1950. The year 1947, it turned out later, was "the year of the depression which never came." Business conditions continued to improve almost without interruption until late 1948. Confidence in the market in 1946 disappeared. Traders and investors were in error as to the facts, but the market broke anyway. The confidence theory was vindicated.

The difficulty of measuring public confidence in the market increases the complexity of stock market analysis. Many traders on technical conditions who attempt to measure confidence by various methods often achieve less than perfect results. Many investors still follow faithfully the conventional theory. Its apparent concreteness and its limitless statistical raw material give it an air of realism which carries great weight. Yet followers of the conventional theory are often perplexed and not a little dazed because their precise calculations often fail to yield the plausible results they anticipate so confidently.

BUSINESS FUNDAMENTALS

Nature of Fundamentals. Fundamental conditions are those economic and political factors outside the market itself that many consider dictate market trends, either for individual stocks, for groups of stocks, or for the market as a whole. They can be divided into two groups: (1) business or economic fundamentals and (2) political fundamentals. There are many thousands of traders and investors in the market at all times, and each is seeking to forecast the trend of prices. Their verdict as to this trend is based mainly on their estimate of fundamental conditions as they affect prices. If a majority believe that fundamental conditions are bullish, stocks will be bought and they will rise; if the reverse, stocks will be sold and price declines will take place.

Stock Prices: 1939–60. A good way to examine the relationship between stock prices and business fundamentals is to study the behavior of stock prices and business fundamentals from 1939 to 1960. For this purpose three years have been arbitrarily chosen: (1) 1939, the end of the Great Depression and the beginning of World War II; (2) 1948, the mid-year of the period 1947–49, once the base period for nearly all economic series; and (3) 1960.

In Table 30–1 stock price changes from 1939 to 1960 are compared with changes for a number of economic series over the same period. References will be made to this table in a number of places in this chapter. At this point a few generalizations seem indicated.

Few business series expand and contract together. Stock prices are no exception. It will be noted that from 1939 to 1948 industrial stock prices showed a notable lag. The 24 per cent rise was less than that of any of the six other series included in the table. The lag behind corporate earnings and dividends is interesting. In the period 1948–60, the situation showed an extreme change. The bull market of 1949 came into being and stock prices showed a very marked expansion. Their advance was far greater than that of any other series with the exception of building contracts. Stock prices noticeably outran the improvement in earnings and dividends. For the entire period 1939–60, stock prices rose less than building contracts, about as much as gross national product, and more than any of the other series.

Table 30–1. Comparative Gains in Stock Prices and Selected Business Series, 1939 to 1960

Series	Percentage Gains		
	1939–48	1948–60	1939–60
Standard & Poor's Industrial Stock Index	24%	307%	406%
Earnings on stocks in this index	158	26	225
Dividends on stocks in this index	60	120	251
Building Contract Awards	161	187	642
Federal Reserve Board Index of Industrial Production	73	59	184
Gross National Product	174	94	431
Wholesale Prices Other Than Farm and Food Products	100	14	129

Although Table 30–1 may be criticized by statisticians who would prefer more complex and refined techniques, it is believed that it serves a useful purpose. It demonstrates rather clearly that stock prices do not fluctuate in unison with other economic series, even corporate profits and dividends. At times they lag; at other times they outrun other series. Over a long period they usually lead other series.

Earnings. Under the conventional theory of stock prices, earnings or corporate profits are considered the most important single fundamental influencing stock prices. Traders and investors buy and sell stock largely on the basis of anticipated earnings. As a result, stock prices are believed to discount or anticipate changes in earnings.

A good theoretical defense can be built up for this premise. Stocks are bought for two purposes: (1) appreciation and (2) yield. A rise in earnings over a period of time causes appreciation in the value of the stock. The yield of stock is determined by the relationship between dividends and the market price. A stock can yield a return to a stockholder only because the company pays out part of the earnings as dividends. Thus, both appreciation and yield are determined by the volume of earnings.

Under this theory it is not too important whether earnings be retained in the company or paid out in dividends. In either case the stockholder gains. If a large proportion is retained as reinvested capital, the company expands. This expansion increases future earnings and hence both future dividends and stock price. A large retention of earnings may be a sign that the company can employ the funds profitably, otherwise they would not have been reinvested. Although a heavy reinvestment of profits may mean a small pay-out in dividends, the stockholder is satisfied because he feels that he owns a "growth stock," and this policy is considered a good indication of growth.

Although it may be argued against this theory that reinvested profits may be lost or wasted or produce only low return, the advocate of this theory is not impressed by the argument. He believes that the past performance of management can be used to test the company's performance. By employing certain ratios, such as the ratio of profits to net worth, invested capital, and sales, he can continually measure the skill of management. As long as profit ratios remain favorable, he believes that his reinvested profits are being put to profitable use.

Sound as this theory appears, stocks are not always highly correlative with earnings. At times stocks move much faster than earnings; at other times they lag behind earnings. Sometimes they actually move in an opposite direction. Hence, even though a skilled follower of the market were to forecast correctly the trend of earnings, there is no assurance that he would be able to forecast correctly the movements of stock prices.

Here are a few examples to demonstrate that stock prices and earnings often show a very poor correlation and, in fact, may actually move in opposite directions for considerable periods. These comparisons are based on the 30-stock Dow-Jones industrial average. From 1938 to 1941 earnings showed a substantial improvement, but stock prices fell. From

1941 to early 1946 earnings showed a decline, but stock prices showed a very sharp rise. From 1946 to 1950 earnings more than doubled, but stock prices remained fairly stable. From 1950 to 1960 earnings on the stocks in the Dow-Jones average rose less than 10 per cent, but the stock prices rose more than 300 per cent. Substantially the same movements are observed in the behavior of the Standard and Poor's index of industrial stocks.

In conclusion, it seems reasonable to state that although earnings are probably the most important long-term, fundamental factor determining stock prices, one must not rely upon the relationship too much. Because of the confidence theory in explaining stock prices, it should be realized that stock prices often over- or underdiscount earnings and frequently move in the opposite direction for short periods.

That there is not a closer relationship between stock prices and earnings is easily explainable. Stock prices over a long period have tended to move ahead of earnings. Hence, changes in earnings come too late to affect stock price movements. In an exhaustive study of statistical indicators in the business cycle, the National Bureau of Economic Research found that common stock prices tended to lead business cycle turns by 4.5 months.[1]

Figure 30–1 shows the earnings of the Dow-Jones industrial average from 1929 to date.

The Price-Earnings Ratio. The most frequently used measurement of the relationship of stock prices and earnings is the price-earnings ratio, which is the current market price divided by annual earnings. For example, a given stock is selling at $60 and earnings per share are $5. It is then said to be selling at a price-earnings ratio of 12 to 1. If earnings were to remain level but the price were to rise to $70, it would then be selling at 14 to 1.

The price-earnings ratio has long been used to measure the value of stock prices. Many years ago a ratio of 10 to 1 was considered standard, and a purchase of a given stock at that ratio or lower was considered a sound investment. Today standards have changed and less and less is heard of sound investments selling at 10-to-1 ratios.

One might assume that a given stock or a given group of stocks would always sell at approximately the same price-earnings ratio. In this way one could determine the true intrinsic value of this stock or group of stocks. If earnings rise, the stock prices should rise accordingly to maintain approximately the same ratio; as they fall, stock prices should drop in sympathy.

---

[1] G. H. Moore (ed.), *Business Cycle Indicators* (2 vols.; Princeton, N.J.: Princeton University Press, 1961) I, e.g., p. 56.

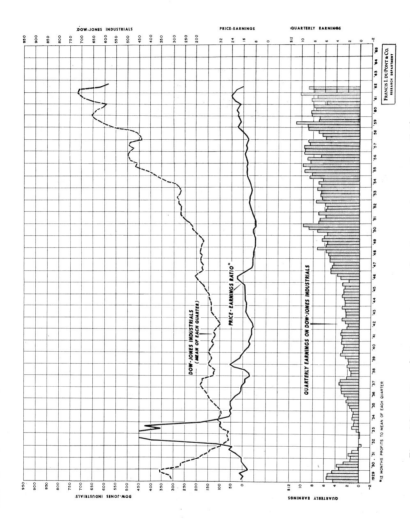

Fig. 30–1. Trends in earnings and price-earnings ratio of the Dow-Jones industrial average.

Actually, the price-earnings ratio fluctuates with amazing frequency and over a wide range. The ratio over the short period of a stock cycle may range from 9 to 1 to more than 15 to 1. Let us take the 30-stock Dow-Jones industrial average as typical for a group of high-grade, blue chip stocks. In the twenty-five-year period from 1936 to 1960, the price-earnings ratio has ranged from as high as 25 to 1 to as low as 7 to 1, as shown in Figure 30–1. For the entire period the ratio averaged 14 to 1.

An indication of the peak of a bull market or the trough of a bear market is the price-earnings ratio. For example, in the bull market of 1929 the Dow-Jones industrial average reached 19 to 1. In 1938 it rose to 25 to 1. In 1946 it was up to 20 to 1. In 1961 it reached 23 to 1. Conversely, the bear market low of 1942 showed a 9-to-1 ratio; the low of 1949 was 7 to 1, while the low of the moderate decline of 1953 was 10 to 1. Under the confidence theory of stock prices, such an amplitude in ratios is entirely logical. During bull markets stock buyers become overoptimistic and bid up stock until the price-earnings ratios are very high, always in excess of 15 to 1. In bear markets they become pessimistic and sell, driving stocks down to very low ratios, always under 10 to 1 for the Dow-Jones industrials.

Stocks should be separated when examining their price-earnings ratios. As indicated, the average ratio for the 30 stocks in the Dow-Jones industrial average has been about 14 to 1 over a considerable period. For strictly growth stocks, such as the chemicals, ratios will normally be substantially higher than these. These frequently sell at ratios of 20 to 1 and 25 to 1. A conservative rule of thumb would be that growth stocks should not be bought, generally, if they sell at more than 20 to 1 and that 25 to 1 should be the upper limit in all cases. On occasion investors will buy stocks at ratios much higher than these mentioned. For example, in 1961 International Business Machines at its high of 607 was selling at 80 times its indicated annual earnings of $7.60.

High price-earnings ratios also seem justified for moderate-growth companies with great stability in earning power, such as food and tobacco companies and public utilities, although ratios in these companies are typically lower than for the more spectacular growth stocks. Ratios of 15 to 1 might be considered satisfactory in such companies. On the other hand, companies subject to large cyclical fluctuations, such as the automobile and steel companies, should sell normally at 10 to 1, the traditional ratio of the sound investment stock of years ago.

In conclusion, price-earnings ratios show wide fluctuations between high and low points of the stock cycle. They also show marked differences between stocks because of the growth factor, size of company, management, trend of earnings, financial strength, and current popularity.

Dividends. In the conventional theory of stock prices, dividends come next to earnings as the basic, fundamental factor in the determination of stock prices. Indeed, many traders and investors are inclined today to attach to this factor just as great importance as to earnings in determining the intrinsic value of stocks. Some give even greater stress to dividends. Various reasons are presented in defense of this attitude. One is that dividends are tangible and concrete. They are here today and represent real assets to the stockholders. There is no danger that earnings reinvested in the company will be lost, wasted, or poorly used, because the stockholder receives them today in the form of cash. This is but a variation of the old axiom, "A bird in the hand is worth two in the bush." The second reason for favoring dividends more highly than retained earnings is that the present value of dividends is greater to the stockholder than future earnings paid out in dividends, even when he may be reasonably certain of receiving them.

The importance of dividends is least in growth stocks, where appreciation is highly important, often bringing a greater ultimate return than dividends.

One must realize that dividends show vast changes over a period of time. For the 30-stock Dow-Jones industrial average during the twenty-five-year period from 1936 to 1960, dividends per share showed a range of 570 per cent from the lowest year to the highest.

Dividends do not move in precise relationship to corporation profits, as indicated in Table 30-1. It will be observed that from 1939 to 1948 profits went up much faster than dividends, while the exact opposite was true from 1948 to 1960.

Of all the factors used by newspaper editors to explain day-to-day fluctuations in the prices of individual stock, dividend news ranks first in importance.

Yields. One way to examine changes in dividends is to study stock yields. The formula for a stock yield, as already indicated, is to divide the annual dividend by the current market price. The one way to find the annual dividend is to add up the last four quarterly dividends.

Stock yields show vast changes in periods of price change. The yields shown by any popular stock average or index will demonstrate this. Let us take the 30-stock Dow-Jones industrial average by quarters for the twenty-five-year period 1936–60. The yield on these 30 high-grade, blue chip stocks was only 3.3 per cent in the second quarter of 1946. Three years later, in the second quarter of 1949, it had risen more than 100 per cent to 6.7. Over the full period the yield on stocks in this average ranged from 3.1 to 6.9 per cent.

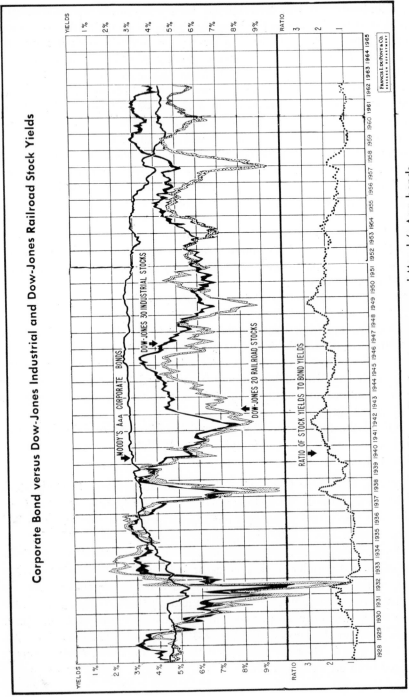

Fig. 30–2. Yields on Dow-Jones average and Moody's Aaa bonds.

Stock yields, like price-earnings ratios, provide one of the simplest tests for measuring the peak of a bull market or the trough of a bear market. At the peak of every bull market from 1929 to 1962, they were close to 3 per cent. At the trough of every bear market during the same period they ranged from 7 to 10 per cent. For the twenty-five-year period from 1936 to 1960, the Dow-Jones industrial average showed an average yield of 5 per cent, based on quarterly computations. Figure 30–2 shows yields on both the industrial and rail averages, and a comparison with yields on Moody's Aaa bonds.

Stock yields show a wide variation among individual stocks. Some growth stocks, such as du Pont and Allied Chemical, have shown yields as low as 3 per cent over long periods, whereas others have yielded over 6 per cent consistently. Many factors—such as growth, status of the company in its industry, size, management, stability and trend of earnings, dividend policies, source of new capital, age of the company, popularity with investors, and risk—explain these variations. An additional factor should be mentioned. Uncertainty about a company's ability to continue dividends at the current rate of payment is frequently a cause of high yield, even in the case of strong, high-grade companies.

In conclusion, stock yields are another useful tool for working with stock valuations. It must be remembered, however, that they show marked changes during the stock cycle and that they vary greatly between stocks. Examined over a period of time, they are very valuable in determining whether stocks are selling at too high a price or at an attractive level.

Stock Splits. One of the most certain stimulants to the market price of a stock is an announcement that the directors intend to split the stock. Although the advantages of stock splits are somewhat illusory, since a stockholder after a split still owns the same percentage of issued stock as before and still receives the same percentage of dividends paid out, such a practice almost invariably stimulates the market for the stock on the expectation that higher earnings and more generous dividends are in prospect. The net effect of an announcement is, therefore, a rise in the price of the stock as soon as the action is announced or even rumored. That a stock split is a reasonable ground for higher stock prices has some justification. Higher earnings often do follow and more generous dividends often are paid.

Interest Rates. Endless hours of research have gone into the study of the relationship between stock prices and interest rates. Do changes in interest rates bring about changes in stock prices? Do interest rates precede changes in the latter series? The results of such investigations are discouraging to the student of the market.

Some have attempted, on a theoretical basis, to justify such a relationship. The theory is that cheap money makes funds available for stock speculation at favorable rates. Speculators can borrow plentiful funds at low rates and make high returns on stock ownership because of the differential between stock yields and the cost of call money; hence, stock will rise. Conversely, when interest rates become high and call money scarce, speculators will contract loans because of tight credit conditions and lack of profit in carrying stocks on margins; stocks will, therefore, fall in price.

A few students of the problem have concluded that changes in interest rates do precede changes in stock prices. Thus, Leonard M. Ayres, who examined twenty-five business cycles over a hundred-year period, concluded that on the upswing of the business cycle, the low point of interest rates was twelve months in advance of the top level of stock prices; on the downswing the top level of interest rates was four months in advance of the low point of stock prices.[2] Ayres' findings, however, are not accepted by later writers.

Owens and Hardy have made probably the most thorough study of the accepted theory that cyclical variations in speculative activity are caused by fluctuations in interest rates. They stated: "The conclusion reached is that neither economic analysis nor historical approach reveals any foundation for the accepted theory."[3] They also noted: "In summary, the data for both periods show clearly that there is a pronounced tendency for the interest rate to lag behind stock prices in their upward and downward movements, with an interval of about twelve months."[4] Moore, in recent years, found that industrial stock prices led bank rates on business loans by 9.5 months, an estimate close to that of Owens and Hardy.[5] Another well-known authority on the stock market, Joseph Mindell, concluded: "There is no direct correlation between the interest rate and stock prices."[6]

High interest rates do not necessarily discourage speculation. They were high in 1928 and early 1929—the highest since 1920—yet a bull market was nearing its crest. Again, they increased during 1954 and 1955, yet the stock market enjoyed one of its best gains on record. Very high price levels were reached in 1960 and 1961 when interest rates were consistently high. Another instance indicating that they appear to have little

---

[2] L. M. Ayres, *Turning Points in Business Cycles* (New York: The Macmillan Co., 1940), p. 67.

[3] R. N. Owens and C. O. Hardy, *Interest Rates and Stock Speculation* (Washington, D.C.: The Brookings Institution, 1930), p. vii.

[4] *Ibid.*, p. 98.

[5] Moore, *op. cit.*, p. 57.

[6] Joseph Mindell, *The Stock Market* (New York: B. C. Forbes & Co., 1948), p. 130.

influence on stock prices is that call loan rates were stabilized at 1 per cent from 1936 to 1946, yet the period witnessed no less than three bull and bear markets.

Stock Yields and Bond Yields. Many students of the market give close attention to the ratio between stock yields and bond yields. This attention stems from a belief that the spread between them has a significant influence upon stock prices. When stock yields are high as compared with bond yields, some investors will keep money invested in stock and place additional funds in stocks as they become available for investment. This acts as a bullish influence on stock prices. On the other hand, when there is a narrow spread, the investors will hesitate to place money in stocks and will turn to bonds because the difference in yield does not conmpensate for the additional risk. A narrow or negative spread is interpreted as bearish.

The ratio between stock yields and bond yields is indicated in Figure 30–2, above. It will be observed that in 1928 the two yields were about the same, while in 1929 stock yields were actually lower until after the crash. In recent years stock yields have been almost three times as large as those on Aaa bonds at the trough of bear markets, while at the peak of bull markets they have been about equal. It is difficult to determine statistically the exact influence of this spread on stock prices. In other words, the theory is still open to proof.

Commodity Prices. A fair theoretical case can be made out to the effect that commodity prices, as indicators of inflation and deflation, influence stock prices. In many mercantile and manufacturing companies, inventories play an important part in the determination of profits. Rising prices mean that inventories can be sold at higher prices than those that prevailed when they were purchased, especially when there is a substantial time lapse. On the other hand, falling prices mean that inventory losses must be assumed. During the depression of the 1930's, many considered stocks as good investments because of the possibility of an inflation in commodity prices. Many accepted the same theory in the post-World War II period of rising prices. Inflation again received much attention in the early months of the Korean War.

Common stocks have been widely considered as hedges against inflation. Not only were they considered to rise as the price level increased, but earnings and dividends would improve at the same or at a greater rate; hence, the stockholder would be protected against the depreciating value of his income dollar. Many corporations have heavy fixed obligations, such as rentals, interest charges, and preferred stock dividends. Since these charges are constant, any gains in net income before these charges would go to the common stockholders.

Whether inflation will benefit the stockholder is dependent upon many conditions. In the industrial corporation the benefit is more probable than it is in the public utility corporation, whose charges are fixed by public regulatory bodies. The traction companies were ruined by the "nickel fare" of World War I. Railroad stocks did poorly during the inflationary period from 1913 to 1920 as rising costs outstripped the gains in revenue.

One difficulty about purchasing stocks in anticipation of inflation is that inflation itself is extremely difficult to forecast. During the depression of the 1930's, wide fears were entertained that the government, through deficit spending and numerous deliberately inflationary policies, would bring on a sharp price rise; many bought stocks on this theory. No great inflation occurred, however, in spite of governmental policies because of the high productive capacity of the country and a large labor force, much of which was unemployed. The efforts to induce inflation, which included a substantial expansion in the monetary supply, simply did not work.

In World War II extreme inflationary forces were present in this country; yet there was no such rise in prices as would seem to have been indicated on the basis of the increase in bank credit and money in circulation, as well as the high level of deficit spending. Investors who would have purchased stocks in 1941 in anticipation of the beneficial effects of commodity inflation on stock prices would have been gravely misled. Commodity prices did rise during the war and particularly after price controls were lifted, but this inflation had no pronounced effect on stock prices.

Stock exchange history is replete with examples of the failure of stock prices to correlate with commodity prices. From 1923 to 1929 a remarkable period of wholesale price stability was present, showing only a slight downward tendency. Yet, in that period, stocks boomed in probably the most publicized bull market on record. Commodity prices rose in 1940, 1941, and 1942, but stock prices receded. In the spring of 1946, commodity price controls were scrapped, and a sharp inflation in prices took place for the rest of the year and continued upward until mid-1948, a steady two-year advance. On the other hand, stock prices began to waver at almost the same date in 1946 that commodity prices began to increase; they fell badly in August and were down substantially for the year. In other words, stock prices collapsed in 1946 at the exact time that the inflationary forces growing out of World War II became greatest.

By January, 1951, the inflationary effects of the Korean War were past. Commodity prices then declined slightly and leveled off until mid-1955. During this period industrial stocks doubled in price.

Commodity prices are unreliable as an indicator of stock prices. The reason is that stock prices move ahead of commodity prices and not after. Moore found that industrial stock prices led changes of the BLS wholesale price index by 5.5 months.[7]

Gross National Product. In recent years the statistical concept of gross national product has loomed large in the study of business conditions. This term refers to the sum total of final goods and services produced in the nation in a given year. It is expressed in dollars and not in physical units. Figures are prepared by the Department of Commerce and released quarterly. Since this is the most inclusive figure released on business activity, it would seem that there should be some definite relationship between the changes in gross national product and in stock prices. The stock trader, however, will find great difficult in correlating the two series.

Gross national product rose almost continuously from 1939 to 1961 with only slight dips in late 1945, 1949, 1954, and 1958. The stock market, however, fell from 1939 to 1942. It collapsed sharply in 1946 and showed no recovery in 1947 and 1948. Both gross national product and stock prices rose from 1949 to 1961 with slight interruptions. The rise in stock prices, however, was far in excess of that noted for gross national product.

The difficulty noted in correlating stock prices with gross national product is that the former precede the latter in the business cycle. Moore's careful study showed that industrial stock prices led gross national product by 4.5 months at cycle turns.[8]

Construction. Construction is one of the nation's leading industries in employment, payrolls, use of investment capital, and demand for materials. Its cyclical movement has a vast effect upon many other industries that supply it. Investment in new plants and equipment is considered one of the most stimulating influences during recovery, while a retrenchment in such expenditures is considered to be a very depressing influence.

Whatever the relationship between building contracts and stock prices may have been in earlier years—and there is dispute about this among business cycle theorists—the relationship has not been close since 1939. Construction contracts rose from 1939 to 1942, while stock prices fell. The reverse was true from 1942 to 1944. Both contracts and prices fell in 1946. Contracts made impressive gains in 1947, 1948, and 1949, but the stock market wavered in uncertainty. On the other hand, contracts and stock prices showed strong gains from 1949 to 1961.

[7] Moore, *op. cit.*, p. 56.
[8] *Ibid.*, p. 56-7.

A careful study of the relationship between the two series showed that on the upturn of the business cycle, residential housing starts and industrial stock prices kept abreast of each other. On the downturn housing starts led by about 1.5 months.[9] Building contracts for commercial and industrial buildings lagged about 2.5 months behind stock prices.

New Orders. New orders received by industry are given careful scrutiny by many traders. These are received by industries some time in advance of production schedules and indicate the potential volume of production in the near future. A rise in orders indicates good business ahead; a reduction means a slump in production. There is no question but that new orders precede changes in business activity. The question is by how much. Moore estimated that at turns of the business cycle, new orders of durable goods industries preceded changes in business activity by 5.0 months and ran 0.5 months ahead of industrial stocks.[10] Plum and Humphrey, however, indicated that new orders led business activity by only three months, which would cause them to lag behind industrial stocks.[11]

There are, however, several limitations to new orders which make them much less useful to market traders than it appears on first observation. The Department of Commerce releases data on new orders about twenty-five days after the close of the calendar month to which they refer. Even if new orders did lead industrial stock prices, the information would not be available before the movement of stocks. If Plum and Humphrey's estimates are correct, there would be a considerable lag of new order data behind stock price movements. There has also been a question raised as to the completeness and reliability of data on new orders, which would further limit their forecasting value. Again, the tendency noted at times of padding orders, canceling orders, and refusing orders also reduces the value of this business series.

Most investigations seem in agreement that on the downturn of the cycle, industrial stock prices lead declines in new orders by several months.

Inventories. There is much discussion in the press about the importance of mercantile, wholesale, and manufacturing inventories. At times, merchants and manufacturers build up heavy inventories in anticipation of better sales. At other times, they attempt to reduce them to keep them in line with forecasts of reduced business. Changes in manufacturers' inventories are given particular attention because of their effects

[9] *Ibid.*, p. 56.

[10] *Loc. cit.*

[11] L. V. Plum and J. H. Humphrey, *Investment Analysis and Management* (Chicago: Richard D. Irwin, Inc., 1951), p. 480.

on production, employment, and payrolls. The drive behind many periods of business recovery is stimulated by decisions of businessmen to build up inventories. After the close of World War II, industry received a great impetus as retailers, wholesalers, and manufacturers sought to "fill the pipelines" with fresh inventories. Again, at the opening of the Korean War in 1950, there was a rush to build up inventories in anticipation of higher prices and shortages. Periods of rising commodity prices tend to stimulate business to increase inventories.

Businessmen and economists interested in inventory trends compare them carefully with production, new orders, and sales to determine whether any favorable or unfavorable trends are developing. Stock traders sometimes do so, but their efforts are not always rewarding. The difficulty is that industrial stock prices usually lead inventory changes. Moore found that the Dow-Jones industrial average tended to lead manufacturers' inventories by 7 months at cycle turns.[12] This largely eliminates the usefulness of inventories as a clue to the future of stock prices.

Strikes. A time-honored axiom in Wall Street is: "Never sell on strike news." The theory stands up well under historical analysis, although there are some exceptions. The belief is that any temporary decline in stock prices should be ignored. Prices will promptly return to previous levels after the strike is over. In many cases the market will refuse to break because of the strike. In either case selling is not justified. The theory is based on two arguments. First, losses in production, sales, and profits during the strike will be made up when the industry gets back into full production. Thus, the steel industry may be operating at only 80 per cent of capacity before the strike; after the strike the plants are speeded up to near capacity operations, and within a few months the loss in production is entirely wiped out. At that time the plants drop back to the pre-strike production level. The second reason that justifies the strike axiom is that manufacturers, wholesalers, and retailers usually have adequate inventories when the strike begins. These may last for one or two months and are sold at the usual profit with no loss in sales. After the strike inventories are replenished.

Business has been able to weather strikes in recent years in such industries as steel, coal, and automobiles with marked equanimity. These industries have very high productive capacities when in full operation and can usually meet pent-up demands after strike settlements within a reasonable time. In fact, these industries often face seasonal declines in production. The strike merely reduces the amount of the seasonal decline. The press gives much attention during a strike to losses in wages and production. Actually, seasonal and cyclical declines have the same

---

[12] Moore, *op. cit.*, p. 56–7.

effect. This explains why management and labor often take their time in settlement of new wage contracts.

Industrial Production. This fundamental economic series is being discussed last because it is the most important industrial series available on a monthly basis. Released by the Federal Reserve Board about fifteen days after the close of a given calendar month, it gives a complete picture of changes in production of all leading industries in the nation. Other useful indexes are published by *Business Week* and *The New York Times*. Stock market followers watch them with great attention.

In the period between World War I and World War II, there was a fairly good correlation between stock prices and industrial production. Gains in stock prices were followed by an improvement in production, while market breaks were followed by a shrinkage in production. Industrial stocks led changes in production by 6.6 months on the upturn of the cycle and by 9.4 months on the downturn.[13] At times, however, there has been a great divergence between the two series. Industrial production rose steadily from 1939 to 1942; stock prices declined. Industrial production dropped somewhat from late 1943 to early 1946; stock prices rose steadily in the same period. Industrial production rose consistently from early 1946 to late 1948, when it reached its best postwar level up to that date. The market, however, broke sharply in 1946 and showed no significant recovery until after June, 1949. Through the 1950's both stock prices and industrial production rose, but prices rose much more sharply. The correlation, however, has been quite high again in the swings of the two series about their respective general trends.

Commenting on the lack of dependable correlation between stock prices and industrial production, two authorities concluded: "After 1940, the cycles are so lacking in synchronism that lead and lag relationships are meaningless."[14] Over a period of forty-seven years, these two authorities found no consistent lead and lag relationship between stock prices and industrial production. From 1919 to 1946 it was found that stock prices showed a lead of as much as 300 days and a lag as great as 185 days.[15] The average lead had very little real meaning.

It is true that the earnings of many corportaions depend upon the level of industrial production, and dividends as well. As production increases, profits rise; as it falls, earnings decline. Hence, the market should discount such changes in production and be greatly influenced by these conditions. The difficulty is, however, that stock prices, as a rule, lead changes in production, and there is no dependable lead and lag rela-

---

[13] *Ibid.*, p. 64.

[14] C. S. Cottle and W. T. Whitman, *Investment Timing: The Formula Plan Approach* (New York: McGraw-Hill Book Co., Inc., 1953), p. 54.

[15] *Ibid.*, p. 56.

tionship. Furthermore, stock prices and industrial production have shown a marked lack of correlation on a number of occasions.

POLITICAL FUNDAMENTALS

Importance. Political fundamentals are those developments in the field of government and politics that affect security prices. In the last quarter of a century, they have assumed an immense importance in the economic life of the country. There has been a great increase in government regulations and controls. In addition, the policies of government spending and taxation have had an immeasurable influence over business conditions. The control of the credit system has been far more widespread than at any time in the nation's history. The federal government has become the largest business in the country, the biggest employer, and the greatest consumer.

War. The importance of war as a political fundamental since 1939 would be difficult to exaggerate. From 1939 to 1945 it was the dominant influence in the world. This dominance, extended to the entire economy, of course had great repercussions in the stock market. This influence has already been examined in Chapter 5. Following the close of World War II, the country suffered a postwar inflation and boom. This began to diminish in 1948 and 1949. A setback to the economy, however, was prevented by the opening of the Korean War, the immediate effects of which were highly stimulating to the economy. After that conflict terminated, the federal government continued a high level of spending, which seems destined to remain for the foreseeable future because of the never-ending "cold war."

Since war is usually an event that cannot be forecast, its effects, once declared, on the stock market are often pronounced and unpredictable. They increase the difficulties of the market follower who seeks to predict stock price changs basd on a normally functioning economic system.

Other Political Fundamentals. The President of the United States has become a political factor of tremendous significance in affecting the stock market. His messages to Congress often influence the market, unless well discounted in advance, as in the case of his recommendations on new taxes, recovery measures, foreign aid, the budget, farm program, public power policies, road program, defense spending, and similar measures. Many industries are affected by government spending programs, an outstanding example being the airplane industry. Even calling Congress into special session has had substantial repercussions in the market. Elections are watched closely to see their effects upon the market. Although presidential elections are supposed to create uncertainty in the market, the effect is usually good. Out of the last sixteen such elections years, there has been a rise in the market in twelve and a decline in only four. Even the health of the President is very important. In the year following the Chief Executive's heart attack in 1955, it affected the market more violently than any other single factor, political or economic.

Acts of Congress are influential in their effects on the stock market. Since Congress holds the purse strings of the federal government, its acts of taxes, recovery programs, foreign aid, defense spending, and similar legislation are watched with great care by market followers.

Various government agencies influence the market with their actions. Rate decisions affect the earnings of railroads and public utilities. Antitrust actions often depress the stocks of companies affected. Corporate mergers may be approved or disapproved by the government. Particularly important in recent years has been the actions of the Federal Reserve Board. Its control over margins often depresses or stimulates the market. Of even greater importance is its control of the banking and credit system, which affects not only the lending and investment policies of all the commercial banks of the country but all business that uses bank credit. The attempts by the Board to stabilize and control the national economy are certain to affect the economic life of the country. The market will evaluate these attempts. Regardless of the success of these attempts and evaluations, there will be market repercussions and effects.

On may occasions the decision of the Supreme Court and the lower courts affect the market when these decisions have a direct bearing on the welfare of a given company or industry.

For these reasons the careful investor and trader in the market must be constantly on the alert for new political developments and must be able to evaluate them in terms of market reaction. He can no more afford to ignore them than he can afford to ignore the latest corporate reports on earnings.

31

Investing and Trading in Common Stocks

This and the following two chapters deal with the basic procedures for investing and trading in common stocks. There is no easy road to riches in the stock market any more than in any other type of business, and none will be described here. The following material deals with procedures and policies that have been found useful by many in the purchase and sale of common stocks.[1]

BASIC CONSIDERATIONS

Introduction. The problems connected with investing and trading in common stocks are so numerous and complex that no attempt will be made in this chapter and the following two to discuss them all. Primary emphasis will be placed upon introducing them to the reader in the hope that he will pursue them further and in greater detail. The first subject to be discussed will be some of the problems involved in stock buying, such as the stock price cycle and the investor's portfolio or investment program. Attention will then be directed to buying stocks by non-formula plans. The following chapters will be devoted to Dow Theory and formula plan buying.

[1] A more comprehensive discussion of investment analysis, wth particular emphasis on analysis of securities in different industries, is available in: Ralph E. Badger, Harold W. Torgerson, and Harry G. Guthmann, *Investment Principles and Practices* (5th ed.; Englewood Cliffs, N.J.: Prentice-Hall, Inc., 1961).

Problems in Buying Stocks. The basic problems connected with carrying out personal investment objectives through purchase of common stocks can be largely summarized with four questions:

1. How many stocks should be purchased?
2. What stocks should be purchased?
3. By what plan should stocks be purchased?
4. When should stocks be purchased

The first question is one of planning one's investment portfolio or program. The second question is one of investment analysis and selection. The next question revolves around the many stock buying plans now available, while the last is concerned with the timing of stock purchases. The last two questions will be treated at some length in this chapter and those following. An extensive discussion of the first two problems can be found in any standard text on investment.

PORTFOLIO OF AN INVESTOR

Characteristics. The term "portfolio" has a technical meaning in the field of investments. It is the investor's program and refers to his holdings of securities. For example, a given investor owns five different bonds and shares of stock in ten corporations with a total valuation of $25,000. That is his portfolio. There are two problems connected with the portfolio: (1) its planning or construction and (2) its management. Decisions must be made on the initial purchases, and the securities must be managed as long as they remain in the portfolio.

The size of a portfolio necessitates a basic decision of policy for the investor. He has at his disposal only limited funds over and above his living expenses, although he may have accumulated wealth that can be invested in securities. His surplus income can be invested in any one or a number of outlets or media, such as a home, other real estate, life insurance, savings accounts and deposits, shares of building and loan associations, issues of investment companies, and stocks and bonds of business corporations.

This basic question of how much money to put into the securities portfolio can be decided only by the investor himself, regardless of how much advice he may obtain from others or from reading books on the subject. For a given individual, it may be nothing or a very large sum; this depends on circumstances.

Certain criteria are useful in making a decision upon the size of the securities portfolio:

1. Income
   a. Size
   b. Sources

    c. Stability
    d. Permanence or expected duration
    e. Future expectations
  2. Number of dependents, degree of dependency, and possibilities
  3. Age and health of the investor and members of family
  4. Insurance status
  5. Tax bracket
  6. Ownership of home
  7. Retirement or pension plan
  8. Accumulated wealth available for investment
  9. Unusual expenses expected in the future
10. Temperament of the investor—his willingness to assume risk
11. Knowledge of and skill in handling investments
12. Time available for management of investments
13. Need for preservation of principal
14. Dependence upon investment income
15. Occupation, business, or profession of the investor

Ideally, an investor's portfolio should be "tailor-made" to fit his individual needs. The fifteen criteria, just mentioned, could be augmented. The combinations of criteria for any particular portfolio are as endless as contract bridge hands. Generally speaking, few investors compute with any degree of precision the amount of surplus family funds that can be put into securities investments. But a decision must be made if there is to be a portfolio. Whether it be $500, $1,000, or $5,000 per year, only the investor can make his own decision. Once this decision is made, certain broad generalizations are possible as to what securities should be purchased and when such purchases should be timed, although even here there is more uncertainty than many laymen realize.

Tests of a Good Investment. There is no such thing as an ideal investment any more than there is anything else in life that is ideal. The reason is that the ideal investment would have to meet a number of tests which are incompatible, even if attainable. All of the qualities of a good investment cannot be combined in any one security. The individual investor must decide on what tests or combinations of tests are most desirable to him and settle for that.

There are a number of possible tests of an ideal investment:

    1. *Safety of principal.* This would mean two things. First, the principal would be safe in dollar values. No one would ever lose the dollar amount of the original investment. In addition, the value of the principal would never lose its purchasing power, regardless of changes in the price level. It should be invulnerable to the twin dangers of inflation and deflation.
    2. *Safety of income.* The investor would always receive an income invulnerable to economic changes.
    3. *Stability of income.* The income would be safe in two ways. It would never fluctuate. In addition, it would have constant purchasing power, regardless of changes in the price level.

4. *Maximum income.* The income should be as large as possible.

5. *Acceptable maturity.* The security should not mature as long as the investor desires to hold it in his portfolio.

6. *Acceptable denomination.* It should not be too expensive to buy or to prevent proper diversification in the portfolio.

7. *Potential appreciation.* The security should have potentialities for future growth.

8. *Freedom from management cares and worry.* The investor should be able to buy it, lay it away in the safe deposit box, and forget it with no other responsibilities than the deposit of the always regular and always generous interest or dividend checks.

9. *Freedom from taxation.* It should be tax free: no federal, state, or local taxes; no income, inheritance, transfer, or property taxes; no tax reports and no inquisitive tax officials.

10. *Marketability or liquidity.* It can always be sold at once at the going market price (which, incidentally, would always be above the original cost).

11. *Non-callable.* The issuer should never have the right to deprive the investor of his ideal investment against his will.

12. *Convertible.* If it is a preferred stock or bond, the investor should always be permitted to convert it into common stock whenever it is profitable to do so.

13. *Low commissions.* Commissions on the purchase or sale should be as low as possible.

14. *Strong issuer.* The issuer should be a growth company; a leader in its field; long established; invulnerable to depression; with strong finances, able management, an enviable and unbroken earnings and dividend record, an excellent sales program, valuable patents, and a research program of high quality, which continuously develops new and better products with a high and continuing demand and better-than-average profit margins.

The above tests were, of course, somewhat exaggerated for purposes of emphasis. Needless to say, however, no one investment can meet all tests of the ideal security. For example, no security is free of all taxes. Again, no security is immune to both inflation and deflation, not even government bonds. The best that the investor can hope for is to combine as many good qualities as possible in his portfolio.

Selection of Investments. Once the investor determines the size of his securities portfolio, he must decide what part should be placed in common stocks. Again, a review of the critera for making a decision on the size of the portfolio will be useful. As indicated in Chapter 2, common stocks have decided advantages and definite limitations. These should be carefully weighed as they concern him.

Once the investor has decided upon the amount of money to be put into common stocks, either at regular intervals or in a lump sum, he must determine what securities he will purchase. Here, the whole field of investment analysis is opened up. It would be well for him to study this field carefully or to consult with a qualified adviser at this point, if he has not already done so, unless he has experience in the field. There are few ways to lose money more quickly than in the purchase of bad common stocks.

The following is a general and by no means complete outline of some of the decisions, problems, and lines of investigation involved in the selection of common stocks:

1. General decisions in advance of stock selection
   a. Degree of risk to be assumed
   b. Priority given to the tests of a good investment
2. Selection of industrial fields
   a. Chemicals
   b. Electronics
   c. Motors
   d. Oils, etc.
3. Analysis of the industrial field
   a. Nature of the industry
   b. Current and potential demand for products
   c. Growth factor
   d. Competition within and from outside the industry
   e. Cyclical influences
4. Selection of the individual company within the industry
5. Analysis of the company
   a. Financial statement analysis
   b. Earnings, dividends, and dividend policy
   c. Capital requirements
   d. Capitalization and senior securities
   e. Company control and financial backing
   f. Financial valuation of the common stock
   g. Position of the company within the industry
   h. Management and management policies
   i. Location, transportation, labor supply, and raw materials
   j. Patent position
   k. Other relevant factors

A thorough analysis of an industrial common stock dictates an investigation of the numerous factors listed above. An examination of stock ratings issued by Standard and Poor's will aid the stock buyer in arriving at his decisions. Brokerage firms will supply much information for making the analysis but are often wary of making recommendations on particular stocks. Financial magazines are sometimes helpful. Some investors prefer to make selections from lists of stocks popular with financial institutions.

Diversification. Investment experts stress the value of diversification in building a good securities portfolio. In simple terms, this means to spread out one's investments as a protection against risk. It is based on the age-old axiom: "Don't put all your eggs in one basket." Diversification gives protection against (1) cyclical movements of business, (2) long-term or secular changes in industry, and (3) losses in the position of individual companies.

Diversification is possible in many ways:

1. Buying issues in different industries
2. Buying issues in different companies
3. Spreading investments over a wide geographical area
4. Buying different kinds of securities, such as bonds, preferred stocks, and common stocks
5. Buying investment company issues with well-diversified portfolios
6. Buying issues of companies with diversified product lines
7. Timing purchases over different periods of the stock cycle
8. Balancing the portfolio as between defensive and aggressive securities, i.e., high-quality, income stocks which do well during a business recession as opposed to cyclical stocks which may bring higher speculative returns when business is expanding

Diversification can be overdone and has its limitations. These include:

1. Increased management problems
2. Increased work of investigation and analysis
3. Increased buying and selling costs
4. Reduced opportunity for better-than-average profits

Within reasonable limits proper diversification is a very sound practice.

THE STOCK CYCLE

Length and Amplitude. Sound investment in common stocks requires some understanding of the length and amplitude of the stock cycle. From the Civil War to the present time, the typical stock cycle has averaged about four years in length, with individual cycles running from two to ten years.

The purchaser of common stocks is warned that too much reliance must not be placed upon the four-year average just indicated. The length of a particular cycle gives no clue as to the length of the succeeding cycle. A five-year cycle can be followed by a two-year cycle, which in turn can be followed by a six-year cycle.

The amplitude of the cycle is its upward and downward swing, the distance between the peak and the trough. Stock cycles vary greatly in amplitude, and to make things more difficult, there is no way in which the amplitude of any given cycle can be forecast in advance. In some cycles the amplitude is small, while in others it is large. The range may be from as few as 24 percentage points to as many as 283.[2]

---

[2] C. S. Cottle and W. T. Whitman, *Investment Timing: The Formula Plan* (New York: McGraw-Hill Book Co., Inc., 1953), p. 4.

To complicate the matter more, it is believed that stock cycles in the last one-third of a century are changing their character and are getting longer in duration and displaying greater amplitude.[3] It is evident, therefore, from this modest discussion of the cycle that the investor must guard against any superficial rules designed to aid him in getting into and out of the market at the right time.

Need for Correct Timing. Because of the pronounced amplitude of stock cycles, it is evident to most investors that some method of correctly timing stock purchases would be highly desirable. Industrial stocks fell 89 per cent after the 1929 crash. They dropped one-third of their value from 1939 to 1942. Again, in 1946 a slump of more than one-fourth took place. Such losses take long periods to recoup. Hence, correct timing becomes a problem requiring the careful attention of all stock owners.

Barometers of Stock Prices. For a number of years now, market analysts have attempted to find barometers of stock prices. A barometer would be a single economic series, such as building contracts, that would move in advance of the stock cycle and thus forecast changes in the stock cycle. There is no such reliable barometer.

As was noted in Chapter 30, practically all economic series lag behind the movement of stock prices on the average; hence, they cannot be used to forecast changes in the market. The only possible exception is dollar liabilities of industrial and commercial failures, which over a period have shown an average lead of 2.5 months over stock prices at the turns of the business cycle.[4] These averages, however, are merely averages; there are individual cycles when the lead and lag relationship just indicated departs sharply from the average.

There is a rather general opinion that no reliable barometer of the business cycle exists; the opinion is even more pronounced in regard to a barometer of stock prices. Cottle and Whitman expressed the consensus of most students when they stated: ". . . there is considerable doubt whether any single barometer would constitute a satisfactory mechanical guide to stock purchases under a formula plan."[5]

NON-FORMULA STOCK BUYING AND SELLING

Nature. In the remainder of the chapter there will be a discussion of a number of leading plans and systems now in vogue for buying and selling common stocks. Some of these are good and some are inferior.

---

[3] *Loc. cit.*

[4] G. H. Moore (ed.), *Business Cycle Indicators* (2 vols.; Princeton: Princeton University Press, 1961), I, 56.

[5] *Ibid.*, p. 63.

Nearly all have their limitations. The intelligent investor will select those that seem to fit his needs. A critical examination of all is recommended.

Trading by Market Axioms. There is a universal love by mankind for the simple axiom which seems to condense the wisdom of the ages into a few precise words. The axiom is simplicity itself; it relieves the mind of the painful mental processes of inductive and deductive reasoning. These digested capsules of wisdom find their place into all branches of human knowledge and into all vocational activities; they honeycomb literature, religion, ethics, marriage, agriculture, philosophy, photography, child-rearing, the arts, and business. It is therefore not illogical that the follower of the stock market is so often an easy victim of the plausible maxim.

The list of market axioms is endless. Many of them appear in books on the stock market written fifty to seventy-five years ago; even at that time they were well established in the lore of profit-making in the market. Perhaps the oldest is one ascribed to Meyer Rothschild founder of the fortune bearing his name. In explaining how he was able to make so much money in securities, he stated in his broken accent, "I buys 'sheep' and sells 'deer.'" He spoke with authority. The Rothschild family acquired vast wealth after the Battle of Waterloo; his remarkable carrier service permitted him to buy vast blocks of securities very cheaply in the London market, when that exchange still believed that Napoleon had won the battle. When the regular carrier service reached London with news of Napoleon's defeat, securities soared in value and the Rothschild fortune was firmly established.

Space permits a listing of only a few of the many market axioms which have long been popular in Wall Street. Some are of unquestioned merit; others are superficial as well as trite. Some of them are directly contradictory to others. A few are entirely sound under certain conditions but entirely misleading under others.

> When to buy and sell is more important than what to buy and sell.
> Don't rely on the advice of "insiders."
> Cut losses and let profits run.
> Sell when the good news is out.
> Never quarrel with the tape.
> There is no need to be always in the market.
> Never put a halo around a stock.
> Avoid too-frequent switching.
> The stock market has no past.
> Never speculate for a specific need.
> Don't try to get the last eighth.
> No one ever went broke taking profits.
> A bull can make money in Wall Street; a bear can make money in Wall Street; but a hog never can.

Buy when others sell; sell when others buy.

Sell on the first margin call.

A margin call is the only sure tip from a broker.

Put half your profits in a safety deposit box.

Never buy a stock after a long decline.

Never answer a margin call.

Many a healthy reaction has proven fatal.

Never sell on strike news.

Stocks look best at the top of a bull market and worst at the bottom of a bear market.

It is not the price you pay for a stock, but the time you buy it that counts.

When in doubt, do nothing.

Learn to take a loss quickly.

Don't buy an egg until it is laid.

When prices close strong, after an all-day advance, the next move is generally downward.

Stocks that have the longest preceding advances have the largest declines.

All stocks move more or less with the general market, but value will tell in the long run.

Value has little to do with temporary fluctuations in stock prices.

Beware of one who has nothing to lose.

The public is always wrong.

If you would not buy a stock, sell it.

Cut back your stocks to the sleeping point.

The market will continue to fluctuate.

An investor is just a disappointed speculator.

Investment Club Buying. A surprising number of stocks are purchased through investment clubs, a new development in the field of investing. The New York Stock Exchange has estimated that their purchases average about 2 per cent of the volume on the Exchange. The members of typical clubs operate under articles of agreement as an unincorporated association. An investment club account is opened with a brokerage firm and the articles filed with it. The association has a regular set of officers. New members are voted in after the initial group has organized. The group meets regularly to discuss the club's investment program. Periodic dollar contributions are made to the club investment fund. Purchases generally are on a cash basis.

The purposes of such clubs are to educate members on the fundamental principles and practices of sound investing, to enable members to invest surplus funds mutually, and to permit members to engage in a regular investment program. Investments are received from members in various units, such as $5, $10, or $25. The liquidating values of these units or shares are computed regularly, such as once a month or before each regular meeting. The club designates one member to act as agent for the group. A member may withdraw from the club upon notice and receive the liquidating value of his shares.

Many clubs have been successful and have performed a useful service to the members. Success depends upon the investment skill, experience, and intelligence of the membership.

Monthly Investment Plan. This plan of buying stocks was developed by the New York Stock Exchange and launched in January, 1954, to stimulate the business of member firms. One effect has been the encouragement of individuals who have not previously bought stock to do so. The substance of the plan is that the individual opens up with his broker an investment program under which he purchases stock regularly, with the advantage of dollar cost averaging (page 552). Payments are made monthly or quarterly with a minimum of $40. This money is sent into the broker who gives immediate credit for it and uses it for the purchase of the selected stock or stocks. The investor decides upon the stocks he wishes to buy and the dollar amount he wishes to send in monthly, quarterly, or periodically, at his convenience. When fully paid for, the shares are withdrawn with accumulated dividends. Dividends can be automatically reinvested during the life of any plan; most investors follow this policy.

The stock is bought at the same commission rates charged on other New York Stock Exchange transactions. There are no starting or management fees, no dues, assessments, interest charges of any kind. If payments are missed, the plan continues in force. It may be discontinued at any time without penalty.

About 100,000 plans were in operation in early 1962. In the first six years of activity, $154 million was invested in 3.7 million shares. Odd-lot transactions and sales of mutual fund plans exceeded those of the monthly investment plan by a wide margin. The investment plan idea continues to grow in importance. Many brokers, however, who also sell mutual fund shares, seem to push the latter issues more strongly since commissions are roughly triple those of the investment plan.

Arguments in favor of the investment plan are: (1) it permits a simple, systematic method of buying stock at regular and convenient intervals; (2) costs are lower than for mutual funds; (3) dividends can be automatically reinvested; (4) high-priced stocks can be purchased on a fractional basis per month, such as one-third of the cost of a $180 per share of stock; and (5) it permits dollar averaging, an advantage discussed fully in the next chapter.

Criticisms of the plan include: (1) some participants in the plan should not be buying common stocks at all; (2) selecting suitable stocks is difficult; (3) there is less diversification than is offered by investment funds; (4) the owners often lack the necessary skill to invest wisely; and (5) there is no protection against buying stocks when they are too high.

These criticisms, of course, could be used against all stock purchase plans. They are not unique to the investment plan.

Special Situations. This plan contemplates the purchase of common stocks in companies where the profit opportunities are exceptionally high. These unusual opportunities are called "special situations" by Wall Street. Such stocks are those of companies that are presently undervalued but destined for sharp gains in the future. These are not growth stocks but have many similar characteristics.

These special situations develop for many reasons. The company may be enjoying a rapid recovery from a successful reorganization. A new management may be making radical changes in policy and operations which are destined to be very profitable. A very heavy volume of new orders may have been received. New products with wide public acceptance may have been introduced. The company may have developed some new natural resource at a great profit, such as uranium.

Three examples are illustrative: The St. Louis and Southwestern Railway common was selling at $1 per share in 1942; its high in 1955 was $320. During this period the company had undergone a successful reorganization. During the depression Zenith Radio sold as low as $0.03 per share; its high in 1961 was in the $80's. Again, Northern Pacific Railway stock rose from 31 in 1951 to 94 in 1952 because of a discovery of oil in the Williston Basin where the road had land holdings.

The advantage, of course, of purchases in special situations before they develop is the immense profits obtainable. Unfortunately, they are not for the average investor or trader. No one on the outside has the knowledge—and probably the luck—to pick these stocks in advance. Only the most skilled analysts can do so. A few investment funds specialize in this type of investing. The management aspect of the special situation is often highly important. The financial group interested in the situation takes over control, installs its own management, and invests new capital which may be required. In effect, the financial group often makes the special situation. It is in the best position to capitalize upon its efforts and it frequently does.

Industry Selection. This term is chosen because there seems to be no better one available. In fact, this method of stock trading is given no name at all by the financial community, although it has been used for years. Traders who follow the industry selection plan base their operations on the expected actions of stocks of particular industries. Certain industries, in their opinion, appear promising in their market outlook in the coming months because of special conditions. A given industry may be enjoying a sharp revival as new orders pour into it. New models may be meeting unusually good public reception. Defense spending may have been creating a heavy volume of new contracts. Business recovery may have resulted in a large gain in freight traffic.

As such situations develop, traders rush into the industry showing such promise over the short run. In a few months, or a year, profit opportunities are past and traders seek other industries with greater promise. Thus, there is a constant shift of trading from oils to steels, to motors, to chemicals, to building materials, to railroads, to road building equipment, to electronics, to aircrafts.

The rewards of this type of trading are substantial for those who can accurately "pick a winner." Gains of 50 per cent or more per year are often possible. The trader who could successfully pick these industries over a long period would reap immense, if not fantastic, profits. In an interesting hypothetical study made by Hugh W. Long and Company, an investment firm, for the period 1915 to 1944, a sum of $100 was turned into one of $70 million by successfully shifting funds from stocks of one industry to another as profit opportunities developed.[6] Hindsight is a wonderful thing.

Trading by industry selection requires the most accurate forecasting possible, as well as perfect timing. A further limitation is that it works against the principle of portfolio diversification; it creates a risk few can assume.

GROWTH STOCKS

Characteristics. These are the glamour stocks of Wall Street. No group of stocks can compare with them in attraction. They are stocks that have shown a much better-than-average appreciation over a period of time. Often they double in value from the crest of one stock cycle to another. Their growth in sales and earnings is much larger than that of common stocks as a whole.

A growth stock is usually considered to be one issued by an expanding company. Generally the company is in an expanding industry. Such companies may be in old-established industries like chemicals and electrical equipment, but many examples are found in very young industries, such as electronics. A growth stock can be looked upon in two ways. First, it can be identified as a stock that has shown very high appreciation in the past. It has now become a strong, well-known blue chip stock, such as du Pont, General Motors, General Electric, or Coca-Cola. Second, it can be identified as a stock that has great potentialities for growth in the future. The two are not the same. Some companies have been growth companies in the past. For others growth is in the future. For still others the growth of the past seems destined to continue into the distant future.

---

[6] *The Thirty Year Bull Market,* Hugh W. Long & Co., New York.

A danger to the investor is that he might buy into a company whose period of growth is past.

Many companies have qualified as issuers of growth stocks in the past. These include outstanding examples as General Electric, Westinghouse, International Business Machines, du Pont, Dow, Monsanto, Union Carbide and Carbon, Sears, Minnesota Mining and Manufacturing, Standard Oil Company (New Jersey), Coca-Cola, General Motors, Ford, Eastman Kodak, and International Paper, to mention only a few. Many of these will doubtless continue in this category.

The type of industries in the growth field changes over a period. Years ago in the 1920's, automobiles, chemicals, radios, and motion pictures were in this classification. Predictions of growth stocks for the future are limitless. Some of the industries listed in this category for coming years include electronics (particularly color television, automatic controls, and business machinery), chemicals, pharmaceuticals, certain synthetic fibers, petrochemicals, plastics, air conditioning, glass, light metals, aviation, uranimum, automatic vending machines, glass fibers and plastics, silicone plastics and products, home freezers, high temperature alloys, and atomic energy.

Looking back over a period of time, outstanding companies in the growth category have been noted for certain rather definite characteristics. Anderson, in an outstanding study of them, found that as a group they were noted for producing goods and services enjoying high and continuous demand; for continuously developing new products with wide appeal and better-than-average profit margins; for large and continuous expenditures in new plant and equipment; for possessing excellent sales programs; for enjoying highly competent management; for having large and high-quality research programs; for possessing the ability to secure adequate amounts of new capital easily; and for flourishing in mass production industries with relatively low labor costs.[7]

Performance. Examples of highly profitable growth stocks are well publicized. A few will suffice here. An investment of $13,000 in 100 shares of du Pont common in 1922 would have grown to $1.5 million by 1961, disregarding more than one-quarter million dollars in dividends received. An investment of $4,320 in 100 shares of Minnesota Mining and Manufacturing stock in 1946 would have been worth $210,000, plus dividends, by 1961. A large firm made a study of 25 typical growth stocks for the period from January, 1939, to September, 1955. A total of $1,000 was placed in each stock. The hypothetical fund of $25,000 increased in the sixteen years to $235,000.[8]

---

[7] Robert W. Anderson, "Unrealized Potentials in Growth Stocks," *Harvard Business Review*, XXXIII (March–April, 1955), 61.

[8] *111 Growth Stocks*, Merrill Lynch, Pierce, Fenner & Smith, 1956, p. 50.

One of the most careful studies of growth stocks ever made was that of Anderson.[9] Twenty-five such stocks were selected to eliminate any advantage due to hindsight. The period was from 1936 to 1954, a period of eighteen years. Yields were found to be only 3.8 per cent or distinctly inferior to the 5.3 per cent rate of the Dow-Jones industrial average. However, when dividends were reinvested and appreciation considered, the portfolio increased 514 per cent for the period in contrast with 400 per cent for the average. In other words, the growth stock portfolio increased 28 per cent faster than the blue chip average. The gain over typical income stocks for the same period was nearly 70 per cent.

Advantages. There are three advantages to buying growth stocks. First, they produce a faster growth in the investment portfolio than the purchase of income stocks or blue chip stocks which characterize the averages. Second, they have a tax advantage to investors in the higher brackets. Dividends are smaller than those on income stocks; hence, there are lower taxes on current income. Appreciation is not taxable until the stock is sold and then only at long-term capital gains rates. Third, the continuous appreciation tends to offset errors in timing of purchases, since they are believed to recover faster from a market decline. Although this was not true after 1929, it seemed evident in 1946.

Criticisms. A number of criticisms have been directed at the purchase of growth stocks. The most important is the difficulty of selection in advance. To secure the largest gains requires that they be purchased when they are undervalued. This means selection before they are recognized as such, when the companies are small and perhaps struggling to get established. It is then difficult to estimate future growth. Even if the industry appears to have growth possibilities, it is not easy to pick the companies that will become leaders in the industry. This selection before growth appears or is well recognized requires the highest possible investment skill.

Second, growth stocks characteristically pay low dividends and give low yields. Hence, an investor interested in high current income finds these stocks unattractive. Eventually, a good growth stock will pay substantial dividends on the original investment, but it may take ten years to reach this stage.

Third, these stocks sell at very high price-earnings ratios. When fully recognized as growth stocks, they are bid up to high prices and sell at such high price-earnings ratios that they represent unusual investment hazards. The market may have discounted future growth and earning

[9] Anderson, *loc. cit.*

power so much and so far in advance that no real profit is obtainable at current prices.

Fourth, growth industries eventually reach a plateau of stability or maturity. Without realizing this, the investor is apt to pay too high a price for the stock and buy a quality which has ceased to exist.

Fifth, there is the danger of competition. Since growth industries make larger-than-average profits, many competitors come into the industry. In the early stages most of the weak units are eliminated until only a handful of major producers remain. The investor runs a big chance of buying into a company which fails to come out on top. The automobile industry is a classic example. Recently, air conditioning showed definite signs of following this pattern.

Sixth, purchase of growth stocks creates a danger of concentration of financial risk as opposed to sound diversification. Growth stocks at their inception are usually highly speculative.

Seventh, investment in growth stocks requires patience. If they are purchased at the period that gives maximum profit, the investor must wait years to realize the full potential growth. In the meantime there is uncertainty and low return, which many buyers are unwilling to assume. If sold too quickly, the return will be less than if income stocks had been purchased.

MANAGEMENT INVESTMENT COMPANIES

Investment companies provide a method by which the investor can purchase common stocks and other securities indirectly. He purchases the shares of the investment company, which in turn invests his funds in the securities of many corporations, often 100 or more.

The growth of investment companies in recent years amounts almost to a phenomenon. In 1961, 515 companies had assets with a market value of $27 billion. Only a brief description of investment companies can be given here. The reader is urged to make a full investigation of them before investing in one. Information is readily available in prospectuses, annual reports, and information statements.

Closed-End Companies. There are about 185 closed-end investment companies in operation. Shares of a few of them are traded on the exchanges; these include Tri-Continental Corporation, Atlas Corporation, and Lehman Corporation, while others are sold in the over-the-counter market. Shares are purchased at the regular commissions. These are stock companies operating with a fixed capital and a fixed number of outstanding shares, whose value fluctuates with the market demand for their shares. Although not pushed by investment houses because there is not the high selling commission obtainable from selling mutual fund shares, their performances have often been very creditable.

Open-End Companies. These companies, commonly known as mutual funds, are the more popular type of investment company today and are growing with great rapidity. There were about 330 in operation in 1962. Each fund is operated by a management group, which is compensated for its services. Investments usually show tremendous diversity. Portfolios consist mostly of common stocks, although certain "balanced funds" purchase bonds and preferred stocks as well. These stocks may be concentrated in a single industry, but broad diversification is typical. Companies operate on the basis of announced policies which do not change. Such objectives may be income, growth, capital gains, or protection of capital. A considerable turnover may take place in any given fund portfolio over a period of time. The portfolio is constantly increased as fund shares are sold to the public. The skill of management, the performance, and the return to stockholders vary widely among individual funds. More and more stress today is put upon management, in part induced by competition and in part by memories of 1929, when investment trusts showed a record of incompetent management verging on the incredible.

The Portfolio. Most funds greatly diversify their portfolios, often owning stocks in more than 100 companies. These portfolios are published quarterly by the companies and by various financial services and can be examined by shareholders and buyers. This high diversification, while a protection against risk, prevents many funds from showing even an average performance as indicated by the market averages.

Management Cost. Funds are managed by a relatively small group of trustees, directors, investment counsellors, or an advisory board, assisted by a staff of analysts. The sponsor of the fund usually is responsible for its management. Compensation comes in two ways. First, the sponsor receives part of the selling commission or "loading charge" unless there is a separate selling organization. This is typically one-fourth to one-third of the total loading charge, which runs from 6 to 9 per cent, but is usually about 8 per cent. The sponsor, therefore, receives about 2 to 3 per cent when the shares are sold to the investor. The fund itself receives only net asset value.

Second, the management retains an annual management fee. This varies but is about $\frac{1}{2}$ of 1 per cent of the assets. This would mean about 10 per cent of the annual income. In addition, the fund charges off certain expenses from gross income before arriving at the total available for dividends, such as taxes, fees, cost of reports. and expenses of paying dividends. Closed-end funds, of course, deduct operating expenses before payment of dividends.

Selling Costs. As just indicated, a rather high commission or loading charge is used in the distribution of mutual fund shares. This averages about 8 per cent. The salesman or sales organization typically receives 6 per cent. This high commission, as compared with stock exchange commissions, helps to explain the great enthusiasm shown by the salesmen for mutual funds, as well as much of the rapid growth of these issues in recent years.

For example, the total selling cost of twenty mutual fund shares at $25 would involve a sale of $500 and result in $40 in commissions. The equivalent purchase on the New York Stock Exchange would involve a commission of only $10. Since mutual funds redeem their own shares, usually without charge, there is no commission as there would be when listed shares are sold. This high loading charge cuts down on the return when mutual fund shares are redeemed in short periods. If they are redeemed within a few years, the actual yield to the buyer may be no better than that which could have been obtained from the purchase of a savings bond or from placing funds in a savings institution, and may be less.

Price Computations. The values of mutual fund shares are computed twice daily by each fund, at 1:00 and 3:30 P.M. The investor can always redeem his shares by selling them back to the fund at the bid price. The offering price quoted in the papers represents the bid price plus the loading charge. The bid price represents the net asset value per share. In other words, it is computed by dividing the total market value of the portfolio by the number of shares outstanding.

Tax and Income Aspects. Registered investment companies are required by law to pay out 90 per cent of their dividends and interest. In addition, they are taxed on any income or capital gains retained. Hence, the general policy is to pay out nearly all of their earnings. They receive two kinds of income or earnings: (1) the ordinary dividends and interest, or net investment income, and (2) the profits from buying and selling securities, or capital gains.

Payments from both sources of income are made to stockholders. The funds must distinguish between the two in their distribution. The stockholder pays the ordinary income tax rate on the net investment income and the capital gains tax rate on the capital gains share of the distribution. In figuring the yield on earnings received, the stockholder is often confused. The yield is based on the net investment income. The capital gains return is really a return of the capital invested in the fund and should not be regarded as a yield. These capital gains are really not spendable income, but a repayment of part of the original investment by the stockholder. It is the same as though an ordinary stockholder in a listed corporation were to sell part of his shares each year and count the capital gains so obtained as dividends on his stock.

Selection of a Fund. The selection of a suitable investment company is no easy matter. Often the danger is that he will buy the shares of the first fund salesman to approach him. Companies vary greatly in their objectives, diversification policies, type of securities issued, reputation, size, and management record. It is possible to check their portfolios, which are reported quarterly. Their performances are a matter of record. Brokers can supply this information. Certain magazines, such as *Barron's*, report quarterly on their performances.

Performances. Salesmen for mutual funds can usually show excellent performance records for these organizations. This has been comparatively easy since 1949 because of the remarkable gains in stock prices since that period. The averages clearly indicate this improvement. Even with no management at all, a well-diversified fund would show an immense increase in asset values. The question then is: Have funds shown a good performance in reaching investment objectives?

A number of studies have been made of the performance of mutual funds. Perhaps the best generalization is that, as a rule, they show a performance somewhat poorer than that of the averages themselves, such as the Dow-Jones industrial average.

Advantages. Diversification is one of the main advantages of purchasing shares of an investment company. All funds have diversification, even those of the special industry type. Generally, the fund has a high degree of diversification by industries and companies, often numbering well over one hundred situations. No small investor can hope to match this unquestionable characteristic of the investment company. The only objection comes from those who can or hope to obtain better-than-average returns. Diversification is obtained more cheaply through investment company shares than through the purchase of individual stocks.

A second advantage is professional management of one's investments. The companies are managed by skilled and experienced investment experts, aided by trained research staffs. Few small investors have the time, skill, and experience to manage their own investments as well as can the board of managers of a fund. Professional skill is, therefore, substituted for amateur skill. For many this is a real gain and well worth the cost involved. It was pointed out earlier that the average fund does no better, and often not as well, as the averages. In justice to the management of the funds, it should be pointed out that high diversification tends to bring average returns. Also conservatism and the purchase of senior securities reduce returns. Some funds, of course, are not well managed. On the other hand, many small investors cannot do as well in their investing as the averages perform, when commissions and taxes are considered.

A third advantage is that the small investor can invest small sums of money regularly and systematically with a minimum of worry, inconvenience, security analysis, and time consumption. To many this is worth paying for.

Criticisms. The first criticism is the high selling cost, which averages 8 per cent, as already indicated. This is very much higher than for buying stocks in round-lots, which comes to about 1 per cent. It is also higher than for odd-lots, except where very small purchases are made. These high loading charges are especially costly in the event the investor redeems his shares within a few years after purchase, since yields are thus greatly reduced.

Another criticism is that successes are overrated by many funds. The average performance, as indicated, is no better than that of the stock averages, in spite of the well-advertised professional management aspect of the investment. Although many amateur investors cannot do as well as the averages, many experienced ones can.

A third criticism is the handling of capital gains. These are paid out to the investor, who must pay taxes on them whether he reinvests them or spends them. If he purchased ordinary corporate shares, he would pay no capital gains tax until his stock was sold. The effect of this investment company policy is that the shareholder's capital is often spent rather than kept in the capital fund.

Another criticism is that there is cause for doubting that present earnings can continue. There was a very strong bull market in stocks for a number of years. This aided funds in making very creditable performances. The question may well be asked: How well can the funds perform in a period of stable or falling markets?

A fifth criticism is that years ago investment trusts rose to prominence by the same arguments of merit, skilled management, and diversification as are heard today, yet their records after 1929 were dismal. Will history be repeated? It is probable, however, that the lessons of 1929 have been well learned. In addition, there is a considerable degree of regulation today which was non-existent many years ago.

A final criticism can be made. The investor in such companies has less control over his investments than if he were to purchase ordinary corporate shares. His investments become inflexible and he becomes locked in with the fortunes of the fund in which he has invested.

A Final Comment. For many small investors, the investment company offers several real advantages, although the cost may be high and the return only average. He could do far worse on his own. For the larger investor, particularly the experienced one, a policy of going it alone has much to be said for it. However, for the large investor, two points are significant: (1) he may be able to acquire a complete portfolio and management relatively inexpensively; and (2) he can liquidate quickly without cost and without individual impact on the market.

32

The Dow Theory

The Dow theory is one that seeks to forecast stock prices by interpretation of the action of the Dow-Jones industrial and rail averages. Its principles were formulated by Charles Dow and S. A. Nelson at the turn of the century and popularized by William P. Hamilton. Both Dow and Hamilton were editors of the *Wall Street Journal*. The theory has a considerable following but appears to have declined greatly in popularity and prestige in the last fifteen or twenty years. It is undoubtedly the best known of all trading plans.

The theory has been extensively defended and criticized, with the criticism in recent years being much more vocal than the defense. It is not a system for "beating the market," and was not so considered by either Dow or Hamilton. Because it was the first widely known trading plan, an understanding of its features is a useful introduction to a study of more modern trading plans.

Much has been written about the theory. Later writers on the theory have attempted to amplify, extend, or modify the original theory as their individual contributions. The discussion that follows, however, will be confined as far as possible to the original theory as first presented by Dow and Nelson, and developed by Hamilton.

Today there is no longer an authoritative voice to discuss the theory. The *Wall Street Journal* no longer carries editorials at frequent intervals to interpret it. No well-known Dow service operates in New York, although there are about four or five important ones located in various cities, mostly in the Middle West. Robert Rhea, perhaps the best-known writer on the subject since Hamilton, has been dead for a number of years.[1]

---

[1] His exhaustive study of the theory was published in *The Dow Theory* (New York: Barron's, 1932).

ORIGIN

Charles Dow. Charles Dow was a New Englander, born in 1851.[2] He was a mild-mannered, undogmatic sort of man, possessed of the characteristic conservatism of his birthplace, according to Hamilton, his close associate.[3] His early newspaper experience was on a Massachusetts paper, *The Springfield Republican*. From this stepping stone he went on to New York in search of greater opportunities. For a time he owned a seat on the New York Stock Exchange. Eventually he left the Exchange and founded the Dow-Jones Company, a financial service. This organization is well known today as the publisher of the *Wall Street Journal*.

During 1900, 1901, and early 1902, Dow was editor of the *Journal* and wrote a number of editorials that dealt with the movement of security prices. It is interesting to note that he never wrote a single editorial devoted exclusively to the Dow theory, nor did he at any time outline it in precise terms or label it as such. The only material he ever wrote on the theory is contained in his editorials.

Nelson and Hamilton. The theory became crystallized in the writings of Nelson and Hamilton. Dow died in early 1902. In the same year a reporter on the *Journal*, S. A. Nelson, prepared and published a modest little volume entitled *The A B C of Speculation*.[4] It was based partly on Dow's editorials and partly upon his experience as a financial reporter in Wall Street. Nelson was the first person to state the principle of the theory in definite form; he also named it "Dow's theory." Later the phrase "the Dow theory" replaced Nelson's nomenclature.

Dow was succeeded as editor of the *Wall Street Journal* by T. F. Woodlock, S. S. Pratt, and, in 1908, by William P. Hamilton. Hamilton held the editorial post until his death in 1929. His editorials continued and refined the development of Dow theory.

Original Purpose. Both Dow and Hamilton believed that changes in the averages anticipated changes in business activity, but the original purpose seems simply to have been measurement of change in stock prices.[5] Later the theory became widely popular because of its alleged ability to forecast trends in the stock market. That the theory could forecast changes in business conditions was thoroughly believed by both

---

[2] For a definitive study of Dow's life and work, see: George W. Bishop, Jr., *Charles H. Dow and the Dow Theory* (New York: Appleton-Century-Crofts, Inc., 1960).

[3] W. P. Hamilton, *The Stock Market Barometer* (New York: Harper & Row, Publishers, 1922), p. 21.

[4] S. A. Nelson, *The A B C of Speculation* (New York: Stock Market Publications, 1934), p. 31. This is a facsimile reproduction of the original work, now out of print.

[5] Bishop, *op. cit.*, pp. 229–30.

men. Said Hamilton: "Our barometer does predict the condition of business many months ahead, and no other index, or combination of indexes, can do that."[6]

Although Hamilton was convinced of the ability of the theory to forecast changes in the stock market, he denied that it was a scheme for "beating the market." It was no "get-rich-quick scheme." Rather, he considered it to be a theory that would benefit the intelligent investor who could find in it a method of protecting himself against changes in the market's trend by a careful study of the action of the averages—the barometer of the market.

BASIC FEATURES

Three Movements in the Market. The theory is based on the fundamental premise that at all times there are three movements in the stock market: (1) the primary, (2) the secondary, and (3) the daily movement; these operate simultaneously.

The first or primary movement is also called the major or primary trend; it is the long-term trend, the major bull or bear market. Coincident with it is the secondary movement, or secondary reaction. This is a sharp and discernible rally in a primary bear market or a steep reaction in a primary bull market. Usually two or three of these will take place in each bull or bear market. The third movement is the day-to-day fluctuation of stock prices. Of the three movements, the first is the most important; the second aids in forecasting the first; the third is unimportant.

Dow conceived of the stock market as having movements very much in the way that the tides of the ocean ebb and flow. The primary movement was the tide; the secondary movements were the waves; the daily movements were the ripples.[7]

His followers have often followed the analogy, which is imaginative but entirely misleading. Few things are as regular and periodic as the tides; few are as uncertain as the movements of the stock market. Various governments have developed the principles of tidal movements so accurately that the tide for any given harbor for any desired period can be predicted far in advance. These predictions are so accurate that variations from actual tide records are so minor as to be without significance. On the other hand, the stock market has no such regularity of movement and any attempt to forecast it upon the basis of a purely mathematical formula is doomed to failure in advance.

Hamilton in his editorials at no time stated his belief in any regular stock cycle. Its duration he felt to be incalculable. The Dow theory is

[6] Hamilton, *op. cit.*, p. 56.
[7] *Wall Street Journal*, January 31, 1901.

based on the assumption that the cycle will be irregular; its only objective is to tell when either a bull or a bear market has terminated; it does not predict how long that market will last.

Forecasting Movements. Dow wrote, as already indicated from 1900 to 1902. At that time his first average, largely a rail one, had been compiled for sixteen years, but his industrial average had been in existence only three years. On this evidence he made certain observations. It was his belief that no one could forecast the length of a major bull or bear market. Said he: "It is impossible to tell the length of any primary movement."[8] Hamilton in his writings also conceded that it was difficult to call the turn of a bull or bear market in advance. As to the length of a primary movement, Dow in his editorials stated that it would last at least a year and generally much longer, perhaps as much as four years. Hamilton, with a much greater volume of statistics, in reviewing the period from 1900 to 1923, concluded that the average bull market ran twenty-seven months and the average bear market extended to only fifteen.

Recent studies of the stock market have increased somewhat these earlier estimates of the length of the stock cycle. A Senate staff report in 1955 computed an average cycle of four years since the Civil War, with individual cycles ranging from two to ten years.[9] In the first fifty years of the twentieth century, the average bull market has been about two and one-half years and the average bear market one and one-half years.

As to the secondary movement, Dow believed that it typically ran "from two weeks to a month or more."[10] Rhea believed that the length was nearer three weeks to three months.[11] Dow's thought was that the secondary reaction would retrace about three-eighths of the prior rise or fall of the primary trend in contrast with Rhea's estimate that the price movement retraces from 33 to 66 per cent of the primary price change of the last preceding secondary reaction.

The secondary reaction is considered a normal and necessary movement in the upward or downward trend of prices. It is a needed correction or a safety valve, growing out of speculation. It often results from the market being overbought or oversold, with resultant attempts by professional traders to cash in on short-term profits. One of the biggest difficulties, incidentally, of trading on the Dow theory, is the

---

[8] *Wall Street Journal,* July 20, 1901.

[9] *Staff Report to the Committee on Banking and Currency, U. S. Senate, 84th Congress,* April 30, 1955, p. 27.

[10] *Wall Street Journal,* December 19, 1900.

[11] *Rhea, op. cit.,* p. 52.

danger of confusing the secondary reaction with the primary trend. Often the distinguishing line is faint and hard to spot.

Secondary reactions are technical reactions in the market caused by profit-taking by professional traders, either "longs" or "shorts." There are no mathematical rules to indicate when they will start or end. Many followers of the theory attempt to discover indications of their approach. For example, some consider that the lack of response to good news in a bull market is a sign of an approaching reaction downward, while the lack of response to bad news in a bear market is a sign of an approaching rally. Steady declines or gains of more than average length are also considered important signals of change.

The day-to-day movements, which may last from several hours to several days, have no significance in the theory. Both Dow and Nelson believed that they "should be disregarded by everybody except traders, who pay no commissions."[12] Followers of the theory, however, daily plot the movements on charts since they eventually develop into the patterns of secondary reactions.

The Dow-Jones Averages. Hamilton used both the Dow-Jones rail and industrial averages as the key to stock market movements. These two averages must corroborate each other to give a positive indication of trend; without such corroboration nothing is indicated by the market's action.

A reasonable justification can be built up for the use of the two averages. The rail average is based upon 20 leading rail stocks; their prices should reflect the present and future business of their respective roads; this traffic affects earnings, which are discounted by market action. The railroads show the movement of goods in commercial and industrial channels. In recent years the use of the rail average has come under much criticism. Railroads are much less important as traffic carriers than they were many years ago. In addition, rail stocks, formerly the most popular of all issues, now account for less than 10 per cent of the trading activity on the New York Stock Exchange. Many Dow theorists today even advocate the elimination of the rail average in the interpretation of the theory.

The industrial average, which is now based on 30 leading stocks, is used as an indicator of the volume of production of the country. Industries in manufacturing and mining operate both upon present orders and anticipated business. Industrial stocks should, therefore, reflect the production level of the country; their prices should discount the earnings of such companies. Hence, the two averages, in theory, will discount

---

[12] Nelson, *op. cit.*, p. 36.

changes in corporate earnings, dividends, production, and the movement of goods. The theory is based on this premise.

There was no Dow-Jones public utility average, of course, until 1929,
the year of Hamilton's death. Dow theorists have never considered the
average as necessary to the interpretation of the theory because utility
stocks are not subject to the same influences as the rails and industrials.

The Averages Discount Everything. Both Dow and Hamilton believed
that the theory needed only the stock averages to operate. No other
averages were necessary; no other economic series was essential. In fact,
both men repeatedly stated that to use any other series was not only
meaningless and a waste of time but absolutely harmful. Many critics
of the theory today, as will be observed later, believe that a series other
than the two averages would be more logical. This premise was early
rejected by Dow and his disciple. Said Hamilton:

> The weakness of every other method is that extraneous matters are taken
> in from their tempting relevance. There have been unnecessary attempts to
> combine the volume of sales and to record the averages with reference to com-
> modity index numbers. But it must be obvious that the averages have already
> taken these things into account, just as a barometer considers everything
> which affects the weather. The price movement represents the aggregate
> knowledge of Wall Street, and above all, its aggregate knowledge of coming
> events. . . . The market represents everything everybody knows, hopes,
> believes, anticipates, with all that knowledge sifted down to what Senator
> Dolliver once called, in quoting a *Wall Street Journal* editorial in the United
> States Senate, the bloodless verdict of the market place.[13]

Since both men were editors of the *Wall Street Journal*, they wrote
about the Dow-Jones averages in the interpretation of their theory.
Hamilton stated in his writings that, although these averages had been
widely imitated, they were still standard, and no other series had proved
to be as satisfactory.

Cyclical Movement in Stock Prices. The stock cycle, according to the
Dow theory, is watched through the closing prices of the industrial and
rail averages of each trading day. These are carefully charted.

The primary movement of stock prices, once established, continues
in the same direction until there is an indication of a change. This upward or downward trend is interrupted at intervals by intermediate or
secondary reactions. Eventually the two averages indicate that a new
primary movement has been established. This, again, continues with
interruptions by secondary reactions until another primary trend is indicated. An entire cycle, as already noted, runs about four years.

[13] Hamilton, *op. cit.*, p. 7.

Confirmation. A basic premise of the Dow theory is that the primary movement is never definitely established until there is a "confirmation." This means that both averages confirm the new primary trend. They must corroborate each other. If one average indicates an upward trend and the other a downward trend, there is no significance to these indications. It is only when both averages go in the same direction that confirmation is possible. One average is then said to confirm the other's action; a new long-term trend is now established.

It was the opinion of both Dow and Hamilton that there was never a primary movement and seldom a secondary reaction in which this confirmation did not take place.

Confirmation may take place in either of two ways: (1) by the averages "making lines" and then showing "break-outs," and (2) by the averages making "new highs or new lows" or by secondary reactions.

Confirmation by Making Lines. Technically speaking, "making a line" is an action that takes place when an average fluctuates within a narrow range for several weeks; e.g., between 160 and 168, or between 500 and 520. Just what is the amplitude of a line is not clear. Many years ago, when the rail average stood at about 80 and the industrial average at about 115, Hamilton considered that a 3-point range would be a line for the former and a 4-point range would be a line for the latter. As prices rose, Hamilton admitted that wider limits were necessary. Rhea defined a line as "a price movement extending two to three weeks or longer, during which the price variation of both averages move within a range of approximately 5 per cent."[14] This definition is as satisfactory as any. In any case, there is no precise mathematical rule to compute the amplitude of a line.

When an average is "making a line," it is in a period of equilibrium or indecision; the buying and selling forces are about equal as the market is being pushed up and down. It should be pointed out that both averages do not need to "make a line" at the same time; these lines may be days or even weeks apart.

Once both averages have pushed above this line, a definitely bullish signal is given. On the other hand, if both averages make a line and then show a "break-out" on the so-called "down side," the indications are very bearish. The signals are meaningless unless one average confirms the signal of the other.

Hamilton considered that lines were useful in indicating a change in the direction of the market at least for secondary, and occasionally for primary, movements.

[14] Rhea, *op. cit.*, p. 79.

Lines have been much criticized by Dow theorists in recent years and mostly have been dropped from discussions because of a belief that they were not dependable.

Figure 32–1 illustrates the action of an average in "making a line" and then confirming a downward movement.

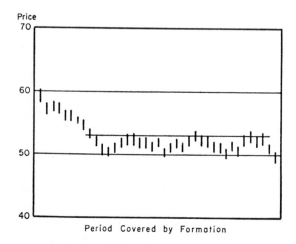

Fig. 32–1. An average making a line.

Confirmation by New Highs and Lows. This type of confirmation is also called confirmation by secondary reactions. This method is the one generally used by Dow theorists in recent years.

Confirmation proceeds in this manner. Let us assume that the primary trend is upward. Each secondary rise of the industrial average is followed by a reaction downward, which in turn is followed by another secondary rise. This wave-like movement continues. An important point to note is that each rise exceeds the previous peak and each decline falls to a point less than the low of the previous decline. In other words, the industrial average makes a new high on every secondary reaction. This average is indicating a continuation of the bull market trend.

At the same time the rail average is showing a similar movement. On each rise the average exceeds the high of the previous secondary movement and each decline carries the average to a point less than the low of the previous decline. Whenever one average makes a new high, followed by a new high for the other average, a confirmation is said to take place. The bull market will continue until one average shows an opposite signal. It is vital to the theory that both averages make a confirmation of a primary trend. If there is no confirmation, the signals are meaningless.

Now, suppose that the industrial average shows a down signal. In other words, on a rally the average fails to make a new high and turns down. This is meaningless unless the other average also fails to make a new high and turns down. When both averages have given down signals, the bull market is over and the confirmation of a bear market is indicated.

Similarly, the end of a bear market is indicated when an intermediate rise goes higher than the previous one and is followed by a decline that does not go as low as the bottom of the previous reaction. Both averages, of course, must confirm the end of the bear market.

Dow described confirmation by new highs and new lows in his editorials, the following statement being typical:

> It is a bull market as long as the average of one high point exceeds that of previous points. It is a bear market when the low point becomes lower than the previous low points.[15]

During what period should one average confirm a primary movement already indicated by the other? This is a vexing question to which there is no answer. No one, even Dow and Hamilton, expected confirmation on the same day, or even in the same week. Rhea did not commit himself. Presumably, there is no maximum period within which confirmation must take place. There have been instances when one average did not confirm the signal of the other average for as long as one year or more; e.g., November, 1935. Such long waits exasperate all but the most devout Dow theorists.

Another problem of confirmation arises: Exactly when does an average make a new high or new low? On December 13, 1961, the Dow-Jones industrial average made a new all-time high, closing at 734.91. At what point would the average be if it were to make another new high? Would it be 734.92; would it be a full point higher, or 735.91; would it be 1 per cent higher, or 742.26? There is no answer since there is today no authority on the matter. Yet the determination of where the new high is located could mean a tremendous difference in determining the signal for another bull market.

Let us illustrate the principle of confirmation by new highs by a simple tabulation; this is shown in Table 32–1 and Figure 32–2, using figures such as were usual in 1961.

In this table it will be observed that the industrial average rose from 710 to 730 and then fell back to 722 in Period C. In Period D it made another new high, since 738 was above the previous high of 730. In Period E it rose still higher to 744, another peak.

At what point did the rail average "confirm" a new upward movement? It rose to 145 in Period B and then fell back to 142 in Period C.

---

[15] *Wall Street Journal*, January 4, 1902.

Table 32–1. Dow Theory Confirmation of New Movement by New Highs

Period	Rail Average	Industrial Average
A	140	710
B	145	730
C	142	722
D	144	738
E	148	744

Although it rose to 144 in Period D, there was no confirmation as yet, since 144 was still under the previous high of 145. In Period E, however, the rail average pushed up to 148, which was another new high, since it was above the previous peak of 145. At Period E, therefore, the rail average is said to have "confirmed" a new upward movement; both averages have now exceeded their previous highs.

The Importance of Volume. The importance of volume, or activity, of the market is a matter of some confusion in the Dow theory. Mr. Dow mentioned volume in his editorials on stock movements without explicit formulation of a relationship. Even Hamilton was guilty of confusion on this aspect. At times he stated that volume was of no importance in interpreting the theory. For example, in one editorial he declared without equivocation: "This is why volume of trading is ignored in these studies. In the quarter of a century of the price movement recorded in

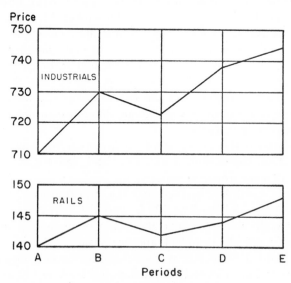

Fig. 32–2. Dow theory confirmation of new movements by new highs.

the Dow-Jones and Company averages, the volume of business has borne little perceptible relation to the tendency of prices."[16] This opinion was repeated with variations many times. However, at other times, he apparently attached importance to volume. For example, in one editorial he stated: "The market became dull on small reactions, showing increased activity on any resumption of the advance. As any professional knows, this is a good indication that strength is still on the buying side."[17] Many variations of this opinion can also be found in Hamilton's editorials. One must conclude, therefore, that Hamilton was very contradictory as to this aspect of the theory. Rhea, however, was a firm believer in volume as an important tool in interpreting the theory, as are many technicians today in interpreting the market, regardless of whether or not they follow the Dow theory.

Charts and Records. Hamilton was no great believer in either charts or records as tools for forecasting the market. He believed that they were not barometers and that they were hazy about the future. He was contemptuous of any theory of action and reaction in the market being equal, as it is in the study of physics. All that one needed was a close study of the averages.

Double Tops and Bottoms. Neither Dow nor Hamilton placed any reliance upon chart formations, such as double tops and bottoms. Said Dow in an editorial: "Those who attempt to trade on this thing alone find a good many exceptions and a good many times when signals are not given."[18] Similarly, Hamilton declared of these formations: "I frankly confess that I have not found them essential or greatly useful."[19]

Summary of Dow Theory. The essential features of the Dow theory, as first presented by Dow, Nelson, and Hamilton, were these:

1. There are three movements in the stock market: (a) the primary movement, (b) the secondary reaction, and (c) the daily fluctuations.
2. The primary movement may be either a long-term bull market or a long-term bear market. These markets are forecast by the action of the Dow-Jones industrial and rail averages.
3. The averages forecast bull and bear markets only when one average confirms the signals of the other. This confirmation may take place either by both averages making lines and then showing a break-out in the same direction or by both averages showing new highs or new lows through secondary reactions.
4. The averages do not forecast how long a primary movement will last, but only indicate when a new bull or bear market is under way.

[16] *Wall Street Journal*, June 4, 1913.
[17] *Wall Street Journal*, February 6, 1911.
[18] *Wall Street Journal*, June 29, 1901.
[19] Hamilton, *op. cit.*, p. 32.

5. The market is forecast solely by the movements of the averages, which discount everything. The importance of volume of trading is not clear from the writings of Hamilton, but is stressed by later students of the theory. No use is made of series other than the averages nor is use made of extensive charts and records. The study of chart formations, such as double tops and double bottoms, is not a part of the theory.

6. The purpose of the theory is to indicate the reversal of primary trends.

7. Primary trends will continue as long as the averages confirm each other as to the direction of the trend.

8. The theory is not a system for "beating the market," but rather one that can benefit the intelligent speculator who wishes to protect himself against changes in primary bull and bear markets.

THE DOW THEORY IN ACTION

The 1929 Signal. In the following illustrations an attempt will be made to evaluate the Dow theory in the light of its ability to forecast the end of a bull or bear market.

The theory was probably put to its greatest test in 1929. The Dow-Jones averages reached their 1929 peaks some time before the October crash. On September 3 the rail average reached its peak for the year, 189; the industrial average reached its peak of 381. Both averages then began to decline. Sharp breaks took place on October 23 and 24. On October 25 the *Wall Street Journal* carried Hamilton's famous editorial, "A Turn in the Tide." In it he stated that the averages by their action on October 23 had signaled the end of the six-year bull market and the beginning of a bear market.

Let us see how well the Dow theory acted in calling "A Turn in the Tide."

Date	Rail Average	Industrial Average
Sept. 3, 1929, close	189	381
Oct. 23, 1929, close	167	306
July 8, 1932, close	13	31

If a trader had followed the Dow signal of October 23, he would have already lost 22 points on the rail average and 75 points on the industrial average, but he would have saved a further loss of 154 on the rail average and 275 on the industrial average. In other words, the theory would have taken him out of the market after it had fallen about 12 per cent of its eventual decline, as measured by the rail average, and 22 per cent by the industrial average.

The 1946 Signal. From 1942 to 1946 the stock market enjoyed a very strong position. The industrial average reached its peak on May 29, 1946, and the rail average on June 13. On August 28 a leading Dow service announced that the bull market was over. By this time the industrial average had fallen 23 points and the rail average 10 points. The trader who sold out on the August signal would have gotten out of the market after it had suffered 46 per cent of its loss for the year, as measured by the industrial average, and 44 per cent, as measured by the rail average.

The 1948 Signal. On May 14, 1948, both averages confirmed a bull market. The market was exceptionally strong for two days and then leveled off for two months and fell sharply on July 17. The signal was entirely false. The market went up 5 points after the signal, whereas it had already gone up 23 points, as measured by the industrial average, in the previous rise from February to May. In other words, 84 per cent of the market rise took place before the bull market signal was given.

From 1938 to 1948 the theory fared badly. If one had placed $10,000 in stocks in 1938 and followed the Dow theory signals in this period, his funds would have grown to $11,903. If he had invested the $10,000, however, in the stocks comprising the average on a "buy-and-hold" policy, his fund would have grown to $13,653.[20] In addition, he would have saved a considerable sum in commissions and received more in dividends. In other words, by doing nothing, our trader would have made substantially more than if he had faithfully followed all Dow signals in the period.

The 1949 Signal. The bull market of 1949 to 1961—the longest on record—began on June 14, 1949. On that date the industrial average stood at 160 and the rail averages at 41. The industrial average gave a bull market signal on August 5, and the rail average on December 2. By that time the industrial average climbed 21 per cent before confirmation took place. The Dow theory worked commendably in the latter part of 1949. Its next performance however, was an unhappy one.

The 1953 Signal. The Dow theory worked very badly in 1953. The industrial average showed a bear market signal in January and the rail average on August 31. Both averages, therefore, by August 31 confirmed a bear market. For the next two weeks there was a baby bear market in which both averages fell about 5 points. The industrial average then reversed its trend and began to rise. It was not until May 7, 1954, however, that the rail average confirmed the bull market trend. By that time the industrial average had climbed from 255 to 321, a gain of 66 points and had covered 35 per cent of the way to the level of 487 on September 26, 1955, when it broke sharply on news of the President's heart attack.

The 1957 Signal. In October, 1957, the industrial average confirmed a bear market signal given by the rail average in August. The industrial

[20] A. W. Jones, "Fashions in Forecasting," *Fortune*, March, 1949, p. 91.

average reached its low in October. Resumption of the bull market was not signaled until November, 1958, by which time the industrial average had risen 160 points and was 75 per cent of the way to its next top.

The 1960 Signal. Both averages affirmed the existence of a bear market in March, 1960. At that time the industrial average was about 620. It subsequently declined to about 570, or 50 points. Although the industrial average then rose 165 points, to the end of 1961, no resumption of a bull market had been signaled. The averages declined in 1962.

Bull Market Confirmations. A few years ago one of the business services released a study of bull market confirmations of the Dow theory over the fifty-year period from 1897 to 1946.[21] In an examination of thirteen bull markets over that period, it was found that the typical rise after confirmation was 44 per cent, with a market increase after each confirmation. This is one of the more favorable studies of the theory. The next study is far more critical.

Cowles Study of Hamilton Editorials. William P. Hamilton, during his long career as editor of the *Wall Street Journal* was, without question, the best known of all Dow theorists. The value of the theory, therefore, can be well tested in the light of his ability to correctly forecast the market. This has been done in a very thorough study of 255 of Hamilton's editorials, published over the twenty-six-year period 1904–29.[22] His editorials were rated as "bullish," "bearish," or "doubtful." In order to add concreteness to the study, it was assumed that an investor bought stocks when forecasts were bullish, sold them when forecasts were bearish, and remained on the sidelines when the forecast was doubtful. As a contrast, the report estimated the profit which would have been made in the same period if an investor had fully invested his money in the stocks represented by the averages for the entire period with no trading. Careful adjustments were made for dividends, stock rights, and brokerage charges.

The study concluded that Hamilton made ninety recommendations of change in position in the twenty-six years: 55 per cent were bullish forecasts; 16 per cent were bearish; and 29 per cent were doubtful. In examining the results, it was noted that forty-five were profitable forecasts and forty-five were unprofitable. In other words, his forecasts were no more successful than if a coin had been flipped for ninety consecutive tosses. These results were for the industrial averages; the forecasts would have been profitable in 41 cases for the rail averages and 49 times unprofitable.

[21] *United Business Service Report,* May 24, 1949, p. 207; computatons by Barbour's Dow Service of Detroit, Michigan.
[22] *Econometrica,* Vol. I, No. 3 (July, 1933).

The most damaging comparison, however, in the study of the performance of the Dow theory during this period was that of the relative gains found in the investment of a given amount of money on a "buy-and-hold" basis and the same amount in issues to be bought and sold as suggested by Hamilton's editorials. Cowles found that the annual return would have been 3.5 per cent better on the "buy-and-hold" basis for the industrials and 2 per cent better for rails than if the money had been put into the market and taken out on the basis of the editorial recommendations.

The survey was made by an able economist, Alfred Cowles III, and presented as a paper before a joint meeting of the Econometric Association and the American Statistical Association. His conclusions are perhaps the most enlightening comments ever made on the validity of the theory.

EVALUATION OF THE THEORY

In Its Defense. Those who defend the theory can often marshal impressive facts to show that it does work. It does not get the trader in at the bottom of the market or out at the top, it is true; yet no one can expect such perfection in a trading method. It is affirmed that it does forecast the turn of the market before it has gone too far; it does permit the trader to make a reasonable profit before the termination of a primary trend. As just noted in the report on thirteen bull market confirmations from 1897 to 1946, the median rise after confirmation was 44 per cent. This defense rests on the "better a half-loaf than none" axiom.

Credit is due Mr. Dow for being the first individual to present a workable plan for studying the action of the market. As a pioneer, his theory may be outmoded by the vast economic changes which have taken place in recent years. His contribution, however, was of value in that it stimulated others to examine the functioning of the market. Many of the theories developed in recent years have been no more successful than the Dow theory in accurately forecasting stock prices.

Indictments of the Theory. A number of adverse criticisms of the theory have developed in recent years. Critics now outnumber defenders by a marked ratio. Few believe that the theory has shown a creditable record since 1938. That many of the criticisms carry conviction is undeniable.

1. *Its successes are overrated.* As already indicated by the Cowles study, ninety forecasts based on its principles and made by the greatest authority on the theory at the time were only 50 per cent successful. A trading policy, based on these forecasts over a twenty-six-year period, would have been less successful than an outright "buy and hold" policy

in the same stocks. The same results were found from 1938 to 1948. The theory has had at least three very marked failures since World War II.

2. *Its superficiality.* The follower of the theory tends to concentrate too much upon surface action of the market as indicated by the averages. Only by a most careful study of fundamental conditions, tempered with a knowledge of technical conditions which may affect it to some extent at all times, can a student perceive the vast, underlying influences that affect stock prices.

3. *Its lack of precision.* There is no agreement as to prices in the theory, even among the most thorough of its students. In measuring confirmation, should a new high exceed a previous one by 0.01, 0.10, or 1.00 points or by 1 per cent? Such hair-splitting distinctions may seem trivial, but new highs or new lows are often dependent on a few cents difference in an average.

4. *Its failure to forecast tops and bottoms.* A very real objection by many practical traders is that the theory does nothing to signal the end of a bull or bear market until a new trend has been definitely established. No one can tell how long a trend will last by studying the averages; the trader would like to know about a turn in the market before it happens and not afterward. It is true, of course, that the theory does not give a signal until the primary trend has run 20 to 30 per cent of its course. On the other hand, a trader is no better off under a system that takes him out of a bull market when it has run only half of its course, as many did in the 1949–61 bull market. One system takes the speculators out of the market too late and the other too early.

5. *The uncertainty of confirmation.* The follower of the theory will often wait days, weeks, or months for one average to confirm the signals of the other. For long periods the averages may give no discernible signals. In the meantime the trader waits impatiently, unable to decide whether to put his money in the market or to take it out. He sees profits disappear or losses accumulate. Even when there is an apparent confirmation, the trader cannot be too sure of his signals because of the lack of precision in measurements. Confirmations are often not as clear cut and as obvious as defenders of the theory would have one assume. The distinction between intermediate fluctuations and primary movements is often indistinct.

6. *It is too slow.* Many critics of the theory become exasperated at the slowness with which confirmation takes place. One average may be dropping sharply and the investor is taking heavy losses, but there is no confirmation of a bear market by the other. By the time confirmation

comes, he may have suffered still greater losses. The trader does not want to read about the turn of the tide after he is engulfed in a tidal wave. To this argument the Dow theorist replies that most of the profits are salvaged—no one can expect perfection. He will also argue that the slowness of confirmation is less dangerous than trading upon early signals which may prove premature, erratic, and expensive.

7. *One cannot buy averages.* A study of the rail and industrial averages throws little light upon the selection of individual issues, unless one accepts the blind philosophy that "all stocks go up and down together." The investor or trader must still consider with great care the purchase of any particular stock. It is true that in a given market the trend may be upward, but great losses are possible by buying the wrong stocks. It is equally true that money can be made in a bear market in certain stocks that are going counter to the trend. Only a majority of stocks go in the direction of the primary trend; there are many exceptions.

Superficially this criticism is true. Yet the same indictment can be made against any trading system or formula plan; none selects individual purchases. This is an entirely different aspect of investment.

8. *Its use of the rail averages.* Many critics point out that the rail averages have lost much of their significance. At one time the railroads were the nearly universal carriers of freight traffic, but today they carry a much smaller percentage. In 1900 rail issues were the popular speculative favorites, while today they account for less than 10 per cent of all trading. It has been suggested that the rail average be abandoned. Some traders actually use the theory with only the industrial average as an indicator. Others have suggested other economic series, but there has been no general agreement as to what series would be acceptable. In any case, a rejection of the rail average would mean a scuttling of the Dow theory; another theory would be established.

9. *It is based on an early economy.* There have been vast changes in the American economy in the last half-century. Our laissez-faire economic system has changed into one with a considerable measure of government control. The old national banking system has given way to a highly integrated Federal Reserve system. The market in earlier days was highly sensitive to changing conditions in banking and the money market and was often a victim of these changes. The situation is much different today. Hence, it can be argued that the Dow theory may have worked under our earlier economy but conditions are now vastly changed. There is more than a little truth to this criticism. A similar situation exists in regard to the ability of the stock market to discount changes in business activity; this ability is much less than it was years ago.

A FINAL COMMENT

The space devoted to the study of the Dow theory is perhaps excessive in view of its present importance as a trading method. The rather extended analysis, however, seems justified in that it indicates the thoroughness that should be used to examine any trading system or formula plan before its general acceptance or rejection.

In the two chapters that follow, many recent systems and plans are discussed. Many will be found wanting when subjected to critical analysis. There are few that have no weaknesses.

The Dow theory has shown poor performance in recent years. Even if its record had been better, one must still ask oneself the question: Should one trade on the general level of stock market prices rather than upon the merits of individual stocks? Trading upon general stock price levels is one of the most hazardous of occupations.

33

Formula Plans

Untold numbers of men have spent untold numbers of hours to reduce the art and science of investing and trading to a plan or formula that would be sound in theory and profitable in practice. Here is a sampling of their efforts and an evaluation of their successes.

Characteristics of Formula Plans. This chapter will deal with a number of representative formula plans that have developed in recent years. All have grown out of a desire by investors and traders to obtain protection against purchases and sales at unfavorable price levels. Stated in another way, the plans were created to obtain better timing, thus avoiding the heavy losses such as were suffered in 1929 and 1946.

It was hoped, and for a time confidently expected, that a successful formula plan would avoid mistakes in judgment. In fact, it was hoped that judgment could be eliminated and that a mechanical set of rules could dictate purchases and sales to assure reasonable profits at all times. In this way the emotional aspect of investing and trading would be eliminated. The buyer would no longer have to trust his own judgment or consult his fears and hopes; the set of rules would take over decision making.

Spurred on by this philosophy, a number of plans were developed. Two general types emerged. The first type consisted of a group of plans that operated without the computation of normal values. The second group operated on the basis of normal values, computed by a number of methods. Selected examples of each classification will be examined later in the chapter.

Before doing so, however, an objection against all such systems should be pointed out. It is the criticism that there are many investors who should not purchase stocks under any of the plans, since all involve dangers that they ought not to assume. Such investors include those who are uninformed about stocks, and those who should not assume the risks of stock ownership. Many economists feel that this group should either stick to more conservative investments, such as savings accounts and savings bonds, or restrict stock purchases to mutual funds.

Classification. No classification of formula plans is entirely satisfactory. The following classification, while not all inclusive, is believed to cover enough plans to be representative and reasonably satisfactory:

I. Non-normal value formula plans
   A. Dollar cost averaging
   B. Constant dollar plan
   C. Constant ratio plan
   D. Ten per cent plan
II. Normal value formula plans with variable ratios
   A. Plans based on price
      1. Moving average plans
      2. Trend plans
   B. Plans based on intrinsic values
      1. Yield plan
      2. Price-earnings plan
      3. Two-signal plan
      4. Earnings-yield plan
      5. Price-dividend plan

More complex classifications than the above are available to those who wish to study formula plans in greater detail than is possible in this chapter.[1]

DOLLAR COST AVERAGING

Characteristics. This is probably the simplest of all formula plans; yet it is without question one of the best. One authority has called it "The unbeatable formula," and with good reason.[2]

The plan consists of investing a constant amount of money in common stocks over a long period, regardless of the level of stock prices. This steady accumulation of stocks proceeds at regular intervals, such as monthly, quarterly or annually. For example, an investor with $1,200 per year would invest $300 each quarter over a period of years.

It is not an in-and-out trading system but a long-term investment program. It is also not a method for investing a large sum at any one

---

[1] The two authoritative works in this field are: Lucile Tomlinson, *Practical Formulas for Successful Investing* (New York: Wilfred Funk, 1953); C. C. Cottle and W. T. Whitman, *Investment Timing: The Formula Plan Approach* (New York: McGraw-Hill Book Co, Inc., 1953).

[2] Tomlinson, *op. cit.*, p. 45. See also: Leonard W. Ascher, "Dollar Averaging in Theory and in Practice," *The Financial Analysts Journal*, XVI (September–October, 1960), 51–3.

time but, rather, one for investing regular amounts out of current income. When the program begins is of no importance, but when it ends is of great importance.

There are two requirements for success. First, the investor must take a long-term point of view. Ten years is considered an excellent length of time, but good results are possible even over five years. Second, the investor should have a steady flow of income to invest, the steadier the better. Given these requirements, the results are highly gratifying.

An Example. There are a number of advantages to the formula. One advantage is that the average cost of stocks is usually less than the average market price of the stocks held in the portfolio. This happens because a constant amount of money buys only a few shares at high prices but many at low prices. This is best illustrated by a simple example. Only two years are necessary. In each year the investor places $1,200 in the shares of a given company. In the first year he buys 40 shares at $30. In the following year he buys 20 shares at $60. His average cost is $2,400 divided by 60 shares, or $40. The market price, however, was $60 in the latter year. The theory is that stocks always can be sold on the average for more than they cost.

Technical Problems. Stocks that fluctuate a great deal give better profits under this formula than those that do not. However, this entails considerable risk and should be avoided by conservative investors. A well-diversified portfolio is best. Shares of mutual funds give excellent diversification and can be used to advantage in dollar cost averaging. It is not necessary to use the same stocks throughout the investment period. The portfolio should be managed just as though no plan were in effect, with elimination of undesirable issues when justified. An important consideration is that stocks with an upward trend be used. Money cannot be made on stocks showing a continuous downward movement. This is the danger of attempting to average on one stock. It may go down and not come back up. This is a danger not present with proper diversification.

The frequency of purchases is not a matter of great importance. Over a ten-year period Tomlinson found little difference between purchases made at one-, three-, or twelve-month intervals.[3] In periods of rising prices, shorter intervals are better, while in periods of declining prices, longer intervals give better results.

The problem of purchases at very high stock price levels presents itself. Strict adherence to the program dictates that regular purchasing policies be continued. Some suggest that purchases be discontinued

[3] *Op. cit.*, p. 68.

when stocks get very high. Such a policy seems reasonable but has three objections: (1) it is difficult to tell when they are "too high"; (2) money not invested is apt to be spent elsewhere; and (3) there is a danger of abandoning the program. If stocks are believed to be very high, the money can be put into "defensive stocks," or those that perform well in a declining market, such as utilities. An opposite situation develops during a period of falling prices. The investor, anticipating still lower prices, withholds purchases. If he is in error, he loses an opportunity to pick up a large number of shares at low prices. However, one suggestion would be that in periods of low prices he concentrate on volatile issues or those with a wide cyclical range. The danger of departing from regular purchases at any time is that the investor will turn into a speculator and never buy except when prices look very low to him. If this happens, his dollar cost averaging program is lost.

In the opinion of many investors, stock buying should be limited to periods when the Dow-Jones industrial average is yielding 4 per cent or better, if possible. In addition, the investor is well advised to buy stocks when the price-earnings ratio is under 18 to 1. These simple precautions, which may cause a delay in purchases at times, would seem to be warranted as a protection against purchases at excessive price levels.

Dividends should be immediately reinvested for maximum gain. The fund will grow probably 40 per cent faster if this is done, since the principle of compound interest operates.

The termination date of a given program is very important. A ten-year program is probably as long as is advisable. In any case, the program should terminate a few years before the total fund is needed, such as for retirement. In this way the investor can wait for a year or two for liquidation in case the stock cycle should be in its trough. There is always, of course, some danger that a plan will terminate at a time when stock prices are low.

Peformance. Studies of dollar cost averaging, based on the behavior of the Dow-Jones industrial average, show uniformly satisfactory results. Tomlinson estimated that a profit of 40 per cent was possible in six years on the average throughout the period 1920 to 1950, with commissions and dividends not taken into account. A program of investing $1,000 per year from 1943 to 1952 produced a fund of $23,615 when dividends were reinvested.[4] Genstein, using five-year programs only, for the period 1929 to 1951, found that no consecutive five-year program in the period produced less than a 12 per cent annual gain.[5]

---

[4] Tomlinson, *op. cit.*, p. 71.
[5] Edgar S. Genstein, *Stock Market Profit Without Forecasting* (South Orange, N.J.: Investment Research Press, 1954), p. 70.

Advantages. The first advantage is that the average cost of shares purchased is always less than the average market price. Another advantage is that it is a very simple plan, involving no computations of normal periods, trend lines, or trading zones. A third advantage is that the investor avoids the danger of buying too many shares when prices are too high. Again, there is the advantage, perhaps the most important of all, that the investor receives the benefit of the long-run appreciation in stock prices and the high yields possible from common stock ownership. To be very conservative, let us assume that the annual appreciation and yield of good industrial stocks total 8 per cent. At compound interest this means a doubling of one's investment in nine years. The corresponding figure for 3 per cent savings bonds is twenty-four years. A fifth advantage is that the plan permits a continuous investment of dividends. A final advantage is that declines in market price not only do not injure the portfolio, but benefit it, because they give an opportunity to buy additional shares at low average costs.

Limitations. The first limitation is the danger of liquidation of the fund during a period of low stock prices, thus causing a portfolio loss. Protection against this danger is much reduced by planning to liquidate the fund several years before it is needed. In this way the investor can defer final liquidation if the level of stock prices is not satisfactory. During this waiting period stock prices will normally rise, permitting liquidation at a satisfactory level. A second criticism is the difficulty of stock selection, a criticism directed against all stock buying plans. Stocks with a downward trend will never show satisfactory results; e.g., the purchase of railroad stocks in the 1920's. In answer to this criticism, it is suggested that the investor adequately diversify his portfolio. Mutual fund issues offer excellent diversification if one's investments are small.

A third limitation is the financial danger of missing purchases. Many investors do not have the stability of income which assures a continuous investment program. In a depression, when salaries are cut and professional income drops off, payments are apt to be reduced or terminated at the very time when stock prices are at their most attractive levels. A fourth limitation is the psychological danger of stopping purchases when stock prices appear too high. Hoping for better prices, the investor stops his buying. He then becomes a speculator. If his judgment is faulty, the results of his program are badly damaged. A fifth danger is that of diverting investment installments into more attractive or urgent channels, such as vacations, new cars, or family weddings. This danger can be lessened by starting a program that can be sustained under adverse conditions or by keeping a liquid reserve, such as a savings account, which can be drawn upon during periods of reduced income.

CONSTANT DOLLAR PLAN

Basic Features. The principle of the constant dollar plan is to keep a constant number of dollars, say $5,000, invested in stocks regardless of the stock price level. The rest of the investor's portfolio should be in bonds or preferred stocks. If stock prices rise, stock should be sold to reduce the stock fund to $5,000. If stock prices fall, so that the stock portfolio is reduced below $5,000, funds should be invested in common stocks to bring it back to the $5,000 level.

Diversification of the stock portfolio would be not only possible but also sound management. However, the plan can be operated for individual stocks, and diversification achieved by having a number of plans in simultaneous operation.

Three basic problems present themselves: (1) the ratio between stocks and bonds, (2) the basis for timing purchases and sales, and (3) the stocks to be used. The last problem, of course, is characteristic of all formula plans and will be discussed no further.

The stock-bond ratio is a question of individual judgment. The usual assumption is that the ratio should be 50–50 at the inception of the plan, which should be started during a period of apparently normal prices. The problem of timing can be settled in several ways. First, purchases and sales can be made at set intervals, one year being a general recommendation. Second, they can be made after stock prices go up or down by a certain percentage, such as 20 or 25 per cent.

An Example. Table 33–1 is an example of a hypothetical fund of $20,000 operating over a four-year period. Shifts in the portfolio are made once a year if stock prices have increased 100 per cent or dropped 50 per cent. The results in this example are gratifying. After one year prices were up 100 per cent, so half of the stock fund was shifted into bonds. At the end of the second year stock prices had fallen 50 per cent, so the stock fund was doubled. In the third year stock prices fell another 50 per cent, so the stock fund was again doubled. In the fourth year stock prices doubled. Although the stock index closed at that time at the same level at which it started, the entire portfolio showed a 50 per cent increase.

Performance. Cottle and Whitman, testing a hypothetical plan over the period 1926–50, found that it produced an annual yield of 5.5 per cent, and an appreciation in the portfolio of 92 per cent more than

Table 33–1. Operation of Hypothetical Constant Dollar Fund

Date	Stock Index	Stock Fund	Bond Fund	Total Fund
Year A	100	$10,000	$10,000	$20,000
Year B	200	20,000	10,000	30,000
		10,000	20,000	30,000
Year C	100	5,000	20,000	25,000
		10,000	15,000	25,000
Year D	50	5,000	15,000	20,000
		10,000	10,000	20,000
Year E	100	20,000	10,000	30,000
		10,000	20,000	30,000

the rise in stock prices.[6] On the other hand, Tomlinson, using five hypothetical tests, found that a "buy-and-hold" policy yielded superior results.[7] Cottle and Whitman saw no basis for recommending such a plan over other formula plans, while Tomlinson found it inferior to the constant ratio plan to be discussed shortly.

Advantages. There are two advantages. The first is the great simplicity of the plan. Stocks are sold as they rise and purchased as they fall on the basis of arbitrary, prearranged signals. There are no calculations of any significant difficulty. The second advantage is that the plan provides for an automatic sale of stocks as they rise in price, thus restraining enthusiasm for stock purchasing at high price levels.

Limitations. The first objection is that the original fund must be started during a period of normal prices, the determination of which is no mean achievement. Otherwise, there is the danger of having too large or too small a stock fund. The second limitation is that for best results a period of substantial fluctuations above and below the original price level is essential. The plan does not work well in a period of continuously rising or falling prices.

CONSTANT RATIO PLAN

Basic Features. This plan is based on the principle of maintaining at all times a constant ratio, such as 50–50, between the value of stocks and the value of bonds held in the portfolio. As stock prices go up, stocks are sold to bring the portfolio back to the original ratio; as they go down,

[6] *Op. cit.*, p. 157.
[7] *Op. cit.*, p. 163.

stocks are purchased to achieve the same result. The result is that stocks are sold as prices rise and the profits are converted into additional bonds. As stocks fall, bonds are sold to take advantage of lower stock prices. Modest profits are, therefore, possible as prices fluctuate above and below the original purchase level.

The first problem involves deciding the basic ratio between stocks and bonds, such as 50–50, 35–65, or 60–40. Cottle and Whitman, after testing several ratios over a considerable period, concluded that a 50–50 ratio was as satisfactory as any.[8]

The second problem is that of a suitable buying and selling schedule. In other words, when should the original ratio, e.g., 50–50, be re-established? Three possible options present themselves: (1) whenever the stock part of the portfolio rises or falls by a certain percentage or amount; (2) whenever a certain change takes place in a selected stock index; and (3) at established time intervals. Cottle and Whitman believed that option (1) was the least satisfactory from the standpoint of cost and administration.

The third problem is that of timing the start of any given plan. This involves forecasting, since the investor must avoid the danger of starting a plan during a period of very high stock prices. Hence, judgment is required when starting the plan.

Some consider that delaying action is desirable, notably when stock prices are declining. Under such a plan stock purchases would be delayed beyond the normal buying schedule as long as stock prices continued to fall. Suggested methods of delaying action include: (1) a requirement that there must be a definite time lapse between successive stock purchases and (2) a requirement that the amount of stock at any one time be limited to a certain percentage of the total fund.

Performance. Tomlinson, using five hypothetical test periods from 1897 to 1951, found that the method produced better results than a "buy-and-hold" plan in only three out of five cases.[9] This is not too convincing a demonstration.

Advantages. The first advantage is that the plan is a very simple one. It is easy to understand and to administer. A second advantage is that small profits seem obtainable when stock prices fluctuate over and under a normal level. A third advantage is that the investor reduces stock holdings when stock prices rise and increases them as they decline, a characteristic of all formula plans except dollar cost averaging. Fourth, it is relatively easy to increase the size of the fund when additional funds are available for investment.

[8] *Op. cit.,* p. 33.
[9] *Op. cit.,* p. 148.

Limitations. First, for best results the plan should be started during a period of normal prices or an adjustment should be made in the initial ratio if prices appear too high or below normal; this involves judgment and forecasting. There is nothing in the plan that defines a normal level of stock prices. Second, the evidence is not conclusive that the plan is superior to other plans, such as "buy-and-hold" or dollar cost averaging.

TEN PER CENT PLAN

Origin. Credit is due Garfield A. Drew for publicizing this method.[10] The plan first appeared in the *London Financial News* and described the operations of an American, Cyrus Hatch, who first employed the rule. He built up a fund of $100,000 from 1882 to $14,400,000 in 1936 by buying and selling stocks upon every 10 per cent reversal in the market. Later it was revealed that "Cyrus Hatch" was mythical.

Basic Features. Under the plan the value of the portfolio is calculated at the end of each week. These weekly figures are then averaged to arrive at a monthly average. Whenever the monthly average declines 10 per cent from the previous highest point, stocks are sold and no purchases are made until the monthly average rises 10 per cent above the lowest point recorded after liquidation. Stocks are then retained until another downturn of 10 per cent takes place, after which a complete liquidation is again in order.

Performance. The results of the original example were gratifying. Drew, however, in using the Dow-Jones industrial average over the same period, found that results were not as satisfactory as those allegedly obtained by Hatch.

George L. Leffler tested the plan from January, 1934, to December, 1955, using the Dow-Jones industrial average and computing all commissions. The gain for the 10 per cent plan was 280 per cent in contrast with 363 per cent for a "buy-and-hold" purchase of the industrial average.

Merits. In view of its inferior performance, just indicated, the plan would seem to have no particular merit as compared with dollar cost averaging, or even to a "buy-and-hold" plan of investing.

NORMAL VALUE PLANS WITH VARIABLE RATIOS

History. Normal value formula plans with variable ratios developed in the investment field in the latter part of the 1930's because of dissatisfaction with the results of portfolio management after the 1937–38 market break. Considerable interest developed among colleges, insurance

[10] Garfield A. Drew, *New Methods for Profit in the Stock Market* (Boston: The Metcalf Press, 1954), p. 54.

companies, trust companies, and some mutual funds. Many individuals adopted the idea in the management of their portfolios, particularly wealthy investors. Interest was quite high in the early 1950's before the 1949–60 bull market reached an advanced stage. Since 1953 enthusiasm has declined greatly, as many plans proved unrealistic and stock prices soared out of the normal pattern to unprecedented highs. Many plans were abandoned after that year because they did not suit the needs of investors, who found that they were "sold out" of common stocks at the very time when stock market profits were at their highest and when there was a continuing need for investment in equities.

Classification. These plans may be divided into two types. The first type consists of those plans that use price as the central or normal value. In this type two main methods are used in arriving at that value: (1) the moving average and (2) the trend line. The second type consists of those plans that use some intrinsic value in arriving at the median value, such as earnings, dividends, or yields.

Basic Theory. All of these plans are aimed at avoiding the worst mistakes of timing. Purchasing takes place when stocks appear low by the formula and are sold when they appear high. In all cases a central or median value is determined. When stocks are selling below this median value, they are purchased; when above, they are sold. Purchasing and selling is done through mechanical rules, rather than judgment. Although these operations do not give the maximum profits possible from buying at the bottom and selling at the top of the market, such plans are defended on the ground that smaller but more assured profits are obtainable with less risk.

The Portfolio. All plans with variable ratios operate through a portfolio divided into two parts. The first part is known as the "defensive" part and consists of bonds and high-grade preferred stocks. The second part is the "aggressive" section and consists of common stocks which move with the general level of stock prices. The first part provides protection against a decline in stock prices, while the second part provides profits during a rising stock cycle.

The various plans differ in the ratio of defensive to aggressive securities, when stock prices are at a normal level. Usually the ratio is 50–50. In some cases, however, the ratio may be as much as 60–40 or 65–35. The ratio is determined by the degree of risk which the investor is willing to assume and the need for current income.

These ratios change as stock prices rise and fall. In some funds the ratio of bonds to total portfolio holdings may range from 100 per cent to 0 per cent. In others it may never be more than 65 per cent or less than 35 per cent.

At this point it seems desirable to divide the discussion into two parts: (1) plans based on price and (2) plans based on intrinsic values.

NORMAL VALUE PLANS BASED ON PRICE

Computation of Normal or Central Value. All formula plans provide for some method of computing the normal or central value for stock prices. In some cases this normal value is called the median value. In most plans the Dow-Jones 30-stock industrial average is the yardstick for measuring the level of stock prices. The first problem is how to find the normal or median value for this average. Two basic approaches are used: (1) the moving average and (2) the trend line.

Let us first consider the moving average. Although various periods are used for the computation of moving averages, ten years or 120 months is considered the most satisfactory. The average for these 120 months becomes the central value. The trouble with using this unadjusted 120-month average is that stock prices over a long period show an upward secular trend, usually estimated at 3 per cent per year. Over a five-year period this would mean that the 120-month average was 15 per cent lower than the normal value for the current year. Hence, a careful adjustment would be to take the 120-month average and raise it by 15 per cent.

The other method of computing normal value is by the use of trend lines. These can be either arithmetic or geometric trend lines. Some plans use one and some the other. There is no general agreement as to which is better, since no analysis of stock prices has ever clearly indicated whether stock prices over a long period increase at an arithmetic or a geometric rate. It is probable that an arithmetic trend line is somewhat superior to a geometric trend line and that either type of trend line is superior to the moving average for measuring the normal value of stock prices.[11] Actually, a good straight line trend, drawn manually and based on careful analysis, may be more realistic than a precise trend line calculated by the most refined statistical formula. The stock market is anything but regular in its movements.

Not all plans calculate trends as straight lines. The Keystone Seven-Point Plan calculates the trend as a central zone which is 15 percentage points wide, as will be explained later.

Zones, Scales, and Action Points. Once the trend line is calculated, it is necessary to determine certain action points above and below the trend line or normal value, so that sales and purchases may be made. The usual method is to draw several zones above and below the trend

11 Cottle and Whitman, *op. cit.*, p. 79.

line or normal value. These zones are based on scales, which may be so many points apart, such as 15 or 20 points, or a certain percentage of the normal value, such as 10 or 15 per cent. These zones then become action points and indicate when buying and selling is in order.

Typically, stocks are never sold until they rise to or above the normal value or trend line and are then sold as they go through each zone or action point. On the way down they are not purchased until they fall to or below the central value and are then purchased as they drop through each zone or action point.

The theory is that during a typical stock cycle stock prices will fluctuate between the top and bottom zones of the formula chart, as they have done historically. The assumption is that stock price behavior in the future can be forecast by the projection of historical trends, an assumption seriously questioned by many students of the market.

Frequency of Trading. There is some difference between the various plans as to the frequency of trading. In some, buying and selling takes place at the exact moment when stock prices pass through a zone or action point. In others, there may be a delay, with buying and selling taking place only at certain intervals, such as at the monthly meeting of the investment committee or at three-month intervals. This delaying action is based on the assumption that stock prices, once they have established a given trend, will continue in that direction for some time.

Advantages of Plans. The first advantage is that such plans permit orderly purchasing and selling without forecasting stock prices. A mechanical set of rules determines buying and selling points in the stock cycle. Thus the element of judgment can be dispensed with and the danger of faulty, emotional decisions is eliminated. Hence, the worry about future price movements is decreased because there is no need for making numerous decisions of when to buy and sell; the formula takes care of that.

The second advantage is that the plans provide for small, but fairly certain, profits over a period of time. By the law of averages, stocks are bought during periods when they are low and sold when they are high, judged by historical standards. Although the maximum profit is not obtainable, the investor hopes to obtain smaller but more certain profit. To him this is justified on the basis of lowered risk.

Limitations of Plans. The danger of miscalculation of the normal value is a frequent criticism. It can be too high or too low. Those trend lines that terminated in the late 1920's would have been far too high, judged by behavior of stocks after 1929. The recent high level of stock prices has convinced many followers of formula plans that historical trend lines are no longer realistic and that the normal level of stock prices is higher than previous calculations would seem to indicate. Many students of the market believe a very great hazard is assumed when an attempt is made to forecast prices by the projection of a trend line based on prices of years ago. The highly mechanistic calculation of future stock prices ignores rational analysis entirely and disregards any changes in economic conditions, such as those that have existed since the close of World War II. The factor that has caused so many plans to be abandoned in recent years has been that present stock prices seem entirely out of line with previous concepts of normal prices. For example, in mid-1956 the normal for one formula plan was about 236. On that date the Dow-Jones industrial average was above 500. To bring prices back to "normal" would have required a bear market with a 53 per cent decline. No reduction approaching that proportion has been witnessed since 1929 and the Dow-Jones industrial average moved nowhere near this "normal" in the five subsequent years.

A second and very important weakness in such plans is that they ignore earnings and dividends. They assume that a stock that was selling at $50 ten years ago is now overpriced because it is selling at $100. High stock prices can be justified if they are accompanied by high earnings and dividends. A $100 stock earning $8 and paying $5 is just as good an investment as a $50 stock earning $4 and paying $2.50. Yet the only thing considered by the formula is the stock price level.

A third criticism is that such plans make it difficult to re-enter the market after an extended rise. This was well illustrated after 1953. At that point many portfolios would have been entirely without stocks; yet there was still a need in the portfolios for dividend income. A literal adherence to formula policy would have prevented any re-entry into the market after 1953.

A fourth limitation is that the plans provide less profit than those that forecast stock prices on the basis of judgment and experience. Granted that such forecasting is difficult, many question whether the reduced profits of formula plans are not too high a price to pay for greater latitude in investment policy.

Another criticism is that such plans prevent the investor from securing maximum protection against inflation. At the very time that inflation gets under way (when prices cross the normal line or zone), the investor begins to sell stocks. He thus loses his protection against inflation at the time inflation becomes the most injurious to him.

A sixth criticism is that such plans are usually complex and require rather formidable statistical calculations. While these may be no great problem to the investment institution, they are a handicap to most investors.

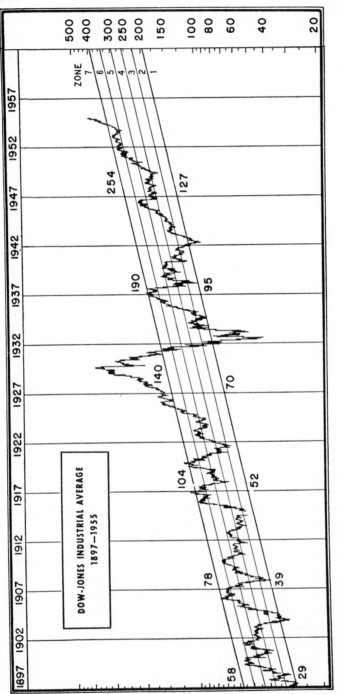

Fig. 33–1. A typical variable ratio stock-and-bond formula plan. (Courtesy of Keystone Custodian Funds, Inc.)

THE KEYSTONE 7-STEP PROGRAM

A final criticism is that they are not practical for the small investor with a limited portfolio. It is not very realistic to expect him to shift his funds from stocks to bonds and back at frequent intervals, as indicated by a formula chart. He will be much more inclined to "buy-and-hold" or to turn his troubles over to a mutual fund.

As in all stock buying plans, there is the inevitable problem of stock selection. It is a weakness of all formula plans.

Keystone Plan. The Keystone Seven-Point Plan, developed by Keystone Custodian Funds, Inc., of Boston, is perhaps the best known of all formula plans.

Figure 33–1 presents the essential features of the plan to 1955 in graph form and illustrates many of the basic features of all similar plans. This plan is based on the Dow-Jones industrial average. The secular, or long-term, trend is plotted as a central zone, known as Zone 4. It is 15 percentage points wide. The trend was manually fitted to stock prices over the period of 1897 to 1940 and then geometrically projected. This channel increases at the rate of 3 per cent per year. Above and below this central channel are three other zones, each representing rises of 15 per cent, making seven zones in all. When stock prices are in Zone 4, the central zone, the portfolio consists of 50 per cent stocks and 50 per cent bonds, and there is no action. The proportion of defensive securities rises as the average goes up, until at Zone 7, the top zone, only 10 per cent of the funds are in stocks, the other 90 per cent being in defensive securities. Conversely, when the average drops into Zone 1, or the lowest zone, the portfolio consists of 90 per cent stocks and 10 per cent bonds.

The plan operated very well from 1940 to 1953, but the Dow-Jones average passed completely out of Zone 7 after that. The question then arose as to whether or not stock prices had made a permanent departure from normal levels calculated for the plan. Managers of the fund in mid-1956 indicated that there was no intention of recalculation of the zones until the current bull market had topped out and a substantial reaction had occurred.[12] In 1960 no fund under this management, however, had the characteristics of the plan indicated by Figure 33–1. One fund, K-1, appeared to place Zone 5 near 600 on the Dow-Jones average.

Vassar Plan. The so-called Vassar Plan was developed by the trustees of Vassar College for the purpose of caring for that part of its investment portfolio tied up in common stocks. It was a variable stock-and-bond formula plan put into operation in 1938 with a fund of $3 million; eventually this common stock fund was raised to $5 million.

The total portfolio was divided into two classes. The first consisted of high-grade bonds and preferred stocks, carried at market values. The

[12] Letter to George L. Leffler, July 12, 1956.

other part consisted of investment grade common stocks with unquestioned liquidity. The plan provided for a range of common stock holdings from 100 per cent to 0 per cent of the total portfolio.

Originally the trend line was calculated from a ten-year moving average; however, the line was later fitted to the Dow-Jones industrial average from 1897 to 1947, with an elimination of abnormal prices beginning in the late 1920's and ending in 1932. No stock purchases are made in a rising market and sales are delayed until the market rises above the normal trend line. As the market rises above normal, sales are made every time prices climb 15 points. The reverse is true in a falling market.

The plan worked very satisfactorily in its early years and received wide and favorable comment because of the fact. Very good results were achieved up to 1946. In that year the fund was entirely in bonds and only nominal losses were taken in the 1946 market crash. However, the College found itself without stocks in 1947 and was compelled to review its plan. Near the start of 1948 it invested $1 million in common stocks independently of the common stock plan. Hence, it seems a fair conclusion that the plan was largely abandoned in that year. In recent years the funds of the institution have been under the continuous supervision of an investment counseling firm.

Yale Plan. The Yale plan was instituted by the endowment fund managers of that university in 1938. The size of the fund was in excess of $85 million at the time it was put into operation. When the plan was started, the trustees decided on a ratio of 70 per cent high-grade bonds and preferred stocks to 30 per cent common stocks. Action was determined by changes in the market value of holdings rather than by changes in any stock average. As stock prices rose, the ratio of stocks to the total fund was permitted to rise to 40 per cent and then cut back to 35 per cent. In a declining market, the ratio of stocks was permitted to drop to 20 per cent of the total fund, and then it was increased to 25 per cent. In 1950 the ratios were somewhat altered.

The formula plan was a very conservative one and necessitated few changes in the portfolio. The plan, however, was abandoned in 1953 or 1954 and has not been used since. The investment policy of the institution was determined by a finance committee of the university, which meets monthly and decides what percentage of the funds is to be invested in common stocks.

Oberlin Plan. This plan, established at Oberlin College in 1944, was for the guidance of the trustees of the $25 million endowment fund of the institution. The plan was a variable ratio plan based on the Dow-Jones industrial average. The normal trend line was an arithmetic trend-line projection of the industrial average, originally based on the period

1897 to 1925 but later changed to 1910–25 and 1934–49, inclusive. The ratio of stocks to bonds was 50–50 when stock prices were normal. During periods of very low prices, the ratio increased to 65–35, while during periods of very high prices the ratio fell to 35–65. Purchases and sales were made with every 10 per cent change in the market.

In its early years the plan was very successful. Substantial profits were made from 1944 to 1946. After the market decline of 1946, stocks were repurchased at substantially lower prices than they had been sold for previously. In 1949 the college made a revision in the plan so that a greater proportion of the fund could be placed in common stocks. It was felt that the original plan was too conservative. The formula plan was considered as an aid in timing purchases and sales and not as a substitute for the exercise of judgment. There has been little change in this attitude over the years.

F. I. du Pont Plan. This formula plan was developed by the brokerage firm of F. I. du Pont and Company for the guidance of institutional investors. It is a variable ratio stock-and-bond plan, based on a ten-year moving average of the monthly mean of the Dow-Jones industrial average. At normal the investment fund is 50–50 in stocks and bonds. There is no maximum or minimum ratio. Under the plan there is a reduction of 10 per cent in the stock portion of the fund every time stock prices rise 10 per cent above normal. Conversely, there is a 10 per cent increase in the stock fund for every 10 per cent decline in stock prices below normal. Thus, there would always be some stocks in the fund and some bonds regardless of stock price levels. Purchases and sales are determined by the movement of the monthly mean of the industrial average. In a rising market no stock sales are made until the market rises to normal. In a falling market no purchases are made until the market falls to normal. The plan calls for a delaying action of one month. In other words, no action is taken unless the mean of the Dow-Jones average continues in the same direction for two successive months.

In one test of the formula over the period 1895 to 1952, it was found that the growth in a hypothetical fund was 6 per cent less than the growth in the fund on a "buy-and-hold" basis, but the fluctuations in value of the fund would have been less extreme.[13]

Modified Scale Trading. The following plan, developed by Leffler for small investors, represents a variation from the previous plans in that the normal or central value is calculated on the basis of annual highs and lows, and not by the use of moving averages or trends.[14] The plan is

[13] Tomlinson, op. cit., p. 219.
[14] For greater detail, see: G. L. Leffler, "Modified Scale Trading," *Barron's,* March 1, 1954, p. 9.

adaptable to one stock only, in contrast to most formula plans, which operate best with a balanced portfolio. The plan is based on the premise that the confidence factor determines the level of stock prices. When confidence is high, a stock will sell close to its annual high for the past four years. When it is low, the stock sells at close to its annual low for the past four years. Calculations are simple. First, the average annual high for the four previous years is calculated; e.g., 42. Then the average annual low for the four previous years is calculated; e.g., 30. In this example, the average of 42 and 30, or 36, becomes the normal value for that stock for the current year. As the price rises above 36, the stock is gradually sold, until there is no investment in it when it reaches 42. If the price falls below 36, the stock is gradually accumulated, until the fund for that stock is fully invested when it reaches 30. When the fund is not invested in the stock, it can be invested defensively, such as in a savings account or in bonds.

A hypothetical testing of the plan from 1944 to 1953 in the shares of United States Steel, General Motors, Radio Corporation of America, and New York Central showed that the plan, after all expenses were computed, produced a profit of 15 per cent per annum during the time the fund was invested in the four stocks.

NORMAL VALUE PLANS BASED ON INTRINSIC VALUES

Basic Theory. These plans are based on the premise that the normal or real values of stocks are not based on price alone but upon other factors. The important thing is not what a stock sold for five, ten, or fifteen years ago—or even yesterday—but what it is worth in terms of earning power, dividends, and yield. An increase in price does not diminish the value of a given stock in investment quality, provided that its intrinsic value increases with the price. Thus, a stock selling at $100 can be just as sound a purchase as when it sold at $25, $50, or $75 if its intrinsic or real value has increased proportionately.

No one, of course, knows exactly what is the intrinsic value of a stock, and there is no agreement on the meaning of the term. Realistically, a stock is worth exactly what it will bring in the market at any given time. On the other hand, a given stock can be overvalued or undervalued at the current market price. Normal value plans, based on intrinsic values, attempt to determine whether or not stocks are overvalued or undervalued.

Stock Yields. Although there has been no publicized formula plan based on stock yields, there is no reason why this important intrinsic value cannot be so used. In the authors' opinion, stock yields are one of the best simple measures of the level of stock prices available to the ordinary investor. Let us take those in the Dow-Jones industrial average. For the twenty-five years ending in 1960, the average yield on a quarterly basis was 4.8 per cent. A simple formula plan would consist of computing a normal yield at 5 per cent, when a fund should be half in stocks and half in defensive investments. At 6 per cent, stocks are very cheap and all the portfolio should be invested in stocks. Since 1937 industrial stock yields have been more than 6 per cent at very favorable buying periods. On the other hand, stocks should not be purchased, or purchased only very cautiously, when yields are less than 4 per cent. One of the best signs of the top of a bull market is when yields are less than 4 per cent. The bull market peaks of 1929, 1939, 1946, and 1961 witnessed yields of 2.9, 3.1, 3.2, and 3.0 per cent, respectively. An exception to the rule that bear markets are characterized by very high yields was found in the periods 1933–36, when an unusual relationship between prices and dividends prevailed.

Price-Earnings Ratios. Another possible formula for intrinsic values would be to use price-earnings ratios. For example, over the twenty-five-year period ending in 1960, the average price-earnings ratio of the Dow-Jones industrial average, computed quarterly, was 14.6 to 1. This figure can be used as normal for an intrinsic value formula. At this level half a portfolio could be invested in stocks and half in defensive securities. At 18 to 1 the entire portfolio, or most of it at least, should be in defensive securities. At 11 to 1 all, or nearly all, of the portfolio should be in stocks. Bull market tops are characterized by ratios in excess of 18 to 1, while bear market lows are always characterized by ratios under 11 to 1. Here again is a good intrinsic value for a formula.

The Two-Signal Intrinsic Value Formula. The following intrinsic value formula plan, devised by Leffler, is presented as a very simple and easy-to-understand method which can be followed by small investors. It involves no computations. The data on yields and price-earnings ratios can be obtained weekly from *Barron's*. For the average investor it is believed to be as workable and practical as any of the more complex variable ratio plans just described.

Its essential features can be presented thus:

Stocks at Very High Level			
Yield:	4.0%	Price-earnings ratio:	18.0 to 1

Stocks at Normal Level			
Yield:	5.0%	Price-earnings ratio:	14.5 to 1

Stocks at Very Low Level			
Yield:	6.0%	Price-earnings ratio:	11.0 to 1

The yields and price-earnings ratios are those of the Dow-Jones industrial average. The formula is based on two signals: (1) a warning signal by yields that stock prices are very high or very low and (2) a warning signal by price-earnings ratios that stock prices are very high or very low. Normal prices are considered to exist when the yield is 5 per cent and the price-earnings ratio is 14½ to 1. If either the yield falls to 4 per cent or the price-earnings ratio rises to 18 to 1, the first definite signal is given that prices are very high. When the other series gives a warning, this constitutes the second signal, or "confirmation," to borrow a term from the Dow theory.

Let us suppose that stocks have been falling. If either the yield increases to 6 per cent or the ratio drops to 11 to 1, a signal is given that prices are very low. When the other series gives a warning, this is the second signal, or "confirmation." At this point an investment can be made in common stocks with a reasonable assurance of profits.

Several performances can be noted. The bull market of 1942–46 began in April, 1942. Confirmation by both series came four months earlier and missed the bear market low by only 18 points. The 1946 high came in May. Confirmation came seventeen months before, or only fourteen months before when allowance is made for the lag in publication of earnings reports. The 1949–60 bull market began in June, 1949. Confirmation by both series came in December, 1948, or six months in advance. Confirmation missed the June low by only 16 points.

Graham Earnings-Yield Formula. Benjamin Graham, a well-known authority on investments, has devised a simple and interesting intrinsic value formula.[15] It is based on a central value computed from the Dow-Jones industrial average and the yield on Aaa bonds. The central value is found by capitalizing the average earnings of the past ten years on a basis equivalent to twice the yield on high-grade bonds. Stocks are purchased when the Dow-Jones average drops to 80 per cent of this central value and sold when the average rises to 120 per cent of the central value.

The following will indicate how the formula works. For the ten years ending in 1955, the average annual earnings were $25.25. In May, 1955, the yield on Moody's Aaa bonds was 3.3 per cent. Twice this yield would be 6.6 per cent. Capitalizing $25.25 by 6.6 per cent would place a central value of 383 for the Dow-Jones average. Under this valuation stocks would be purchased when the average fell to 306 and sold when they reached 460. The average during that year ranged from 408 to 480.

[15] Benjamin Graham, *The Intelligent Investor* (New York: Harper & Row, Publishers, 1949), p. 264.

In 1961, although the average earnings and the Moody bond yield rates had both risen, the range computed under this formula would have been lower than in 1955. The industrial average was well outside the range.

Viewed historically, it is interesting to note that the formula failed to get the investor out of the market during 1946, when the market showed a decline of more than 25 per cent. This would seem to have been a major performance error.

Genstein Price-Dividend Formula. Another intrinsic value formula has been developed by Edgar S. Genstein.[16] The central value is a self-adjusting median, based on a normal price-dividend ratio. Three preliminary figures from the Dow-Jones industrial average are necessary: (1) the average price for the past ten years, (2) the average dividends for the past ten years, and (3) current dividends. The central value is found by dividing (1) by (2) and multiplying by (3). Stocks are purchased when they fall to 80 per cent of this central value and sold when they rise to 125 per cent.

The formula may be illustrated with an example for the first quarter of 1956. For the ten years ending in 1955, the average price of the Dow-Jones average (computed on a quarterly basis) was 256.3. Average dividends were $14.41. The price-dividend ratio was, therefore,, 17.8 to 1. Dividends for the twelve months ending December, 1955, were $21.58. Multiplying 21.58 by 17.8 gives a central value of 384. The formula would indicate buying when the Dow-Jones industrial average was below 80 per cent of this figure, or 307, and selling when it was 125 per cent, or 481. During the quarter the range of the average was 462.35 to 513.03. Thus, strict adherence to the formula would have led an investor to sell his stocks during this quarter. Had he done so, and had he continued to adhere to the formula, he would not have purchased stocks again (to mid-1962).

If an investor had decided that a rise in the average above the upper limit of the formula should persist at least one quarter of a year before the sell signal was acted on, he would not have sold out in the first quarter of 1956. The average returned within the formula range in the second quarter and remained there until the third quarter of 1958. This investor, however, would have sold out in the fourth quarter of 1958 and would not have purchased any stock in later years (to mid-1962). In the second quarter of 1962, the range computed by the Genstein formula was 443 to 693. The average had re-entered the range for the first time since 1958 but, at mid-year, was still well above the buying point.

16 *Op. cit.*, p. 40.

A FINAL COMMENT

An ancient Roman proverb read: *Caveat emptor*—Let the buyer beware! It could be called the oldest of market maxims. The saying is untarnished after two thousand years, as far as the investor and trader in stocks is concerned. It stands as a reminder that care and common sense are requisite qualities in investment operations.

34

Technical Analysis of Stock Prices

Technical analysis of stock prices deals primarily with the interpretation of stock price movements over short periods. Few forms of speculation are more illusive in their rationale or more dangerous for public investors than trading to obtain short-term profits.

Nature of Technical Analysis. Technical analysis of the market contrasts with fundamental analysis. In fundamental analysis the investor seeks to ascertain the action of the market as determined by fundamental economic and political conditions—by forces outside the market. He is interested not only in the movement of the market as a whole but also in the investment merits of individual stocks. He seeks to find the intrinsic values of stocks or what he considers their real worth. He is an investor, but is interested in appreciation as well as income. His primary viewpoint is for the long run.

On the contrary, the technical analyst of the market usually is a short-run trader. His chief interest is in capital gains, whether they be obtained in a day, a week, a month, or six months. Technical conditions to him are highly important. These are factors or conditions that arise in the market itself as contrasted to fundamental conditions that develop outside the market. Technical conditions result from activities of professional, speculative, and investment interests.

Technical conditions develop because of the activities of all traders and investors who seek profits in the market. They may be either buyers or sellers. Although a few are short sellers, the overwhelming majority buy and sell "long." Both margin and cash traders are found in this group.

Their objective is always the same: to capitalize on daily and secondary fluctuations of the market, regardless of whether the primary trend is upward or downward.

Timing is the keynote of technical analysis. When to buy and sell as well as what to buy and sell is the objective. Concentration, therefore, is upon those technical factors or conditions that affect, or are supposed to affect, stock prices generally, and individual issues particularly. Timing is a fascinating subject but one that requires the highest analytical skill. Many methods have been developed over a long period. Many have been complete failures. All have shown weaknesses from time to time.

Advantages of Trading on Technical Conditions. The technical analyst justifies his activity on several grounds.[1] First, it is believed that short-term fluctuations in the market are much more important than long-term trends and, therefore, are more profitable upon which to trade. A long-term, upward trend of the industrial average, for example, may total 50 points. The technical analyst believes that the market will go forward, decline, and retrace itself many more points—perhaps 100 to 150—in making that total gain. There are many more trading opportunities in this total movement. The trader can buy at the bottom of each decline and sell at the top of each rally. Hence, his profit will exceed that of the investor who obtains only the profit on a major trend and perhaps not the entire amount.

A second alleged advantage is that information on fundamental conditions comes too slowly for maximum profit. The investor gets into the market only after he obtains basic or fundamental statistics on earnings, dividends, sales, orders, policy changes, and similar factors. By that time the market has discounted these news items and made a substantial advance or suffered a serious loss. The trader on technical conditions, however, seeks to capitalize instantly on any change in stock prices, even before the news is publicly available. He operates on trends in the current market rather than upon historical records of earnings and dividends. The technical analyst believes that no other published economic series can be used as a barometer of changes in stock prices, since stock prices typically precede movements of other series. He is then forced to forecast changes in stock prices by watching their behavior and to ignore changes in fundamentals outside the market.

This second defense of technical analysis makes the technical trader and analyst the supreme isolationist. Some extremists operate as though in a vacuum. Ignoring all outside factors, influences, and conditions, they

[1] For example, see: Joseph E. Granville, *A Strategy of Daily Stock Market Timing for Maximum Profit* (Englewood Cliffs, N.J.: Prentice-Hall, Inc., 1960).

concentrate solely on what the market is doing and not why it is doing so. If technical analysis were more scientific than it is, perhaps such operations could be fully justified, but that is not the case. Both the fundamental and technical approaches to stock price analysis suffer from limitations.

Traders on Technical Conditions. Although myriad traders on technical conditions are found in the ranks of the general public, it is believed that such activity should be confined to those with ample funds, long experience in the market, willingness to take substantial losses, and plenty of time to follow the market. It is no business for the novice, but rather a field best suited to the qualifications and resources of the professional.

The technical analyst and trader may be a member of an exchange; he may be a full-time trader who spends much time in board rooms and at his desk; he may be a wealthy investor or speculator who has intimate contacts with the market at all times; he may represent some financial organization that has large market commitments. In any event, to be successful he must have adequate information on technical conditions, much of which is not quickly and generally available at the time to the general trading public.

Relative Importance of Technical Conditions. There is no accurate way of measuring the comparative influences of technical conditions and fundamental factors upon the market. In the daily analysis of the market, the newspaper columnists mix the two at will, often with results that confuse not a few readers. A favorite theory of these column writers uses technical conditions as a basis of explanation for any short-term reversal of the market. Since technical conditions can change from day to day, it requires no great exercise of logic to explain why the market is very strong one day and very weak the next, even though fundamental conditions were exactly the same on both days.

Certainly, over the last quarter of a century there have been many factors that have reduced the importance of technical influences affecting stock prices. Manipulation, once a dominant factor in the market, is gone. No longer do pools and corners influence the market. "Bear raiding" is unknown. Changes in the costs and supply of call money have little influence on price movements. Short selling is less influential in the market than it was many years ago.

Margins are so large that call loans are no longer called to protect lenders. "Daylight trading" has been restricted by exchange rules. The old-time market plunger of the Jesse Livermore type is no longer an important factor, nor is the professional trader who would buy 5,000 to 10,000 shares in the morning and wipe out his position before the market closed.

Strength and Weakness. The technical analysis of the market concentrates largely on determining the strength or weakness of the market at any given time. When analysis indicates that the market is "technically strong," stocks should be bought; when it is "technically weak," they should be sold. Hence, technical analysis is used to determine whether the market is strong or weak. Many methods are employed for this purpose, a representative number of which will be discussed in this chapter.

Volume. Without question, volume occupies more of the attention of technical analysts than any other factor. The heart of the analysis is an old market axiom, "Volume goes with the trend." Volume is supposed to increase on rallies in a bull market and to decline on reactions. In a bear market volume should increase on reactions and shrink on rallies. Heavy volume at the end of a considerable movement in prices is believed to indicate the end of that trend and the turning point in prices.

In precise form, the popular theory of volume may be stated this way: (1) the market is technically strong when volume increases on rallies and declines on reactions; (2) the market is technically weak when volume increases on reactions and declines on rallies.

If volume increases as prices advance, the theory is that demand is still greater than supply, or, in other words, buying forces are stronger than selling forces. This is why traders like to see increasing volume on a rising market. On the other hand, in a bull market, if volume drops off as prices decline, this is a good sign. It indicates that the supply is falling off at lower prices and owners are unwilling to sell.

In a genuine bear market, volume is supposed to increase as prices drop, since supply is increasing and stockholders want to unload. This shows the market is weak. If volume drops off on temporary rallies, the market is still weak because no large amount of buying is entering the market.

This theory of volume probably obtained its first prominence in the early years of the Dow theory. As indicated in Chapter 32, however, Hamilton's thinking on the importance of volume was very confusing, since he stressed volume in some editorials, while minimizing it in others.

Technical analysts today use volume for short periods of analysis, such as a few days, or one day, or hourly. When the theory of volume is subjected to analysis on a monthly basis over an entire stock cycle, it shows a doubtful validity. In an exhaustive statistical investigation over the period 1934 to 1955, one author found a very poor correlation between volume and stock prices.[2] In five bull markets in that period, the coefficient of correlation was only 0.4482. A correlation of 1.00 would have been perfect; such perfection, however, is seldom found in corre-

[2] G. L. Leffler and R. H. Dennis, "Faulty Gauge," *Barron's*, May 16, 1955, p. 9.

lations. This meant that there was only a fair amount of correlation between the two series and that the relationship had little practical value. In the five bull markets the only good correlation was from 1953 to 1955. The correlation in the four bear markets in that period was 0.2422, which had no value at all.

Breadth of the Market. Many technical analysts stress the breadth of the market. This refers to the number of issues being traded. There are somewhat more than 1,500 stocks traded on the New York Stock Exchange. The number of these that advance or decline in a given day is considered by many to be very significant. For example, if on a given day 600 advanced, 400 declined, and 200 remained unchanged, the market would be considered to be technically strong. Many consider these data more important than the averages, since they show what is happening to the supply and demand for all stock and not merely for a few high-grade blue chips. An example of extreme technical weakness in the market occurred on September 26, 1955, the first day the market was open after the President's heart attack. On that day, there were 1,247 declines and only 38 advances, a situation without precedent.

An increase in the breadth or number of issues traded is considered a favorable sign in a rising market and an unfavorable one in a falling market.

New Highs and Lows. Keen interest is shown by many in the number of new highs and lows being reported on the New York Stock Exchange each day. One criticism made is that the averages represent a faulty sampling of the market and consist largely of a few blue chip stocks. Hence, an average may make a new high or new low and yet not mean too much. To those who subscribe to this viewpoint, the number of new highs or lows attains much importance. For example, on a given day the market may show 10 new highs for the year, but 100 new lows. This would be interpreted as a sign of great technical weakness. On the day just mentioned, September 26, 1955, the market made 1 new high and 131 new lows for the year.

Unfortunately, this technical factor sometimes plays tricks on its followers. On April 9, 1956, the Dow-Jones industrial average reached 524.37, a new all-time high. During the week 277 new highs had been made as against 155 new lows. Despite this technical strength, the average was down 60 points in seven weeks.

Short Interest. Short selling at the time it occurs is supposed to be a sign of technical weakness in the market, since the normal amount of stock offered for sale is augmented by that of the short sellers. Conversely, short covering is alleged to be a sign of strength, since the short sellers repurchase the stock previously sold. A large short interest is supposed to make the market technically strong, since short sellers must cover eventually, thus bringing buying power into the market. On the other hand, a light short interest makes the market weak, since there is not this support under the market.

Too much reliance must not be placed on short selling and the short interest as technical factors. There are several reasons for this conclusion. First, the amount of short selling and consequent short interest is rather small. Less than 1 per cent of the shares outstanding in listed issues on the New York Stock Exchange were held in short position in recent years. Hence, their importance can be minimized as compared to margin buying, which amounted to almost 20 per cent of volume. Second, much short selling is done for reasons other than speculation; as such it has no speculative significance. Third, short sellers make some incredibly bad decisions as to when short sales should be made. There was little short selling when stocks were overpriced in 1946, whereas the short interest was high in 1949, just before the start of the 1949–61 bull market rise. Because of this bad timing, it is difficult to tell the precise effect of short selling and the short interest upon the market. Finally, there appears to be little correlation between the volume of short selling and the movement of stock prices, either for individual stocks or for the market as a whole, as indicated in Chapter 12.

Theory of Contrary Opinion. Some traders approach technical analysis from the standpoint of psychology. Their belief is that "the public is always wrong" and that success in forecasting stock prices is achieved by determining the buying and selling moods of the public and then doing just exactly the opposite. This, of course, is a very old theory, going back nearly 150 years to the days of Baron Meyer Rothschild, who operated on the basis of buying when others sold and selling when others bought. This theory is based on the analysis of mass psychology in the market. It stresses the fact that stock prices are determined by the emotional decisions of thousands of traders and investors who often trade without sound knowledge of the market. These errors of judgment are not confined to the general public but are often made by professional advisers and forecasters of the market.

On the basis of this premise, a successful trader on technical conditions would sell when mass optimism about stock prices was high and buy when it was low. He would be a good psychologist rather than a good economist. There is no little truth in the theory. The difficulty comes from the lack of precise measurements of public psychology. It is easier to indict the public for bad judgment after a market error than before.

Behavior of Odd-Lot Public. A theory of technical analysis similar to the theory of contrary opinion is that of trading on the behavior of the odd-lot public. Garfield A. Drew has stressed this aspect perhaps more than any other analyst.[3] Trading under this theory is dictated by changes in the volume of buying and selling of the odd-lot public. Elaborate indexes have been developed which measure these changes and signal market movements to be followed by more informed traders. Drew's theory is not based on the well-known axiom, "The public is always wrong," but upon the premise that the market can be forecast by watching for periods when the odd-lot public changes its on-balance buying to on-balance selling or vice versa.

Whether or not the actions of the odd-lot public can be used to predict stock price movements has been the subject of much controversy. Hardy, as already indicated in Chapter 14, concluded that any correlation between market actions and those of the odd-lot public would have slight forecasting value. The odd-lot public may be wrong at times, just as professional traders are sometimes wrong, but it is not always wrong. And it may be right just often enough to make faulty any predictions based on its behavior. The actions of no class of traders are so consistent as to be infallible guides to market behavior. In addition, the behavior of the odd-lot public may be such as to indicate no trading signals at all.

Low-Priced and High-Priced Stocks. Another relationship watched by technical analysts is that between the actions of low- and high-priced stocks in bull markets. Briefly, the theory is that low-priced stocks, percentagewise, will show greater gains in a bull market than high-priced ones. The speculative public will purchase these in preference to the high-priced, sound blue chips, which appear to offer less opportunities for large profits. A point profit on a $10 stock is 10 per cent, but is only 1 per cent on a $100 issue. The theory of the uninformed public is that the $10 stock in a bull market is likely to go up 10 per cent more quickly than the $100 stock.

Timing plays an important part in this theory. It is believed that in the early stages of a bull market, attention is directed to sound investment stocks. As the market advances and the general public enters in large numbers, attention focuses more and more on the highly speculative issues. At, or even before, the crest of the market, speculation in them is very intense. As the market reaches its peak, public confidence declines rapidly in the speculative issues, which drop with great speed.

Some services, such as Standard and Poor's, regularly publish indexes of both low-priced speculative stocks and high-grade investment issues. Technical analysts can thus watch the action of these two series.

[3] Garfield A. Drew, *New Methods for Profit in the Stock Market* (Boston: The Metcalf Press, 1954). Especially Sec. VI.

The theory is well supported by the facts. A close examination of a chart of the action of low-priced and high-grade stocks since 1926 reveals that low-priced stocks clearly outperformed high-grade issues in 1929, 1933–34, 1937, 1946, 1949, 1955, and 1959. Such uniformity is rare for a technical factor.

Reaction to News. Some technical analysts are interested in the reaction of the market to good and bad news. If the market fails to react favorably to good news, it is believed to be a sign of technical weakness because it does not induce buying. If the market, on the other hand, fails to decline on bad news, that is believed to be a sign of strength because it does not induce selling. Traders, however, would be wise to reject such a simple analysis with reservations. The market is often able to discount news successfully a considerable period in advance. The effect of the good or bad news has already been discounted by the market in such cases. No further action is to be expected. "Sell when the good news is out" was a market axiom long ago.

Seasonal Movements of the Market. The question is often asked: Does the market show a seasonal pattern? The answers vary. Theoretically, such a pattern could not exist if it were of any significant size. Let us suppose that stocks always rose strongly from November to December. To take advantage of this rise, well-informed traders would always buy in November in order to sell in December at a profit. This early action would entirely destroy the pattern.

There is no question but that there is a slight seasonal pattern, which can be explained. Using the Dow-Jones industrial average as an example, it is found that over the period from 1897 to the present, the market has tended to go up in certain months. It is more likely to go up than down in January, July, August, and December. Hence, one hears of "the summer rise" and "the December rise."

One must not take these variations too seriously, nor can one use them as reliable indicators of profit-making opportunities. They are too small and too erratic to justify risking one's money on them. Even if the pattern were sharp enough to permit a profit, as indicated by the 30-stock Dow-Jones average, the trader has no assurance that there would be any profit in a particular stock he might own.

Let us take the month of December, a month of rising prices. At this time of year, income taxpayers have typically sold issues carrying losses for the year, so that these losses could be established in the computation of capital gains taxes. They have now re-entered the market to place idle funds at work. This continues into January. One could logically expect some improvement in prices at this time.

From 1897 to 1961, a period of sixty-five years, the Dow-Jones industrial average has shown a gain from the end of November to the end of

December in nearly three out of four years. The odds are, therefore, about 75 out of 100 that prices will rise in this period. Much of this improvement has absolutely nothing to do with seasonal change. The Dow-Jones industrial average went from about 30 to 700 in that period. Its long-term trend, month by month, was upward. A majority of these gains from November to December were nothing more or less than an expression of the long-term, upward trend. The same reasoning explains why ten months out of every year show a rise in the average. It is merely showing its upward trend.

Let us reduce the seasonal pattern to a realistic trading signal. In a study by Leffler, four leading industrial averages were used to determine the seasonal pattern in stocks.[4] The averages were those of Dow-Jones, *The New York Times*, Moody's, and Standard and Poor's. The period used was from 1946 to 1952. During this period all four averages and indexes showed gains from November to December and from December to January, the best increases of the year. The indicated movement from the end of November to the end of January was 3.5 per cent. Can one profit on this rise? The answer is no. Let us use an example.

Our hypothetical seasonal trader buys 100 shares at 50 on November 30. He sells them on January 31. He does this for four years. In three of them he captures the seasonal rise of 3.5 per cent. On the fourth year he loses 3.5 per cent. This is as good as he can expect. On this assumption, he will have made a gross profit of $350. His commissions and taxes on the four transactions will be $360. Our trader never again trades on the seasonal pattern.

Sequent Price Movements. Stocks appear to show some sequence in movements. In other words, once a short-term movement has been established, it continues for some time in the same direction. A study by Alfred Cowles III, covering 1,200 monthly sequences from 1836 to 1935, showed that the market trend succeeded itself 62½ times out of 100 and reversed itself 37½ times.[5] Blind acceptance of this tendency might be profitable if employed over a long-enough period, but it might be expensive in commissions and taxes because of the number of times that the trader would be "whip-sawed" in and out of the market.

CHARTS AND CHART READING

Their Use. Charts are used by all types of traders and investors, professional and amateur. They can be employed for long-term investment planning, based on fundamentals, or for short-term technical analysis of

---

[4] "Seasonal Pattern," *Barron's*, March 30, 1953, p. 27.
[5] Alfred Jones, "Fashions in Forecasting," *Fortune*, March, 1949, p. 180. See also: Sidney S. Alexander, "Price Movement in Speculative Markets: Trends or Random Walks," *Industrial Management Review*, May, 1961, pp. 7–26.

the market. They are introduced at this point only because of their special significance in technical analysis, with which this chapter deals.

Nature of Charts. Charts are graphic pictures of numerical data. If they are well prepared, they enable the market analyst to grasp in a moment significant changes in stock prices and trends over a considerable period. Rightly used, they can be of substantial worth in interpreting market changes.

Chart construction methods are now well standardized. There are two basic types of stock chart. The first is constructed with an arithmetic scale and is almost universally used. Equal changes in absolute values are represented by equal spaces; thus, on equidistant horizontal lines one would find stocks priced at $10, $20, $30, $40, $50, $60, etc. The individual trader can easily construct such charts with the aid of ruled paper purchased at any stationery store. Paper that is divided into eight spaces to the inch is very practical for plotting daily stock prices. Any good textbook on statistics will be a convenient guide in the construction of well-designed charts.

On occasion it is desirable to construct a ratio chart, technically known as a chart with a "semi-logarithmic scale." These are difficult to construct unless one is trained in statistics. The great advantage of these charts is that they show rates of changes instead of differences in amount. On a ratio chart, if a stock is rising at a rate of change of 10 per cent per year, the chart will show a straight trend line. If two stocks are plotted, the one showing a greater percentage gain will show a steeper line than the other. Once the principle of the ratio chart is grasped, its advantages for skilled analysis are readily apparent. It does not require any knowledge of higher mathematics or logarithms to understand such charts.

A third type of chart is viewed with favor by certain analysts, many of them connected with large financial organizations. It is called the "point-and-figure chart." It consists of plotting prices over a given period, not in the form of a continuous line, but by a series of x's. Prices are given in rounded-off digits, such as 50, 50, 51, 52, 51, 51, 49. For example, closing prices of 50, 50¼, 50⅝, and 50⅞ would all be plotted as prices of 50. The chart ignores minor fluctuations and concentrates on the development of formations and patterns showing major price movements. Many question whether or not such charts show anything not revealed in the standard line chart.

One of the biggest problems of the chart follower who constructs his own charts is that of selection. There are endless charts which may be made; the averages; charts for major industries, such as steel, motor, oil, chemical, equipment, food, amusement stocks; charts for individual companies, such as General Motors, Allied Chemical, Westinghouse. If a trader is following a few stocks, these may be the only ones needed for his charts. Perhaps the best advice to a trader who specializes in only a few stocks is to plot them on the same chart as one of the better-known averages; thus he can compare the performance of his own stocks with that of the market as a whole.

There is no reason why a chart reader needs to construct his own charts if he is willing to purchase them. All of the leading financial pages publish charts on averages; e.g., the *Wall Street Journal, The New York Times,* and the *New York Herald Tribune.* There are a number of excellent chart services that publish charts on hundreds of leading stocks; transparent work-sheets enable the reader to compare the performance of any stock with market averages; comparisons are also possible with stocks in entire industries, such as steel, motors, oils, and farm machinery.[6] The Federal Reserve Board publishes a monthly chart book, which contains many charts on the market and business; it is invaluable as a reference book.

Value of Charts. Some traders have elevated chart reading to the status of a cult. By endless study of formations, trends, resistance levels, reversal patterns, channels, gaps, and trend-lines, they hope to reduce their study to a science; on this basis they hope to forecast the market. Their operations are based on the principle that history repeats itself and that the past actions of the market will predict the future. Their theory is that if a stock is weak, the chart will show it; if the stock is strong, that also will be indicated. All study of fundamental conditions may be disregarded in this blind faith in the revelations of the chart. Perhaps the follower of the Dow theory is the greatest devotee of this fad. Such blind faith is not only unjustified but is apt to lead to financial loss. History never exactly repeats itself, either in the field of politics or in the market. There is a considerable amount of truth in the market axioms that "The market has no past" and "The market can do anything."

Charts tell one where the market has been but not necessarily where it is going. They may be compared to the famous story of the blind man who traveled all day over very rough country—up hill and down dale. He knew where he had been but had no conception whatever of where he was going. Charts deal with the past; the successful speculator wants to forecast the future. Charts do not and cannot forecast the future; they are a valuable aid in forecasting the future but cannot take the place of well-considered judgment. This is not to disparage the use of charts. The best-informed and most skilled investment analysts in the nation are constant users of charts; there are few tools of the statistician that give

[6] See Chapter 38 for references to chart services.

as quick and sound a grasp of numerical data. Nevertheless, they must be used with caution and reservations.

There are endless chart formations and many excellent books on the construction, use, and interpretation of charts.[7] In the brief space allotted to this subject, the reader can only be introduced to a few of the important aspects of chart reading.

Chart Formation. There are many chart formations. To give an idea of the elaborations developed by chartists, here are some types:

Head-and-shoulders top	Broadening top
Head-and-shoulders bottom	Broadening bottom
Double top	Dormant bottom
Triple top	Right angle triangle
Double bottom	Ascending triangle
Triple bottom	Descending triangle
Rectangle	Exhaustion gap
Diamond	Island reversal
Rising wedge	Double trend-line
Falling wedge	Trend channel
Flag	Intermediate down trend
Pennant	Major down trend
Scallop and saucer	Major trend channel
Common or area gap	Spiral or coil
Continuation or runaway gap	Complex top

The list of thirty formations could be extended. For purposes of illustration, only two will be given and explained. They are the so-called "head-and-shoulders top" and the "triple top."

Head-and-Shoulders Top. This is one of the best-known and respected formations used by chart readers; it is shown in Figure 34–1. The formation is known as a reversal pattern and indicates the end of an upward movement in stock prices. As the curve forms the right shoulder, it fails to recover as high as the head and then turns down again. When the curve penetrates the neckline after forming the right shoulder, this confirmation or breakout is supposed to be a definite indication of a downward movement. Some writers believe that the breakout should proceed 3 per cent below the neckline for a positive signal.

---

[7] Representative books on various aspects of charts include: R. D. Edwards and John Magee, Jr., *Technical Analysis of Stock Trends* (Springfield, Mass.: Stock Trend Service, 1948); A. W. Cohen, *The Chartcraft Method of Point and Figure Trading,* (Larchmont, N.Y.: Chartcraft, Inc., 1961); G. A. Drew, *New Methods for Profit in the Stock Market* (Boston: The Metcalf Press, 1954); C. S. Cottle and W. T. Whitman, *Investment Timing: The Formula Plan Approach* (New York: McGraw-Hill Book Co., Inc., 1953). Any standard college text on statistics will be adequate for chart construction technique.

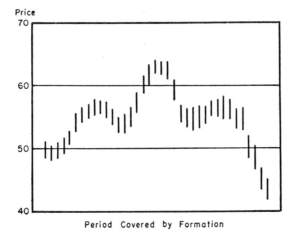

Fig. 34–1. Head-and-shoulders top.

The head-and-shoulders bottom (not illustrated) is the exact reverse of the head-and-shoulders top; it allegedly indicates the reversal of a downward trend and is, therefore, a bullish signal.

Triple Top. This is indicated in Figure 34–2. Double and triple tops differ, of course, only in the number of tops. The principle is the same in both formations. The formation indicates a resistance level above which a stock will not penetrate. When the stock reaches that level, distribution is supposed to take place and it is thrown on the market by sellers who believe it to be overpriced. The double and triple tops, therefore, are signs of weakness in a stock.

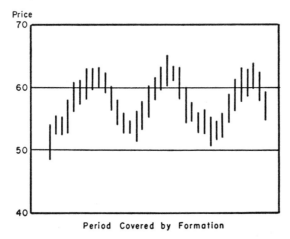

Fig. 34–2. Triple top.

Nearly perfect examples of triple tops are found not infrequently. For example, the Dow-Jones industrial average touched 489.94 in September, 1955, and then receded. It rose to 490.75 in November and then declined. In January, 1956, it made the triple top of 490.92 and then dropped. Yet despite this unmistakable signal of weakness, the average made a new all-time high of 521.05 in the following April.

Double and triple bottoms are the reverse of tops; they are considered signs of strength. When the stock reaches a bottom, accumulation by "strong hands" is believed to begin; the stock has met a resistance level. If the stock should penetrate a double or triple bottom, that, of course, would indicate a new sign of weakness.

A FINAL COMMENT

There are many technical conditions of interest to the short-term analyst and trader. Most of the leading ones have been mentioned in this chapter. No follower of technical conditions relies upon one factor alone. It is only when a number of factors confirm a given condition that an analysis is considered reliable, and even then it is accepted with caution.

The uninformed member of the general public usually is not, and does not have time to become, adept at technical analysis, which even the most experienced students of the market find difficult. When trading on short-term movements of the market on the basis of his technical evaluations, he will not be playing with loaded dice, as he often was in the old market, when manipulation was prevalent, but he is likely to be playing with a loaded pistol.

35

Securities Options—
Puts and Calls

Securities options, as the term is used in this chapter, refers to those options commonly known as puts, calls, spreads, straddles, strips, and straps. These options are bought and sold by about twenty-eight specialized put and call dealers and brokers. The use of options is not too well known to the general public, but they account nevertheless for a substantial volume of business during the course of a year.[1]

Trading in puts and calls has a long history. Reports of their use run back as far as 1694, before the London Stock Exchange was founded, which did not begin operations until 1773. Options of various types have had use in business for many years. Perhaps the best known are those connected with oil and mining properties and the sale of real estate. They are used extensively in the entertainment field in contracting for services of ball players, actors, and musicians. Their use in the securities business is simply another aspect.

Securities options as they are now written were in extensive use in the late 1920's. In the speculative markets of that era, the use of options by insiders and by members of pools in the manipulation of stock prices gave the instruments themselves a rather bad reputation. Some of that reaction still remains in investors' minds.

Two other factors appear to have affected public interest in options, perhaps more strongly, in recent years. First, the large number of new

[1] For a more complete discussion of this business written by a specialist in it, see: Herbert Filer, Sr., *Understanding Put and Call Options* (New York: Crown Publishers, Inc., 1959).

shareowners includes many not familiar with the put and call business. This is made more significant because many of the new registered representatives in broker-dealer organizations are also unfamiliar with this aspect of the securities business. Second, despite the small sum involved in a purchase of an individual option, trading through this medium can be expensive.

Nevertheless, the business is a substantial one. It is carried out on an international basis. Much option business is done between New York and Switzerland, England and France, and between other countries. The best method for measuring its present importance domestically is comparison of option volume to volume of stock sales on the New York Stock Exchange. The number of shares handled rose from 0.49 per cent to 1.12 per cent of the volume of stock trading on the New York Stock Exchange between 1943 and 1960. Options on 3.7 million shares were outstanding at June 1, 1959.[2] By 1961 the amounts outstanding were about three times that figure.[3]

NATURE OF THE OPTION BUSINESS[4]

Put and call dealers stand ready to buy or sell options. Each option is a contract granting the holder the right to buy, or sell, a given number of shares of a specified issue of stock at a predetermined price at any time within a stated period of time.

Terminology. Six types of option contract can be distinguished in the present market:

A *put* may be defined as a negotiable contract, given for an agreed premium, entitling the owner thereof, at his option, to sell, on or before a fixed date, a specified number of shares at a predetermined price.

A *call* is a negotiable contract for an agreed premium that entitles the holder thereof, at his option, to buy, on or before a fixed date, a specified number of shares at a predetermined price.

A *spread* consists of two separate options, one a call and one a put. Both contracts are identical as to stock and time expiration. The spread is priced at points away from the market, which means that the put may be exercised at points below the market, while the call may be exercised at points above the market.

A *straddle* also consists of two separate options, one a call and one a put. Both the put and call contracts are identical as to stock, contract price, and time of expiration. The contract price usually is the market

---

[2] SEC, *Report on Put and Call Options*, August, 1961, p. 5.

[3] Statement by Herbert Filer, Sr., March, 1962.

[4] In addition to the sources referred to previously, see: Anthony M. Reinach, *The Nature of Puts and Calls* (New York: The Bookmailer, 1961).

price at the time the contracts are drawn, which means that either the put or the call may be exercised at that market price and not points away from it, as in a spread. Many options are written as straddles but few are sold in this form. The usual buyer of an option is either bullish, and wants the call, or bearish, and wants the put, but has not the ambivalence to desire both.

A *strap* combines two calls with one put.

A *strip* combines two puts with one call.

Brokers and Dealers. The business of handling options is carried on through the medium of the put and call broker and dealer. There are about fifteen active firms. They are among the twenty-eight member firms organized as the Put and Call Brokers and Dealers Association. Some years ago the number of brokers and dealers was close to fifty. The purpose of the association is to promote trading in puts and calls, to assure trade practices beneficial to the members and the public, and to settle disputes which may arise among the members. The firms operate in rather small offices which have little contact with customers except over the telephone. It is rare for a firm to have a membership on a stock exchange.

The function of the put and call broker-dealer is to get the maker and the buyer of puts and calls together. For this service he receives compensation as a broker in the form of a commission which is charged to the maker of the option, or as a dealer he obtains profit from the difference between the price paid and the price received for the option. The compensation usually runs from as low as $\frac{1}{8}$ point on a low-priced stock to $\frac{1}{2}$ point on average-priced shares. If the premium is large, as it would be on an option covering high-priced shares, the compensation for the broker or dealer may be $1\frac{1}{2}$ points or more. The broker-dealer does not endorse or guarantee the option; this is done by a member or member organization of the New York Stock Exchange. The put and call broker-dealer acts only as an intermediary, without obligation to the holder, who accepts the option on this understanding.

CHARACTERISTICS OF PUTS AND CALLS

Parties. In every option contract there are four parties. The first, as already noted, is the put and call broker-dealer, whose function is to bring the maker and holder together.

The second party is the maker, writer, or seller. He is the party who sells the contract and must be willing to receive or deliver stock according to the terms of the contract. For writing the contract he receives a premium.

The third party to the contract is the purchaser or holder, who has the option or privilege of exercising the contract within its terms. This is done either through buying the stock from the maker or delivery of stock to that party. Options, of course, may be allowed to lapse without exercise or may be sold before exercise.

The final party is the endorser, a member or member organization of the New York Stock Exchange. The endorser guarantees that the maker of the contract will carry through the contract; thus he protects the purchaser against failure of the maker to perform his obligation. The endorser guarantees that the contract will be carried out, since he requires an adequate margin from the maker for this purpose, as will be found later.

Type of Stocks. For the most part, trading in puts and calls is carried on in the active market leaders. There is, however, some trading in the less-active stocks. As many as fifty active market leaders may be advertised by a put and call dealer at any one time.

Contracts. The Put and Call Brokers and Dealers Association uses a uniform, standard contract form for its operations. Puts and calls require separate forms, which are about 3½ by 9 inches and resemble a bank draft or promissory note. The contract indicates the date the contract is made, the number of shares (100), the name of the stock, the contract price per share, and the duration of the option. The name of neither the maker nor holder appears on the contract. The contract is a bearer instrument and is transferable. The holder is identified merely as the bearer. The contract is signed by the put and call broker-dealer who sold it. It is endorsed on the reverse side by a member or member organization of the New York Stock Exchange. An example of a call option is shown in Figure 35–1.

Endorsement. All put and call options dealt in by members of the Put and Call Brokers and Dealers Association must be endorsed by members or member organizations of the New York Stock Exchange for the protection of buyers. This endorsement, as indicated, is the guarantee of performance of the contract by the maker.

Types. There are two types of contract written. The first is called the market option, or option "at the market." The second is called the "points away," or wide-priced, or differential option. This latter has some historical importance but little present significance, and will be described briefly after consideration of the market option.

The Market Option. As has just been indicated, the more popular option today is the market option, or option at the market. There are three common maturities: sixty days, ninety days, and six months. Tech-

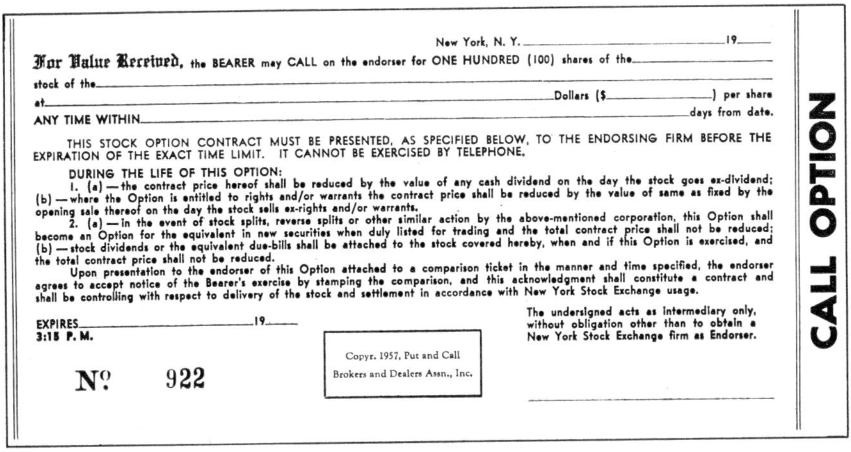
New York, N. Y. ______ 19____

For Value Received, the BEARER may CALL on the endorser for ONE HUNDRED (100) shares of the ______

stock of the ______

at ______ Dollars ($______) per share

ANY TIME WITHIN ______ days from date.

THIS STOCK OPTION CONTRACT MUST BE PRESENTED, AS SPECIFIED BELOW, TO THE ENDORSING FIRM BEFORE THE EXPIRATION OF THE EXACT TIME LIMIT. IT CANNOT BE EXERCISED BY TELEPHONE.

DURING THE LIFE OF THIS OPTION:

1. (a)—the contract price hereof shall be reduced by the value of any cash dividend on the day the stock goes ex-dividend; (b)—where the Option is entitled to rights and/or warrants the contract price shall be reduced by the value of same as fixed by the opening sale thereof on the day the stock sells ex-rights and/or warrants.

2. (a)—in the event of stock splits, reverse splits or other similar action by the above-mentioned corporation, this Option shall become an Option for the equivalent in new securities when duly listed for trading and the total contract price shall not be reduced; (b)—stock dividends or the equivalent due-bills shall be attached to the stock covered hereby, when and if this Option is exercised, and the total contract price shall not be reduced.

Upon presentation to the endorser of this Option attached to a comparison ticket in the manner and time specified, the endorser agrees to accept notice of the Bearer's exercise by stamping the comparison, and this acknowledgment shall constitute a contract and shall be controlling with respect to delivery of the stock and settlement in accordance with New York Stock Exchange usage.

EXPIRES ______ 19____
3:15 P. M.

Copyr. 1957, Put and Call Brokers and Dealers Assn., Inc.

The undersigned acts as intermediary only, without obligation other than to obtain a New York Stock Exchange firm as Endorser.

Nº 922

CALL OPTION

Fig. 35–1. A call option.

nically, the six-month option is written for six months and ten days. This may allow the taxpayer to treat gains and losses made upon such trading as long-term capital gains and losses rather than short-term ones subject to the full amount of the income tax. Options for as long as one year or more are written occasionally, and odd maturities often appear in lists of "special options" advertised in the press. "Special options" usually represent inventory of the dealer, who hopes and expects that market fluctuation will enable him to sell at a profit.

A put at the market can be exercised at any time in the allowed period at the market price current when the contract was written; e.g., 50. The call also may be exercised at any time during the life of the option at the current market price just indicated, of 50. Hence, the holder is not penalized by paying more than the market price at the date of contract when exercising a call or getting less than that market price when exercising a put. This, however, is offset by another factor; namely, the premium on the market option.

The premiums on market options range from as low as $100 for 100 shares to well over $1,000. Premiums on calls are nearly always higher than on puts. The difference depends on market conditions but ordinarily runs from $50 to $75 per 100 shares on ninety-day options and $75 to $100 on six-month options. It would seem that six-month options should carry premiums double those on ninety-day options. The usual differential, however, is about 40 per cent. A call that would cost $400 for ninety days, for instance, would probably cost $550 for six months and ten days.

Table 35–1 shows examples of premiums for various options on a number of stocks on June 20, 1962. The stocks in the table are listed in order, based on market price per share. The average price of the shares in these issues was $43.

Table 35–1. Premiums on Ninety-Day and Six-Month Puts and Calls, Priced at the Market, June 20, 1962

		Premiums			
Stock Issue	Market Price	90-Day Put	90-Day Call	6-Month Put	6-month Call
American Tel. & Tel. ...	$104	$650	$700	$850	$950
Kennecott Copper	70	550	600	750	875
General Electric	61	400	475	625	700
International Nickel ...	59	500	550	625	775
United States Steel	46	425	475	600	700
Chrysler	43	325	400	500	575
United Aircraft	42	350	425	500	625
Anaconda Copper	40	275	325	375	425
International Tel. & Tel.	39	350	375	475	500
Bethlehem Steel	34	275	325	375	450
Celanese	33	300	325	425	475
Atchison, Topeka & Santa Fe	23	225	250	325	350
Shenley Industries	19	200	225	300	325
American Motors	13	150	175	187½	225
New York Central	12	175	200	250	275
Average	$ 43	$345	$391	$479	$553

Source: Filer, Schmidt & Co.

Several generalizations about the premiums are apparent. First, there is general correlation between size of premium and market price. However, volatility, or the rate at which price change might be expected, was also a factor. Note the higher premiums on New York Central in comparison with American Motors, and the obviously less than proportional increase in premium on American Telephone and Telegraph in comparison with Kennecott Copper and General Electric. Second, call premiums are larger than put premiums. This is consistently true in the figures in the table, and reflects the generally greater demand for calls. Stockholders and option buyers are usually bullish. Third, the premium for six-month contracts were larger than those for ninety-day contracts by about 40 per cent.

Cash Dividends, Rights, and Stock Dividends. The contract price on a put or a call option is reduced on the ex-date for a distribution of a cash dividend or right to the shareholder by the market value of that distribution if the ex-date falls within the option period. For example, a holder of a call on 100 shares of American Telephone and Telegraph might have a contract price of 103. When the stock sells ex-dividend on the New York Stock Exchange, this price is lowered $0.90, the amount of the dividend, to $102.10 per share. If the option had been a put with a contract price of $98 per share, for example, the new price would have been $97.10 per share. If rights to buy new securities had been authorized, these prices would have been reduced by the market value of such rights on the ex-rights date set by the New York Stock Exchange.

Stock dividends are treated in somewhat different fashion but the result is similar. If an option is exercised after an issue has been traded ex-stock-dividend, the amount of shares involved is increased by the fraction of the stock dividend. For example, suppose a company declared a 5 per cent stock dividend, or a dividend of 5 shares for each 100 held. On or after the ex-dividend date, the holder of a put would be required to deliver 105 shares if he exercised his option. If he sold the option back to a put and call broker-dealer, as many option holders do, he would have been paid a price based on the market value of 105 shares. In other words, the stock dividend goes with the stock.

Margin. The maker, or writer, of an option must put up a margin at the time the contract is written in order to assure the endorsing member or member organization of the New York Stock Exchange that he will be able to carry out his obligation under the contract.

The margin requirement that is minimum under New York Stock Exchange rules for the sale of a put is 25 per cent of the put, or contract, price. After the date of initial sale, the margin is increased by the amount of loss or decreased by the amount of gain for the writer on the option at that contract price. A member or member organization may, of course, require its clients to maintain a higher percentage of margin.

If the option is a call, no margin is required on this transaction provided the writer has the stock and it is in the broker's custody. If the writer of a call does not have the stock, however, the transaction is considered a short sale and the minimum margin requirement is 30 per cent. After the date of the contract, this requirement also is increased by the full amount of any loss or decreased by the amount of any gain to the writer on the contract at its contract price in the current market.

Different rules apply to call options on low-priced shares (Rule 431).

The buyer of an option is not required to put up a margin at the time he buys it, since its exercise is solely at his initiative. It should recognized, however, that this means that no payment over and above the full premium on the option is required. Options have no loan value in general accounts.

When a buyer does exercise an option, the transaction must be margined. If he has no debit balance or security position with the organization at the time, the amount of margin will depend on the order of his operations. If, in exercising a call option, he first calls and then sells the stock in the market on the same day, the minimum maintenance margin required by the Exchange applies; i.e., 25 per cent of the market value of the stock or $1,000, whichever is greater. If he makes a short sale of stock first and subsequently calls the stock on option, the minimum required margin is that for a short sale, usually 30 per cent of the market value of the stock involved.

If a buyer exercises a put by tendering the stock first and then buying in the market, the 30 per cent minimum applies. If he buys first and then tenders the stock to the option writer, the 25 per cent margin requirement applies. In these cases the organization may, of course, require more margin, and the short sale requirement is different on low-priced shares.

The above statements apply, too, only to "daylight" trades, or those on which the transaction in the market and the exercise of the option both occur on the same day. If they occur on different days, the initial margin requirements of the Federal Reserve Board, expressed in Regulation T, apply.

Commissions and Transfer Taxes. If the holder of an option does not exercise his option, there is no commission payable by him to anyone at any time (excepting the unlikely possibility that his brokerage firm acquires the option for him on a "net" basis plus commission). If he does exercise his option, he will pay one New York Stock Exchange commission for the calling or putting of the stock under the contract and a second commission for the corresponding trade in the market. The commissions are the regular, round-lot commissions of the Exchange membership and are paid to the member organization handling the transactions for the option holder. On occasion the holder of a put may deliver stock from his box and, on that, pay no commission at the time of delivery.

There are no transfer taxes on puts. On calls, however, the same taxes are levied by the federal and New York State governments that would be levied on regular sales of stock at the contract price. The rates are identical to those on stock transfers. The tax may run as high as $0.12 per share, or $12.00 per option. The taxes are paid by the buyer, or holder, of the option at the time he acquires it.

Income Tax Status. Profits or losses arising from ownership of options are, of course, subject to federal income tax. In general, profits or losses resulting from the ownership of an option alone and a final liquidation by sale of the option itself (or evidence of its worthlessness) are taxable as capital gains or losses. They are short- or long-term gains, or losses, depending on the period of ownership of the option. For options exercised, the problems become more complex. The advice of tax authorities can be helpful. In any event the cost of an option is a cost of investing for tax purposes.

Wide-priced Options. These comments on the standard options of today apply generally to the type of option called "wide-priced." The primary difference is that the wide-priced option is written with a contract price that is points away from the market price on the date the contract is made up. The number of points away will depend largely on the maker's notion of the likelihood of a price change of a given amount. Wide-priced options, which were popular in the 1920's, usually have a standard premium of $137.50 for a thirty-day option. The adjustments for risk and share price level are made by establishing the number of points away from the existing market price of the shares rather than by changing the premium. Puts are written at points below the market, of course, so that some price decline must occur before the option becomes effective. In reverse, calls are written at points above the market. Some thirty-day, wide-priced options are sold today. They are of little significance in the market.

USES FOR PUTS AND CALLS

The New York Stock Exchange does not permit trading in puts and calls on the floor of the Exchange. It does permit members and member organizations to act as endorsers for such options, and the rules require that accounts of option writers or of option holders that exercise their options be adequately margined. In an approximate sense, there is an over-the-counter market for puts and calls. Put and call broker-dealers will reacquire options during their period of effectiveness at prices reflecting the market value of the stock under contract, and they may resell such options as well as some other special options they acquire in the marketing process.

Makers of Options. Puts and calls usually are written by individual security owners and traders or securities houses. Some wealthy stockholders who own stock for income purposes are willing to write options. The premiums on the options not exercised are income for them in addition to the dividends and other forms of income earned on their portfolios. Investment and financial institutions, such as investment clubs, insurance companies, and funds with large portfolios, might be willing to write options for the same reason but they are not an important source.

Most makers of options are owners of substantial blocks of securities, although many of them engage in the business on a frankly speculative basis. A minimum capital of $50,000 is usually appropriate. Broker-dealers hesitate to deal with makers with less capital. Profits from option-writing can be quite high; rates of return of 10 to 25 per cent after allowance for losses are earned—unless the market is quite unfavorable. In this, as in other investment operations, losses are sustained and may be severe.

Reasons for Writing Options.[5] A basic reason for writing options was mentioned above. The writer obtains premiums ranging in amount from $25 to over $1,000 on an option. If the option is not exercised, this is income to him. The premium on a ninety-day option may well exceed the dividend income for a full year. An investor expecting a rising market can write puts, which will be converted to calls, as explained below, for sale to similarly minded option buyers. If his forecast is good, the premiums are his. If he expected price for certain shares to decline but there was a demand for calls in the market, he could write calls. If his forecast were correct, the premiums would be his. There will be errors of judgment, of course, but a continuing program of writing options is quite likely to provide income in this fashion. Less than half of the options written are exercised.[6]

The exercise of options must be anticipated, however. Without attempting to catalog all of the strategies a writer might perceive, reference to two situations may indicate why writers find the making of options reasonable in another sense. First, assume that a writer has decided to buy 100 shares of a certain stock issue. He expects the price to rise, but not rapidly, and believes it may decline in the near future. He may write a put against this issue. If the price does rise, he can buy and his cost will be the price paid minus the premium on the put—which, of course, will not be exercised. If the price falls, he buys the stock at the contract price minus the premium on the put, which gives him a net acquisition price several points below the market price on the day he sold the put.

Again, assume that a writer has decided to sell 100 shares of stock in his portfolio. He expects the price to fall but thinks there may be a short-term upward change in the near future. He sells a call. If the price does fall, he can sell the stock and obtain a net return equal to the price at which he does sell plus the premium on the call. If it does rise, the option holder calls the stock at the contract price. The writer receives the price in the market on the day he made his decision plus the premium on the call option.

[5] For more explanation than feasible here, see: Reinach, op. cit., pp. 43–85.
[6] SEC, op. cit., p. 45 ff.

In both instances rapid change in price over a considerable range could make these very nice statements of opportunity ludicrous, and option writers must expect their forecasts to show error at times.

Conversion is a specialized writing function, mostly for professionals. The problem usually is to turn a put into a call. It is accomplished in the following way. The converter buys a put from an option writer at, say, $250. At the same time he sells a call to a buyer at, say, $325. He owns 100 shares of the stock or buys it on the same day at the same price entered into both option contracts. There are three possible outcomes: (1) the price of the stock falls, he puts it at the contract price, and has the difference of $75 between the price paid for the put and the price received from the call as a gain; (2) the price of the stock rises and it is called from him at the contract price, which was identical to the price he paid or is higher than the price he had paid at some earlier time, and he has the difference of $75 as a gain; (3) the price fluctuates somewhat but ends up identical to the contract price, neither put nor call is exercised, and he has the difference of $75 as a gain. Conversion permits makers holding bullish forecasts to write puts and sell them for somewhat less than they might if bearish forecasts were generally held.

Multiple options have a peculiar advantage. Assume a maker writes a strap, two puts, and one call, in a situation in which generally bullish forecasts are held. He receives a substantially greater premium than he could obtain by writing a call alone. If the call is exercised, he sells his stock at the contract price plus this premium. If the price of the stock falls, he may receive 200 shares of the stock when the puts are exercised but his purchase price is the contract price less one-half of the strap premium on each round-lot. In the happy circumstance of small, indecisive price changes, he might end up with three options unexercised and the full premium as income. This is unlikely. At least one side, either put or call, of the options in a multiple contract is exercised.

Reasons for Buying Options. The motivations of buyers of puts and calls are various, and the following paragraphs serve merely to indicate some of them. It is well to remember that a buyer enters the market with a personal concept of investment objective and a personal forecast of probable market price changes. He wants either puts or calls, but not both. The motives described below are in many instances alternatives for different buyers or the same buyer at different times.

1. *To enter the market at low cost.* A speculator, believing that a given stock will rise 10 points in three months, may buy a call. His initial expenses are the premium and the transfer taxes. Let us assume that the stock is selling at 50. To secure a ninety-day market call option, he would pay a premium of perhaps $400 plus $6 in transfer taxes, a total of $406.

To buy such stock on a 70 per cent margin would require an investment of $3,500 plus a commission of $44, a total of $3,544. On such a purchase, then, he has $3,544 at risk, much of which might be lost if the price of the stock should drop precipitously. If the stock fails to rise, he loses $406; if it does rise, he loses less or makes a profit, and on a substantial rise his profit may be very handsome indeed when measured as a rate of return on this initial investment. In the booming bull market of the 1950's, some speculators obtained high profits on well-bought calls.

2. *To enter the market at a future date.* A speculator, believing strongly that a given stock will increase in price but, for example, lacking sufficient funds to buy at the moment, may buy a call. The market price at the time is, say, 40. If the stock price does rise as anticipated, the trader may enter the market later, when he has funds, at the call price—or he may sell the option itself at a capital gain.

3. *To make a speculative profit on a call.* Many speculators buy calls for the same reason that they buy stocks outright or on margin. They hope for an increase in prices; in such a case they exercise the call and sell the stock in excess of the call price.

4. *To make a speculative profit on a put.* The principle here is the same as for the short sale. The speculator, believing that a stock will decline, purchases, a put. The stock, having fallen in price, is purchased in the open market at less than the put price and delivered to the maker of the put at the specified price, the difference representing the gross profit.

5. *To protect a profit on a long position.* A trader purchases stock and holds until it has risen to a profitable selling price. Uncertain as to the future, he buys a put. If the stock continues to rise, he can liquidate his long position at a profit and disregard the put option. If it declines, however, he falls back on his hedge and sells the stock to the maker at the agreed contract price.

6. *To protect a profit on a short position.* A trader has short sold 100 shares. The stock has declined, giving him a substantial paper profit. He may now decide to purchase a call. In case the market again rises, he can exercise the option and protect much of the profit previously obtained, since he can obtain stock from the maker and cover at a fixed price.

7. *To protect purchase at time of commitment.* A trader at the time of purchasing stock may wish to hedge against a possible market reversal. A purchase of a put at that time will protect his investment against such an eventuality, the cost being the expense of the option.

8. *To protect a short sale at time of commitment.* Similarly, a short seller, at the time he makes his original short sale, may purchase a call. This will protect his commitment against a rising market, since he can always cover at the price specified in the option.

The above reasons may be reduced to two main ones: (1) to make a speculative profit and (2) to hedge against a market position. Although brokers generally agree that these are the two main objectives in buying puts and calls, there is reason to believe the first is most often important.[7]

Number of Trades Against Options. A very important and interesting fact about a put or call is that, although the holder may exercise it only once, he may trade against it as many times as circumstances permit. Once an option has been exercised, the contract is ended. However, the broker may buy and sell the stock a number of times during the life of the option if profit opportunities exist. The reason for this is that, in case the trader errs in his operations, it is always possible to fall back upon the option to limit his losses. This situation may be illustrated by an example.

Let us suppose that a stock is priced at 60. The trader buys a put, priced at the market. His premium is, perhaps, $380. The stock falls to 55; at that point he goes long 100 shares. The stock rises to 59 and he sells at a 4-point gross profit. He could have exercised the put, but that would have ended its usefulness. The stock again falls, this time to 54. He again goes long 100 shares at that price. The stock now increases to 61, and he sells at a 7-point profit. He has now made two complete "round-turns" with a gross profit of 11 points without touching his option. Let us suppose that on his third "round-term" he buys on a decline to 56 and is unable to liquidate at a profit within the period of the option. He now proceeds to exercise the option and deliver the stock to the maker at 60.

Exercising the Option. There is no need for the owner to exercise the option at any particular time in the option period. It may be exercised on or before the termination date specified in the contract. The privilege is exercised only if it is to the advantage of the holder to do so; there is no compulsion. In exercising a call, it is ordinarily assumed that the option will not be exercised unless the holder can resell the stock for more than the expenses involved. This is not necessarily so. Let us assume that the holder is already out $406 for the premium and tax on a call. If the option is not exercised, this is a loss. However, the holder may be able to exercise the option without profit but can reduce that loss to a lesser figure; e.g., $200. He would then exercise the option even though it meant a net loss of this amount. Similiarly, in a put there may

[7] SEC, *op. cit.,* pp. 76–7.

be no real profit on exercising it; yet the loss of the premium may be reduced by exercising the privilege.

Comparison with Stop Orders. The option has a great similarity to the stop order and can be used for the same purpose to some extent. As has been indicated, a prime purpose of the option is to protect the security holder against losses. Let us suppose that a security holder has 100 shares valued at 50. He has, so far, obtained a 10-point paper profit on the stock but is fearful that a market reaction may wipe out his profits. He now has two alternatives: (1) to buy a put with a specified price of 50 or (2) to place a stop order to sell at 48. Which should be his choice? There are advantages to both alternatives.

The option has an advantage in that it gives a longer period of execution and protects the security holder until its expiration. The market price may reach the stop limit many times during the life of the option. In the case of the option, the market may reverse itself and a price rise will turn a loss into profit. Hence, a number of trades may be possible at a time when a market is continuously reversing itself. On the other hand, the stop order protects the holder only until the market reaches the stop price; at that time it becomes effective and is executed at the best possible price. Thereafter it gives no more protection. In summary, the option protects against a market reversal throughout its life in contrast to the stop order which protects only until the market reaches the stop price. Calls have the same advantage over stop orders in short selling.

The second advantage of the option is that it gives greater protection than does the stop order. A stop order assures a security holder no definite price upon execution; the broker fills the order at the best possible price, which may be at, above, or below the stop price. In the option, however, the holder is assured the price specified in the option contract. In the example just cited, the holder was guaranteed a price of 50 for his stock, whereas a stop order at 48 assured no such figure.

The stop order, on the other hand, does have one distinct advantage over the option. It is cheaper. In the case of a stop order to sell, the only expense of execution, exclusive of taxes, is the commission, whereas the put carries two commissions plus whatever premium may have been paid to the maker of the option. The premium may have been $472.50 for a ninety-day option. The heavy premiums paid for options tend to counterbalance their advantages.

Expenses and Profits of Options. In order to illustrate more clearly the expense and profit aspect of options, two examples will be given. In the first example, a trader believes that a certain railroad stock selling at 56 will go up 10 points in ninety days. It carries a $100 par value.

The premium on the call is $380. The trader is correct in his forecast. At the end of three months the stock is selling at 66. He exercises his call and sells the stock at that price. His net profit is $516.78, as the following figures will indicate:

Sale of 100 shares at 66		$6,600.00
Expenses:		
Premium on call	$ 380.00	
Transfer taxes on call	6.24	
Cost of 100 shares at 56	5,600.00	
Commission on purchase	44.60	
Commission on sale	45.60	
Transfer taxes on sale	6.64	
SEC fee on sale	.14	6,083.22
		$ 516.78

In a second example, a stockholder wishes to speculate on his belief that a given industrial stock will fall 6 points in the next half-year. The stock is selling around 31. He buys a put, priced at 31, and pays the $300 premium. His judgment was wrong and the stock stood at 27 at the end of six months. This is the way he came out.

Sale of 100 shares at 31 to the maker		$3,100.00
Expenses:		
Premium on put	$ 300.00	
Cost of 100 shares at 27	2,700.00	
Commission on buying stock	32.50	
Commission on putting stock	34.50	
Transfer tax on put	5.24	3,072.24
		$ 27.76

It is interesting to note in this transaction that even if the stock had fallen to only 28, it would still have paid him to exercise the option. He is already out $300. By exercising the option when the market was at 28, he could have reduced this loss.

Merits of Puts and Calls. Without question, there are certain advantages to the use of puts and calls, especially to the protective use of such options. On the other hand, the buyer should carefully weigh the costs involved, such as premiums, taxes, and in the case of wide-price options, the number of points away from the market. These total overhead costs may range from as low as 2 to as many as 5, 6, or more points. A given stock must, therefore, move as much as this amount of overhead before the option can show a profit to the holder. Unless such a market movement is indicated, the prospective buyer may find that the use of market and stop orders is better fitted to his requirements.

On occasion holders of puts and calls may make very large profits on these options. In such cases the market may decline more than the general expectation at the time the put is written or rise more than the expectation in the case of a call. Holders of calls in the 1950's were fortunate in this way. During that period they were more fortunate than the writers of calls.

DOUBLE OPTIONS

Spreads. As indicated earlier in the chapter, a spread is a double option or combined put and call. The holder may exercise both options, one and not the other, or neither, as circumstances dictate. The spread is priced at "points away from the market." For example, if the market were 60, the put could be exercised at 57 and the call could be exercised at, perhaps, 63½. The buyer pays a large premium for such options, roughly the same as on a put and call combined. The question may then be asked: Why not buy the put and call separately? The answer is that it would be entirely practical to do so except that the points away on the spread are likely to be less than the points away on puts and calls purchased separately.

The alleged advantage of the spread is that the trader, not certain of which way the market may go, hedges against both market advances and declines. The objection to the spread, of course, is that the cost in premiums and points away from the market is great. The possibility of profit is correspondingly reduced.

Spreads are not popular in that most speculators are convinced, in their own minds at least, that they know which way the market will go. Hence, they will buy calls if they believe the market is going up, and puts if they believe the market is due for a decline.

Spreads are not currently being quoted in the market.

Straddles. A straddle is the other form of double option. It also consists of two separate options, one a put and one a call. Both contracts are identical as to stock, contract price, and time expiration. The contract price for both options is usually the current market price for the stock. Few are sold as such to option buyers today. Put and call dealers buy straddles from makers and then sell the options separately. Few buyers are both bullish and bearish at the same time.

The holder of the straddle may exercise either one or both sides of the option at any time during the life of the contract. Exercising one option, such as the put, does not affect in any way the right to exercise the other option, nor does it cancel it.

Since the straddle is priced at the market, the premium must be high to compensate the maker. There is a danger of loss regardless of which way the market goes. One side of a straddle in practice is almost always exercised by the holder of that option unless the price remains practically unchanged. If the stock should rise by enough to cover the expenses of calling the stock and selling in the market at a profit, the call option holder will call. If the stock should fall by enough to cover the costs of putting the stock and show a profit, the put option holder will exercise the put. Thus, the chances that the maker may retain the entire premium as profit are rare. Equally infrequent is the exercise of the put and call at the same price, which would again result in the entire premium being a profit.

Of the two-way options, straddles have the higher premiums. These offset the higher overhead cost in trading in this type of option. Besides their high cost, straddles are also unpopular with buyers of options for the same reasons indicated for spreads; namely, the belief of the trader that the market will go only one way.

Strips and Straps. Each of these consists of options on 300 shares. A strap combines two calls with one put: a strip reverses the combination. Buyers of option seldom interest themselves in these combinations. They are of more significance to writers who feel they can increase their opportunities for profit from this form of business by having more options on one side of the market.

36

Stock Rights

Many investors from time to time receive rights to subscribe to stock or bonds in the companies in which they have a stockholder interest. These rights are options, not unlike the call options described in the last chapter, to buy a stated number of shares of stock or a stated par amount of bonds at a predetermined price during a specified period of time. Experienced investors are aware of the value of such rights and the different ways stockholders may profit from them.

Rights are issued to stockholders of record on a date set by the board of directors of a company. They are in the form of stock, or bond, subscription warrants, one of which is shown in Figure 36–1. The stockholders may exercise these rights by returning them to the corporation with the required funds to pay for the new security. In case the stockholders do not wish to exercise the rights, they may sell them in the market. A very considerable amount of trading in rights usually takes place during the period in which they may be exercised.

Rights are issued under a procedure known as a privileged subscription. By this is meant a procedure by which existing stockholders are given priority in subscribing for the new shares at a price lower than the current market price. This privilege, popularly considered a favor to the stockholders, may have much less value than popular opinion accords it.

Legal Aspects of Privileged Subscriptions. The law on privileged subscriptions has undergone a considerable change over the years. Under the interpretation of the common law by the courts, stockholders are entitled to privileged subscriptions under what is known as the "pre-emptive right." This is the right of stockholders to buy new stock before it is offered for cash to non-stockholders. Two arguments are used to justify the pre-emptive right.

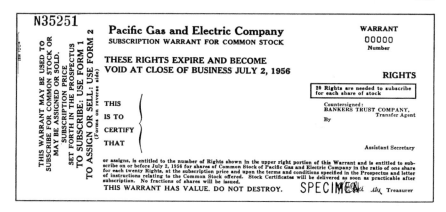

Fig. 36–1. A stock subscription warrant.

The first is that each stockholder is entitled to preserve or maintain a proportionate voting interest in the corporation. A substantial block of new stock sold to outsiders might cause a marked change in the voting control of the corporation. Control might shift from one group to another. Under the pre-emptive right, however, a given stockholder or group of stockholders could subscribe to new stock in the ratio to current holdings and maintain the same degree of control as before.

The second is that each stockholder is entitled to maintain a proportionate share in the assets of the corporation, or, to put it another way, to maintain his proportionate share in the net worth or equity of the common stockholders. Stock issued under privileged subscription typically is sold at a price substantially below the current market price. Thus, book value of each old share is diluted and the stock tends to fall in value after the issue of new shares. The stockholder is entitled to protection against such a decline. Protection is secured by the right to buy new stock before an offer to and on more favorable terms than accorded other purchasers.

The common law justification for the pre-emptive right has been altered by legislation over the years. A considerable variation, therefore, exists now among the several states. Some states, such as California, Indiana, and Pennsylvania, have abolished the pre-emptive right entirely unless it is specifically introduced into the charter, or articles of incorporation, by the founders. In other states a corporation may be formed and the founders are free to include or exclude the pre-emptive right in the charter as they see fit. States such as Delaware, California, Indiana, New Jersey, Ohio, and Pennsylvania permit a majority of the stockholders of a company to amend the charter and deny pre-emptive rights.

Although many corporations have amended their charters to permit the directors to issue stock without the pre-emptive right, this option is not always taken. In 1961, for example, American Telephone and Telegraph chose to issue new stock through privileged subscription although this is not a charter provision.

The SEC has also recognized a changing concept with respect to the pre-emptive right. In earlier years, in interpretation of the Public Utility Holding Company Act, the SEC held that stockholders were entitled to pre-emptive rights. In more recent years the Commission has not insisted on the principle when it appeared that the management could obtain funds on more favorable terms by selling stock under competitive bidding.

The absence of the pre-emptive right no doubt increases the freedom of directors in choice of new security issues. Whether this negation is sound policy, however, and fair to the stockholders, is debatable.

Purpose of Issuing Rights. Rights are offered to stockholders when the directors believe this to be the best method of raising additional funds. Long-term, or capital, funds may be secured by selling common stock, preferred stock, or bonds. If a company wishes to secure more funds from common stockholders, it may issue rights even though the pre-emptive right is waived under the charter, as before indicated. The rights are a vehicle facilitating subscription to the new stock. The immediate recipients may sell their rights to others; but ultimately, barring nonsense destruction of the warrants, or a drastic price decline, these rights will end in the hands of individuals who will exercise them and buy the stock.

Pricing the New Stock. In all privileged subscriptions, the directors set a subscription price which is below the current market price of the stock at the time the rights are issued. This is not benevolence on the part of directors. It is part of a policy designed to make the new issue a success. No board of directors expects present stockholders to make a significant financial sacrifice to buy new stock. Indeed, they expect them to buy the stock only if the issue is made sufficiently attractive through a price discount.

The pricing of new stock requires exercise of care. Decision on the exact subscription price may be deferred until a day or two before the public announcement, which follows the release of the issue by the SEC. The market price may be 25 to 40 per cent higher than the subscription price chosen, particularly if the issue is not underwritten. The offering price, of course, must equal or exceed the par value of the stock, if it has one. A substantial spread between market and subscription price is justified on two grounds. First, the risk is reduced that market price will fall during the subscription period enough to jeopardize the success of the issue. Second, a substantial spread "sweetens" the issue, in the sense that it gives the stockholders the sense of a bargain and increases the willingness to accept the new issue.

Procedure in Issuing Rights. A number of steps must be followed by the board of directors in issuing rights. First, the directors must authorize issue of the new stock through a formal resolution. If the company does not have enough unissued stock for this purpose, an amendment to the charter by the stockholders will be needed before the additional shares can be issued.

Second, approval of the new issue by the stockholders is required. Usually, a special meeting of the stockholders is called. Approval by vote of holders of two-thirds of the stock present at the meeting is a usual requirement. Some corporate laws, however, permit authorization of new stock issues at a regular meeting of the stockholders.

In calling a meeting of the stockholders, the directors send to them a special letter and a proxy statement with complete details of the proposed financing and its justification. The company also releases items to newspapers during the period before the stockholders' meeting in order to increase the likelihood of understanding and, hence, of acceptance of the proposal. Such proposals of directors usually are approved by the stockholders with a very large majority vote.

The Securities Act of 1933 requires that all non-exempt issues be registered with the SEC before a public offering. A registration statement is prepared and submitted to the Commission. At the same time a preliminary, or "red herring," prospectus—minus some important items, such as price—may be printed and released to the securities industry. The Act requires a twenty-day waiting period before public sale. Shortly before the end of this period, a decision is made as to the subscription price, unless such a decision was made earlier.

As soon as an issue is released for sale by the SEC, there is a rush to issue the subscription warrants. A date of record is decided upon by the directors prior to this time. This date, ordinarily, is the same as the date on which the registration is declared effective by the SEC. As soon as the stockholders of record on this specified date are properly identified from the stock record books, subscription warrants are prepared in their names and mailed to them. This is a complex and expensive process, since thousands of stockholders must be reached. Commonly, a company starts days ahead in preparing stockholder lists and then makes corrections up to the date of record from later information. In view of the short duration of the offering period in most rights distributions, companies begin mailing warrants within twenty-four hours of the date of record. Very large companies, however, may take one to two weeks to complete the process.

To avoid errors and possible loss by stockholders, subscription warrants are prepared to look like instruments of value, even though most are now in the form of punch cards used in machine accounting systems. Each warrant shows the number of rights represented by the warrant. Blank spaces permit the holder to subscribe for the new stock or endorse the warrant for sale of these rights. Warrants may be exercised by surrendering them to the company or to the warrant agent with the proper funds needed to buy the new stock. If the holder wishes to sell them, he may do so through any broker. Often the corporation appoints a bank or trust company to act as its agent; the holder does business through this agent if he cares to do so.

FULL INSTRUCTIONS FOR USE OF FORMS APPEAR IN THE LETTER ACCOMPANYING THIS WARRANT

Payment of this amount must accompany Subscription. Check must be payable to the order of Pacific Gas and Electric Company in United States dollars and drawn on a bank in Continental United States.

This Warrant is transferable, in the same manner and with the same effect as in the case of a negotiable instrument payable to a specified person, upon due execution of the assignment form. If and when this Warrant is assigned in blank, the Company and the Subscription Agents may thereafter treat the bearer hereof as the absolute owner of this Warrant for all purposes and neither the Company nor said Agents shall be affected by any notice to the contrary.

This Warrant is transferable in San Francisco or New York

FORM 1 — SUBSCRIPTION: I hereby subscribe for Common Stock as indicated below, on the terms specified in the Prospectus relating thereto, receipt of which is hereby acknowledged, and request American Trust Company or Bankers Trust Company to purchase any additional Rights needed to complete this subscription or to sell any Rights in excess of the number needed for this subscription. I understand that I will be sent a bill for Rights purchased or a check for proceeds of Rights sold.

Number of full shares subscribed for.......... ______ shares

Total Rights required for this subscription. ______ Rights

Total cost of shares subscribed for..........$ ______
(Number of shares times the Subscription Price)

Total Rights surrendered herewith ______ Rights

______ Date ______
(Subscriber's Signature)

FORM 2 To ASSIGN or SELL these Rights mark ONE box to indicate your instructions.

ASSIGNMENT: For value received, I hereby assign the Rights represented by this Warrant to:

☐ ______

SALE: ☐ I hereby request American Trust Company or Bankers Trust Company to sell all Rights represented by this Warrant and send me a check for the net proceeds. Receipt of the Prospectus relating to the Common Stock offered is hereby acknowledged.

Address for mailing certificates if other than imprinted on face

Street

Town State

______ Date ______

______
(Signature of Registered Owner)
Signature must correspond with name as shown on face of Warrant.

Fig. 36–2. Instructions on back of subscription warrant.

When the stockholder receives his warrant, he also receives detailed instructions from the company. An illustration of such instructions is shown in Figure 36–2, the reverse side of the warrant shown in Figure 36–1. This gives complete details on the number of shares which may be purchased, the subscription price, the date when the subscription period expires, how new stock may be purchased, and how the rights may be sold. In case the warrant does not represent the exact number of rights needed to buy an integral number of shares, additional rights can be purchased or the excess rights may be sold. For example, if the company were to require twenty rights to buy one new share and the stockholder had twenty-five rights, he could either sell five of his rights or buy an additional fifteen rights in order to buy one more share.

As soon as the stockholder receives his warrant, he is faced with this question of what he should do with it. The company has provided the opportunity for him to surrender the warrant and subscribe to new stock. He may, however, prefer to sell his rights. His decision may be based on any of a number of things, such as his investment funds, the merits of the stock as an investment or speculation, the size of his present holdings in the company, the relative profits in buying the stock or disposing of the rights, or his forecast of the market. A number of alternatives are open to him; they will be examined shortly.

Meaning of a Right. A right is the privilege attaching to one old share of stock. Each outstanding share is given one right; the number of old shares and the number of rights are identical. If a stockholder owns 10 shares, he will receive ten rights. If he possesses 200 shares, he will receive two hundred. This is the so-called "New York plan," now generally used in privileged subscriptions.

Rights Needed to Buy New Stocks. The directors, in setting forth the terms of the privileged subscription, always state in clear language the number of rights needed to buy one new share. Three, five, ten, or twenty rights, for example, may be necessary. If the stockholder owns 50 old shares and ten rights are necessary to acquire one new share, he may subscribe for 5 new shares.

A simple method is used by the company to decide how many new rights are necessary to subscribe for one new share. Let us suppose that a company has 1 million shares outstanding and proposes to issue 50,000 new shares. One million rights will be issued. The directors do not want to sell more than 50,000 shares. Hence they decide that twenty rights must be surrendered in the purchase of each new share. All of the rights will have been exercised by the time the offer of 50,000 shares is fully subscribed.

Trading in Rights. Rights on the New York Stock Exchange are traded as soon as registration of the issue is effective under the 1933 act. The Department of Stock List announces when this activity may begin. Before trading is approved, the Department must be certain that all details of the new issue have been approved by the directors and by the stockholders, if required; that they have been effectively registered with the SEC; and that they are approved by any other governmental body with regulatory jurisdiction. The additional shares or new issue must be approved by the Department and the Board of Governors of the Exchange.

Rights are traded on a "when issued" basis until they are mailed out to stockholders by the company. Thereafter they are traded "regular way." The period in which "when issued" trading in rights continues will vary. It may be from one day to several weeks. There are instances where it has been as long as five weeks. The deciding factor is how quickly the warrants can be processed and mailed to the stockholders. In the issue of rights by American Telephone and Telegraph in 1961, the period of "when issued" trading ran sixteen business (twenty-five calendar) days. The Pacific Gas and Electric issue of the same year had "when issued" trading for only three business days. For the majority of smaller issues, "when issued" trading is limited to a single day.

The original issue trades ex-rights usually on the first business day following the first day of trading in the rights, but not earlier than the third business day before the date of record. The stock is said to be selling "cum rights" or "rights on" before it goes ex-rights.

From this date until the end of the privileged subscription period, the rights are freely bought and sold separately from the stock. The stock transactions are ex-rights and the buyers and sellers understand that no rights go with it. Trading in the rights themselves continues until noon on the day when the right to subscribe expires.

The time schedule described above can be illustrated by reference to the American Telephone and Telegraph issue of 1961. On December 23, 1960, the directors announced that rights would be issued to stockholders of record at the close of business on February 23, 1961, and that twenty rights would be required to buy one new share. On January 26 the registration statement was filed with the SEC. On February 17 (three full business days before the date of record) the stock went ex-rights. The twenty-day waiting period ended on February 15; a subscription price of $86 per share was announced; trading in rights on a "when issued" basis began at 10 A.M., February 16. Warrants were mailed on Thursday, March 9, and trading on a "when issued" basis ceased on March 10, the next businesss day. Trading in rights "regular way" began with the opening of the market on Monday, March 13. On April 14 the rights expired; trading in the rights was suspended at noon, and they traded on "cash" contracts during the morning session.

A final word about "when issued" contracts. Each brokerage house has its own printed forms for such trading but follows the form prescribed by the Exchange. "When issued" contracts are settled by delivery of the rights and payment therefor on a date fixed by a special ruling of the Department of Stock List. This date varies with circumstances, a common one being three days after the trading in rights on this basis ceases. It was March 16 in the American Telephone and Telegraph case.

Value of Rights. Many speculators and traders in rights use some formula to determine the theoretical value of such rights. Interest in the subject is probably overstressed, but the figure usually computed is one below which arbitraging is profitable and, therefore, investors generally may expect it to be the lowest price in the market for rights. Two formulas have some use in figuring theoretical value: (1) before the stock goes ex-rights and (2) after it goes ex-rights. These are given below.

To find the theoretical value of one right *before the stock goes ex-rights,* the formula below is used.

$$V = \frac{M - S}{N + 1}$$

where V is the value of one right
    M is the market price of the old stock
    S is the subscription price of the new stock
    N is the number of rights necessary to buy one new share

Let us take two examples and find the theoretical value of a right. First, a stock is selling at 40 in the market; it is offered to the stockholders at 30; nine rights are necessary to subscribe for one new share. The value of the right is $1.

$$\frac{40 - 30}{9 + 1} = \$1$$

In the next example, the stock is selling at 95; the subscription price is 75; seven rights are necessary to buy one new share.

$$\frac{95 - 75}{7 + 1} = \$2.50$$

The reader may be puzzled as to why the figure "1" is added each time, and he may wish proof that the rights are worth the figures indicated. Let us go back to our first example.

Nine old shares worth $40 each	$360
Plus one new share contributing $30	30
Total value of 10 shares	390
Value of each of the 10 shares	39
Theoretical value of stock after subscriptions	39
Cost of the new share	30
Profit made in owning 9 old shares	$ 9
Profit made on each old share	$ 1

In other words, the company now has 10 shares outstanding instead of 9; there are $390 in assets and earning power behind each of the 10 shares of $39 each. The new share was purchased for $30. The stockholder realized $9 profit but had to own 9 shares to obtain it. Each right was worth, therefore, $1.

A formula for finding the value of the rights *after* the stock goes ex-rights is as follows:

$$V = \frac{M - S}{N}$$

After the stock goes ex-rights, it is not as valuable as before; its market value falls approximately the amount equal to the theoretical value of the right. In our first example, above, this new value is $39; the value of one right is still $1.

$$\frac{39 - 30}{9} = \$1$$

Market and Theoretical Values of Rights. In practice, the actual or market value of a right and its theoretical value are seldom precisely the same. The market value may fluctuate above and below the theoretical value. It is very interesting, however, how close together the two values remain most of the time. For example, in the American Telephone and Telegraph issue referred to above, the rights were selling at $1.50 at the close of the first week of "when issued" trading; the theoretical value at that time was $1⅜. Five weeks later the rights were selling at $1⁵⁄₁₆, a figure identical to the theoretical value. The early trading in Pacific Gas and Electric rights was at $⅜ when the theoretical value was $¹⁰⁄₃₂. Two weeks later the rights sold at $¼, a figure identical to the theoretical value.

An Illusion—The Privileged Subscription. Many stockholders are pleased to be invited to buy new stock at subscription prices substantially below the market price. The differential of, perhaps, $5 to $30 appears to be a genuine source of profit and the low subscription price a definite bargain. From a theoretical standpoint, there is no profit and the stock is no bargain. The profit made by buying the stock at the subscription price is exactly offset by the decline in the market value of the stock after the operation is ended. There are more shares outstanding and less equity behind each share. Theoretically, the company cannot earn as much per share as it did before and the stock will fall.

In the first example just cited, let us suppose that the stockholder had 9 shares worth $40 each and $30 in cash; his total assets are $390. If he were to buy the one new share for $30, he would now possess 10 shares worth $39 each; his assets are still $390. If he were to sell his rights at $1 each, he would now possess 9 shares worth $351, his original $30 in cash, and $9 received from the sale of nine rights; his assets are still $390. Either way he comes out with the same total assets in the end; there has been no real profit.

In actual practice, stockholders often do not accept this analysis. Since many investors do not realize the effect of any issue of new stock upon per share earnings, dividends, and assets, they consider the proceeds from the sale of rights a real income or profit, even though the stock may slump in value. Other stockholders are of the opinion that the company will probably maintain the same dividend rate and, hence, the stock should go back to its original market price. It is believed that companies that issue additional stock through privileged subscriptions are growing companies and will be able to put the new money to work to good advantage. The profits made from the sale of rights are considered by numerous stockholders as merely additional dividends or income from ownership.

Market Value of Rights. The most difficult problem connected with trading in rights is that they may sell above, at, or below their theoretical value. To make things more difficult, they fluctuate constantly; they may be worth more at the beginning, in the middle, or at the end of the subscription period. The holder, therefore, has the difficult decision to make as to the timing of the sale of rights, if he wishes to dispose of them.

"Sell rights early" has for years been an axiom among speculators. It it based on the theory that rights are worth more when the plan is proposed or when rights are first available for sale than at the close of the subscription period when, it is believed, rights will be dumped on the market by holders who do not care to put up the cash to subscribe to new stock; they will force the value of the rights to a low level. The trouble with this theory is that if everyone believes it, it will not work out this way. If everyone sells at once, the rights will immediately touch bottom and will not go any further. This, of course, does not happen.

There is little published material to indicate at what point in the subscription period rights sell at their highest level. Dewing, an authority in the field of finance, made several unpublished studies many years ago. In a study of 191 privileged subscriptions of railroads, public utilities, and industrials from 1918 to 1929, he found that rights sold at their highest in 46 per cent of the cases at the beginning of the subscription period, in 15 per cent of the cases at the middle of the period, and in 39 per cent of the cases at the end of the period.[1] Other studies by him in earlier years showed substantially the same distribution. It seems a fair conclusion, therefore, that the axiom "Sell rights early" is something less than a solid foundation for success in trading in stock rights. A very important factor governing the value of rights during the subscription

[1] A. S. Dewing, *Financial Policy of Corporations* (5th ed.; New York: The Ronald Press Co., 1953), p. 1159.

period is the trend of the market. A rising market will cause the rights to sell at their highest at the end of the period; the reverse is also true.

Alternatives Offered Holders of Rights. The holder of rights have a number of options. The first one is disposal in the waste basket, or no action. It is surprising how many stockholders take no action when receiving rights and how much money is lost this way each year. During another privileged subscription of American Telephone and Telegraph, in 1955, 280,000 rights, or ½ of 1 per cent of the total, were not exercised; the loss was about $960,000. In the same year, during the privileged subscription of General Motors, 1,329,000 rights, or 1½ per cent of the total, were not exercised; the loss was $1,500,000. Losses this way run from ½ to 2½ per cent of the total rights offered. Many companies go to great lengths to prevent this and often engage in an extended educational campaign over a period of years. Repeated attempts are made to get stockholders to exercise or sell their rights, yet the irreducible minimum in losses appears to be about ½ of 1 per cent.[2]

The option desired by the company is the surrender of the rights and subscription to the new stock. Many stockholders, however, do not do this. In the 1955 American Telephone and Telegraph issue, which was a fine success otherwise, only 38 per cent of the original holders exercised the rights and purchased new stock.

The third option is the sale of the rights on a "when issued" basis. This is done through a contract handled by the broker. The Exchange determines when such trading may begin and when it terminates, as stated earlier. The Exchange also fixes the date when the rights must be delivered and payment made therefor. This option is used by those who subscribe to the theory that rights sell at their highest when first announced. A very heavy volume of trading takes place this way in privileged subscriptions of large companies. In the General Motors issue of 1955 referred to above, 2,100,000 rights were sold on this basis; the total issue was in excess of 88 million.

The fourth option is to sell them the "regular way." This is done by selling the warrant when received by the stockholder. This is the simplest and cheapest alternative and a highly popular one.

The fifth option is to sell the stock with "rights on," or "cum rights" as it is sometimes called. This means selling the stock before it goes ex-rights. Here the stock and the rights are both sold together. The action is based on the previously stated theory that one should "sell rights early." After the stock goes ex-rights, it can be replaced at the pleasure of the former stockholder. It can now be purchased cheaper

[2] C. James Pilcher, *Raising Capital with Convertble Securities* (Ann Arbor: University of Michigan Press, 1955), p. 105.

than when sold; the difference is a profit. In doing this, the owner should realize that he pays the regular selling and buying commissions and transfer taxes on the stock. This makes it more expensive than merely selling rights the "regular way."

The sixth option is similar to the fifth. Here the stockholder sells the stock with "rights on," or "cum rights," before the stock goes ex-rights. The difference is the method of replacement. In this case the owner buys enough rights to replace the amount of stock sold. He does this on the belief that rights may be picked up cheaply in the market near the end of the subscription period. For example, he has 100 shares of stock. New stock may be purchased by the surrender of ten rights for each new share. During the subscription period, 1,000 rights are purchased and used to buy the new stock. All the previously sold stock has now been replaced. The difference between the sale of the stock with "rights on" and the cost of the rights plus the subscription price is the gross profit on the deal.

Arbitrage in Rights. Some professional trading takes place in rights on an arbitrage basis. For example, a trader may find that rights are selling too low on the basis of the market price of the stock. He may then sell 100 shares short, buy enough rights to subscribe for 100 shares, purchase the stock, and cover by delivering the subscribed stock which he will obtain in due time. Such action reduces the market price of the stock and increases that of the rights; thus the two are kept on a parity with each other. This arbitrage requires very close cost calculations; it is no business for the amateur.

37

Convertible Securities

Convertible securities appear to be highly attractive as investments. In some mysterious way they seem to have both the strength of a senior security and the speculative possibilities of a common stock. Everything has its price, however, and the convertible security is no exception.

Nature. Convertible securities have so many speculative aspects and are so closely tied in with common stocks that it seems desirable to discuss them at greater length than was possible in Chapter 2.

A convertible security is one that permits the holder, at his option and under certain conditions, to exchange such an issue for another security of the same company. The holder may exercise this option of exchange if and when a profit opportunity presents itself.

Convertible securities are, as a rule, either junior bonds or preferred stocks. Senior bonds, such as the first mortgage type, seldom carry the privilege. This chapter will deal mostly with convertible bonds. The same principles, in general, apply to convertible preferred stocks. Hence, a detailed treatment of both types of securities is unnecessary.

Importance of Convertible Security Financing. Many comparisons are possible to show the importance of this type of financing. Over a twenty-year period, 1933–52, only 1 per cent of senior securities privately placed had this feature, whereas 20 per cent of all such securities offered publicly had it.[1] During this period one-third of all preferred stocks issued to raise capital were of this type but only 10 per cent of bonds were convertible. Industrial corporations tend to use the conversion feature four times as often as do utilities, railroads, banks, and insurance com-

---

[1] C. James Pilcher, *Raising Capital with Convertible Securities* (Ann Arbor: University of Michigan, 1955), p. 8.

panies. Industrials, as a group, find it harder to raise new capital than the other groups just mentioned; hence, the convertible feature is especially popular in this type of financing.

The volume of convertible security financing is very large in the aggregate. During periods of bull markets, many such issues appear. In 1955, for example, the most spectacular post-war issue was the $637 million offer of American Telephone and Telegraph. More and more convertible issues were used in private placements, especially in financing growing enterprise, during later stages of the boom.

Reasons for Financing with Convertibles. Corporations never add extra features to bond indentures or stock contracts without a purpose. A number of reasons justify corporations in making certain issues convertible. The chief reason is apparently to raise additional equity capital. This is particularly true for large corporations. In a survey of seventy-five American companies, 63 per cent reported that this was the reason for this type of financing.[2] A word of explanation is needed here. A given company wishes to raise a certain amount of new capital. It is believed that the time is not propitious to issue common stock, although the company would prefer this method of financing. It sells, therefore, an issue of convertible bonds. Eventually the bonds are converted. The capitalization has changed from bonded indebtedness to equity capital. The company has, in effect, raised funds today at tomorrow's higher stock prices. This is just the opposite of raising capital by selling common stock under a privileged subscription. In this instance the company raises equity capital by selling stock at less than today's stock prices, since the subscription price is typically under the market price by a substantial margin.

A second reason for convertible security financing is the desire to make the issue more salable, or, in the words of the trade, to "sweeten" the issue. Debenture bonds and preferred stocks are often hard to sell. This additional feature often makes an issue a very attractive one to investors, who wish to combine speculation and investment in the purchase of a single security. This reason seems particularly important in the financing of small companies. Pilcher found this factor to be the most important in about 23 per cent of all convertible security financing.[3] This reason is especially powerful during a weak bond market or during a bull stock market, when so many investors are interested in common stocks.

Another factor in favor of this type of financing is that it can result in a lower rate of interest on the bonds or in a higher offering price,

[2] *Ibid.,* p. 138.
[3] *Loc. cit.*

which means one and the same thing in terms of cost. Again, it may be argued that the company benefits upon conversion, since fixed charges are eliminated at that time. A minor advantage, perhaps, is that conversion often results in additional stockholders for the company, an objective often of considerable importance in the eyes of corporate boards.

Everything is said to have its price. This can certainly be said of conversion security financing. If convertible bonds are held by those who are not common stockholders, there is always the possibility of a shift in voting control upon conversion. Extensive conversion dilutes the per-share earnings of the common stock, since more common shares are issued upon conversion. It also reduces the advantage to the corporation of trading on the equity, which means that the company is no longer borrowing money at a low cost but at the higher cost of common stock dividends. Conversion also increases the income tax load, since interest payments on convertible bonds are regarded as expenses, while dividends are not. Finally, a large conversion issue overhanging the market tends to depress the price of the common stock. To the extent that these disadvantages affect the corporation they also affect the common stockholders in the corporation.

Type of Companies Using Convertibles. All types of companies—large and small, strong and weak—use convertible security financing. American Telephone and Telegraph, by far the largest American corporation, relies heavily upon convertibles. Thousands of small and weak companies also use them. Companies that have long reached maturity issue them. Even "growth" companies employ them. No generalization can be made as to the credit standing of companies that issue these securities.

Attraction to Investors. Convertible securities have an irresistible attraction to many investors, based on the natural desire to "have your cake and eat it too." Some investors view a convertible bond as a very desirable security. It appears to give the safety of a bond plus the speculative possibilities of a common stock. As long as one holds on to the bond, he possesses a secure investment with a fixed return. If the company becomes very prosperous, he may convert the bond into common stock and benefit by the company's increased earning power.

A second reason for the convertible security's attraction is that it has been suggested as a hedge against inflation. As long as the price level remains stable, the bond can be retained. If inflation occurs and the purchasing power of fixed interest payments declines, the rising dividends of stock obtained upon conversion will offset the increase in living costs. The principal will also rise if the conversion is effected.

In practice, the investor may be disappointed on one or both grounds. If the conversion clause is worth anything, it means that the purchaser of the convertible will have to take a smaller yield on the issue—the coupon will be less or the offering price will be higher. If the clause were added to the issue to sell it, obviously the company received more for the security than it would have otherwise. Again, the common stock may never rise enough to make conversion profitable.

However, in the bull market that started in 1949 and ran longer than any other of record, owners of convertibles obtained handsome profits because of the sustained and substantial rise in stock prices. This market benefited the holders of both convertible bonds and convertible preferred stocks. In those years the buyers of convertible bonds issued by American Telephone and Telegraph, for example, were able to obtain almost immediate profits under the terms covering its large isuses.

The Pre-emptive Right. Common stockholders are generally given the pre-emptive right to buy new convertible bonds whenever this privilege is accorded these security owners in the purchase of additional common stock. The theory is that common stockholders should be allowed to subscribe for the new bonds, since their sale to others might result in a shift in the distribution of voting control upon conversion and because conversion tends to dilute the equity behind each share of common stock. Pre-emptive rights are accorded stockholders generally under the common law. Under present statutes, however, some states deny the pre-emptive right to common stockholders unless expressly reserved in the charter; others make it optional with the company to use the right; while in some states a charter may be amended to deny the right even though it was in the original articles of incorporation.

In probably half the cases or less, corporations are required to accord the right of privileged subscriptions to common stockholders. In the rest the use of the privileged subscription is voluntary or optional with the company directors.[4] Even where there is no necessity to give the stockholders this right, it is often considered shrewd policy to do so.

Securities Given the Conversion Privilege. As already indicated, the practice is to give junior or unsecured bonds the privilege rather than the well-secured issues. The debenture or unsecured bond is a favorite security to be made convertible. Nearly all industrial and utility issues are of this type, and railroad convertible issues are usually junior mortgage bonds. During the 1920's it was generally believed by investment experts that convertibles were weak securities and that the feature was used to compensate for inadequate security.[5] This opinion is not so

[4] Pilcher, *op. cit.*, p. 98.
[5] Benjamin Graham and David L. Dodd, *Security Analysis* (1st ed.; New York: McGraw-Hill Book Co., Inc., 1934), p. 242.

prevalent today. Investors, however, will do well to investigate the relationship between bond quality and the conversion right when buying such securities.

The Conversion Period. This important part of the conversion feature indicates when the privilege begins and ends. Extreme variations are found in this respect as in most other features of convertible securities. The privilege may be limited or unlimited. If unlimited, it extends throughout the life of the bonds; if limited, there is a cutoff date, which is often from ten to fifteen years after the issue of the bonds. For preferred stock the privilege typically is unlimited.

The privilege may be delayed from a month to several years after the date of issue. Such delay permits the company to put the invested funds to work before it is necessary to issue more stock.

The Conversion Security. Any of a variety of securities may be the type of security received upon exercise of the conversion privilege. The usual provision permits the conversion of a senior security into common stock. This is the practice in the issue of utility and industrial bonds. In railroad finance, in some instances, bonds may be convertible into preferred stock. There are also examples of one class of common convertible into another—as Citizens Utilities A is convertible into the B stock.

The Redemption Clause. Convertible bonds frequently give the company the right to redeem or call the securities before maturity. If they are called by the company, the investor has no alternative but to turn in his security and receive cash. The call feature is typical of bond financing today. The advantages to the company are overwhelming; there are none to the investor. The provision has two effects upon the holder of a conversion issue. First, it limits the possible profits to the holder, since the security may be called before the common stock has reached its highest point in a bull-market. Second, it may force the investor to convert at a time not to his liking.

The investor is usually given a reasonable notice that the company is to redeem the issue. The period is usually thirty days. The holder may convert until about five to ten days before the call date.

Protection Against Dilution. An interesting problem relative to the conversion clause is that of dilution. This can take place where the company increases the number of shares without a corresponding increase in the assets or earning power of the company. Examples would include stock splits, stock dividends, issuance of new shares at less than the market price under a privileged subscription, issue of new convertible securities, merger, consolidation, and sale of assets. Most convertible issues have "anti-dilution" clauses which protect the investor, but there are exceptions. The investor should be certain that he is adequately protected against procedures that would dilute his conversion right.

Let us take an example. Let us suppose that a given bond with $1,000 par value can be converted into 10 shares of common stock. The company declares a 100 per cent stock dividend. Each share of stock is now worth only half what it was before the dividend. Full protection against this dilution would be provided if the company were to change the number of shares from 10 to 20 receivable upon conversion.

The Conversion Ratio or Rate. The language of the financier and writer in the description of conversion security operations is often indefinite. There is no uniform terminology. Hence, one encounters such terms as conversion rate, conversion ratio, conversion price, and parity price often used interchangeably.

For the purposes of this description, the term "conversion rate or ratio" refers to the rate at which a $1,000 par value bond may be converted into shares of common stock. This ratio may be 10, 20, 25, or 50 shares, or any other rate set by the company. The ratio is definite and can easily be verified by the examination of the indenture. The formula for determination is to divide $1,000 in par value by the conversion price, next to be described.

The Conversion Price. This may be defined as the amount of par value exchangeable for 1 share of common stock. For each such unit of par value surrendered to the company, 1 share will be issued. A few examples will clarify the definition.

Let us suppose that the conversion price is $50. This sum divided into $1,000 indicates that the holder will receive 20 shares upon conversion. Again, let us suppose the price is $100. The holder is entitled to 10 shares. Finally, let us suppose that the price is $125. The holder will receive 8 shares if he converts.

The simplest form of conversion contract has a converison price that is constant throughout the conversion period. There are, however, issues where the price changes during the conversion period. Two kinds of change are common: (1) increasing the price with the passage of time and (2) increasing the price as the amount of conversion increases.

In the first situation, the conversion price might be $100 for the first five years, $105 for the next five years, $110 for the next five years, and $115 for the final five years of a twenty-year issue.

In the second situation, the conversion price might rise with the volume of conversions. Thus the price might be $100 until 25 per cent of the convertible issue had been converted, $105 until 50 per cent was converted, $110 until 75 per cent was converted, and $115 for the remaining life of the issue. This form of step-up is substantially less common than the first, and both are relatively uncommon in convertible financing.

The effect of stepped-up ratios is a tendency to force conversion and a reduction in the dilution of the equity of other stockholders. The value of a conversion privilege falls on the date that a step-up in the conversion price occurs. It is as though the security sold ex-right. An investor should be thoroughly familiar with the conversion clause in any issue he purchases or owns.

Uneven Conversion. A technical problem arises when bonds do not convert into an even number of shares of stock. Such a situation develops under some indentures where there are changing conversion terms. For example, a bond is convertible at $100, then at $105, then at $110. Let us suppose that a given investor is ready to convert when the price is stepped up to $110, which means that $110 in par value is exchanged for 1 share of common stock. On a $1,000 par value bond, such an exchange would result in the holder's receiving 9 shares with $10 in par value left over. What becomes of this $10 which is not converted?

There are four possible plans the company may use in the indenture. One permits the issue of warrants or scrip by the company; in this method, the company would issue a $10 warrant to the bondholder. This could be sold or used together with other scrip purchased to buy an additional share. This is fair to the investor and is the usual plan. A second plan would permit a cash payment by the investor. In our example, the individual could deposit $100 in cash plus the $10 in unused par value and secure another share. A third plan is one in which the company requires even conversion. In other words, the investor loses the unused portion of his bond unless enough par value is deposited to secure an even number of shares. In the present example, the holder would have to turn in $11,000 in par value or eleven bonds to obtain an even conversion of 100 shares. A final plan would be one in which the company would redeem in cash the unused part of the bond, in this case, $10.

Cash Payments Upon Conversion. The typical conversion provision permits conversion of a bond into a certain number of shares of stock by an exchange. However, some companies require the surrender of the convertible bond plus a payment of cash to obtain the additional stock. The leading exponent of this practice is American Telephone and Telegraph. The conversion price on most post-war issues has been $100, which means the holder received 10 shares for each $1,000 bond. However, the holder was required to pay additional cash per share. For example, in the $637 million issue of 1955, the conversion price was $100, while the additional cash payment was $48 per share, making a total cost of $148.

The Adjusted Stock Price. Professional traders in convertible securities often go into very precise adjustments in making conversions, since profits are small and costs must be calculated within close limits. One such adjustment would be the computation of the adjusted stock price.

Since bonds are quoted by a different method from stocks, the stock price should be adjusted to obtain an equality with the convertible bond. The problem is to adjust the prices of the two securities. It will be recalled that stocks are sold "flat" and bonds "with interest." This means that the stock quotation includes accumulated income, while the bond quotation excludes it. In buying a bond, one pays the quoted price plus interest. For example, if a given stock is quoted at 104, that is all that one pays, even though the company may be ready to pay a $1 dividend in a few weeks. If a bond is quoted at 104, one pays $1,040, plus, perhaps, $4, $10, or $15 accumulated interest.

To place these two securities in the same basis, it is necessary to subtract the accumulated dividend on the stock; this, of course, is exactly what has already been done with the interest in the bond quotation. Accumulated dividends are figured on the basis of three hundred and sixty-five days per year to the nearest $1/8$ point. Adjustment tables permit easy calculations for those who have access to them.

Let us take an example. A given stock pays a dividend of $6 per year. Two months have elapsed since the last dividend date. The current market price is $104\frac{3}{8}$. Since the dividend rate is $1.50 per quarter, or $0.50 per month, it is obvious that dividends of $1.00 have accumulated. The adjusted stock price is, therefore, $103\frac{3}{8}$.

Another example may be useful. A stock is paying dividends at an annual rate of $2.40; its market price is $40\frac{1}{8}$; it went ex-dividend twenty days ago; find the adjusted stock price. The dividend rate is $0.20 per month. Since two-thirds of a month have elapsed, a dividend of $0.13 has accrued. The nearest fractional point is $1/8$. Hence, the adjusted stock price is $40\frac{1}{8}$ minus $1/8$, or 40.

Conversion Equivalent. This may be defined as the adjusted price at which the stock must sell to be on an exact equality with the bond. If one disregards taxes and commissions, the stock received is worth exactly as much as the bond given at conversion; the investor would "break even" if he were to convert. It should be carefully noted at this point that the conversion equivalent is based upon the adjusted stock price and not the actual market price.

This formula will permit easy calculation of the equivalent:

$$\text{Conversion Equivalent} = \frac{\text{Market Price of Bond}}{\text{Number of Shares Received}}$$

Let us take a few examples. The bond is selling at 104½ and is convertible at 100, or par for par. Since 10 shares are received upon conversion, the conversion equivalent is found by dividing the value of the bond, $1,045 by 10; the result is 104½.

In a second example, the bond is selling at 104; it is convertible at 25. The stock is selling at 28½ with a ½ point accumulated dividend. The investor buys a bond and converts. What is his gross profit if taxes and commission are disregarded? The answer is $80, as the solution will show:

$$\$25 \overline{|\$1,000}$$
40 shares received

$$40 \overline{|\$1,040}$$
$26—the conversion equivalent

Market price of stock	$28.50
Less: Accumulated dividend	.50
Adjusted stock price	28.00
Less: Conversion equivalent	26.00
Profit per share	2.00
Multiply by 40 shares	×40
Gross profit	$80.00

In other words, the stock costs the investor $26 per share or the conversion equivalent. The stock, less the accumulated dividend, can be sold for $28. Since he receives 40 shares upon conversion, his gross profit is $80. If the adjusted stock price had been only $26, he would have neither lost nor gained on the transaction, provided taxes and commissions were ignored. Obviously, in practice, if the stock price rose above $26, the bond price would rise also. A profit on conversion is extremely rare.

Price Movements. Under certain conditions there is a very close relationship between the price movements of a convertible bond and the conversion security. If the stock is selling below the conversion equivalent, there is no profit in converting the bond; hence, the price of the stock has no effect on the market value of the bond. In such a case the bond sells strictly on its merits as an investment issue.

Let us suppose, however, that the stock rises sufficiently to warrant a profit to bondholders upon conversion. The conversion security is then said to exercise "sympathetic price control" over the market value of the bond. If the stock increases above the lowest conversion equivalent, the bond will automatically rise because of transactions by arbitragers. These arbitragers, who see a profit opportunity, will buy the bonds and convert into stock through an arbitrage transaction. Conversion equivalence will be maintained as the stock price rises further.

For example, let us suppose that the conversion price of a given issue were $100. The stock rises to $125. The bond might easily rise to 125, since 10 shares of stock upon conversion would be worth $1,250. In a situation such as this, the investor would need to be sure he converted the bond into stock if the company called the issue.

Rapidity of Conversion. The question here is how soon after a convertible issue is sold may the investor expect to realize a conversion profit. These are three possibilities: (1) quickly, (2) in a number of years, and (3) never.

There are few instances in which the investor may expect to realize quick profits. The conversion price is usually so high that there is no immediate chance of conversion at a profit. American Telephone and Telegraph convertibles are a marked exception. Such issues permit an immediate profit as soon as the conversion privilege begins, which is typically in two to four months after the close of subscriptions for the issue. Investors know that immediate profits are possible at the end of this short waiting period. The result is a great stimulus to the sale of the convertibles. For example, in the $637 million issue of 1955, the earliest day of exchange was two months after the close of the subscription period. An immediate profit was possible. As a result, a total of $250 million was converted on the first day, with 295,000 of 525,000 subscribers taking advantage of this opportunity.

In most cases, however, much time elapses before the common stock is high enough to permit profitable conversion. A bull market, such as the one that started in 1949, however, may shorten this time. In numerous instances there is never a time when there is a profit upon conversion, and the bonds will be called or retired without being converted.

Arbitrage Profits. An arbitrage profit becomes possible in a convertible bond whenever the adjusted stock price is higher than the conversion equivalent by the amount of taxes and commissions involved in the transaction. Let us take a simple example. A bond is selling at 100 and can be converted into 10 shares of stock, the adjusted price of which is 104. The difference between the selling price of 10 shares of stock, or $1,040, and the cost of the bond, or $1,000, represents the gross profit from which must be deducted the commissions and taxes involved in the entire operation.

There are three ways in which to take advantage of such a situation. The first is to buy the bond at 100 in anticipation that it will rise to about 104 because of "sympathetic price control." The price would be forced upward by speculators. After this happens, the bond could be disposed of by sale without any conversion. This method has an element of risk in that the stock may fall instead and the profit never be realized.

The second way is to sell the stock short, the technique of the professional. At the instant a professional arbitrager or bond trader sees a profit differential, he will buy the bond and sell short the number of shares to be received upon conversion. This operation guarantees him an immediate gross profit which is the difference between the stock price, say, 104, and the cost of the bond, or 100. Such opportunities exist only momentarily. The gain, however, is certain.

The final method is to purchase the bond, convert into stock, and sell the stock. If the bond were purchased at $1,000 and the stock were sold at $1,040, there is a $40 gross profit. The danger of this method is that by the time the bond is purchased, delivered, and converted into the equivalent number of shares, the profit differential may have disappeared.

Interest and Dividend Adjustment. In some cases the company makes adjustments for accrued interest on the converted bonds or accumulated dividends on preferred stock when conversion takes place, but this is not the practice today.

Convertible Preferred Stocks. The principles and practices governing the issuance of convertible bonds are applicable for the most part to convertible preferred stocks; hence, only limited discussion of them is necessary at this point. An examination of nearly 500 public offerings of such stock issued from 1933 to 1952 showed that 35 per cent were convertible.[6] On the other hand, private placements rarely carry the convertible feature. Industrials use convertibles much more extensively than do utilities or railroads. Nearly half their issues during a twenty-year period carried the provision. The life of the privilege is typically unlimited. In some cases, however, the right of conversion is delayed. In practically all cases the conversion security is common stock. The conversion price, as a rule, is constant as long as the preferred issue is outstanding. An examination of 424 preferred stocks listed on the New York Stock Exchange in early 1956 showed that 89, or 21 per cent, were convertible.

A number of holders of convertible preferred stocks were able to make large profits after the close of World War II. For example, in 1947 American Cyanamid Company gave the stockholders the right to buy convertible preferred stock at 102. The conversion price was $21.25, or a ratio of about 5 shares of common for each preferred share. This is an

[6] Pilcher, *op. cit.*, p. 7.

excellent case of "sympathetic price control." During the period 1947 to 1953, the common stock showed a striking advance in price. The preferred stock rose to 229 and was called in 1953. Dow preferred stock showed an almost identical performance in this same period.

Examples of Convertible Securities. In the description of convertible issues, it was believed unwise to burden the reader with repeated examples of these securities. Eight typical issues are given at this point to indicate representative features of these bonds and stocks.

1. Boeing Airplane Company 4½'s, 1980, are convertible into 2 shares of the common stock.
2. Food Fair Stores, Inc., 4's, 1979, are convertible into 2.38 shares of the common stock until 1969.
3. International Minerals and Chemicals Corporation 3.65's, 1977, are convertible into 1.82 shares of the common stock until 1962 and into 1.67 shares until 1967.
4. Rohr Aircraft Corporation 5¼'s, 1977, are convertible into 5.41 shares of the common stock.
5. Consolidated Sun Ray, Inc., 5% preferred stock is convertible into 5 shares of the common stock.
6. Electronic Communications Company 6% preferred stock is convertible into 1½ shares of the common stock.
7. Public Service Company of Indiana $4.80 preferred stock is convertible into 2½ shares of the common stock.
8. United Industrial Corporation $0.42½ Series A perferred stock is convertible into ½ share of the common stock.

38

Sources of Information and Security Rating

The purpose of this chapter is to indicate the chief sources of information available to the investor or trader; they are his ever-present tools. Few will read and study them all, but everyone should be familiar with them and their contributions to the study of the stock market. The last section of the chapter will deal with the subject of rating securities.

SOURCES OF INFORMATION

The Financial Page. Without question, the first and most accessible source of information for nearly all followers of the market is the financial page. A well-edited financial page will summarize the chief business and financial news of the day and provide a substantial amount of interpretation. It is, of course, heavily weighted with "spot news" or current developments and many times it may be lacking in long-run interpretations. Nevertheless, it should be the first source of information for anyone who wishes to keep abreast of current events as they affect the market.

There are many excellent financial pages in the country. Those in the eastern part of the country that are especially popular with market followers include those of the *Wall Street Journal, Journal of Commerce, The New York Times* and *New York Herald Tribune.* Each has a large following; the editorial approach varies somewhat from paper to paper; all are generally excellent. A student of the market would do well to examine a number of leading daily papers and then select one that appears to satisfy his needs best.

News Ticker. There is one financial news ticker service in the country. It is owned and operated by Dow Jones & Company, which also publishes the *Wall Street Journal.* This printing telegraph operates continuously throughout the day, and may be found in many brokerage houses. Its chief value is that it carries the leading "spot news" items of the day in the world of commerce, industry, finance, and politics. Since many "spot news" items are immediately evaluated by the market, the value of such a service is obvious. Sometimes this service is called the "broad tape"; it is often watched with the same concentration that characterizes the study of the stock ticker tape.

A great many of the items appearing on the Dow-Jones financial news ticker service eventually find their way to the financial pages of the *Wall Street Journal* and other papers.

The great press associations also have teletype service and carry much financial news. At least one brokerage house has its own news ticker service and others carry news on their multipurpose wire networks.

Bank Letters. Several of the leading banks of the country release each month so-called "bank letters." Actually, they are fairly large bulletins and are available upon request to anyone interested in being placed on the mailing list. Their chief function is the interpretation of business and economic developments, often from a long-run point of view. Generally well edited, they give a more detached and objective interpretation of news than is often possible in the daily press. They do not deal directly with the stock market but aid one in understanding the basic and underlying currents of the business situation. Probably the best known of such publications are those published by the First National City Bank of New York, the Morgan-Guaranty Trust Company of New York, the Cleveland Trust Company, the Federal Reserve Bank of New York, and the Security First National Bank of Los Angeles. There are several excellent Canadian bank letters, that of the Bank of Montreal being a good example. Many of the Federal Reserve banks publish monthly bulletins which cover thoroughly and concisely the business conditions within their own districts.

Newsletters. Several newsletters have an extensive following. These reports, which go only to paid subscribers, summarize the latest news developments, particularly of a political character, together with an interpretation. Forecasts of coming political happenings play a significant part in the composition of such letters. The Kiplinger and Whaley-Eaton letters are examples.

Financial Magazines. There are a number of financial magazines available. These vary widely in editorial approach, subject matter, and format. Generally, they stress these current business news and its effect upon the stock market and the business situation. Some give regular forecasts of the stock market with an evaluation of underlying factors of strength and weakness. A frequent feature is the selection of certain stocks that appear to be particularly promising investments or speculations. Other magazines are largely chronicles of financial news with little attempt at advising the market trader or investor. Some periodicals are heavily weighted with stock and bond tables and earnings reports; others feature long articles on business conditions or case histories of leading corporations. No two of these magazines are exactly alike; each seeks to attract a particular audience. A student of the market will do well to examine a number of such periodicals and determine for himself the contribution which each can make to his understanding of securities markets. Magazines in this group include *Bank and Quotation Record, Barron's, Commercial and Financial Chronicle, Financial World, Forbes, Fortune, Magazine of Wall Street,* and *The Exchange.*

Other Magazines. Several magazines of a somewhat broader character than the group of financial magazines just examined are well worth reading by the investor or trader. Although not edited with this class of reader specifically in mind, they often contain carefully written articles on finance or the markets. Since the market is at all times sensitive to world events, political as well as economic, their interpretation of non-financial news is useful. Examples of such periodicals would be *Business Week, Time,* and *Newsweek.*

Federal Publications. The federal government and the Board of Governors of the Federal Reserve System release several publications of considerable value to the investor or speculator. The *Statistical Abstract* of the Department of Commerce is an annual volume which contains a great mass of statistical material on production, consumption, sales, employment, finance, population, taxation, prices, government expenditures, debts, banking, business conditions, and agriculture. The data are largely on an annual basis. For certain purposes the volume is invaluable.

The *Survey of Current Business,* also published by the Department of Commerce, is a monthly periodical which is unique. The magazine is largely a tabulation of monthly business statistics which are covered both in the form of actual figures and as index numbers. Examples of topics covered include general business indicators, commodity prices, constructions and real estate, domestic trade, employment and population, finance, international transactions, transportation and communications, and manufacturing. The publication also presents each month several outstanding articles on the business situation.

The Board of Governors of the Federal Reserve System publishes two periodicals of significance to the student of economic conditions. The

Federal Reserve Bulletin, a monthly release, emphasizes mainly the banking and financial conditions of the country; the banking statistics are particularly complete. Much of the material on general business appears in the *Survey of Current Business.* The magazine also carries a considerable volume of editorial comment on the banking, fiscal, and business situation. The Board also publishes a chart book monthly covering the principle series of data in the *Bulletin.*

A fourth statistical service of the federal government is called *Economic Indicators.* Prepared by the Joint Committee on the Economic Report by the Council of Economic Advisers, it presents tables and charts on current economic conditions, such as output, income, and spending; employment, unemployment, and wages; production and business activity; prices; currency, credit, and security markets; and federal finance. It is very useful for those interested in the latest data on these series.

Yet another service of the Federal government, called *Business Cycle Developments,* prepared monthly by the Bureau of the Census, provides data for those series most helpful in determining the peaks and valleys of economic fluctuation. It is a development following from the work of Geoffrey H. Moore and his colleagues at the National Bureau of Economic Research, to which reference has been made in several preceding chapters.

Corporations. The stockholders of corporations and the general public are furnished a great deal of information about corporate affairs. Many annual reports to stockholders are outstanding as sources of information. A stockholder of any company with securities registered for trading on a national stock exchange, and others, receive copies by mail routinely. They are usually available to inquirers by writing the secretary of the company. The reports vary widely in format, editorial treatment, presentation of figures on finances, and clarity. Much can be learned from these reports. One of the outstanding changes in these reports in recent years has been a genuine attempt to present the report in popular style, easily understandable by the layman. This is in distinct contrast to former reports, which were clear only to accountants and professional investors and often not even to them. Accounting terminology is also becoming more and more standardized, a reform much needed for many years. Even the appearance of the reports has been radically changed. The use of color and attractive design provides sharp contrast to the drab affairs of a few years ago. Annual reports stand high as a source of information and cannot be ignored by any student of the market. Many of the corporations with securities registered for trading on a national stock exchange release quarterly reports of sales and earnings.

Trade Associations. Many of the large industries of the country have trade associations, often identified by such a phrase as "institute." From time to time these associations prepare and release reports on their particular industries. Since these associations are the public relations representatives of their industries, it is also necessary to remember that they are presenting a certain point of view in the hope of its favorable acceptance. Examples of well-known trade associations are the American Iron and Steel Institute, American Petroleum Institute, Cotton Textile Institute, National Association of Wool Manufacturers, National Retail Dry Goods Association, National Brass and Copper Association, and the Edison Electric Institute.

Trade Journals. There is a seemingly endless list of trade journals. These may be privately published or prepared by trade associations. Typically, they cover business conditions, production, sales, new developments, and personalities in their special fields. If well edited, they give a good presentation of the current economic situation in a given industry. A few examples are *Railway Age, Textile World, Food Industries, Electrical World, Machinery, Oil and Gas Journal, Chain Store Age, Iron Age, Steel,* and *Chemical and Metallurgical Engineering.*

Commercial Banks. A good customer of a commercial bank or trust company may often obtain valuable advice about the securities markets from the bank officers. Because banks are large holders of bonds, these officers are often particularly competent to advise on this class of investment. Many trust companies and trust departments, of course, are willing to handle customer investment portfolios on a fee basis.

Securities Houses. In many cases securities houses are the chief source of personal contact that their customers have for investment information and advice. Well-managed organizations are in a position to give service to customers along a great many different lines. Personal conferences with partners and registered representatives are often very useful to the customer in supplying him with advice and information about buying and selling stocks and bonds. Many firms will examine without charge a customer's portfolio and advise as to its merits. The broker, of course, hopes that such a procedure will result in more business; nevertheless, the service may be of considerable value to the customer.

A good brokerage firm will ordinarily answer any reasonable query of a customer made by letter or over the telephone; in some cases a considerable amount of research will be undertaken to answer such requests. Many brokerage offices have stock and news tickers, and customers are encouraged to use them. A well-equipped firm will also have one or more of the statistical services; these may be used by customers or a representative of the firm will secure such information as may be requested from them.

Firms differ considerably in the amount of research and publishing which they initiate themselves. Some of the larger firms have highly qualified staffs which turn out a continuous stream of reports on the market, on corporations, on various industries, and on business conditions. These reports may take the form of market letters, industry reports, investor bulletins, special investigations of particular corporations, bulletins on how to trade or invest, reports on attractive stocks, studies of dividend-paying stocks, etc. In recent years such reports have expanded greatly in number and scope over those of the 1920's; they also tend to stress the investment side of the market more than they did some years ago. If the firm is an underwriter of a new security issue, it can also supply the prospectus for interested customers.

Many years ago the market letter was the typical and often the sole release of the brokerage firm. It dealt with the day-to-day aspects of the market, largely from the standpoint of the in-and-out trader; it was often hastily and poorly edited and frequently was highly superficial. Although a number of firms still release such daily or weekly letters in mimeographed, multilithed, or printed form, they are considerably less importance than they were at one time. The market analysis of a good financial page will contain about the same information.

Securities and Exchange Commission. The SEC in its Washington and regional offices receives from registered corporations a great deal of information useful to the investor. This takes the form of registration statements for securities being underwritten or sold, periodic reports to the Commission, and reports of companies registered on national securities exchanges. The reports are mandatory under the Securities Act of 1933, the Securities Exchange Act of 1934, the Public Utility Holding Company Act of 1935, and the Investment Company Act of 1940. These reports are available for public inspection; an extensive use of them is made by the various commercial statistical services, which secure primary data from them. The average investor, however, will find it much simpler to secure such data from secondary sources, such as a brokerage firm, a registration prospectus, or a securities manual.

The monthly *Statistical Bulletin* and the *Annual Report* of the SEC are invaluable aids for serious students of the securities markets and general economic activity analysis.

Chart Services. There are a number of chart services which have attained popularity with market followers. These services have a great similarity in format and composition. Essentially, they seek to chart the stocks of many leading corporations of the country, largely those listed on the New York Stock Exchange. The number of charts varies from over 200 to nearly 1,000; each chart covers a number of years. They may cover earnings, dividends, volume of trading, prices, and price ranges. New additions appear monthly or bimonthly. Each chart in a given service is the same size as every other chart; this makes it easier to compare the performance of one stock with another. A very significant feature of some of the chart services is a transparent work-sheet, which may show, for example, the Dow-Jones industrial average. This work sheet may be superimposed over the chart of any particular company, and a careful study may indicate how well that company's stock is conducting itself as compared with the market averages. The value of the services, therefore, is that the user may be able to select certain stocks that apparently show promise as either investments or speculations or, conversely, to sell those already owned that are doing poorly in the market.

Typical examples of such services are the M. C. Horsey Company, Robert Mansfield and Company, the Securities Research Corporation, and the F. W. Stephens Company. There are many other chart services; a number of which attempt to evaluate the market in terms of the Dow Theory.

Advisory Services and Investment Counselors. The number of individuals and firms in the securities field that attempt to advise speculators and investors is legion. They vary from some of the most-respected organizations in the field with excellent staffs and long records of reputable service to fleeting individuals or organizations that flourish with each market rise and disappear with each major decline. It goes without saying that a most careful investigation of such a service should be made by anyone before subscribing to it.

The Statistical Services. One of the most widely used sources of information available to securities owners is the statistical service. At the present time there are three such well-known organizations: Moody's Investors Service, Standard & Poor's Corporation, and the Fitch Publishing Company, Inc. In addition to security rating, which will be described shortly, the three services gather and publish a vast amount of statistical information on corporate stocks and bonds.

Perhaps the best known of these services are the large manuals of corporation records. They are usually too expensive for the individual investor to purchase, but they are generally available at banks, libraries, and brokerage houses. The manuals are either bound or in loose-leaf form; in any case, they are kept up to date by frequent reports. For ease of reference the large annual volumes are often broken down into rails, utilities, industrials, governments, and banks and finance. The services report on nearly all large companies in which there is a definite investment interest. Typically, the report for a given company will contain a short description of the company's business, its industry position, its income account and balance sheet, its securities, the security ratings, the dividends and earnings per share, and the market price of the securities. The statistical information may be carried back from five to ten years for comparative purposes.

Weekly or semiweekly reports, as already indicated, keep the annual volumes from becoming obsolete. They contain the latest figures on earnings, dividends, calls, rights, new offerings, ratings changes, securities matured, etc.

The services also publish stock and bond surveys. There are separate reports for each, and publication is often once a week. A typical stock survey or report will contain such topics as the near-term prospect for stocks, the longer prospect, individual issues, business outlook, business and the market, and stock groups. These reports also feature opinions on individual stocks, such as a general market opinion, fundamental position, dividend forecast, earnings prospects, recent developments, finances, recommendations for buying and selling. Such a service is, therefore, of a definitely advisory character.

The bond survey also keeps investors informed of the latest developments in the bond business, such as market outlook, construction activity, new offerings, yields, new government issues, and financing. All important factors, economic, financial, or political, that determine and affect security prices are discussed in the stock and bond surveys.

In summary, the three statistical services gather and release a large amount of statistical information on nearly all important companies, listed and unlisted, together with analyses and interpretations of the positions of those companies and their securities. The reports are factual, analytical, and advisory.

Investment Company Manuals. Several organizations issue manuals and interim reports providing data on investment company portfolios and performance. Perhaps the most widely known is that of Arthur Wiesenberger and Company, *Investment Companies,* published annually. The quarterly analysis of investment company portfolios in *Barron's* also are well known.

Forecasting Services. Perhaps the most recurrent question in the entire field of speculation is: What is the market going to do? Everyone would like to know the course of security prices; the answer would provide an invaluable road map to certain wealth. To provide such forecasts is a popular and profitable pursuit of many informational services, whether they be periodicals, advisory services, columnists, brokerage houses, security dealers, or forecasting services. The value of such advice depends, of course, upon its accuracy.

Two rather thorough studies have been made of the reliability of financial services in forecasting the stock market. The first was made by a distinguished economist and statistician, Alfred Cowles III, and published in 1933.[1] He examined sixteen financial services over a period from January 1, 1928, to July 1, 1932. In that period 7,500 recommendations were made on common stocks for investment. His conclusion was that the stock recommended by these services showed an annual record of gain for the stockholders which was on the average 1.4 per cent poorer than the average common stock.

In addition, Cowles investigated twenty-four financial publications and their ability to forecast the stock market during the same period. He found that during this four-and-a-half year period the group failed by 4 per cent to achieve a result as good as the average of purely random performance. In other words, their forecasts were little better than those that could be expected from pure chance.

The second study of forecasting accuracy was conducted by the SEC in its study on *Stock Trading on the New York Stock Exchange on September 3, 1946*. On that day the market fell sharply; the average price decline of 945 issues in the 100-share market was $3.40. The bear market continued downward and share prices did not rise again to the 1946 high until 1950. The SEC examined 896 different pieces of literature disseminated by 166 investment advisers, brokers, and dealers from August 26 to September 3, the week that immediately preceded the break. These were market letters, bulletins, news items, flash reports, and other forms of market comment.

A total of 489 forecasts was made on the long-term market outlook at that time. About 260, or nearly 60 per cent, were bullish at the time without qualification; only 20, or 4 per cent, were definitely bearish or advised selling at least part of holdings. The rest were cautious or uncertain.

Ninety-five forecasts were made on the day-to-day outlook: 55 were bullish; 34 were cautious; and 6 were bearish. As to the outlook for specific industries and companies at that time, 272 forecasts were bullish; 10 were bearish; 17 were mixed; and 13 were inconclusive.

SECURITY RATING

Nature. Security rating is a process by which a statistical service prepares various ratings, identified by symbols, which are indicators of the investment quality of the securities so rated. The best quality secu-

---

[1] "Can Stock Market Forecasters Forecast?" *Econometrica*, (July, 1933), 314–16.

rities are rated "A," the next best "B," and the poorest "C" or "D." The three services, just described, rate bonds in this manner. Standard & Poor's Corporation rates stocks.

History. Four rating concerns have in the past achieved enough importance in the field of security rating to be classed as leaders.[2] The first security ratings were published by John Moody during 1909 in his *Analyses of Railroad Investments.* Poor's Publishing Company entered the field in 1916; it was followed by the Standard Statistics Company in 1922. These two companies later merged and are now known as the Standard & Poor's Corporation. The fourth company to enter the field was the Fitch Publishing Company in 1924. The first security ratings were received with considerable enthusiasm by investors but were bitterly opposed by many corporations and investment bankers who objected to inferior ratings for their securities. The opposition was similar to that which characterized the early history of commercial credit ratings.

Use of Ratings. Many institutions and investors find the rating system a useful one. Banks, particularly the smaller ones, find ratings helpful in the selection of their portfolios; the larger banks also use them as a check on their own investigations. Brokers generally employ them for investment opinions and as a service for their customers. Insurance companies use them in the purchase of their bonds, even though their own staffs prepare investment analyses. They are also used by trust companies, trust funds, investment companies, and endowed institutions as a significant type of information in security management. Although not too many individuals can afford the heavy expense of the complete services, unless they are relatively large investors, countless persons have access to them through banks and libraries and utilize them accordingly. They are also available through brokers.

The rating services have even been accorded public recognition by both federal and state banking authorities in the evaluation of bank portfolios. Some years ago the Comptroller of Currency issued a ruling that national banks could carry at cost only bonds rated at Baa or the equivalent; fractional write-offs were necessary for other securities.[3] Later a retreat was made from the ruling, but the bond ratings of the services are still important in the management of bank portfolios; they would be even more so were it not for the fact that, in recent years, banks have held large amounts of government securities.

Information for Ratings. The services apparently obtain their data for ratings from very much the same source as indicated in the earlier

---

[2] Gilbert Harold, *Bond Ratings as an Investment Guide* (New York: The Ronald Press Co., 1938), p. 9.

[3] Cited by Harold, *op. cit.,* p. 25.

part of the chapter, namely, such official and primary sources as annual and quarterly reports of companies and data filed with the SEC. Primary reliance would appear to be upon the financial statement; the services, of course, do not reveal how the information is obtained or used, except to release broad statements to the effect that information from "all sources" is considered.

Rating Symbols. The rating services employ nearly identical symbols; each symbol means approximately the same thing as to investment rating. These are tabulated in Table 38–1.

Table 38–1. Comparative Bond Ratings of Three Statistical Services

Moody	Standard & Poor's	Fitch	Interpretation
Aaa	AAA	AAA	Highest grade
Aa	AA	AA	High grade
A	A	A	Upper medium; medium grade; sound
Baa	BBB	BBB	Medium; good grade; some uncertainty
Ba	BB	BB	Fair to good; lower medium; uncertainty
B	B	B	Fair; speculative features
Caa		CCC	Outright speculations; poor standing
Ca	C	CC	Outright speculations; marked weakness
C		C	Best defaulted isuses; highly speculative
		DDD	In default
		DD	Assets of little value
		D	No apparent value

In the "A" group the services are uniform in their appraisals; each subgroup carries the same meaning. These are bonds of the highest grade; they are characterized by maximum safety as to principal and income. They are protected by ample assets; they have a large margin of earnings to protect interest payments; changes in business conditions have little effect upon their security. These are the "gilt-edged" bonds of the seasoned companies; they are characterized by low yields. Changes in interest rates are more important than changes in business conditions.

The "B" group might be called "businessmen's investments." They are attractive investments for men who are skilled in the purchase of investments; individuals who are willing to accept some uncertainty will receive higher yields than those who buy only "A"-rated issues. They are affected by some uncertainty as to interest, security, and stability; their values are influenced markedly by changes in business conditions. Since they are characterized by more or less uncertainty, they need very capable selection and management.

The "C" and "D" groups must be considered together, since neither the Moody Service or Standard & Poor's has a so-called "D" group. Taken as a whole, the two groups range from outright speculations at the top with a poor statistical standing and great uncertainty down to worthless issues with no apparent value at the bottom. The issues in these two bottom groups are gambles at best; usually they are in default; only the most promising issues have any prospect of recovery. In no sense can either group be considered an investment.

The Rating of Bonds. Bond rating it considered a more scientific procedure than the rating of stock. A few fundamental factors are used in determining ratings. Chief among these are earning power, asset value, security of income, and stability of income. Certain intangible factors, such as management and company prospects, also play a part.

Moody Bond Ratings. The Moody's Investors Service at the present time rates well over 5,000 issues in the corporate and tax-exempt areas. It does not rate real estate bonds, obligations of financial companies, non-profit corporations, issues sold privately, or issues of less than $600,000. Ratings are long-run judgments designed to show protection at the low point of the business cycle. They are not raised and lowered with changes in business conditions. The ratings are raised and lowered only when fundamental conditions affecting a particular issue change, such as when a borrower is gaining or losing ground in relation to other parts of industry or when the amount of debt is substantially reduced or increased.

The organization employs the usual tests of the ordinary income account and balance sheet analysis, but does not set up arbitrary standards in this analysis. The ratings are not mechanical ratings, the service believing that there are no mechanical means to true judgment.

In addition to the usual statistical analysis, the service considers non-statistical factors, particularly long-run industry trends. Financial practices and policies are examined, such as dividend policy in relation to financial needs. Another non-statistical factor examined is the amplitude of cyclical fluctuations in the industry of the particular issuer. Intangibles, such as franchises, leases, and patents, are studied. Another factor is the indenture and its features, such as call feature, sinking fund, power of issuer to create additional indebtedness, after-acquired clause, indebtedness of subsidiaries, and right of the issuer to sell or lease its property.

The service stresses the fact that no single formula is used in rating bonds and that judgment plays a highly important part in the final determination of all ratings.

Standard & Poor's Bond Ratings. This organization determines its bond ratings on statistical tests and upon economic and trade developments. Prices are not a part of their rating system, but they are used to indicate whether or not a given issue requires a complete new study.

In their work of arriving at ratings of bond quality, the organization relies upon all information available about the company and the industry in which it operates. This information varies, of course, with industrials, public utilities, and railroads. The following material relative to the rating of industrial issues is illustrative.

Five major classes of information are evaluated in the rating of industrial bonds. The first is earnings. These are evaluated from the standpoint of earnings prospect, immediate and long term; present earnings; past record; reputation of products and position of company in trade; character of trade; and quality of management as indicated by reputation, earnings record, sales trend, operating ratios, efficiency, depreciation practices, and dividend policy.

Other factors included in the analysis of industrial issues include protection from fixed assets, protection from net current assets, protection from cash resources alone, and adequacy of working capital.

Fitch Bond Ratings. Factors considered by Fitch in its rating of bonds are very similar to those of the two services just described. In addition to reliance upon the analysis of profit-and-loss statements and balance sheets, the organization considers all factors bearing on immediate and more distant prospects of the issuer. The current position of the company is studied with special consideration to net working capital, floating debt, and approaching maturities of bonded debt. An examination is made of the nature of the industry in which the company is located and the position of the issuer in the industry. An important factor is the legal nature of the debt, such as the degree of lien, and whether the issue is a collateral trust issue, or an unsecured issue. Guarantees, call provisions, and sinking fund features have an influence upon ratings.

In addition, the service examines the outlook for prompt payment of the security at maturity, the possibilities of refunding, its banking connections, and financial plans for the future. Many ratios are used by the service, such as debt to equity capital and the current ratio. For industrials stress is also placed upon such ratios as sales to inventory, operating ratio, depreciation, net available for common to invested capital, common profit margin, common earnings to property, and price-earnings ratio. Although statistics play a very important part in arriving at ratings, this service also places much stress upon non-statistical factors.

Stock Ratings. As already indicated, stocks are rated today only by Standard & Poor's Corporation.

Many have contended that stock rating is not satisfactory because stocks lack many of the characteristics of a good investment. They are unstable in price; their income is not secure; and their asset value is often not important. Since dividends are not fixed charges, it is impossible to estimate the number of times charges are earned, which is a basic factor used in determining the safety of a bond. The common stock is a residual legatee of a company's earnings; hence, such earnings become highly conjectural. Stocks are, therefore, less adaptable to rating systems than are bonds. It is doubtful whether stock ratings have the validity that has become so accepted in the field of bond investments.

In contrast to its system of rating bonds, this service is frank to admit that its stock ratings are based on a formula, which is fully described in its *Stock Guide*. The formula judges the quality of common and preferred stocks upon two factors alone: earnings and dividends.

In the rating of stocks, the service discards the usual criteria used in the analysis of bonds, such as financial position, capital structure, cash resources, asset values, depreciation policies, and profit margins. It maintains that there are no common denominators for many of these elements in the rating of stocks. It is their contention that all of the elements that make for a high- or low-quality stock are ultimately reflected in per-share earnings and dividends.

Earnings are examined over the previous eight years. Earnings stability is a key factor in the earnings record. A basic score is given for each year in which net earning per share are equal to, or greater than, those for the preceding year, while the score is reduced in any year were a decline takes place. The average of these eight annual scores becomes the basic earnings index. This stability index is then multiplied by a growth index, based on the square root of the percentage by which earnings increased between the base years 1946–49 and the three most recent years. This stability of the particular company is compared with that of the general economy to see whether the company is doing as well as, better, or poorer than the economy as a whole.

Dividend stability is the other factor used in the formula. For determining this, a twenty-year period is examined with weights increased for more recent years. The result is also multiplied by a growth factor similar to that for earnings, but for a longer period.

These two factors, earnings and dividends, are then combined into a single numerical rating. All stocks are then divided into seven classes, which range from highest to lowest as follows:

A+ Excellent	B+ Average
A Good	B Below Average
A− Above Average	B− Low
C	Lowest

The ratings are not market recommendations and do not indicate whether or not a given stock is overpriced or underpriced. They are not intended to be substitutes for analysis. Certain highly speculative stocks, dependent upon unusual factors, such as airplane contracts, are not rated.

Value of Ratings. That ratings possess a considerable value to the investment community would seem to be indicated by the very extensive use made of them by many institutional and individual investors over a long period. Even organizations with their own extensive staffs utilize them in cross-checking their investigations. They are a quick, easy reference available to most investors; when used with care, they are a valuable source of information to supplement other data available.

Limitations of Ratings. Certain limitations are evident in the ratings. Based as they must be on the element of judgment, especially as to forecasting the future, they must be considered as only tentative. The fact that many changes occur in the ratings would seem to indicate that finality is impossible. They cannot be used as a recommendation to purchase, since the ratings are not based upon price. An "A"-rated bond may or may not be a bargain at any particular quotation. Because of the great number of securities rated, it is doubtful whether the services can or do consider more than the chief factors in any one rating. For this reason the investor will do well to examine the primary sources of information on all investments which are purchased. Ratings, as far as they are obtained from statistical data, must look to the past. This immediately limits the value of ratings to some extent. Many of the strongest companies become insecure under the impact of economic change; e.g., the railroads and the traction companies. On the other hand, many of the most promising industries rise from highly uncertain origins. Management is important in all companies, particularly industrials; it is often more important than assets or even past earnings. Yet its valuation without the most intimate study is often mere conjecture.

Index